THE Musician's BUSINESS AND LEGAL GUIDE

4TH EDITION

COMPILED AND EDITED BY

MARK HALLORAN, ESQ.

A PRESENTATION OF THE
BEVERLY HILLS BAR ASSOCIATION COMMITTEE FOR THE ARTS

PEARSON

Prentice
Hall

Upper Saddle River, New Jersey 07458

Cataloging-in-Publication Data is available from the Library of Congress

A Division of Pearson Education
Upper Saddle River, NJ 07458

Pearson Prentice Hall is a trademark of Pearson Education, Inc.
Pearson® is a registered trademark of Pearson plc.
Prentice Hall® is a registered trademark of Pearson Education, Inc.

Produced by
Jerome Headlands Press, Inc.
Hines, Oregon 97738

Art direction—Julie Sullivan
Cover design—Mary Ross
Still-life photography—Michael Thompson
Production—Girlvibe, Inc.
Editor—George Glassman
Index—Rebecca R. Plunkett Indexing Services

Manufactured in the United States of America

10 9 8 7 6 5 4 3

ISBN 0-13-228127-9 and 978-0-13-228127-0

Pearson Education Ltd.
Pearson Education Australia PTY, Ltd.
Pearson Education Singapore, Pte. Ltd.
Pearson Education, Canada, Ltd.
Pearson Educatión de Mexico, S.A. de C.V
Pearson Education Malaysia, Pte. Ltd.

Disclaimer of Liability

This publication is intended to provide accurate and authoritative information regarding the subject matter covered.
It is sold with the understanding that Jerome Headlands Press, Inc., Prentice-Hall, Inc. and the Committee for the
Arts of the Beverly Hills Bar Association are not engaged in rendering legal, accounting or other professional service.
The information in this book is subject to change at any time without notice and should not be relied upon as
a substitute for professional legal advice. Neither the publisher, distributor nor the authors make any guarantees or
warranties, express or implied, concerning the information in this publication. The information contained in this book
does not constitute legal advice. If legal advice or other expert assistance is required, the services of a competent,
experienced professional person should be sought.

Contents

Preface

Welcome to the latest edition of this book. Since our last edition, the music business has undergone unprecedented change in our digital age. With these changes in mind we have updated all the information and have added three new chapters, "Protect Your Copyrights: Do Lunch *AND* Contracts," "Music Licensing: A Primer" and "Talent Agents: New Thinking on an Old Business." However, the basic messages from the previous editions remain constant. At some point in your professional music career, you will learn that there are legal questions implicit in almost everything you do. Whether you write, record, perform or sell a song, your actions give rise to rights and obligations that you should consider. The time to learn is now.

The purpose of this book is to demystify the music business and the seemingly indecipherable body of law that shapes it. And to help you "make it" by explaining the industry and the laws that govern it.

This book is a collection of chapters written by people that work in the music industry. Many are lawyers; some are musicians. We have tried to make our information comprehensible to everyone and have avoided presupposing a lot of knowledge on your part.

At this point, we must present a few warnings. First, there is no substitute for obtaining competent help as you build your career. Talent agents, personal managers, lawyers and business managers are trained to guide you. Their expertise costs money, but that cost is more palatable if you consider that these expenses are an investment in your career. Also, the chapters written by lawyers are primarily designed to identify problems, not to give specific solutions that apply to your situation. If you have a legal problem, do not rely on the information contained in this book; see an attorney. The chapters in this book are not the law but merely describe legal applications, in general terms, for the music industry. Additionally, before you photocopy our forms for submittal, check with the organizations to which you are submitting—they may require you to fill out their original forms. In many cases, these forms can now be downloaded and submitted via the Internet.

There has been a radical change in the way musicians can access information since our last edition—the Internet. The U.S. Copyright Office and virtually all other major organizations involved in the music business now have Web sites that make their information instantly available and up-to-date.

The Internet is also a new source of distribution of both songs and sound recordings and as acts as an advertising and promotional tool for musicians. There has been a flurry of lawsuits against those that have given away the music you create. Thankfully, the music copyright owners have either prevailed in court or have negotiated settlements—but regulating the Internet in a way to protect your works and have their use paid for remains the greatest current challenge facing musicians.

One final note—although this book is a useful tool, musicians should write music, not contracts. Unless you devote your time and energy to developing and exploiting your talent, this book does not matter. Make it matter.

Mark Halloran, Esq.
Coauthor and Editor

Acknowledgments

This book was originally compiled from materials prepared for a Beverly Hills Bar Association Committee for the Arts Symposium for Musicians held in 1979. Since then, the book has been updated many times and now has a life of its own.

Initially, my thanks to Jordan Kerner (cofounder and cochair, along with Evanne Levin, of the Committee for the Arts) and Norman Beil (Committee for the Arts member), who invited my participation.

I also wish to thank Gunnar Erickson and Ned Hearn with whom I cowrote *The Musician's Guide to Copyright* for Bay Area Lawyers for the Arts in 1978.

Although I have contributed chapters, this book is the sum total of the contributions of many authors. With this in mind, I thank the following authors that made contributions to prior editions: John Braheny, Wayne Coleman, William Dobishinski, Richard Flohil, Steven Gardner, Marshall Gelfand, Todd Gelfand, Brad Gelfond, Ronald Gertz, Peter Paterno and Peter Spellman.

It often takes more energy and effort to update a chapter than to write one from scratch. Thus, I offer kudos to the following authors that spent their precious time in revising their chapters for this edition: Stephen Bigger, Steven Ames Brown, Bartley Day, Robert Dudnik, Ned Hearn, E. Scott Johnson, Neville Johnson, Christopher Knab, Evanne Levin, Linda Newmark, Jack Phillips, Bernard Resnick, Margaret Robley, Alfred Schlesinger, James Sedivy, Madeleine Seltzer, Gregory Victoroff and Thomas White.

The vitality of this book has been augmented by the following authors that contributed new chapters to this edition: Matthew Burrows, Diane Rapaport and Kathleen Williamson.

Thank you to Bernard M. Resnick for his coauthorship, together with Neville Johnson, of the revisions to "Music Publishing"; "Analysis of a Personal Management Agreement"; and "Practical Aspects of Securing a Record Deal with a Major Label."

Thank you to Lawrence Blake and Daniel Stuart who chose to analyze a new contract for their chapter, "Analysis of a Recording Contract."

For their assistance with compiling and updating the Resource Directory, I would like to thank Diane Rapaport and Sue Tillman; and for their help on earlier versions, Committee for the Arts volunteer, William Vu Tam Anh; Marianne Borselle, Debra Graff, Peter Spellman, Harris Tulchin, Sue Tillman and Gregory Victoroff.

Thanks to my assistant, Kelly Choo for her administrative assistance.

Combining the styles of so many authors into one cohesive unit is always a challenge. I would like to thank our editor George Glassman for his help in creating a clear and comprehensible book.

Thanks also to Julie Sullivan for art direction and Mary Ross for the *Guide's* updated cover; Lisa Petty of Girlvibe, Inc. for production assistance; and to Rebecca Plunkett for providing an excellent index.

This book would not exist in its current form without the help of Diane Rapaport and Sue Tillman of Jerome Headlands Press. Their contribution in coordinating the revisions and design is incalculable.

Lastly, Prentice Hall has done a terrific job in distributing the book and my thanks to them.

Mark Halloran, Esq.

Introduction

When I began my entertainment law practice in the early 1980s, I was very pleased and relieved to discover that the Beverly Hills Bar Association had published a series of books for musicians, screenwriters, visual artists and other talent in the various areas of the entertainment industry. What was particularly wonderful was that these books not only helped artists but simultaneously provided legal practitioners with practical business and legal guidance. Today, as *The Musician's Business and Legal Guide* is republished in its fourth edition, the Beverly Hills Bar Association continues to provide cogent, comprehensive and clear information to artists and their representatives.

The Beverly Hills Bar Association is pleased and proud to have the premiere Entertainment Law Section in the nation. It is from that large pool of eminent attorneys (along with important nonlawyer contributors) that The Committee for the Arts first created the books and we continue to periodically update them so they contain the most current and useful guidance. In addition to thanking all the authors listed in the acknowledgement section, I want especially to recognize and thank Mark Halloran and Gregory Victoroff, the original creators and guiding lights.

We are also grateful to you for your interest in this new and revised guide. Whether you are a musician, an attorney or merely curious, I know that you will find this book to be among your most worthwhile and valuable resources.

Marc Staenberg
Executive Director, The Beverly Hills Bar Association

Getting Started: Music as a Business

ENTERTAINMENT GROUP NAMES:
SELECTION AND PROTECTION

BUSINESS ENTITIES

HOW TO SET UP A MONEY DEAL

MUSIC ATTORNEYS

MEDIATION FOR MUSICIANS

PROTECT YOUR COPYRIGHTS:
DO LUNCH *AND* CONTRACTS

Entertainment Group Names: Selection and Protection

BY STEPHEN BIGGER

The first rule in selecting a name for an entertainment group is a simple one: *be original.* It can, however, be quite difficult to put this rule into practice, since the field is very crowded. A brief check of a trade reference such as the *Billboard International Talent & Touring Directory* shows, for example, three different groups called Dixie Cups, The Dixie Cups and The Dixie Kups.

It is important to create an entirely original name to avoid being sued for infringing someone else's name. Rights in a group name or trademark usually derive from priority of use. This means that a prior group, even a small one, can successfully stop a new and more successful group from using the same name, at least in the area of the prior group's reputation. It is also easier to protect the name if you are the first one to use it. If you know that there is already a group called The Sledgehammers, it would be a poor choice to call your group The Sledgehammer Band.

SERVICE MARKS

A group name used for entertainment services is legally known as a service mark. The difference between a service mark and a trademark is that a trademark is a brand name used for a product. A trademark can be a word, a logo design or both together. A service mark is also a brand name but is used for services rather than for physical goods. A service mark can also be used as a trademark. For example, a group name can be used as a trademark for such things as T-shirts, toys, games or other merchandising items. However, use of a group name as a service mark for entertainment services will not necessarily entitle you to use the same mark as a trademark for goods. Again, in the United States, trademark and service mark rights are usually created by use and therefore, in order to create rights in a trademark for a product, it is usually necessary to use the mark by actually selling the product bearing the trademark to the public.

Although the owner of a trademark for a particular product or service generally cannot stop someone else from using the same or similar name on a completely different type of product or service, there are exceptions for famous names and trademarks. It would not be a good idea to call your new group something like Pepsi-Cola, since to do so would be inviting a lawsuit from the owners of this famous name. No one would confuse a bottle of rum with a diamond ring, but the owners of the famous

Bacardi name were able to stop someone else from using that name on jewelry.

It is best for a group to find a completely original name so that no confusion can occur with an existing record label, group or publishing company.

The title of a song or record album can usually coexist with the same or similar name of an entertainment group, especially if the words are commonplace and the group name is not famous. A federal court ruled on just such an issue in the case where a little-known rock band named Pump, composed of a group of singing body-builders, sued the famous Aerosmith entertainment group to stop their sale of an album of the same name. At the time the lawsuit was filed, Aerosmith had already sold over one million copies of their *Pump* album in the U.S. and 600,000 copies abroad. Although the band had a federal registration for the word Pump combined with a barbell design covering entertainment services and had played at a few local high school concerts in the New England area, the court held that the *Bigfoot* case (see The Little Guy Prevails on page 5) did not apply, since no likelihood of confusion had been established between the group and the Aerosmith record album title. The attorneys for the Aerosmith group presented a number of examples where group names had peace-fully coexisted, without confusion, with similar album or song titles. A song and album named *The Kiss* coexisted with the Kiss group name and the album *Rumors* (by Fleetwood Mac) coexisted with The Rumors group name. This does not mean that the little-known group named Pump could, by the same token, issue a record album titled *Aerosmith*. The extensive fame and reputation of the Aerosmith group name precludes it. In cases of this kind, where it is *not* a question of group name versus group name but rather group name versus something else, the relative fame of the group name is an important and probably crucial factor.

Special problems arise when a group name is used with the name of a star per-former. Some thought must be given as to whether the star should have any rights in the group name or should that name belong separately to the group, whether or not it continues to perform with the star.

Previously, it was not possible to obtain a federal service mark registration (granted by the U.S. Patent and Trademark Office) for the name of an individual performer. That was changed some years ago when Johnny Carson was able to convince the Patent Office that he was entitled to register his name but only upon proving that the name was used together with the words "in concert" in connection with entertainment services.

A common question is whether anyone can use his or her own name as a performer, even if it may conflict with the name of someone famous. The answer is, not necessarily. If your name happens to be Neil Diamond, you would have a difficult time convincing a court that you were entitled to use that name, as a singer, in view of the likelihood of confusion with the famous Neil Diamond.

RESEARCHING THE NAME

As soon as you have selected a name for the group and before it is used, a search should be conducted to see whether the proposed name conflicts with any prior name. As mentioned above, rights in a group name or trademark usually derive from priority of use. Therefore, if a prior group has used the same or a similar name, it is entitled to object to your use of that name, at least in the area of its reputation.

Trade references that are easily checked include the *Billboard International Talent and Touring Directory* (performing artists section), which lists active performing groups but includes only those that request to be listed (via response to an annual questionnaire). Record stores generally have databases that can be searched for current recordings by artist or by group name. Many book and record stores now have a customer accessed computerized service named RedDotNet—where you can easily check the names of current recording artists and group names (although this may not turn up variant names with different spellings).

Check sources on the Internet to help in clearing your group name. You can use search engines such as AltaVista *(www.altavista.com)* or Yahoo! *(www.yahoo.com)* to see what similar group names pop up. Check music Web sites such as CDnow *(www.cdnow.com)*, All Music Guide *(www.allmusic.com)* and Ultimate Band List *(www.ubl.com)*. It is important to note that the absence of a band name on the Internet does not mean that the name is available for you to use. It is still important to conduct a regular trademark search of the kind mentioned below.

A search should be conducted through a professional searching bureau to see whether the name has been registered as a trademark or service mark with either the U.S. Patent and Trademark Office in Washington, DC (federal registration) or with the Secretary of State in any of the 50 states (state registration). A comprehensive search by a professional searching bureau costs about $500 to $900, depending on the complexity of the search and number of classes of goods or services and covers the federal trademark register, all of the state trademark registers and common law rights (that is, trademarks and names in use but not necessarily registered) reflected in trade directories, as well as Internet references including domain names, etc. It is advisable to have the results of such a search reviewed by an attorney who is experienced in trademark law to give you some sense of the relative importance of the various references turned up in the search.

Professional searching bureaus are listed in the telephone directory yellow pages under "Trademark Agents" and "Trademark Consultants."

After you have satisfied yourself as best you can that the use of the proposed name will not infringe on the rights of some other group, the most important thing you can do is to use the name publicly so that you create rights in the name. Keep a careful record of performance places, dates and publicity, so that you can prove that you used the name, in what territory and for how long. Use it consistently and with some continuity. If the name is unused for a period of time and you no longer have a public reputation in the name, you have lost your rights in that name.

Finally, you can stand up for your rights once you have used the name, notwithstanding any big group that comes along later and tries to bluff you into discontinuing the name because they are famous and you are not. Do not let your group be pushed around if, in fact, you are the prior user. As the prior user, you have superior rights, at least for the area of your reputation, and you can enforce them against any subsequent user no matter how big or famous.

CREATING RIGHTS IN THE NAME

In the United States, rights in a group name, trademark or service mark are usually created by use and not by registration or any other kind of filing or claim. However, you can "reserve" a name before you use it by filing a federal "intent to use" trademark or service mark application (see the section titled U.S. Trademark Registration).

Reserving a name for incorporation with the Secretary of State of your particular state, or filing a fictitious business name statement will not create any rights in the name

THE LITTLE GUY PREVAILS

- In the landmark *Bigfoot* case, a large tire company knew of a smaller company on the West Coast that had been using the trademark Bigfoot. They very effectively wiped out the reputation of the smaller company by blitzing the media on a nationwide basis, so that by the time they were through, Bigfoot meant only one thing to the public and that was the tire sold by the larger company. When the case came before the court, it resulted in the largest award ever given in a U.S. trademark case: over $19,000,000 in damages, in view of the deliberate infringement, by the larger company, of the smaller company's trademark rights. (In the trial court, there was a punitive damage award by the jury of $16,800,000 and an actual damage award of $2,800,000, both of which were upheld on posttrial motions. However, on appeal, the higher court reduced the awards to something over $4,000,000 for punitive damages and $600,000 for actual damages.)

- In a more recent decision, which cited the *Bigfoot* case, a court awarded $250,000 in damages to a little-known group called The Rubberband, which had prior use and a federal registration and had objected to a later use of the name by the well-known group, Bootsy's Rubber Band. The court noted that the later group's fame had effectively wiped out any reputation that the earlier group had and held that the little-known group was entitled to receive all of the profits earned by the willful infringement of their name, although the newcomer was allowed to keep its name.

- Another pertinent case concerned the right to use the group name Flash. A California group by that name had performed in the San Francisco Bay Area but had never recorded an album. There was also an English group called Flash, which had recorded with a major company. When the records bearing their group name were distributed in the San Francisco area, the unrecorded Bay Area group was able to stop distribution of them based on their prior use and reputation for that territory.

that you can enforce against the first commercial user of the same or a similar name. Likewise, the mere fact of registering a domain name on the Internet will not create any protectable rights in the name. (For further details, see Rights in Cyberspace below.)

The United States is a common law jurisdiction where you acquire trademark rights by using the mark, quite apart from any statutory registration procedure. In several European and Latin American countries, however, trademark rights are created solely by registration. The U.S. system is designed to protect the person who has created some reputation in a name by using it even if he or she cannot afford to register the name. This positive aspect, whereby prior users cannot lose their rights as long as they continue to use the name, despite any subsequent user who may be bigger or more famous, also includes an element of uncertainty. Even if you conduct an extensive search, you cannot be absolutely certain that you are not infringing on the rights of some prior group that is performing in some backwater. There is nothing you can do to dislodge the rights of such a group, provided that they continue to use the name and maintain some kind of public reputation.

If you search the name you wish to use and find another group with the same or a similar name you have two choices: (1) use a different name or (2) try to buy the rights to the name from the prior group. Do not ignore the rights of the prior group, even if you are about to sign a big recording contract and they have never recorded their music. To try to roll over a prior, relatively unknown, group because you are bigger, more famous or better financed, could be a fatal mistake.

If there is a prior group of the same or similar name but they are no longer performing it could still be very dangerous to use the name without coming to terms with them, either by obtaining their permission to use the name or (preferably) by an assignment of their rights. Rights in a group name, like other property rights, can be sold or transferred.

In a case involving the group name The Buckinghams, the court protected the residual reputation of a group that had been disbanded for five years. Although the group had not performed for that period of time, the members had no intention to abandon the name, and they continued to collect royalties from their records that were currently being sold. The Buckinghams were, therefore, entitled to stop another group from using the name, even though they had stopped performing and making records.

Territoriality

Another basic concept in trademark and service mark law is that of "territoriality." In the entertainment area, this means that it is possible for two groups to operate under the same name in different parts of the country and for each of them to own the name in its own territory. Of course, everyone wants to own their own group name for the entire country, if not the entire world. However, if two groups, each without knowledge of the other, independently adopt the same name, then both are entitled to use it in their respective territories. It is even possible for each of the parties to obtain a separate federal registration, with an appropriate limitation as to the area of the group's reputation. If, however, you are aware of a group in another part of the country that has the name you wish to use, then you cannot, without risking a lawsuit, use the name in the other group's territory, either by performing there, distributing records or engaging in advertising or promotional activities for your group. Since every group hopes to be successful nationwide and to perform and distribute records on a national basis, it makes no sense to pick a name used by another group even if it is purely local, unrecorded and in a different part of the country. Further, if it can be shown that you were aware of the other group's name before you began use of that name, your adoption of the name was not "innocent," and a court may rule against your right to use the name even in your own territory.

Ownership of the Name

After selecting the name and searching it, the next important step in protecting the name is to decide who is going to own it and to put this decision in writing. Even if you cannot afford a lawyer, confirm your agreement in writing. This can be as simple as a signed and dated statement that says that if Tom, Dick or Harry leaves the group, then the departing member will have no right to use the group name, which shall continue to be owned by the remaining members of the group. A simple agreement along these lines can help avoid complicated hassles and problems in the future. It would also be advisable to include a similar statement in any management or recording contracts in order to make clear that the group name is owned by the group and not by the management or recording company.

The person who thought up the group name does not own it. The group name is like a brand name for a product. It identifies to the public the services provided by the group. Rights in the name are only created when it is used to create a public reputation. (With the single exception of a federal intent-to-use trademark or service mark application that must be validated by actual commercial use of the name before registration is granted.) If one member of the group thinks up the group name that person does not, individually, own the name. Ordinarily, the entity that actually uses the name owns it, subject to some agreement to the contrary. It would be possible, although not usual, for some other party to own the group name, such as the manager of the group, the record company or the financial backer. However, any such unusual ownership arrangement should be confirmed by a written agreement. If there is nothing in writing to the contrary, the general assumption is that the members of the group, as a whole, own the group name and any member or members leaving the group would have no further rights in the use of the name.

There are some interesting decisions in this area. In the *Rare Earth* case, a federal district court held that in the event of a group breakup, where the group was organized as a corporation, the faction having working corporate control would prevail in a dispute over the right to use the name. In a Michigan state court decision involving The Dramatics name, the court held that upon dissolution, where a partnership made no advanced disposition of the group name, the group name became "the property of the partners in common and belongs to each of them with a right to use it in common but not the exclusion of the other partners." In other words, after the breakup of the group, you could have three or four different individuals calling themselves The Dramatics. Such a result seems in the interests of no one and underlines the advisability of having a written agreement, at the outset, as to the ownership of the group name.

Typically, a group starts out as a partnership and the members own the group name in common. In other words, they have the right to use the group name together but not separately. The question of ownership can be simplified to some degree by having the members of the group form a corporation that will own the name. Then, if a federal registration is obtained in the name of the corporation, the departure of one or more members will not affect the title to the registration.

A situation that can become complicated is when a solo performer works with a group and the performer and the group use separate names. The solo performer may believe, if there is no agreement to the contrary, that he or she has some rights to the ownership of the group name. Imagine that a solo performer named Lucky Starr and a backup group called The Sledgehammers perform together. They sign their first contract with a record company, and the record company designs a composite logo for the entire performing unit including the words Lucky Starr & the Sledgehammers. Together, the solo performer and the group obtain a federal registration for the composite mark (including both names and the logo design). If the parties have a falling-out, you can imagine how difficult it will be to answer the question of who owns what.

On the question of ownership of the copyright in a logo design prepared, for example, by an artist hired by the record company, it would be advisable to have an agreement with the artist and the record company confirming that the ownership in the copyright for the logo design belongs to the group or at least that the record company makes no claim to the words that are included in the logo design. Otherwise, if there is a disagreement between the record company and the group, the record company may claim that it owns the logo design. Generally though, the fact that the record company's artist designed the logo would not give it any ownership rights in the name, since the group owns the name in whatever form it is depicted.

Rights in Cyberspace

It is a good idea to register the group name as a domain name in order (among other things) to prevent someone else from doing so later, once your group becomes famous. A domain name can be registered through one of many different registrars—such as Network Solutions *(www.networksolutions.com)*. Typically, a domain name is registered for a term of one to nine years. A good benchmark is a three-year-term of protection, which costs about $35 per year via Network Solutions and possibly less via other services such as Go Daddy and Domains Priced Right. You need to list an administrative contact for the maintenance of the domain name. Select someone who is responsible about business affairs and has a permanent e-mail address. After the domain name is registered, the registrar will usually send a notice in advance to the administrative contact address you have designated concerning renewal of the domain name before it expires.

Registering a domain name on the Internet does not automatically give you any rights in the name. A domain name registration will, however, block someone else from registering exactly the same domain name—but not some minor variation thereof. If, for example, your group name is The Sledgehammers, and someone else has registered the domain name "sledgehammers.com," that would not prevent you from registering a domain name like "sledgehammersband.com." Accordingly, unless someone else is actually trying to steal your group name, it may be best to simply avoid the problem entirely by selecting a slightly different domain name. Usually, no one would want to intentionally copy your name unless your group is already famous. The trick is to register your group's domain name before you become famous in order to avoid problems later. Consider alternatives to a .com domain name such as .biz or .org if the name you want is not available at a .com address.

If, however, your group becomes famous overnight, and someone else beat you to the punch with a domain name registration, you can possibly "recapture" the name through various legal procedures that are now available to protect well-known names against cyberpiracy. Recent successful recapture cases include the "mariahcarey.com" and "juliaroberts.com" domain names. In the latter case, the famous actress recaptured her domain name under a new procedure called the Uniform Dispute Resolution Policy (UDRP), which involves a special tribunal designed to settle domain name disputes of this kind. The arbitration panel in that case found that the actress Julia Roberts has a common law trademark right in her name, i.e., she has rights in the name even though it was not registered as a trademark, and they also found that the person who had registered her name was acting in bad faith with the intent of profiting from the unauthorized registration. Generally, if someone tries to hijack your group name in cyberspace, you will need a lawyer to sue them to recapture the name or to utilize the special UDRP procedure mentioned above (generally much less expensive than filing a lawsuit).

There is also a federal law that protects against "cybersquatting" or the hijacking of domain names, entitled the Anticybersquatting Consumer Protection Act (ACPA), effective in 1999. Both the ACPA and UDRP procedures apply essentially the same standards for achieving similar results. Generally, however, the UDRP procedure is faster and less costly. Under the ACPA procedure, a court action is required—but this can provide broader relief in the forms of awards of monetary damages or court injunctions that go beyond the simple recapture of the domain name and prevent the use of unauthorized content on the objectionable Web site.

U.S. TRADEMARK REGISTRATION

Although U.S. trademark rights are usually created and must be maintained by use rather than by registration, it is advisable to register a trademark. State trademark registrations are obtained from the local Secretary of State and a federal registration may be obtained at the U.S. Patent and Trademark Office in Washington, DC. The rights conferred by federal registration are so much wider than those afforded by a state registration that normally a federal registration, which covers the entire country, is the only registration of the group name that you need. A state trademark registration might be considered as an alternative in special cases where a federal registration is not available or if some kind of registered protection was needed in a hurry to take action against infringements in a limited area restricted to a particular state.

Since the amendment of the U.S. Federal Trademark Law in 1989, it is possible to reserve a name in advance of any actual commercial use by filing an intent-to-use trademark or service mark application for federal registration—so long as there is a bona fide intention to use the mark on the specific goods or services covered by the application. The simple filing of such an application will create superior rights in the name, even if some other party begins later use of the same or a similar name before the applicant begins commercial use. For this reason, it is now very important to search a group name to see whether a federal application for registration has been filed for the same or a similar name (even in the absence of any public use by the applicant), which may bar the use of a new group name. The intent-to-use trademark or service mark application must be validated by filing evidence of actual commercial use of the name before the registration is granted. If such evidence is not filed within four years, the application will be declared invalid.

A federal trademark or service mark registration provides very important rights in court, including the right to sue for trademark infringement in federal district court. It provides an arsenal of procedural weapons that can be used against an infringer, including extensive discovery procedures that allow you to discover the evidence and information available to the other side. Significantly, a federal registration also provides "constructive notice," so that any subsequent user of the same or a similar name is deemed to have knowledge of your rights. Someone with constructive notice cannot claim that he or she innocently adopted the name and is entitled to use it notwithstanding your prior registration. Only a federal registration entitles the owner to use the ® symbol denoting a federally registered mark.

The ™ symbol is unofficial and without any legal meaning or definition under federal or state statutes. It has been used on an optional basis to indicate a claim to trademark ownership for an unregistered trademark. Sometimes the ™ symbol is used to indicate a service mark. It is not essential to use either symbol and, in fact, their use is not especially popular in the entertainment world, except on merchandising items. However, it is advisable to use the ® symbol if you have a federally registered mark since it puts other parties on actual notice of your federal registration and may affect the question of damages (i.e., whether the damages should be counted from the beginning of the infringement or from when the infringer was notified in writing by you or your lawyer).

Registration Procedure

The procedure for obtaining a federal trademark or service mark registration begins with the filing of an application for registration with the U.S. Patent and Trademark Office in Washington, DC. Before that application can be filed, it is necessary to have used the mark in interstate commerce (that is, commerce across state lines)—or to base the application on a bona fide intent to use the mark on the goods or services specified in the application. This requirement of use in interstate commerce for a federal application is met if there is a public performance by the group under the group name in a place that attracts an interstate clientele or where the group performance is advertised in a newspaper or publication that crosses state lines. When based on preapplication use, a federal application requires the submission of specimens showing the use of the name. Usually, this would be in the form of advertisements or promotional materials for the public performance of the group. The Patent Office *does not* accept album covers bearing the group name as specimens of use for entertainment services. This narrow view is established practice at the Patent Office. Hopefully, someday someone will challenge this practice by an appeal to the Trademark Trial and Appeal Board or to the courts and win. The good news is that the Patent Office will now accept, as specimens of trademark use, printouts from the Internet for both entertainment services (in the form of an advertisement for upcoming concerts or tours) and for merchandise such as clothing (provided that the Web site provides some way to order the merchandise).

If no problems are encountered, it takes about one year to obtain a federal registration after filing the application. The application procedure has two stages. The first involves an official examination by the Patent Office for both registrability of the mark and any prior registrations for similar marks, which may be cited against the new application as barring registration. The second stage is the opposition period, during which the application is published in the *U.S. Official Gazette* (Trademark Section) and may be opposed by any party wishing to do so within 30 days following the publication date. The *U.S. Official Gazette* is issued weekly and may be ordered by writing to the Superintendent of Documents, Government Printing Office, Washington, DC 20402.

The cost of obtaining a federal registration (excluding special problems) is $900 or more, depending on the number of classes of goods and services, which includes official filing fees and legal fees. If a determined adversary opposes an application, the defense of the application is tantamount to fighting a lawsuit in federal court. This could cost thousands of dollars. The applicant, of course, has the option of defending against the opposition or withdrawing the application without incurring any additional expense.

After a federal registration is obtained, it is necessary to continue use of the name in order to preserve the validity of the registration. A federal registration may be canceled for abandonment of the name. The statute provides (effective 1996) that three years' nonuse constitutes prima facie (a legally sufficient case on its face) abandonment. Further, after the fifth anniversary of the registration, it is necessary to file (within one year) an affidavit that confirms that the use of the name has been continued. An affidavit of incontestability should be filed at the same time, provided that the name has been used continuously for the past five years. This will make the registration incontestable (it cannot be canceled by someone else based on a prior registration or on a claim of prior use). Renewal of the registration is required every 10 years and costs $900 or so, depending on the number of classes covered by the registration.

Foreign Registration

Generally, you want foreign registration for only those countries where you have or believe you will have, some real commercial interest. Frequently, new groups will search their chosen name in the United States and Canada at the same time, and if the name is clear, file in both countries. A more expansive plan of initial protection includes a trademark application in the European Community that covers, in just one application, all 25 member countries of the European Union (EU) as follows: Austria, Benelux (Belgium, the Netherlands and Luxembourg), Cyprus, the Czech Republic, Denmark, Estonia, Finland, France, Germany, Great Britain, Greece, Hungary, Ireland, Italy, Latvia, Lithuania, Malta, Poland, Portugal, the Slovak Republic, Slovenia, Spain and Sweden.

The United States is a member country of the Paris Convention, the Magna Carta of the international patent and trademark field. It is possible, under this convention, to file foreign applications within a six-month term following the filing of a U.S. application, claiming the priority date of the U.S. application. This can be very helpful for a group that becomes famous overnight and is faced with infringements in countries where others try to register the name before the group has had the opportunity to get applications on file. There are approximately 175 trademark jurisdictions in the world. The cost of registering a name as a trademark or service mark in all of these jurisdictions, without any special problems, is about $250,000. If there are Patent Office or third-party objections, the cost could escalate to over $500,000. Approximately 125 countries provide for the registration of service marks, which is what you really want, rather than a trademark registration. Some jurisdictions have no provisions for the registration of service marks, although the trend is towards the adoption of registered service mark protection.

The U.S. has also recently joined an international convention named the Madrid Protocol where a single trademark application may be filed for an international registration extending to many (but not all) countries—based on a corresponding U.S. trademark application or registration. Depending on the number of countries that are selected for an application for international registration, there may be some significant cost savings in filing under the Madrid Protocol. There are, however, some disadvantages in following this procedure (during the pendency stage after the application has been filed) and, for example, the international application will be dependent on the fate of the U.S. application for registration, which, if it runs into difficulty, may undermine the entire international application. Also, if the Madrid Protocol procedure is followed, the foreign application has to be restricted to the relatively narrow U.S. specification of goods and services—while otherwise the foreign application could be filed for much broader specifications in many of the jurisdictions concerned.

The Latin American countries and a number of countries in Europe (including France, Germany, Italy and Spain) are "first-to-file" countries, where trademark and service mark rights derive from registration rather than from use. In other words, the first to register the name is the one who owns it. There are exceptions for famous names (if they can be proven by evidence of local reputation), which are, under the Paris Convention, entitled to special protection even in the absence of registration.

If someone has filed for your group name, prior to you, in a first-to-file country such as France and you try to perform or sell records in that country, the owner of the registration would be entitled to stop you from performing in France under that name and stop you from selling records bearing that group name.

Prior use is not required for filing trademark or service mark applications in most foreign countries. In Australia, Canada and the United States, an application can be filed based on either prior use or proposed use. You may reserve a name in foreign countries by filing a trademark or service mark application, even before you use the name. However, many of these countries have user requirements after registration, so that if you do not use the name within a certain period of time, your registration can be canceled for nonuse.

WHEN YOU BECOME FAMOUS

If you have just become famous and have signed a big recording contract, you must decide how extensively you should protect the group name by way of registration. Focus on those foreign jurisdictions where service marks can be registered for entertainment services. The most important are Australia, the Benelux countries, Brazil, Canada, Denmark, Finland, France, Germany, Great Britain, Italy, Japan, Mexico, Norway, South Africa, Spain, Sweden and Switzerland. You can file a single trademark application in the European Community, which covers all 25 EU nations. If you want protection in a large number of countries, consider filing a single application for an international registration under the Madrid Protocol, if you have a basic U.S. application or registration already in place.

You can obtain trademark registrations in jurisdictions such as the Bahamas, Antigua and the Netherlands Antilles, where service mark registrations are not available, to cover merchandising items like T-shirts, toys, games, etc. Generally, however, it is not worthwhile to spend the money on trademark registrations for merchandising items unless you have a real commercial interest in merchandising the name in those jurisdictions. Many of these countries have user requirements, so that a registration is subject to cancellation after five years (or some lesser period) of nonuse.

If you do intend to actively merchandise the group name, obtain trademark registrations for the merchandising items, especially in those jurisdictions where trademark rights derive from registration rather than from use. Without a trademark registration for the goods concerned, you have nothing to license to another party for manufacturing the goods and selling them in the local jurisdiction.

Consider defensive merchandising, registering the mark for merchandising items, simply to prevent someone else from doing so. For example, a famous performer may not wish to merchandise his or her name in order to sell T-shirts but may be plagued by unscrupulous persons that capitalize on the name by emblazoning it on T-shirts anyway. The famous performer has two choices in these cases, ignore the infringements or try to stop them.

The most effective way of stopping infringements of this kind is to register the name for merchandising items and then license the name on a selective basis to create trademark rights in the area of most active infringements. A case in point is that of the unauthorized sale, in Great Britain, of T-shirts bearing the group name Abba. In that case, the merchandising company representing the famous Swedish group was not able to stop the sale of the T-shirts, since they were being sold by the first user, despite the fact that there was no connection with or authorization from the famous group. The English court indicated (in 1976) that the fame of the Abba name for entertainment services in Great Britain (where service marks were not yet registrable) was not enough to entitle the group or its merchandising company to prevent use of the name on T-shirts by the unauthorized party.

Since the amendment of the UK Trademark Law in 1994, the registration of an entertainment group name provides a basis for stopping the unauthorized use of the name on the same kind of goods or services covered by the registration. There is also a provision in the new law that protects registered marks, which are well-known in the UK, against use of the same name on dissimilar goods or services if such use would take unfair advantage of or be detrimental to, the character of the well-known mark. In order to take advantage of this expanded protection, however, it is crucial to obtain a UK registration of the name for the goods or services for which the name has become well known. If, however, you obtain a European Community trademark registration, you do not need a separate national UK registration.

There is some question about whether the use of a group name on only the front (or back) of a T-shirt is, in fact, trademark use. It is better, from the standpoint of trademark protection, if the group name also appears on the neck label, indicating that it is the brand name for the shirt itself. Otherwise, an infringer may be able to claim that the use of the group name on only the front of the shirt is an ornamental use (open to anyone) and not a trademark, which only the trademark owner is entitled to use or authorize. Also, adding the ™ symbol to the name on the front of the shirt (or the ® symbol if the name is federally registered as a trademark for shirts) helps to show that trademark rights are being claimed.

Finally, a maximum approach to protection of a group name should include a system to watch for infringements. There are trademark surveillance services that survey trademark journals, where applications are published for opposition purposes, which are available in at least 150 countries. Costs average $500 per year for surveillance on an international basis. In this way, you will be informed if someone in Peru or France or Sweden files to appropriate your group's name for entertainment services, merchandising items or whatever, and you will have the opportunity to oppose the applications or obtain cancellation of the resulting registration before it can be used to damage or block your rights in the name in that country.

Business Entities

BY EDWARD (NED) R. HEARN

There are mainly four forms of business that can be used to organize your music business affairs. These are (1) sole proprietorship (a single self-employed individual running the business); (2) partnership (two or more self-employed people running the business); (3) corporation (which can be owned by one or more individuals and is organized under specific state laws); or (4) a limited liability company, which has elements of a partnership and a corporation. Each of these forms has special features that should be examined when making a decision about how to organize your business. These features include, among others, expenses, personal liability and taxes. You should seek professional advice to determine the best form for your particular situation before investing too much time and money in your enterprise. The cost of planning to minimize problems is much less than the cost of trying to cure those problems after they have materialized.

SOLE PROPRIETORSHIP

A sole proprietorship is a business conducted by one individual who is the sole owner. If you have your own business for the purpose of making money, whether by making or selling records, writing and publishing songs, operating a recording studio or performing solo, you have a proprietorship business, and this material applies to you.

A proprietorship is the simplest form of business to start because it generally requires no contracts (contracts require at least two people) and only a few special papers have to be prepared. These papers include a fictitious business name statement, commonly called a DBA ("doing business as"), which identifies you as the owner by your name and address and the name under which you are doing business. Note, however, that a DBA generally needs to be filed only if you use a name other than your own to do business. That statement must be filed with the county recorder located in your local county courthouse. After filing with the county recorder, you must publish a legal notice statement of your doing business. Inquire at your county recorder's office to find out which local newspapers publish the notices and have the least expensive legal notice rates. Certain local governments may require the proprietor to obtain a separate business license or that license may be covered by the fictitious business name filing. Your county recorder's office can fill you in on this.

If you sell goods at retail, you will need a permit issued by the appropriate tax authority. This is discussed later in this chapter in the section titled, General Business Obligations.

You, as the sole proprietor, are the only one who makes decisions on how the business should operate and what its focus should be. With a proprietorship, you enjoy all the profits but must absorb all the losses. Employees do not participate in the ownership. A proprietor who has employees must withhold income and social security taxes, unemployment and other insurances required by state and federal law and must submit the withheld sums to the appropriate government agencies. While a proprietorship usually has fewer regulatory and record-keeping requirements than a partnership or corporation, you must focus on the reports to be filed with the local, state and federal taxing authorities. If you are going to hire employees, be certain to contact each of those authorities to obtain the required forms and instructional booklets that tell you what to do. A good bookkeeper or accountant will be able to assist you with that part of your business. These requirements are discussed in more detail later in this chapter.

As a proprietorship, you are responsible for your acts and, in general, the acts of your employees. If, for example, you or one of your employees should injure someone in a car accident while promoting your record to radio stations, you would be responsible for compensating the injured party. A judgment against you would enable the judgment creditor (the person who won the suit and to whom you owe the money) to look to all your assets, both business and personal, to recover on the judgment. You should obtain insurance to provide coverage from the liabilities that can occur in running a business.

The entire income of a proprietor is taxable income, but business expenses and losses are deductible from income. Proprietors, as self-employed, must file quarterly estimated income tax returns and make prepayment of anticipated taxes with the Internal Revenue Service and the state tax authorities. The estimated tax is based on a projection of expected income during your first year of business and thereafter on your prior years taxes. You should consult an accountant who has a tax orientation to assist you in these matters.

PARTNERSHIPS

If your band of one, or your one-person record or publishing company has grown to two or more people that share the profits and losses, and you plan to stay in business for a while, you have a partnership. A partnership is defined as an association of two or more persons conducting a business on a continuing basis as co-owners for profit. Usually, the relationship among the partners is governed by a written partnership agreement that details the rights and responsibilities of each partner. Although you do not need a written contract to be considered a partnership, obtaining a written partnership agreement is recommended. If there is no written partnership agreement, state statutes control the relations of the partners with each other. The partners can be individuals, other partnerships, corporations, limited liability companies or any combination of these. Each partner contributes property, services or money to the business of the partnership. Partners also may loan property, money or services to the partnership.

General Partnership

In a partnership, each of the partners has an undivided equal interest in all of the partnership property, unless, by contract, they provide for their interests to be unequal. Essentially, each partner owns the assets in common with the other partners and has a duty to each of the other partners to take care of that property and not to dispose of it without the consent of the other partners.

WHEN THERE ARE NO WRITTEN PARTNERSHIP AGREEMENTS

A frequently raised issue is how to structure the business arrangements among the members of a band. Whenever two or more musicians form a band, they have formed a general partnership. While it is important to have a written agreement at some point, most struggling bands cannot afford to hire a lawyer to prepare one for them. If this is the case, it is important for the members of the band to work out answers among themselves. Communicate with each other. Seek professional help. Follow your instincts on what seems fair and reasonable to you. A good issue on which to focus is to determine at what point your band should make an effort to have a written agreement. It is far less expensive to plan your business properly in the beginning than it is to resolve problems after the fact, especially if the resolution takes the form of expensive litigation. If you cannot reach an agreement, maybe that is a sign you should not be in business together.

Legal Presumptions

If the members of a band have formed a partnership by working together but do not have a written agreement, state statutes presume that certain conditions apply to the band's arrangements. These conditions are that each partner (a) has an equal vote in the affairs of the partnership and a majority vote determines the decision of the partners; (b) owns an equal share in the assets of the partnership, which include equipment purchased by the band, the name of the band and income; (c) shares equally in the profits and losses of the partnership; and (d) is responsible for the acts of all of the other partners performed in pursuing the partnership business. If a partner, for example, delivers the band's independently produced recording to record stores for sale and in the course of making a delivery has a car accident, then all of the partners are liable for any damages.

Leaving Members

When there is no written agreement and a partner leaves the partnership, whether willingly or at the demand of the other partners, then the band's partnership terminates automatically. The band has a responsibility to pay all of the debts of the partnership and, if necessary, sell the partnership's assets to do so. If thereafter, the remaining members of the partnership wish to continue performing as a band they may, but in effect, they form a new partnership and start over. If the band's creditors cooperate, it may be able to avoid having to liquidate assets so long as the remaining band members continue paying the creditors. You need to work out with the departing members their continuing responsibility to make payments owed or to receive payments due. If you do not want to deal with a dissolution and liquidation under these circumstances you need a written partnership agreement.

Taxes

At income tax time, the partnership files an informational tax return (Federal Partnership Return of Income Form 1065) that describes losses or profits, but the partnership itself pays no taxes. Rather, the losses or profits are passed through to the individual partners for reporting on their individual tax returns (thus, a partnership is often described as a tax conduit) and again, unless the agreement provides otherwise, losses or profits are shared equally. As with a proprietorship, the partners must file quarterly returns and personal income tax prepayments.

PARTNERSHIPS: CRITICAL WRITTEN AGREEMENT DECISIONS

Acquired Property

When a band acquires property, such as a sound or lighting system, each of its members assumes a share of that system's cost. The partners should be aware of their payment responsibilities and what happens if somebody leaves the band. For example, will the departing member have to continue to make payments? Do the remaining members of the band have any obligation to pay the departing member for the equipment based on its market value or the money paid by the departing member, if the band is going to keep that equipment?

Name

If the band becomes well known and its name is recognizable to a large audience, who will have the rights in the name if the band breaks up or individual members leave the band? Partnership agreements generally state that the group, as a whole, owns the name. A provision should be included in the agreement stating that if any member leaves the group, whether voluntarily or otherwise, that member surrenders the right to use the band name, which will stay with the remaining members of the group. Any incoming member would have to acknowledge in writing that the name of the band does belong to the partnership and the new member does not own any rights in the band's name greater than the partnership interests allocated to that new member.

The partnership agreement could provide that none of the band members may use the name if the group should completely disband, or that any one of the members could buy from the others the right to use the name at a value to be established by binding arbitration with expert testimony, if the members cannot agree among themselves.

Leaving Members

Prior to signing long-term contracts such as recording or publishing agreements, the band should determine how to resolve the issues regarding the rights of departing and new band members concerning services already performed or commitments that have to be met under those agreements and the sharing of recoupable costs for projects predating and postdating the leaving and new band members.

Song Rights

Can the departing member take his or her songs when they leave the group? If the songs were cowritten with remaining band members, the band can continue to use the songs and record them, as can the departing member, but each will have to report to the other their respective shares of income earned from such usages. When the departing member is the sole author of certain compositions, the band could be prevented from recording them, if they had not already been released on commercially distributed phonorecords, and from performing them if they had not yet been licensed to a performing rights society like BMI or ASCAP. Sometimes bands form a publishing company as part of the assets of the partnership, which will control what happens when a writer member leaves the band. Usually the band will continue to be able to use the songs as will the departing member.

Each person who is a partner may act on behalf of the partnership and that act binds all of the partners in the partnership. Each person in the partnership is liable for the business obligations of the partnership incurred by any of the partners. In other words, if your partner signs a business commitment to pay for advertising for the business, you as a partner are responsible with the other partners for making payment. On contract actions, the creditor can sue all of the partners, but cannot single out any one partner to sue exclusive of the others. A tort claim (inflicting harm on another person or property) for injuries is different. If, for example, a partner runs a car through a record store display window while delivering records in the normal course of partnership business, each partner is severally (individually) liable and the store owner could sue any individual partner or all the partners in the partnership.

The personal assets of the partners can be taken by the creditors of the business only after all of the partnership assets have been taken and the personal creditors of the individual partners have satisfied their claims out of the partners' personal assets. For example, the business creditors must exhaust all of the property and money of the partnership before they can look to your car, stereo or instrument, and the person you still owe for the car, stereo or instrument has to be paid before the business creditor can claim any of these prized items. Some states' laws will allow certain "necessary" property of the debtor to be exempt from creditors' claims, such as food and clothing.

Death or withdrawal of a partner (or some other specified event set out in a partnership agreement) will dissolve the partnership. By written agreement, however, the partners can provide that the partnership will continue despite a partner's death or withdrawal. In that case, the agreement establishes distribution rules to determine how the departing partner is to be compensated (this is called a buy out) and how the partnership is to continue without the deceased or withdrawn partner.

As with a proprietorship, a partnership must file a fictitious business name statement (if all the partners' surnames are not in the partnership name) and publish a DBA statement in a local county newspaper. You also must file a form SS-4 with the Internal Revenue Service to obtain an employer identification tax number *even if you do not employ anybody.* These forms can be obtained by calling, faxing, writing or e-mailing to your regional Internal Revenue Service center. The performing rights organizations, ASCAP, BMI and SESAC, ask publisher members to include their employer identification tax numbers on their membership applications. You must also secure any required local licenses and permits.

In a general partnership, all of the partners participate in the control of the business. Partners may agree among themselves to assign specific duties according to ability. Voting on business decisions may be equal or may be weighted according to capital contribution (money and property contributed to making the partnership work) or on some other basis.

The profits, losses and risks are shared equally among the partners unless they agree, in writing, to a different division.

On dissolution of the partnership, the assets of the partnership are liquidated (turned into cash) and the creditors of the partnership are paid first. The balance of the liquidated assets, if any, is distributed to the partners, first to repay loans by any of the partners to the partnership, secondly to return any money or assets contributed by the partners and finally, to the partners according to how they share profits.

Joint Venture

A joint venture is a form of business relationship that consists of an association of two or more persons, partnerships, corporations, limited liability companies or some combination thereof, for the purpose of accomplishing a single or limited series of business transactions for profit, rather than carrying on a continuous business. A joint venture is a partnership with respect to all the applicable rules discussed above and the terms of the relationship should be governed by a written agreement. Examples of a musical joint venture include recording a single album, producing one video or promoting a concert.

Limited Partnership

A limited partnership functions as a financing vehicle to raise capital to fund identified business goals. It consists of a least two people, corporations, partnerships or some combination thereof. A limited partnership requires at least one general partner, whether a person, another partnership or a corporation and one or more limited partners as investors. The limited partners contribute capital but take no part in the management of the business and have no liability beyond the amount of money that each contributed to the partnership and any profits owed to them under the limited partnership. Should a limited partner become involved in the management of the business then he or she would lose this limited liability status. Generally, a limited partnership is for an established duration and must be set out in a written limited partnership agreement. State and federal securities laws that regulate investments apply to limited partnerships and a discussion of these laws is found in the chapter, "How to Set Up a Money Deal."

CORPORATIONS

At some point in your career, you may decide that it is time to incorporate, either because you have reached a high income level or because you wish to protect your personal assets from the claims of your business creditors. Frequently, successful entertainers form what in the business is known as a "loan-out" corporation. In other words, you have yourself incorporated and that corporation agrees to make your services available to other parties (for example, record companies) in any particular deal.

What does it mean to be a corporation? Corporations differ substantially from proprietorships and partnerships. A corporation is an artificial, separate, legal entity recognized by state law, the formation of which is regulated by procedures established by state law. Ownership of a corporation is obtained by buying shares of stock for value. A corporation can be owned by one or more persons (including a partnership) or other corporations. A corporation can be owned privately (the stock is not traded on the stock market) or publicly (the corporation's stock is sold on the stock market and is held by the public at large).

The corporation is a separate legal entity with a life apart from the persons that own and operate it. Corporations raise capital by selling shares. The issuance of shares in the corporation is a security subject to state and, under some circumstance, federal securities laws. Like an individual or a partnership, a corporation can own, buy or sell property in its own name, enter into contracts, borrow money, raise capital and do the various kinds of activities that a proprietorship and partnership can do.

The corporation is governed by a board of directors elected by the shareholders. In turn, the corporation is managed by officers (such as a president and treasurer) that are employees of the corporation hired by the board of directors. In loan-out corporations, the officers and directors usually are the individuals that form the corporation and are the shareholders. If the corporation was formed by one person, then that person usually holds all of the officer positions and is the sole director.

Risks of the business are borne by the corporation. The shareholders' liabilities are limited to the amounts invested in the corporation and their share of the profits. The investments are usually evidenced by issued shares (stock).

The corporation must file annual tax returns and pay taxes on profits. After taxes, profits can be retained for operating capital or distributed to shareholders as dividends, which are taxable as income. Profits are shared among shareholders in proportion to their ownership participation. Unlike partnerships, there is no passing of profits and losses from a corporation to the individual owners of shares, except in a Chapter S corporation.

With a Chapter S corporation, the shareholders get the benefits of a partnership by having profits and losses passed through to them for tax purposes, while they retain the benefit of the corporation's limited liability status. Losses passed through to the shareholders cannot exceed the amounts invested by the shareholders.

A corporation is brought into existence by filing a document known as the articles of incorporation (or charter or articles of association in some states), the filing of which, for example, costs $100 in California, plus a prepayment of an annual minimum franchise tax payment, currently $800. Forming a corporation, however, will cost more than this because of attorneys' fees to organize the corporation and prepare shareholder and buy/sell agreements concerning the stock issued to the shareholders. In addition, there may be local fees for permits and business licenses.

Shares of publicly held companies are generally transferable from one owner to a subsequent owner on the open market. With nonpublic corporations, there is no ready market for the shares and the shareholders have to seek out specific buyers. Also, the law often restricts the sale of shares and requires that certain procedures, established by state and federal statutes, be followed before they can be sold. Also, the shareholders may have agreements among themselves, or the corporation may have provisions in its bylaws that put limitations on a shareholder's transfer of stock. This is a complex area that requires professional counsel on securities, tax and accounting issues and is too involved a topic to examine in this chapter. These are considerations that require some attention and you will need professional advice when it comes time to focus on them.

THE CASE OF DEEP PURPLE

An example of the issues involved when a group disbands but its product still sells involved the group Deep Purple, which had not been performing as a band for many years. Its records, however, still sold. One of the original members of that band formed a new group. None of the other members of that new group had been members of the original Deep Purple.

This new group began to perform under the name Deep Purple. The corporation, owned by the original members of Deep Purple and their management, still owned the rights to the name Deep Purple. They sued the new Deep Purple to stop them from performing under that name and were awarded damages of $672,000; compensatory damages (actual damages suffered by the corporation) were $168,000 and $504,000 was for punitive damages.

Since then, the authorized Deep Purple has reformed and resumed performing and recording. This situation is one of many that can happen when a group disbands.

The rules that govern the operation of the corporation are known as the bylaws and these are adopted at the beginning of the life of the corporation. Generally, the officers of the corporation are empowered to operate the daily affairs of the corporation, subject to approval or disapproval by the board of directors, which in turn answers to the shareholders. The board of directors will hold periodic meetings to review the acts of the officers. The shareholders will hold periodic meetings to review the board of directors.

Voting among shareholders is based on the number of shares owned—generally one vote per share. Shareholders are sometimes divided into different classes. Some classes of shares may be nonvoting. Some corporations' bylaws provide for "cumulative" voting for the directors of the board. In other words, a shareholder can multiply the number of his or her shares (e.g., 100 out of 500) by the number of board positions (e.g., three) and apply all of the total (300) to one candidate on the board and thereby increase that shareholder's assurance of placing a representative on the board.

The corporation's existence is perpetual unless the shareholders vote to terminate the corporation or the corporation cannot continue financially. On dissolution, creditors, such as banks, trade creditors, employees and taxing bodies are paid first. Then shareholders receive a return of capital (that is, they get back what they paid for their shares if the dissolved corporation has sufficient funds) and finally, a distribution of assets and profits, if any.

LIMITED LIABILITY COMPANIES (LLCS)

A limited liability company (LLC) has elements of both a partnership and a corporation. It can be advantageous for entertainers that work in a group, such as a performing and recording band. Discuss with your attorney the pros and cons of structuring your business as an LLC, instead of as a partnership or regular corporation (usually a Chapter S).

An LLC is an organization in which the owners (members) have an interest in the LLC and are parties to a contract, known as the operating agreement, which details the rights and duties of the members and acts as the guiding rules for the LLC. Some state statutes require that the operating agreement be in writing. Generally, a written agreement better serves the interests and needs of the members regardless of statutes.

There are two types of LLCs, member-managed, in which members, by statute, have the agency and authority to make management decisions; and manager-managed, in which the members are not the agents of the LLC and have the authority to make only major decisions, leaving the authority to exercise day-to-day management decisions to the managers. For the most part, bands that organize as an LLC should be member-managed.

LLCs provide limited liability (as do corporations) and a greater and more flexible freedom to establish ownership and management relationships, as in partnerships, based on the contract of the members, which is known as an Operating Agreement. LLCs are treated in the same way as partnerships for tax purposes and they are currently the preferred form of business for performing and recording groups.

The members of the LLC are not individually liable for the obligations and liabilities of the organization. This also extends to the relationships among members. While general partners in a partnership have an obligation to contribute to the partnership and indemnify other partners for losses and obligations incurred in carrying on the business, no such individual obligations exist for members in an LLC. Generally, the LLC will be required to indemnify a member for obligations incurred by the members in carrying on the business of the LLC. But, if the LLC does not have sufficient assets to fully indemnify the member, the member may not look to the individual assets of other members for contribution, as may a partner in a general partnership.

Under most LLC statutes, members have the right to withdraw at any time and demand payment for their interest. This right to return an interest to a member of the LLC is similar to the rule that applies to partnerships. Some state statutes limit members' rights to withdraw or to demand that the LLC purchase their interests, unless the members have agreed otherwise. Consequently, like a partnership (or like shareholder agreements with a corporation), the operating agreement among the members of the LLC should specify the conditions under which the LLC is obligated to purchase the interests of a leaving member. The disassociation from the LLC by a member, due to death, bankruptcy, dissolution or some other event, will cause the dissolution of the LLC unless the remaining members consent to continue the business. Structuring the operating agreement so that an LLC does not dissolve upon the disassociation by a member is especially helpful when the organization holds title to property, like copyrights or rights to income, such as advances and royalty payments under a recording agreement, which might be adversely affected by the dissolution and reformation of the business that technically accompanies the withdrawal of a member.

The need to get professional counsel when you begin your own business cannot be stressed too strongly. Your lawyer or accountant will help you determine which form will be best for your situation and, thereafter, will monitor the operation of your business to decide whether you should switch to another form as your needs change.

LEGAL OBLIGATIONS OF EMPLOYERS AND BUSINESS

As an individual involved in the music business, you may find it necessary to hire others to work for you. If you hire employees, you must satisfy certain obligations imposed on employers by state and federal laws. This section briefly identifies those obligations and others of which you should be aware. If you start your own business and hire employees, consult with an attorney or accountant or at least with the appropriate government officials, to make certain that the federal and state laws regarding wages, benefits, hours, compensation, insurance, taxes, licenses and other matters are satisfied.

Employers' Tax Obligations

Becoming an employer imposes a host of form-filing obligations. One of the first things an employer must do is obtain an employer identification number from the Internal Revenue Service. This number must be shown on all federal tax returns, statements, and other documents. Application for this number is made on form SS-4, which may be obtained from and filed with your local IRS office.

Generally, employers must withhold federal income and social security taxes as well as state income taxes and other state taxes from the wages they pay to their employees. Contact your nearest IRS office and the local office of your state taxing bureau to obtain the necessary information on the procedures for withholding such taxes.

The employer must have all employees complete the employee withholding allowance certificate (form W-4). If the employee had no federal income tax liability for the preceding year and anticipates no liability for the current year, the employee withholding exemption certificate form W-4E should be completed. These forms should be returned to your local IRS office. Based on the information contained in the W-4 forms and in tax tables (which should be included in the information you receive from the federal and state taxing authorities) you will be able to determine the amount of income and social security taxes to be withheld from each wage payment and the amount of the employer's matching contributions for social security taxes.

The withheld income and social security taxes are deposited along with federal tax deposit form 8109 at an authorized commercial bank depository or the Federal Reserve Bank in your area. The deposits are required on a monthly, semimonthly or quarterly basis, depending on the amount of the tax involved. Form 941, which describes the amounts withheld, must be filed on a quarterly basis.

The employer must furnish to each employee two copies of the annual wage and tax statement form W-2 for the calendar year no later than January 31 following the end of the calendar tax year, including a federal copy, state copy, city copy (for certain jurisdictions that impose a city income tax, like New York and California) and employee record copy. If the service of the employee is terminated before the end of the year, the W-2 form must be submitted to the employee not later than 30 days after the last payment of wages to that employee. This W-2 form is an informational one for the purpose of advising the employee how much tax money was withheld and it may be combined with state and city withholding statements. It must be used by the employee in filing annual income tax returns.

It is important to remember that if you are the person responsible for withholding taxes on behalf of employees (yourself or others), you may become personally liable for a 100% penalty on the amount that should have been withheld if you fail to comply with these obligations.

Note also that the employer may be subject to federal and state unemployment taxes and to withholding on state disability insurance taxes. You should consult your accountant or the local office of the IRS, the state unemployment compensation bureau and the state disability insurance office to find out the details on unemployment taxes and disability insurance. Generally, the procedures for withholding money for these programs are similar to those for withholding federal and state income taxes and social security taxes.

If you hire independent contractors that will be responsible for making their own tax payments, it should be clear that they are operating their own businesses, have been retained by you to perform services, are not under your control or direction and will be performing the same or similar services for others. Also, you should file a 1099 form with the IRS by February 28th of each year identifying the independent contractors and the amounts paid for the services. Examples of independent contractors include someone to set up and engineer the sound for a showcase concert; a producer to oversee and produce a recording of the masters for your albums; an arranger to arrange your original compositions for your album. The IRS is particularly interested in independent contractors you retain that perhaps should have been treated as employees, so be sure to review with your accountant the current rules and regulations that distinguish employees from independent contractors.

Other Employer Obligations

Most employers are subject to state workers' compensation laws. These laws impose liability on the employer for industrial accidents sustained by employees regardless of the employer's negligence. They provide a schedule of benefits to be paid to the employees for injuries or to their heirs if the employees are killed in an accident. It is important that you obtain sufficient workers' compensation liability insurance from an authorized insurer or a certificate of consent from your state's director of industrial relations if you are going to self-insure. Generally, insurance coverage can be obtained through the local office of your state's compensation insurance fund or through a private licensed workers' compensation carrier.

Both state and federal laws impose minimum obligations on the employer concerning wages, hours and working conditions. You can obtain detailed information by contacting the Department of Labor, Department of Industrial Welfare or Department of Industrial Relations in your state as well as the U.S. Department of Labor. Both state and federal laws impose obligations on the employer to refrain from discrimination in hiring and in the conditions of employment. You must be careful to comply with these laws.

GENERAL BUSINESS OBLIGATIONS

As a business, you have certain additional obligations. We will not go into detail here, but will simply identify problem areas with the advice that you become aware of them either by consulting with your local, state and federal authorities or with an attorney.

If you engage in retail sales to consumers, you must comply with state sales and use taxes. Generally, this tax is imposed on the consumer but the seller is obligated to collect the tax. On the seller's failure to collect, he or she will be obligated to pay the sums to the state that should have been collected from the consumer. Also, as a seller of retail goods, you must obtain a seller's permit from the local office of your state taxing authority. If you sell your product to a distributor who will in turn sell to retailers or if you sell directly to a retailer, then you need to obtain a resale tax exemption certificate from the state.

Note that businesses in most states must pay personal property tax on certain items of personal property that the business owns or possesses at a certain time in each calendar year. You must file a property statement with the county assessor within the period of time required by state law. You should check with your accountant or state's business property tax department to obtain the necessary information to enable you to comply with the state's laws on such taxes.

It is advisable to obtain casualty and public liability insurance and you should consult with local insurance agents to give you advice on this matter.

Many trades, occupations and businesses are required to obtain state and sometimes local business licenses. Again, consult with your local and state authorities to determine what your obligations are.

It should be clear from the items discussed here that starting a business involves numerous filings and much record keeping. These requirements are unquestionably a burden, particularly for a small business. While it may be possible to ignore them and "fly below radar" for awhile, the odds are against doing it for long. The more successful the enterprise, the sooner it will become visible.

The recommended approach is to comply from the outset. If the requirements seem confusing or you do not have sufficient business experience to feel confident that you have undertaken all the proper steps, have an accountant, businessperson or lawyer look over what you have done and advise you. Once your bookkeeping and reporting systems are established, they are not difficult to maintain.

How to Set Up a Money Deal

BY EDWARD (NED) R. HEARN

This chapter explores some of the forms of financing that are available and shows how to analyze and structure a financial package to obtain the money for your project. The examples used will draw on the music industry, but the concepts and ways of structuring deals apply whether you are a musician, writer, actor, or, for that matter, if you want to establish your own instrument manufacturing company.

DEVELOPING THE BUSINESS PLAN

A business plan tells potential investors who you are. It describes your professional goals, what you plan to do to achieve those goals, and how that achievement can generate income to pay back the investor and further finance your career. An outline of the general headings of a business plan is at the end of this article.

Identifying Your Goals

The first and most important thing to be done is to identify the reasons you need to raise money. To establish a clear focus, you must determine your career goals, your immediate project goals and your strengths and weaknesses. Identifying your goals, such as securing a recording contract or getting a name artist to record your songs, will assist you in determining a feasible project to undertake to achieve that end. The project might be producing an independent record so you can market it and demonstrate that there is an audience for your product or it could be preparing a publishing demo to shop your songs.

You need to analyze your strengths and weaknesses. What is your best selling point? Pinpointing your strongest talents will assist in determining the project that would be most appropriate to achieve your goals. If your best skill is songwriting, perhaps you should raise funds to do a publishing demo of some of your songs to send to publishers and to performers that record material written by others. If your best talent is performance skill, perhaps you should develop a video package that will show the style you use to slay your audience. Money can be raised for other projects as well, such as producing a master sound recording, backing a tour for promotional or showcase purposes, buying equipment to enhance your stage show, or hiring a publicist to orchestrate a media blitz before you storm into Los Angeles.

Reaching a final decision on your goals and the projects designed to achieve them is a precondition to figuring out how much money you must raise and what kind of information to include in the business plan you will present to prospective investors.

Preparing the Budget

Once you have decided on the project, your next step is to determine its costs. You must develop a budget that shows the amount of money you need and how it will be spent. To do this, you must research the cost of each of the various elements of your project. If you plan to produce your own recording, you must budget the cost of studio time, tape, musicians, arrangers, producer and engineer, mixing, mastering, manufacturing, cover art, design, packaging, distribution, advertising and marketing. Each project has its own cost items. It is your responsibility to develop a clear and accurate picture of what those costs will be. The section in this chapter entitled, Identifying and Evaluating Sources of Income, discusses analyzing future sources of income to be used in scheduling payback arrangements with investors.

Preparing the Proposal

Once you have established your goals, the project, and the amount of money you will need, you must reduce all that information to a proposal or business plan to submit to individuals that may have an interest in funding your project. The proposal should itemize the elements we have just explored, explain what the end product will be, how your business operates, how marketing the product or implementing the service will assist you in developing your career, and how money will be earned to repay the investors. The proposal should also contain information on your background and the current status of your career, and a clear statement of your goals. There is no better way to force yourself to develop a clear focus than having to articulate it to others, especially if you are asking them for money.

RAISING CAPITAL

Your project, most likely, will be financed by one of three methods: self-financing, borrowing or profit sharing. This section will discuss these methods and the advantages and drawbacks inherent in each.

Self-Financing

The best way to retain full control of your project is to use your own money. It is the only technique that allows you to be free of financial obligations to lenders and gives you maximum artistic and financial control. Although it means that you must bear all the risk of the project, it also means that you will enjoy all the benefits.

Self-financing also minimizes the paperwork, record keeping, and other business complications involved in other ways of raising money.

Borrowing

If you are not in a position to self-finance, borrowing is the second basic technique for raising funds. Borrowing means accepting a loan for a fixed sum and agreeing to repay that sum plus a specified percentage of interest by a certain time. Arrangements where the return to the lender depends on the success of the project will be discussed under the section on investments and profit sharing.

Loans are usually absolute obligations that must be repaid whether or not the project is successful. If the rate of interest is high, you will have to earn a substantial amount of money from the project before you make any profit. For example, on a loan of $10,000 at 12% annual simple interest payable in two years, your interest obligation would be $2,400. To pay back the principal and interest on a self-produced recording that sells for $7.25 (average wholesale price), you would have to sell about 1710 recordings, plus an additional number to cover your cost of sales. Only then would you be able to sell for a profit. As costs climb, of course, the number of recordings you must sell to break even also rises.

Loan Sources

There are several possible sources of loans. The first are commercial sources. They include banks, finance companies, savings and loan associations, and credit cards with cash advance provisions.

Interest on commercial loans, secured by such collateral as a home, auto, recording or performing equipment or even the cosignature of a person in whom the bank has confidence will usually be lower than interest on unsecured loans. The reason is obvious: the risk is lower. Loans backed with collateral or the cosignature of a creditworthy individual are also easier to secure.

In deciding whether or not to give you a personal loan, a bank will look at your credit rating and at whether you own property that can be used as collateral for the loan. Unfortunately, musicians' credit ratings are not always good, because of the fluctuating conditions of their employment. But if you have a credit card or two and have lived in the same place for a couple of years without having trouble paying the rent, you may be able to convince a bank to loan you a modest amount of money (e.g., $5,000). Some banks will loan more than this amount if the borrower's credit rating is good. Banks may want to see your income tax returns for the last couple of years.

Some banks refuse to make a personal loan of more than $5,000 unless it is secured by collateral, such as a house in which you have equity. If you are looking for a loan to buy new keyboard equipment, you will find that banks generally will not consider securing the equipment itself as collateral. Some banks will let you use an automobile as collateral, however, provided you have title to it.

In the event you do not qualify for a personal loan yourself, you can ask a relative or a friend to act as a cosigner, which means they promise to make the payments if you are unable to. The bank will be more concerned with their credit rating than with yours, but will still want to make sure that you actually have the ability to make the payments.

In addition to personal loans, banks regularly make commercial loans to businesses. You may feel that since music is your business, you belong in this category, but you will find that commercial loans have their own rules and regulations. If you have a solidly established band with ongoing income, a commercial loan might be your best option. But if what you have in mind is borrowing money to start a project, you will probably have to go with a personal loan. When you become more established, some banks, especially those with operating offices in Los Angeles or New York, may lend money secured by the copyrights in your songs, master recordings and other intellectual property.

A commercial loan package usually contains your business plan, the profit and loss statements of your business, tax returns for the last two or three years and a personal financial statement. Banks will check your credit history. They need to know you have a sound financial plan and that you are financially responsible. They will generally insist that you put up as much as 50% of the money for improving the business out of your own pocket, with the loan supplying the balance.

Since commercial lenders make money lending money, you should shop for the best deal. This should also apply to loans from individuals that lend money to you for your project as a business venture, even if they are personal friends.

A second source for loans is family and friends. Usually, they will lend money at a rate lower than that of a commercial lender. The important thing to consider when borrowing from friends is that strong pressure for timely repayment may result, which often is more burdensome (because of the personal nature of the debt) than the legal obligation to repay.

When you borrow from friends, the usury laws of most states come into play. These statutes limit the amount of interest a private lender can charge a borrower. Banks and other commercial lenders are generally exempt from the usury limits and can charge higher rates.

Whether you borrow from friends or from commercial lenders, you will want to structure a written repayment plan that states the amount of money that was borrowed, the rate of interest, and the method of repayment.

This can be a simple written promissory note: "On or before June 15, 2010, John Debtor promises to pay Sally Lender the sum of $2,500 plus 9% interest per annum from January 1, 2007, (signed) John Debtor."

The note from a commercial lender is more complex, but it will contain similar elements. Sometimes commercial loans are structured so that you pay a smaller monthly amount the first two years and a larger one the next two to three years. Once again, you should shop for the most favorable terms, interest and monthly pay back amounts.

INVESTMENTS/PROFIT SHARING

If self-financing is not an option and you have not been able to obtain a loan, the third option is to find candidates to fund your project, such as investors, and offer them a profit share. The arrangement can take several forms, depending on whether the investor is "active" or "passive." The different alternatives are discussed below.

Active Investors

Active investors are individuals that put up money to finance a project for another person and become involved in the project (or fail to take adequate action to insulate themselves from responsibility). They assume all of the risks of the business, including financial liability for all losses, even if the losses go beyond the amount invested. Generally, such persons are responsible for the obligations of the business even if they have not given their approval or have not been involved in incurring business debts.

The forms of businesses in which the financing participants are active include general partnerships, joint ventures, corporations and limited liability companies. The profits or losses of such businesses are shared among the participants according to the nature of their agreement. These business structures are discussed more fully in the chapter, "Business Entities."

A general partnership is co-ownership of an ongoing enterprise in which the partners share both control and profits. A joint venture is a general partnership that either has a very short term or a limited purpose. For example, the production of a single recording by a group of people could be structured as a joint venture.

The general partners and the joint venturers are each personally liable for all the debts of the enterprise. The liability is not limited to the amount that they invested or to the debts that were incurred with their approval. All of the personal assets of each of the general partners or joint venturers are liable for repayment of the debts incurred by the enterprise.

If a corporation or a limited liability company is formed, then even if the project is a total failure, only the assets of the corporation or the limited liability company are vulnerable to the business creditors. A corporation is a separate entity formed under state laws. This also is the case for a limited liability company. The ownership of corporation is divided among its shareholders, and the ownership of a limited liability company is divided among its members. A corporate structure provides limited liability to the shareholders. This also is the case for a limited liability company. If you are thinking about setting up a corporation or a limited liability company, you will need some sound legal advice.

Passive Investors

A more complex category of investments is that in which backers provide money for the project but take no role in the management and affairs of the project. Such backers are passive investors whose return is based on the success of the project.

The primary advantage of profit sharing arrangements, from the point of view of the person getting the money, is that the downside risks are shared. If a project fails to recoup the money invested, you are not obligated to repay the investors. Offsetting this advantage are several problems that make profit sharing the most complicated form of financing a project.

The foremost problem is security law requirements. Any time one enters into an agreement in which people give money for a project with the understanding that part of the profits are to be shared with them and the investors do not actively participate in the management of the funds or the operation of the business, a "security" has been sold. A security can be a promissory note, stock, points or any other form of participation in a profit sharing arrangement, either written or oral, where the investor's role in the business is passive. The investments of a general partner or joint venturer may be treated as a security, but they are a different class of security because those investors are actively involved in the business. The level of protection required for active investors is less stringent than for passive investors. Active investors are liable for the debts of the business beyond just the amount of their investment, while passive investors are only responsible for the debts of a business up to the amount of their investment.

Limited partnerships, promissory notes structured with profit sharing, corporate stock, limited liability company membership and contracts providing for points participation, where the persons that put up the money are not active in your business, are all securities, and state and federal securities statutes must be satisfied when these types of funding are used. Failure to comply may have serious civil and, in extreme circumstances involving fraud, even criminal consequences.

What does this legal talk mean to you? Why should you have to worry about it if all you want to do is raise some money to record some music or finance a performance tour? The securities laws were enacted to protect investors from being harmed by the fraud of others or by their own lack of sophistication or even their inability to afford to lose the money they invest in the project. The legal burden falls on the one seeking to raise the money to make certain the investors are getting a fair deal and fully understand the risks involved. "Let the seller beware," is the rule that operates.

If you want people to invest money without allowing them a hand in controlling the project, then you should be willing to accept some responsibility to them. Willing or not, state and federal statutes place responsibility on you.

Investment Loans Conditional on the Success of the Venture

In these types of loans, the debt is evidenced by a promissory note and repayment is conditional on the success of the funded project. The note should set out the terms of repayment, including interest rates and payment schedules.

A common form of this kind of loan is a "point" arrangement in which a percentage (points) of sales from the funded project are shared with an investor who puts in only time or with some other investor who puts in only money. Another form is a percent interest in the income (or losses) generated by the business. This arrangement can be provided in a written contract rather than in the form of a conditional promissory note.

Limited Partnerships

Like a general partnership, a limited partnership has co-ownership and shared profits, but only some of the participants are entitled to control or manage the enterprise. Those persons are termed the general partners. The other investors are called limited partners and their only involvement is the passive one of putting funds into the project.

A partner receives that percentage of the business profits or losses set out in the agreement between the partners, for example, 20% of the net profits up to $10,000 and 10% of the net profits after the first $10,000. The term of the limited partnership is often limited to a specified period. If the project has not earned the hoped for return by the end of the term, the investor has to absorb the loss.

There are rules in the federal law and in several states that apply to limited partnerships and other security investments that are structured as private offerings (i.e., to only a small number of people), which are easier to qualify under than the laws regarding public offerings (i.e., to the general public).

Corporate Shares and Limited Liability Company Memberships

Another way to raise investment capital is through the sale of shares in a corporation or memberships in a limited liability company. Corporate shares and limited liability company memberships are securities that usually are sold for a stated number of dollars per share or membership. That money is used to operate the business or pay for a specific project. Shareholders or members own whatever percentage of the corporation or limited liability company their shares represent in relation to the total number of shares sold.

Shareholders or members participate in the profits of the corporation or limited liability company when they are distributed as dividends and vote on shareholder or member issues according to their percentage of ownership.

Whatever method of financing you use, it is wise to check with your lawyer and set up a good financial record keeping system with your bookkeeper.

COMPLYING WITH LEGAL STATUTES

After deciding on the legal structure to use in raising the money for your project, you must make certain that your efforts comply with state and federal law. California statutes require that (unless an exemption applies), the party raising and accepting investment capital must file documents with the Commissioner of Corporations explaining, in part, the proposed investment project, how the money will be used, all of the risks in the venture, the financial ability of the investors and the background of the persons seeking the funding. The commissioner must conclude that the proposed offer and sale is "fair, just and equitable." On an affirmative finding, the commissioner will issue a permit authorizing the sale. A negative conclusion will bar the sale. Most states have statutes imposing similar requirements.

Fundamental in any offering of a security (whether public or nonpublic), is the disclosure, to potential investors, of all the risks involved in the project, including the risk that the project may fail, that no profit may be made, and that the investors may never have their investment returned. In seeking investment money, you must disclose, in writing, the risks, the background of the principals (the people starting and running the business), the nature of the proposed business, the manner in which the money will be used and the way that the investor will share in any profits (or losses). Also, the offer and sale of securities that involves an interstate transaction may require registration of those securities with the Securities and Exchange Commission (SEC) in Washington, DC. Knowledgeable legal counsel should be obtained before seeking to offer any securities.

State Law Exemptions

Under the securities statutes and regulations of most states, there are certain exemptions from the requirement to obtain a permit. These exemptions occur only in very specific situations. Three common exemptions are the nonpublic partnership interest, the limited number of shareholder exemptions for corporations and the nonpublic debt security (note for a loan). In California, a limited partnership interest or other security will be presumed to be a nonpublic offering not requiring a permit from the commissioner provided that (1) there is no advertising of the investment; (2) there are no more than 35 investors contributing to the project; (3) the investor represents that he or she is purchasing the interest for his or her own account and not with the intent to distribute the interest to others; and (4) either the persons investing the money have a preexisting business or personal relationship with you, or their professional financial advisor can reasonably be presumed to have the ability to protect their interests because of the advisor's business experience. Also, a notice detailing information about the investment must be filed with the Commissioner's Office, which office establishes the kind of information that must be presented.

If the financing arrangement is to be in the form of a debt that is secured by a note with payment to the investor to come from the proceeds, if any, of the venture, then the requirements just described must be met to qualify the arrangement as an exempt nonpublic debt offering under California law. However, the investments may not be taken from more than 10 persons. This description is overly simplified and is not intended to be a full explanation of all the nuances and requirements of the security statutes and regulations. Its purpose is merely to give you a sense of how the laws operate.

IDENTIFYING AND EVALUATING SOURCES OF INCOME

If you lack your own money for your project, and do not have the credit necessary to borrow money, then you must face the reality of raising investment capital and complying with the appropriate securities statutes discussed above. Probably the most frustrating aspect of this will be your quest to identify the angel who will give you the money you need. Frequently, investors are attracted by the idea of putting money into entertainment projects because of the mistaken impression that it is a glamorous business and they desire to be associated with the glamour, or they have read that the entertainment industry can generate a substantial amount of money and wish to gamble that they will earn a great return if your project is successful.

For the most part, the money usually comes from family, friends or interested persons that have seen your talents and wish to be involved in developing your potential. If the money does come from family and friends, however, it is critical that you act in a businesslike manner to help preserve your personal relationships.

Unfortunately, there is no magic source of money. It will be up to you to identify who has enough faith in your talents and future to make their money available. Other possible sources of money are investment counselors and accountants that are searching for reasonable business opportunities for their clients. In reviewing proposals for investments, financial advisors analyze the possibilities of eventual return on the investment and the tax benefits, if any, that may be made available to the investors.

Educating Investors About Risk

Once you have identified individuals that are willing to put money into your project, it is very important that you examine their expectations and compare them with your own perspective. It is crucial for you to educate your investors about the risks, the rewards and all the problems and variables that can arise over which you may have little or no control. Investors need to know how much money is required for your project in order to evaluate whether they can afford it. If they have any reservations, you should uncover them. If the reservations cannot be resolved, you should not accept money from them. Spend time talking with them and make certain that you really understand each other and that they are people to whom you want to be committed.

Fair Return/Profit Sharing

In discussing payback, essentially as profit sharing, with the investor, you need to identify and explore three specific areas. What will be the share of the investor's participation? For how long will the investor participate? And from what sources of income will the investor be repaid? The argument that the investor can make, and it is a good one, is that he or she is taking a substantial risk in putting money into your project that could be invested in other ways for a more certain return. As a consequence, the investor will insist on a very healthy return. This is not unreasonable, provided it leaves you with enough to continue your life and career.

Measuring a fair return or profit sharing with the investor is a function of how badly you need the money and how eager the investor is to put money into your project. This will frequently determine how much each side is willing to offer. Investors generally have alternative places to put their money for a good return, and if you have no other source of income for a project, you may not be in a position to do a lot of arguing. If you have to give up an amount that you feel will hurt your business or your ability to fund your career, then you should not accept the money; go look for another investor.

A more constructive way of measuring a reasonable return is to look at the amount of risk assumed by the investor in relation to the amount of money invested; the smaller the number of dollars and the smaller the risk of failure, the smaller the return. For example, if your project cost $2,000 it would be hard to justify returning 10% of your income for life to an investor. A more fair return would be the return of the money plus an additional percentage, e.g., 50%. If however, the investor put $200,000 into your project, it is easy to justify committing a reasonable percentage of your income (e.g., 10% to 15%) to the investor (after out-of-pocket deductions for payments to certain third parties, such as managers and business creditors) for a substantial period of time (e.g., five years to seven years) or until a return of a multiple of the amount of the investment (e.g., two to four times), whichever happens first, at which time the participation stops. If the investment is for a specific project, e.g., a full CD of your recorded musical performances, first dollars in could be used to reimburse the investor, with additional money being split evenly until the investor has gotten two to three times the investment, and thereafter a reduced percentage, e.g., 20% to 25%, to the investor for so long as that recorded project is generating income, without any restrictions in time.

You can determine the proper percentage to offer to an investor by looking at how much you can afford to give up. Remember, there are only so many slices in the money pie, and if you give up too many slices there will be little for you to eat. Consequently, you should identify all of your existing commitments, such as those to managers, attorneys, other investors, partners and the like. After you pay those people, you will still need money to run your business and support your personal needs. You must carefully analyze your income potential and anticipated expenses.

It is important to specify the sources of income from which the investor will be repaid. Will the money be coming from the revenue generated by the project itself or will it be coming from other sources such as record sales, live performances, music publishing, or merchandising? These points must be clearly and carefully thought out before you commit to a participation with an investor.

CONCLUSION

There are no simple answers. Deals can be structured in many ways. Your decisions depend on a business analysis of your funding sources, the urgency of your needs, the risks the investors are taking, their alternative investment possibilities, and your other money commitments. Do your homework and be very careful about the commitments you make. When in doubt, seek advice. If the deal does not make sense or does not feel good to you, trust your instincts and walk away. Do not be pressured into a commitment that may later hinder your career. In any event, be honest with yourself; figure out your goals, your value system and what you are willing and not willing to give up. Only by taking all these factors into account can you arrive at a financial package that will work for you. Once you set up such a package, however, you may be able to accomplish career objectives otherwise beyond your reach.

BUSINESS PLAN OUTLINE

Here are the topics usually covered in business plans. Even if you are not using a business plan to find financing for your project, it will help identify your goals, outline the strengths and weaknesses of your project and help determine when your project will make a profit. In short, a business plan is the map that shows how to get from an idea stage to project completion and profit.

When you want to obtain investment money, the business plan is a vital sales tool that can impress prospective investors with your planning ability and general competence as a manager.

1. Summary of your project, including the money you need to successfully launch it and reach your market.

2. Company description (history, background and management).

3. Description of your background.

4. Description of industry you are operating in.

5. Project description and planning schedule.

6. Description of the market for your project.
    A. Market size
    B. Market trends
    C. Competition

7. Marketing plan.
    A. Estimated sales and market share
    B. Strategy
    C. Pricing
    D. Sales and distribution
    E. Publicity and advertising

8. Operations (If project is a product [i.e., a compact disc or new software], describe how it will be produced, manufactured, marketed and distributed).

9. Project timeline.

10. Critical risks and problems.

11. Financial information.
    A. Financing required
    B. Current financial statements
    C. Financial projection (three-year profit and loss, cash flow and balance sheet projections).

Music Attorneys

BY MARK HALLORAN

Musicians can face myriad legal issues throughout their careers. Only a competent attorney, knowledgeable in the music business, can help a musician effectively solve these problems. The following will discuss music attorneys—who they are, what they do, what they cost, what their obligations are to you and how to best work together.

An attorney (lawyer) is a professional with legal training who is licensed to practice law in a particular state or states. Typically, an attorney must be a college and law school graduate. Full-time law schools have broad-based curriculums that last three years—there are no "majors" in law school. After graduation, the student must pass a state's bar exam. The bar is a state sponsored monopoly—only attorneys can practice law. The traditional professional activities of lawyers fall into roughly four categories: consulting with clients; drafting and negotiating legal documents; representing clients before the courts; and insuring compliance, by clients, with local, state and national laws and contracts (such as union agreements), which govern the client's business activities. For musicians, the most important of these four functions is the lawyer's drafting and negotiating legal agreements.

SPECIALIZATION

Most attorneys specialize. The primary reason for specialization is the ever-increasing complexity of the legal problems that confront the professional and the sophistication and training necessary to apply the correct problem-solving tools. The law is far too complex and fast changing for a lawyer to have adequate competence in all areas. Specialists can do a better job for their clients because of their acquired experience in particular areas, including both legal and business issues.

Due to the growth and complexity of the entertainment field, a legal specialty, called entertainment law, has arisen. Music lawyers are entertainment lawyers who specialize in the legal and business aspects of the music business.

A recent trend is the certification of lawyers that practice a specialty. In California, for example, there are five certified specialties: criminal law, workers' compensation, taxation, patent law, and family law. Entertainment law is not one of the certified specialties. Thus, at this time, there are no state certified music lawyers in California (or elsewhere). This does not mean lawyers cannot specialize in representing music industry clients. They can and do. What distinguishes a music attorney, then, is not certification, but that he or she has experience in solving the problems musicians encounter. It is not necessary for an attorney to specialize exclusively in music to have enough expertise to help you. In fact, only a handful of lawyers (mostly in Los Angeles, New York and Nashville) are exclusively music attorneys.

MUSIC ATTORNEY FUNCTIONS

Recording and publishing agreements can be incredibly complex, and proper negotiating and drafting require superior legal skills and a thorough knowledge of music business practice. This is especially true since recording and publishing agreements can last for many years, and the typical artist's career, at least at the top, is short.

In addition to negotiating and drafting a wide variety of agreements for songwriters, recording artists, record companies, music publishers, record producers, personal managers and music investors, a few select music attorneys solicit deals for their clients by "shopping" (distributing) demo tapes. Over time they develop relationships with people and companies in the industry, and their recommendation of a music client is sometimes influential in obtaining a contract. Most music attorneys, however, do not find deals for their clients. That task is left to the musicians and their managers. The attorney's foremost functions are structuring, negotiating and documenting deals to maximize benefits to their client.

Another important function of the music attorney is to act as a business hub, coordinating the activities of your agent, personal manager and business manager. Because music attorneys deal with these representatives, they develop a working knowledge of their functions in the music industry and help to insure that they act in your best interests.

Music attorneys are sometimes empowered to be attorneys-in-fact for their clients with respect to collecting money. In this regard, they collect and receive monies due you or your companies from all sources, based on your agreements with them. They deposit, into a client trust account, checks and monies payable to you and your companies and deduct any fees for attorney compensation before remitting the remainder.

A music attorney may also provide general career advice, such as you would expect from a personal manager. This can be crucial in the early stages of your career, as it is often difficult to attract competent, experienced personal managers until you are signed to a major label. Some music attorneys also act officially as managers, although this is unusual.

FINDING A MUSIC ATTORNEY

Music attorneys may work alone (sole practitioners), or as part of a law firm. Entertainment divisions of large firms are often divided into two departments: TV/film and music. Generally, the more experienced lawyers (often partners that are owners of the firm), negotiate the big deals, while the nonpartners (associates) negotiate the small ones. Associates also usually do the lion's share of drafting agreements.

In recent years, the large firms have lost many of their clients to smaller "boutique" entertainment law firms, which typically have 10 to 20 lawyers. Many boutique entertainment firms charge either a flat amount or 5% of the dollar value of the deal negotiated, rather than bill on an hourly basis. Although percentage arrangements may be advantageous when you are unable to afford hourly rates, you may end up paying more than the hourly rate. Remember that your income is also diminished by your personal manager (10% to 25%), agent (10%) and your business manager (5%), and then by federal, state and sometimes local income taxes.

Few music lawyers will take clients "on the come" (work free until the client is successful). Attorneys must cover their overhead and the music industry is overcrowded and fiercely competitive. The odds are a music lawyer will never collect delayed fees from an aspiring client.

You should interview a number of lawyers before retaining one. It is important to retain an attorney who specializes in entertainment law and knows how the industry works. A working knowledge of the standard (and nonstandard) contracts is mandatory—attorneys who do not have this knowledge will spend a lot of your money researching or buying time from another entertainment attorney, or even steering you wrong. Do not be afraid to interview a lawyer, but be sure to make your intention clear when making the appointment, and confirm you will not be charged for the time. Be prepared to ask pointed (but not confrontational) questions about the lawyer's music business experience. Do not try to use the interview as a ruse for getting free legal help—that is not fair and will put off the attorney. Talk to successful musicians and managers that can recommend lawyers. The fact that you know someone who has an ongoing relationship with the attorney should help you get in the door.

There are various ways to find a music attorney. Some well-known practitioners, such as John Branca (Aerosmith), Don Passman (Janet Jackson), Lee Phillips (Barbra Streisand) and Alan Grubman (Madonna), command coverage in the music industry press—but they are inundated by potential clients.

Another way to meet music lawyers is to attend music conferences. Prominent music attorneys are often invited to appear at music symposia, and some business relationships are started as a result of meetings at such functions. However, it may not be advisable to retain an attorney who is far beyond your status in the industry, because high-powered music lawyers will first serve their successful clients—if it's your telephone call or Michael Jackson's, their choice is clear!

Lawyer Referral Services

Many lawyer referral services have been established that will discuss problems and refer the caller to an attorney on the service's referral panel. This attorney will interview the referred client for a moderate fee. After the first interview, fee arrangements and the legal services to be rendered are left up to the lawyer and client. Sometimes, fees are split between the referral panel and the lawyer. In California the best-known referral service is California Lawyers for the Arts (CLA). This nonprofit organization, based in San Francisco, is devoted exclusively to the arts. CLA has been authorized by the California State Bar Association to refer clients statewide.

In Los Angeles, you can call the Lawyer Referral Service of the Los Angeles County Bar Association for recommendations. The Beverly Hills Bar Association Committee for the Arts Lawyer Referral and Information Service offers lawyer referrals to those with entertainment-related legal problems. These referral panels only provide you with the name of an attorney, registered with them, who claims to have some experience in your area of concern. The panels do not rate lawyers or guarantee that the attorney will have the skills and experience you need. It should also be noted that the "heavyweights" usually are not on these panels.

If you live outside California, check with your state or local bar association for lawyer referral services.

WHEN TO SEE A MUSIC ATTORNEY

The cardinal rule is—see a lawyer before you sign anything except autographs. In essence, when you sign a contract, you are setting up law with the other party that will govern your relationship. Even though in some instances a lawyer may not be able to negotiate more favorable contract terms for you, at the very least he or she can explain the agreement so you know what you are getting into. Most likely, however, your lawyer can help by negotiating terms more favorable to you. These terms might include higher advances and royalty rates in recording contracts, partial ownership of your copyright and a participation in the publisher's share of revenue in publishing contracts, and perhaps a way to get you released from a contract if it does not work out. You should consult with an attorney when establishing contracts with your other advisors, such as your talent agent, your business manager and especially your personal manager. Do not sign a contract and assume you can get out of it.

Be wary of people that give you form or standard contracts to sign, saying that "everybody accepts these terms." Although standard contracts exist, they are drafted by attorneys that are out to protect their clients' interests, not yours. Odds are that your attorney also has a standard contract—but it's much more favorable to you. The negotiating process consists of each side making specific demands and seeing if the other side will agree. If you retain a lawyer, the other side may give in to at least some of your demands. Together, the opposing lawyers can identify issues and potential problems. The result is a contract that is different from the form contract and more favorable to you.

First Meeting

Your first meeting with an attorney will probably be arranged over the phone or by e-mail. You should be prepared to talk about two things at that meeting: your specific legal needs and your fee arrangement with the attorney.

Fees

Lawyers cost money. Many lawyers cost a lot. Fees can exceed $400 an hour. Nonsuperstar music attorneys normally charge $150 to $300 per hour. The legal fee for negotiating an agreement with a major record company, even by a relatively low-priced attorney, will be $3,000 to $10,000.

Lawyers sell services. They must cover their overhead, which often exceeds 50% of the billing rate, and make a decent profit.

You should realize that in retaining a lawyer you are making a contract, even if your agreement is not written. In return for a fee, your lawyer promises to render legal services on your behalf and both parties should do their best to fulfill their obligations.

It is preferable for the fee agreement to be written. In California, if the bill will likely exceed $1,000, or is based on a percentage, the fee arrangement must be written.

Not all lawyers charge on a per hour basis. Some will charge a set fee, such as $5,000, to negotiate or draft a contract. Others will charge a percentage of the money you receive under contracts they negotiate. This fee generally runs 5% of the deal, although the percentages and structures of these types of arrangements vary greatly. You should check around to see if the fee arrangement proposed by the lawyer is competitive, although price (whether low or high) is not necessarily an accurate indication of the value or quality of the attorney's work. Cautious lawyers will remind you that you have the right to seek the advice of another lawyer as to the propriety of the fee arrangement. Many lawyers will represent you on a percentage basis for negotiating only a specific contract. Additional services, such as tax advice, formation of corporations, etc., will have separate and additional charges.

Lawyers generally ask reimbursement for their out-of-pocket costs, which may include long-distance telephone calls, photocopies, word processing, postage, messenger service, fax, etc. These expenses typically are not considered part of the hourly fee, which only covers the lawyer's services.

Fee Payment

The quickest way to sour your attorney-client relationship is to not pay your bill. Lawyers that bill on an hourly basis will render a monthly statement that sets out the services rendered, date of services, costs, and the total bill. If you cannot pay the bill, at least call to say so and arrange some payment schedule. Some music attorneys will accept partial payment and continue to **work** for you.

In the good old days lawyers rarely sued their clients for nonpayment. Now they are doing so with increasing regularity. In California, you have the right to a fee arbitration if the lawyer's claim exceeds $5,000 (the small claims court limit). The lawyer will send a notice to you, advising you of your right to arbitrate. You must respond within 30 days or lose your arbitration right.

Retainers

Many lawyers require a retainer (initial payment). Most retainers are credited against your bill, but make sure that is your agreement. Thus, if you retain an attorney with $2,500 it is usual for that $2,500 to be credited to your account. These funds are typically held "in trust" for you until your lawyer renders sufficient legal services to earn them. For example, in the first month your attorney negotiates a publishing contract and spends ten hours at $300 an hour doing it. You will get a bill showing $2,500 received and $3,000 for services rendered. Thus, you owe $500 at that point. Some attorneys require that you keep replenishing the retainer. In the foregoing example, you would be billed $3,000 so the retainer would be brought back up to $2,500. Keep a record of all legal bills so you can try to deduct them as business expenses. You should also keep copies of all documents and correspondence.

Conflicts of Interest

In return for the monopoly on practicing law, lawyers are constrained by very special ethical obligations. Like all agents, lawyers have a "fiduciary" obligation to their "principal"—you. The heart of this obligation is that they must act with your best interests as the goal in all situations.

As part of this obligation lawyers have an ethical duty to avoid so-called conflicts of interest. If you think your attorney may be representing conflicting interests you should seriously contemplate retaining a different lawyer. Closely scrutinize the conflict, especially in recording contract situations. The most prevalent conflict of interest occurs when a lawyer concurrently represents multiple clients with potentially adverse interests. For example, assume your attorney represents XYZ Records and XYZ Records wants to sign you to a recording contract. XYZ wants to give you as little as they can; you want as much as you can get. This is a conflict of interest, as your interest and XYZ's interest are opposed to one another, or "adverse."

Under the California Rules of Professional Conduct (3-310), if this type of conflict arises, the lawyer must disclose his or her relationship with the adverse party and obtain both clients' written consent to dual representation. A lawyer cannot represent both parties except with the written consent of all parties concerned. Lawyers violating this rule are subject to discipline by the state bar, as well as malpractice claims by clients whose interests are damaged by the lawyer with the conflict. Similar legal controls are in effect in other states.

A lawyer may represent multiple clients with adverse interests if (1) it is obvious that he or she can adequately represent the interests of each; and (2) each client consents to the representation after full disclosure of the possible effect of such representation on the exercise of the lawyer's independent professional judgment on behalf of each. The conflict of interest situation extends to all members of a law firm. Under the American Bar Association's Code of Professional Responsibility, a lawyer cannot avoid a conflict by referring you to someone else in the firm.

TIPS FOR DEVELOPING A GOOD WORKING RELATIONSHIP WITH YOUR LAWYER

- Remember, your lawyer's time is money. If you are organized in your legal and business affairs, it makes your lawyer's job easier and less expensive for you.
- Keep accurate records and communicate in *writing*. People read faster than they talk and written communications provide records.
- Always be honest with your lawyer. They operate more efficiently on facts than on lies.
- Pay your bills on time.
- Keep your lawyer informed. An ounce of prevention is worth a pound of cure in music business legal affairs.
- Prepare for meetings with your lawyer. Bring all documents that might be useful, such as letters and your calendar.
- Do not sign anything until your lawyer has reviewed it.
- E-mails are usually more efficient than phone calls.

In our previous hypothetical situation, it may be that the attorney for XYZ Records can adequately represent you in your negotiations with XYZ. After discussing the conflict, he or she may present you with what is known as a "conflict" letter. This letter will say: (1) the lawyer informed you of the conflict; (2) it is suggested you seek independent counsel; (3) the agreement is fair to you; (4) you consent to your lawyer's representation of the other party; and (5) you will not claim in the future that your lawyer breached his or her fiduciary duty (trust) to you in regard to the conflict. This letter, at least in theory, protects the attorney from your future claim that you were not fairly represented. The ethical lawyer will act in accordance with the terms of the conflict letter, which you will be asked to sign. You should feel free to have another lawyer look at it.

If the conflict cannot be overcome, you have to get another lawyer. The lawyer with the conflict may suggest specific counsel, or, preferably, provide you with a list of competent lawyers and leave the choice to you. The fact you are referred to another lawyer does not mean the lawyer with the conflict cannot subsequently represent you. He or she just cannot represent you with regard to the conflict situation.

Confidentiality
Your lawyer is under a duty to keep your communications confidential. Frequently, negotiations are secret and it is in your best interest to keep them that way. News can

get out, though, as when the trades note that a particular record company is negotiating with a specific act. Conceivably, this can help you if more than one company is interested in you. Your lawyer can play them one against the other. However, your lawyer needs your consent to leak information.

Changing Lawyers

Although many attorney-client relationships are long lasting, you may find that you want to change attorneys. If you do, you should inform your new attorney of your previous relationship. Your new lawyer cannot simultaneously represent you in a matter that is being handled by another lawyer.

The technical description used by the bar is that you "discharge" your lawyer. By law, a client has an absolute right to discharge an attorney at any time, regardless of the reason. This does not mean that you do not have to pay the discharged lawyer for the services already provided. As an initial step, your new lawyer will want to obtain your previous files. The fact you owe your old lawyer money is irrelevant as far as turning over the files is concerned. Your previous lawyer still has a duty to represent your best interests, which includes turning over the files and cooperating with your new lawyer.

You should note that your attorney can also sever this relationship (except in litigation where court permission is sometimes required), but must avoid prejudicing your rights by giving you notice and time to hire another lawyer. And all your papers and any unearned retainer must be delivered to you.

CONCLUSION

Developing an effective lawyer-musician relationship can be a valuable step in your career. Your decision in selecting an attorney is crucial—it should be an informed decision and should be done as early in your career as possible.

ATTORNEY-CLIENT FEE LETTER AGREEMENT
HOURLY ARRANGEMENT

Dear Client:

It is a pleasure to undertake your representation in connection with the above referenced matter.

We are writing this letter to set forth the basis under which our firm will represent you, your related entities and any other persons or entities that you request us to represent with respect to this matter.

Our fees on all matters will be based on the guidelines set forth in the Rules of Professional Conduct of the State Bar of California. Our hourly rates range between $80 and $350 per hour, depending on which attorney or paralegal performs the work. Fees for services will be charged on a minimum quarter-hourly basis and, when services are rendered outside our office, you will be charged on a portal-to-portal basis. We will be sending you itemized monthly statements, which will be due upon receipt and will include our costs advanced in connection with your representation. Such cost charges include, but are not limited to, messenger service, shipping, postage, copying expenses and telephone charges.

An initial retainer fee in the sum of $_____ is due at the commencement of our representation.★ The retainer will be applied to fees and costs as they are incurred. You will not receive any interest on the retainer, and upon completion of our work, any remaining balance will be either refunded to you or applied toward future legal services rendered by our firm on your behalf. At this time, the services contemplated will encompass representing you in connection with:

(Specific contract or project is outlined here.)

It is the policy of our firm to look to clients jointly and severally regarding any fees incurred either on their behalf or at their direction on behalf of any person, firm or entity for which our clients request we render services. This firm reserves the right to withdraw from this matter at any time should fees and costs not be paid as agreed. In the event it becomes necessary for this firm to take legal action for the collection of fees and costs due, the prevailing party in such action shall be entitled to collect attorneys' fees from the other party.

If the foregoing agrees with your understanding, please execute the enclosed copy of this letter and return it in the envelope provided, together with your check in the sum of $_____ as our retainer, as explained above.

If you have any questions concerning this agreement, please do not hesitate to contact me. Additionally, if at any time you have questions regarding anything relating to our services or fees charged, we encourage you to bring such matters to our attention so that we may discuss and resolve them at once.

We look forward to the opportunity of working with you on this matter.

Yours truly,

★(Optional—We acknowledge receipt of the sum of $_____ and will proceed on your behalf at once.)

PERCENTAGE FEE LETTER AGREEMENT

Dear Client:

This letter will confirm our agreement with you whereby we agree to render our services as your attorneys in connection with your professional career.

You engage us during the period of this agreement as your attorneys and will cause any companies connected with your professional career in which you have any controlling interest to engage us as their attorneys in connection with all legal matters pertaining to your professional career in the entertainment industry. The term of this agreement shall commence on the date hereof, and shall continue until terminated by either of us by written notice, which shall be personally delivered, sent by facsimile, or mailed by certified or registered mail, postage prepaid, to the respective address set forth on this page (or to such other address as either of us may notify the other of). No termination shall affect our right to be paid our percentage fee described below.

For our services to be rendered during the term of this agreement you and each of your companies (but not both regarding the same gross consideration) will pay us as and when received by you or such companies, respectively, beginning as of the date hereof, five percent (5%) of all gross consideration (including salaries, bonuses, percentages, commissions, royalties, profit shares, stock interests, and all other forms of compensation of any nature and from any source), prior to any withholding or deductions, earned, accrued, paid or payable (directly or indirectly) to you or your companies from and after the date hereof, for your services or the services of such companies in connection with any facet of your professional career in the entertainment industry rendered during the term hereof, or for such services rendered by you or such companies pursuant to any agreement (oral or written) (and any extensions, renewals, substitutions, or resumptions thereof) substantially negotiated or entered into during the term hereof (irrespective of when such services under such agreement were or are to be rendered), whether such gross consideration is received by you or your companies (or any third party on your or their behalf) during or after the term hereof.

Notwithstanding anything in the preceding paragraph to the contrary, the aforesaid percentage shall be ten percent (10%) (not five percent [5%]) with respect to gross consideration as defined above that is not subject to being commissioned by a licensed artist's manager (commonly referred to as an "agent"). Our additional compensation with respect to such uncommissioned gross consideration arises out of situations where no licensed artist's manager is involved, resulting in greater responsibility on our part in connection with the negotiations in connection therewith. There shall be no inference from this increase that we in any way agree to seek personal employment for you.

The services that we shall be expected to render in return for the above compensation shall include reviewing, drafting, modifying, negotiating and otherwise assisting you in connection with all agreements, contracts or other legal matters in connection with your professional career in the entertainment industry, and consulting with you and advising you regarding all other legal aspects of your professional career in the entertainment industry; but the services we shall be expected to render in return for the above compensation shall not include matters that involve litigation, arbitration or other contested proceedings, planning or the preparation of tax returns, preparation or administration of pension or profit sharing plans, or matters pertaining to your personal life or other businesses as opposed to your professional career.

You understand, of course, if we represent you in any such matter involving litigation, arbitration or other contested proceedings, the preparation or administration of profit sharing plans, or matters pertaining to your personal life or other businesses, as opposed to your professional career, we shall be paid an additional reasonable fee for such services, to be agreed upon between us, and costs reasonably incurred in connection therewith.

You are hereby authorizing us and empower us, and appoint us as your attorneys-in-fact and as attorneys-in-fact for your companies to collect and receive all monies due you or your companies from all sources relating to this agreement, to negotiate and endorse your (or your companies') name(s) upon and deposit into our clients' trust account all checks and other monies payable to you or your companies, to deduct therefrom our compensation as set forth above, together with any costs advanced by us and to remit the remainder to you or your companies as the case may be.

The terms "you" and "your," as used herein, shall refer to you or any firm, partnership, corporation or other entity owned or controlled by you.

If the foregoing meets with your approval, please sign and return the original and one copy of this letter; the other copy is for your files.

Inasmuch as this letter constitutes an agreement between us, we cannot, of course, advise you concerning it, and we suggest that you retain outside counsel to advise you concerning this agreement.

Yours truly,

ATTORNEY CONFLICT OF INTEREST
WAIVER LETTER

Dear Attorney:

We understand that you have been representing and continue to represent each of us in connection with a variety of matters. We also understand that you have and may in the future represent one of us in matters involving the other and in which the other has been or will be represented by his own counsel.

We would like your firm to represent us in connection with the following matters: (Description of project/contract, etc.)

In connection with the above, you have advised us of the following terms of the provisions of Section 3-310 of the California State Rules of Professional Conduct:★

"(A) If a member has or had a relationship with another party interested in the representation, or has an interest in its subject matter, the member shall not accept or continue such representation without all affected clients' informed written consent."

"(B) A member shall not concurrently represent clients whose interests conflict, except with their informed written consent."

You have also advised us of the following provisions of California Evidence Code Section 962 relating to the attorney-client privilege:

"Where two or more clients have retained or consulted a lawyer upon a matter of common interest, none of them, nor the successor in interest of any of them, may claim a privilege under this article as to a communication made in the course of that relationship when such communication is offered in a civil proceeding between one of such clients (or his successor in interest) and another of such clients (or his successor in interest)."

Notwithstanding such joint representation and any actual or potential conflict of interest, we hereby request that you represent both of us in connection with the aforesaid matters and consent to such representation. Furthermore, we acknowledge and agree that at no time will your representation of us be construed, claimed or deemed to be a breach of a fiduciary relationship, a conflict of interest or a violation of any other obligation to either of us. We each agree that at no time shall we claim or contend that you should be or are disqualified from representing either of us in connection with said matter or any other matter, related or unrelated.

Yours truly,

★(These are similar to other states' rules of professional conduct.)

Mediation for Musicians

BY MADELEINE E. SELTZER

Inherent in any agreement is the possibility of disagreement. When the relationship between a musician or composer and his or her manager, agent, record company, producer, etc., breaks down, or a dispute arises, it may be advisable to consider mediation as a means of resolving the problem. Mediation is usually superior to the traditional manner of settling disputes in our society—litigation in the courts—for a variety of reasons. It is particularly well-suited for resolving disputes involving musicians and composers because of its unique characteristics and should be considered before other options are pursued.

GENERAL PRINCIPLES

Mediation is a form of alternative dispute resolution (resolving disagreements outside of the court system). It differs from other alternative dispute resolution methods in that the parties themselves craft their own settlement. Ideally, mediation removes the adversary structure of the conflict in which only one party comes out the winner. Instead of a judge or arbitrator imposing a decision, a neutral third party, the mediator, assists them in the process of determining solutions. Because the parties deal directly with each other, set their own agenda, and work out their own resolution, mediation allows them to explore their relationship and the difficulties that led to their conflicts and helps them to reach creative solutions.

Mediation has other attractive features. First, it is low risk because it is voluntary and nonbinding. If it does not result in a mutually agreeable settlement of the dispute, the parties are free to pursue other courses of action, including litigation. Second, it is flexible, adaptable and applicable to almost any kind of dispute; it can be utilized at any stage of a conflict; and the parties can choose any available mediator. Third, it is informal—there are few structural or substantive rules such as rules of evidence or procedure, or legal precedents that must be followed. Finally, it is cost-effective—legal fees are minimized, and mediation takes much less time to conclude than other methods of dispute resolution. Also, the nonadversarial and cooperative nature of mediation helps avoid the costs associated with the damage or destruction of the business relationship, enabling it to continue profitably. In addition, the emotional costs of litigation are avoided; agreements arrived at through mediation are usually quite durable, thereby minimizing the possibility of future disputes.

HOW MEDIATION WORKS

Mediation may involve two individuals, several individuals, or even groups, and one mediator or two comediators. Mediators try to facilitate discussion among the parties and create an environment that allows them to communicate effectively, express their grievances and discover their own road to settlement of their conflict. The mediator may also help by articulating a potential agreement that the parties are close to reaching: that is, the mediator may help to draft an agreement that fairly, fully and specifically incorporates the parties' intentions.

The mediation process is quite simple. It usually begins with each party giving his or her account of the situation that led to the mediation. Then, with the help of the mediator, the parties set an agenda as to how they want the mediation to proceed. Issues are narrowed, and with the use of various devices employed by the mediator, such as private meetings with the individual parties (caucusing), the resolution process begins. The goal is to reach a written agreement as to some, if not all, of the matters in dispute. Such agreements are usually enforceable as contracts in courts of law.

In order to encourage free and uninhibited dialogue among the parties, it is imperative that all oral and written information presented in a mediation be treated as confidential. Therefore, the parties are encouraged to enter into a confidentiality agreement before the commencement of the mediation to ensure that the information provided will not be used in a subsequent legal proceeding. Some states, such as California, Colorado and Virginia have enacted legislation ensuring confidentiality. For example,

ARTS ARBITRATION AND MEDIATION SERVICES: A MODEL PROGRAM

The California Lawyers for the Arts (CLA), a non-profit organization that has served and promoted the interests of artists, including musicians and composers, in California for many years, established Arts Arbitration and Mediation Services (AAMS) in 1980. It was the first program in the country to offer alternative dispute resolution services to artists and it has served as a model for similar services in other states. These programs are now part of Arts Resolution Services, a national mediation program for the arts. The national hotline number is 1-800-526-8252.

Since its inception, AAMS has resolved over 1100 cases with the help of a panel of specially trained volunteer mediators and arbitrators whose backgrounds include the arts, the music industry, law, and business. According to a spokesperson for the Southern California office of CLA, many of the disputes involve musicians and composers and include such issues as copyright, royalties, personality conflicts, negotiating collaborations, contracts and payment for work. The majority of these matters are resolved to the satisfaction of all the parties.

according to California Code, "Evidence of anything said or of any admission made in the course of the mediation is not admissible in evidence or subject to discovery, and disclosure of this evidence shall not be compelled, in any action or proceeding in which, pursuant to law, testimony can be compelled to be given." This rule also applies to documents. In addition, the statute pronounces that, "When persons agree to conduct or participate in mediation for the sole purpose of compromising, settling, or resolving a dispute . . . all communications, negotiations, or settlement discussions by and between participants or mediators in the mediation shall remain confidential."

Because of all of the advantages of mediation described here, it is advisable that mediation clauses be included in standard agreements. By so doing, the parties will be required to employ mediation before other methods of dispute resolution are used.

MEDIATION: A PROCESS OF BEST RESORT

There is often an emotional undercurrent in disputes that involve musicians and composers, particularly when their work is at issue. These issues may include the content of the work; credit for work performed; and the factors that contributed to the production of the work. Mediation allows for the airing of feelings and enables the intangible and even irrational elements of a situation to be given as much weight as the tangible and rational. Rules of law and other external standards such as the market value of the services or work produced need not control the result in a mediation. The parties create their own rules to fashion their own particular resolution. The musician or composer retains the power that he or she may have historically relinquished to other representatives or lawyers. This gives them dignity and a sense of control that they may not otherwise have. Unlike judges and arbitrators whose function is to impose their will and decide the matter, the mediator is there to facilitate the process. If the parties have not entered into a written contract it makes the enforcement of their rights and obligations very difficult using traditional means and the relatively inexpensive cost of mediation makes it an extremely attractive alternative to litigation. Finally, since mediation tends to preserve rather than destroy relationships, it is preferable to other forms of dispute resolution.

Protect Your Copyrights:
Do Lunch *AND* Contracts

BY KATHLEEN G. WILLIAMSON

"Moviemakers do lunch, not contracts."

With this statement, a California judge summed up his frustration with the entertainment industry's practice of verbal agreements that deal with copyright protected works. He added, "Common sense tells us that agreements should routinely be put in writing." This chapter explains why and how you should protect your copyright interests by using written contracts. A few illustrative and interesting court cases are found at the end of the chapter.

Much of the entertainment industry is built on social relationships. At best, participants prefer to present themselves as groovy and trusting and do not want to blow deals by seeming uptight or waiting for written contracts. Asking for an agreement in writing can seem socially awkward. It may be perceived as uncool or a symptom of mistrust. Hence, the discussion about fine-tuning and memorializing agreements gets postponed indefinitely or is completely avoided. However, an implied contract is usually not any more helpful to you than an implied lunch.

Do not buy into those appearances and assumptions. Adopt a professional attitude and expect the same from others. A written agreement does not have to be an elaborate legal document. The guidance of a lawyer is always preferable, but if you cannot afford one, simply write down the terms of the agreement as the discussion happens. Then ask the other side to read it and clarify or correct it. Signatures of both sides are preferable, but even a short memo or letter outlining the agreement and delivered within a reasonable time after the agreement is reached and before the work begins can suffice to protect you. The sending party should keep a copy for his or her records. At a minimum, this writing will serve as a reminder if memories falter, promises are broken or as evidence of the agreement in court. First class mail is acceptable in court but a signature on a return receipt is better.

A contract is *any* situation in which somebody offers X in exchange for Y (what is called "consideration" in legal parlance), whether it is money or trade. By the time a label or big agency signs you or your band, you will already have committed yourself to scores of contracts and legal relationships. Contractual relations and questions extend even to your band members: you enter into business relationships as you create the band (a business joint venture and legal identity), the distinguishing name and logos (protected under trademarks), and the musical works and recordings (protected under copyrights) that constitute your band's substance. If you do not clarify and write down your understandings, you may fight later over who gets to use the band name and who really wrote the songs or arrangements.

There are perils specific to copyrights when agreements are not clarified and committed to writing. Your career and economic future depends on the quality of your artistic work and the protection of your copyrights. It is a relatively small thing to not get paid what you orally agreed upon for the gig you did last Friday night. It is a bigger deal, however, to realize that you unintentionally transferred rights to your musical creations without adequate compensation and reduced your future earnings or ability to license your work to others.

Here is an example scenario that you want to avoid. You and a television producer make a fast deal over a good-humored lunch. The agreement is that you will compose something (maybe an entire soundtrack, a song, hero's theme or musical cues) that will be used for what you think is a limited purpose, for example, 10 episodes of a show. You agree on what you think is a fair price based on the amount of your time, talent and what you think the boss will gross for the ten shows. You deliver the work, add it to your resume, get paid and that is the end of the story, right? Nope.

What if the show becomes an international cult success and airs for five more years, is syndicated and broadcasted repeatedly, your music is reproduced in millions of CDs, DVDs, downloads, ringtones, and there is talk of a major motion picture? Are you getting paid for any of this? It depends: if you do not intend to sell that much of your future copyrights when you sell your music, it is important to get it in writing.

A professional or aspiring professional musician or songwriter should have legal counsel in addition to the many services they already purchase, such as Web design, graphic design and recording engineering. Get, at least, a minimal amount of help with contracts. However, for the starving artist who does it all, educate yourself as best as you can with books like this and carefully write out your agreements in confirmation letters or contracts. If you do not, the entity that commissions your music may get to gobble up future profits from the use of your creativity, while you are still starving.

TYPICAL REASONS TO WRITE A CONTRACT

Most contracts, such as performance contracts, which will not take over a year to complete, are enforceable whether they are written or not. This is true especially if one or both parties relied and acted on the promises made.

However, written contracts are extremely helpful for remembering and enforcing the specific terms of agreements. There is a cultural admiration for handshake agreements between people who possess such high degrees of memory, mental clarity and integrity that promises need not be written. With oral contracts, however, the parties have a much harder time convincing a judge that theirs is the accurate or truthful version. Memories can get cloudy, even those of honest and well-intentioned parties.

Even the best of such agreements can suffer legal battles, such as those occasioned by future third parties or unforeseen technologies. Unlike real property, intellectual property has a chameleon-like life. It changes form and potential as new technologies and uses develop or as new parties exploit or adapt it, thus opening new avenues of litigation. A good contract can help to ensure payment for your work in a changing world.

Written contracts are common between the big players when long-term projects are involved (such as record and publishing deals), but handshake contracts involving artistic services still happen too often. This is true whether it is between people just starting a band, midlevel record producers stealing the musical ideas of contributing recording artists, radio stations buying jingles or major television shows that exploit musical creations for years.

Even if you finally win your case in court or settle out of court, you do not want the expense and stress of litigation when a written memo could have protected you and ensured a quick resolution to a dispute. Jefferson Airplane, John Fogarty and others had disputes that wound up in courts for decades. Unlike them, however, you cannot afford attorneys for that amount of time and, because of that, most musicians lose before a battle has even been waged.

It is important to commit contracts to writing at the earliest stages of the business relationship in order to (1) avoid uncertainties over what the court will interpret after a dispute arises; (2) know the copyright status and respective rights for which the parties bargained; and (3) to avoid unnecessary and costly lawyer fees and the stresses of litigation.

INTELLECTUAL PROPERTY OWNERSHIP AND TRANSFERS

Creative expressions involve two basic realities: the long life of intellectual property rights (life of the author plus 70 years) and the unforeseeability of its value, which is whether the work will enjoy economic success and, if so, when, how, to what degree and for how long.

You should guard your intellectual property as you would your real or personal property: your home, land or any significant investment. As an analogy, real property involves your ownership and right to the exclusive use of the home you own. You have a bundle of rights as the owner; you decide whether to rent or sell all or some of it; use it exclusively or share it; and you can kick people out for trespassing and sue or prosecute them for stealing or damaging it. If you rent property, you can negotiate for exclusive or nonexclusive use of it or to sublease it.

Think of intellectual property in the same way. Once you have put your creative idea in some "fixed," e.g., recorded or written form, you, the "author" in copyright law, automatically become the owner of *all* the copyrights. These include the rights to reproduce, distribute, perform and adapt the work (what is referred to as a derivative work). If you created it alone, you own these rights exclusively. If you cocreated it, you share these rights with the other authors, unless you have a written contract stating otherwise. The status of any contributions should be made clear in writing.

You can sell some or all of these rights or you can rent them by what the law calls "licensing" to another party to use them either exclusively or nonexclusively with yourself or others. You can limit the rights you license or sell to a certain duration or region. On the other hand, you may want to license or buy rights from other musicians, such as a compulsory or synchronization license to record someone else's song for your album, concert DVD, or to license some music segment for sampling. The copyright ownership or various exclusive rights can also be bought outright at any time, provided it is in writing.

WORKS FOR HIRE

Sometimes a work is owned, at its inception, by a person or corporation other than the artist if it falls under the work-for-hire category. Under the Copyright Act, one type of work for hire is a work prepared by an employee if the work was done within the scope of the employment and the parties *have not agreed otherwise in writing.*

Congress did not define "employ" or "employment," which has resulted in a body of case law involving a wide variety of explicit and implicit work-for-hire relationships. An employee is thus defined by the courts under the common law rules of agency and on a case-by-case basis. A second type of work-for-hire transfer of copyright ownership is achieved by commissioning a work. This can only happen *if the parties agree in writing* and the work falls under the specific list of purposes listed in the Act. Copyright ownership of a work for hire is presumed to vest in the employer or commissioner of the work. Generally, the rules of thumb for work-for-hire copyright transfers are (1) writing prevents automatic transfer of employees' copyrights to the employers; but (2) a writing is required in order to transfer the copyright ownership to the person commissioning certain types of listed works.

For our purposes here, it is important to know that work-for-hire copyright ownership can be transferred for commissions that are audiovisual works but, to dispel a common studio myth, not works that are solely audio works, or what the copyright statute calls "phonorecords" or "sound recordings." Technically, one cannot legally achieve work-for-hire status from contracted or commissioned musicians for audio works, even with a writing.

TRANSFERRING LICENSES TO USE THE WORK

An exclusive or nonexclusive license to use the work may be used instead of an attempted work-for-hire agreement but should be put to writing, along with other terms and conditions, by the producer and the musician.

The Copyright Act specifically requires that a transfer of an exclusive license be in writing because exclusive licenses are defined as a form of copyright ownership and are freely transferable. A nonexclusive license, however, is not required to be committed to writing. Unlike ownership, unless limited to a shorter term in writing, any licenses, exclusive or nonexclusive, may be terminated by the author or the heirs but not before a 35-year period expires.

IF YOU DO NOT WRITE IT, THE COURT WILL

Under the Copyright Act, only nonexclusive licenses can be transferred without a writing, and as the *Xena* case shows (see page 54), the court may rule that such a right was implied by the parties' contractual type of behavior when a writing is not accomplished. If there is no writing, the court may find an implied nonexclusive license, which has become the default method for the courts to allow another to use your work without limits and in all mediums, invented or not yet invented, with no further payments to you.

Work-for-hire status is often one of the arguments made in oral contract copyright cases. The facts for these two doctrines, work for hire and implied nonexclusive licenses, usually overlap. The court often finds that there was a nonexclusive implied license when a work-for-hire argument is rejected or vice versa. The Copyright Act's work-for-hire section 204(a) writing requirement does not apply to nonexclusive licenses because they are considered to be personal property interests and therefore may be granted without a written contract and may be implied by the contractual type of behavior between the parties. Before the 1976 Copyright Act, it was work-for-hire transfers that did not require a writing and the courts would create an "implied work-for-hire" transfer of ownership when the parties did not write down their agreement.

Since the 1976 Act, however, the only nonemployee transfer of a copyright interest that does not require writing is the nonexclusive license.

Thus, the "implied nonexclusive license" is the current court remedy to transfer usage of intellectual property without a written contract.

Importantly, the courts have given the implied nonexclusive license a broad scope. If supported by consideration, i.e., sufficient payment or trade as is required for any contract, the oral contract may be interpreted as the transfer of the nonexclusive use of all the types of copyright and may be irrevocable. An implied nonexclusive license may grant much more than the copyright owner intended to convey or would have conveyed if he or she had put their intentions in writing.

By contrast, in a negotiated and properly drafted agreement, the scope of an exclusive or nonexclusive license can be limited to a territory, particular use, duration or quantity, and it can be made nontransferable.

CONCLUSION

The practical results of the case law for the people in the fast moving entertainment industry can be perplexing. The bottom line is simply to be fair and get an agreement in writing as early as possible.

Your basic, everyday negotiations do not require a highly technical expensive document and neither does the Copyright Act. A written contract can be a brief signed memo outlining the basic understandings with little formality. For example—

> Dear So and So,
>
> I have listed below what we agreed to at lunch yesterday. If you need to correct or add anything please do so and send this back to me as soon as possible. If you are in agreement, please countersign and send one copy back to me before the work is scheduled to begin.

The extent to which the parties do or do not want to convey copyright ownership or licenses should be in writing. At a minimum, there will be some written evidence that will outlast the other party's shaky memory. Spell things out in detail as best as you can. If you want to reserve any rights, list them. Perhaps, for example, you want to have the option to use your work in different or future technologies. Failure to limit your transfer could make it completely unconditional.

When a contract is complex or copyrights are involved, it is preferable to get the advice of a lawyer. Many states, especially those with sizeable entertainment industries, have pro bono or reduced fee legal help available through their state bar organizations. New York, California and other states also have excellent Volunteer Lawyer-for-the-Arts nonprofit organizations (e.g., *www.vlany.org*). Find out about them and use them. You can benefit greatly by going to *www.copyright.gov* and reading the Copyright Act yourself. It is downloadable and you can quickly search for keywords. It is a lot to digest, but knowing about copyright law will prevent a lot of heartburn and result in more money for celebratory dinners.

Remember that no matter who prevails in litigation that could have been avoided by using written contracts, very few are real winners after so much stress, project delay and expenses for court costs and attorneys' fees.

HOW THE COURTS DEAL WITH THE PROBLEMS OF UNWRITTEN COPYRIGHT AGREEMENTS

The Xena TV Cues/Music Case
Kolton v. Universal Studios, Inc.

Joseph LoDuca owns a business that composes music for movies, commercials and other audiovisual productions. The plaintiff, Dan Kolton, was employed there from 1993 to 1999 to compose musical cues for television shows, specifically the popular *Xena* and *Hercules* episodes. *There were no written contracts between Kolton and LoDuca.* Kolton earned cumulatively over $300,000 for his work during this six-year relationship with LoDuca. The television and cable network companies, that Kolton also sued, bought the soundtracks from LoDuca by using a written work-for-hire agreement to get the copyrights from LoDuca. *Xena* was a huge success and the shows spawned ongoing reruns, as well as the sale of videos, DVDs and CD soundtracks (and, later, ringtones!). During the initial TV showings, Kolton was aware that his contributions were nationally broadcasted with sole credits to LoDuca as composer. Kolton did not object but did seek royalties in two failed renegotiations with LoDuca. Kolton eventually quit after five seasons and sued for copyright infringement. He asserted that the intent of the oral agreement was for an exclusive license of his music limited to the first run of *Xena* and *Hercules* episodes. However, the Copyright Act requires that an exclusive license be in writing. The *Kolton* court decided there was an implied nonexclusive license, because of the following unwritten but contractual type of conduct by the parties: (1) there was adequate consideration in return for the plaintiff's delivery of music; (2) the plaintiff had knowledge that LoDuca was receiving full screen credits; and (3) the plaintiff never rescinded his contract or withdrew his consent to use the music during the five-year period he was working and being paid. During that time, the plaintiff did not complain of copyright infringement, did not demand screen credits or claim any copyright interest. The court specified that the two radical actions taken by Kolton, which were quitting his employment and filing a lawsuit, did not act as rescissions or terminations of his implied license to allow the use of the works.

The court found another bone to pick. Kolton argued that even if an implied nonexclusive license did exist, the defendants went beyond its limits when they published the work on cable networks and on DVD. Regardless of Kolton's stated intent to convey a limited use of the compositions, the court further diminished Kolton's copyrights and value by ruling that the implied nonexclusive license to the works was irrevocable, unlimited in scope and was applicable to the new media technologies. The court ruled that the nonexclusive license conveyed all the rights of copyright ownership, including unrestricted performance rights, rights to copy and distribute for sale and rights to prepare derivative works. The court basically granted unlimited scope of the license. In cases of written contracts, courts are known to scrutinize the scope of licenses, especially where future technologies and uses are concerned. Regardless, the court found that Kolton's unwritten contract with LoDuca permitted the use of any rights consistent with copyright ownership, including making and distributing copies of Kolton's musical cues and compositions in any medium or new formats.

If you ever think you would prefer to have the court write your contract for you, think again. You cannot rely on courts to protect interests you did not bother to protect for yourself.

Lulirama: Jingles
Lulirama Ltd. v. Axcess Broadcast Services

The plaintiff, Lulirama Ltd., Inc., was hired by Axcess Broadcast Services, Inc. to create jingles for radio and, potentially, television ads. The parties had written and signed a work-for-hire agreement. A dispute arose; Lulirama quit, and forbade any further use of the jingles. The defendant, the hiring party, used the jingles anyway. Lulirama sued for infringement.

The court rejected the defense argument that Axcess owned the copyrights pursuant to a written and signed work-for-hire contract. The court reasoned that up to the date of its writing, the jingles were only used for radio, or auditory purposes; therefore, the use did not fall under the audiovisual works classification listed under section 101 of the Copyright Act's definition for commissioned works for hire. That requires that in order for sound recordings to be commissioned as works for hire, they must be "part of a motion picture or other audiovisual work." The jingles were just music, so the court had to find another basis to allow the defendants' ongoing use of the compositions. Since the work-for-hire agreement was invalid, the court looked to the parties' behavior as if there was no written contract and tried to enforce what it thought the parties intended to exchange with each other. The court found that the parties conducted themselves consistent with an implied nonexclusive license. (Remember, the court cannot create an implied exclusive license, since an exclusive copyright license must be in writing under the copyright statute. The court cannot ignore the requirements of the statute.) Interestingly, the Lulirama court explicitly gave the implied license an unlimited scope because that is what the defendants would have had if the work-for-hire agreement had been valid. The court did try to give the parties what they originally intended to convey to each other. It is easier for a judge to define the scope of a license or intent of the parties if they put it in writing, even with the wrong name for the agreement.

Ulloa Case: The Spontaneous Contribution at the Recording Studio
Ulloa v. Universal Music & Video Distrib. Corp.

This is another case involving a failure to write any agreement. Here, the plaintiff/artist had a good claim for copyright infringement. The court, looking to the behavior of the parties, refused to benefit the defendant/record producer and refused to give him an implied nonexclusive license.

In 2001, Demme Ulloa was invited to a recording session where she spontaneously composed and recorded a significant vocal countermelody to the main hook of a major industry recording for defendants Universal Music and Video Distribution Corp., Island Def Jam Music Group, Roc-Λ-Fella Records, LLC, and Shawn Carter (aka Jay Z). Over the course of that day's discussions with the producers, Ms. Ulloa made it clear that she would like credits and perhaps an appearance on a music video if her contribution was used. Ulloa attempted on several more occasions to negotiate these terms for the use of her work but was either ignored or told that the recording was not going to be used. Ultimately, the song was released with her compositional contribution and vocal recording on it. At one point, because she was repeatedly ignored, Ulloa attempted to

CONTINUED ON NEXT PAGE

CONTINUED FROM PREVIOUS PAGE

communicate with the producers through the American Federation of Television and Radio Artists (AFTRA), a national labor union that resolves disputes. The AFTRA also contacted and requested payment from the producers to no avail. Finally, after several communications from an attorney, the producers sent a minimal check to the AFTRA. Ulloa returned the check and filed suit.

Because the defendants withheld taxes on the check to the AFTRA, they tried to raise a frivolous work-for-hire employment defense, which was rejected by the court. The defendants then argued that Ms. Ulloa gave them an implied nonexclusive license in the hopes that they would get all of the unlimited uses discussed in such cases as *Kolton* and *Lulirama* (above).

The court ruled, however, that an implied license will only be found where a party created a work at another's request and delivered it with the intention that it would be copied and distributed by the other. Clearly, those were the intentions of both musicians, Lulirama and Kolton, when they composed their works.

Furthermore, the *Ulloa* court ruled that even if there was an implied license, the plaintiff revoked it prior to filing a lawsuit. In the *Kolton* case, the plaintiff did nothing to revoke his implied license to LoDuca. This makes sense when you remember that where the contract is not in writing, the court will look to the parties' conduct in the exchange to determine who will get what copyrights or licenses. Kolton, the Xena cues composer, was paid $300,000 and Ms. Ulloa was blatantly ripped off.

Ulloa subjected the music producer to the possibility that the platinum-certified album could be pulled from retail sale and her contribution deleted from a remanufactured and redistributed version. The costs to the label (and artist/producer who has to recoup before being paid!) would have been astronomical. After the court denied summary judgment against the defendants, the parties reached a settlement instead of taking it to trial, definitely for a lot more than what Ulloa originally requested. Most artists, however, would not have had Ulloa's tenacity or resources to litigate so strenuously, a fact upon which the producers and distributors relied to their detriment. Since most musicians are often also indie music producers, the *Ulloa* case shows us that it is a good idea to be fair and get your agreements in writing no matter what task you are trying to accomplish and whether you are attempting to obtain, convey or reserve any copyright interests.

Protecting
Your Compositions

COPYRIGHTS: THE LAW AND YOU

COPYRIGHT INFRINGEMENT

SAMPLING

COLLABORATOR/SONGWRITER AGREEMENTS

DIGITAL DOWNLOADS AND STREAMING: COPYRIGHT AND DISTRIBUTION ISSUES

INTERNATIONAL COPYRIGHT

Copyrights: The Law and You

BY MARK HALLORAN

$\mathbf{A}$ copyright is a property right, comprised of a set of legally enforceable privileges, granted for a limited term by law to creators of artistic works such as songs and recordings. These privileges ("exclusive rights") vary depending on the type of creation. The most important of these exclusive rights to musicians are the exclusive right to make and sell copies of the creation and the exclusive right to publicly perform it. Copyright owners make money by selling or licensing these rights to others or by exploiting the rights themselves. Copyright law is based on the public policy, as stated in the U.S. Constitution, that the law should promote the creation of artistic works.

Although the copyright law recognizes that artistic creations ("works") other than music are copyrightable, the most important artistic creation for a musician is what the law terms a "musical work," that is, a musical composition such as a song or instrumental piece. For simplicity's sake, we will refer to a musical work as a "song." The other important work is a "sound recording" (i.e., the recording of the song).

Two prerequisites must be met before a song can be protected by copyright. The song must be original to the author and fixed in a tangible medium of expression. "Original" means that you yourself created the work (rather than copied it). "Fixed in a tangible medium of expression" means you put your song on paper, tape or any other medium from which it can be perceived either directly or with the aid of a machine or device (such as a CD player) for more than a very short period of time. Singing a song in a club does not fix that song for you to have a copyright in it. However, once you have recorded a demo or written a lead

THE BUNDLE OF RIGHTS COMPRISING A COPYRIGHT

The U.S. Copyright Act gives copyright owners the right to control the use of their compositions in the following ways:

- Reproduction of the work in copies or phonorecords

- Distribution of the work for sale to the public

- Public performance of the work

- The creation of derivative works based upon the copyrighted work

- Display of the work in printed form, such as sheet music

sheet, the song is fixed. Copyright law terms you the "author" of the song, and you are the initial owner of the copyright in the song.

The recording of a song is called a "sound recording." Sound recordings have separate copyrights from songs, as discussed below.

Arrangements of copyrighted material may be copyrighted only when made by the owner(s) of the copyright or with their consent.

If you cowrite a song with the intention of making an inseparable whole, you have created a "joint work." Unless you agree otherwise, the writers own the song prorata (e.g., if two writers, the split is fifty-fifty; three writers, one-third each). The issues peculiar to joint works are discussed in the chapter, "Collaborator/Songwriter Agreements."

Ideas are not copyrightable. The originators of rap could not copyright one rap song and then say that everyone is forbidden to write rap songs. Only the expression of the idea, that is, what has been put on paper, disc or tape, is protected. Thus, you are free to write a rap song even if you did not originate the rap mode. You cannot, however, steal a previous rap song note for note, beat for beat and word for word, without opening yourself to legal liability.

Song titles are not copyrightable, as they do not possess sufficient expressive content. However, this does not mean you could write a new song and entitle it "Like a Rolling Stone" with total impunity. The owners of "Like a Rolling Stone" may have legal recourse, but this recourse is under laws other than copyright law.

PUBLIC DOMAIN SONGS

Not all songs are protected by copyright. Songs whose copyright terms have lapsed fall into the "public domain"; the public owns them. You are free to use a song in the public domain in any way you choose. Many new songs take material liberally from the public domain.

New material added to public domain songs makes these compositions eligible for copyright to the extent new material is added—the public domain portion is not resurrected to copyright status. New material includes new lyrics, changes in melodies, arrangements, and compilations of versions of the same song. In the copyright form PA, line 5, "Previous Registration" and line 6, "Derivative Work or Compilation" ask you to furnish pertinent information regarding any public domain work upon which you may base your song.

New copyrights based on public domain material make it possible for writers and publishers to receive performance monies and mechanical license fees from record companies.

If you are unsure as to whether a song is public domain, you can have the Copyright Office or a private search service check the copyright status. The Copyright Office charges $150 per hour (and normally takes six weeks to do a search). Private services may charge on a sliding scale but are quicker than the Copyright Office.

For information on copyright searches, you can call the Reference and Bibliography Section of the Copyright Office or search the Copyright Office Web site.

You should be aware that even if a song or recording is in the public domain in the United States, it may still be protected by copyright overseas. To be used worldwide without permission, a public domain song must be cleared worldwide.

You can call ASCAP or BMI to determine the publisher of a song, or search their Web sites. CD labels typically list songwriters and publishers, as well as the record company that owns the recording.

COPYRIGHTS, PATENTS AND TRADEMARKS

Copyright protects works that are artistic in nature, such as songs and sound recordings. Patents protect new and useful inventions, such as new processes and machines. Trademarks are words or symbols used in association with products or services, which distinguish those goods or services in the marketplace. A registered trademark's notice is ®. Do not confuse it with the copyright notices, which include the symbols © and ℗.

Copyrights, patents and trademarks make up the bulk of what is known as "intellectual property law." This body of law recognizes that the products of people's minds that are in tangible form have a value that should be protected.

Generally, in the music field, you can get a copyright for two types of creations: musical works and sound recordings. Although dramatic works (such as a musical play, e.g., *The Phantom of the Opera*) may include accompanying music, they are beyond the scope of this discussion.

Interestingly, the copyright law does not define "musical works." However, what most people consider a song is a musical work. Both the music and the lyrics (or each of them separately) can constitute a musical work.

A sound recording is a work comprised of a series of recorded sounds. Thus, the sounds recorded on a compact disc constitute a sound recording. You must distinguish between the musical work and the sound recording. Mariah Carey's version of The Jackson Five song "I'll Be There," which you hear when her *MTV Unplugged* album is played, is a sound recording. However, "I'll Be There" the musical work, is distinct from Carey's performance as embodied in the sound recording.

Sound recordings are comprised of the efforts of many people—the instrumentalists, vocalists, engineers and producers—all of whom may be considered to have constituted copyrightable elements of a sound recording. The Copyright Act does not legislate how the authorship and ownership in sound recordings is to be divided. It is clear the featured vocalist is initially an "author," but unclear whether the instrumentalists, back-up vocalists, and the producer are "authors," which is determined on a case-by-case basis.

The distinction between musical works and sound recordings is important when it comes to public performance income (i.e., fees paid for the public performance of copyrighted material by users such as television broadcasters and radio stations). In the United States, there is no exclusive right to publicly perform a sound recording (except for digital audio recordings, discussed below), even if you own it, but there is as to a musical work. Accordingly, public performance royalties (distributed by ASCAP, BMI and SESAC) are paid to the writer and publisher of the musical work, not the performer or owner of the sound recording. Thus, the public performance income generated by Mariah Carey's version of "I'll Be There" is paid to the writer and publisher of the song, not to Mariah or her record company.

Congress has considered but not passed, bills that would create a general public performance right in sound recordings. Systems similar to those of ASCAP and BMI could be used to compute frequency of performances, and the money would be distributed by the licensing agency among record companies, producers and performers. It should be noted that public performance income from the exploitation of sound recordings is currently paid in some countries outside the United States, but it is not yet a significant source of revenue to U.S. record companies and recording artists.

Many provisions of the Copyright Act refer to "phonorecords." A phonorecord is the physical object (tape, cassette, record, compact disc or other device) that embodies both a musical work and a sound recording. However, although you may purchase and therefore own the compact disc, you do not own the sound recording or the musical work—the copyright owner has only parted with the physical embodiment of the copyrighted works, not ownership in the sound recording or the musical work.

COPYRIGHT REGISTRATION AND NOTICE OF CLAIM TO COPYRIGHT

Some people are under the misapprehension that you send to Washington, DC to get a copyright. What you send for is not a "copyright"—which you get as soon as you fix the work in a tangible medium of expression—but a copyright registration certificate, a very valuable piece of paper that is not only evidence of your claim to copyright, but also makes it easier for you to sue if someone infringes your copyright. In general, failure to register does not invalidate the copyright, and as of March 1, 1989, you are no longer legally required to put a copyright notice on published copies.

The fastest way to get copyright registration forms is to download them from the Copyright Office Web site (*www.copyright.gov*). You can also get free copyright registration forms by writing to the Library of Congress, Washington, DC 20559 or calling the Copyright Office at (202) 707-3000 (if you are not sure which form you need) or (202) 707-9100 (if you know the specific form you want). Allow at least two to four weeks for delivery. This time does vary, however, so ask the person at the Copyright Office how long you will have to wait. The Copyright Office is very helpful with questions regarding registration. Sample forms are duplicated at the end of this chapter. You should keep at least one original form on file so you can photocopy it. You may also order Copyright Office circulars, which are written in plain English and are very helpful, either by Internet, letter or phone.

REGISTERING COLLECTIONS

A group of unpublished songs may be registered as a collection under the following conditions:

- The elements of the collection are assembled in an orderly form.

- The combined elements bear a single title identifying the collection as a whole.

- The copyright claimant in all the elements and in the collection as a whole is the same.

- All of the elements are by the same author, or, if they are by different authors, at least one of the authors has contributed copyrightable authorship to each element.

(From Circular 1 "Copyright Basics," available at no charge from the U.S. Copyright Office.)

What to Submit

To register a copyright in a song, you submit the appropriate form plus one lead sheet, CD or cassette if the work is not published (i.e., copies have not been distributed to the public). The CD or cassette need only contain words, basic melody and rhythm; it does not have to be a fully arranged and beautifully produced demo. You must submit two lead sheets, or two CDs or cassettes if the work is published. The appropriate forms for registering a song are form PA (performing arts) or SR (sound recording). When you are the copyright owner of all the songs on the sound recording, form SR covers both the copyright of the songs and the copyright in the sound recording. Please note that the Copyright Office keeps the materials you submit and stores them as a national artistic treasure of the Library of Congress.

Registering Collections

You may register many songs for a single fee by putting them on a CD or tape and registering them as a collection by using form PA. The biggest drawback to this method is that since the songs are clumped together as one work under one title it is difficult to identify just one of the songs. If you want to pull out one of the songs, you can do so by filing form CA (correction and amplification) or by registering a separate form PA for the song.

Alternative Registration

At the outset, it must be emphasized that no alternative means of registration will protect your songs to the extent that formal registration with the Copyright Office does. Because of the high cost of copyright registration (currently $45 per song) and the technical requirements of the Copyright Office, alternative forms of registration have arisen. The primary reason for using an alternative registration method is to provide proof of the date of creation (fixation) of a song, which is crucial in determining who first created copyright in the song.

So-called poor man's copyright consists of enclosing a copy of your song in an envelope, sending it by registered mail to yourself and not opening the envelope. The postmark serves as proof as to the date of creation of the song. Some variations of the poor man's copyright theme include having a notary public notarize a lead sheet with their signature and date, placing lead sheets or tapes of the song in a safe deposit box and having people listen to a song so that they can testify that the song had been created as of a certain date. Virtually all these methods are anachronistic in our digital age, and most digital files, which are dated, can be very useful proof of time of creation.

PROPER COPYRIGHT NOTICE

Proper notice of a claim to copyright in a song or sound recording is a useful step in protecting your rights, since it puts people on notice that you claim the copyright. Failure to attach proper notice to published copies, however, no longer invalidates your copyright. There are separate symbols for notice of copyright in songs (sheet music, written lyrics) © and in sound recordings (CDs, cassettes, etc.) ℗. The copyright notices for songs and sound recordings must include three elements: the symbol © or ℗, the year of publication, and the name of the copyright owner. The word "Copyright," or the abbreviation "Copr.," may be used instead of the symbol ©. Proper notices are illustrated below.

A copyright notice for a song fixed on sheet music should look something like this:

© 2007 Sally Songwriter.
All Rights Reserved.

Notices that vary from this form are common. A popular one is "Copyright © 2007 Sally Songwriter," or "© Copr. Sally Songwriter 2007." All the law requires is that these three symbols "give reasonable notice of the claim of copyright."

U.S. copyright law does not suggest the words "All Rights Reserved," but they are recommended because they provide additional copyright protection in certain South American countries.

The copyright notice for sound recordings fixed in tapes, records or CDs looks something like this:

℗ 2007 XYZ Records.
All Rights Reserved.

This notice may be put on the surface, label or container of the phonorecord.

Omission of Notice
Under the pre-1978 U.S. Copyright Law, omission of a copyright notice on published copies was fatal to a claim of copyright. This is not true under the present law.

Copyright Notice on Demos
Legally you do not have to put any copyright notice on unpublished lead sheets, or demonstration tapes or CDs. However, the prudent thing to do is to put the appropriate notice on every one of your songs, CDs and tapes.

Put a © notice on every lead sheet or lyric sheet as soon as you write it down. Put a ℗ notice on every tape or record you submit or loan. This puts people on notice that you are claiming copyright in your songs and recordings and that you take your craft seriously.

PUBLICATION
A song is published when it is distributed to the public by sale or by some other means. The most common way songs are first published is through the distribution of records containing them. Be sure the appropriate copyright notice is affixed to the records, tapes, sheet music or other physical embodiments of the work that are publicly distributed.

RECORDING A COPYRIGHTED SONG
The copyright law gives the owner of a copyrighted song the exclusive right to make the first sound recording of the song. However, once the song has been recorded and distributed to the public, others are entitled to make their own recordings of that work and distribute them in phonorecords. Thus, The Jackson Five (or the publisher) could not prevent Mariah Carey from redoing "I'll Be There."

If you want to record a song, you have two alternatives: you may negotiate a "mechanical license" from the copyright owner; or you may use the "compulsory mechanical license" provision of the copyright law, which does not require that you gain permission of the copyright holder but does require you to account to the copyright holder and to pay fixed rates per song for each record manufactured and sold. In practice, however, the vast majority of mechanical licenses are negotiated through The Harry Fox Agency in New York. Mechanical license fees are paid to that agency, which deducts its administration fees and remits the balance to the copyright holder (usually a publisher) on a quarterly basis.

DURATION OF COPYRIGHTS
Copyright protection begins on the date of creation (i.e., fixation in a tangible medium of expression) and as of 1998, in most cases, lasts for the lifetime of the author plus 70 years. Thus, if you write a song in 2007 and die in the year 2020, the copyright

lasts until 2090. If there is a coauthor or authors, then the 70 years are measured from the last surviving author's death.

"Works made for hire" (discussed below) are protected for 95 years from the date of publication or for 120 years from the date of creation (fixation), whichever is shorter.

TRANSFER AND LICENSING OF COPYRIGHTS

Copyrights, like other property, can be divided, bought and sold. When you license ASCAP to collect public performance royalties you have, in effect, given part of your copyright to ASCAP. You still own the rest of the copyright, however. Also, in typical music publishing and record deals, you transfer your copyright to the label or publisher, in return for their promise to pay you royalties.

You can give permission to someone to exploit your copyright without transferring ownership. This is called a "license." For example, someone may record and distribute your song under a mechanical license—but you still own the song. Another common license is a "synchronization license," whereby you or your publisher gives permission for your song to be included in a film or television program.

If you transfer (as opposed to license) your copyright or any exclusive right under copyright, the transfer of ownership must be in writing and be signed by the copyright owner (you). The transfer should be recorded in the Copyright Office, but it is not legally required. Recording of the transfer document is important to the person to whom the copyright is transferred, as it is a prerequisite for bringing a copyright infringement suit. Also, conflicts may emerge between persons that claim the same copyright. In such cases, the first to record the transfer will prevail in a lawsuit arising from a dispute over copyright ownership. Failure to register the transfer, however, does not invalidate the transfer.

Reacquiring Copyright

The present law provides that an author or author's heirs may reacquire a copyright between the 35th and 40th year after transfer by serving a written notice on the person who, at that time, holds the copyright. They then regain ownership of the copyright for the rest of its duration. This does not apply to works made for hire as your employer or the person commissioning the song is deemed the author and owner of the song.

Obviously, for you or your heir to take advantage of this provision you must keep good records and a prospective calendar.

WORKS MADE FOR HIRE

Songwriters are frequently hired to write songs. In such cases, they are described as "employees for hire" or "writers for hire," in songwriting contracts. The significance of this is that the employer (person who hired the writer) is deemed to be the author of the song, and owns the song unless the contract states otherwise. If a song is not produced by an employee in the course of his or her employment, it will be considered a work made for hire only if there is a written agreement to consider it such and the song falls into the specific list of "specially ordered or commissioned works" found in the Copyright Act. Remember, in the work-made-for-hire situation, you do not have copyright in the song as your employer or commissioner is the author of the song. The Copyright Act lists the following uses as specially ordered or commissioned works—a contribution to a collective work; a part of a motion picture or other audiovisual work; a translation; a supplementary work; a compilation; an instructional text; a test; answer material for a test; or an atlas. The same analysis applies when you create sound recordings for record labels.

In 1998, at the behest of the record labels, the Copyright Act was amended to include sound recordings as specially ordered or commissioned works. However, after a battle between the record companies and recording artists, sound recordings were deleted from the list of specifically ordered or commissioned works in late 2000. Notwithstanding this deletion, record companies still take the position in their contracts that the sound recordings are works made for hire as a contribution to a collective work. The significance to recording artists is that they or their heirs may have the ability to terminate the transfer of their sound recordings to record companies in the window from 35 to 40 years after assignment if the transfer was indeed an assignment and not a work made for hire. There is no termination right for works made for hire. The issue of whether sound recordings under recording contracts are subject to termination has not been adjudicated yet but it surely will, starting no later than 2013 (35 years after January 1, 1978, when the 1976 Copyright Act came into effect).

COPYRIGHT INFRINGEMENT

A work is infringed when any of the exclusive rights in a copyright are violated. Persons that infringe copyrights are subject to both civil and criminal penalties. Here are some examples:

You write a song, and the sheet music is sold in a store. An infringer purchases the sheet music, duplicates it and sells it. This is an infringement of your right to reproduce the work and of your exclusive right to distribute copies of the work to the public.

You record an album containing your songs, and an infringer reproduces hundreds of CDs of your album and sells them. This violates your exclusive reproduction and distribution rights and infringes your rights in both the songs and the sound recordings fixed in the album. Consequently, you and your record company can sue for infringement.

Infringement need not be intentional. George Harrison was found to have infringed the Chiffons' 1962 classic "He's So Fine" with his 1970 hit "My Sweet Lord." The court found the music of the two songs to be identical. Even though the lyrics and concepts of his song were different, and Harrison only subconsciously took from "He's So Fine," it was still an infringement.

Statute of Limitations

The copyright law has a statute of limitations (i.e., a time limit during which you can sue). In cases of infringement, you have three years from the initial date of infringement to bring suit. Any delay, however, can harm you. See a lawyer as soon as you learn of an unauthorized use of your song or recording.

Imitating a Performer

As long as you have permission to rerecord a song (whether from the copyright owner or by filing the compulsory mechanical license), you can try to make the song sound like the original recording of the song. As discussed above, you get permission to record the song by getting a compulsory license through complying with copyright law formalities, or by obtaining a negotiated license from the owner of the copyright in the song. You do not have to have the permission of the original performer unless that performer happens to have the rights to the song. If you record "Born in the U.S.A." you can try to sound like Bruce Springsteen, but you must have permission to record the song.

You should be careful, however, if an advertising agency hires you to imitate the sound of a well-known performer. Cases involving Bette Midler and Tom Waits resulted in substantial judgments against advertising agencies that deliberately had singers imitate their voices.

Infringement Remedies

The remedies provided by law in an infringement suit include injunctions, impounding infringing articles and money damages. If you prove infringement at a preliminary stage of the suit, the court will order the infringer to stop, even before the formal trial.

This is a form of injunction—that is, a court order against the infringer. The court can also order the impoundment of the allegedly infringing copies or phonorecords as well as the machinery that produced them.

Since proving money damages is difficult the law sets "statutory damages," which generally run from $750 to $30,000 for a single act of copyright infringement and up to $150,000 if the infringement is willful.

If you win your infringement suit you may elect to receive either the actual damages you suffered plus the profits the infringer earned from the infringement or statutory damages. In certain instances, the court will also award court costs and attorneys' fees. Remember, statutory damages and attorneys' fees will be awarded only if you make timely registration of your copyright with the Copyright Office. Additionally, you must always keep in mind that if you *lose* your copyright infringement action the court can order that you pay the defendant the court costs and legal fees, which could be hundreds of thousands of dollars

The copyright law also provides for criminal penalties.

FAIR USE

Generally, a person who wishes to use copyrighted material must seek permission of the copyright holder. However, the law recognizes certain limited uses of copyrighted material without permission as "fair use." In broad terms, the doctrine of fair use means that in some circumstances, where the use is reasonable and not harmful to the copyright owner's rights, copyrighted material may be used, to a limited extent, without permission of the copyright owner. Under this doctrine, critics have been held to be free to publish short extracts or quotations for purposes of illustration or comment, and record reviewers may quote from songs. Also, in a high-profile case, 2 Live Crew was found not to have infringed a song by doing a parody of it.

The line between fair use and infringement is unclear and not easily defined. There is no specific number of words, lines or notes that can be safely taken without permission. Acknowledging the source of the copyrighted material does not avoid infringement. The safe course is to get permission before using copyrighted material. The Copyright Office cannot give this permission. It will supply information regarding copyright ownership as disclosed by a search of its records.

Use of copyrighted material without permission (even in a parody), should be avoided unless it is clear that the doctrine of fair use would apply to the situation. If there is any doubt, consult an attorney.

We all know that new songs frequently incorporate parts of old ones. A pervasive myth is that you can graft four bars from a copyrighted song without subjecting yourself to a lawsuit by the copyright owner, as taking four bars is a fair use. In fact, there is no such provision in the law. The test is whether the amount taken from the old song was substantial. A judge or jury applies this rather loose standard when they listen to your song. Remember, there is no standard measure of how much music, or how many lyrics can be incorporated in a new song without infringing the old. Vanilla Ice found out the hard way when he stole the hook to the Queen/Bowie hit "Under Pressure" as the basis to his notorious rip-off "Ice, Ice, Baby."

DIGITAL AUDIO RECORDING TECHNOLOGY (DART) ACT

On October 7, 1992, Congress passed the Digital Audio Recording Technology (DART) Act. The act requires manufacturers and importers of digital audio recording devices and media that distribute these products in the United States to pay a set percentage royalty of the transfer price to the Licensing Division of the Copyright Office, which invests the fees in U.S. Treasury securities until royalties are distributed by the Copyright Royalty Board and its three-member panel of Copyright Royalty Judges (CRJs). The royalty for digital audio devices is 2% of the transfer price and for recording media it is 3% of the transfer price. The transfer price, in the case of an imported product, is defined in the Act as "the actual entered value at U.S. Customs (exclusive of freight, insurance and applicable duty)." In the case of a domestic product, the transfer price is defined as "the manufacturer's transfer price (FOB the manufacturer, and exclusive of any direct sales taxes or excise taxes incurred in connection with the sale)."

The law also requires manufacturers of digital audio equipment to install serial copy-prevention systems that permit copies to be made from original recordings but not from copies, thereby preventing unauthorized mass duplication.

DART is an attempt to balance the concerns of copyright owners and music publishers about unlawful infringement (unauthorized tape duplication and distribution) with the public's demand for DAT technology. The act includes a special provision that protects consumers against infringement actions when they use the technology to create digital copies for private noncommercial use.

The fees are distributed according to the following percentages: 4% of the fund is allocated to nonfeatured musicians and vocalists. Of the remaining 96%, two-thirds (66.6%) is distributed to the Sound Recordings Fund, which is subdivided into a Featured Artists subfund and a Copyright Owners subfund; and one-third (33.3%) to the Musical Works Fund, which is subdivided into a Writers subfund and a Publishers subfund.

The 4% of the Sound Recordings Fund that is earmarked for nonfeatured musicians is distributed directly to an independent administrator that is appointed jointly by the record companies and the American Federation of Musicians (AFM). Similarly, in the case of the nonfeatured vocalists, the independent administrator is appointed jointly by record companies and the American Federation of Television and Radio Artists (AFTRA). Historically, the independent administrator has been the same in both cases.

The Copyright Royalty Board and the CRJs determine how much a particular claimant is entitled to with respect to the other four subfunds. In order to be eligible for a share of these fees, any entity/person entitled to receive a share of the funds must file a claim to each subfund in which they are interested copyright parties. Negotiations then occur among the claimants within a particular subfund. If claimants within a subfund agree on the distribution then the Copyright Royalty Board will make the distribution according to that agreement. However, if the claimants within a subfund cannot agree, the Copyright Royalty Board then conducts a hearing to determine how to allocate the funds among the claimants in that subfund.

Negotiations about how these subfunds are actually distributed between the majority of featured artists and owners of sound recordings are handled by the Alliance of Artists and Recording Companies (AARC) on behalf of member record companies. Record companies that are not members of the AARC can make their claims directly to the Copyright Royalty Board.

Negotiations about how writer subfunds are distributed are administered by ASCAP, BMI and SESAC; and the music publisher subfunds are administered by the Harry Fox Agency (HFA) on behalf of member publishing companies. Publishers that are not administered by the HFA may file claims directly to the Copyright Office.

For more information, call the Copyright Royalty Board, (202) 707-7658.

CONCLUSION

Musicians and songwriters should have a basic understanding of copyright law. When you write or record a song, you have certain valuable rights in that song that you can exploit. By knowing your rights you can protect them but you should always consult an attorney for guidance.

SUMMARY OF NOTICES THAT APPEAR ON RECORDINGS

Item	Location	Purpose
℗ year, owner	Typically on label and packaging	Gives notices of owner of sound recording.
© year, owner	Label, packaging	Provides notice of ownership of the art and text on the label and packaging when the owner of the sound recording is the same.
© year, owner	Beside specific text or art on packaging	Identifies ownership of specific text or art when they are owned by another.
© year, owner	At end of written lyric	Provides notice of ownership of songs.
All Rights Reserved	After each © notice	Provides notice required for copyright protection in certain foreign countries.
Used by permission	After certain © notices	Typically used when permission to use another's copyrighted work has been granted.
Unauthorized reproduction prohibited, etc.	Packaging	Optional warning designed to deter infringement; can take various forms.*
Songwriters' names	Adjacent to song titles	Not required by copyright law, but customarily added as a matter of courtesy or as required by contract to facilitate payment of songwriter royalties.
BMI/ASCAP/SESAC	Next to song title	Not part of the copyright notice, but identifies the performing rights society that licenses the song for public performances and collects royalties on behalf of the songwriter and publisher.
Playing time	Next to song title	Not part of the copyright notice but convenient for disc jockeys.

*(i.e., "_WARNING_: Unauthorized reproduction of this recording is prohibited by federal law and is subject to criminal prosecution" or "Unauthorized duplication is a violation of applicable laws.")

Copyright Office fees are subject to change. For current fees, check the Copyright Office website at *www.copyright.gov*, write the Copyright Office, or call (202) 707-3000.

Form PA
For a Work of Performing Arts
UNITED STATES COPYRIGHT OFFICE

REGISTRATION NUMBER

PA   PAU

EFFECTIVE DATE OF REGISTRATION

Month   Day   Year

DO NOT WRITE ABOVE THIS LINE. IF YOU NEED MORE SPACE, USE A SEPARATE CONTINUATION SHEET.

1 TITLE OF THIS WORK ▼

PREVIOUS OR ALTERNATIVE TITLES ▼

NATURE OF THIS WORK ▼ See instructions

2 **a** NAME OF AUTHOR ▼

DATES OF BIRTH AND DEATH
Year Born ▼   Year Died ▼

Was this contribution to the work a "work made for hire"?
☐ Yes
☐ No

AUTHOR'S NATIONALITY OR DOMICILE
Name of Country
OR { Citizen of
Domiciled in

WAS THIS AUTHOR'S CONTRIBUTION TO THE WORK
Anonymous?   ☐ Yes ☐ No
Pseudonymous?   ☐ Yes ☐ No

If the answer to either of these questions is "Yes," see detailed instructions.

NATURE OF AUTHORSHIP Briefly describe nature of material created by this author in which copyright is claimed. ▼

NOTE
Under the law, the "author" of a "work made for hire" is generally the employer, not the employee (see instructions). For any part of this work that was "made for hire" check "Yes" in the space provided, give the employer (or other person for whom the work was prepared) as "Author" of that part, and leave the space for dates of birth and death blank.

b NAME OF AUTHOR ▼

DATES OF BIRTH AND DEATH
Year Born ▼   Year Died ▼

Was this contribution to the work a "work made for hire"?
☐ Yes
☐ No

AUTHOR'S NATIONALITY OR DOMICILE
Name of Country
OR { Citizen of
Domiciled in

WAS THIS AUTHOR'S CONTRIBUTION TO THE WORK
Anonymous?   ☐ Yes ☐ No
Pseudonymous?   ☐ Yes ☐ No

If the answer to either of these questions is "Yes," see detailed instructions.

NATURE OF AUTHORSHIP Briefly describe nature of material created by this author in which copyright is claimed. ▼

c NAME OF AUTHOR ▼

DATES OF BIRTH AND DEATH
Year Born ▼   Year Died ▼

Was this contribution to the work a "work made for hire"?
☐ Yes
☐ No

AUTHOR'S NATIONALITY OR DOMICILE
Name of Country
OR { Citizen of
Domiciled in

WAS THIS AUTHOR'S CONTRIBUTION TO THE WORK
Anonymous?   ☐ Yes ☐ No
Pseudonymous?   ☐ Yes ☐ No

If the answer to either of these questions is "Yes," see detailed instructions.

NATURE OF AUTHORSHIP Briefly describe nature of material created by this author in which copyright is claimed. ▼

3 **a** YEAR IN WHICH CREATION OF THIS WORK WAS COMPLETED This information must be given Year in all cases.

b DATE AND NATION OF FIRST PUBLICATION OF THIS PARTICULAR WORK Complete this information ONLY if this work has been published. Month   Day   Year   Nation

4 COPYRIGHT CLAIMANT(S) Name and address must be given even if the claimant is the same as the author given in space 2. ▼

See instructions before completing this space.

TRANSFER If the claimant(s) named here in space 4 is (are) different from the author(s) named in space 2, give a brief statement of how the claimant(s) obtained ownership of the copyright. ▼

APPLICATION RECEIVED
ONE DEPOSIT RECEIVED
TWO DEPOSITS RECEIVED
FUNDS RECEIVED
DO NOT WRITE HERE OFFICE USE ONLY

MORE ON BACK ▶ • Complete all applicable spaces (numbers 5-9) on the reverse side of this page.
• See detailed instructions. • Sign the form at line 8.

DO NOT WRITE HERE
Page 1 of   pages

EXAMINED BY

CHECKED BY

CORRESPONDENCE
Yes

FORM PA

FOR
COPYRIGHT
OFFICE
USE
ONLY

DO NOT WRITE ABOVE THIS LINE. IF YOU NEED MORE SPACE, USE A SEPARATE CONTINUATION SHEET.

PREVIOUS REGISTRATION Has registration for this work, or for an earlier version of this work, already been made in the Copyright Office?

☐ **Yes** ☐ **No** If your answer is "Yes," why is another registration being sought? (Check appropriate box.) ▼ If your answer is No, do **not** check box A, B, or C.

a. ☐ This is the first published edition of a work previously registered in unpublished form.

b. ☐ This is the first application submitted by this author as copyright claimant.

c. ☐ This is a changed version of the work, as shown by space 6 on this application.

If your answer is "Yes," give: **Previous Registration Number** ▼   **Year of Registration** ▼

5

DERIVATIVE WORK OR COMPILATION Complete both space 6a and 6b for a derivative work; complete only 6b for a compilation.
Preexisting Material Identify any preexisting work or works that this work is based on or incorporates. ▼

Material Added to This Work Give a brief, general statement of the material that has been added to this work and in which copyright is claimed. ▼

a
6
b

See instructions before completing this space.

DEPOSIT ACCOUNT If the registration fee is to be charged to a Deposit Account established in the Copyright Office, give name and number of Account.
Name ▼   **Account Number** ▼

a
7

CORRESPONDENCE Give name and address to which correspondence about this application should be sent. Name/Address/Apt/City/State/Zip▼

b

Area code and daytime telephone number   (   )   Fax number   (   )
Email

CERTIFICATION* I, the undersigned, hereby certify that I am the

Check only one {
☐ author
☐ other copyright claimant
☐ owner of exclusive right(s)
☐ authorized agent of

8

Name of author or other copyright claimant, or owner of exclusive right(s) ▲

of the work identified in this application and that the statements made by me in this application are correct to the best of my knowledge.

Typed or printed name and date ▼ If this application gives a date of publication in space 3, do not sign and submit it before that date.

Date

Handwritten signature (X) ▼

x _____

Certificate will be mailed in window envelope to this address:

Name ▼

Number/Street/Apt ▼

City/State/Zip ▼

YOU MUST:
• Complete all necessary spaces
• Sign your application in space 8
SEND ALL 3 ELEMENTS IN THE SAME PACKAGE:
1. Application form
2. Nonrefundable filing fee in check or money order payable to *Register of Copyrights*
3. Deposit material
MAIL TO:
Library of Congress
Copyright Office
101 Independence Avenue SE
Washington, DC 20559-6000

9

*17 *USC* §506(e): Any person who knowingly makes a false representation of a material fact in the application for copyright registration provided for by section 409, or in any written statement filed in connection with the application, shall be fined not more than $2,500.

Form PA – Full   Rev: 07/2006   Print: 07/2006 — xx,000   Printed on recycled paper   U.S. Government Printing Office: 2006-xxx-xxx/60,xxx

Copyright Office fees are subject to change. For current fees, check the Copyright Office website at *www.copyright.gov*, write the Copyright Office, or call (202) 707-3000.

Form SR
For a Sound Recording
UNITED STATES COPYRIGHT OFFICE

REGISTRATION NUMBER

_____

SR   SRU

EFFECTIVE DATE OF REGISTRATION

_____

Month   Day   Year

DO NOT WRITE ABOVE THIS LINE. IF YOU NEED MORE SPACE, USE A SEPARATE CONTINUATION SHEET.

1

TITLE OF THIS WORK ▼

PREVIOUS, ALTERNATIVE, OR CONTENTS TITLES (CIRCLE ONE) ▼

2

a

NAME OF AUTHOR ▼

DATES OF BIRTH AND DEATH
Year Born ▼   Year Died ▼

Was this contribution to the work a "work made for hire"?
☐ Yes
☐ No

AUTHOR'S NATIONALITY OR DOMICILE
Name of Country
OR { Citizen of ▶
      Domiciled in ▶

WAS THIS AUTHOR'S CONTRIBUTION TO THE WORK
Anonymous? ☐ Yes ☐ No
Pseudonymous? ☐ Yes ☐ No

If the answer to either of these questions is "Yes," see detailed instructions.

NATURE OF AUTHORSHIP Briefly describe nature of material created by this author in which copyright is claimed. ▼

NOTE

Under the law, the "author" of a "work made for hire" is generally the employer, not the employee (see instructions). For any part of this work that was "made for hire," check "Yes" in the space provided, give the employer (or other person for whom the work was prepared) as "Author" of that part, and leave the space for dates of birth and death blank.

b

NAME OF AUTHOR ▼

DATES OF BIRTH AND DEATH
Year Born ▼   Year Died ▼

Was this contribution to the work a "work made for hire"?
☐ Yes
☐ No

AUTHOR'S NATIONALITY OR DOMICILE
Name of Country
OR { Citizen of ▶
      Domiciled in ▶

WAS THIS AUTHOR'S CONTRIBUTION TO THE WORK
Anonymous? ☐ Yes ☐ No
Pseudonymous? ☐ Yes ☐ No

If the answer to either of these questions is "Yes," see detailed instructions.

NATURE OF AUTHORSHIP Briefly describe nature of material created by this author in which copyright is claimed. ▼

c

NAME OF AUTHOR ▼

DATES OF BIRTH AND DEATH
Year Born ▼   Year Died ▼

Was this contribution to the work a "work made for hire"?
☐ Yes
☐ No

AUTHOR'S NATIONALITY OR DOMICILE
Name of Country
OR { Citizen of ▶
      Domiciled in ▶

WAS THIS AUTHOR'S CONTRIBUTION TO THE WORK
Anonymous? ☐ Yes ☐ No
Pseudonymous? ☐ Yes ☐ No

If the answer to either of these questions is "Yes," see detailed instructions.

NATURE OF AUTHORSHIP Briefly describe nature of material created by this author in which copyright is claimed. ▼

3

a
YEAR IN WHICH CREATION OF THIS WORK WAS COMPLETED
This information must be given in all cases.
◀ Year

b
DATE AND NATION OF FIRST PUBLICATION OF THIS PARTICULAR WORK
Complete this information ONLY if this work has been published.
Month ▶   Day ▶   Year ▶   ◀ Nation

4

a

COPYRIGHT CLAIMANT(S) Name and address must be given even if the claimant is the same as the author given in space 2. ▼

See instructions before completing this space.

b

TRANSFER If the claimant(s) named here in space 4 is (are) different from the author(s) named in space 2, give a brief statement of how the claimant(s) obtained ownership of the copyright. ▼

APPLICATION RECEIVED

ONE DEPOSIT RECEIVED

TWO DEPOSITS RECEIVED

FUNDS RECEIVED

DO NOT WRITE HERE
OFFICE USE ONLY

MORE ON BACK ▶
• Complete all applicable spaces (numbers 5–9) on the reverse side of this page.
• See detailed instructions.
• Sign the form at line 8.

DO NOT WRITE HERE
Page 1 of _____ pages

EXAMINED BY	FORM SR
CHECKED BY	
CORRESPONDENCE ❏ Yes	FOR COPYRIGHT OFFICE USE ONLY

DO NOT WRITE ABOVE THIS LINE. IF YOU NEED MORE SPACE, USE A SEPARATE CONTINUATION SHEET.

PREVIOUS REGISTRATION Has registration for this work, or for an earlier version of this work, already been made in the Copyright Office?

❏ **Yes** ❏ **No** If your answer is "Yes," why is another registration being sought? (Check appropriate box) ▼

a. ❏ This work was previously registered in unpublished form and now has been published for the first time.

b. ❏ This is the first application submitted by this author as copyright claimant.

c. ❏ This is a changed version of the work, as shown by space 6 on this application.

If your answer is "Yes," give: **Previous Registration Number** ▼   **Year of Registration** ▼

5

DERIVATIVE WORK OR COMPILATION
Preexisting Material Identify any preexisting work or works that this work is based on or incorporates. ▼

a

6

See instructions before completing this space.

Material Added to This Work Give a brief, general statement of the material that has been added to this work and in which copyright is claimed. ▼

b

DEPOSIT ACCOUNT If the registration fee is to be charged to a deposit account established in the Copyright Office, give name and number of Account.
Name ▼   **Account Number** ▼

a

7

CORRESPONDENCE Give name and address to which correspondence about this application should be sent. Name/Address/Apt/City/State/Zip ▼

b

Area code and daytime telephone number   Fax number
Email

CERTIFICATION* I, the undersigned, hereby certify that I am the

Check only one ▼

❏ author   ❏ owner of exclusive right(s)

❏ other copyright claimant   ❏ authorized agent of

Name of author or other copyright claimant, or owner of exclusive right(s) ▲

8

of the work identified in this application and that the statements made by me in this application are correct to the best of my knowledge.

Typed or printed name and date ▼ If this application gives a date of publication in space 3, do not sign and submit it before that date.

Date

Handwritten signature (x) ▼

X _

Certificate will be mailed in window envelope to this address	Name ▼	**YOU MUST:** • Complete all necessary spaces • Sign your application in space 8
	Number/Street/Apt ▼	**SEND ALL 3 ELEMENTS IN THE SAME PACKAGE:** 1. Application form 2. Nonrefundable filing fee in check or money order payable to *Register of Copyrights* 3. Deposit material
	City/State/Zip ▼	**MAIL TO:** Library of Congress Copyright Office 101 Independence Avenue SE Washington, DC 20559-6000

9

*17 *USC* §506(e): Any person who knowingly makes a false representation of a material fact in the application for copyright registration provided for by section 409, or in any written statement filed in connection with the application, shall be fined not more than $2,500.

Form SR   Rev: 07/2006   Print: 07/2006— xx,000   Printed on recycled paper   U.S. Government Printing Office: 2005-xxx-xxx/60,xxx

Copyright Infringement

BY ROBERT M. DUDNIK

To establish a claim of copyright infringement, the plaintiff (person who files the lawsuit) must first demonstrate either ownership of the copyright of the song that was supposedly copied, or ownership of a copyright interest in that song, such as an exclusive license. The plaintiff must then demonstrate that the composer of defendant's song in fact copied from plaintiff's song and that the material that was copied results in a finding of copyright infringement. Once infringement is established, then the question becomes what remedies are available to the plaintiff.★

ESTABLISHING OWNERSHIP

Copyright of a song is established when the work is first fixed in a tangible form—for example, notated on paper or recorded digitally or on tape. Registration of the song with the Copyright Office is not a prerequisite to the song being protected by copyright. However, before an infringement case may be filed in court, the owner of the copyright must, as a general rule, register the song with the Copyright Office. Prompt registration after creation of the song will be beneficial in terms of remedies in the event the song is infringed after it is registered.

Typically, the copyright owner will be either the composer of the song, the employer of the composer (if the composer wrote the song during the course and scope of employment as a work for hire) or a person or company to whom the original owner of the copyright in the song transferred the copyright or a copyright interest in the song by means of a written instrument.

Proof of ownership may become complicated where the plaintiff is not the composer of the song but, instead, claims ownership either as the employer of the composer or by virtue of a transfer in ownership. Further, the fact that the plaintiff has registered the song with the Copyright Office and has claimed ownership of the song on the registration certificate does not conclusively establish that the plaintiff is, in fact, the true owner of the copyright in the song.

ESTABLISHING THE ACT OF COPYING

A composer who is charged with copyright infringement rarely admits copying from the plaintiff's song. And it is very unusual for there to be what the law calls "direct"

★ *This chapter does not deal with peer-to-peer/piracy issues or sampling.*

evidence of copying, such as testimony by a witness who observed the composer listening to the plaintiff's song while writing the defendant's.

Since admissions of plagiarism as well as other forms of direct evidence of copying are hard to come by, the law permits a copyright plaintiff to prove copying through "circumstantial" evidence—by showing that the composer of defendant's song had "access" to plaintiff's song and that the two songs in issue are "substantially similar."

Access

Access means that there is a "reasonable possibility" that the composer of defendant's song heard plaintiff's song or saw a print version of it before writing defendant's song. If the plaintiff can establish only that there is a "bare possibility" that the composer of defendant's song heard or viewed a printed version of the song before defendant's song was written, then plaintiff has not established access and, with one exception discussed below, plaintiff's case will be dismissed from court.

A plaintiff can establish access under this reasonable possibility test by showing that the composer of defendant's song, as a member of the general public, had a reasonable opportunity to have been exposed to plaintiff's song. For example, where plaintiff's song was a major hit before defendant's song was written, access would ordinarily be established. This is true even if the composer of defendant's song denies having heard plaintiff's song since, in the eyes of the law, there is a reasonable possibility that the composer of defendant's song heard plaintiff's song on the radio or on television and is either lying or has forgotten that he heard it. If, on the other hand, plaintiff's song received only limited airplay in one region of the country and little other exposure, and the composer of defendant's song could show that he never visited that region while plaintiff's song was being played, access would, ordinarily, not be established. As another example, if plaintiff's song was played during only a few club dates, access would ordinarily not be established unless it could be shown that the composer of defendant's song frequented one or more of the clubs where plaintiff's song was performed.

There is a second way of establishing access. If the plaintiff can establish that plaintiff's song was auditioned for or submitted to the composer of defendant's song before defendant's song was written, then access would be established. Access might also be established where plaintiff's song was auditioned for or submitted to a close business associate or close friend of the composer of defendant's song or the composer's boss. More difficult questions arise where plaintiff's song was auditioned for or submitted to a large company, such as a major record label, with which the composer of defendant's song has a business relationship.

In the end, the question of whether access is established is usually one of degree, which raises interesting and difficult issues for lawyers and judges. However, it is clear that the stronger the showing of access, the greater the chance the plaintiff will have of proving copying by circumstantial evidence.

Substantial Similarity

As mentioned above, to prove copying by circumstantial evidence, the plaintiff must, ordinarily, show not only access but also that there are elements in the two songs in issue that are substantially similar. Those elements may consist of melody, harmony or lyrics or a combination of them and may be found in one or more sections of the songs, such as the chorus, verse or bridge.

There is no precise definition of substantially similar. Clearly, it means something less than identical and something more than a little bit alike. Probably the best way of defining substantially similar is "so similar that an ordinary listener to music would believe that there was a strong possibility that one song or at least an important part of it, was copied from the other."

As discussed above, even where the two songs in issue are substantially similar, the plaintiff's case will ordinarily be dismissed from court if the plaintiff cannot also present evidence of access. There is, however, one very narrow exception to the general rule that both access and substantial similarity must be proved to establish copying by circumstantial evidence. Where an expert witness will testify that the similarity between plaintiff's song and defendant's song is so overwhelming that there is no explanation for the similarity between them other than that one was copied from the other, access will be "inferred" from the similarity and the plaintiff will not be required to present any other evidence showing access, so long as there is some evidence that plaintiff's song was written before defendant's. It should, however, be pointed out that it is a rare case where this exception—known as the "striking similarity doctrine"—to the general rule would be applicable.

ESTABLISHING INDEPENDENT CREATION

It is important to keep in mind that the plaintiff does not conclusively establish copying just by presenting evidence showing both access and substantial similarity. Presentation of this evidence merely means that the issue of copying will be presented to the jury. Even if the plaintiff proves both access and substantial similarity, the defendant can win by convincing the jury that defendant's song was created independently of plaintiff's song. Regardless of how similar the songs in issue are, if the defendant did not in fact copy from the plaintiff's song, there can be no finding of copyright infringement. This is true even if the songs are virtually identical, since without copying there cannot be infringement. This is the law's way of recognizing that two composers could conceivably compose the very same song without either having heard the other's composition.

To establish independent creation (lack of copying), defendant will attempt to show a number of things. First, defendant will try to prove that the composer of defendant's song had solid musical training and a substantial background in music. This supports the conclusion that the composer of defendant's song had no need to copy from anything to write a good song.

Second, defendant will attempt to show that the composer of defendant's song wrote several hit songs before writing defendant's song. This supports the conclusion that the composer is skilled and successful and had no motivation or need to copy.

Third, and important in persuading a jury that the similarity between the songs in issue did not result from copying, defendant will try to present expert witnesses that can testify, using examples, that several songs or other musical works, written prior to plaintiff's and defendant's songs, are similar to both of them. This evidence is used to show that the musical elements that result in the similarity between the two songs are elements commonly used by composers of popular music. This increases the likelihood that the similarities between the songs are coincidental and, thus, decreases the likelihood that defendant's song was copied from plaintiff's.

The law has long recognized that there are limits on the abilities of songwriters to combine notes, chords and rhythms so as to make music that will be relatively easy for most musicians to play and be both pleasing and accessible to the public. Because of these limits, courts recognize that simple musical phrases are likely to recur in popular songs spontaneously—not as the result of one composer copying from another. Consequently, defendant will attempt to prove (using expert witnesses) that the musical elements of defendant's song upon which the plaintiff's claim of copying is based, are simple musical elements that are pleasing to the musically-unsophisticated audience for contemporary popular music and are relatively easy for most musicians to perform.

Finally, defendant will attempt to show that the composer of defendant's song previously wrote one or more songs that also contained the musical elements that were supposedly copied from plaintiff's song. If the composer of defendant's song had used these same elements in songs written before there was a possibility of hearing plaintiff's song, it would be unlikely that defendant's song was copied from plaintiff's. It is, after all, ordinarily permissible to use material from one's own compositions, and composers of contemporary music often write songs that, in terms of the music, are very much like their earlier songs. If, however, a composer uses material from one of his or her songs that is owned by someone else, a problem may arise.

In the final analysis, assuming that plaintiff puts on evidence sufficient to make a showing of access and substantial similarity, and defendant then puts on evidence of independent creation, it will be for the jury to determine whether the composer of defendant's song in fact copied from plaintiff's.

ESTABLISHING INFRINGEMENT

Even if the plaintiff establishes ownership of plaintiff's song and that the composer of defendant's song copied from it, still more must be shown to establish infringement.

The plaintiff must show that more than a minimal amount of material contained in defendant's song was copied from plaintiff's. However, contrary to what many musicians believe, there is no legal rule stating that a composer may freely borrow four bars, or six notes, or any other set amount of material from a copyrighted work without being found liable for infringement. Indeed, the copying of a very brief musical passage from plaintiff's song may result in a finding of infringement if that passage is qualitatively important to both songs in issue. For example, the copying of a brief melodic "hook" might well result in infringement if that hook is the centerpiece of plaintiff's song and is important in defendant's.

Defendant will not avoid liability for infringement by showing that there is much material in defendant's song that is not in any way similar to, and thus not copied from, plaintiff's song. For example, if the basis of plaintiff's claim is a strong musical similarity between the choruses of the two songs, defendant cannot avoid a finding of infringement by showing that the verses and bridges of the songs are totally dissimilar and there is no similarity in lyrics.

Copyright law does not protect ideas, only their expression. Accordingly, to establish infringement, plaintiff must demonstrate that the composer of defendant's song copied not just the musical ideas but also the manner in which the composer of plaintiff's song expressed those ideas. The distinction between a musical idea and the manner in which it is expressed is quite puzzling to musicians, lawyers and judges. Nevertheless, it is a distinction that is central to United States copyright law.

The material that was copied from the plaintiff's song must have been "original" to its composer and not commonplace for there to be infringement. That is so because the copyright in a song protects only those musical elements, and combinations of musical elements, that are original to its composer. If certain elements of a copyrighted song were original and others were commonplace or copied from an earlier song, the copyright in the song is valid, but copyright protection in the song extends only to those elements that were original to its composer.

The fair use doctrine may provide a defense even where the composer of defendant's song is found to have copied from plaintiff's song. However, this defense—which involves the weighing of several factors—is rarely useful in music infringement cases except where the defendant's song is a parody.

The plaintiff is not required to show that the composer of defendant's song deliberately infringed the copyright in plaintiff's song. In fact, plaintiff need not even establish that the copying was a conscious act. Subconscious copying will result in a finding of infringement.

Significantly, if defendant's song is found by the jury to infringe plaintiff's song, everyone who commercially exploits defendant's song will be liable for infringement, regardless of whether they had any reason to suspect that defendant's song infringed plaintiff's. For example, a record company that innocently distributes an album containing a performance of an infringing song is liable for copyright infringement even if it has no possible way of knowing that the song is infringing, and even if the person or company supplying the recording represented and warranted that the song did not infringe any other musical work. The same is true with respect to a motion picture company that innocently includes defendant's song in the soundtrack of one of its films, and a manufacturer that innocently employs defendant's song in a television commercial.

The fact that companies in this position are treated as infringers, despite their lack of knowledge, is of great consequence, since the remedies available to a winning plaintiff apply to these companies.

REMEDIES

It is important to note that, after being charged with infringement, a losing defendant cannot avoid the remedies discussed below by expressing a desire to negotiate a "fair" license to use plaintiff's song or a willingness to pay plaintiff the prevailing "statutory rate" for a compulsory mechanical license.

The four most important remedies available to a winning plaintiff are (1) injunctive relief, (2) statutory damages, (3) actual damages, and (4) the profits of each of the infringing defendants that is attributable to their use of infringing musical material (often perceived as the pot of gold at the end of the rainbow).

Injunctive Relief

Injunctive relief is a court order enjoining (i.e., prohibiting) each of the defendants from further distributing and selling works, such as recordings, which contain material that infringes plaintiff's song. For example, if one of the defendants is a record company that has released a recording containing a song that is found to infringe plaintiff's song, the record company may be enjoined from further distributing and selling the recording until the infringing song is removed. Similarly, if one of the defendants is a motion picture company that has released a film containing infringing music, the company may be ordered to discontinue distribution and exhibition of the film unless the infringing music is removed from the soundtrack. If, however, the amount of infringing material in a work is insignificant when compared to all of the noninfringing material and it would be difficult to delete the infringing material without destroying the commercial appeal of the work, it is unlikely that the court would issue an injunction order.

Where a plaintiff is able to obtain an order enjoining a defendant from commercially exploiting a work—such as a successful recording or film—which is producing substantial revenues for that defendant, plaintiff will have enormous economic leverage, permitting plaintiff to dictate the terms of a monetary settlement with that defendant.

Statutory Damages

Statutory damages are a form of damages provided for in the Copyright Act. They are calculated by multiplying a set amount of money, which varies depending on certain factors, times the number of infringements. This calculation can, however, become very complicated. Ordinarily, statutory damages are not nearly as meaningful to a plaintiff as any of the other remedies. Nevertheless, if an infringement action is contemplated or pursued, the option of statutory damages should be examined carefully, especially where it would be difficult to prove actual damages and the defendants' profits were minimal or nonexistent. The timing of the filing of the plaintiff's application for registration with the Copyright Office may preclude the plaintiff from obtaining an award of statutory damages.

Actual Damages

Actual damages are those damages actually suffered by the plaintiff as the result of the infringement of plaintiff's song. For example, if defendant's song was comprised of music copied from plaintiff's song, coupled with obscene or distasteful lyrics added by the defendant, plaintiff might find it difficult to thereafter commercially exploit the song. Or if a song that infringed plaintiff's song was included on the soundtrack of a successful film, plaintiff might well find it difficult to license the song to a motion picture company. In sum, any use of an infringing song that tends either to make plaintiff's song "old news" or to tarnish it is damaging to the plaintiff, and the plaintiff (generally through the use of expert witnesses) will attempt to prove the monetary extent of those claimed damages, and the defendant likely will challenge the claimed damages as being too speculative to support an award.

Award of Profits

Often the most significant remedy available to a prevailing plaintiff is an award of the profits of each of the defendants that are attributable to the use of the infringing material. Profits, simply put, mean revenues minus properly deductible costs and expenses, including, in some cases, income taxes. The issues that relate to the calculation of an award of profits are among the most challenging faced by lawyers involved in copyright cases.

In establishing the profits of an infringing defendant, the plaintiff is only required to present proof of the gross revenues realized by the defendant from its exploitation of the infringing song or, where the infringing song is embodied in a larger work, such as a motion picture or an album containing a number of other songs, from defendant's exploitation of that larger work. Defendant is then required to prove its properly deductible costs and expenses, which gives rise to a series of complicated accounting questions involving such matters as overhead, which are too complex to be treated in this chapter.

Since a prevailing plaintiff is entitled only to the profits attributable to the use of infringing material, two separate issues frequently arise. First, a determination must be made as to what extent the popularity and commercial appeal of the infringing song is attributable to its inclusion of infringing material, as distinguished from other factors, for example, the song's inclusion of noninfringing material, such as the lyrics, or the performance of the artist who sings it or the production of the recording that embodies it. This question will often be the subject of expert testimony, with the plaintiff trying to prove that the infringing material was crucial to the popularity of the infringing song, and the defendant trying to prove that the infringing material played an insignificant role in the infringing song's success.

Second, where the infringing song is embodied in a work (such as a CD or a motion picture) that includes other material that has no connection with plaintiff's song, another question becomes how much of the profits realized from the exploitation of that work is attributable to the infringing song and how much to the other material? For example, where the infringing song is one of 10 cuts on a recording, more than 10% of the profits realized by the record company from its sales of that recording would be attributable to the infringing song if it was the hit, or one of the hits, which drove up sales, and less than 10% if it was not one of the hits and therefore received little airplay.

Where an infringing song is used on the soundtrack of a motion picture, how much of the motion picture studio's profits from its distribution of the film were attributable to the song's presence on the soundtrack? If the infringing song's inclusion on the soundtrack constituted an incidental or minor use, only a minuscule percentage of the film's profits would be attributable to its inclusion. If, on the other hand, the song was the film's title song, which was released on a recording that was successfully used to promote the film and keep the radio-listening public reminded that the film was in theaters, the plaintiff's case for profits would be much better.

A very difficult question arises where an infringing song is used in a commercial for a product, such as a beer. The question then becomes how much of the company's profits from beer sales were attributable to the use of the song in the commercial?

In dealing with the difficult questions regarding apportionment of profits discussed above, both plaintiff and defendant will rely upon statistics, sales figures and expert testimony in their attempts to maximize (in the case of the plaintiff) or minimize (in the defendant's case) the significance of the song in "selling" the recording, the film or the beer.

Punitive Damages/Attorneys' Fees

Finally, there is the question of whether punitive damages and attorneys' fees are available as remedies. The Copyright Act does not provide for punitive damages and the prevailing view is that punitive damages are not a remedy available to a successful plaintiff. However, unlike most cases filed in U.S. courts, the prevailing (winning) party in an infringement case may be entitled to an award of his, her or its attorneys' fees. A number of factors are considered in determining whether the prevailing party will be awarded fees and the courts are presently grappling on a case-by-case basis with the issue of whether the prevailing party will receive such an award. It is important to note that as with the case of statutory damages discussed above, the date the plaintiff filed its application for registration will govern whether it may obtain an award of attorneys' fees, even if it establishes infringement. Thus, a plaintiff that did not file its application before the infringement first started will be in the unenviable position of possibly having to pay the defendant's attorneys' fees if it loses the case and not be able to collect its fees if it wins.

Sampling

BY GREGORY T. VICTOROFF, ESQ.

At its best, sampling benefits society by creating valuable new contributions to modern music literature. At its worst, sampling is vandalism and stealing; chopping up and ripping off songs and recordings by other artists without permission or payment and fraudulently passing off the joint work as the work of a single artist, without giving credit to the sampled work or the unwilling collaborators. The practice is not new. In the 19th century, Rachmaninoff, Brahams and Liszt "borrowed" material from contemporary Niccolo Paganini's "Caprice No. 24 in A" for use in their own compositions.

With the advent of digital technology and the increasing capabilities of cell phones and portable digital recording devices, more refined MIDI programs, affordable off-the-shelf sampling software and hardware and the almost universal use of personal computers, sampling sounds and manipulating them has become relatively easy. As a result, sampling has opened a Pandora's box of old and new sound combinations, and with that, the necessity for new interpretations of the issues of copyright infringement, privacy rights and unfair competition.

COPYRIGHT INFRINGEMENT

Copyright owners have the exclusive right to authorize the making of copies and derivative works based on the original work, whether a musical composition or a recording. Unauthorized sampling violates these rights.

The music publisher, by itself or together with the songwriter(s), usually owns the copyright in the song. Previously, under traditional recording contracts, the recording company owned the copyright in the sound recording. Today, as the quality and affordability of home recording and mixing equipment improves, many more artists, whether distributed by small independent labels or major music conglomerates, own and retain the copyrights in their recordings or "masters." In December 1999, Congress amended section 101 of the Copyright Act to include *sound recordings* among the nine categories of works that may be owned by an employer or commission party as works made for hire. The amendment caused a firestorm of controversy from recording artists. Sheryl Crow and many other artists testified against the amendment at congressional hearings and as a result, a year later Congress passed "The Work Made For Hire Copyright Correction Act of 2000" that repealed the 1999 amendment. Today, sound recordings are not enumerated in section 101 of the U.S. Copyright Act as qualifying as works made for hire. However, Congress specifically left undecided the issue of whether sound recordings could qualify as works made for hire.

BREACHES OF CONTRACT
Warranties

Copyright infringement from illegal sampling may breach warranty provisions in recording contracts. Provisions called "Warranties," "Representations" and "Indemnifications" are almost always found in contracts between musicians and record companies; musicians and producers; producers and record companies; music publishers and record companies; songwriters and music publishers; record companies and distributors; and between distributors and record stores. According to these clauses, the person who provides the product (e.g., the songs, recordings, publishing rights, records, tapes, CDs) promises the person buying or licensing the product (the record company, Web site or record store) that the recordings do not infringe anyone's copyrights or other rights.

If a lawsuit for illegal sampling is filed, it could result in lawsuits for "breach of warranty" between each person that sells the illegally sampled product. Claims apply from person to person along the record-making and marketing chain, creating a duty to indemnify each other person along the chain. Unless expressly disclaimed, the same chain of written and implied indemnities applies to transmissions of digital sound recordings via the Internet. Final legal responsibility may lie with the recording artist. The indemnification rights that exist between each person or company in the process trigger one another like a chain reaction. This can result in hundreds of thousands of dollars in liability to the artist that uses an unauthorized sample.

Indemnification provisions require the record distributor to pay the retailer's damages and attorneys' fees, the record company is required to pay the distributor's fees and damages, the producer pays the record company's fees and damages and the artist may be technically liable for everyone's attorneys' fees and damages.

Unsatisfactory Masters

Another potential problem for musicians that sample is that most recording contracts give the record company the right to reject unsatisfactory masters. Masters that infringe copyrights of other sound recordings or musical compositions can be so rejected.

Artists are required to obtain copyright licenses (clearances) from the owners of sampled material or deliver substitute masters, which do not contain samples, to satisfy contract obligations to record companies.

Failure to comply with a record company's master delivery requirements could result in the artist having to repay recording fund advances and defending legal claims for breach of contract.

Fair Use Defense

The defense of fair use permits reasonable unauthorized copying from a copyrighted work, when the copying does not substantially impair present or potential value of the original work, and in some way advances the public benefit.

One rationale for the so-called fair use defense to copyright infringement is that only a small portion of the copyrighted work is copied. For many years there was a popular myth among musicians and producers that up to eight bars of a song was fair use and could be copied without constituting copyright infringement. This is not true. The rules determining which uses are fair uses, and not copyright infringement are not clear or simple. Many different economic and artistic factors go into determining whether or not a given use will be a productive and fair use. All of the circumstances of each case must be considered. The fair use standard for sound recordings is, however, generally stricter than for fair uses of musical compositions.

The reason for this difference is that U.S. copyright law only protects the expression of ideas, not the idea itself. Since there are a limited number of musical notes, copyright law treats single notes like ideas, and does not protect them. For this reason, it is safe to say that borrowing one note from a song will usually be a fair use of the copyright in the song, and not an actionable infringement. Borrowing more than one note, however, could be trouble. Lawsuits have involved copying as few as four notes from "I Love New York" and three words from "I Got Rhythm."

By selecting and arranging several notes in a particular sequence, composers create copyrightable musical compositions or songs. Songs are the expression of the composer's creativity and are protected by copyright.

But different fair use standards apply to sound recordings. Since there is virtually an unlimited number of sounds that can be recorded, sound recordings are, by definition, comprised of pure, copyrightable expression.

For musicians, engineers and producers, the practical effect of the two different fair use standards is that sampling a small portion of a musical composition may sometimes be fair use because copying a small portion may borrow uncopyrightable single notes like uncopyrightable ideas. But recent court decisions have held that the owner of the sound recording copyright has an exclusive right to grant licenses to sample the recording, and any unauthorized use, no matter how small, constitutes an infringement. Thus, sampling even a fraction of a second of a sound recording is copying of pure, copyrightable expression, constituting copyright infringement.

One way some producers and engineers that sample attempt to reduce the chances of a successful copyright infringement lawsuit is by electronically processing (camouflaging) portions of the sampled sounds beyond the point of their being easily recognizable. Filtering, synthesizing, or distorting recorded sounds can help conceal the sampled material while still retaining the essence of an instrumental lick or vocal phrase embodied in a few seconds of sound. Adding newly created sounds to the underlying sampling further dilutes the material. This is an attempt to change the sampled materials so that even though material was illegally *copied,* there is no substantial similarity, thus avoiding a suit for copyright infringement.

UNFAIR COMPETITION

State and federal unfair competition laws apply when the record buying public is misled as to the source or true origin of recordings that contain sampled material.

The Lanham Act is a federal law that punishes deceptive trade practices that mislead consumers about what they are buying or who made the product.

If a consumer is confused by hearing sampled vocal tracks of James Brown, or sampled guitar licks by Eddie Van Halen, and mistakenly buys a record only to discover that he or she has bought a recording by a different artist, the consumer has been deceived by the sampling. Such confusion and deception is a form of unfair competition, which can give rise to legal claims for Lanham Act violations that can be brought in state or federal court, or unfair competition claims that may be brought in state court. All of the previous warnings about the costs of litigation apply here as well.

LANDMARK LAWSUITS

In one of the most publicized sampling cases, the publisher of songwriter Gilbert O'Sullivan's song "Alone Again (Naturally)" successfully sued rap artist Biz Markie, Warner Brothers Records and others for sampling three words and a small portion of music from O'Sullivan's song without permission for Markie's rap tune "Alone Again."

A lawsuit involving the unauthorized use of drumbeats sought strict enforcement of copyright laws against sampling. Tuff City Records sued Sony Music and Def Jam Records claiming that two singles by rap artist L. L. Cool J ("Around the Way Girl" and "Six Minutes of Pleasure") contained drum track samples from "Impeach the Presidents," a 1973 song by the Honeydrippers and that another Def Jam Record, "Give the People" included vocal samples from the same Honeydrippers song.

The case is important because the common practice of sampling drumbeats is often overlooked as a minor use, too insignificant to bother clearing. This lawsuit reinforces the rule that any sampling of a sound recording may lead to a lawsuit for copyright infringement. Courts have also found a particular harmony or the repetition of the word "uh-oh" in a distinctive rhythm sufficiently original to be protectable by copyright.

A lawsuit testing the limits of the fair use defense was brought by the Ireland-based rock group U2. The band, its recording company, Island Records, and music publisher Warner-Chappell Music sued the group Negativland for sampling a part of the U2 song, "I Still Haven't Found What I'm Looking For" without the group's permission. While attorneys for U2 claimed that the sampling was consumer fraud, Negativland maintained that the use was parody, satire and cultural criticism and was therefore protected under the fair use doctrine. The case was settled out of court. Negativland agreed to recall the single and return copies to Island Records for destruction.

Jarvis v. A&M Records was a lawsuit over the taking of eight words ("Ooh ooh ooh ooh...move...free your body") and a keyboard line. The sampling party argued that the amount of material taken was too insignificant to constitute copyright infringement. The federal district court in New Jersey disagreed and refused to dismiss the suit, ruling that even similarity of fragmented portions of the song could constitute infringement if the portions taken were qualitatively important.

Recently, in Tennessee, the publisher of the musical composition and the owner of the sound recording of "Get Up Off Your Ass and Jam" by George Clinton and the Funkadelics each sued the Miramax and Dimension film companies over the inclusion of a two-second sample from the guitar solo that was lowered in pitch, "looped" and extended to 16 beats lasting seven seconds in the composition "100 Miles" in the soundtrack of the film *I Got the Hookup*. After several interim rulings, the court's final decision was that the portion of the musical composition used (a three-note arpeggiated chord repeated several times) was insufficiently original to constitute infringement of the musical composition. However, the court applied an entirely different standard to the admitted use of the sound recording, holding that for a sound recording to be infringed, the two recordings need not be "substantially similar." Rather, the party bringing suit need only prove that the original sound recording was used without authorization.

PRE-1972 SOUND RECORDINGS

Because U.S. copyrights in sound recordings were not recognized under federal law until February 15, 1972, in lieu of federal copyright protection, state common law copyright laws and state unfair competition statutes provide grounds to prosecute unauthorized samples of pre-1972 sound recordings.

RIGHTS OF PRIVACY VIOLATIONS

When sampled material incorporates a person's voice, statutory, and common-law rights of privacy ("rights of publicity") may be violated. In California, Civil Code section 3344 establishes civil liability for the unauthorized commercial use of any living person's voice. Such a use would include sampling.

Although current federal moral rights legislation does not protect sound recordings or voices, such protection may be available in the future. Meanwhile, many state laws make unauthorized sampling of voices a violation of state right-of-publicity laws. Further, if the sampled voice was originally recorded without the vocalist's permission, sampling such an unauthorized recording may violate other state privacy laws as well.

FEDERAL ANTIBOOTLEGGING STATUTES

Effective December 8, 1994 the adoption of the Uruguay Round Agreements Act by the U.S. Congress amended U.S. law by adding both civil and criminal penalties for the unauthorized recording or videotaping of live musical performances.

Any person who recorded or sampled in the past, or records or samples in the future, any part of any live musical performance without the performer's consent, can be sued under federal law for the same statutory damages, actual damages and attorneys' fees that are available in a traditional copyright infringement suit.

Previously, unauthorized recording of live performances was prohibited only under certain state laws.

Federal copyright law (17 U.S.C. §1101 *et seq.*) currently contains provisions which apply to so-called bootleggers that secretly record or sample live musical performances, or copy such illegal recordings by including sampled portions in new recordings. This strict law also prohibits selling or even transporting bootlegged recordings.

Remarkably, the law is retroactive, protecting even pre-1994 recordings if they are currently being sold or distributed, and has no statute of limitations, so that arguably suit can be brought against bootleggers and sellers of bootlegged recordings 10, 20, even 100 years after the unauthorized recording was made, if the unauthorized recordings are sold or distributed after the effective date of the Act. Unlike copyrights, which usually only last for the life of the author plus 70 years, the new federal musical performance rights are perpetual, lasting forever. Moreover, the defense of fair use may not apply to such unauthorized recordings because the fair use defense in section 107 of the Copyright Act was not incorporated into the statute.

Recent court decisions have held the antibootlegging statute to be unconstitutional because live musical performances are not "fixed" and thus are not "writings" subject to copyright protection and because the protection afforded under the statute is perpetual and not limited in time.

Of even greater concern are criminal penalties (18 U.S.C. §2319A) of forfeiture, seizure, destruction, and up to ten years imprisonment for knowingly, for profit, making or distributing copies of illegally recorded performances, transmitting an illegally recorded performance, or distributing, selling, renting, or even transporting illegally recorded performances, even if the performance occurred outside the United States!

Notwithstanding the possible unconstitutionality of the antibootlegging statute, the serious ramifications of outlaw sampling are obvious. Sampling any part of a live performance, or any part of an unauthorized recording of a live musical performance triggers a minefield of federal civil and criminal penalties. Great care should be taken to avoid using such bootlegged recordings in any way.

NO ELECTRONIC THEFT ACT

Both civil and criminal liability may result from sampling preexisting recordings or compositions acquired from unauthorized MP3-type files in electronic or digital form using the global computer network, commonly referred to as the Internet. In late 1999, Jeffrey Gerard Levy, a 22-year-old University of Oregon student was sentenced to two years probation after pleading guilty to illegally distributing copyrighted materials including MP3 files, movie clips, and software. As the first person convicted under the No Electronic Theft (NET) Act, Levy could have been sentenced to three years in prison and fined up to $250,000.

PENALTIES

Attorneys are always expensive. Entertainment attorneys usually charge $100 to $400 per hour. Those that are experienced in federal court copyright litigation often charge even more. Court costs and one side's attorneys' fees in a copyright trial average about $350,000. If you lose the trial you will have to pay the judgment against you, which could be as high as $100,000 for a single willful infringement (higher if there are substantial profits involved). An appeal of a judgment against you involves still more attorneys' fees and sometimes requires the posting of a bond.

In some cases a copyright infringer may have to pay the winning party's attorneys' fees. Copyright law also authorizes injunctions against the sale of CDs, tapes, and records containing illegally sampled material, seizure and destruction of infringing matter, and other criminal penalties.

In short, defending a copyright infringement lawsuit is a substantial expense and a risky proposition, exposing one to the possibility of hundreds of thousands of dollars in legal fees and costs.

Even if a particular sampling does not constitute copyright infringement, and is a fair use, it must still avoid violation of state and federal unfair competition laws.

COPYRIGHT CLEARANCES

Obtaining advance permission, copyright licenses or clearances from owners of both the musical composition and the sound recording you want to sample is the best way to avoid the problems and expenses that can result from illegal sampling.

Many factors affect whether and when musicians should request and pay for clearances for samples. Although copyright laws and general music industry practices do not give rise to a lawsuit in every sampling situation, the enormous expenses of any sampling dispute should be avoided whenever possible.

In many cases, it is wise to clear samples early in the recording process even if, eventually, they are not used, because when the record is finished and the sample must be cleared, the artist will have little leverage in negotiating clearance fees.

In some cities, special music clearance firms routinely request, negotiate, prepare, and process clearances for sampled materials for a fee. They know reasonable rates for clearances and will prepare valid copyright licenses for less cost to the requesting party than will most music attorneys.

Clearance Costs: Royalties

The cost of clearances is a major consideration in deciding whether to sample. Generally, record companies will not pay an artist more than the full statutory mechanical license fee for permission to sell recordings of the artist's composition. In 2006, the statutory rate was 9.1¢ per unit, for up to five minutes of a recording. However, most record companies and others typically negotiate mechanical license fees of only 50% to 75% of the statutory rate to record an entire composition. Out of that mechanical license fee, the sampling artist must pay the owners of any sampled material. If the clearance fees for the sampled material are too high, none of the mechanical license fee will be left for the sampling artist, and the sampled cut may end up costing the artist more than is earned by the entire composition.

Sampling royalty rates for musical compositions can range from 10% to 25% of the statutory rate. Sampling royalty rates for sound recordings range from .5¢ to 5¢ per unit sold.

Clearance costs double or triple when more than one sampled track is included in a recording. Imagine, for example, a composition containing Phil Collins' snare drum sound, Jimi Hendrix's guitar sound, Phil Lesh's bass, and Little Richard's voice. In this case, combined sampling clearance fees could make the multitrack recording impossibly expensive.

Sampling clearance practices vary widely throughout the music industry. Fees are affected by both the quantity of material being sampled (a second or less is a "minor use," five seconds is a "major use") and the quality of the sampled material (i.e., a highly recognizable lyric sung by a famous artist would be more expensive than an anonymous bass drum track). Certain artists demand exorbitant fees to discourage sampling. On the other hand, some music publishers offer compositions in their catalogs and actively encourage sampling. Prices are affected by the popularity and prestige of the sampling artist and the uniqueness and value of the sampled sounds.

Clearance Costs: Buyouts and Co-Ownership

A percentage of the mechanical license fee (royalty) is one type of clearance fee. Another is a one-time flat-fee payment (buyout) for the use of sampled material. Buyout fees range from $250 to $10,000, depending on the demands of the copyright owners. Up to $50,000 or more may be charged for a major use of a famous artist's performance or song. An upper limit on the number of units embodying the sampled material that may be sold may be imposed by some licensors, requiring additional payment at a higher royalty rate or an entirely new license if the maximum is exceeded.

More frequently, music publishers and record companies demand to be co-owners of the new composition as a condition of granting permission to sample. The option of assigning a share of the publishing (i.e., the copyright) in the song containing the sampled material to a publisher or record company may be helpful to the sampling artist, particularly when a buyout of all rights is not possible. Assigning a portion of the copyright in lieu of a cash advance may be less of a financial burden on an artist, enabling a song to be released where the cost or unavailability of a license would otherwise preclude the record from being distributed legally. If you license the sample for a percentage of the statutory rate, and you later want to license your song with the sample in it for a film, the film producer must obtain separate permission from the publisher who has granted the license. That publisher must always be consulted in new licensing situations. On the other hand, if you negotiate a buyout, you are free from any continuing obligation to the publisher. Similarly, if you negotiate income participation, which is to sell a percentage of your song in return for permission to sample, the publisher becomes a part owner of your song, and may or may not have approval rights in future licensing of the new work depending on the administration terms in the sampling license. Percentage of income participation ranges from 5% for a minimal use within the song to as much as 75% if the sample has been utilized throughout the song and is an integral part of the work.

GUIDANCE FOR NONFAMOUS ARTISTS THAT WANT TO NEGOTIATE SAMPLING RIGHTS FROM LARGE COMPANIES

For the aspiring recording artist, the most efficient and least expensive way to include high-quality samples without risking a lawsuit or sacrificing royalties is to purchase commercially available sampling software. Various "precleared" or public domain instrumental sounds and effects are available for unrestricted use. These may be incorporated into recordings without payment of any royalty or fee beyond the initial cost of the program.

If you are determined to use a sample of a recording owned by a major label or publisher, the following suggestions may improve your chances of obtaining a sampling license at an affordable rate.

Send a written request for a sample license either to the publisher of the musical composition or to the record company. Publishers and record companies may be more willing to grant low-cost licenses to sample dormant catalog artists that are not currently enjoying significant sales, than for their hottest artists with records on the charts.

Include an explanation of how the intended sample will be used, the length of the proposed sample and other facts that would encourage the granting of the license. For example, if your most recent recording had good sales or positive reviews, this may be helpful. If you are not signed to a record company and the sampled recording will not be distributed commercially, for example, a demo tape or a soundtrack for a student film, this fact may convince the publisher or record company to issue a free or low-cost "festival" or "demo" license that permits the sample as long as the demo or film are not commercially distributed. If you later want to sell or distribute the film or demo or publicly perform it on radio or TV, you will have to return to the licensor and negotiate a license at current commercial rates.

AMERICAN FEDERATION OF MUSICIANS PAYMENTS

Under certain circumstances, the American Federation of Musicians (AFM) collects fees for its member musicians when a record company uses a sample of a preexisting recording in a new recording. When a portion of a recording containing the performance of a "covered musician," i.e., an AFM member, who is a "nonroyalty artist" (a musician who plays on the recording but does not receive record royalties) and is not a self-contained royalty group or symphonic musician, is sampled under the following AFM definition, the company owning the recording that is being sampled makes a one-time lump sum payment of $400 for the first sample (regardless of how many times it is used in the new recording) and a one-time lump sum payment of $250 for each additional sample from the same recording, plus 2% of the gross revenue received by the company in excess of $25,000, less the lump sum payments that have already been made. These payments are made to the Sound Recording Special Payments Fund, which are then distributed to the musician members. The AFM's definition of a sample is "the encoding of a portion of a phonograph record containing the performance of a Covered Musician(s) into a digital sampler, computer, digital hard drive storage unit or any other device for subsequent playback on a digital synthesizer or other play-back device for use in another song; however, a re-mix or re-edit of the new song shall not be considered a sample for purposes hereunder." Note that the definition includes not only samples embodied in traditional tapes and CDs, but also includes samples embodied on synthesizers, samplers, and other playback devices.

SOUNDTRACK SAMPLING

Occasionally, artists sample things other than music, such as audio bytes from feature films, television shows, or news footage. In these cases, permission must be obtained from the owner of the footage. Fees range from $1000 to $8000 per minute for buyouts, which must be negotiated directly with the representative for the actor whose voice is being sampled. The minimum fee for such use is the Screen Actors Guild's full day rate, which is currently $737 in Los Angeles (subject to change yearly). Private licensing agents such as CMG in Indianapolis, Indiana may charge far more for permission to sample the voice of someone of the caliber of Elvis Presley or Marilyn Monroe. If a film or television program is used, payments may also be due to the writers' and directors' guilds and to the American Federation of Musicians.

CONCLUSION

Throughout history, every new development in music has been greeted with suspicion by the music establishment of the day. Polyphony (playing harmonies) was considered demonic in medieval times, and was punishable by burning at the stake. As modern musicians explore innovative chord progressions, syncopated rhythms, and new electronic instruments, we all learn more about the musical landscape around us. Only time will tell whether samplers will be viewed as musical innovators or plagiarists.

SAMPLE USE AGREEMENTS

The Master Sample Use License Agreement and Mechanical License are short-form examples of licenses to incorporate or sample portions of a recording of a musical composition. Permission to sample the musical composition is granted by the music publisher(s) in the Mechanical License; permission to sample the recording of the musical composition is granted by the record company in the Master Sample Use License Agreement.

Fees for using the master and the musical composition are expressed as a one-time flat fee or buyout and perpetual, worldwide rights are granted. As discussed above, such extensive rights may not always be granted. Limits on the term, territory or number of units that may be sold, co-ownership and coadministration of the recording and co-ownership of the musical composition embodying the sampled material, or statutory compulsory license fees on every copy sold, may be required by certain record companies and music publishers.

MASTER SAMPLE USE LICENSE AGREEMENT

In consideration of either (the sum of $ _____ which covers ____ % of the copyright) or (granting ____ % of the copyright and publishing right [and coadministration rights]) for the rights and license herein granted thereto, _____ (Record Company), hereinafter referred to as "Licensor," hereby grants to _____ (sampling Artist and/or recording company), hereinafter referred to as "Licensee," the nonexclusive, limited right, license, privilege and authority, but not the obligation, to use a portion of the Master Recording, defined below (hereinafter referred to as the "Master"), as embodied in the tape approved by Licensor, with no greater usage of the Master than is contained in the approved tape (the "Usage"), in the manufacture, distribution, and sale of any phonorecord (as that term is defined in Section 101 of the Copyright Act) entitled "_____" ("Album"), performed by _____ ("Artist") embodying the recording _____ ("Master") as performed by _____ ("Sample Artist"), and produced by _____ ("Producer"). Licensor additionally grants to Licensee the right to exploit, advertise, publicize, and promote such Master, as embodied in the phonorecord, in all media, markets, and formats now known or hereafter devised.

1. The term of this agreement ("Term") will begin on the date hereof and shall continue in perpetuity.

2. The territory covered by this agreement is _____.

3. It is expressly understood and agreed that any compensation to be paid herein to Licensor is wholly contingent upon the embodiment of the Master within the phonorecord and that nothing herein shall obligate or require Licensee to commit to such usage. However, such compensation shall in no way be reduced by a lesser use of the Recording than the Usage provided for herein.

4. Licensor warrants only that it has the legal right to grant the aforesaid master recording use rights subject to the terms, conditions, limitations, restrictions, and reservations herein contained, and that this license is given and accepted without any other warranty or recourse. In the event said warranty is breached, Licensor's total liability

shall not exceed the lesser of the actual damages incurred by Licensee or the total consideration paid hereunder to Licensor.

5. Licensor reserves unto itself all rights and uses of every kind and nature whatsoever in and to the Master other than the limited rights specifically licensed hereunder, including the sole right to exercise and to authorize others to exercise such rights at any and all times and places without limitation.

6. This license is binding upon and shall inure to the benefit of the respective successors and assigns of the parties hereto.

7. This contract is entered into in the State of California and its validity, construction, interpretation, and legal effect shall be governed by the laws of the State of California applicable to contracts entered into and performed entirely therein.

8. This agreement contains the entire understanding of the parties relating to the subject matter herein contained.

IN WITNESS WHEREOF, the parties have caused the foregoing to be executed as of this _____ day of _____ , 200___.

AGREED TO AND ACCEPTED:

_____   _____
LICENSOR (COMPANY NAME)   LICENSEE (COMPANY NAME)

_____   _____
BY (SIGNATURE)   BY (SIGNATURE)

_____   _____
NAME AND TITLE (AN AUTHORIZED SIGNATORY)   NAME AND TITLE (AN AUTHORIZED SIGNATORY)

_____   _____
FEDERAL I.D./SS#   FEDERAL I.D./SS#

MECHANICAL LICENSE

In consideration of the sum of $ _____ which covers _____ % of the copyright and full payment for the rights and license herein granted thereto, _____ ("Licensor") hereby grants to _____ ("Licensee") the nonexclusive right, license, privilege, and authority to use, in whole or in part, the copyrighted musical composition known as _____ written by _____ and _____ (hereinafter referred to as the "Composition"):

1. In the recording, making, and distribution of phonorecords (as that term is defined in Section 101 of the Copyright Act) to be made and distributed throughout the world in accordance with the provisions of Section 115 of the Copyright Act of the United States (the "Act"), except it is agreed that: (1) Licensee need not serve or file the notices required under the Act; (2) consideration for such license shall be in the form of a one-time flat-fee buyout; (3) Licensee shall have the unlimited right to utilize the Composition, or any portion thereof, as embodied in the phonorecord, in

any and all media now known or hereafter devised for the purpose of promoting the sale of the phonorecord which is the subject of this agreement; and (4) this license shall be worldwide.

2. This license permits the use of the Composition or any portion thereof, in the particular recordings made in connection with the sound recording _____ ("Album") by _____ ("Artist"), and permits the use of such recording in any phonorecord in which the recording may be embodied in whatever form now known or hereafter devised. This license includes the privilege of making a musical arrangement of the Composition to the extent necessary to conform it to the style or manner of interpretation of the performance involved.

3. Licensor warrants and represents that it has the right to enter into this agreement and to grant to Licensee all of the rights granted herein, and that the exercise by Licensee of any and all of the rights granted to Licensee in this agreement will not violate or infringe upon any common-law or statutory rights of any person, firm, or corporation including, without limitation, contractual rights, copyrights, and rights of privacy.

4. This license is binding upon and shall inure to the benefit of the respective successors, assigns, and sublicensees of the parties hereto.

5. This agreement sets forth the entire understanding of the parties with respect to the subject matter hereof, and may not be modified or amended except by written agreement executed by the parties.

6. This license may not be terminated for any reason, is entered into in the State of California, and its validity, construction, interpretation, and legal effect shall be governed by the laws of the State of California applicable to contracts entered into and performed entirely therein.

IN WITNESS WHEREOF, the parties have entered into this license agreement as of this _____ day of _____ , 200__.

AGREED TO AND ACCEPTED:

LICENSOR (COMPANY NAME)	LICENSEE (COMPANY NAME)
BY (SIGNATURE)	BY (SIGNATURE)
NAME AND TITLE (AN AUTHORIZED SIGNATORY)	NAME AND TITLE (AN AUTHORIZED SIGNATORY)
FEDERAL I.D./SS#	FEDERAL I.D./SS#

Special thanks to Suzy Vaughan, Esq., and Ron McGowan for their generous assistance in the preparation of these agreements.

Collaborator/Songwriter Agreements

BY MARK HALLORAN AND EDWARD (NED) R. HEARN

If you cowrite a song with someone, both of you own the song as "joint owners" in what the copyright law calls a "joint work." This is irrespective of whether one of you writes the music and the other the lyrics, or you both write music and lyrics. Both of you have an "undivided" ownership in the song (i.e., you each own 50% of the whole song). There is not a separate copyright in the music and lyrics. There is one copyright in both.

The essence of cowriting is writing together to create a single song, regardless of who contributes what. This does not mean that you have to work together, or that your creative contribution be equal in quality or quantity. You also do not need to have an express "collaboration agreement," although it is a good idea, given the myriad issues that can arise.

One of the most famous cowriting teams is Bernie Taupin and Elton John. Bernie, on his own, first writes the lyrics. John, on his own, then writes the music. Since both Bernie and Elton intend that their work be a united whole, the result is a joint work, which they co-own fifty-fifty.

PERCENTAGE OWNERSHIP

As joint owners you and your cowriter can divide your song ownership in whatever proportion you want. In the absence of an agreement you share equally, even if it is clear that your contributions are not equal. Thus, if there are two songwriters, you own the song fifty-fifty; three songwriters, one-third each; etc. Dividing the ownership ratably is also the most common way to divide ownership in a written collaboration agreement.

One common benchmark in dividing ownership is that the lyrics are worth 50% and the music 50%. For example, if two people write the music and one person writes the lyrics, they may agree to divide the ownership 25% each for the two music writers, with the lyricist retaining the remaining 50%. However, if there is no such agreement, each would own 33.3% of the song.

GRANT OF RIGHTS

Now that we have determined who owns the song, who controls it? It is crucial to the exploitation of the song that there be a central place to license the work and collect money.

Coadministration of Licenses

It is usually more convenient for one music publisher to collect and divide all the income. Licensing can become complicated when a licensee has to seek the approval of, and document permission from, multiple publishers. However, many cowriters prefer that there be separate administration among the various publishing companies. This has its advantages. You have control over the scope of the licenses, to whom licenses are granted, how much is charged, how the money is collected and what costs are incurred.

As joint owner (in the United States), you may exploit the song yourself and also grant nonexclusive licenses. Still, you must account to your cowriters for the money that is generated from the nonexclusive licenses.

A license is permission to use a work. It is not a transfer of copyright ownership, which requires the written permission of all songwriters (although you could transfer just your share to another without affecting the ownership interests of the other cowriters/co-owners). (See discussion below.)

- Public Performances. Public performances agreements must be entered into with ASCAP, BMI or SESAC. Typically, they are done in the name of the song-writer's publishing company. If cowriters want to use one company, they may use that company and divide the publisher's share of the income. Or, each of the separate publishing companies may enter into a performance agreement for its share with ASCAP, BMI or SESAC with each collecting its respective percentage of the publisher's share of the public performance income. Writers should join ASCAP, BMI or SESAC, to collect their portion of the songwriters' shares of the public performance income.

- Mechanical Licenses. Mechanical licenses are nonexclusive; any cowriter can grant them but must account to and pay the other cowriters, or instruct the licensed party that the cowriter's shares be paid directly to them.

- Print Rights. These agreements are usually exclusive, and all cowriters must agree in writing.

- Subpublishing Rights. Foreign subpublishing deals are usually exclusive, and all cowriters must agree in writing. Additionally, most foreign jurisdictions require that all co-owners agree to licensing, so the subpublishers are going to want to have all cowriters sign. If agreement cannot be reached on a shared subpublisher, you can, however, still make arrangements with one to represent just your interest share in the songs' copyrights.

DIVISION OF INCOME

Just as a contributing author is entitled to a ratable share of ownership, the coauthor is also entitled to the same ratable share of income, absent an agreement to the contrary.

PURSUIT OF INFRINGEMENT

One obligation that cowriters have together is to protect the copyright. This includes pursuing infringers. Can you sue even if a co-owner does not want to sue? The answer appears to be yes, at least with respect to your interest in the copyright. However, the court may require that you bring in the cowriter(s) as a coplaintiff, so it is best that you decide to sue together.

What if you have to sue a co-owner, for example, for failure to account to and pay you? You may, but you do not have to, bring in all the other co-owners in order to sue.

COPYRIGHT DURATION

The basic rule is that the copyright of a song written after January 1, 1976 lasts for the life of the author plus 70 years. In the case of a joint work, the copyright lasts for the life of the last surviving author plus 70 years.

COPYRIGHT TRANSFERS

Each collaborator, independently of the other collaborators, has the right to transfer his or her copyright ownership to another party. That transfer may be for the full copyright share of the collaborator to a publisher, or a partial copyright transfer to a copublisher. A collaborator may also grant all administration and supervision rights of that collaborator's share to a third party as the publishing administrator, while still retaining ownership of the copyright.

If one collaborator transfers his or her copyright interests to a third party, but the second collaborator does not do the same, then the third party would co-own the copyright with the other collaborator. At the same time, the second collaborator has the option to transfer his or her copyright interest, in the whole or in part, or just the administration rights, to the same new owner as did the first collaborator or to a different party.

Unless either collaborator has granted to the other collaborator the administration rights in the copyright for the song, the new co-owner will have to share decision-making and the publisher's income share with the collaborator who did not transfer his or her interests. The accounting can become cumbersome if income sharing and accounting procedures are not coordinated.

DIFFERENT PERFORMING RIGHTS SOCIETY AFFILIATIONS

It is also possible for each coauthor to belong to a different performing rights society, namely ASCAP, BMI or SESAC. If that is the case, then a share of the performance income collection would be allocated to each collaborator's affiliated performing rights society. For example, if the song is performed as a part of a soundtrack to a television program, then, with the performance rights for that song being divided between two different performing rights groups, the performance fee also would be so divided. Each performing rights group would receive its allocated share and distribute it to the collaborator affiliated with it. It is quite possible that one collaborator, being paid by a different performing rights society, would not receive the same amount of writer and publisher performance income as the other, since each of the performing rights societies uses a different reporting mechanism.

SONGWRITERS AS MEMBERS OF DIFFERENT BANDS

In the event one of the collaborating songwriters is a member of a band and the other is not, the collaborator who is a member of the band will have the authority to allow the band to rehearse and perform the collaborated song in live concerts and to record the song for release on phonorecords. While, technically, it is best to have both writers approve and issue a combined use license, e.g., a mechanical license to reproduce the song on phonorecords, each has the authority to do so, but must account to the collaborator who is not a band member for their share of writer and publisher income.

Most record labels will want to get both coauthors and copublishers to provide written authorization for the initial reproduction of that song on phonorecords. After the first release of the phonorecords, a compulsory mechanical license procedure may apply to any future recordings of that song, whether by that same or any other band.

CONTROLLED COMPOSITION CLAUSE

Of particular significance is the situation where one of the coauthors is a band member (while the other is not) and has a recording agreement with a record label that requires the writer/band member to agree to a controlled composition clause in the recording agreement. This clause authorizes the record company to pay a reduced mechanical royalty, usually 75% of the prevailing statutory mechanical rate, as the royalty fee for the right to reproduce the song on phonorecords that are sold to the public.

Generally, the recording artist/collaborating writer will be required by the record company to represent that he or she has obtained permission from the collaborating writer who is not the band member and not a signatory to the recording agreement to issue a mechanical license for the reduced rate. But often, the recording artist/collaborating writer cannot guarantee that, and most likely will not be able to provide the record label with written authorization from the collaborator accepting a reduced mechanical royalty rate. In those situations, the record company will have to pay the collaborating writer who is not a member of the band nor a signatory to the recording agreement that cowriter's share of mechanicals, both as writer and copublisher, at full statutory rate, while paying the collaborator, who is a signatory, the reduced rate. It is also possible that the rate for the recording artist/collaborating writer will be reduced even further, given the need to pay the unsigned collaborator the higher amount, which will reduce the amount available to pay the recording artist/collaborating writer.

By way of illustration, assume that the maximum pool of mechanical royalties for all of the songs on the recording artist's album is 68.25¢ (75% of 91.1¢ or 75% of 0.091 x 10 songs), as distinct from the current statutory rate of 9.1¢ per song, which would earn 91¢ if ten songs are on the album. The payout to the collaborating coauthor who is not a signatory to the recording agreement will reduce the overall pool available for mechanical royalties, causing the amount payable to the collaborator/band member to be even less than the 75% fractional statutory rate. For example, if that nonsignatory collaborating coauthor has contributed half of the material on four different songs, he/she will get full statutory for his/her share of those songs, .5 x 9.1¢ x 4 = 18.2¢, which will be deducted from the maximum pool of 68.25¢, leaving 50.05¢ to be allocated to the signatory collaborating songwriters for the other six songs that were fully written by them and for the other four coauthored by them with the nonsignatory collaborator.

COACCOUNTING

Any income that either collaborating writer receives from the commercial exploitation of the song, whether it is from their own use or from use by an authorized third party, must be accounted for and apportioned to the other collaborating songwriter. Such payments should be made in a timely manner, for example, no less than 30 days after receipt. Also, statements that accompany the payments to the first collaborator should be copied and forwarded with the payment to the other collaborator.

FUTURE GENERATIONS

The rights of each deceased coauthor will pass on to the benefit of the heir(s) and descendant(s) of that coauthor, either by way of a will (testate) or without a will (intestate). If there is no will, the distribution will be governed by state statutes, usually to surviving spouses and children, on a first priority basis, before other relatives. It then would be the heir or the executor of the estate of the deceased who will have the authority to grant and make decisions with respect to the use of a collaborated composition. By the same token, the surviving collaborator will have the authority to continue to exploit the song while having a reporting and payment sharing obligation to the deceased's descendants or executor. The estate of the deceased collaborator can exploit the song too, and must account to the surviving coauthor.

PHANTOM COWRITERS

Some songwriters have complained that they have been forced to acknowledge songwriters that did not make a significant (or is some cases any) contribution to a song. This group of "phantom" songwriters has allegedly included label heads, producers and nonwriting band members. The exact contribution to a song is often a subjective measurement; once a songwriter acknowledges a cowriter it is virtually impossible to undo. If the price to place a song on a record of a multiplatinum artist is sharing writing credit this pressure is difficult if not impossible to resist. It's impossible to measure the prevalence of this practice, but most acknowledge, off the record, that it goes on. Prominent songwriters rarely if ever share credit in this context, and surely your goal should be to not share credit with phantom cowriters.

Digital Downloads and Streaming: Copyright and Distribution Issues

BY EDWARD (NED) R. HEARN

Important: **An updated copy of this chapter by Edward Hearn can be downloaded for free at http://www.internetmedialaw.com/articles.html**

In the prior version of this chapter, written in 2001, we explored how the development of digital compression technology, concurrent with the wide acceptance of the Internet created an environment that shook up many of the old rules of the music industry and challenged the traditional music business to adapt to changes in consumer preferences. There have been many changes since that time, including continued development of digital delivery technology, statutes, court cases, contractual agreements and new economic models, creating a whole new paradigm on how to provide consumers with recorded music, with music publishers and record companies attempting to control the economic returns due to them and to the creators of music and sound recordings. This chapter discusses the rights of master owners, recording artists, music publishers and composers in this ever-evolving landscape. It will explain how the recent changes to the Copyright Act, including relevant recent litigation and business developments, are working to create a mechanism to provide an economic return for music and recordings in the digital media world.

In viewing the evolution of the digital marketplace, it is interesting to compare physical sales with digital sales. In the first six months of 2005, there were approximately 282 million physical albums sold in the United States as compared to 270 million physical albums sold in the first six months of 2006. During the same period, there were approximately 158 million digital tracks sold in the United States in the first six months of 2005 as compared to 281 million in the first half of 2006. Consistently, over the past five years, the sale of physical product has decreased while the sale of digital product has increased. The latter is still a substantially small percentage of the overall recorded music market, but it is steadily growing, while the physical market is steadily decreasing, and the physical retail stores are working harder and harder at just trying to survive in business.

DIGITAL PERFORMANCE OF SOUND RECORDINGS

When you compose and record music, you essentially create two properties, both of which are protected by the copyright laws—the music you write and the musical performances you record.

As the copyright owner of the music and the sound recording, you have the exclusive right to reproduce, distribute, display, perform and create derivative works with those properties, with the sole exception that, in the United States you have no exclusive rights to perform the sound recording (as distinct from the performance of the music on the sound recording), namely anyone can perform the sound recording without having to make any payment to you for it. Examples of performing the sound recording include playing, broadcasting or transmitting those sound recordings over radio or television. This situation is the result of effective lobbying by the broadcast industry when sound recordings first became subject to federal copyright protection in 1972. The broadcast industry was able to get Congress to exclude from the exclusive rights of the owner of sound recordings the right to perform those works, since the broadcast industry already was paying the music publishers royalties for the performance of the music contained on the recordings (namely, the payments collected by BMI, ASCAP and SESAC). These royalties are distinct from synchronization fees paid for the right to fix and reproduce the music and the sound recording on the soundtrack of an audiovisual production.

The record companies were determined not to let their experience with the performance of sound recordings on radio or television be repeated in the digital world. Consequently, amendments to the Copyright Act were enacted in 1995, namely the Digital Performance Right in Sound Recordings Act (DPRSRA) and in 1998, the Digital Millennium Copyright Act (DMCA). The DPRSRA vests in the owner of the sound recording the exclusive right to control the *digital* performance of the sound recordings over cable and satellite. The DMCA applies the same exclusive right to the owner of the sound recording with respect to webcasting over the Internet or wirelessly. Under each of these Acts, fees must be paid for the performance of the sound recording in the digital medium. The companies that wish to perform the sound recording digitally must get either a voluntary license for interactive streaming and conditional downloads (consumers can choose what they want to listen to whenever they want to listen to it) or a compulsory license for noninteractive streaming (consumers get to listen only to whatever selections the transmitting entity decides to program) if they are to avoid copyright infringement claims. Examples of companies that rely on the compulsory licensing opportunities are the satellite services, such as XM and Sirius, cable systems like Music Choice, and the Internet radio station features of the webcasters, such as RealNetworks' Rhapsody. These entities also get voluntary licenses from the record companies for their features that do not fall within the scope of the compulsory license. The provisions of both acts are very complex, and at the end of this chapter there is a description of the requirements that must be satisfied for cable, satellite companies and webcasters to qualify for a compulsory license; i.e., getting permission from the record companies and owners of the sound recordings to digitally perform them is not necessary so long as the intent to rely on the compulsory license procedure for noninteractive streaming is filed with the Copyright Office and the rules that regulate the scope of performances under the compulsory parameters are satisfied.

If the cable and satellite industries and webcasters do not satisfy the compulsory license provisions provided for the digitally transmitted performance of the sound recordings in a noninteractive manner, then they must get permission from the owners of the sound recordings. The granting of such permission is voluntary and the owners can set their own rates based on negotiations with the digital music service providers, as further described below in the section on digital phonorecord deliveries of sound recordings.

With regard to the compulsory licensing under the DPRSRA for noninteractive streaming, the record, cable and satellite industries tried to negotiate and establish the rates that would be used to compute the fees to be paid. They could not reach agreement and an arbitration panel, under the auspices of the Copyright Office, reviewed the matter and set the rates. The record companies were arguing for a royalty of 15% to 20% of the receipts of the cable and satellite companies, and the latter were offering 1% to 2% of their revenues. The final license fee imposed on the cable and satellite industries was 6.5% of their gross revenues. The fees paid, based on that percentage, are allocated 50% to the record company (i.e., the owner of the sound recording), 45% to the featured artist, 2.5% to nonfeatured musicians and 2.5% to nonfeatured vocalists. There have been millions of dollars collected to date under the DPRSRA, which have been paid to SoundExchange *(www.soundexchange.com)* as the representative of the sound recording copyright owners and artists. SoundExchange disburses that money to the labels and to the recording artists in their respective shares on a quarterly basis.

A similar situation occurred under the DMCA with respect to webcasters for noninteractive streaming. The disparity in fees sought by the labels and offered by the webcasters paralleled the same positions experienced between the record companies and the satellite and cable companies. As the representatives of the record and webcasting industries were not able to settle on fees, the matter was submitted to arbitration under the auspices of the Copyright Office. Eventually the Copyright Office issued its findings and directed that the rate to be paid to the record companies by webcasters for noninteractive subscription and nonsubscription services is 0.0762¢ per performance or 0.88¢ per aggregate tuning hour (i.e., a measurement of the period of time that a consumer user is logged onto the service and streaming the music) for simulcast broadcast, or 1.17¢ per aggregate tuning hour for programming other than simulcast broadcast, or a proportionate share of 10.9% of the subscription service revenues, but not less than 27¢ per month per subscriber. The rates schedule also requires that the digital audio service providers pay minimum annual fees of between $200 and $5,000 per channel against the per performance and per tuning hour rates described above. The amount collected by SoundExchange between April 1, 2003 and March 31, 2004 (the last publicly filed report as of the writing of this article) for this category of fees is $15.6 million. It is expected that this amount of money will grow as these services to consumers become more established and expand.

Keep in mind that the rates described for the various categories of digital audio services are subject to ongoing changes. The rates were scheduled to change in 2006, but those adjustments were still pending as of fall 2006. As a result, the 2004 to 2005 rates still applied to 2006, subject to a retroactive adjustment once the 2006 rates are set (scheduled to be announced in January, 2007). To get an updated report on what rates are being charged, visit the SoundExchange Web site, which provides a substantial source of information on the rates that apply and the requirements to be met by the cablecasters and webcasters.

DIGITAL PERFORMANCE OF MUSIC

In addition to fees for the streaming of sound recordings by satellite, cable or webcasting, the streaming companies must sign license agreements with the music performance rights societies, BMI, ASCAP and SESAC, for the performance of the music embodied on the sound recordings. The performing rights societies will allocate those fees as collected and make payment to the publishers and writers. There has been no dispute about the right of the performing rights societies to collect such sums nor any dispute about the obligation of the satellite, cable and webcasting companies to obtain licenses and pay. The issue has been how much to pay. The Web sites of the performing rights societies provide details on how they compute the fees for the performance of music over the Internet. Fees have been negotiated on a case-by-case basis. Most cable and satellite companies, and webcasters and streaming media companies, such as MusicNet, Yahoo!/Musicmatch/Launch, and AOL/MusicNow, have obtained licenses from the performing rights societies.

Note also that the National Music Publishers Association (NMPA) takes the position that a digital delivery or download of a phonorecord containing music requires payment of a performance fee as well as a mechanical royalty. That issue is still unresolved.

DIGITAL PHONORECORD DELIVERIES OF SOUND RECORDINGS

Since the right to reproduce and distribute copies of sound recordings is recognized as an exclusive right of the copyright owner, the DPRSRA and the DMCA did not have to address the rules that would apply to digital phonorecord deliveries as they relate to sound recordings. Rather, the economics of digital phonorecord delivery is evolving based on marketplace experiments and contractual arrangements between recording companies and other owners of sound recordings and artists, and the third parties that license those sound recordings to distribute them digitally to consumers. Sound recordings can be digitally delivered directly to consumers' computers over the Web, wirelessly through carriers to mobile devices and through kiosks at retail outlets that have connections to the Internet or have the masters stored on servers at the retailer. At the kiosks, consumers can download masters and have them burned into compact discs or loaded into portable MP3 players.

The real birth of the significant digital download market happened in the spring of 2003, when Apple launched its iTunes store. Apple was the first company to convince the major labels to make their masters available for digital downloads to consumers' desktop and laptop computers and now to mobile devices. This undertaking coincided with Apple's launch of the iPod, which has been the dominant product in the portable digital marketplace. That arrangement between Apple and the majors opened the door for other companies to pursue being digital suppliers to consumers in this market and for other labels to get their content into the digital distributed mediums. Since the launch, Apple has extended its reach beyond the United States to Canada, the UK, Europe, Japan and Australia. As of early 2006, over a billion downloads had occurred through the Apple iTunes system. While, on its face, that is a significant number, representing about 84 million albums, it is only 5% of the total number of physical albums, over 1.6 billion, sold in the United States during that first three years of iTunes. This is not to say that the initiative that has been launched by Apple is not significant, but rather it underscores that we are still in the very early stages of the digital distribution revolution. On the other hand, billions upon billions of illegal downloads have occurred through P2P file sharing systems, which is where the real revolution has been occurring with substantial impact on the recorded music industry and the artists, labels, publishers and writers that depend on it for their livelihood.

The other significant players involved in the digital distribution content include MusicNet, AOL/MusicNow, Yahoo!/Musicmatch/Launch, MTV's Urge, RealNetworks' Rhapsody, Microsoft's MSN and its intended iPod competitor, Zune, Liquid (which services Wal-Mart), Sony Connect and Napster (which is the successor-in-interest in name only to the original Napster, having purchased that mark from the bankrupt original Napster). Amazon.com also has announced its intent to participate in this market. With reference to Napster, SanDisk, a Milpitas, California based company that manufactures flash memory cards and MP3 players, currently makes the second most popular MP3 player behind the iPod. In the summer of 2006, it announced that it was in negotiations to acquire the Napster service to create its own player/service ecosystem to compete with Apple's iPod and Microsoft's newly announced Zune player. Unlike Napster, which has to rely on its digital download and subscription services as its sole income source, SanDisk, like Apple, can rely on selling its hardware and using the content side as a marketing device to spur sales. As of the submission of this chapter for printing, however, this transaction with SanDisk had not been reported as having progressed any further. Each of these companies, and the many dozens of other companies that have been started and that will be started to serve the digital distribution market, has its own economic model, but as that model is applied to consumers, record labels, music publishers, artists and composers, the economic profiles are similar.

In the most common model for so-called digital phonorecord deliveries (i.e., downloads to computers and certain mobile devices), the average retail price to the consumer for a single track is 99¢. On average, album downloads are sold at $9.99. From that 99¢, the digital distributor will pay the label between 60¢ and 70¢ as a wholesale price (or $6 to $7 for an album), and sometimes a bit higher with regard to major label superstars, and will keep the difference as its share. From that wholesale payment, the label will pay the mechanical royalties, 9.1¢ per download through December 31, 2007, and a royalty to the artist and producer, which is usually based on the royalty rate paid to the artist/producer on the retail sale price of physical product. For artists/producers with a 12% royalty, they would see 12¢. Occasionally, a label may treat the artist/producer so that he/she would share fifty-fifty or some other percentage of the wholesale price paid for the download minus mechanicals. That, however, is the exception rather than the rule. Most labels will not take packaging deductions or free goods allowances on the downloads, since there obviously is no packaging and there are no free goods, unless the artist and the label have agreed to distribute a track at no cost as a promotional device.

Some digital distributors, such as eMusic, have a subscription system for permanent downloads that will allow a certain number of downloads for a monthly subscription fee. In those situations, the average download price per master, inclusive of mechanical, would be as low as 22¢ (90 downloads for $19.99 per month), which is a lot less than the per download fee paid under the arrangements that Apple and its competitors have with the major and independent labels. Of course, if the eMusic subscriber does not download the full monthly allocation, then the value attributed to each track actually downloaded is higher. Generally, eMusic will share with the label on a fifty-fifty basis the accounted for value per download based on the actual number of downloads from the allowable subscription allocation, after deduction of the mechanicals payable to publishers and other costs that are defined in the agreement between eMusic and the labels. From the 50% share of that net amount received by the label, the label must pay the artist and producer royalties.

A number of the companies, in addition to the download model, also have subscription streaming and conditional download programs. Streaming is like listening to the radio, but occurs over the Internet, as for example, RealNetworks' Rhapsody. A conditional download is a temporary download, i.e., it only lasts for the period of time that the consumer maintains a subscription. Based on negotiations, labels receive a percentage of the subscription revenue, which they share with the artists and producers. Usually, the digital music service providers for streaming and conditional downloads pay around 40% of gross subscription revenue, often including advertising income, or 50% of the net with deductions somewhere in the range of 15% to 20%, into a pool that is distributed to the labels based on the percentage of their content that is streamed or delivered to the consumer as a conditional download in proportion to the total number of the content of all labels that is streamed and conditionally downloaded. In lieu of that formula approach, some digital music service providers will pay anywhere from a fraction of a penny to a full penny per stream. Subscriptions can range from as little as $6 per month to as much as $15 per month. The higher monthly rates usually accompany those subscription services that enable the customer to port the conditional downloads from their computer to a portable device so they can take their rented music library with them when they leave the home. If the monthly subscription lapses, then any content in the conditional download library is erased. The labels must compensate the artists/producers from the labels' share of these subscription fees, with the most common approach being done on a fifty-fifty split.

In addition to the download of audio content, most digital music service providers also provide video content in their services. The average charge to the consumer for the download of a video is $1.99. An average wholesale price to the label of that video content is $1.40. From that $1.40, the label must cover publishing costs (which, in the video medium, includes synchronization, as well as mechanical rights), artist, producer and other video content supplier royalty participants, with the balance being retained by the label for itself. These same companies are also providing video streaming as part of their subscription service, with payments to the labels and arrangements with the consumers being similar to those provided for audio content.

The other development of significance in the digital distribution market is the delivery of content directly to mobile devices, including ringtones, which include (1) monophonics (cover recordings that have only a single melodic line of the song); (2) polyphonics (cover recordings that have both the melody and harmony of the song); and (3) mastertones (digital sound recordings of the original master recording of the song). There are also ringbacks (recordings of songs that the caller hears while waiting for the person being called to answer the call); OTAs (over-the-air download of full tracks and videos); as well as audio and video streaming. While the major labels have the depth and breadth of catalog to be able to do direct deals with carriers (i.e., the companies with the "pipes" to do the deliveries), few of the independent labels, let alone individual artists, have that capacity, and thus must go through aggregators to get into the ringtone and OTA market. There is a group of aggregator companies with which the carriers will deal in accessing such nonmajor label content, such as Moderati, Mobile Streams, Jamster, Zingy, Hudson, Xringer, Qmobile, Infospace, and others. These companies license from labels the rights for mastertones, OTAs and video, to sell such content to the consumer for downloads to cell phones. These companies also will make deals with the carriers to be able to utilize the carriers' platforms to use the delivery pipes for the sales to the consumer. The economics of these arrangements are described below, with the carriers and the labels getting a major share of the income and the aggregators getting a small percentage to cover their cost of business and relatively slim profit margins. Consumers, in turn, in purchasing ringtone downloads may do it à la carte or they may subscribe for a monthly fee that enables them to download a finite number of ringtones. These services also have gotten into the market of selling "wallpaper" (i.e., visual images) and voice tones (for example, personality announcements), either à la carte or as part of the subscription menu.

The economics of the mobile delivery marketplace are different than the more traditional economics of digital distribution to computers and laptops, which work off of the 99¢ per track model (and the $9.99 per album model). The significant difference is that there is a carrier delivering the content, which puts an additional party into the mix, and the retail prices with ringtones and ringbacks are higher even though the content is much less, namely just a clip to be used as a ringer on your phone. An average price for a download of a ringtone is $2.49, with some content priced at $1.99 and other content at $2.99. From this amount, the carriers will take 30% to 50%, with the principal carriers being Verizon, Sprint and Cingular. Major labels generally will get 45% to 50% of the retail price against a minimum of between 75¢ to $1.25 per download. Independents will get 30% to 40% of the retail price against a minimum of 35¢ to 50¢. The balance is kept by the aggregator. From the label's share, it has to cover mechanicals and artist and producer royalties. Most labels apply the same royalty calculation approach to ringtones for the artists/producers as they apply to full track downloads for an Apple iTunes or other download company, namely the percentage of the retail price equal to the percentage paid by the label to the artist on the sale of physical product. See the section below, Digital Phonorecord Deliveries of Music, for a discussion of mechanical royalties on ringtones.

With regard to OTAs, an average retail price is $1.99, with the carrier, again, getting between 35% to 50% and the label getting 30% to 50%, usually against a minimum to the label of 60¢ to 95¢ per OTA download. The balance goes to the aggregator company that is selling the OTA. Often, OTA consists of a "dual" download, namely a low-bit file delivery to the cell phone or other mobile device and a high-bit file downloaded to that same consumer's PC. On these OTA downloads, the label generally would have to pay mechanicals twice to the publisher, at least for noncontrolled compositions, since from the publisher's perspective, two copies of the song have been delivered and a mechanical royalty should be paid for each. A single master royalty would be paid to the artist/producer. Similar economics apply to the video delivered to a mobile device.

Keep your eye on a litigation that has been filed by counsel for the Allman Brothers and Cheap Trick against Sony BMG, claiming that the royalty to be paid for digital downloads, or an OTA or master ringtone, whether through Apple, a ringtone company, or any other digital music service provider should be 50% of the price paid to the label by the downloading company after deduction of mechanicals. The theory is that these deals are not sales in the traditional sense of sales in the physical market, but are really licenses, since a third party is authorized by the label to do the actual reproduction and delivery to the consumer, not unlike the licensing of a track to a third party to include a master on a compilation album for which it would pay a royalty to the label, which the label would then share fifty-fifty with itself and the artist/producer. The obvious economic differences are significant. Counsel for these plaintiffs are endeavoring to make the case what is known as a class action case that would incorporate into a single lawsuit similar artists with suits against various record labels in pursuit of a remedy that is more economically advantageous to the artists. Certainly, the labels will resist this, since their profit margins on digital downloads are substantial, and relatively speaking, better than their profit margin in the physical world, even though the latter is still their principal income source.

DEVELOPMENT OF AGGREGATORS

Just as there is a network of independent distributors that labels and artists use to get their physical product into stores, there are specialized distributors that facilitate the ability of smaller labels and artists to get their content distributed digitally to consumers through the digital music service providers. Initially, such distribution was available for the independents and artists under direct deals with Apple iTunes, MusicNet, RealNetworks, Napster and others, but making individual deals with the thousands and thousands of independent labels and artists became administratively inefficient for them. Also, the work that must be done by the labels and the artists to service the initial delivery and the ongoing submission of their content with the digital music service providers can be quite a burden, not just with regard to the major digital music service providers, but also because of the rapid increase in alternative outlets through which the independent labels and artists can have their content delivered to the consumer. As a result, a new kind of digital distributor known as "aggregators" has developed. They act as the conduit to get content from the independent labels and artists into the numerous digital music service providers that are available, including the majors, such as Apple iTunes, as well as the multiplicity of smaller outlets that deal with digital downloads, streaming, ringtones, OTAs, and even in-store kiosks and direct deals with manufacturers of high-tech equipment that preload their hardware with musical content. Significant players in the aggregator market include IODA *(www.iodalliance.com)*, DRA *(www.digitalrightsagency.com)* and The Orchard *(www.theorchard.com)*, as well as a number of others. For many smaller labels and artists, getting into the digital music service provider platforms can now only be done through such aggregators. Generally, a deal with an aggregator is done on an exclusive basis, usually for a term of one to three years. Unlike distributors in the physical market, however, the aggregator companies are much better at collecting payments, making timely payments to the labels and artists they represent, and are reasonably accurate in their reporting. In turn, many of the digital music service provider companies that do the digital delivery to the consumers, such as Apple iTunes and Yahoo!, make timely accountings and payment to the aggregators.

Generally, the aggregators, for a reasonable percentage, with the average being 15% of receipts, will take the content of the labels and artists, encode and format it for delivery to the digital music service providers, make the delivery, and collect and make timely payment based on receipts from those digital music service providers. Accounting to the labels and artists is generally done on a monthly basis, usually by no later than the end of the month following the month during which the aggregators receive payment. Since the digital music service providers generally account to the aggregators in the same time frame, i.e., within a month of the month during which the download commerce activity occurs, the labels and the artists actually receive payment on average within a couple of months from the time of the download. This is unheard of in the physical market.

DIGITAL PHONORECORD DELIVERIES OF MUSIC

When a record is manufactured and sold, the record company must pay a mechanical royalty to the publisher for the reproduction of the music on the phonorecords. Likewise, the DPRSRA provides that a mechanical royalty must be paid for music that is digitally downloaded just as the mechanical royalty is paid for music on phonorecords sold in hard medium. Most record contracts try to limit the statutory rate that has to be paid for the reproduction of music on phonorecords written by the recording artist (i.e., a controlled composition) to 75% of the statutory rate, often with a cap of 10 to 12 songs per album as opposed to the actual number of compositions on an album, if there are more than that. Under the directives of the DPRSRA, the RIAA and the NMPA agreed that the same mechanical royalty rate would apply to both physical phonorecords and digital phonorecord deliveries (DPDs). A new mechanical rate was to be negotiated for music on digital phonorecord deliveries made after December 31, 2000, but new rates have yet to be established, although the common practice is to charge the statutory rate from time to time in place (i.e., the mechanical royalty rates periodically change, so the rate is not fixed as a forever amount). Through December 31, 2007, the current rate is 9.1¢ per song or 1.75¢ per minute for songs greater than five minutes. The various industry players also have asked the Copyright Office to determine mechanical royalty rates for "conditional downloads" or "incidental" DPDs, e.g., digital phonorecord deliveries that time out or that are streamed on demand and temporarily buffered or cached in that process. The determination of those rates is still not resolved, just as an industry agreement or a Copyright Office determination on mechanical royalties for digital phonorecord deliveries is still to be resolved.

For mechanical royalties on ringtones, record labels and ringtone aggregators have negotiated royalty rates with the publishers in the range of 10% of the retail selling price per download against a minimum of 10¢ to 12.5¢ per download, plus a one-time fixing fee of $25 per composition to store the music on the ringtone company's servers. These terms are usually on a favored nations basis. The publishers' position has been that ringtones are not phonorecords and therefore are not subject to the compulsory licensing provisions of the United States Copyright Act for statutory mechanicals, and thus the publishers could quote any fee they wanted for granting the right to use their music on the ringtones, and even to withhold permission if they wanted. The record companies (even though the majors also own publishing companies) took exception, and asked the United States Copyright Office, with opposition from the publishers, to render an opinion on whether ringtones were phonorecords and subject to the statutory mechanical compulsory licensing provisions of the United States Copyright Act. In response, the United States Copyright Office has ruled that ringtones are phonorecords, and that compositions used for ringtones do fall under the compulsory licensing provisions of the United States Copyright Act. As such, the publishers are not free to withhold permission to use their compositions or to negotiate rates with the record companies for the royalties to be paid for ringtones. With this ruling, the Copyright Royalty Board will need to hold hearings to determine the mechanical rates to set for ringtones. The publishers may challenge this ruling, which could be a lengthy process, so this matter may stay at issue for some time. Accessing the United States Copyright Office's Web site *(www.copyright.gov)* is a good way to monitor what the Copyright Royalty Board finally proposes for these rates and what actions the publishers may take to oppose this decision and what actions the record companies and digital music service providers take to support the United States Copyright Office's findings.

For the compositions used for the ringtones to be subject to the compulsory licensing provisions of the United States Copyright Act, the ringtones may not recast, transform, or adapt the music, or include additional material, in a way that it becomes an original act of authorship, i.e., a derivative work. If it does, then a license must be negotiated with the publisher.

The decision of the United States Copyright Office also makes the portion of a composition that has been recorded and sold only as a ringtone, even if it has never been released on a physical phonorecord or sold as a full track permanent download, subject to a compulsory license for use by others, as it will be deemed to have been recorded and distributed to the public as a "phonorecord" with authorization from the copyright owner, which is the condition precedent for allowing use of the statutory compulsory mechanical license.

Under the DPRSRA, contractual efforts to impose a fractional limit on mechanical royalties for music on digitally delivered phonorecords that is written or controlled by an artist is not permitted, except for agreements that predate June 22, 1995 or agreements made after that date when the songs in question were recorded with the artist/songwriter thereafter agreeing, in writing, to a reduced rate. Absent these qualifications, the full statutory mechanical royalty rate must be paid for music on digital phonorecord deliveries. The representatives of the record and music publishing industries must meet, determine, and submit to the Copyright Office for approval mutually agreed to schedules for the mechanical rates for physical product and digital deliveries that will apply commencing January 1, 2008.

One area of adjustments to the Copyright Act about which to stay aware affects Section 115, which deals with mechanical licenses for the reproduction of music in phonorecords. Legislation has been proposed to amend this provision of the Copyright Act to apply the concept of compulsory blanket licensing, utilize designated collection agents, and provide fixed royalty rates to music that is digitally distributed. Effectively, this would extend the compulsory mechanical licensing mechanism used for music with physical product to the digital world by allowing applications to be filed for blanket licenses by digital music service providers, record companies and others to download music as embodied on masters as permanent downloads, streams and conditional downloads. This adjustment, if made, certainly would facilitate the administration of the businesses in the digital distribution market. Issues have been raised with the proposed legislation, however, because of what has been referred to as the "General Designated Agent." That "Agent" most likely would be The Harry Fox Agency. It also could be others, but only if they represent the rights of at least 15% of all published compositions. This would make The Harry Fox Agency or a major publisher, such as EMI Music or Warner Chappell, the enshrined controllers or gatekeepers with regard to being able to access royalties for such digital uses of music and eliminate the ability of smaller publishers to represent their own interests. Basically, they would be required to align with The Harry Fox Agency or another "Agent" that satisfied the minimum percentage control requirement in order to have any expectation of receiving payments that would be due. There is certain to be much lobbying with regard to this proposed legislation before final enactment occurs, but given the size of the companies who are supporting it, some form of this legislation most likely will pass. Supporters include the RIAA, the National Music Publishers Association, the Digital Music Association, the major webcasters and digital music service providers, including AOL, Yahoo! and RealNetworks.

LITIGATION

In the earlier edition of this article, there was a lengthy description of litigations that were happening at that time involving Napster and MP3.com. Those litigations are long resolved, and as a result, neither of those companies are now in existence, with the courts having found that their conduct constituted infringements in clear violation of Copyright Law. The economic repercussions of those adverse judgments essentially put those companies out of business. The most interesting recent development in terms of litigation has been the decision by the United States Supreme Court in 2005, finding that Grokster and StreamCast could be found guilty of copyright infringement in the dissemination of their P2P software, the principal, if not sole purpose of which, was to facilitate the unauthorized reproduction and mass distribution of copyrighted content, principally master recordings and the music on those master recordings. The Court concluded that if it was determined by the facts that the companies perpetuating the P2P software intended that their software be used to infringe copyrights and if they undertook the promotion of that software's ability to do just that, even if the software could also be used for noninfringing purposes, those companies could be found to be liable for copyright infringement as contributors to such infringement and for having "vicariously facilitated" such infringement. The Australian Supreme Court came to a similar conclusion in a case brought against Sharman for its use of the Kazaa P2P software. Effectively, each of those companies likely will soon be out of business, transform their business models or be absorbed by another company, and the representatives of the recording industry are pursuing similar companies, such as Limewire and eDonkey. Of course, the reality of this P2P software is that it is essentially impossible to eradicate, and so it is likely that there will always be a parallel universe of illegal file sharing alongside the growing legitimate world of legally authorized file distribution. Some P2P companies are actually trying to adapt their systems to facilitate only authorized P2P sharing, with technology provided by a company called Snocap, which was started, among others, by the same person who started the original Napster, Shawn Fanning. Whether these efforts to monetize the world of P2P file sharing will succeed is still to be determined.

Given the speed with which technology evolves and how it is always ahead of the status of the laws and the economic models put into place to try to get commercial benefit from the use of the technology, change will be a constant, and substantial adjustments to what was discussed in this article are a given. One current real-life example is the dispute between XM Satellite and the record labels on whether the new XM portable device, which allows about four to five hours of content programming to be captured in the device, is a copying that requires the payment of a fee for the masters and the music, just as a download from Apple iTunes would, or whether this merely is a "temporary storage," comparable to using Tivo technology or a video recorder to copy a television program to watch at a later time. Sirius Satellite released a similar device, and under pressure from the labels agreed to pay a royalty to the labels for its device. The short of it is that technology will continue to provide ways to expand how the consumer can access content. The creators and owners of the content need to stay alert on how to translate those technological enhancements into commerce so that their creativity, marketing and distribution efforts can be sufficiently rewarded to support and encourage their continued efforts.

QUALIFICATIONS FOR COMPULSORY LICENSE UNDER THE DIGITAL PERFORMANCE RIGHT IN SOUND RECORDINGS ACT OF 1995 (DPRSRA)

In 1995, the DPRSRA provided a public performance right in a sound recording for the copyright owner, for the first time in the United States (amending Section 106 and Section 114 of the Copyright Act). This grant applied, however, only in certain limited circumstances, as detailed below.

- Public performance by means of digital audio interactive and on-demand transmissions for which a voluntary license is required; therefore, it is the exclusive right of the sound recording owner (i.e., the record company) to decide whether to issue a license permitting interactive transmissions.

- Public performance by means of subscription noninteractive transmission—for which a compulsory blanket license applies; i.e., a voluntary license is not required from the sound recording owner. (This legislation fostered a debate on whether the DPRSRA applied to Internet webcasters and resulted in a provision being included in the Digital Millennium Copyright Act of 1998.)

- DPRSRA does not apply to digital broadcasters (i.e., transmissions by FCC licensed terrestrial broadcast stations), which are exempt from needing a public performance license (whether voluntary or compulsory) for sound recordings. The DMCA does apply to the simulcast of such stations' programs over the Internet.

The following are the conditions that must be met for a Web broadcaster to qualify for compulsory license, without which transmission would be an infringement of copyright:

- Must not exceed "sound recording performance complement"; i.e., over a three-hour period, cannot transmit more than two consecutive or three total selections from one sound recording; or more than four songs, or three in a row, from the same artist.

- Must transmit owner encoded copyright information with recordings; i.e., must identify sound recordings, the album and featured artist.

- Prior announcements are not permitted, cannot publish a program guide.

- Looped or continuous programs may not be less than three hours in duration; and programs of less than one hour and performed at scheduled times may be performed only three times in a two-week period, or four times in a two-week period if one hour or more in duration.

- Archived programs (i.e., previously performed programs or series of programs) may not be less than five hours in duration and may reside on the Web site for no more than a total of two weeks.

1998 DIGITAL MILLENNIUM COPYRIGHT ACT (DMCA-SECTION 405)

The DMCA further amends Section 114 of the Copyright Act by granting a public performance license for digital transmission or streaming of sound recordings by webcasters, i.e., playing or performing (as distinct from a digital download) of audio musical sound recordings over the Internet. This activity does not fall directly within the categories addressed by the DPRSRA, and Section 405 of the DMCA amended the DPRSRA to expand the statutory (compulsory) license for nonsubscription transmission to include webcasting as a new category of eligible transmission, and therefore subject to a compulsory license. As such, the sound recording's copyright owner cannot prevent the webcasting provided that all of the criteria required by the statute (see below) are satisfied by the webcaster and it has timely filed for a compulsory license.

Webcasters took the position that the DPRSRA did not apply to them as their conduct was a "nonsubscription transmission" and "noninteractive," and therefore exempt from requiring the permission of sound recording copyright owners.

RIAA's position was that webcasters were required to get licenses from the sound recording copyright owners (i.e., the DPRSRA's exemptions were only available to FCC terrestrial licensed broadcasters).

The DMCA confirmed that a license, either compulsory or voluntary, was required, by providing that the sound recording copyright owners have the exclusive right to control online or Internet delivery of their sound recordings.

The statutory license applies, however, only to certain noninteractive subscription and nonsubscription transmissions. Interactive service is defined in the DMCA to exclude transmission of songs specifically requested by and for a particular user, and programming that is specifically designed for a particular user.

To be eligible for the statutory license, a webcaster's service and programming must meet several criteria. Services that do not meet the criteria must obtain (i.e., negotiate) voluntary licenses directly from the recording companies.

The eligibility criteria for the compulsory license includes the following:

1. Programming must comply with limitations designed to assure the sound recording copyright owner that webcasting (which generally occurs as uninterrupted programming) does not displace sales of records. As a condition for eligibility—

    a) programming should comply with the "sound recording performance complement," which is defined under current law (as provided in the DPRSRA), to provide that over a three-hour period, a service should not intentionally program more than three songs or more than two in a row from the same recording, or four songs or more than three in a row from the same recording artist or anthology;

    b) archived programs that, when accessed, always start in the same place and play in the same order should be at least five hours long and should not be available for more than two weeks at a time;

CONTINUED ON NEXT PAGE

CONTINUED FROM PREVIOUS PAGE

c) continuous looped programs that always perform in the same order, but are accessed in a continuous play stream should be at least three hours long; and

d) rebroadcasts of programs can occur at scheduled times three times in a two-week period for programs of less than an hour and four times for programs of an hour or more.

2. The webcaster is not permitted to publish advance program guides or use other means to announce when particular sound recordings will be played.

3. The webcaster must use only sound recordings that are authorized for performance in the United States (e.g., not play bootleg recordings).

4. Webcasters must provide some means for end users to identify the song, artist and album title of the recording as it is being played.

5. Any identification or technological protection information included in the sound recording must be passed through, as long as it does not impose substantial costs or burdens on the webcaster, or create any audible or visible effects for the end user.

6. The webcaster must not deploy or support technological means to evade these requirements.

7. To the extent it is technologically available, the webcaster must set transmissions so that receiving software will inhibit the end user from doing any direct digital copying of the transmitted data and must not explicitly encourage home taping.

International Copyright

BY E. SCOTT JOHNSON, ESQ.

There is no such thing as international copyright. Copyright protection exists only under the laws of individual countries, and those laws vary as to categories of works protected, rights protected, duration of protection and remedies for infringement. Even though you cannot register an "international copyright" as such, your music is automatically protected under the copyright laws of foreign countries with which your home country has copyright treaty or convention relations. That includes almost every country in the world for U.S. nationals, and every country with a significant music market has agreed to extend the same copyright protection to U.S. works that it accords to its own citizens. This is known as "national treatment."

Copyright law typically protects the right to reproduce, distribute, publicly perform and prepare "derivative works," including arrangements. These are "economic rights" and do not always include "authorization rights." For example, in the United States, once a song has been released on records, tapes or CDs, another recording artist may release a cover version of that song without first securing authorization from the copyright owner, under the compulsory licensing provisions of the U.S. Copyright Act. The song's owner may not refuse to grant a mechanical license, so long as the song is not significantly altered (stylistic interpretations are okay), payment required under the statute is made (i.e., the copyright owner's economic right is satisfied) and the other requirements of the compulsory licensing provisions of the U.S. Copyright Act are met. Despite the lack of an authorization right for cover recordings, the copyright owner could refuse to authorize synchronization of the song in a television commercial. In that case, there is no compulsory license under U.S. copyright law, so the copyright owner enjoys both an economic right *and* an authorization right. Countries vary in scope of the authorization rights granted to copyright owners, as reflected in differing approaches to legal principles such as "fair use," "compulsory license" and "moral rights."

Some countries provide strong moral rights or *droit morale* laws, according creators (generally referred to as "authors"—whether of music, literature, artwork or any other copyrightable work) special rights above and beyond the economic and authorization rights incident to copyright ownership. Moral rights generally belong to the author irrespective of who owns the copyright and may include a number of special rights, including the right to require name credit on copies ("paternity") and to prevent unauthorized changes to a work ("integrity"). Following its accession to the Berne

Convention in 1989, the United States added limited moral rights provisions to the U.S. Copyright Act, applicable only to certain works of visual art. United States copyright law does not accord moral rights to composers or performers of musical compositions. In fact, U.S. recording artists are often asked to waive moral rights through special provisions in recording contracts, intended to divest them of moral rights that may apply in foreign countries. It is beyond the scope of this chapter to assess whether a contractual waiver of moral rights in a U.S. contract would be effective under the domestic laws of any particular foreign country.

NATIONAL TREATMENT

The common feature of the important copyright conventions and treaties and of the GATT Accord on Trade-Related Aspects of Intellectual Property Rights (TRIPS) is the requirement that each signatory country accord works from other signatory countries national treatment under the domestic copyright law of the country in which protection is sought. This means, for example, that a U.S. songwriter's music will be protected automatically under Italian copyright law on the same basis as if the songwriter was an Italian citizen or first published the music in Italy. Likewise, Italian songwriters are entitled to protection under U.S. copyright law, because both countries are members of the Berne Convention, which requires national treatment as a condition of membership. This is good news for U.S. copyright owners, because copyright protection in foreign countries is automatic and often more favorable to authors than U.S. copyright law.

Domestic copyright law generally does not protect you abroad. If your copyright is infringed in a foreign country, you usually cannot bring your infringement case in a U.S. court or seek remedies under U.S. copyright law in a foreign court. In most instances, you will need to bring your copyright infringement claim in a court in the foreign country where the infringement occurred, under that country's laws. If the infringing product is distributed worldwide, you may have separate infringement claims in each country where the product is distributed. But even for a product released only abroad, a basis may exist for a U.S. claim. If, for example, a videotape distributed in Germany was produced in the United States, where your music was recorded onto the video master without your permission, that act of unauthorized copying within the United States would infringe at least one of your exclusive rights under U.S. copyright law, and you could bring an infringement claim in a U.S. federal court against the U.S. producer, in addition to any claim you may have in Germany under German law. Moreover, you might be able to recover the U.S. defendant's *German* profits in a U.S. court, as a remedy for its infringing activities in the United States.

Unlike patent law, which requires formal filings within strict time frames and the timely payment of fees to secure patent protection in each country, protection under the copyright laws of foreign countries is generally automatic. The Berne Convention, of which the United States is a member, prohibits such formal barriers to protection and requires national treatment and minimum standards of protection as a condition of adherence. Where a U.S. patent owner would have to make timely filings and pay governmental fees to secure and maintain patent protection in France, for example, a U.S. copyright owner need merely assert copyright ownership and establish the work's status as a "Berne work" in order to secure copyright protection in France.

National treatment does not guarantee that the copyright laws in every foreign country will provide protection equivalent to United States copyright law. For example, in some countries, the term of protection for sound recordings, photographs and certain other works may be shorter than in the United States. Sound recordings in the United States are often treated as works made for hire for record companies, and the term of protection for a U.S. work-made-for-hire sound recording is the shorter of 95 years from date of publication or 120 years from date of creation, just like other works protected under copyright. If owned by an individual producer or artist, the term of protection for U.S. sound recordings is the life of the last surviving author plus 70 years. But in many countries, sound recordings are protected for only 50 years. Not every country protects sound recordings under copyright law; many countries treat them as a separate category of property right—called in international copyright parlance a "neighboring right" or "related right" law. The Rome Convention, among others, contemplates reciprocal protection for sound recordings under related rights laws of its signatories.

There are permitted exceptions to the national treatment principle. A common exception concerns duration of copyright protection. Many countries follow the "rule of the shorter term," which provides that copyright protection will last for the shorter of (1) the term of protection available for the work under the national laws of the foreign country where protection is sought or (2) the term of protection afforded to the work in the home country. The rule of the shorter term is part of the copyright law of many (but not all) countries, on the theory that a country ought not be required to protect foreign works longer than the foreign author's home country protects such works. The rule of the shorter term may operate to deny protection for pre-1978 United States copyrights, which are protected under U.S. law for a term of years following the registration or first publication date, rather than a term of years after the death of the author. Pre-1978 U.S. copyrights may lapse in the United States prior to expiration of the term of protection that would apply to the same work in foreign countries, which generally provide copyright terms measured by the "life of the author" plus 50, 60, 70 or more years. So, for example, if a songwriter's U.S. copyrights expired in 1995, but the songwriter died in 1960, in foreign countries that do *not* apply the rule or the shorter term, the songs would remain in copyright until 2010 or later (2030 in many cases, because the term now is life plus 70 years throughout most of Europe and elsewhere). If the songwriter had been an Italian citizen, for example, the song would ordinarily be protected under the national laws of Italy for the life-plus-70-years term, but under the rule of the shorter term followed in Italian copyright law, a pre-1978 U.S. song for which the U.S. copyright had expired, generally would not be protected under Italian copyright law, even if the composer is still alive. That seems simple enough, but this can be a complex area, not easily susceptible to hard-and-fast rules. For example, if a pre-1989 (year of U.S. Berne accession) U.S. song qualified for protection in a non-Universal Copyright Convention Berne country (in UCC countries, the United States would be the home country for purposes of applying the rule of the shorter term) by the back-door-to-Berne procedure discussed below, the song would be treated as originating from the Berne country in which it was "simultaneously" (or first) published, which would have provided a copyright term of at least life plus 50 years, potentially longer than the U.S. term of protection.

While there are few examples of U.S. songwriters that outlive their full-term renewed copyrights (Irving Berlin comes to mind—he lived to 101 and began writing as a young man), it happened more often than you might think prior to 1992, when the U.S. Copyright Act was amended to prevent works from being thrust into the public domain for failure to file a renewal application. Prior to 1972, many songs fell into the U.S. public domain prematurely due to a failure to file for renewal of the U.S. copyright during the 28th year, and in those cases songwriters may well have outlived their U.S. copyright.

U.S. songwriters do not have to worry about outliving their copyrights for works composed after 1978, because the copyright term is no longer determined by a set number of years from registration or publication (except works made for hire, which are accorded a set number of years from creation or publication) but rather, is based on the life of the author plus 70 years. However, if you are recording a song that is in the public domain in the United States, you may still need to determine whether it is in the public domain worldwide. Because not every country follows the rule of the shorter term (Canada and the United Kingdom, for example, do not), a song that is in the public domain in the United States *may* still be protected under copyright in certain foreign countries. Irving Berlin's songs are a case in point. In 1911, Berlin had a hit with "Alexander's Ragtime Band." Copyright was renewed in 1939, and the song entered the U.S. public domain at the end of 1986. However, because Irving Berlin lived until 1989, and because Canada (a Berne country) provides a term of protection measured by the life of the author plus 50 years, and because Irving Berlin met the then-applicable requirements for protection in Berne Convention countries (by simultaneously publishing the work in a Berne Convention country) distribution of recordings embodying the Irving Berlin song "Alexander's Ragtime Band" in Canada will infringe Irving Berlin's publisher's rights in that song under Canadian copyright law (unless a mechanical license for Canada is obtained) until 2039, even though by then the song will have been out of copyright in the United States for 53 years!

FORMALITIES

The United States has a long history of imposing technical conditions on copyright protection, such as notice, renewal, deposit and manufacturing requirements ("formalities" in international copyright parlance), and while many formalities in the U.S. Copyright Act have been eliminated or defanged in recent years, some still persist. For example, one may not sue for copyright infringement in the United States unless the infringed work has first been registered with the U.S. Copyright Office and a registration certificate obtained. It is more advantageous for the U.S. songwriter to receive national treatment under the laws of France, for example, at least with respect to the registration requirement, than it is in the United States. A United States citizen who failed to register his or her copyright in the United States—a prerequisite to filing suit for copyright infringement in the United States—could nevertheless sue for copyright infringement in France, which has no comparable requirement.

The registration requirement is an easily met "soft" formality (because the registration can be secured at any time during the life of the copyright), compared to the harsh formalities that for many years dominated United States copyright law. Prior to 1992, if you failed to renew a pre-1978 copyrighted song during the 28th year of the copyright term, the song automatically lost U.S. copyright protection. Instead of 75 years of protection, the copyright owner enjoyed only 28 years of protection. "Rockin' Robin" by Jimmie Thomas, one of the great pop hits of the 1950s, is such a song. The U.S. copyright notice requirement was even harsher then. If copies of a song were published before 1978 without a proper copyright notice, the song was automatically injected into the U.S. public domain. Many foreign authors published works without copyright notice, not realizing that this omission would result in a permanent forfeiture of copyright protection in the United States. These are harsh penalties for hypertechnical mistakes, and the unfairness of loss of copyright for these and other technical failings under U.S. law was roundly condemned for years by the international copyright community and was impermissible under the Berne Convention. The United States was ineligible to join the Berne Convention until 1989, when it finally committed to basic revisions in U.S. copyright law to eliminate formalities as a condition of copyright protection and to provide Berne's minimum standards to Berne works. Following Berne adherence and subsequent trade negotiations resulting in the NAFTA and TRIPS Agreements, many copyrights in foreign works have been "revived" through retroactive restoration of copyright protection in works that lost copyright protection for failure to comply with formalities. Fortunately, not long after the United States joined the Berne Convention, the U.S. Copyright Act was amended to provide that a failure to renew copyright, even by a U.S. national, would not inject the work into the public domain.

BERNE CONVENTION

The Berne Convention for the Protection of Literary and Artistic Works (referred to as the "Berne Convention" or "Berne") is the most important international copyright convention. Established in 1886, the Berne Convention is the oldest copyright convention in which reciprocal protections are granted to member countries. A number of countries are signatory to both the Berne Convention and the Universal Copyright Convention as well as other regional or bilateral treaties. Berne is the premier copyright convention, however, by virtue of the minimum standards its members must agree to accord to works of other Berne nationals and its prohibition on formalities as barriers to protection. The other preeminent copyright convention, the Universal Copyright Convention (UCC), explicitly grants priority to Berne in relations between UCC members that are also Berne members. The United States was late to join the Berne Convention, finally joining in 1989, after many years of lobbying by members of Congress, trade groups, copyright owners and others that believed that the United States could not lead in international trade negotiations if it did not afford the minimum standards required by Berne to the works of Berne member countries.

Even though the United States did not join Berne until 1989, works by U.S. songwriters could qualify for copyright protection and national treatment in Berne Convention countries by a procedure that became known as "back door to Berne." To qualify for protection in Berne countries, a U.S. work had to be simultaneously published in a Berne country, which generally meant publication in a Berne member nation within 30 days of the original publication date in the non-Berne country. Printed sheet music copies of U.S. songs were routinely published in a Berne country within the prescribed time frame by authorization of the U.S. publisher, in order to obtain protection for the song in all Berne Convention countries. Many criticized this procedure as unfairly obtaining for U.S. works the benefits of Berne protection without providing reciprocal benefits to Berne Convention works in the United States.

If a work qualifies as a "Berne Convention work," it will be protected under the national laws of all Berne countries. A Berne Convention work is defined under U.S. law as a work (1) created by at least one author who has an "habitual place of residence" in a nation adhering to the Berne Convention, (2) published works of which at least one author is a national of a Berne signatory on the date of the first publication, (3) works first published in at least one Berne country, (4) pictorial, graphic or sculptural works incorporated in buildings or other structures located in a Berne country, and (5) audiovisual works created by at least one legal entity headquartered in a Berne country or at least one individual author who is a national of a Berne country. It is still possible for non-Berne countries to obtain protection in Berne Convention countries through the back-door-to-Berne procedure, much like United States publishers followed prior to 1989.

The Berne Convention provisions are not "self-executing" in the United States (in some countries they are); that is, a foreign author cannot go into a U.S. court and expect it to enforce the minimum protections required under the Berne Convention. United States law had to be brought into accordance (to the extent it was not already in accordance) with Berne Convention minimum standards of protection and had to remove barriers to protection, by implementing legislation. In the United States, this has been done piecemeal over the years since U.S. law is still not in full compliance with all the provisions of Berne.

An interesting limitation on the Berne minimum standards obligation is that a Berne member must accord the minimum standards of protection to works from other Berne countries but is not required to accord the minimum standards to its own authors. Although resulting from trade agreements and not directly from Berne, retroactive restoration of copyright is one area in which foreign authors are given preferential treatment under U.S. copyright law. The U.S. Copyright Act has been amended in recent years (in accordance with NAFTA and GATT Agreements) to restore copyright protection for Berne and certain other foreign works for which U.S. copyrights had lapsed or failed to vest initially due to failure to comply with U.S. formalities. However, these amendments did not restore copyright protection for U.S. works for which copyright protection had lapsed or failed to vest initially for the same reasons.

UNIVERSAL COPYRIGHT CONVENTION

Many countries are signatories to the Universal Copyright Convention, in addition to the Berne Convention. In 1955, the United States ratified the UCC, becoming a founding member of this international copyright convention administered by the United Nations Educational, Scientific and Cultural Organization (UNESCO). Berne is administered by the World Intellectual Property Organization (WIPO). The UCC requires member countries to accord national treatment to works from other member countries but does not require that its members meet the rigorous minimum standards Berne requires. Berne countries that wanted to bring the United States and other countries with formalities prohibited under Berne into the world copyright community sponsored UCC originally.

The Universal Copyright Convention actually prescribes use of a copyright notice (the symbol ©, the name of the copyright owner and the year of first publication) as the condition for obtaining certain Convention benefits in UCC countries. While notice is not a prerequisite for protection, any formalities that any UCC member nation may impose upon its nationals, such as deposit, registration or first publication requirements, are deemed satisfied if the foreign (UCC) work bears the prescribed copyright notice. The "free pass" on compliance with formalities does not apply to nationals of the country in which the exemption is sought. Of course, most countries today do not impose formalities as prerequisites for copyright protection, and many UCC member countries are also members of the Berne Convention and may not impose formalities in any case, so the UCC's relevance has been greatly diminished in recent years. A number of countries (primarily Eastern European countries) however, do not belong to Berne but do belong to the Universal Copyright Convention. For that reason and because under U.S. copyright law, failure to provide copyright notice can provide an infringer with a potential "innocent infringement" defense (an element of which is "lack of notice"), most copyright owners continue to use copyright notices. In addition to the standard, "© 2007 by (copyright owner)," it is common practice to include the words "All Rights Reserved," for reasons discussed below.

BUENOS AIRES CONVENTION

The Buenos Aires Convention was executed in 1910 by the United States, Argentina, Brazil, Chili, Columbia, Costa Rica, Dominican Republic, Ecuador, Guatemala, Haiti, Honduras, Nicaragua, Panama, Paraguay, Peru and Uruguay. The essential requirement for protection in all Buenos Aires member countries is compliance with copyright law in the home country and the use of a statement that indicates the reservation of the property right. While the copyright notice required under the Universal Copyright Convention: "© (year of publication) by (copyright owner)" arguably satisfies the reservation of the property right requirement of the Buenos Aires Convention, to ensure compliance, copyright owners have adopted the practice of combining the UCC copyright notice with the words "All Rights Reserved." Some believe that the notice "all rights reserved" alone would fulfill the requirement under the Buenos Aires Convention. However, because most of the Buenos Aires Convention countries later joined the Universal Copyright Convention, which requires a full copyright notice to secure Convention benefits, the full notice is generally given. Honduras is the only Buenos Aires Convention member country that is not a signatory of the Universal Copyright Convention. The Buenos Aires Convention superseded the Mexico City Convention, a multilateral Pan American treaty to which the United States was a signatory. All of the signatories of the Mexico City Convention signed the Buenos Aires Convention except El Salvador.

In 1974, the United States joined the Geneva Phonogram Convention, formerly known as the Geneva Convention of October 29, 1971, for the Protection of Producers of Phonograms Against Unauthorized Duplication. This is an agreement between countries to protect sound recordings ("phonograms" in international intellectual property parlance) of member countries against bootlegging. Not every member country protects sound recordings under copyright. In many countries, sound recordings are protected under a neighboring right—a related intellectual property or unfair competition law.

Another international treaty according national treatment and protection to owners of sound recordings is the International Convention for the Protection of Performers, Producers of Phonograms and Broadcasting Organizations (1961), commonly referred to as the Rome Convention.

WORLD INTELLECTUAL PROPERTY ORGANIZATION

The World Intellectual Property Organization (WIPO) is an agency of the United Nations System of Organizations, with the mission of promoting the protection of intellectual property throughout the world through cooperation among the countries of the world, and for the administration of various multilateral treaties, especially the Berne Convention. WIPO is concerned not only with copyrights but with trademarks, industrial designs and patentable inventions.

COLLECTING PUBLISHING ROYALTIES ABROAD

Songwriters collect royalties from foreign territories for the public performance of their music and for mechanical reproduction of their songs on compact discs, tapes and other sound devices. Public performances primarily consist of radio and television broadcasts, although Internet streaming, live performances, music-on-hold, theatrical performances and "storecasts" account for a portion of revenues that flow to collecting societies for distribution to the publishers and writers that own copyrights in musical compositions. In the United States, music publishers and songwriters do not receive income from movie theater performances of their music contained in films, but in other countries, such theatrical performances are licensed by the local performing rights organizations.

In the United States, ASCAP, BMI and SESAC license virtually all public perform-ances of music. Comparable performing rights organizations exist in most countries, although the United States is unusual in having three competitive performing rights organizations. In most countries, a single rights organization collects all public per-formance royalties and through reciprocal arrangements with the U.S. performing rights organizations, funnels royalties to their members. Some of the major overseas performing rights collecting organizations (some, but not all of which also collect mechanical royalties) include PRS in the United Kingdom, SACEM in France, GEMA in Germany, SIAE in Italy, and JASRAC in Japan. In the United States, The Harry Fox Agency represents the majority of music publishers in collecting mechanical royalties from record companies, and it maintains reciprocal arrangements with foreign mechanical rights collecting societies. Even though reciprocal arrangements exist between collecting organizations for the collection of public performance royalties and mechanical royalties, it is prudent to have a publisher with foreign affiliates or subpublishers to oversee the collection of foreign royalties.

The Recording Industry Association of America has formed SoundExchange, a royalty collecting organization, to assist record companies and recording artists in collecting royalties for certain digital transmissions. At present, earnings are relatively small, but this should change. Phonorecord sales are in global decline, while revenues from digital transmissions and other secondary licensing revenues are becoming increasingly important. SoundExchange has negotiated reciprocal royalty agreements with several international performance rights organizations, including Phonographic Performance Limited (PPL), the UK rights collection organization that administers the sound recording performance rights of UK record companies and recording artists, Mexico's SOMEXFON and the Netherlands' SENA. To clarify, PPL is an industry organization that collects and distributes public performance royalties for sound recording copyrights, similar to SoundExchange in the United States. This is contrasted to PRS, which is an organization that collects and distributes public performance royalties for musical work copyrights, similar to ASCAP in the United States.

ALL TOGETHER NOW: HARMONIZE

In the international copyright arena there is a global harmonization of national copyright and related rights laws. The goal is to ensure that similar protections and enforcement mechanisms exist globally for copyrighted works. For example, the European Union Commission has issued a Directive that required all EU member countries to provide a term of copyright protection for most copyrighted works, measured by the life of the author plus 70 years. Previously, some EU countries protected copyrights for the life of the author plus 50 years, while others provided protection for the life of the author plus 70 years, which resulted in disharmony between the EU countries' national copyright laws and potentially inhibited the free movement of goods within the European Union. The Commission has issued a number of Directives to its member countries that require harmonization of domestic copyright laws. While stopping short of requiring a European Union-wide uniform copyright code, certain substantive norms like "life plus 70" have been required, since the Commission concluded that uniformity of law is necessary to advance the goal of free movement of goods within the European Union.

Global harmonization drove the U.S.'s enactment of the Sonny Bono Copyright Term Extension Act of 1998, which extended copyright protection under U.S. copyright law by 20 years, from life plus 50 to life plus 70. Because of the economic benefits to U.S. copyright interests, due in large part to the operation of the rule of the shorter term, many argued that the United States needed to extend the terms of copyright protection in order to increase the value of U.S. copyrights, by securing protection in foreign countries that would continue to protect U.S. works for the life of the author plus 70 years, unless the copyrights had expired in the United States. The U.S. Term Extension Act harmonized U.S. law with European Union law.

Similarly, the U.S. Digital Millennium Copyright Act (DMCA) was passed in 1998 to implement provisions of the WIPO Copyright Treaty and the Performances and Phonograms Treaty. Its intent is to harmonize copyright laws in the international arena by raising minimum standards of protection for copyrighted works, including Internet commerce protection and new digital-era protections for sound recordings. Passage of the DMCA enabled the United States to ratify the WIPO treaties. The United States, which was already substantially in compliance with treaty standards, needed to enhance protection in two areas to come into full compliance, by enacting "anticircumvention" provisions (to prevent electronic theft of digital works) and prohibitions against alteration of copyright management information. Under the WIPO treaties, signatory countries must provide "adequate legal protection and effective legal remedies" against the circumvention of technological measures, such as encryption technology, used to restrict unauthorized or unlawful copying. Among other things, the DMCA prohibits the sale of "black boxes" used to circumvent anticopying technology. Both of the new WIPO treaties require signatory countries to protect the integrity of copyright management information. This includes "digital watermarking" information that identifies the work, the author of the work and the owner of any right in the work, as well as any information about the terms and conditions of its use and any numbers or codes representing such information, when any of this information is digitally "attached" to a copy of the work or appears in connection with the communication of the work to the public. Congress added Chapter 12 to the U.S. Copyright Act, which provides civil remedies and criminal penalties for violations of either the anticircumvention provision or the alteration of copyright management information provision.

The member nations of the World Trade Organization (WTO) adopted the TRIPS Agreement, which imposes new substantive minimum requirements, both on subject matter and nature of the rights protected, as well as specific provisions relating to enforcement of copyright laws. The TRIPS Accord requires all WTO members to pass and enforce copyright, patent and trademark laws, and to meet minimum standards for protection. The TRIPS Agreement adopts the WTO dispute settlement procedures, and the United States initiated the first TRIPS-related dispute in a case against Japan in 1996 and has since initiated more cases, including a case against Ireland for failing to pass a TRIPS-consistent copyright law.

The Office of the U.S. Trade Representative has announced that one of its top priorities is to ensure full implementation of the WTO commitments on intellectual property, specifically requiring compliance by all members of the WTO with the enforcement provision of TRIPS, which goes further than Berne. It requires that members of the WTO accord protection to more categories of works and addresses other specific protections that enhance Berne's minimum protections. The 1996 WIPO Copyright Treaty (WCT) included additional substantive minimum standards, including anticircumvention of encryption technology laws, which increased harmonization of signatory countries. The United States has already adopted anticircumvention of encryption technology laws in its Digital Millennium Copyright Act.

The Internet is driving the need for international harmonization of laws, to facilitate the global management of copyrights and to deter infringement. File-sharing technologies, which do not recognize national borders, emphasize the need for global harmonization of copyright and antipiracy laws to support encryption and other technology to protect copyrighted works. Ultimately, the answers will be found both in technology, through sophisticated copyright management systems and encryption technology and in the law, such as anticircumvention of encryption technology laws, like the DMCA. Conventions and treaties promoted by WIPO and the WTO, initiatives put forth by the International Federation of the Phonographic Industry (IFPI), an international music industry association that represents about 1450 companies in 75 countries, and alliances between domestic collecting societies and their counterparts in other countries, are paving the way for a global technology-based system of rights management with enforcement mechanisms and laws to back them up.

Many governments have recognized and shut down the better known of the first generation file-sharing sites that provided centralized facilities for file storage, e.g., Napster and Gnutella. However, people were quick to adapt technologies in attempts to circumvent the law and prevent detection. Now individual countries, often in concert with industry trade groups and entertainment companies, have begun to crack down on the next generation of online file-sharing programs that use decentralized technologies, e.g., BitTorrent, to gather and assemble pieces of files from various locations (potentially worldwide) to provide users with coherent and usable, albeit illegal, files. International efforts to curb illegal online music sharing have accelerated in the past few years. In the United States, the Supreme Court held in the *Grokster* case that software service providers of these newer file-sharing technologies could be liable for the copyright infringement of their users, even in the absence of a centralized source of illegal files. Recently, the IFPI and Swedish officials shut down one of the world's largest BitTorrent sites, Pirate Bay. Likewise, in the largest illegal file-sharing action to date, Germany brought criminal charges and member companies of the IFPI brought civil suits against 3,500 individuals for uploading files to peer-to-peer networks, specifically the eDonkey network. While many countries are taking action to prevent online copyright infringement and other forms of music piracy, others are the subject of increasing scrutiny and pressure from the international community to do more to protect copyrights. In a recent report to Congress, the U.S. Trade representative noted that 48 countries have inadequate laws for protection of intellectual property, with China and Russia among the worst offenders. Despite problems along the way in particular territories, international treaties, conventions, trade agreements and EU Commission Directives are leading toward global harmonization of copyright and related rights laws, by establishing international norms of protection and enforcement. While variations in the national laws of countries will persist, and there may never be an international copyright per se, the expectation is that a work protected in one country will be similarly protected in others. This is increasingly important as the significance of national borders declines in the digital era.

Music Publishing

Performing Rights Organizations: An Overview

BY MARK HALLORAN AND DIANE RAPAPORT

If you write songs that are commercially exploited, you must join a performing rights organization to collect money for the public performance of your songs. Which organization you join is one of the most important business decisions you will make in your career, so a basic understanding of them is crucial.

This chapter provides an overview of the three U.S. performing rights organizations—the American Society of Composers, Authors and Publishers (ASCAP), Broadcast Music, Inc. (BMI) and SESAC. The vast majority of U.S. copyrighted songs are in the repertoires of either ASCAP (over 8,000,000 songs) or BMI (more than 6,500,000 songs). We will discuss performing rights, the issue of nondramatic versus dramatic public performance rights, how television and blanket licenses work, the agreements you enter, collaboration, how money is generated and divided and grievance procedures.

COPYRIGHT LAW UNDERPINNING

To understand exactly how performing rights organizations work, you must understand one fundamental tenet of copyright law: a copyright owner in a musical work (song) has the exclusive right to perform the work publicly. The concept "performance" includes live performances and the rendering of previous performances that are fixed in records, videotape or film. When a radio station broadcasts a song it is being publicly performed, even though the recording artist is not performing live. Thus, the radio station must be licensed by the copyright owner to play the song. Radio stations pay fees to obtain public performance licenses from ASCAP, BMI and SESAC. The same is true for songs in television programs. When a television program is broadcast, the songs in the program are being publicly performed. The network or local station must be licensed to publicly perform those songs.

Radio and television stations that make music available via the Internet via webcasts, satellite, cable-wired music services and podcasts, must obtain performance licenses from ASCAP, BMI and SESAC. Companies that offer ringtones and ringbacks must also obtain performance licenses.

CLUB PERFORMANCES

Radio and TV are not the only kinds of public performance. When you are dancing to "We Are Family" by Sister Sledge in a nightclub, the playing of that song and recording by the disc jockey is a public performance. Equally, when a band performs it live in a nightclub that is a public performance as well. But, at this point you should consider what performance the performing rights organizations license. The performance of the musical composition in the record is licensed, not the performance of the sound recording. (A sound recording is a series of sounds. Its copyright is separate from the copyright in the song.) When the disc jockey is playing "We Are Family," the *musical composition* "We Are Family" is licensed, not Sister Sledge's recording. Therefore, regardless of who makes a record with "We Are Family" on it, if it is played publicly, the writer and publisher of the *musical composition* "We Are Family" earn performance royalties, not the performers on the record or the record label.

In the United States, there is no public performance right in a sound recording that applies to nightclubs. To perform a song that has been embodied in a sound recording without violating copyright law, the nightclub must have a license to publicly perform this song.

That is where ASCAP, BMI and SESAC step in. They negotiate licenses (permissions) with nightclubs, cabarets, discos and the like that enable them to use the musical compositions contained in the performing rights organizations' catalogs—whether the song is performed live or is being played by a DJ.

The essence of the agreements between performing rights organizations and night-clubs is simple: the performing rights organizations grant the right to the nightclubs to use the songs (perform them publicly), and the performing rights organizations are paid fees by nightclubs. These fees are ultimately divided among the songwriters and publishers that create and publish the songs. The company that publishes "We Are Family" and the song's writers must authorize ASCAP, BMI or SESAC to license the public performance.

The performing rights organizations will sue broadcasters, clubs and others that publicly perform songs without a license. Pursuing lawsuits under the copyright law is one of their most important functions.

PUBLIC PERFORMANCE OF SOUND RECORDINGS

For many years, owners of sound recordings (e.g., record labels) and featured artists lobbied for payment of public performance royalties, arguing that their performance and interpretation of the songs were equal in importance to their creation. Record companies argued that their copyrights in sound recordings gave them a right to performance royalties.

In 1995, the U.S. Congress passed the Digital Performance Right in Sound Recordings Act (DPRSRA), which amends the U.S. Copyright Act. The DPRSRA provides the owners of copyrights in sound recordings and the artists that perform on them the right to be paid public performance royalties for the streaming of sound recordings via satellite and cable. In 1998, the U.S. Congress passed the Digital Millennium Copyright Act (DMCA) that gave owners of sound recordings, featured artists and nonfeatured artists the rights to be paid royalties for webcasts and other Internet transmissions. The U.S. Copyright Office designated SoundExchange, Inc., to administer the distribution of royalties. (More information is found in the chapter, "Digital Downloads and Streaming: Copyright and Distribution Issues.")

Thus, the owners of the sound recording and featured performers are now entitled to public performance royalties that arise from digital transmissions.

Music Played In Movie Theaters

As a result of an antitrust case brought on behalf of theater owners, ASCAP, BMI and SESAC do not license the public performance of musical works in U.S. motion picture theaters. However, certain foreign performing rights organizations do so in their respective territories.

Performance rights organizations distribute performance royalties on behalf of songwriters and publishers when films that contain their music are aired on television and cable programs in the United States.

DRAMATIC VERSUS NONDRAMATIC RIGHTS

ASCAP, BMI and SESAC do not license dramatic performance rights ("grand rights"). The Copyright Act grants the exclusive right to perform publicly a dramatic work to the copyright owner. Dramatic works include, among other things, plays (both musicals and dramas) and dramatic scripts for radio, television, ballets and operas. A musical composition (a song), in and of itself, is a nondramatic work.

Drawing the line between a dramatic and nondramatic performance is sometimes difficult, if not impossible. The standard ASCAP, BMI and SESAC contracts state they license only nondramatic performances of the compositions they administer. Thus, radio and television licensees must be careful to make sure their blanket license covers their use of a song from a play or opera. The industry practice is that radio stations may play unlimited numbers of instrumentals from cast albums or play a sequence of up to two vocals and an instrumental from a cast album. Some record companies and publishers, however, avoid this licensing problem by obtaining clearance from the copyright holder for unrestricted radio use of songs from cast albums and notify broadcasters of such.

Dramatic performances are usually licensed directly from the writers (or their agents) of the music, lyrics and book of the play. Writers usually reserve dramatic rights in their contracts with publishers. For example, if a theater company wants to stage *The Phantom of the Opera,* they must seek permission directly from the writers of the play to perform the play and the accompanying music. On the other hand, if a radio station wants to play only the song "Music of the Night" from *The Phantom of the Opera* cast album, this is not a dramatic performance, and ASCAP, BMI and SESAC license that.

WHAT PERFORMING RIGHTS SOCIETIES DO NOT DO

Performing rights societies do not issue licenses for records (mechanical licenses); the synchronization of music works in audiovisual words (such as films and television programs); nor do they authorize the printing and sale of sheet music. They do not register songs for copyright, which only the United States Copyright Office can do. And, as discussed above, they do not license dramatic performance rights.

ASCAP

In 1914, Victor Herbert and a handful of other composers organized ASCAP because performances of copyrighted music for profit were so numerous, widespread and fleeting that it was impossible for individual copyright owners to negotiate with and license music users and detect unauthorized public performances of their songs. ASCAP was organized to serve as a clearinghouse for copyright owners and users and to solve those problems. Today, ASCAP is a membership society that represents over 260,000 composers, songwriters, lyricists and publishers. ASCAP collected more than $750,000,000 in 2005, and distributed over $646,000,000 to its members. ASCAP represents such songwriters as Bruce Springsteen, Stevie Wonder, Madonna, Beck and Irving Berlin.

BMI

BMI is a nonprofit corporation, organized in 1939, whose stock is owned by members of the broadcasting industry. BMI represents more than 300,000 publishing companies, songwriters and composers and operates in much the same manner as ASCAP. In fiscal year 2005–2006, BMI collected more than $779,000,000 and distributed over $676,000,000 to its affiliates. BMI represents such songwriters as Mariah Carey, The Black Eyed Peas and Kanye West.

SESAC

SESAC, formed in 1930, is a privately held corporation and represents approximately 270,000 songs for some 11,000 writers and publishers (affiliates). SESAC differs from ASCAP and BMI in that it is much smaller and offers affiliates efficient and personalized services, including catalog consultation and collaboration recommendations. SESAC represents such songwriter/performers as Bob Dylan and Neil Diamond, as well as songwriters that compose songs for artists such as Mariah Carey, Justin Timberlake, Nelly Furtado and Beyoncé.

PERFORMANCE LICENSES

The bulk of money paid to the performing rights organizations comes from radio and television broadcasters. These fees vary according to how many people are reached by a particular medium. For example, network television stations are charged far higher license fees than radio stations and nightclubs because they reach wider audiences.

Blanket Licenses

Most radio and television stations pay blanket licenses (one annual fee) to ASCAP, BMI and SESAC that cover all the works in their catalogs. Thus, television and radio stations do not have to clear the music before it is broadcast—stations can be confident the song being played is somewhere in the performing rights organizations' catalogs. The granting of blanket licenses makes sense when you consider the vast number of songs in those catalogs. If users had to individually negotiate with the copyright holder each time a song was played, chaos would result. Blanket licenses also benefit writers and publishers, as they do not have the means to enforce their exclusive right to public performance of their songs.

After a performing rights organization issues its blanket license, the license holder may use any of the works of any of the members of that organization as often as desired during the license term. The performing rights organizations use sampling techniques to figure out to whom the money should go and compute the division of income based on the frequency and the kind of public performance of songs. The computation and payment of royalties is discussed more fully below.

Per Program Licenses

Stations can choose a "per program" use fee in lieu of blanket licenses. Typically these are all-talk or news stations where music is seldom played.

MEMBERSHIP

To become an ASCAP or BMI writer member, you must have written or cowritten a song that has been or is about to be commercially recorded (CD, record, tape, etc.) or written or cowritten a song that is or is likely to be performed on television, film, cable or is available for sale or rental. Once released into the commercial marketplace, songs are considered published and have the potential to earn income from a variety of sources, which include performances on radio, television, live concerts, nightclubs and jukeboxes.

As performing rights organizations pay writers and publishers separately, both must join. Writers can only belong to one performing rights organization at a time. Even when writers are affiliated with publishing companies, they should join performing rights organizations so that they can directly receive any royalties that are due.

Publishers always have separate ASCAP, BMI and SESAC-affiliated legal entities (e.g., A Tunes [ASCAP], B Tunes [BMI] and C Tunes [SESAC]). Each organization has name clearance procedures to avoid name duplication or the confusion of similar names.

If you are an ASCAP writer and a publisher administers your song, it will be handled by the entity of the publisher that is affiliated with ASCAP.

There is no cost to join ASCAP and there are no annual dues. BMI has no dues or cost to join for writer members, but it charges publisher members a one-time processing fee of $150 for individually owned businesses and $250 for partnerships, limited liability companies (LLCs) and corporations.

Unlike the other performing rights organizations, SESAC has a selection process it uses to grant affiliation to songwriters and publishers. Submissions are reviewed by SESAC's writer/publisher relations staff and membership is by invitation only. There is no fee to affiliate with SESAC for writers or publishers.

COLLABORATION

If an ASCAP writer collaborates with a BMI or SESAC writer, the song is licensed concurrently by both organizations. Thus, you will notice that on some record albums some songs have more than one organization listed.

REGISTRATION OF COMPOSITIONS

Prior to choosing which performing rights organization to join, you should register your songs with the U.S. Copyright Office in order to establish authorship and ownership.

It is essential to collecting royalties that you or your publisher registers every composition that is published with your performance right society. ASCAP, BMI and SESAC provide forms for registering musical works and members may also file this information on line.

CONTRACTS WITH SONGWRITERS AND PUBLISHERS

Once you qualify for membership in ASCAP, BMI or SESAC you will enter into a contract with one of them. Basically, once a song is published, you can join ASCAP or BMI. (As mentioned above, SESAC's membership process is different.) In so doing, you give that organization the right to license the public performance of songs that you write in return for their promise to pay you royalties for the reported performances.

Publishers also join ASCAP, BMI or SESAC. Their contracts are much the same as for writers.

HOW PUBLIC PERFORMANCES ARE MONITORED
Radio

ASCAP samples some 500,000 hours of AM and FM radio per year in order to produce their model for the distribution of performance royalties. It samples larger stations more heavily. Weighted multipliers are then applied to calculate radio royalties payable to songwriters and publishers. ASCAP also uses information provided by Mediaguide's "audio fingerprint" technology (broadcasts are identified by matching them to a database that contains compact representations of audio content [fingerprints] of registered works); station logs of actual works performed; and recorded tapes of broadcasts.

BMI requires that all licensed stations provide detailed logs of the music they have scheduled for airplay during a three-day period each year, with different stations logging each day of the year. This provides BMI with over 4,000,000 hours of logs to be surveyed. In addition, BMI surveys radio performance data obtained from third-party providers such as MediaBase and Broadcast Data Systems (BDS). This information is used to create a statistically reliable projection of all feature performances on all commercial music format radio stations throughout the country

ASCAP uses actual "off-the-air" audiotapes to avoid any potential alterations (as could occur with a log). There is no consensus as to whether the ASCAP or BMI sampling system is more accurate.

The number of surveyed performances of the compositions, not their chart position, determines the amount of performance royalties paid. These royalties fluctuate depending on the music category (e.g., pop, country, rhythm and blues, religious, gospel, symphonic) and also whether the composition "crosses over" to other music charts or categories.

Most SESAC performances are surveyed on a census basis from information obtained through BDS as well as directly from licensees. Payment for performances is based on the license fees collected and the number of payable performances occurring in each quarter.

ASCAP, BMI and SESAC also track and pay royalties on a variety of cable and satellite radio services.

Network Television

To track network television performances, ASCAP, BMI and SESAC receive cue sheets submitted by the networks' program producers, which detail each second of music used in network programs and the types of use. All three organizations also tape network shows to spot check information that is provided on the cue sheets.

Local Television

ASCAP uses cue sheets, program schedules, station logs and tapes to cover all movies and syndicated programs broadcast on local television stations to sample about 30,000 hours of local television programming yearly. As with radio, this sampling is then multiplied, using statistical models, to calculate local television royalties. BMI and SESAC use similar techniques. They compile cue sheets, complete computerized accounts of regional *TV Guides* and program listings from local television stations.

TELEVISION MUSIC

There are three main categories of television music—theme, background and feature performances. Performing rights organizations pay different rates for each. They factor in the number of stations that air the performance, the type of station (e.g., network, local, cable or public television) and the duration of the performance. Payments are also made for music used for promotional purposes or for jingles.

Theme music appears at the opening or closing of a television program and during segments within programs. Background music is played to enhance the program but is not intended as the focus of the program. There is typically about 10 (although some animated programs often contain up to 20) minutes of background music in a 30-minute program. A feature performance is music that is the visual focus of the program. For example, a composition sung on camera is considered a feature performance. Rates fluctuate depending on many factors, including whether the show is network or syndicated, time of day and program type (e.g., series, soaps, quiz shows, movies).

PAYMENT OF ROYALTIES

The amount of royalties paid varies between ASCAP, BMI and SESAC due to many factors, the most significant of which are differences in rates and survey methods. Generally, each organization divides and pays the revenues derived from licenses and fees 50% to publisher and 50% to writer. ASCAP and BMI assign various credit values to publishers, factoring in the size and dollar value of their catalogs but do not do so for writers.

Nightclubs

With few exceptions, it is impractical for ASCAP and BMI to monitor and pay for performances in bars or nightclubs. There are no significant royalties paid for non-television/nonradio performances. Royalties for radio and television performances come from licensing fees from radio and television. The fees collected from bars and nightclubs are allocated to the same funding pool that pays songwriters and publishers for radio and television performances.

SESAC is the only performing rights organization that pays royalties for all reported live performances. SESAC affiliates can claim payments for performances occurring in all "live" music venues, such as arenas, stadiums, concert halls, theatres and nightclubs by completing the Live Performance Notification Form. The form asks for such data as performance date, venue information and songs performed. Payments vary based on the performance and the licensing fees collected from music venue owners, the number of tickets sold and whether or not the performance occurs during the opening act's or headlining act's performance.

ASCAP

ASCAP's method of paying royalties is to "follow the dollar" (e.g., television licensing fees are paid out only as television royalties). ASCAP calculates royalties on a quarterly basis. Songs that have generated high amounts of feature performances over time (e.g., 20,000 feature performances over a five-year survey period) are called "qualifying works" and are assigned higher credit values than performance royalties for background music.

BMI

BMI pays quarterly, six to seven months after the end of the calendar quarter in which the performance occurs. Royalty payments vary from quarter to quarter depending upon the amount of license fees collected and the total dollar amount available for each quarterly distribution. Royalties are paid simultaneously to writer and publisher in equal lump sums. In the absence of a publisher, payment of the full amount of royalties may be made to the writer or by agreement between the writer and publisher, payment maybe split unequally, with the writer receiving the larger share (but not vice versa).

BMI recognizes frequently performed works by awarding hit song bonuses to both writers and publishers for songs that reach a high number of current-quarter performances and standards bonuses for songs with a high number of cumulative performances.

Neither ASCAP nor BMI pay writer royalties to anyone other than the writer, unless such royalties have been assigned by the writer to legitimate creditors.

SESAC

Distributions of domestic performance royalties are made to SESAC writer and publisher affiliates four times per year. Royalty distributions are made 90 days after the close of each quarter and are based on a quarterly review and analysis of each affiliate's catalog and its performance activity.

ADVANCES

Until the early 1980s, both ASCAP and BMI routinely paid advances (nonrefundable prepayments of estimated future royalties) to writers and publishers in an effort to stabilize their incomes and entice major musical stars to join their respective organizations. However, due to legal challenges to syndicated television blanket licenses and the resulting concern about future royalties, advances were discontinued and both organizations remain wary of them.

To replace advances, both ASCAP and BMI allow assignments of royalties as collateral against bank loans to composers and publishers. BMI and ASCAP also accept assignment of writer royalties against advances made to the writer by the writer's publisher. As the documentation for such assignments is complex, assignments are usually only cost-effective for composers and publishers with substantial projected royalties.

SESAC offers advances as part of their campaign to encourage successful ASCAP and BMI affiliates to join and to entice promising unaffiliated writers and publishers.

FOREIGN INCOME PAYMENTS

Foreign performing rights organizations monitor foreign performances of compositions in the ASCAP/BMI/SESAC domestic repertoires and pay royalties for such performances to U.S. writers and publishers through them. The lag in payment of foreign royalties can be as long as five years.

One constant problem is that U.S. writers' or publishers' foreign performing rights royalties are often diluted by the payment of royalties to translators of popular American songs by the foreign performing rights organization. Monies that are collected from U.S. songs, which are not distributed to ASCAP, BMI and SESAC are generally forfeited to the foreign organization's general fund (the infamous so-called black box) for disbursement to the members of the foreign society. To avoid the black box and accelerate payments, most publishers prefer to have their foreign royalties collected "at the source" by their foreign publishers (i.e., subpublishers). Writer royalties, however, still flow from the foreign performing rights organizations to the domestic ones.

GRIEVANCE PROCEDURES

If you have a dispute with ASCAP, BMI or SESAC (for example, you do not agree with your royalty statement), you have recourse through their grievance procedures. The ASCAP grievance procedure is set out in their articles of association. ASCAP provides these articles to you when you join. BMI grievances are submitted to the American Arbitration Association in New York City. SESAC must receive royalty adjustment claims for domestic performances within one year of the date of the performance. Foreign adjustment requests must be submitted to SESAC within nine months of the applicable foreign distribution. SESAC evaluates grievances on a case-by-case basis.

Music Licensing: A Primer

BY DIANE RAPAPORT

The bundle of rights given to copyright owners is protected through the issuance of licenses to businesses or individuals that want to use their compositions. Licenses are issued to users by composers and publishers when their music is

- Recorded, reproduced and sold as sound recordings (mechanical licenses)

- Recorded and sold as permanent downloads from the Internet (mechanical licenses)

- Used as segues in radio and television shows (mechanical licenses)

- Used to create derivative works (mechanical licenses)

- Used to create ringtones, excerpts of musical compositions embodied in a digital file and rendered into audio (mechanical licenses)

- Played publicly on radio, television, the Internet, on jukeboxes, performed live in concerts, bars and restaurants, etc. (performance rights licenses)

- Used in film, video, TV and video games (synchronization licenses)

- Used in advertising commercials (synchronization licenses)

- Sold as sheet music (sheet music licenses)

The use of a song in one medium, such as a CD, does not automatically confer the use on another CD, such as a compilation CD or another use, such as a film. Licenses are issued for each use, which results in multiple sources of income.

COMPULSORY MECHANICAL LICENSES

According to the provisions of the U.S. Copyright Act, once compositions are published (sold to the public), publishers must issue compulsory mechanical licenses (statutory licenses) to record companies for their use on recordings sold in the United States.

The right to reproduce (record) songs for the first time belongs to composers. They can exercise that right in one of two ways: they can record the songs themselves or they can transfer that copyright to someone else via a written contract. In either case, publishing companies will issue mechanical licenses to record companies for use in songs.

The U.S. Copyright Office establishes the compulsory mechanical license rate. From January 1, 2006 to December 31, 2007, the rate is 9.1¢ per song or 1.75¢ per minute, whichever is larger.

The Harry Fox Agency (HFA) is used by many U. S publishers to issue mechanical and other licenses. It collects and distributes fees to the publishers.

The income from mechanical licenses is divided between the publishing companies and songwriters according to the contracts they have signed.

PERFORMANCE LICENSES

The issuance of licenses for public performance of an artist's work is the domain of public performance rights organizations and societies such as ASCAP, BMI and SESAC. These organizations have established fees for users (radio stations, TV stations, webcasters, jukeboxes, concert presenters, ringtone aggregators, etc.). The performance rights societies collect these fees and distribute them to publishers and artists. There is no practical way for an artist to license the right for public performance without joining one of the performance rights organizations.

SYNCHRONIZATION LICENSES

The integration of music in audiovisual works, such as films, television programs, video games and advertising is referred to as synchronization (timed to the picture). Producers that want to use music in audiovisual mediums must obtain synchronization (synch) licenses from publishers, unless they have commissioned the music under a work-for-hire agreement. Additionally, a separate mechanical license must be obtained if the music is to be reproduced in a sound recording, video game, etc.

The U.S. Copyright Act does not provide guidelines for the amount of synch license fees. These fees must be negotiated between users and publishers.

Income from synch licenses is divided between publishing companies and composers according to the contracts they have with each other.

Individual synch licenses must be obtained for each medium that a song will be used in, such as film documentary, network television and pay (subscription) television. Sometimes, blanket synch licenses are negotiated for all mediums.

SHEET MUSIC LICENSES

Use licenses must be obtained for including copyrighted songs in print mediums, such as songbooks, band arrangements and reprints of lyrics in books or magazines. The fees are negotiated, but in practice, print publishers pay music publishers a 12% to 25% percentage of the retail price for each copy that is sold and paid for.

Income from sheet music licenses is divided between publishing companies and composers according to the contracts they have with each other.

THE ROLE OF PUBLISHERS

With the exception of fees for mechanical licenses, which are established by the U.S. Copyright Act, publishers and the HFA negotiate use fees and other terms for licenses. In effect, publishers have become gatekeepers between the artists and businesses that want to license their works. Publishers try to negotiate the highest licensing fees possible for commercial uses.

Some potential users may find it difficult to obtain synch and other licenses from large publishers because they either cannot afford the fees or their earnings potential is too small to warrant a publisher's time and attention.

Here are a few examples:

- An author is writing a book on the art of writing lyrics and wants permission to include examples of lyrics of well-known songwriters. The book is not expected to sell more than 5000 copies. The author writes/calls/e-mails and gets little or no response.

- An amateur or documentary videographer wants to use a published work of a major label artist in their film or video but cannot afford the high fees that the publisher wants.

- An amateur, noncommercial podcaster or blogger wishes to use snippets of lyrics/videos, etc, and cannot get past the secretary of the licensing firm.

Songwriters may have no knowledge of how many requests are ignored by their publishers, and even when they do know, there is not much they can do about it, because they have ceded negotiation of licenses to the publishers.

Songwriters that have not signed contracts with major or established publishing companies find it difficult to exploit their compositions in commercial media. Several nonprofit and commercial organizations, such as TAXI *(www.taxi.com)*, have been formed to help songwriters that do not have publishers.

CREATIVE COMMONS LICENSES

Creative Commons *(www.creativecommons.org)*, a nonprofit organization, was created in 2002 to offer some practical licensing alternatives to songwriters and other artists that wished to share their published works more freely in order to gain greater exposure and distribution for their works. This alternative is not available to songwriters that have contracts with publishers, unless they have reserved some of their rights to pursue licensing alternatives.

A Creative Commons license can apply to all works that are protected by the U.S. Copyright Act. The license, which is available free to artists and users from Creative Commons, allows musicians to clearly mark their songs as free to download and share while it protects their commercial and other rights. The license also helps musicians tag their works digitally, which allows the Creative Commons search engine to index them from the Web site. This makes it easy for musicians that want to share their music and for fans that want to legally download it, to find each other.

Songwriters can choose to issue six types of Creative Commons licenses, three of them for strictly noncommercial use and three that allow commercial use. Songwriters can limit the term of the license. Creative Commons also offers a set of other licenses for more specialized applications, such as sampling. Below are the six types of Creative Commons licenses.

1. Attribution Noncommercial No Derivatives (by-nc-nd)

Allows users to download a work and share it with others as long as they mention the artist and link back to them. The user cannot change the work in any way or use it commercially.

2. Attribution Noncommercial Share Alike (by-nc-sa)

Allows users to remix, tweak and build upon a work noncommercially, as long as they credit the artist and license their new creations under identical terms. Users can download and redistribute a work just like the by-nc-nd license, but they can also translate, make remixes and produce new stories based on the work. All new work will carry the same license, so any derivatives will also be noncommercial.

3. Attribution Noncommercial (by-nc)

Allows users to remix, tweak and build upon a work noncommercially, although the new work must also acknowledge the artist and be noncommercial, the user does not have to license their derivative works on the same terms.

4. Attribution No Derivatives (by-nd)

Allows users to redistribute the work, commercially and noncommercially, as long as it is passed along unchanged and in whole, with credit to the artist.

5. Attribution Share Alike (by-sa)

This license lets others remix, tweak and build upon the work even for commercial reasons, as long as they credit the artist and license their new creations under the identical terms. This license is often compared to open source software licenses. All new works based on the original carry the same license, so any derivatives must also allow commercial use.

6. Attribution (by)

Lets users distribute, remix, tweak and build upon the work, including commercially, as long as they credit the songwriter(s) and license their new work under the identical terms.

CONCLUSION

The issuance of licenses is the mechanism that songwriters and publishers use to protect their copyrights and exploit the commercial values of their works. Licenses are issued for each commercial use, which results in multiple sources of income. Songwriters should consult their attorneys before issuing any licenses or signing publishing contracts that cede the rights to publishers to negotiate licenses on their behalf.

Music Publishing

BY NEVILLE L. JOHNSON AND BERNARD M. RESNICK

The wise professional songwriter understands the dynamics and economics of song exploitation: failure to do so can be perilous. This chapter explores the types of income that are generated in the music publishing industry and the kinds of deals that are commonly struck between publishers and songwriters. The attributes of a good publisher are summarized, suggestions for obtaining a publisher are made, and typical music publishing agreements are examined.

Music publishing has been the major source of revenue for songwriters since the turn of the 20th century, when vaudeville was the primary vehicle for exploiting songs. Music publishers of that era worked to persuade entertainers to publicly perform musical compositions to stimulate the sale of printed editions and player piano rolls. Over the years, the technology for merchandising music has expanded with inventions such as the phonograph record, radio, motion pictures, television, videotape, CDs and DVDs. Now, digital transmission is rapidly becoming the dominant way by which music is distributed. Songwriters and publishers have benefited from each of those new sources of income. As the complexity and size of the music publishing industry increases, so does the amount of money that can be earned within it. Today, one hit song can make a songwriter very wealthy.

Music publishing is a beautiful way to make money because the company that uses the music ordinarily does the marketing and promotion—which is the hardest part of selling music. The costs of music publishing have traditionally been dwarfed by the massive manufacturing and promotion costs of selling music to the public. The economics of music publishing are that the songs in the catalog are, in a sense, promoted by the publishing company's own customers. Record companies, film and television companies, video game manufacturers and advertising agencies dedicate large amounts of funds to promote sales of their respective products, which cannot exist without the songs they have licensed from the music publisher. Therefore, the company licensing a song helps the music publisher fulfill its goal of marketing its catalog, at little or no cost to the publisher. This is why publishing catalogs have become so valuable and currently sell for eight to fifteen times their average annual income (calculated on an average, weighted basis of the preceding few years). Some catalogs and songs are sold at even higher multiples. Major financial institutional investors are always on the hunt for music publishing catalogs. Songs are like oil wells; they keep pumping revenues year after year.

Music industry expert Alan Rubens has stated that music publishing is the "real estate of the record business." This analogy is quite apt, because, like real estate, music publishing catalogs—

- generally increase in value over time;

- are generally not affected by short-term market fluctuations;

- can be used to borrow money against the future income of the catalog (similar to a mortgage on real estate) because of the steady, predictable flow of income over time;

- have a predictable tax basis;

- can be used to make money in multiple ways at the same time; and

- have the potential to realize sudden, large gains in value due to market conditions.

One advantage of music publishing catalogs, compared with real estate, is the low maintenance costs of the catalog, once the initial purchase price has been paid. Once the music publishing company has paid the songwriter the advance cost of obtaining the rights to the song, exploitation costs for that song are rather low.

Because of the digital revolution, the music industry is in a state of flux. Nowadays, an artist can get distribution digitally and the need for "hard product," CDs in particular, is diminishing. The traditional retail record industry is dying; but the music industry is not going to disappear, it is simply changing, and music publishing will continue to prosper, though it too will change as the new technologies continue to take hold.

With sites such as myspace.com, recording acts can self-market and develop a grassroots base. Still, there is no substitute for the marketing machines of the major record companies, which spend millions of dollars breaking acts.

Increasingly, nontraditional methods of promotion are intersecting the music industry: video games, television shows, advertising tie-ins and peer-to-peer sharing are shaking the foundations of the music business. As the music world goes almost entirely digital, the tracking of income will become almost entirely electronic, making it easier for songwriters and publishers to monitor and collect their income. Some argue that this will make traditional publishers increasingly irrelevant or less necessary as the function of collecting becomes easier, and the collection of music revenues will become something that the ordinary songwriter and musician can understand and control on his or her own.

TYPES OF INCOME

There are eight major categories of music publishing income. The first seven categories are each referred to as "small rights" (nondramatic public performing rights); the eighth is known as "grand rights" (dramatic performing rights). Foreign income can be derived from all eight categories.

Mechanical Royalties

Mechanical royalties are paid to songwriters by record companies based upon the number of units sold to the public that contain songs written by those songwriters.

The current statutory rate for mechanicals is 9.1¢ per song or 1.75¢ per minute, whichever is greater. The U.S. Copyright Royalty Board adjusts the mechanical royalty rate every two years, with such adjustments normally rising 5% to 10% for the ensuing two years, in accordance with the rise in the cost of living. In other words, if the song is longer than 5 minutes and 12 seconds, the writer is entitled to more than 9.1¢ per unit sold. For example, if a song were included on a platinum album (1,000,000 units sold), the songwriters would normally be entitled to $91,000. This is for just one song—if, for example, five songs were written, the amount would be $455,000. This would be divided amongst the songwriters in proportion to their respective writer's shares. If a songwriter is a 50% cowriter of one of those songs, he or she would get $45,500.

Normally, each time a new artist records a new version (cover) of the song, the original writers receive mechanical royalties at the full statutory rate, based on the number of sales of the new artist's recordings. All songs contained on an album are paid the same amount of mechanical royalties; it does not matter whether or not the song is the single or is made into a music video.

It is common for songwriters that are also recording artists or producers to give a 25% discount from the statutory mechanical rate to their record companies when the record companies release records containing songs written by them. Songs subject to this discount are known as "controlled compositions." Controlled compositions do not exist in other countries and have been eliminated to some extent by legislation with respect to digital delivery of songs. The Copyright Act at 17 United States Code §115 prohibits any diminishment of the rate otherwise payable under a compulsory license for agreements entered into after June 22, 1995 and prohibits the addition of new songs to controlled composition limits when such agreements are modified.

As the music industry goes digital, the concept of albums becomes irrelevant since consumers can purchase/download/stream songs on an individual basis. The controlled composition discount generally reduces the amount payable by the record company from 9.1¢ to 6.825¢ per unit sold. Further, it is common for a record company to set a cap of 10 or 11 on the number of controlled compositions on an album for which it will pay mechanical royalties. In cases where songwriter/artists compose all of the songs on albums that are subject to a 25% rate discount and an 11-song cap, they will receive approximately 75¢ per album in mechanical royalty payments.

Once a songwriter has signed a contract with a music publisher, the publisher takes over the responsibility of collecting all mechanical royalties due, either by issuing licenses and collecting royalties itself or by using an agency such as The Harry Fox Agency, Inc. In the United States, mechanical income is paid to the publisher of a composition by the record company that manufactures recordings of the composition pursuant to a contract between them called a mechanical license. A mechanical license is granted in lieu of a statutory "compulsory license," which can be obtained via the United States Copyright Office after a song has first been recorded. Very few compulsory licenses have been obtained in the past for manufactured product; whether this methodology will be used for digital distribution remains to be seen. Under a mechanical license, the record company is required to account to the publisher (render a written statement which details the amounts collected and accompanies a royalty payment to the publisher) on a quarterly basis, and audits are permitted.

In most foreign countries, mechanical rights income is computed differently than in the United States. Instead of a flat rate per song, the royalty is computed on a basis that is usually 6% to 8% of the selling price of the recordings (usually referred to as "published price to dealers"). Mechanical income is allocated evenly among the compositions on the recording. This income is collected and distributed by mechanical rights societies, which exist in most countries of the world. The entity closest to a mechanical rights society, in the United States, is The Harry Fox Agency, Inc. *(www.harryfox.com),* headquartered in New York City. Although many American publishers issue their own mechanical licenses, many prefer to use this company, which, for a 6.75% fee (this fee fluctuates yearly based on their expenses), issues mechanical licenses to American record companies and to digital distributors and conducts audits of such companies to insure that proper payments are made. The Harry Fox Agency collects fees for synchronization licenses granted prior to 2002 and collects monies due from imported sound recordings. The Harry Fox Agency has a market share in excess of 60% of all income collected from this sector. It is owned by the National Music Publishers Association. An excellent resource for understanding this area is the book *Kohn on Music Licensing,* by Al Kohn and Bob Kohn (2002, Aspen Publishers).

Performance Rights and Income

The copyright laws in the United States and similar laws in virtually every other country of the world require that compensation be paid to copyright owners for the public performance of their music. Concert promoters, nightclubs, radio stations and TV stations pay fees to performance rights societies in exchange for the right to publicly perform or broadcast music. Performing rights organizations exist because it is impractical for copyright owners to license the right to publicly perform their compositions to every music user separately; likewise, it is impractical for music users to keep track of copyright owners and negotiate individual licenses to authorize the performance of each copyrighted work.

Music users throughout the world are licensed by, and make payments to, performing rights organizations. After deducting their costs of administration, these organizations distribute revenue to copyright owners and their publishers.

The United States has three performing rights organizations. ASCAP (American Society of Composers, Authors and Publishers), BMI (Broadcast Music, Inc.) and SESAC, which is much smaller than the other two organizations. These organizations collect public performance income and distribute it in proportion to the success of each composition they license.

The performing rights organizations divide performance income so that 50% is paid directly to the composer (writer's share) and 50% is paid to the publisher (publisher's share). The performance rights societies collect the fees, then divide the money and distribute it directly to their member songwriters and publishers, based on the number of public performances of each particular song as discerned through a combination of "census surveys" (complete counts of public performances) and sample surveys. One anomaly of the United States compared to the rest of the world is that performance revenues are not paid for performances in motion picture theaters. This is the result of a case, *Alden-Rochelle, Inc. v. ASCAP,* 80 F. Supp. 888 (SDNY 1948), which occurred because ASCAP was found to have acted in a monopolistic fashion. The right to grant performance and synchronization licenses was taken from ASCAP (and subsequently BMI pursuant to a consent decree with the U. S. Department of Justice) and given to music publishers. Since then, the motion picture companies have refused to bargain with composers regarding rates that would be competitive with those paid to foreign composers.

Foreign countries have their own performance rights societies, such as GEMA in Germany, PRS in England and SACEM in France. The U.S. societies generally have reciprocal agreements with overseas societies, which allow them to collect overseas performance rights income on behalf of their members, and almost all writers receive their worldwide performance income from one society. Almost all domestic publishers have subpublishers—some of which are wholly owned subsidiaries—that collect performance and all other income in the foreign territories. Some publishers sign directly with foreign societies and their companies are administered by the subpublishers; they do so to obtain such benefits as unallocated income, also known as "black box" revenues, which are available only to members of the foreign collecting societies.

Songwriters join a performing rights organization when they get their first recording or placement in a film, commercial, TV program or video. It is the publisher's job to register musical compositions with the performance rights society. The registration process is quick, painless and can be done electronically. See the chapter, "Performing Rights Organizations: An Overview," for more information.

Samples/Interpolations

Samples occur when other artists incorporate some or all of a songwriter's song into their new work by using a digital recorder/sampler. "Interpolations" occur when other artists incorporate some or all of a songwriter's song into their new work by replaying and rerecording some or all of the original work. The creator of the new work must get the original songwriter's permission to include a sample or interpolation, and this is usually accompanied by a negotiated, up-front license fee and a percentage share of ownership of the new composition. Sample and interpolation license fees can range from $2,500 to $50,000, depending on the depth of the use and the relative negotiating leverage of the parties. It is also customary for the party requesting the sample clearance to grant a percentage of ownership of the copyright (and a corresponding share of the new composition's future income) to the party being sampled. Once a songwriter has signed a contract with a music publisher, the publisher takes over the responsibility of clearing samples and interpolations. Clearance procedures consist of negotiating the sample and interpolation license fees, drafting the license agreements and collecting all funds due. There are clearance companies that will do this for artists, producers and record companies.

Synchronization

Synchronization income is the money paid by motion picture and television production companies and advertising agencies for the right to use compositions in motion pictures or in dramatic presentations on television. The "synch right" for a composition to be contained in a major motion picture can vary from zero to hundreds of thousands of dollars, and the attendant exposure can stimulate the generation of additional revenue from those areas discussed above. Television commercials can be particularly lucrative for a songwriter, and fees in the range of $50,000 to seven figures for TV commercial synchronization rights for well-known songs occur. Typically, the synchronization fee will be on a most favored nations (equal) basis with the master recording that will be licensed contemporaneously.

When films, television shows, multimedia CD-ROMs, video games, Internet Web sites, and other audiovisual media, use a songwriter's music to accompany the pictures contained in their productions, they must get permission to do so, and this is usually accompanied by a negotiated, up-front license fee. Major film company synchronization payments are as low as $5,000. However, in the case of major recording stars, the synchronization fees can be in the mid six figures and more. Television programs generally pay synchronization license fees in the range of $500 to $5,000 per use. Video game synchronization fees average approximately $1,000 to $5,000 per use. Once a songwriter has signed a contract with a music publisher, the publisher takes over the responsibility of clearing synchronization. Clearance procedures consist of negotiating the synchronization license fees, drafting the license agreements, and collecting all funds due.

Synchronization uses invariably mean that there will be performance royalties as the work is performed on television and movie theaters other than in the United States.

Print Rights

Sheet music is more common in jazz, classical and pop music than in hip-hop, R&B and country and western. Once a songwriter has signed a contract with a music publisher, the publisher takes over the responsibility of soliciting and arranging for sheet music manufacturing, through agencies and other companies that specialize in this task. The publisher hires the sheet music manufacturer, negotiates the license fees, drafts the license agreement and collects all funds due.

Printed music can contribute substantial earnings to a songwriter. Today the industry is concentrated in a few companies that manufacture and distribute printed music across the United States. There are three major print music companies in the United States: Alfred/Warner Publications, Hal Leonard and Music Sales. Cherry Lane is also a substantial print music company, which distributes through Hal Leonard.

The publisher that licenses to one of the major print outfits usually makes 20% of the suggested Retail Selling Price (RSP) for pop single sheets. The RSP in 2006 was $3.95. Print music is generally sold at the wholesale price of 45% to 50% of the RSP. Thus, the publisher earns approximately 80¢ per sheet sold for its songwriter client, and half of that would go to the songwriter.

A publisher that does not print and manufacture its own edition but licenses such rights to another company, is customarily paid 20% of the wholesale selling price, which is split fifty-fifty with the writer.

For general folios, songwriters are generally paid 12.5% of the wholesale selling price of the edition (though some contracts pay on the retail selling price). Education and compilation editions usually bear a royalty of 10% to 12.5% of the retail selling price. Electronic sheet music is now available, although this business has yet to show great financial returns and it is doubtful that it will have much impact until a device that can replay the score on an electronic device is successfully marketed.

Lyric Reprints

A negotiated fee is paid to songwriters for permission to reprint song lyrics, either in album liner notes, on Web sites, in sheet music folios, concert programs and wherever else lyrics are printed or used. Once a songwriter has signed a contract with a music publisher, the publisher takes over the responsibility of clearing lyric reprints. Clearance procedures consist of negotiating the reprint license fee, drafting the license agreement and collecting all funds due.

New Media

New uses of copyrighted materials are being developed at a rapid pace, and these new, generally digital uses can generate additional royalties and fees for owners of copyrights. These new uses include, but are not limited to, items such as mobile telephone "monophonic ringtones," "polyphonic ringtones," "ringbacks," "master ringtones" and "digital downloads." In some cases, publishers in the U.S. can collect on behalf of their songwriters for these new uses in a traditional way. For example, The Harry Fox Agency, which has traditionally dealt with mechanical licenses covering CDs, records and tapes, has also begun issuing licenses and collecting royalties for "Digital Licenses" including full downloads, limited-use downloads, on-demand streaming and CD burning; and the performance rights societies now license songs for use on Web sites and as ringtones (however, they are still establishing policies for calculating performances and distributing royalties). In other circumstances, publishers are currently sailing in uncharted waters as they negotiate fees for these new types of licenses of digitized music. The laws governing the World Wide Web and digital transmission of information vary widely from nation to nation, thus further complicating this category. Because these rights are still developing, and hard bargaining is occurring on a daily basis, it is too early to state with any certainty what the model will be for calculation and payment of royalties in these nascent income centers. The publisher is responsible for issuing all licenses regarding musical compositions; the owner of the sound recordings is responsible for licensing the sound recordings to the digital service. Many of the digital services have sought to make the sound recording licensor responsible for the payment of music publishing royalties. Whether this will become the model for the future is unclear as there are legislative "solutions" being introduced, litigation in this area, and there is no consensus as to how licenses will hereafter be granted for music publishing in the digital context. Given the success of the medium, songwriters are advised to reserve for themselves the right to grant licenses on services such as myspace.com or other Web portals where they may wish to stream or allow downloads gratis. Because the methodology is still evolving, any licenses granted should be limited in time; we recommend three years.

In October, 2006, the Register of Copyrights of the U.S. Copyright Office issued an administrative ruling that held that ringtones (including monophonic ringtones, polyphonic ringtones and master ringtones) are subject to compulsory licenses. The amount of the compulsory license fee was not yet announced at the time of printing of this book, however we expect this administrative ruling to dramatically drive down the rates that publishers have previously been obtaining for ringtone licenses. Another effect of the Copyright Office ruling (assuming it is upheld) is that it will become much easier for record companies to license ringtones derived from their master recordings.

Immediately following the announcement of the Copyright Office's ruling, The Harry Fox Agency announced its disappointment with the ruling, as well as its intention to evaluate its legal options with respect to that ruling. This ruling will affect the future process of ringtone clearance and license fees, but the details are not yet known. Further, the administrative ruling has a potential effect on thousands of previously-negotiated contracts that serve to license hundreds of thousands of ringtones, which will no doubt give owners of the master recordings, songwriters, music publishers and their attorneys lots of work to do in order to adjust these prior agreements.

Grand Rights

A negotiated fee is paid to songwriters for permission to publicly perform, in whole or in part, dramatic works that combine musical works with dramatic settings (for example, together with staging, dialogue, costuming, special lighting or choreography). This includes musical comedies, operas, operettas and ballets, in which there is a definite plot depicted by action and in which such performance of the composition is woven into and carries forward the plot and its accompanying action. Once a songwriter has signed a contract with a music publisher, the publisher takes over the responsibility of clearing grand rights. Clearance procedures consist of negotiating the license fees, drafting the license agreements and collecting all funds due.

Foreign Income

The foregoing sources of income occur throughout the world. Domestic publishers enter into foreign licensing or subpublishing agreements with music publishers that operate outside the United States. (Canada is often treated as the "51st state," and U.S. publishers usually obtain Canadian rights when they obtain U.S. rights.) Shrewd and successful commercial songwriters often retain foreign rights and make their own subpublishing deals, which can provide substantial supplemental income.

TYPES OF MUSIC PUBLISHING CONTRACTS
Full Publishing Deal

The traditional division of income between the songwriter and publisher is a fifty-fifty split. If we assume that there is $1 of value in a songwriter's catalog, this means that the so-called writer's share of income equals 50¢, as does the so-called publisher's share. No matter what happens, writers always keep their writer's share. A full publishing contract gives the publisher sole ownership of the copyrights contained in the songwriter's catalog, for the total length of the copyright. Full publishing deals are rare today; most songwriters' attorneys negotiate for copublishing deals, as described below.

These transactions come in two species—single-song agreements and long-term agreements. (See also the chapter, "Exclusive Term Songwriter and Copublishing Agreements.") Under these agreements, the income is generally split as follows:

- Mechanical Income. Publisher collects all mechanical income and pays 50% to composer.

- Performance Income. Publisher receives and retains all of publisher's share of performance income. Composer is paid directly by the performing rights organization and retains all such writer's share of performance income.

- Print Income. Publisher collects all revenue and pays writer 50% of 20% of the Retail Selling Price per piano-vocal sheet music and 50% of the publisher's receipts on folios and other multiple-composition editions where licensed to a third party.

- Synchronization Income. Publisher collects income and splits fifty-fifty with composer.

- Foreign Income. Net receipts (that amount received by or credited to publisher from subpublisher) are split fifty-fifty with composer. Most deals are now "at source" or modified receipts, meaning that the foreign share is computed as being received in the country where the revenue is earned, i.e., without additional subpublishing or other administrative charges being deducted. A subpublisher typically should not take more than 10% to 25% of monies earned in that sub-publisher's country.

In a single-song deal, the publisher owns the copyright in the composition for the term of its copyright, subject to the possibility of its reversion to its composer 35 years after its publication (its first commercial distribution) or 40 years after its assignment (transfer), whichever is earlier. Some long-term songwriter's agreements provide that compositions created pursuant to such agreements are works for hire for the publisher and, hence, incapable of being recaptured by the composer. However, the trend over the last decade is to provide that the songs will revert to the writer after a period of time, somewhere in the range of seven to twelve years. If the songwriter is not also a recording artist, then it will be difficult to negotiate reversions. Normally such agreements last for one year, with two to four one-year options being held by the publisher. The publisher owns and controls all compositions created by the songwriter during the term.

Under most such agreements, the writer is paid a cash advance on signing the deal, as well as additional cash each time the publisher exercises a subsequent renewal option. Some publishers and writers opt to pay the advance in the form of a weekly salary rather than in a lump sum. In 2006, these deals start as low at $10,000 to $15,000 for a three-year deal, with additional advances being paid when recoupment occurs. However, in the past few years, the trend has been for deals to diminish in terms of advances.

Writers want these deals because they offer security and ideally, promotion of their songs. Long-term writer deals and copublishing deals are commonplace in Nashville, where cover recordings more commonly occur. In Nashville, typical deals for incipient writers start at $10,000 to $15,000 per year. Outside that locale, there are few long-term songwriter agreements these days for creators who do not also have record deals with major companies or regular success getting their music recorded by others. Music publishers want publishing deals with writers, producers and artists that can create "pipeline income" by getting songs "placed" (recorded and released to the public). Top producers that write or can obtain publishing rights on songs that they record are also highly sought after by publishing companies.

Single-song agreements are entered into with or without advances paid to the songwriter: there is no common industry standard.

Under both types of agreement, the publisher administers the compositions subject to them. "Administration" means that the publisher issues all documents and contracts affecting such compositions and collects all income (other than the writer's share of performance income) earned by the compositions.

Copublishing Deal

These days it is common, indeed the norm, for writers to hold onto half of the ownership of the copyrights in their catalogs, in addition to half of the publisher's share of income (25% of the total value of the catalog), which in this example is 25¢ of each dollar. This means that the writer usually ends up with 75% of the pie (all of the writer's share, which is 50% of the total, plus half of the publisher's share, which is 25% of the total). The music publisher usually ends up with 25% of the total funds to be collected (half of the publisher's share). This is known as a copublishing deal.

Under copublishing agreements, as in standard agreements, the publisher administers the compositions subject to such agreements. However, the songwriter not only receives the writer's share of publishing income, or roughly 50% of the gross revenues (except print revenues) of the composition, but also shares in that portion of what traditionally was the publisher's share of music publishing income. Thus, under such agreements, the songwriter is ordinarily paid 75% of the mechanical income, print income, and synchronization income derived from the composition and, in addition to the writer's share of performance income, receives 50% of the publisher's share of performance income. Usually, the publisher and songwriter own copyrights to the compositions jointly—but what really counts is who administers the composition, who has the right to collect income therefrom. Often, the publisher will charge an administration fee of 5% to 10% for services rendered.

Copublishing agreements can encompass one song, a number of stated songs or all compositions written over a period of years, as in a long-term songwriter's agreement.

Many modern copublishing deals provide for a reversion of the copyrights to the songwriter anywhere from 7 to 12 years after the song is first delivered to the publisher and provided the publisher has recouped any advances to the songwriter. The advances are in the same range as discussed above. Superstar acts and writers can get advances in the high six or even seven figures.

Administration Deal

Many songwriters enter into administration deals. In an administration deal, the publisher does not share in ownership of the songwriter's copyrights. Therefore, the pie is not divided, and the songwriter retains 100% of the catalog. The administrator is merely responsible for negotiating contracts, collecting monies and accounting to the writer based on these collections. Some administrators will also solicit uses of the music in the catalog (known as "pitching songs"). The administration fee generally varies from 10% to 20% of the amount collected by the administrator. Administration deals usually have terms of three to ten years. Many administration agreements provide that if the administrator secures a cover recording, the administrator will retain administration rights for a longer period of time (which could include the life of the copyright) and obtain a higher percentage of the income generated by the cover secured by the administrator.

Administration agreements are difficult to obtain for songwriters that have no independent means of exploiting compositions that would be subject to such an arrangement. For singer-songwriters that have recording deals or songwriters that can get their songs covered, such transactions are often the most beneficial for their long-term financial prospects. The major music publishers rarely enter into administration deals, except for superstar writers, because they prefer the full publishing or copublishing deals mentioned above. However, there are administrators in Los Angeles, Nashville and New York that will do so; the market leaders in this category are Bug Music and The Royalty Network.

POINTS OF NEGOTIATION

Royalties and advances are always negotiable. Under any type of deal, a songwriter will commonly ask the publisher to pay an advance on the songwriter's future earnings in order to obtain the exclusive rights described above. The amount of the advance that a music publisher is willing to pay to obtain a catalog (or the exclusive right to publish works to be created in the future by a songwriter) depends on whether—

- the songs contained in the catalog are already earning income;

- there is as yet uncollected income for previously-contracted uses of the songs in the catalog ("pipeline income");

- the songwriter has a proven history of writing "hit" songs;

- the songwriter is willing and able to collaborate with other songwriters or artists;

- the songwriter is also a recording artist, and signed to a recording contract with a major record company;

- the songwriter is able to write songs that can be recorded and performed by multiple artists, either on recordings or in the live concert setting; and

- whether the publisher will take an ownership stake in the catalog and if so, whether the stake will be a full publishing 100% stake or a copublishing 50% stake.

The more "yes" answers that are given to the above questions and the higher a publisher's evaluation of the songwriter's future income potential, the higher the advance. The publisher is always entitled to recoup all advances, dollar for dollar, from all income derived from the songwriter's catalog. The contracts between songwriters and music publishers also allow publishers to cross-collateralize all earnings from a given songwriter's catalog against all advances to that songwriter. Therefore, a publisher's risk, which is limited to the advance paid and other promotional costs, is spread over all songs contained in a songwriter's catalog, and no further advances are due until full recoupment is achieved.

A songwriter should always attempt to obtain a reversion of any composition subject to a single-song, long-term publishing or copublishing agreement when any such composition has not been commercially exploited within a specified time period. A composer should only allow translations of, or the addition of new lyrics to, any composition with his or her prior written consent (or at the very least be notified of the same), since in some countries a translator or lyricist may register and receive income from a translation that is never performed, sold or even recorded due to the nationalistic policies and regulations of various performing rights societies. The translator and subpublisher may receive compensation from performances of the original version and/or share in "black box" or general unallocated income, which can be sizeable. (Italy is one notable example where this can occur.) As to new lyrics, a writer should know the reasons for having such written; the writer would want the opportunity to write such lyrics in any language in which he or she is fluent. Some writers are touchy about the use in commercials of their materials and would want to approve alterations that might devalue the work. A clause permitting translations, as long as there is no diminution income by the writer should be acceptable to most writers. But be careful, if the song is written "words and music" by two songwriters, and the contribution of each is separate, one for music, and one for the lyrics, then the song should be registered this way as the composer of the music will not suffer if there are translations, while the lyricist may. Despite these potential financial consequences, some teams prefer to share the "words and music" attribution. When two or more people collaborate to write a song, each owns a share of the whole, but it is very unusual to have one cowriter allow changes or translations without the approval of all other cowriters, even if only one writer contributed lyrics.

Points in publishing contracts vary in importance among publishing companies. Similarly, songwriters differ on the priorities of the numerous issues involved in a songwriting agreement. Songwriters should have advisors, such as attorneys, personal managers and business managers, to counsel them on the best methods of navigating the intricacies of music publishing.

SELF-PUBLISHING

Some composers are capable of creating and administering their catalogs. The music publishing industry is not so difficult that its mechanics would confound an attentive student. It is difficult, however, to obtain the commercial exploitation of compositions. For composers interested in and capable of properly administering and promoting the products of their artistry, self-publishing can be a viable alternative to the traditional arrangements with publishers, but in practice, few writers are successful going it alone.

When a record is released on an independent label, financed by the artist, self-publishing makes sense. Universal copyrights are valuable assets—it is inadvisable to transfer or lessen these rights without a good reason.

FINDING A GOOD PUBLISHER

Music publishers play an important role in today's music industry. First, they have the best success at securing covers. Moreover, a songwriter usually needs a go-between, critic, cheerleader and business manager. Good music publishers are enthusiastic and knowledgeable about their artists and their music. They have competent royalty departments and reputations for honesty; pay for or advance money for demos; have aggressive professional managers that work to get songs to record producers and their artists; are responsive to the needs, suggestions and questions of their writers; and they deal with the foreign territories.

Finding a publisher is not an easy task for a songwriter, especially if that writer's songs are not already being played on the radio, contained on a hit album or generating thousands of downloads on an Internet site. Many publications such as *The Songwriter's Market, The Musician's Atlas, The A&R Registry, Billboard Magazine, Billboard's Guide to Touring and Promotion, Pollstar* and *New On The Charts,* have extensive listings for publishing companies. Nevertheless, most songwriters have a difficult time getting music publishers to consider them. Songwriters can attend music industry conferences and conventions such as MIDEM, South by Southwest, Independent Music Conference, NEMO, Millennium, NARM, Atlantis, *Billboard Magazine's* R&B and Hip-Hop Conference and dozens of others. Generally, it is the songwriter's responsibility to solicit the talent scouts and garner interest. More often than not, these talent scouts are so inundated with demonstration recordings and solicitations that they will not accept material directly from songwriters they do not already know. Accordingly, in many instances songwriters need intermediaries such as managers, booking agents or lawyers to present material to publishing companies.

The major publishers are Universal Music Publishing Group, Warner-Chappell Music, EMI Music Publishing, Sony Music Publishing, Famous Music Publishing, Rykomusic and peermusic. These are huge companies, some with over a million songs in their catalogs. (As this book goes to press, BMG Music Publishing, another major publisher, is being acquired by Vivendi [Universal Music Publishing Group] pending regulatory approval.) They are generally considered to be weak on promotion, but they do promote some of their works and sometimes have spectacular success. There are many smaller publishers that are very effective.

Songwriters, with their advisors, should work out a strategy to find a good publisher and to enter an advantageous agreement. Some personal managers are capable of finding reputable publishers and subsequently obtaining satisfactory agreements. The song-writer's music attorney may be able to open doors to publishing companies. Representatives of ASCAP, BMI and SESAC can be helpful, as can the recommendations of other songwriters.

Because music publishing agreements can be extremely technical, a music attorney should always be consulted to review any agreement *before* a composer signs. Most importantly, composers should investigate carefully before choosing their advisors and business partners.

RESOURCES FOR SONGWRITERS AND PUBLISHERS

Nashville Songwriters Association International (NSAI)

(www.nashvillesongwriters.com)

1710 Roy Acuff Place

Nashville, TN 37203

(800) 321-6008 or (615) 256-3354

We highly recommend NSAI, the world's largest not-for-profit songwriters' trade organization dedicated to the service of amateur and professional songwriters.

Songwriters Guild of America (SGA)

(www.songwritersguild.com)

SGA East Coast

1560 Broadway, Suite 408

New York, NY 10036

(212) 768-7902

SGA West Coast (Los Angeles)

6430 Sunset Boulevard, Suite 705

Hollywood, CA 90028

(323) 462-1108

SGA Central

209 10th Avenue South, Suite 534

Nashville, TN 37203

(615) 742-9945

SGA is the oldest of the songwriters associations and is reinventing itself. It is not as active and vibrant as NSAI, but it is doing good work. It collects royalties for some composers.

SongwriterUniverse

(www.songwriteruniverse.com)

11684 Ventura Boulevard, Suite 975

Studio City, CA 91604

This is an interesting site with lots of good information for songwriters.

The following two organizations have regular meetings on topics of interest for publishers. Both are recommended.

Association of Independent Music Publishers (AIMP)

(www.aimp.org)

AIMP West Coast

P.O. Box 69473

Los Angeles, California 90069

(818) 771-7301

AIMP East Coast

5 West 37th Street

New York, NY 10018

(212) 391-2532

California Copyright Conference

(www.theccc.org)

P.O. Box 57962

Sherman Oaks CA 91413

(818) 379-3312

This is a typical mechanical license issued by one of the major companies. Mechanical licenses must be tailored for the needs of the particular company. For example, the applicable law should be the state of the principal office of the publisher.

MECHANICAL LICENSE

TO:_____   LICENSE NUMBER: _____

DATE: _____

We, [name of publishing company] _____, are the publisher that controls _____ percent (__%) of the copyrighted work listed below.

You have advised us as publisher that you wish to obtain a nonexclusive mechanical license to make and distribute phonorecords of the copyrighted work listed below, under the mechanical license provision of Section 115 (c) (2) of the Copyright Act.

SONG TITLE: _____   WRITER(S): _____

PUBLISHER: _____   RELEASE TITLE:_____

ARTIST: _____   RECORD LABEL: _____

RECORD #: _____   FORMAT: _____

RELEASE DATE:_____   TIME OF RECORDING:_____

ROYALTY RATE: Statutory

Upon your doing so, you shall have all the rights which are granted to, and all the obligations which are imposed upon, users of said copyrighted work under the compulsory mechanical license provision of the Copyright Act, after phonorecords of the copyrighted work have been distributed to the public in the United States, provided that—

1. Within forty-five (45) days after the end of each calendar quarter, you shall account to us in detail for the number of phonorecords made and distributed during said quarter and shall pay us the royalties due at the same time.

2. This mechanical license covers and is limited to one particular recording of said copyrighted work as performed by the artist and on the phonorecord number identified above and this mechanical license does not supersede nor in any way affect any prior agreements now in effect respecting mechanical reproduction or other uses of said copyrighted work.

3. With respect to all such phonorecords manufactured and sold in the United States for domestic sales, the royalty rate hereunder shall be the compulsory mechanical rate as contained in the Copyright Act that is in effect at the time such phonorecords are distributed (the "Statutory Rate"). In the event the Statutory Rate is hereinafter increased, then with respect to all such phonorecords distributed from and after the effective date of such increase, the royalty rate hereunder shall be such increased Statutory Rate.

4. This license includes the privilege of making a musical arrangement of the copyrighted work to the extent necessary to conform it to the style or manner of interpretation of the performance involved but the arrangement made (i) may not change the basic melody or fundamental character of the copyrighted work; (ii) shall not be subject to protection under the Copyright Act by you as a derivative work; and (iii) all copyrights and other rights in and to any such arrangement shall automatically vest in the owners of the copyrighted work upon the creation of such arrangement.

5. If more than one musical work is licensed hereunder, each such license of each such work shall be for all purposes treated as if (and deemed to be) a separate license and, without in any way limiting the foregoing, there shall be no right of offset between such licenses or otherwise in connection herewith.

6. You shall permit us, our chartered accountant or certified public accountant or any other representative of ours, within thirty (30) days from the date of written notice, to inspect, at your place of business and during usual business hours, upon written notice, all books, records and other documents relating to the manufacturing and distribution of phonorecords pursuant to this license. We shall have the right to make copies of such books, records and other documents as same may relate to the subject matter of this license. The cost of such audit shall be our responsibility. Notwithstanding the foregoing or anything set forth to the contrary in this license, if any such audit reflects an underpayment to us of ten percent (10%) or more for the periods audited (i) you shall pay the costs of such audit plus interest on any sums due at the prime rate at leading New York City banks at the time plus two percent (2%); and (ii) we shall have the right to terminate this license immediately by giving written notice to you. We shall not have the right to examine your books, records and other documents more than once per calendar year.

7. In the event you fail to account and/or pay royalties to us as herein provided for, we may give written notice to you that, unless the default is remedied within thirty (30) days from the date of such notice, this license shall terminate without further notice. Such termination shall render either the making or the distribution or both, of all phonorecords for which royalties have not been paid, actionable as acts of infringement under and fully subject to the remedies provided by the Copyright Act. Notwithstanding revocation of the license, you shall remain liable to us for all monies previously accrued hereunder.

8. You need not serve or file the notices required by the Copyright Act.

9. This license is limited to the United States, its territories and possessions and specifically excludes those phonorecords manufactured and sold in the United States for export.

10. In the event we are required to institute any legal proceedings against you in connection with this license, in addition to any damages awarded us, we shall be entitled to our attorneys' fees and you shall abide by any ruling made by the Court with respect to the payment of costs and reasonable attorneys' fees in connection therewith.

11. This license sets forth the entire agreement between the parties and may only be modified or amended by means of a written amendment, designated as such and signed by one of our authorized signers.

12. Neither this license nor any of the rights granted to you hereunder may be assigned by you to any party without our prior written consent, but we may assign this license and/or any of the rights granted to us hereunder at any time and for any reason.

13. You agree that our total liability and the total liability of the owner(s) of the copyrighted work shall not exceed, under any circumstances the royalties paid to us pursuant to this license.

14. This license shall be binding upon the earlier of your countersigning at least one copy hereof in the place provided below or your causing or permitting the release of, in the United States of America, the phonorecord referred to above.

15. You further agree that all sums indicated as due and owing on statements rendered hereunder shall bear interest at the rate of one percent (1%) per month from the date due if not paid within thirty (30) days after the date due and payable.

16. This license does not authorize the reproduction or exploitation of the said copyrighted work in any manner not specified hereunder, including, but not limited to, devices embodying sound synchronization with visual images.

17. The validity, construction, interpretation and legal effect of this license shall be governed by both the Copyright Law of the United States and the laws of the State of New York applicable to contracts entered into and to be fully performed therein.

AGREED TO AND ACCEPTED:

_____
BY (AN AUTHORIZED SIGNATORY)

_____
BY (AN AUTHORIZED SIGNATORY)

_____
FEDERAL I.D./SS#

_____
FEDERAL I.D./SS#

Exclusive Term Songwriter and Copublishing Agreements

BY EVANNE L. LEVIN

The agreement that follows is an example of an exclusive term songwriter agreement (ESA) entered into between a songwriter (writer) and a music publisher (publisher). It provides that 100% of the ownership (copyright) in the compositions written during a stated period of time will belong to the publisher. In many cases, an agreement of this type, either alone, or with a copublishing agreement (CPA) (see sample following this agreement), is used to acquire the musical works of a writer who is also a recording or performing artist.

Why are term agreements desirable? Although songwriters are required to relinquish part or all ownership in the musical compositions covered by this type of agreement, they seek term agreements for two basic reasons. First, the periodic advance and maybe a weekly salary provides a financial foundation that enables the songwriter to dedicate more time and energy to writing and, with the assistance of the publisher's professional staff, develop the skills shared by successful songwriters. Second, the publisher will introduce the writer's material to a broad network of performers and record producers, increasing the likelihood of the songs being recorded. Note that negotiations for a term agreement typically take place only after a writer has had songs recorded by recording artists or concurrently with negotiating an exclusive recording agreement with a writer who will be recording his or her own material.

There is no standard term agreement. Even a term agreement that is a particular publisher's standardized form is subject to modification by your legal representative. A term agreement is distinguished from a single-song agreement by the addition of provisions that may include—advances payable to the songwriter; a period of time the songwriter is employed to write and deliver original songs; tying the duration of the initial term and option terms to the release of recordings of the original songs; the writer's exclusivity to the publisher; a guaranteed annual or periodic minimum advance compensation option; and the scope of the writer's earnings to be withheld for claims brought by others against the publisher. At the heart of the negotiation is the publisher's interest in acquiring the maximum rights and control in the maximum number of songs for the least amount of money versus the writer's interest in relinquishing the minimum of rights and control in fewer compositions for the maximum consideration.

Given the complexity of and variations in this type of agreement, it is recommended that a writer not sign a term agreement without first seeking the advice of an attorney familiar with the subject matter.

EXCLUSIVE TERM SONGWRITER AGREEMENT

AGREEMENT ("Agreement") effective as of the _____ day of _____ 20___ , by and between _____ hereinafter referred to as "PUBLISHER" (an affiliate of [ASCAP/BMI/SESAC]), located at _____ , and _____ hereinafter (collectively) referred to as "WRITER" (an affiliate of [ASCAP/BMI/SESAC]), located at _____ .

In consideration of the mutual covenants and undertakings herein set forth, the parties do hereby agree as follows:

1. SERVICES

Publisher hereby engages Writer to render his or her services as a songwriter and composer and otherwise as may be hereinafter set forth. Writer hereby accepts such engagement and agrees to render such services exclusively for Publisher during the term hereof, upon the terms and conditions set forth herein.

Although the writer is not the publisher's employee, for the term of the agreement the writer is considered like an exclusive employee of the publisher, and as such, cannot write for anyone else.

2. TERM

The term of this Agreement shall commence with the date hereof and shall continue in force for a period coterminous with the term of that certain Exclusive Recording Artist Agreement between Writer and Publisher, entered into concurrently with this Agreement, as same is renewed, extended, amended or substituted.

Performers that record their own material often enter into term songwriter agreements with their record label's affiliated publishing company. In these instances, the writer should limit the term of the songwriter agreement to the length of the term of the record deal. Once the recording agreement is over the writer will want any new material to be available to negotiate a stronger agreement with the next record company, and by that time may be in a better position to keep some or all of the copyright in the new songs and a portion of the publisher's share of income. In instances where the songwriter agreement is not tied to a record deal, the term is usually three years with an initial term of one year and two one-year options, exercisable by the publisher. The songwriter may want to try to obtain some measure of performance by the publisher, such as obtaining a certain number of cover recordings, especially if little or no advances are paid, as a condition to the publisher's exercise of its option to extend the term.
As a practical matter, the greater the advances, the less likely an option to extend the term will be exercised unless the publisher has been successful in exploiting the material.

On the other hand, a publisher will, as a condition of any sizable advance, require inclusion of two provisions:

> *1) Delivery during each term of a minimum number of 100% of copyright, totally original compositions; and*
>
> *2) a minimum number of commercial releases in the United States.*

The number of songs to be delivered, as well as the number of covers and in which territories, is an important area of negotiations. It is not unusual for the one-year term of an agreement to stretch into several actual years due to nonfulfillment of contractual commitments for commercial releases. For example if the commercial release requirement is three songs per year, but all three songs are cowritten, the writer would have to obtain six commercial releases in one year before moving to the next term of the agreement.

There are pros and cons to a performer-writer entering into a songwriting agreement with their record company's publishing affiliate. Since the publishing company knows that the writer's material will be recorded and released by its affiliated record company, it is not taking a great risk that it will not earn back advances paid. Moreover, since the parent company will be earning money from two sources with each record sold (profits on the record and the publisher's share of mechanical royalties for the writer's compositions on the record), the writer should be able to negotiate a more favorable advance in exchange for the publisher's share of the compositions. The writer may also insist that in exchange for signing with the affiliated publishing company, the record company must pay a full mechanical royalty rather than the usual 75% rate on the writer's compositions included on the record. The publishing company will also benefit to the extent it has acquired a copyright in the recorded songs. Finally, the affiliated companies have a double incentive to promote the writer and material.

Other considerations may suggest that the writer's best interests would be served by entering into a term songwriter agreement elsewhere. The record company's publishing arm may not be offering the best terms or may not be the best publisher for that writer's material. Are the recording contract and term songwriter contract cross-collateralized in any way, so that advances or other costs incurred by one company under one contract can be recovered from the writer's income under the other contract? How do the different publishing companies measure up in various territories? The writer may be one whose material has tremendous foreign income potential in certain major markets where a different publisher would do a better job for the writer. The writer may wish to refrain from entering into any ESA until the record is released, to be in a position to negotiate a better deal with competing suitors (if the record catches on).

Many times, however, the writer has cash flow problems and is anxious to receive the publisher's advance and cannot or will not adopt the riskier, but potentially more profitable, "wait and see what happens" posture.

The current trend is away from the publisher retaining 100% of the copyright in favor of sharing the copyright (that carries with it sharing the publisher's portion of the income) in some split with the writer. (See, Copublishing and Administration Agreement and discussion on page 174.)

3. GRANT OF RIGHTS

(a) Writer hereby irrevocably and absolutely assigns, transfers, sets over and grants to Publisher, its successors and assigns each and every and all rights and interests of every kind, nature and description in and to the results and proceeds of Writer's services hereunder, including but not limited to the titles, words and music of any and all original musical compositions in any and all forms and original arrangements of musical compositions in any and all forms, and all rights and interests existing under all agreements and licenses relating thereto, together with all worldwide copyrights (and any renewals or extensions thereof), which musical works have been written, composed, created or conceived, in whole or in part, by Writer alone or in collaboration with another or others, and which may hereafter, during the term hereof, be written, composed, created or conceived by Writer, in whole or in part, alone or in collaboration with another or others, and which are now owned or controlled and which may, during their term hereof, be acquired, owned or controlled, directly or indirectly, by Writer, alone or with others, or as the employer or transferee, directly or indirectly, of the writers or composers thereof, including the title, words and music of each such composition, and all worldwide copyrights (and renewals and extensions thereof), all of which Writer does hereby represent, are and shall at all times be Publisher's sole and exclusive property as the sole owner thereof, free from any adverse claims or rights therein by any other person, firm or corporation.

Note that the writer is assigning 100% of the compositions to the publisher even if owned with others. The writer should be required to give the publisher only the writer's share, since the cowriter(s) or joint owner(s) will want the right to decide what to do with their share and may even have their own term songwriter agreement with another publisher that contains an identical provision. Unless the other writers give you permission to give your publisher their share of the copyright, you may be in breach of your agreement with your publisher if you cannot grant 100% of the copyright in songs you cowrite. The prudent way to handle this common dilemma is to limit the publisher's ownership in the material to your share. It would also be acceptable to require you to use "reasonable efforts" to obtain the cowriter's copyright share. (For more information regarding cowritten compositions, see the chapter, "Collaborator/Songwriter Agreements," on page 94.)

Requiring the writer to also give the publisher ownership of all songs written before the term is unfair, unless the publisher is paying additional money for these. Post term reversion clauses are becoming more acceptable. These provisions may involve one or both of the following:

1) A post term reversion of all unrecorded songs, at a term of one to five years following the term, provided the publisher has recouped all outstanding advances to the writer; and

2) a post term reassignment of administration rights to a portion of each composition, five to seven years following expiration of the term, again only if the writer is fully recouped. This latter provision is more likely to be an issue where there is a copublishing agreement, i.e., where the publisher and writer jointly own the copyright and divide the 50% publisher's share.

A similar reversion should also apply to songs written during the term if the advances are low. "Advances" refers to both money received by the writer at the beginning of each year or other term of the contract and money paid out on a regular basis like a paycheck.

A concept having far-reaching effects on writers' future rights in their compositions is embedded in this provision. It is most significant that this provision, while assigning the writer's copyright in the compositions for the minimum copyright term, does not include specific language describing the writer as creating the compositions "within the scope of Publisher's employment of Writer's personal services" whereby the writer would be deemed the publisher's so-called employee for hire and the publisher would be "deemed the author of the Compositions initially created during the Term." When this language is used, the compositions are deemed works made for hire under U.S. copyright laws and the publisher is considered the writer and original copyright owner of the compositions. This would preclude the writer from having any right to reclaim the copyright in these songs after 35 years, which writers can do if they have written the material prior to the term of the ESA, or the language of the agreement provides for the writer to assign copyrights to the publisher without saying more about the publisher being considered the author from the outset or including the works-made-for-hire language. Even where employee/writer-for-hire language has been used, writers have succeeded in challenging the status of "author" claimed by their publishers by proving that the publisher was not in a position to actually control the development of the songs to be written. The control element is one factor considered by courts in characterizing whether a composition was written (1) independent of the publisher or (2) under the direction of the publisher. The publisher might need to demonstrate that it was involved in the creation of the song by having critiqued the material and having instructed the writer to make changes, as well as having given the writer direction about the compositions it expected to be written. The opposite of this would be a writer delivering completed songs written without input from the publisher that were done on the writer's own time at a location other than the publisher's offices.

If the publisher agrees to allow the writer to keep a share of the copyright or publisher's share of income (roughly 50¢ on each dollar generated from exploiting the composition), it is generally handled by the writer first assigning the entire copyright to the publisher and the publisher then assigning back to the writer a part of the copyright or publisher's share of income, if the publisher wants to maintain sole ownership and control of the copyright but is willing to share part of the 50% income that comes to the copyright owner. This can be accomplished by adding a provision to the end of this agreement assigning back to the writer a percentage of the copyright or providing for payment of a percentage of the publisher's share of income to the writer.

A separate agreement called a "Copublishing Agreement" often accompanies the ESA and spells out the writer's interest in the songs as a publisher, as distinguished from a writer. This represents an additional source of income from the songs but generally does not provide any additional control over if or how the copyrights will be used. See the Copublishing and Administration Agreement that follows this discussion of the ESA.

(b) Writer acknowledges that, included within the rights and interests hereinabove referred to, but without limiting the generality of the foregoing, is Writer's irrevocable grant to Publisher, its successors, licensees, sublicensees and assigns, of the sole and exclusive right, license, privilege and authority throughout the entire world with respect to the said original musical compositions and original arrangements of compositions in the public domain, whether now in existence or hereafter created during the term hereof, as follows:

The publisher should have to give the writer the first opportunity to make changes in the material.

(i) To perform said musical compositions publicly for profit by means of public and private performance, radio broadcasting, television or any and all other means, whether now known or which may hereafter come into existence;

(ii) To substitute a new title or titles for said compositions and to make any arrangement, adaptation, translation, dramatization and transposition of said compositions, in whole or in part, and in connection with any other musical, literary or dramatic material as Publisher may deem expedient or desirable;

The writer should seek to limit the changes that can be made without reasonable prior consent, at least title and lyric changes in English. Writer can also ask to be given the first opportunity to make the changes desired by the publisher. Moreover, the songwriter may suffer a substantial decrease in his or her share of the revenue if another writer is added at the unilateral discretion of the publisher. Translations are a special problem, as songwriters frequently lose considerable portions of revenue to translators that write versions that are not successful commercially. Translations should not be registered with any foreign performing or mechanical rights society until a commercial recording of the translation has been released. All major changes and additions should be made with the consent of the songwriter.

(iii) To secure copyright registration and protection of said compositions in Publisher's name or otherwise as Publisher may desire, at Publisher's own cost and expense and at Publisher's election, including any and all renewals and extensions of copyright under any present or future laws throughout the world, and to have and to hold said copyrights, renewals, extensions and all rights of whatsoever nature thereunder existing, for and during the full term of all said copyrights and all renewals and extensions thereof;

Writers should attempt to require the publisher to secure valid copyright protection for the songs throughout the world wherever such protection is recognized. Although formal registration with the U.S. Copyright Office is no longer mandatory to claim ownership in a work, it establishes proof of ownership and is required in order to maintain a claim against another for copyright infringement of the work. The $45 registration fee should not be a problem for the publisher. Since the United States recently joined the Berne Convention, registration in this country will be recognized by all other member countries. The specific requirements for establishing and maintaining a valid copyright are beyond the scope of this chapter but are covered in the chapter, "Copyrights: The Law and You."

(iv) To make or cause to be made, master records, transcriptions, sound tracks, pressings, and any other mechanical, electrical or other reproductions of said compositions, in whole or in part, in such form or manner and as frequently as Publisher's sole and uncontrolled discretion shall determine, including the right to synchronize the same with sound motion pictures and the right to manufacture, advertise, license or sell such reproductions for any and all purposes, including, but not limited to, private performances and public performances, by broadcasting, television, sound motion pictures, wired radio, audio devices, so-called new technologies such as streaming, permanent downloads, satellite radio transmissions, video games, cell phone rings, and any and all other means or devices whether now known or hereafter conceived or developed;

Writers can protect the integrity of their music by requiring prior consent to its use in X-rated films or those taking an overt political, religious or moral stand. Writers may also seek to require their consent for the use of their music in commercials since the product or service advertised may be one that the writer feels is inappropriate and may diminish the value of the copyright by being associated with it.

(v) To print, publish and sell sheet music orchestration, arrangements and other editions of the said compositions in all forms, including the right to include any or all of said compositions in song folios or lyric magazines with or without music, and the right to license others to include any or all of said compositions in song folios or lyric magazines with or without music; and

The mandatory printing of sheet music or a folio can sometimes be tied to a song reaching a certain level on the Billboard *sales charts, although this is not typically a significant source of income and is not equally suited to all types of music.*

(vi) Any and all other rights of every and any nature now or hereafter existing under and by virtue of any common law rights and any copyrights (and renewals and extensions thereof) in any and all of such compositions.

Again, prior consent for the use of the song for merchandising purposes might be desired by the writer to prevent identification of the song with some ridiculous product or service. The publisher will want to limit such consent since it has a financial investment in the writer and will claim expertise as compared to the writer in determining the best use of the songs. A compromise can be reached by listing the types of goods or services that would reasonably require the writer's consent. These typically include alcoholic beverages, personal care products, firearms and tobacco products. In addition, writers may try to exclude what are called "grand" rights (the use of the musical material in combination with a dramatic rendition, such as a drama, play or opera).

(c) Writer grants to Publisher, without any compensation other than as specified herein, the perpetual right to use and publish and to permit another to use and publish Writer's name (including any professional name heretofore or hereafter adopted by Writer), likeness, voice and sound effects and biographical material, or any reproduction or simulation thereof and titles of all compositions here-under in connection with the printing, sale, advertising, distribution and exploitation of music, folios, recordings, performances, player rolls and otherwise concerning any of the compositions hereunder, and for any other purpose related to the compositions hereunder, and for any other purpose related to the business of Publisher, its affiliated and related companies, or to refrain therefrom. This right shall be exclusive during the term hereof and nonexclusive thereafter. Writer will not authorize or permit the use of his name, likeness, biographical material concerning Writer, or the identification of Writer, or any reproduction or simulation thereof, for or in connection with any musical composition or works, in any manner or for any purpose, other than by or for Publisher. Writer further grants to Publisher the right to refer to Writer as "Publisher's Exclusive Songwriter and Composer" or other similar appropriate appellation.

The clause "any other purpose related to the business of Publisher, its associates, affiliates and subsidiaries," is too broad and should be deleted. The writer should be able to negotiate for reasonable approval of his pictures and biographical material. All uses of the writer's name and likeness, which are reasonably related to the compositions, have already been covered. In addition, the prohibition against writers allowing their names or information about them to be used in connection with any composition not covered by this agreement is overreaching and unfair since the agreement may not cover preexisting material or new material not accepted by the publisher. The designation "Publisher's Exclusive Songwriter and Composer" is merely descriptive of the writer's status and is standard in exclusive term agreements.

4. EXCLUSIVITY

From the date hereof and during the term of this Agreement, Writer will not write or compose, or furnish or dispose of, any musical compositions, titles, lyrics or music, or any rights or interests therein whatsoever, nor participate in any manner with regard to the same for any person, firm or corporation other than Publisher, nor permit the use of their name or likeness as the writer or cowriter of any musical composition by any person, firm or corporation other than Publisher.

This exclusivity provision should be qualified to state the writer retains ownership of material written before the term of the agreement. In addition, the material written during the term should be evaluated by the publisher and either accepted or rejected as commercially viable within a reasonable period of time after delivery—30 to 60 days is fair. Rejected songs should be given back to the writer since the publisher does not believe in them and therefore will not promote them.

5. WARRANTIES AND REPRESENTATIONS

Writer hereby warrants and represents to Publisher that:

(a) Writer has the full right, power and authority to enter into and perform this Agreement and to grant to and vest in Publisher all the rights herein set forth, free and clear of any and all claims, rights and obligations whatsoever.

(b) All the results and proceeds of the services of Writer hereunder, including all of the titles, lyrics, music and musical compositions, and each and every part thereof, delivered and to be delivered by Writer hereunder are and shall be new and original and capable of copyright protection throughout the entire world.

(c) No part thereof shall be an imitation or copy of, or shall infringe any other original material.

(d) Writer has not and will not sell, assign, lease, license or in any other way dispose of or encumber the rights herein granted to Publisher.

(e) Writer warrants that each composition contains no unlicensed "samples" of other copyrighted material, or if so, that all such samples have been previously licensed from the owner of the sampled material.

The writer should try to limit the warranties to "the best of Writer's knowledge." Of course, the song must be noninfringing and not the property of someone else—this is the heart of the agreement. Virtually all publishing agreements contain language of the above nature. In any event, if the song is infringing or has been previously sold to a third party, the songwriter is liable.

6. ATTORNEY IN FACT

Writer does hereby irrevocably constitute, authorize, empower and appoint Publisher, or any of its officers, Writer's true and lawful attorney (with full power of substitution and delegation) in Writer's name, and in Writer's place and stead, or in Publisher's name, to take and do such action, and to make, sign, execute, acknowledge and deliver any and all instruments or documents which Publisher, from time to time, may deem desirable or necessary to vest in Publisher, its successors, assigns and licensees, any of the rights or interests granted by Writer hereunder, including but not limited to such documents required to secure to Publisher the renewals and extensions of copyrights throughout the world of musical compositions written or composed by Writer and owner by Publisher, and also such documents necessary to assign to Publisher, its successors and assigns, such renewal copyrights, and all rights therein for the terms of such renewals and extensions for the use and benefit of Publisher, its successors and assigns.

This common boilerplate provision gives the publisher the authority to act on behalf of the writer to secure and protect the rights it has obtained from the writer. The power of attorney should be exercisable only if the writer fails to sign the requested documents within a reasonable period of time. Ten business days is typical.

7. ADVANCES; ANNUAL GUARANTEES

Conditioned upon, and in consideration of, the full and faithful performance by Writer of all of the terms and provisions hereof, Publisher shall pay to Writer the following annual amounts, in equal monthly installments, all of which shall be recoupable by Publisher from any and all royalties payable to Writer under this or any other agreement between Writer and Publisher:

(a) (amount) ($_____) during the initial term hereof.

(b) (amount) ($_____) during the first renewal term hereof.

(c) (amount) ($_____) during the second renewal term hereof.

The range of yearly advances for songwriter agreements of this type, where the songwriter is not already a recording artist, is anywhere from zero to $15,000 the first year.

A more experienced writer, depending on the level of prior success, should start at anywhere from $25,000 to $100,000, and would probably be able to insist on retaining part of the copyright in the songs by entering into either a separate CPA or a more comprehensive CPA that encompasses both the publishing and songwriter's share of revenue, as well as many of the financial terms found in this ESA, such as advances, recoupment, reversion and any restrictions on commercial exploitation. A new writer's advances in option years would likely increase EITHER a flat amount (e.g., $2,500, or 10% of the first year's advance) each year for years two and three, with a possible bonus of at least $5,000 for the first song each year that hits the top 20 on Billboard's record sale charts, OR an amount equal to 75% of the actual earnings in the prior year of the songs covered by the agreement, subject to some minimums and maximums, as follows:

YEAR	MINIMUM	MAXIMUM
(a) first renewal term	*$12,500*	*$25,000*
(b) second renewal term	*$15,000*	*$30,000*

If the writer is also a recording artist, there will probably be no set advances as a songwriter. Instead, advances will be contingent on delivery and release in the United States by the record company of recordings of the writer's performance of the material, and will cover a wide range of amounts, with $25,000 to $75,000 fairly typical for an unknown group's first album.

8. ROYALTIES

Provided that Writer shall faithfully and completely perform the terms, covenants and conditions of this Agreement, Publisher hereby agrees to pay Writer for the services to be rendered by Writer under this Agreement and for the rights acquired and to be acquired hereunder, the following compensation based on the musical compositions which are the subject hereof.

(a) Ten percent (10%) of the wholesale selling price per copy for each and every regular piano copy and for each and every dance orchestration sold by Publisher and paid for, after deduction of each and every return, in the United States.

Few publishers print and distribute sheet music themselves. If so, the rate should have a floor of 15¢ per copy, but the trend is to pay the writer 50% of the publisher's net on all print exploitation, the same as is paid for the exploitation of other rights such as mechanical rights, electrical transcription and reproduction rights, motion picture synchronization and television rights, etc., enumerated in (c), below.

This rate is far too low; 15¢ per edition is reasonable, with increases tied to the Consumer Price Index. Many publishers now simply split their net receipts fifty-fifty from single editions with the songwriter, in the same way that they split their receipts from other revenue streams such as mechanical rights, synchronization licenses, etc. See (c) below.

(b) Ten (10%) percent of the wholesale selling price upon each and every printed copy of each and every other arrangement and edition thereof printed, published and sold by Publisher and paid for, after deduction of each and every return, in the United States, except that in the event that such composition shall be used or caused to be used, in whole or in part, in conjunction with one or more other musical compositions in a folio or album, Writer shall be entitled to receive that proportion of said ten (10%) percent which the subject musical composition shall bear to the total number of musical compositions contained in such folio or album.

Again, the writer should try for 50% of the net of what the publisher receives but in any event at least 15% to 20% of the wholesale selling price or its retail equivalent (roughly twice the wholesale price). Proration for use in folios with material by other writers should be limited to copyrighted, royalty-bearing compositions. An additional 5% of wholesale to 5% of retail should be paid for use of the writer's name and likeness in a personality folio.

(c) Fifty (50%) percent of any and all net sums actually received (less any costs for collection) by Publisher from mechanical rights, electrical transcription and reproduction rights, motion picture synchronization and television rights, so-called new technology rights such as streaming, permanent downloads, satellite radio transmission, video games, cell phone rings, and all other rights (excepting public performing rights) therein, including the use thereof in song lyric folios, magazines or any other editions whatsoever sold by licensees of Publisher in the United States.

While the equal split stated is fair, the agreement should also provide that the writer receive 50% of any nonreturnable and earned advances the publisher receives with respect to the composition(s). Also, since the publisher is the administrator of the compositions, collection costs should be charged against the publisher's share rather than the writer's share, if possible. This comment applies wherever collection costs are referred to in the agreement. The writer should see to it that he or she is paid on monies credited to the publisher wherever the agreement refers to the writer receiving a share of monies received by the publisher.

(d) Writer shall receive his public performance royalties throughout the world directly from his own affiliated performing rights society and shall have no claim whatsoever against Publisher for any royalties received by Publisher from any performing rights society which makes payment directly (or indirectly other than through Publisher) to writers, authors and composers.

This is correct. The writer's performing rights society (usually ASCAP, BMI or SESAC) pays the writer's share of public performance income directly to the writer.

(e) Fifty (50%) percent of any and all net sums, after deduction of foreign taxes, actually received (less any costs for collection) by Publisher from sales and uses directly related to subject musical compositions in countries outside of the United States (other than public performance royalties as hereinabove mentioned in paragraph 8(d).

Income generated through subpublishers (licensees of original publisher) or foreign affiliates of the publisher may far exceed United States income. It is important to establish ceilings that a subpublisher or affiliate of the publisher can charge. The collection fee charged by a subpublisher for obtaining a cover record (local version) of the writer's composition is usually greater than the fee charged for mechanical license and other income generated from the original recording in the territory involved. The fee should not exceed 30% to 40% (depending on the territory) of what the publisher would otherwise receive before paying the writer for income attributable to the cover recording and 20% to 25% for original recording income. The split between the publisher and subpublisher (i.e., before the writer's share is computed) is often stated in songwriter agreements as "80/20," "75/25," etc., representing the publisher and subpublisher's shares of gross income from its origin.

(f) Publisher shall not be required to pay any royalties on professional or complimentary copies or any copies or mechanical derivatives which are distributed gratuitously to performing artists, orchestra leaders, disc jockeys or for advertising or exploitation purposes. Furthermore, no royalties shall be payable to Writer on consigned copies unless paid for, and not until such time as an accounting therefor can be properly made.

(g) Royalties as specified hereinabove shall be payable solely to Writer in instances where Writer is the sole author of the entire composition, including the words and music thereof. If this Agreement with Publisher is made and executed by more than one person in the capacity of Writer, the royalties as hereinabove specified shall be payable solely to the particular Writer or Writers who are the authors of the entire composition, including words and music thereof, and such royalties shall be divided equally among the particular Writers of such composition unless another division is agreed upon in writing between the Writers. However, in the event that one or more other songwriters are authors along with Writer on any composition, then the foregoing royalties shall be divided equally between Writer and the other songwriters of such composition unless another division of royalties is agreed upon in writing between the parties concerned.

(h) Except as herein expressly provided, no other royalties or moneys shall be paid to Writer.

Provision should be made for advances to be paid to the writer under any term songwriter agreement. Here, the publisher is requiring the writer to write exclusively for it and in exchange is paying the writer only the royalties noted above, while retaining complete ownership of the songs and keeping 100% of the publisher's share of income, and there is no guarantee that the publisher will successfully exploit any of the writer's material, in which case the writer will see no income.

Advances are typically paid (1) in one lump sum on execution of the agreement and at the beginning of each succeeding year of the term or (2) in regular installments over the term, like a weekly or semimonthly paycheck. Small, independent publishers typically pay less in advances than large publishing companies but contend that more time will be devoted to promoting their staff writers since they have fewer of them.

The amount of the advance typically escalates 10% to 20% for each succeeding year of the term, and may be boosted by additional advances triggered by a song's commercial success. This is commonly done by tying increases to Billboard chart positions achieved or sales levels reached by previous albums. All advances are recoupable from both the writer's share and publisher's share of royalties otherwise payable to the writer (ASCAP/BMI/SESAC royalties excluded).

A publisher that pays an advance to a writer will require the delivery of a specified minimum number of compositions written by the writer. Fifteen to twenty "Wholly Owned Compositions" is typical, with songs cowritten receiving partial credit. For example, if the writer writes a song with two other writers, the publisher will give the writer credit for one-third of a wholly owned composition toward the minimum delivery requirement. If the writer fails to deliver the minimum number of songs required during any contract year, the publisher will have the right to extend the term without having to increase the advances beyond the agreed amount until a sufficient number of songs are delivered. The writer should object to any provision giving the publisher the right to suspend advances in addition to extending the term.

In any event (h) is meaningless and should be deleted, since the rest of paragraph 8 provides for payment to the writer for all types of uses.

9. ACCOUNTING

Publisher will compute the royalties earned by Writer pursuant to this Agreement within ninety (90) days after the first day of January and the first day of July of each year for the preceding six (6) month period, and will remit to Writer the net amount of such royalties, if any, after deducting any and all unrecouped advances and chargeable costs under this Agreement, together with the detailed royalty statement, within such ninety (90) days. All royalty statements rendered by Publisher to Writer shall be binding upon Writer and not subject to any objection by Writer for any reason unless specific objection is made, in writing, stating the basis thereof, to Publisher within one (1) year from the date rendered. Writer shall have the right, upon the giving of at least thirty (30) days written notice to Publisher, to inspect the books and records of Publisher, insofar as the same concerns Writer, at the expense of Writer, at reasonable times during normal business hours, for the purpose of verifying the accuracy of any royalty statement rendered to Writer hereunder.

> *Mechanical income should be paid on a quarterly basis since record companies usually account for mechanical income quarterly. Forty-five to sixty days after the close of an accounting period should be enough time for statements to be rendered. The writer should have at least two and preferably three years from the time rendered to object to a statement.*

10. COLLABORATIONS

Whenever Writer shall collaborate with any other person in the creation of any musical composition, any such musical composition shall be subject to the terms and conditions of this Agreement and Writer warrants and represents that prior to the collaboration with any other person, such other person shall be advised prior to the collaboration of this exclusive agreement and that all such compositions must be published by Publisher in accordance with the terms and provisions hereunder. In the event of such collaboration with any other person, Writer shall notify Publisher of the extent that such other person may have in any such musical composition and Writer shall cause such other person to execute a separate songwriter's agreement with respect thereto, which agreement shall set forth the division of the songwriter's share of income between Writer and such other person, and Publisher shall make payment accordingly. If Publisher so desires, Publisher may request Writer to execute a separate agreement in Publisher's customary form with respect to each musical composition hereunder. Upon such request, Writer will promptly execute such agreement. Publisher shall have the right, pursuant to the terms and conditions hereof, to execute such agreement on behalf of Writer hereunder. Such agreement shall supplement and not supersede this Agreement. In the event of any conflict between the provisions of such agreement and this Agreement, the provisions of this Agreement shall govern.

> *This language is not consistent with the reality that writers do collaborate without regard to existing exclusive writer agreements and is detrimental to the natural collaborative creative process. A better approach would be to require that the publisher be entitled to its own writer's entire ownership share of the song and perhaps the ownership share of any cowriter not similarly signed to a publisher. If a lyricist and composer have written the song, their respective contributions should be delineated. The lyricist should not suffer if the music is infringing and vice versa with respect to the composer if the lyrics infringe. Further, it is the lyricist, not the composer, who may suffer a loss in income from translations, which the composer may not wish to share. In the absence of an agreement to the contrary, all creators are equal owners, irrespective of the amount*

of the contribution. If these roles are delineated, the composer of the music will not share lyric reprint royalties, and the lyricist will not share royalties on instrumental versions, unless the parties agree otherwise.

Moreover, paragraph 10 should state, "Writer shall use best efforts to cause such other person to execute a separate songwriter's agreement" with respect to cowritten compositions. Finally, writers should never authorize others to sign agreements in their name, except possibly to the extent necessary to allow the publisher to secure and protect the copyright share obtained from them, as discussed in paragraph 6 above.

11. DEMOS

Writer will deliver a manuscript copy of each musical composition hereunder immediately upon the completion or acquisition of such musical composition. Publisher shall advance reasonable costs for the production of demonstration records and one-half (¹/₂) of such costs shall be deemed an advance which shall be deducted from royalties payable to Writer by Publisher under this Agreement. All recordings and reproductions made at demonstration recording sessions hereunder shall become the sole and exclusive property of Publisher, free of any claims whatsoever by Writer or any person deriving any rights from Writer.

It is unfair, but traditional, for publishers to recover one-half the demo costs from the writer's royalties. The writer should try to get this deleted, especially if they are not receiving part of the publisher's share of income. The writer should be able to keep copies of demos of songs that are rejected by the publisher and can offer to reimburse publisher the unrecouped share of demo costs if they are successful in exploiting the song on their own.

Better yet, would be for the publisher to provide a development fund, at least during the initial term, if the writer is also a recording artist but does not already have a recording agreement. The fund is used for expenses incurred to showcase and market the writer for the purpose of securing an exclusive recording agreement. Development fund expenditures are considered additional advances recoupable from royalties.

12. INJUNCTION

Writer acknowledges that the services rendered hereunder are of a special, unique, unusual, extraordinary and intellectual character which gives them a peculiar value, the loss of which cannot be reasonably or adequately compensated in damages in an action at law, and that a breach by Writer of any of the provisions of this Agreement will cause Publisher great and irreparable injury and damage. Writer expressly agrees that Publisher shall be entitled to remedies of injunction and other equitable relief to prevent a breach of this Agreement or any provision hereof, which relief shall be in addition to any other remedies, for damages or otherwise, which may be available to Publisher.

This standard provision allows the publisher to get a court order to prevent the writer from writing for any other publisher if the writer becomes dissatisfied and wants to terminate the deal with the current publisher and write for someone else. It is doubtful, however, that a court would issue an injunction just because this clause is in the contract.

This provision should only allow the publisher to seek an injunction from the court so that the publisher would be required to prove that a money judgment would not be sufficient. In addition, this kind of relief should be available only if the writer's action or failure goes to the essence of the agreement, such as failing to deliver the songs required or refusing to turn over the demos to the publisher.

It is also important to know that, for contracts governed by California law, the publisher cannot obtain an injunction against the writer unless it has agreed to pay certain annual minimums. The amounts for a three-year agreement are $6,000; $9,000; and $12,000, for years one through three, respectively. As all other advances, these are fully recoupable against writer's royalties.

13. REVERSION

If Publisher fails to secure a cover recording of the Compositions within the term of this Agreement, Writer may, during the fifteen (15) days following the expiration of said term, demand the return of the Compositions in writing and if Publisher receives such notice within said period, Publisher agrees to reassign the compositions and all Publisher's rights therein to Writer and to execute any documents necessary to effect such reconveyance. Notwithstanding the foregoing, Publisher shall not be obliged to reassign the Compositions to Writer until such time as Writer shall repay to Publisher any advances or unrecouped demonstration recording costs chargeable to Writer.

The maximum period of time possible for the writer to come up with the money to reacquire the compositions should be negotiated—two years is probably the most a publisher will allow. The writer should additionally have the right to recapture even those compositions that are covered but are not commercially released on a major label. Even better, but harder to obtain unless the writer has a measure of bargaining power, is requiring that the recording be by a major artist or achieve a certain chart position. Top 50 is a reasonable target to request. In addition, the publisher may require at least a year following the term for exploitation of those songs delivered during the last year or two of the term so as to have at least two or three years to record them. A new writer may have to settle for reversion after four or five years after the term, but this still offers an opportunity to breathe new life into compositions that would otherwise languish in the publisher's archives and be lost to the world. Be sure that the reversion is at the writer's option if repayment of advances is tied to reversion; there is no point in being required to buy back those compositions that are not winners even in the writer's eyes. Finally, only unrecouped advances should be repaid.

14. ACTIONS; INDEMNITY

(a) Publisher may take such action as it deems necessary, either in Writer's name or in its own name, against any person to protect all rights and interest acquired by Publisher hereunder. Writer will at Publisher's request, cooperate fully with Publisher in any controversy which may arise or litigation which may be brought concerning Publisher's rights and interests obtained hereunder. Publisher shall have the right, in its absolute discretion, to employ attorneys and to institute or defend any action or proceeding and to take any other proper steps to protect the rights, title and interest of Publisher in and to each musical composition hereunder and every portion thereof and in that connection, to settle, compromise or in any other manner dispose of any matter, claim, action or proceeding and to satisfy any judgment that may be rendered, in any manner as Publisher in its sole discretion may determine. Any legal action brought by Publisher against any alleged infringer of any musical composition hereunder shall be initiated and prosecuted by Publisher, and if there is any recovery made by Publisher as a result thereof, after the deduction of the expense of litigation, including but not limited to attorneys' fees and court costs, a sum equal to fifty (50%) percent of such net proceeds shall be paid to Writer.

(b) If a claim is presented against Publisher in respect to any musical composition hereunder, and because thereof Publisher is jeopardized, Publisher shall have the right thereafter, until said claim has been finally adjudicated or settled, to withhold any and all royalties or other sums that may be or become due with respect to such compositions pending the final adjudication or settlement of such claim. Publisher, in addition, may withhold from any and all royalties or other sums that may be due and payable to Writer hereunder, an amount that Publisher deems sufficient to reimburse Publisher for any contemplated damages, including court costs and attorneys' fees and costs resulting therefrom. Upon the final adjudication or settlement of each and every claim hereunder, all moneys withheld shall then be disbursed in accordance with the final adjudication or settlement of said claim.

This version is actually fairer to the writer in several respects than some other boilerplate indemnity provisions. This provision clarifies that the writer shares in any recovery obtained against infringers, limits the amount of money withheld from the writer to a sum related to the anticipated cost of the claim and continues payment to the writer for income from compositions not involved in the claim. Since many claims are made by third parties and are not pursued, the agreement should also provide that any monies withheld from the writer by the publisher when a claim is made against the publisher bear interest and be released to the writer if no formal lawsuit is filed within six months after the monies are first withheld. The writer should also have the right to be represented by his or her own attorney and to consent to at least those settlements in excess of a few thousand dollars. In addition, since the publisher has acquired the copyright and controls the compositions, the publisher should have not only the right but also the obligation to protect the copyrights by taking action against infringers and bear all costs of defending or instituting claims.

15. NOTICES

Any written notice, statement, payment or matter required or desired to be given to Publisher or Writer pursuant to this Agreement shall be given by addressing the same to the addresses of the respective parties referred to herein, or to such other address as either party shall designate in writing, and such notice shall be deemed to have been given on the date when same shall be deposited, so addressed, postage prepaid, in the United States mail.

Be sure that the contract includes complete addresses for both parties. A copy of notices given by the publisher should also be sent to the writer's attorney and so stated in the ESA so she or he can answer any questions by the writer that might arise from the notice. Providing for a copy of statements to the writer's attorney and accountant is advisable for the same reason, and these professionals might readily detect any apparent reporting errors. Notices that exercise an option or claim that a breach has occurred should be by certified mail with a return receipt. Notification by fax transmission, verifiable by receipt, may also be included, providing that it shall be confirmed by mailed copy. The effective notice date should be 48 to 72 hours from deposit in the mail since it may take several days to arrive.

16. ENTIRE AGREEMENT

This Agreement supersedes any and all prior negotiations, understandings and agreements between the parties hereto with respect to the subject matter hereof. Each of the parties acknowledges and agrees that neither party has made any representations or promises in connection with this Agreement or the subject matter hereof not contained herein.

17. MISCELLANEOUS

This Agreement may not be canceled, altered, modified, amended or waived, in whole or in part, in any way, except by an instrument in writing signed by both Publisher and Writer. The waiver by Publisher of any breach of this Agreement in any one or more instances, shall in no way be construed as a waiver of any subsequent breach (whether or not of a similar nature) of this Agreement by Writer. If any part of this Agreement shall be held to be void, invalid or unenforceable, it shall not affect the validity of the balance of this Agreement. This Agreement shall be governed by and construed under the law of the State of New York applicable to agreements executed in and to be wholly performed there.

> *If the writer or the attorney reside in California, it would be better for California law to apply since it is more familiar and may be more favorable to the artist inasmuch as this state's legislature and courts have adopted a role somewhat more protective of artists than have other states.*

18. BREACH; NOTICE

No breach of this Agreement on the part of Publisher shall be deemed material, unless Writer shall have given Publisher notice of such breach and Publisher shall fail to discontinue the practice complained of (if a practice of Publisher is the basis of the claim of breach) or otherwise cure such breach, within sixty (60) days after receipt of such notice, if such breach is reasonably capable of being fully cured within such sixty (60) day period, or, if such breach is not reasonably capable of being fully cured within such sixty (60) day period, if Publisher commences to cure such breach within such sixty (60) day period and proceeds with reasonable diligence to complete the curing of such breach.

> *The writer should be given the same opportunity to cure breaches.*

19. ASSIGNMENT

This Agreement may not be assigned by Writer. Subject to the foregoing, this Agreement shall inure to the benefit of and be binding upon each of the parties hereto and their respective successors, assigns, heirs, executors, administrators and legal and personal representatives.

> *The agreement is silent regarding the publisher's right to assign either the entire agreement or any of its rights or obligations. The publisher should be allowed to assign only to a person or entity acquiring all or substantially all of the assets of the publisher without the writer's consent. The writer should be allowed to purchase the song at the same price at which it is sold to any third party (if it is part of a catalog, an independent appraiser can be appointed), but few publishers will agree to this.*

IN WITNESS WHEREOF, the parties hereto have executed this Agreement as of the day and year first above written.

AGREED TO AND ACCEPTED:

_____   _____
(WRITER)   (PUBLISHER)

_____   _____
NAME AND TITLE (AN AUTHORIZED SIGNATORY)   NAME AND TITLE (AN AUTHORIZED SIGNATORY)

_____   _____
FEDERAL I.D./SS#   FEDERAL I.D./SS#

COPUBLISHING AND ADMINISTRATION AGREEMENT

THIS AGREEMENT ("Agreement") made as of the_____ day of
_____20___ , by and between [name of Publishing Company]
(hereinafter referred to as "Company"), an affiliate of [ASCAP/BMI/SESAC], located
at _____ and [name of copublisher], an affiliate of
[ASCAP/BMI/SESAC], located at _____ (hereinafter referred
to as "Copublisher").

*Both this agreement (sometimes referred to in discussions in the ESA agreement and
here as "CPA") and the ESA agreement previously analyzed state that the agreement
is made "as of" the agreed date. This is done because sometimes the agreement goes into
effect before the formal contract is fully executed. The parties may be relying on an
abbreviated agreement of the major deal points, called a "deal memo" or "deal letter."*

*It is a good idea to include which performing rights association the parties belong
to (circle the one that applies) and a mailing address. Later, in the notices provision, I
recommend adding the songwriter's law firm or accounting firm where statements and
payments can be sent. It is also preferable for the writer (copublisher) to form his or her
publishing company as a DBA rather than a corporation or LLC as it can be difficult
to transfer copyrights, and there is the question of whom besides the songwriter may
have any interest in the corporation or LLC. Typically, the songwriter's publishing
company is not actively engaged in administering the copyrights or marketing the
music—that is what the established publishing company is set up for and paid to do.
Rather, the songwriter's publishing company is a vehicle for the songwriter to retain
partial ownership of the copyright and share in the publisher's share of the income.
"Company" is the established music publishing company such as Warner/Chappell Music.*

WHEREAS, it is the intention of Company and Copublisher that they shall jointly
own the musical compositions (hereinafter individually referred to as "Composition"
and collectively referred to as "Compositions") acquired by Company pursuant to
Company's exclusive songwriter's agreement of even date herewith with [name of
songwriter] ("Exclusive Songwriter's Agreement," or "ESA"), so that the entire worldwide right, title and interest, including the copyright, the right to copyright and any
and all renewal rights, in and to the Compositions shall be owned by Company and by
Copublisher in the percentages described below:

TITLE:	PERCENTAGE to Company:	PERCENTAGE to Copublisher:
	[e.g., 50%]	[e.g., 50%]

*Until recently, the most common split was fifty-fifty, but there are many exceptions
depending on the relative strength of the parties, number of songwriters, the size of
advances, recoupment terms and other financial terms. Instead of listing song titles here
it may be easier to refer to an attached schedule that includes this information. Note
that this list will not include titles not yet written but that will be written and shared
over the course of the ESA and this agreement or a stand-alone copublishing agreement
if used without an ESA. It is good practice to update and submit the list periodically,
perhaps with each release of new titles or on an annual basis to include material that*

has not or may not be released but is nonetheless co-owned by the terms of the agreement. Recall from the discussion in the ESA that the songwriter should have a right of recapture of any songs not commercially released during or within a specified period following the expiration of the agreement.

WHEREAS, the Compositions shall be registered for copyright in the names of Company and Copublisher in the Copyright Office of the United States of America;

I recommend specifying who will register the compositions—it is usually the company.

NOW, THEREFORE, for good and valuable consideration the receipt of which is hereby acknowledged by each party hereto, it is agreed as follows:

1. Company and Copublisher shall jointly own the Compositions, in the shares above described, including all the worldwide right, title and interest, including the copyrights, the right to copyright and any renewal rights, therein and thereto.

Specify how long the term is, once delivered. This would be in perpetuity or at least as long as any copyright law anywhere in the territory is applicable.

2. The Compositions shall be registered for copyright by Company in the names of Company and Copublisher in the office of the Register of Copyrights of the United States of America. If any Composition has heretofore been registered for copyright in the name of Composer or other writers, Copublisher shall simultaneously herewith cause Composer or such other writers to deliver to Company and Copublisher an assignment thereof, in form acceptable to Company. If any Composition has heretofore been registered for copyright in the name of Copublisher, Copublisher shall simultaneously herewith deliver to Company an assignment of the appropriate interest therein, in form acceptable to Company.

3. Company has the sole, exclusive and worldwide right to administer and exploit the Compositions, to print, publish, sell, dramatize, use and license any and all uses of the Compositions, to execute in its own name any and all licenses and agreements whatsoever affecting or respecting the Compositions, including but not limited to licenses for mechanical reproduction, public performance, dramatic uses, synchronization uses and subpublication, and to assign or license such rights to others. This statement of exclusive rights is only in clarification and amplification of the rights of Company and not in limitation thereof.

All of the company's rights are subject to any restrictions in the ESA, such as prohibiting licensing where excessive violence or explicit sex is involved, limiting or prohibiting commercial licenses (tobacco, cigarettes, hygiene products, pharmaceuticals, etc.) as moral rights, and any moral rights restrictions (if required by a country outside the U.S. where moral rights or droit moral, are recognized).

4. Company is entitled to receive and collect and shall receive and collect all gross receipts derived from the Compositions. "Gross Receipts" is defined as any and all revenue, income and sums derived and actually received by Company in the United States (after deduction of any collection or other fees charged by The Harry Fox

Agency, Inc., CMRRA or any other such collection agent that may be used by the Company in the United States and Canada, and after deduction of any collection fee or share of royalties charged by any collection agent or subpublisher used by Company outside the United States and Canada) from the exploitation of the Compositions, including, without limitation, mechanical royalties, synchronization fees, dramatic use fees, printing income and the publisher's share of public performance fees. In the event Company or its subsidiaries or affiliates in the United States or Canada shall print and sell any printed editions of any of the Compositions, gross receipts with respect thereto, for the purposes of this Agreement, shall be deemed to be a royalty on the net paid sales of each printed edition, which royalty shall be equal to the then current royalty generally being paid by print licensees in the United States to unrelated music publishers.

> *While the HFA is widely used, it may be bypassed by the company that issues its own licenses to avoid HFA charges and keep better track of the money, especially where major catalogs are involved.*

5. Company shall pay to Copublisher [e.g., fifty] percent [e.g., (50%)] of the net income derived by Company from the Compositions, and shall retain the remaining net income for its own account. "Net Income" is defined as the gross receipts less the following:
    (a) An administration fee of [e.g., ten] percent [e.g., (10%)] of the gross receipts, which Company shall retain for its own account;
    (b) Royalties which shall be paid by Company to Composer pursuant to the ESA, and royalties which shall be paid by Company to any other writers of Compositions pursuant to any songwriter's agreements between Copublisher and any such other writers (true copies of which latter agreements shall be submitted by Copublisher to Company promptly upon execution thereof), it being understood that in no event shall any royalties exceed the royalties provided for in Clause 7 of the ESA;

> *Royalties are credited but not paid, until advances are recouped.*

(c) Administrative and exploitation expenses of Company with respect to the Compositions including, without limitation, registration fees, advertising and promotion expenses directly related to the Compositions, the costs of producing demonstration records to the extent such costs are not recoupable from Composer's or other writers' royalties; and

> *Legal fees, demo costs and general overhead in particular, are highly negotiated these days. The outcome depends on the relative strength of the parties.*

(d) Attorneys' fees, if any, actually paid by Company for any agreements (other than the within agreement) affecting solely the Compositions or any of them.

> *If there is no separate ESA, the songwriter's share of income would be included here and the percentages above adjusted accordingly. Broadly speaking, out of each dollar (and forgetting about various deductions for now), the songwriter's share is one-half and the total publisher's share is one-half—here shared fifty-fifty—so 25% to the company and 25% to the copublisher). The combined share payable to the songwriter/copublisher would then be 50% + 25% = 75% of net revenues for most forms of exploitation.*

6. Small performing rights in the Compositions, to the extent permitted by law, shall be assigned to and licensed by the performing rights society to which both parties belong. Said society shall be and is hereby authorized to collect and receive all monies earned from the public performance of the Compositions in the United States and Canada and shall be and is hereby directed to pay directly to Company the entire amount allocated by said society as the publisher's share of public performance fees for the Compositions for the United States and Canada.

7. Mechanical royalties for the Compositions for the United States and Canada shall be collectible by The Harry Fox Agency, Inc., CMRRA or any other collection agent which may be designated by Company, provided, however, that Company shall, in the case of any record company in the United States or Canada affiliated with Company, issue the mechanical licenses directly to said record company at the then current statutory rate (with such reduced rates for special types of sales or distribution for which Company customarily grants reduced rates to nonaffiliated record companies) and collect mechanical royalties directly therefrom, in which case there shall be no collection fee as referred to in Clause 4 above.

An additional clause that provides for the collection by the company of all fees, royalties and other payments relating to the exploitation of the compositions by any means not specifically mentioned in this agreement should be added. This would read "including, but not by limitation, so-called new technologies such as streaming, permanent downloads, satellite radio transmissions, video games, cell phone rings," etc. Since new technology is ongoing it is important to include "and means, now or hereafter known," to ensure capture of new sources of revenue not yet known or listed.

8. Statements as to monies payable hereunder shall be sent by Company to Copublisher semiannually within ninety (90) days after the end of each semiannual calendar period. Statements shall be accompanied by appropriate payments. Upon the submission of each statement, Company shall have the right to retain, as a reserve against subsequent charges, credits or returns, such portion of payable monies hereunder with respect to print sales by Company or its affiliates as shall be necessary and appropriate in its best business judgment. Copublisher shall be deemed to have consented to all royalty statements and other accounts rendered by Company to Copublisher, and said statements and other accounts shall be binding upon Copublisher and not subject to any objection for any reason, unless specific objection in writing, setting forth the basis thereof, is given by Copublisher to Company within two (2) years from the date rendered. Copublisher or a certified public accountant in its behalf may, at reasonable intervals, examine the books of Company pertaining to the Compositions, during Company's usual business hours and upon reasonable notice. Said books relating to activities and receipts during any accounting period may only be examined as aforesaid during the two (2) year period following service by Company of the statement for said accounting period.

Quarterly payments are better, if you can get them, and should be sufficiently detailed and formulated in accordance with standard accounting practices, not some obtuse method used by the company that is difficult, if not impossible, to follow. It is also important that the statement include only the account balance as of the end of the accounting period, such as June 30, regardless of the date that the copublisher actually receives the statement. There are instances where major publishing companies have paid an advance after the accounting cut-off period but before the statement was sent, then subtracted the advance in that royalty statement, reducing or eliminating the payment of any royalties that should have been due the songwriter for that period. Some record companies have done the same.

9. Each party hereto shall give the other the equal benefits of any warranties or representations that it obtained or shall obtain under any agreements affecting the Compositions except for the ESA.

10. Company shall have the sole right but not the obligation to prosecute, defend, settle and compromise all suits and actions respecting the Compositions, and generally to do and perform all things necessary concerning the same and the copyrights therein, to prevent and restrain the infringement of copyrights or other rights with respect to the Compositions. In the event of the recovery by Company of any monies as a result of a judgment or settlement, such monies shall be divided between Company and Copublisher in the same shares as provided in Clause 5 above, after first deducting the expenses of obtaining said monies, including counsel fees, and paying any necessary share thereof to Composer or any other writers. Copublisher shall have the right to provide counsel for itself, but at its own expense, to assist in any such matter. Any judgments against Company and any settlements by Company of claims against it respecting any of the Compositions, together with costs and expenses, including counsel fees, shall be covered by the indemnity provisions of Clause 15 hereof, and Copublisher's indemnity payment thereunder shall be paid to Company promptly upon demand and may also be recouped by Company from any and all sums that may become due to Copublisher hereunder.

See the comments to the indemnity provision in paragraph 14 of the ESA.

11. Copublisher shall not sell, transfer, assign or otherwise dispose of any interest in the copyright of any Composition without first offering to Company the right to buy or acquire such interest at the same bona fide price and pursuant to the same bona fide terms as may be offered to Copublisher by any responsible and unrelated third party, which terms may, however, only provide for payment of cash in lump sum or installments. Copublisher agrees to give Company written notice of any such bona fide and acceptable offer as described above (which notice shall set forth the name of the prospective purchaser, the price, and all other terms of such offer), and Company shall have ten (10) business days after receipt of such notice in which to notify Copublisher whether or not it desires to acquire such interest in the copyright of such Composition at the price and pursuant to the terms set forth in the notice. If Company fails to give Copublisher written notice within the ten (10) business day period that it is exercising its option to buy or acquire such interest, Copublisher shall have the right to accept the bona fide offer by the prospective purchaser, but only as set forth in Copublisher's notice to Company, provided, that if Copublisher does not accept such bona fide offer from such prospective purchaser within sixty (60) days after expiration of the ten (10) business day period, the procedure set forth in this clause shall again be followed by Copublisher before Copublisher may dispose of such interest in the copyright of such Composition.

Lawyers that represent the copublisher often try to delete this requirement but if the company's advances to the copublisher are significant, it will feel entitled to this right. This provision may prevent the copublisher from taking the song to another publisher that may be better suited for the material.

12. The rights of the parties hereto in and to each Composition shall extend for the full term of the copyright of said Composition and of any derivative copyrights herein in the United States of America and throughout the rest of the world and for the terms of any and all renewals or extensions thereof in the United States of America and throughout the rest of the world. Each composition is a work made for hire under the U. S. Copyright Law.

If used with an ESA, be sure that the work-for-hire language is consistent in both documents. See discussion elsewhere in this book about when a work should be classified a work for hire as distinguished from the copyright being initially held by the songwriter/copublisher and 50% of it then assigned to the company.

13. Copublisher hereby warrants and represents that it has the right to enter into this Agreement and to grant to Company any rights granted herein, and that the exercise by Company of any and all rights with respect to the Compositions will not violate or infringe upon any common law or statutory rights of any person, firm or corporation, including, without limitation, contractual rights, copyrights and rights of privacy. The rights granted herein are free and clear of any claims, demands, liens or encumbrances. Copublisher acknowledges that Company has the right to administer and publish compositions other than the Compositions.

See comments to the representations and warranties provision found in paragraph 5 of the ESA.

14. Copublisher hereby indemnifies, saves and holds Company, its assigns, licensees and its and their directors, officers, shareholders, agents and employees harmless from any and all liability, claims, demands, loss and damage (including counsel fees and court costs) arising out of or connected with any claim or action by a third party which is inconsistent with any of the warranties, representations or agreements made by Copublisher in this Agreement or by Composer in the ESA. Company shall give Copublisher prompt written notice of any claim or action covered by said indemnity, and pending the disposition of any such claim or action Company shall have the right to withhold payment of such portion or any and all monies hereunder as shall be reasonably related to the amount of the claim and estimated counsel fees and costs.

Additionally, it is common to limit the indemnification to claims that have been reduced to final court judgment or settled with the reasonable consent of the company after consultation with the copublisher. If no claim is filed with a court within a certain period of time, any funds withheld should be released. Attorney fees should be "reasonable," as measured by current fees charged in that community. Also, see comments found in paragraph 14 of the ESA.

15. The initial term of this Agreement shall commence upon the date hereof and continue for the initial term of the ESA. It is the intention of the parties hereto that

the term hereof shall be coterminous with the term of the ESA, as same may be renewed or extended from time to time. Accordingly, each extension or renewal of the term of the ESA shall automatically extend or renew the term hereof for the same period. The phrase "the term hereof" or "the term of this Agreement" as used in this Agreement, shall refer to the initial and any extension or renewal terms hereof in accordance with the foregoing.

> *If this agreement is used without a companion ESA, the term here would be defined in a similar manner as in the sample ESA, i.e., tied to the term of the recording agreement. Each term will typically require that a specified minimum of songs featured on each album be new, wholly controlled compositions written by the writer/copublisher. Remember that while the initial and option terms of the agreement end at some point, the company's copyright and administration rights continue.*

16. The respective addresses of Company and Copublisher for all purposes of this Agreement shall be as set forth below, until written notice of a new address shall be duly given: [names and addresses of Company and Copublisher]. All notices shall be in writing and shall either be delivered by certified mail (return receipt requested), postage prepaid, or by electronic communication (fax, e-mail), provided that such transmission is supported by proof of transmission. The date of mailing or confirmed transmission shall be deemed the date of service.

> *See paragraph 15 of the ESA for comments regarding notices. Additionally, statements are typically sent by regular First-Class Mail.*

17. This Agreement shall not be deemed to give any right or remedy to any third party whatsoever unless said right or remedy is specifically granted to such third party by the terms hereof.

18. The parties hereto shall execute any further documents including, without limitation, assignments of copyrights, and do all acts necessary to fully effectuate the terms and provisions of this Agreement.

19. This Agreement sets forth the entire understanding between the parties, and cannot be changed, modified or cancelled except by an instrument signed by the party sought to be bound. This Agreement shall be governed by and construed under the laws of the State of California applicable to agreements wholly performed therein.

20. Company may enter into subpublishing or collection agreements with, and license or assign this Agreement and any of its rights hereunder and delegate any of its obligations hereunder to, any persons, firms or corporations for any one or more countries of the world. If Company is or shall be a party to any subpublishing, collection or administration agreement for any country of the world with a subsidiary or affiliate, such agreement shall be deemed to be an agreement with an unrelated third party and, for the purposes of this Agreement, such agreement shall be deemed to be on a basis no less favorable to Company than an agreement providing for the American publisher to receive fifty percent (50%) of the mechanical royalties computed at the source, fifty percent (50%) of public performance royalties computed at the source and ten percent (10%) of suggested retail selling price on printed editions.

All other sources of income relating to the compositions should be added. This is a good, arms-length provision for the treatment of assigning rights to sister companies on sweetheart terms between the affiliates.

21. This Agreement shall not be binding upon Company until duly executed by Copublisher and duly executed by Company. Nothing herein contained shall constitute a partnership between or a joint venture by Company and Copublisher. Neither party hereto shall hold itself out contrary to the terms of this clause, and neither party shall become liable for any obligation, act or omission of the other party contrary to the provisions hereof. If any provision of this Agreement shall be declared invalid, same shall not affect the validity of the remaining provisions hereof. No waiver of any provision of this Agreement or of any default hereunder shall affect the waiving party's rights thereafter to enforce such provision or to exercise any right or remedy in the event of any other default, whether or not similar.

22. Annexed hereto as Schedule "A" is the form of letter of direction and assignment from Copublisher to [name of performing rights society, e.g., BMI, ASCAP or SESAC] which shall effectuate the provisions of Clause 6 above. Copublisher shall sign and deliver to Company copies of said letter simultaneously herewith, and in default thereof Company is hereby authorized and empowered by Copublisher to sign copies of this letter for and on behalf of Copublisher and submit same to the appropriate society.

23. If any musical composition acquired in whole or in part by Copublisher during the term hereof or by Company under the provisions or the ESA shall have been written or cowritten by a member of a performing rights society other than the society to which the parties hereto belong, said musical composition or the appropriate share thereof shall be a composition hereunder, co-owned by an affiliate of Company which shall be a member of said other society and by an affiliate of Copublisher which shall be a member of said other society, and administered by Company's affiliate.

It will be difficult to hold anyone except the songwriter/copublisher to this clause. Try to take it out if you are the copublisher.

General Comments
Also, see the ESA comments, particularly paragraphs 7, 8, 9, 11 and 13, with regard to advances and development fund provisions that would appear in a stand-alone CPA.

Sometimes the copublisher is referred to as "Participant" in form contracts. This is accurate if the writer is participating in the publisher's share of income but has no copyright ownership in the songs. It is clearer and more accurate to use "Copublisher" whenever the writer retains any share of his or her copyrights.

IN WITNESS WHEREOF, the parties have executed this Agreement the day and year above set forth.

BY	BY
TITLE	TITLE

SCHEDULE A (BMI)

Letter of Direction and Assignment

Dated: _____

Clearance Department
Broadcast Music, Inc.
320 West 57th Street
New York, NY 10019

Gentlemen:

This is to advise BMI that we have entered into an agreement with another BMI publisher for the administration of the following work(s) previously cleared with BMI on our behalf, and that BMI's records should be marked to reflect the agreement as follows:

1. Title(s): _____

2. Name of BMI publisher acting as our administrator: _____

3. Effective date of Agreement: _____

CHECK ONE

___Immediately, i.e., effective with the first calendar quarter as of which BMI can change its records.
___Effective with performances on and after _____, 20 ____.
___Must be as of the beginning of a calendar quarter (i.e., Jan. 1, April 1, July 1, or Oct. 1).

4. Territory:
___World
___United States
___United States and Canada
___(Other) _____

5. Checks for all our BMI royalties earned by the work(s) in the territory indicated should be made payable to the administrator and should be sent together with statements and all other correspondence regarding the work(s) to the administrator at its address on BMI's records.

We understand that BMI cannot mark its records at this time so as to indicate the termination date of the Agreement and that, therefore, the above information will continue to be reflected on BMI's records until such time as we or the administrator notifies BMI that the administration Agreement is about to terminate and advises how the work(s) should be credited thereafter.

Very truly yours,

SCHEDULE A (ASCAP)

Letter of Direction and Assignment

Dated: _____

American Society of Composers, Authors & Publishers
One Lincoln Plaza
New York, NY 10023

Gentlemen:

You are hereby authorized and directed to pay our administrator [name] ("Administrator") at [address] and we hereby assign to Administrator, all monies payable from and after the date hereof (regardless of when earned) as the publisher's share of public performance royalties with respect to the compositions described below:

All musical compositions that are or shall be co-owned by Administrator and the undersigned.

The foregoing authorization and direction shall remain in full force and effect until modified or terminated by both the undersigned and Administrator.

Very truly yours,

It is helpful to identify the specific agreement by the names and addresses of both the administrator ("Company") and the copublisher ("undersigned"), the date and the name of the agreement (e.g., "Copublishing and Administration Agreement").

Special thanks to Gerald Rosenblatt, Esq., for contributing revisions and updates to this chapter for the fourth edition of The Musician's Business and Legal Guide.

Contemporary Songs and Recordings for Soundtracks

BY MARK HALLORAN AND THOMAS A. WHITE

In recent years, successful pop/rock song-writers and recording artists have moved, seemingly en masse, into motion picture soundtrack songwriting and performing. Some, such as Jessica Simpson, have had star acting careers, and some actors, such as Jennifer Lopez, have used acting careers as the platform for a music career. However, these are exceptions. Typically, songwriters and recording artists do not act in the film but are hired by film studios during or after the film is shot to write and record individual musical compositions specifically for the film. The songs are then synchronized with the picture and may be used in promotional trailers and television spots; included in a soundtrack album; and released as downloads and MTV promotional videos. This chapter examines relevant issues when nonactor writers/performers are commissioned to create individual songs for a film. The primary focus is on practices at major Hollywood studios, although we also discuss practices at the nonmajors and in the independent film world. (When we say "major Hollywood studios," we mean 20th Century Fox, Warner Bros., Universal, Sony Pictures Entertainment [Columbia Pictures and TriStar], Paramount/Dreamworks and Disney.) You should be aware that much of the music used in films is preexisting. These preexisting songs are typically licensed from music publishers for fees, which are split between the publishers and songwriters. Similarly, preexisting recordings are typically licensed from record companies for fees, which are split between the record companies and the performers. We are not discussing film composers or orchestral scores. Orchestral scores typically are the background music and do not include individual songs. But there are exceptions to this rule, too. James Horner's theme for *Titanic* was adapted into an individual song and was a huge international hit for Celine Dion.

CURRENT PRACTICE IN WRITING AND RECORDING SOUNDTRACK MUSIC

When you are asked by a studio or producer to write and record an original song for a motion picture there are fundamental business and legal concerns. How much money will you be paid initially? How will your music publisher and record label be involved in the deal? What controls, concerning the use of the song and the recording, will you have? How much money can you expect later from the exploitation of the song and the recording? We will first look at the studio's viewpoint to better understand its motives.

The Creative Choices

The filmmaking team—the studio, the producer and the director—usually chooses the songs and performing artists and collectively they must reach a creative and business consensus. Most major studios have music departments that are headed by creative music executives that, combined with the filmmaking team, represent the studio's music interests and are available to its film producers for consultation referrals and other general music services, including recommending songs, recordings and artists. Absent a consensus, the amount of clout the individual members of the filmmaking team wield will determine the choice of songs and performers. When dealing with high-powered, experienced, successful film producers and directors, the studio will often defer to their creative choices, but will still insist on consultation or approval of both the musical talent and their deal. Some directors have so-called final cut of the film, which may or may not include final determination of the musical talent and music in the film.

In some instances, a music supervisor, who reports to the director and producer and represents their interests, is hired. Music supervisors have gained prominence because filmmakers have recognized that well-known songs and recordings stimulate box office sales and have seen the necessity for a bridge between filmmakers, the music community, the studios and the soundtrack record labels. Soundtrack singles/downloads are routinely released in advance of a picture so that its opening coincides with demand created by the record label's marketing efforts and the studio's film advertising, which are coordinated to maximize public awareness of the film and its music (the classic example is the Bee Gees' "Staying Alive" from *Saturday Night Fever)*. Music supervisors have varying degrees of involvement in the music that is commissioned or selected for films. The extent of their job is defined by how the filmmakers perceive their own abilities as music experts and how "connected" the music supervisor is in the contemporary music world. Music supervisors are almost never delegated decision-making authority, but instead gather and present choices to the filmmakers.

Some music supervisors offer only creative services (e.g., suggesting possible songs and artists or producing records). Others provide primarily business or sales services (e.g., publishing administration, music clearance, soundtrack placement, music production coordination). The studio's music business affairs department, or the filmmaker's music counsel usually handles business affairs (i.e., deal making and documentation). Although film music is a diverse and specialized field, virtually anyone who has ever worked in the music business may offer their services as a music supervisor. Consequently, competence varies greatly. Because the market has an excess of prospective music supervisors, most practitioners are not engaged in such services on an exclusive, full-time basis.

The main concern of the filmmaking team is whether the choice of a song and artist will enhance the dramatic and commercial impact of their picture. They cast the songwriters and performers as they would any theatrical talent, by subjectively evaluating whether the writer's or act's musical contribution will enhance the look, feel and profit of their picture.

Budgets

Major studios usually stick with top pop writers whose songs have sold millions of records and have had successful chart histories. On independent motion pictures, however, producers have less financing available and they use less recognized writers and artists that have not had hit records. Accordingly, they pay less.

Exhibit 1 compares what major studios and independent producers typically spend. The bottom line is that independent producers pay less up-front money than the major studios. Major studios are frequently tied in with labels that own national branch distribution systems and they invest far greater sums than nonmajors in promoting their films and music. Back-end revenue potential is therefore usually higher at major studios.

Even studios that defer to the creative choices of filmmakers must approve the writer/performer deal because of the large investment. The studio intends to protect its multimillion-dollar investment, of which music is an important, but relatively minor, part. Average production budgets of major studios are around $60 million and can reach $200 to $250 million for "tent poles" (big budget films with large advertising budgets that are released during peak Christmas and summer seasons); exploitation budgets (principally ads) average $36 million and can exceed $100 million on tent poles. Music budgets usually range from 2% to 5% of the film budget.

The most pervasive myth regarding songs that are written for soundtracks is that in some cases the studio makes more money from the music than from distribution of the film. Although it has been true that an unsuccessful film has spawned a successful album *(FM* with music by Steely Dan), the authors are unaware of any case in which a film generated less money to a studio than did the film music. In contrast to this myth, there are some basic truths. One is that ultimately major studios view film music, except in the rarest cases (perhaps *Flashdance),* as a less-than-integral part of the film and more of a promotional tool and ancillary market for the film. If a teenager has $10 to spend for entertainment and has a choice between seeing a film or buying the soundtrack album, the studio would much rather the money be spent on a theater ticket. The studio can expect to receive approximately half of the $10 spent at the theater but is lucky if it nets 30¢ to 50¢ from the sale of a CD and even less from a download.

The studio protects its investment by insisting that broad exploitation rights be obtained in the song and the recording. A studio's incentives for acquiring all rights to songs and recordings include (1) complete freedom of use and exploitation (including royalty-free use in other studio productions) without consultation, approval or further payment; (2) optimum duration of copyright ownership; (3) avoidance of third-party claims and controls; (4) actual profit from music revenues; (5) increased cash flow; and (6) the building of a publishing catalog as a perennial, liquid and salable asset.

Limiting the Studio's Investment: Spec Writing Deals

Studios and filmmakers like to have the opportunity to choose songs that are not specifically commissioned and that require no guaranteed up-front payment. There is quite a lot of speculative songwriting for film soundtracks. By speculative we mean songs that are written or reworked for the film and submitted for consideration without the studio being committed to use or pay for the song. If the studio likes the song, a deal is negotiated. Some songwriters will not write spec songs since their time is valuable and they consider it an insult to their artistic integrity to be asked to write a song without a financial commitment. On the other hand, many songwriters are happy to have their song considered in this manner.

A variation of spec writing is the so-called songwriter's step or option deal. This means there will be an intermediate step after the song is written but before it is used in the film when the studio can decline to proceed further by not making further payment for the song. For example, in a step deal the studio may pay the songwriter $5,000 for a song to be written and demoed. If the studio approves the song and synchronizes it in the movie, the writer receives another $20,000.

Probably the most contentious point on step deals is whether or not the writer gets back rights to rejected songs and under what conditions. Although the usual outcome is that the songwriter keeps the rights, studios may take the position that they will return the song provided it is subject to a lien for recovery of the amount the studio has invested. In the example above, if the studio were to reject the song and the song reverted to the songwriter, and it was subsequently exploited, the studio would receive the first $5,000. A variation of this is that the studio may retain a continuing financial participation in the publisher's share of music income, irrespective of recoupment of its investment. Alternatively, the writer may buy back the rights by reimbursing the studio for its out-of-pocket costs.

STUDIO/RECORD LABEL DEAL

The studio, as owner of the soundtrack album rights, makes the basic arrangement for the production and distribution of the soundtrack with the label. If we assume a contemporary soundtrack, rather than an orchestral one, the following delineate the basic issues.

Advances

Advances typically reflect record companies' perceptions of anticipated sales in the domestic territory and can range from a nominal amount to, in extraordinary cases, $1 million or more. What makes the negotiations difficult is that soundtrack albums are usually one-shots, and the label cannot recover losses from subsequent product like they can do for an artist with a multirecord deal. Another difficulty is that typically the final music choices have not yet been made. A graduated scale may be created to remedy this, e.g., $150,000 with an additional $50,000 per platinum-certified artist and $25,000 per gold-certified artist, with a cap of $300,000.

Royalty Rate

Royalty rate negotiation is very similar to that for a normal recording contract. The range for a basic royalty is 10% to 20% of retail. The studio hopes to maintain a minimum royalty override in the 4% to 6% range; thus, in a 16% of retail deal, 10% to 12% of royalty would be available to third-party recording artists.

Product

The record company is going to want to know what they are buying. Also, the record company would prefer a contemporary soundtrack with higher sales potential rather than an orchestral soundtrack, although in many cases the two are combined.

Promotion Fund

Oftentimes the record company will look to the studio to put up a matching fund for promotion of the soundtrack CD under the theory that both the studio and the record company will profit.

Singles

The releasing label will always want separate singles/download rights. The singles/downloads are used as promotional tools to sell the CDs, which is where the real money is. If singles/downloads rights are not available, the record company will probably cut its advance.

Guaranteed Release

Studios will often insist that as long as the necessary materials are delivered on time, the record company will be required to release the CD no later than the theatrical release of the film.

Ownership

The studio will continue to own the underlying musical compositions and the sound recordings as embodied in the film. The record company will want to assert ownership over the sound recordings as embodied in records. The record company will want worldwide rights. Split territory deals with major labels are rare but not unprecedented.

ARTIST VIEWPOINT: PREEXISTING AGREEMENTS

The following are major concerns when a studio approaches you to write and perform a soundtrack song. The threshold issue is whether you can grant the rights in the song and the recording that the studio requires.

Preexisting Term Songwriter's Agreement

If you are signed to a term songwriting deal, the publisher has the exclusive right to your songwriting services during the term and owns and administers the songs you compose or cowrite during the term, subject to paying the usually inviolate writer's share of music income. However, studios have music publishing holdings too. In these agreements, administration means the management of the copyright for purposes of collection and distribution of income. Like other music publishers, studios often insist on copyright ownership and administration of the song, and they normally retain all or part of the publisher's share of music income. Usually any conflict of rights between the songwriter's publisher and the studio is settled during initial discussions. In some cases, the studio's publishing arm and the songwriter's publisher will split the publisher's share of music income between the writer's publisher and the studio.

In order to avoid potential publisher/studio conflict and to freely shop their songs for soundtracks, a very few established writers have negotiated a fixed number of songs per year that are excluded from their exclusive term songwriting deal. If you are not signed to a term songwriting deal, have negotiated an exclusion or have already reached the maximum number of songs required under the term songwriting deal, you are free to work out whatever arrangements you desire with the studio.

If you do not have a lot of clout, the studio will end up owning and administering the song, and you will be entitled to approximately 50% of the income generated from the song as the writer's share, plus whatever nonrecoupable creative fee is negotiated (the studio will grant itself a free synchronization license in connection with the use of the song in the film and in-home video devices, so you will receive no further synchronization income from these sources). Studios typically insist on free synchronization licenses for product based on the initial film, such as remakes, sequels and television programs that they produce or distribute and even for totally unrelated properties that they produce or distribute. However, the writer retains the writer's share of public performance income.

Preexisting Recording Agreement

If you are signed to a term or multiple album recording contract, the label typically has the right to your exclusive recording services during the term for master recordings and phonorecords (e.g., vinyl records, cassettes, CDs and DVDs). Recording contracts usually define phonorecords as including "sight and sound devices," so unless you are the rare superstar artist who has a soundtrack exclusion (i.e., a provision excluding soundtrack recordings from the record deal), the label must grant a waiver of its services exclusivity for theatrical synchronization, home video and phonorecords.

Record companies are understandably jealous of the services of their artists. Major record companies can invest $1 million or more to break in a new recording act. It is estimated that on average, minimum sales of 300,000 CD units are necessary for a major label to break even on a typical artist investment. Such costs include advances and royalties to artists, producers and production companies; recording costs; manufacturing and distribution; marketing, including record promotion and advertising; mechanical licenses; video clip production; general overhead; legal expenses; salaries; taxes; product returns; etc.

In order to receive a return on their investments, some record companies insist on an override royalty (a royalty in addition to or to be deducted from the recording artist's royalty) from the studio as a condition to granting permission for the artist's soundtrack services. For example, if your deal with the studio is a basic album royalty of 10% of retail prorated, and you have two of ten cuts on a soundtrack album, the label may ask for a 1% override on your 2% of retail royalty. Your royalty will be about 20¢ per CD, and the label's royalty will be about 10¢ per CD.

Most studios, however, insist that the artist and the label work out the royalty arrangement between themselves. Some labels may require a 75% (artist)/25% (label) split of the prorated royalty for the sales of soundtrack records. The label retains its share and either credits the artist's royalty account or pays the 75% directly to the artist. For an illustration, see Exhibit 2. Also, just as major studios are music publishers, some major studios have record company divisions. Universal (Universal Records) is the leading example.

In some cases, major labels insist that the entire royalty (and even part or all of the artist's up-front cash creative fee) be paid directly to them for their services exclusivity waiver, especially if the artist's royalty account is unrecouped. However, the artist more typically keeps the creative fee from the studio, which is deemed a fee for motion picture services rather than a recording advance.

RECORDING ARTIST AND STUDIO ISSUES

Assuming the artist and label make their arrangement, the next step is to sort out the soundtrack recording issues between the record company and its artist and the studio. These issues follow.

Marketing Fund

This is a guaranteed fund to be spent by the studio (and perhaps a matching amount by the label) to promote the soundtrack album and singles, the aggregate of which can be $100,000 to $500,000.

Video Ownership

Regardless of the investment issue, both studios and labels compete for music video ownership. The studio wants to control the exploitation of the video, especially in conjunction with marketing the film, although promotion of the video is often a joint effort by the label and studio. Because of uncertainty about the impact of commercial exploitation under union agreements, studios rarely give record companies rights, other than for promotional use, if the video contains film clips and they try to limit the promotional use to the period when the film is in active distribution.

Singles/Download Rights

The principal issue centers on prohibition of release of the recording as a single/download by any label other than the artist's label. Since the label distributing the soundtrack CD wants to use singles and downloads as a selling tool for the CD, retention of singles rights by the artist's nondistributing label can diminish the attractiveness of the CD to the distributing label. Additionally, the studio is anxious to use the single and downloads to promote the theatrical release of the film. This noncompetition restriction allows the artist and the label to reap full benefit by ensuring that a potential single and downloads used in a film are included on, and stimulate the sale of, the artist's own album, rather than a soundtrack album containing other artist's recordings that yields a prorated royalty to each.

THE ARTIST/STUDIO DEAL: MAJOR POINTS

The following is a list of the major deal issues that will be discussed between artist's counsel and the studio that commissions a song and record. Exhibit 1 provides a comparison on typical deals for major studios and independents.

Cash Creative Fee

Compensation for writing and recording can be structured either as a cash creative fee, not including recording costs, or an all-inclusive recording fund that includes writing, performing, producing and recording costs. Writing fees per song range from a nominal amount for an unknown writer to $50,000 to $100,000 for a superstar's work. Recording fees are in the range of $10,000 to $50,000 per track for major performers.

If the deal is structured as a recording fund, the studio will pay a flat sum for delivery of the song and master, with the artist being responsible for all recording costs and keeping any balance as the creative fee. The all-in fee per song for a top writer/performer ranges from $100,000 to $250,000 and for a midlevel writer/performer from $50,000 to $100,000. New acts may receive $10,000 to $25,000. The all-in structure is an inducement for the artist to limit recording costs and caps the studio's investment. However, the studio has no contractual assurance the money is being allocated judiciously. Problems sometimes arise when the studio is dissatisfied with the song or recording and asks the artist to rework it. Recording fund deals are particularly attractive to acts that own recording studios and computer-based music technology, since they can keep recording costs down.

Song Royalties

The writer's share of royalties for songwriting services is negotiated the same as with a nonfilm song agreement, i.e., the writer basically receives 50% of the income, except for sheet music, which typically generates 8¢ to 12¢ per piano copy and 10% to 12.5% of wholesale for nonpiano copies. The writer may seek to guarantee a full statutory mechanical rate for the soundtrack CD or single (currently 9.1¢ per song). Most studios resist guaranteeing a full mechanical rate since the label will seek to limit the mechanical rate for CDs to 10 times 75% of statutory, which comes to 68.25¢ per CD, and for singles to 75% of statutory for each side.

If you have a lot of clout or are signed exclusively to a publisher, you may be able to structure a copublishing agreement in which song ownership and administration are shared. This allows the artist to participate in a percentage of the publisher's share of music income. Independent producers typically pay less up-front money and do not have affiliated music publishing arms, and they are more likely than major studios to agree to grant a participation in the publisher's share. Assuming a fifty-fifty participation arrangement, the artist will receive approximately 75% of the total music income (the full writer's share and half of the publisher's share).

The split of copyright known as copublishing is considerably less common than financial participation in the publisher's share of income. In participation deals, the participant has little or no control over the use or exploitation of the copyright. Major writers/performers receive a participation in the publisher's share of income that ranges up to 50%.

Also, the publisher's share of income that is subject to participation is reducible if the studio or its music publishing arm charges an administration fee on income, if collected. For example, if there were a 15% administration fee, the publisher's net share would be reduced to about 42.5% of the total income derived from the song.

In extraordinary cases, superstars that both write and perform have been able to keep both copyright ownership (and administration) and all of the publisher's share of music publishing income, subject always to a free synchronization license to the studio for use of the song in the film and home video devices.

Major writers/artists are much more likely to share in publishing revenue than writers that do not perform their own material, since successful artists are perceived to add great promotional value to the song and the film. However, to the extent the artist participates in the publisher's share of income, the up-front cash fee may decline correspondingly, because the studio is forgoing all or a portion of the publisher's share of income from which it hopes to recover its investment and make some profit. However, for superstars, studios have a hard time reducing the cash creative fee, even if the publisher's share is relinquished or split.

Record Royalties

Record royalties, like music royalties, are negotiated much in the same manner as a normal recording agreement. However, there are a few points that are particularly important in soundtrack agreements.

Studios usually insist that the artist royalty be all-in, i.e., inclusive of all others that might be entitled to royalties with respect to the artist's recording, such as the record producer and the artist's label.

The royalty is usually subject to two forms of proration. First, it will be prorated for length, either by playing time or more typically by number of cuts. For example, if you have two out of the 10 cuts on the CD, and receive a prorated 10% of retail royalty, your basic royalty will be .2 x 10% (2%). Second, the royalty is prorated by the number of artists on the cut. For example, if on the cuts the act performs together with a second recording act, the act's royalty will be cut in half, .5 x .2 x 10% (1%).

CD Override

Heavyweight artists ask for a CD override, e.g., an additional 2% on the entire CD, regardless of proration. This may be fair when the soundtrack CD consists of filler that does not sell CDs or promote the film.

Royalty Allocation

Studios try to keep the aggregate artist royalties in check so they retain an appropriate net portion of the overall royalty from the soundtrack CD. For example, if the studio gets 16% of retail from the record company, they may allocate 10% to 12% to all royalty participants, retaining 4% to 6% for themselves. One way the studios try to contain royalties is to give the same royalty deal to every artist, e.g., 10% to 12% prorated.

Singles

The artists that anticipate release of their master as an A-side single may try to insulate themselves from royalty reduction for the B-side of the single to assure a full single record royalty. Singles royalties are not as heavily negotiated as CD royalties.

Recoupment

Smart artist representatives insist that the only recording costs the studio or label can recoup from the artist royalty account before royalties are paid are those paid solely in connection with the soundtrack CD, as opposed to the picture, since the studio pays recording costs whether or not there is a soundtrack CD. These nonpicture recording costs are called "soundtrack conversion costs" and usually include guild new use fees and occasionally, remixing. This point can have a major financial impact on the artist royalty. If not limited to nonpicture costs, the artist royalty account could be charged with film-related recording costs. For example, if the act's royalty is 10% of retail prorated on a cut, and they have one cut of ten, the royalty per CD sold would be .1 x 10%, or 1% of retail (about 10¢ per CD). If the label sells 100,000 CD units, the artist's royalty account would be credited with $10,000. To the extent the studio recoups soundtrack conversion costs, they are deducted from the royalty. Recoupment of recording creative fees from the artist's royalty account is negotiable. New acts often have their creative fee recouped from their royalties; established acts face this less often.

Song and Master Ownership

The studio's attitude is "we own what we pay for." The studio will insist on acquiring the song and master recording copyrights as works made for hire. As discussed above, superstars may occasionally succeed in sharing ownership and administration of the song and master recording. Artists' ownership of master recordings may be allowed in rare cases when a superstar's recording services are furnished by their own production companies.

Use of Master on Artist's Label

An act may succeed in getting a license from the studio for use of the master recording on the act's own records. The master might then be released both on the soundtrack CD and on the artist's CD. As a condition to granting the license, the studio may ask for an override royalty from the artist's label on CDs embodying the master. In any event, the studio will insist that any release of such master by the artist's label not compete with the studio's soundtrack CD by conditioning the licensing grant on a holdback from release. This mostly applies from four to twelve months after release of the soundtrack CD, so that the record-buying public associates the soundtrack song and master with the film and is motivated to buy the soundtrack CD. Studios are finding it more difficult, at least with major acts, to negotiate a holdback on the release of the master on the artist's home label.

Approval of Record Producer

Many established acts produce themselves or insist on using a record producer they approve. Studios rarely try to interfere with the artist's producer selection or the artist/producer creative relationship, especially if the deal is the typical recording fund deal, which makes the artist responsible for the producer's compensation. However, if the studio pays the producer's cash advance or royalty separately, they insist on approving the producer deal.

Credits

As long as the song is used in the film, most studios will agree to give an "end title" screen credit in the form of "[Song Title], written by [Artist], performed by [Artist]." Sometimes credit in the form of, "courtesy of [Label]" is accorded the artist's record company. Only rarely does an artist receive main title credit (where the writer, director, producer and other major creative elements get credit).

Paid ad credits that promote the film, e.g., credits in newspapers, magazines and the like, are usually not granted to writers/performers by major studios, except for main title songs or when the prestige of the soundtrack artist is considered a significant marketing benefit. Independent producers tend to grant paid ad credits to writers/performers more frequently than major studios.

Record jacket credit is a different matter. Studios rarely refuse to give the recording act credit on the jackets of soundtrack CDs since this is a selling tool. Sometimes, if there are multiple recording artists, all the acts get credit in alphabetical order. In contrast to the normal competition among actors, directors, and producers for large and prominent credit, the act and label may try to keep the credit small so the soundtrack CD does not look like it is the act's own CD, which might compete with and thereby diminish sales of the act's own records. This makes sense because the act receives the entire royalty on their own CDs (subject to recoupment of recording costs by the label) and, if they write, they receive the mechanical royalties on the entire CD (always the writer's share and sometimes a portion of the publisher's share).

Additional Artist/Studio Deal Points

One issue to consider is that the studio will also insist on a provision whereby they are not obligated to use the song or the recording (whether in the film, soundtrack CD or as a single), although they may have to pay whether or not they use the song. From the studio perspective, the filmmaking team must be allowed the freedom to add and subtract songs and recordings during the editing process. In some instances the artist will be paid whether or not their work is actually used. If the artist is not paid, the song and recording usually revert to the artist.

Also, since music videos are an important selling tool, studios normally insist that the act provide music video services, usually at no additional cost or at minimum union scale. MTV prefers concept videos to film-clip-only videos.

Finally, songwriters and soundtrack performers that do not perform onscreen are never granted a participation in the nonmusic receipts of a film. These participations are usually divided between the actors, director, producers and the studio. However, music artists have a distinct advantage as to the payment of royalties—they do not have to wait until the studio earns back its investment before songwriter royalties are paid. The same is true for artist royalties from the soundtrack CD. Usually, only relatively minimal nonpicture soundtrack conversion costs are recouped before the artist is paid for record sales.

INCOME

Let us assume you make a deal at a major film studio. You are a writer/performer/producer who writes a title song and records a title song master. You are paid $25,000 for the song and $25,000 to record. You retain the writer's share but the studio retains the publisher's share. You receive a royalty of 12% of 130% of the wholesale price in the U.S., prorated, on CDs. Depending on the record company, you might be paid on less than all of units sold (e.g., 85%), but we have not assumed that here. Your master is three minutes long. The picture is a blockbuster. Your recording hits number one on *Billboard's* Hot 100 Chart. The soundtrack CD, on which you have one of the ten cuts, sells 500,000 copies in the United States and 375,000 copies overseas. Exhibit 3 gives you an idea of what your earnings might be.

CONCLUSION

The writing and recording of songs for films involves complex financial and business arrangements with studios, record labels and music publishers. The advantages to both new and established songwriters and recording acts in participating in soundtracks are numerous. The song and its recording may be exposed to millions of people, it may be included in the soundtrack album, and, in the best case, be released as a single and MTV video. The downside is that the artist has very little, if any, input as to how the song is used in the film. You may write and record a beautiful four-minute ballad that is blared from a radio for only a few seconds, but that is the risk you take.

The most important advice to a new writer or recording act, however, is to not play prima donna if approached by a studio to work on a soundtrack. Only major acts have this luxury. Your goal should be to get the song considered and accepted. Nonestablished writers/performers should not expect the same sort of terms that Paul McCartney gets. Do not blow the deal. Once you get your foot in the door and make a positive contribution to a soundtrack, you will have taken a substantial step in your writing and performing careers.

EXHIBIT 1
TYPICAL MUSIC ACQUISITION PRACTICES FOR EACH COMMISSIONED SONG

	MAJOR STUDIOS	INDEPENDENT PRODUCERS
Songwriter's fee	up to $100,000	zero to $10,000
Participation in publisher's share of income	zero to 50%	zero to 100%
Writer/Artist recognition level	Major label (recently signed) to superstar	Unsigned to recognized label artists
Artist's fee (off-camera)	$10,000 to $100,000	zero to $15,000
Recording budget	$25,000 to $100,000	$500 to $10,000
Copyright proprietor (occasionally writer)	Major studio	Independent producer
Artist's & producer's soundtrack royalty (subject to proration)	12% to 14% (foreign reduced)	6% to 12% (foreign reduced)
Copyright administrator	Major studio	Outside publisher
Music producer's fee (if negotiated separately)	$10,000 to $25,000	None (usually artist or supervisor produced)

EXHIBIT 2
ARTIST'S ROYALTY STATEMENT

Sales for original soundtrack of *Century City Blues* cat. no. 14899

Statement Date: September 30, 200_

Country of Sale: United States

Period of Sales: Second-Half 200_

Release Date: April 5, 200_

Distributing Label: Megabite Records, Inc.

Film Company Behemoth Studios, Inc.

PRORATA PER UNIT

Configuration	Pkg. Deduct	SRLP	Royalty	Share	Royalty	Sales	Earnings
CD singles	25%	4.98	8%	4 on 4	.29880	2,500	$747
CD album	25%	15.98	10%	2 on 10	.23970	1,000,000	$239,700

Gross Earnings This Period	$240,447
Less Soundtrack Conversion	($6,000)
Total Payable This Period	**$234,447**

$175,835.25 remittance to artist (75%) enclosed

$58,611.75 remittance to artist's label (25%)

EXHIBIT 3
ROUGH INCOME SUMMARY

The following rough income summary is designed to alert you to sources of income rather than to provide exact figures. Digital downloads will eventually replace physical product.

A. WRITER

1. Writing Fee (nonrecoupable)	$25,000
2. Song Synchronization License For Film	0
3. Performance Income (worldwide)	
(a) From Film In Theaters	
(i) United States	0
(ii) Foreign	$20,000
(b) Radio Performances	$100,000
(c) Home Video	0
(d) Pay TV	$3,000
(e) Free TV	
(i) U.S. Network TV (two runs)	$4,000
(ii) U.S. Syndicated TV (two runs 150 stations)	$1,500
(iii) Foreign	$5,000
4. Sheet Music (40,000 copies @ 10¢/copy)	$4,000
5. Mechanicals	
(a) United States (75% of statutory)	
(i) CD (500,000 x 6.825¢)	$34,125
(b) Foreign	
(i) CD (375,000 x 10¢)	$37,500
Total	**$234,125**

B. RECORDING ARTIST

1. Recording Fee (nonrecoupable)	$25,000
2. Master License For Film	0
3. United States Record Sales	
(a) CDs (500,000 x 9.8802¢)	$49,401
4. Foreign Record Sales	
(a) CDs (375,000 copies x 7.26¢)	$27,225
Less Soundtrack Conversion Costs	($3,000)
Total	**$98,626**

Managers, Agents and Unions

WHAT A MANAGER DOES

**ANALYSIS OF A PERSONAL
MANAGEMENT AGREEMENT**

BUSINESS MANAGERS

**TALENT AGENTS: NEW THINKING
ON AN OLD BUSINESS**

CLUB CONTRACTS

MUSIC UNIONS

What a Manager Does

BY ALFRED SCHLESINGER

Let us say you are an artist who says to a prospective manager, "OK, I'm a talent, this is what I look like, here is what I do. Are you interested?" And the manager says, "Yes!"

First, your manager will probably say to you, "Look, all of our energies have to go toward getting a record contract. Anything else we do is avoiding the main issue. You are not going to make it, you are not going to become a star, you will not make good money and nothing monumental will happen to you as a musical performer without a record. Let's get a record contract!"

This is still true in the era of the Internet, inasmuch as you have to look upon Internet sites as retail stores. It is quite simple to have your own Web site, as well as a number of links. But in order to have someone choose your record and have it move off the Internet "shelf," as opposed to the many thousands of others offered on the Internet, the demand for your record must be created by extensive promotion and marketing. That is where the record company machinery is needed.

WHAT TO LOOK FOR IN A MANAGER

The manager, whether an individual or a company, must have honesty and integrity, knowledge and capability. If any one of these attributes is missing, the manager will not be effective.

Your manager represents, advises and works for you. This person or organization handles all of your day-to-day business while you create, and for that receives a percentage of your earnings. If you make money, your manager makes money. If not, your manager will have spent an awful lot of time and effort for nothing.

When considering managers, check out their reputations. People have reputations because they have earned them. Nobody can be liked by everybody, but if a person is spoken of as being genuine and honest, you can assume this is probably true.

However, a good reputation means nothing unless there is a trust and good feeling between artist and manager. I do not see how anyone can have a personal manager they dislike.

The manager's enthusiasm and belief in you are essential for a successful relationship. A manager cannot and should not represent you if he or she does not understand your motives, priorities, beliefs, way of life, and what is important to you.

The personality of the manager must be considered. Some managers can break down doors (literally and figuratively), scream, holler, demand and be very effective. Some artists like that, others might want someone more laid back. The object is to enable the artist to write, rehearse and perform; to create with a free and clear mind. The idea is not, however, to remove artists from business entirely, but rather to free them from the nitty-gritty work-a-day affairs. Artists should know what is going on with their careers and be familiar with the agent, record company personnel, business manager, attorney, public relations people, and whoever else has a hand in their success or failure. Managing an artist is a difficult, time consuming job; artists choosing to do it for themselves will have great difficulty finding time to create music and run their business.

THE MANAGER'S ROLE

A manager provides knowledge, judgment and objectivity in the following key areas:

Record Companies

It is a manager's job to know the record companies and the people at those companies. It is up to the manager to know the strengths and weaknesses of each company and whether a company is right for his or her artist. Some companies do extremely well in one genre of music and are unsuccessful in others. Since distribution is of primary importance, the manager will normally look for a deal with a major record company (one that has its own distribution branches), an affiliate of a major, or an independent record company distributed by a major. (Another option is to sign with an independent record company that is distributed by a successful national distributor.)

The record companies usually want to hear a tape of the artist performing three or four songs, as well as see the artist perform live before they will consider signing that artist. It is up to the manager to make sure that the demo tape shows the artist's direction and makes a statement about the artist's music. The manager also has to make sure that the artist's live performance will grab an audience. Since touring is the best promotion for an artist's album, and there is a definite correlation between touring and record sales, the record company will normally not sign an artist unless the live performance will greatly help record sales.

Once the record deal has been made, the manager will often play an important role in the selection of the producer. The manager will also be heavily involved in the artwork that is going to be part of the package. Artwork is critical to the artist, as it portrays the image of the artist in an "image" business. The album artwork is also used in advertising, as poster art and on all types of merchandise, such as T-shirts and jackets. Prior to the release of an album, and until the album has run its course, the manager will be in constant contact with the promotion and marketing departments of the record company and the distribution branches to make certain his or her artist is being properly promoted and marketed.

Scheduling

It is important for a manager to help schedule an artist's life by structuring recording and performing contracts appropriately. Some performers want to schedule 16 months of activity into a year. There is no way that can be done. A manager has to help the artist plan ahead, sometimes a year or more at a time. Time should be set aside for creative activity, vacation, recording and for touring. To help do that, the manager has to be very sensitive to the artist's habits and needs. For example, if the artist is a songwriter, the manager must realize that songs take a certain amount of time to produce. It is difficult for some artists to write songs while recording, while on the road or on vacation. It is important to set aside enough time out of the year for this kind of creativity.

Recording Habits

A manager must understand the artist's recording habits and should know how long a recording is likely to take. Some artists can spend two days at a recording studio and come out with 10 tracks for a flawless, marvelous album. Others will take up to 18 months in the studio. One of the most devastating things that can happen to a recording artist is having a manager obtain a very heavy commitment from a record company to release a certain number of albums in a short period of time when the artist cannot handle that many albums or that kind of pressure. That contract can wind up lasting for most of the recording artist's professional life.

For example, you could be committed to deliver one album a year for seven years. If it takes 18 months to deliver each album, you could actually be under contract to that record company for more than 10 years.

Objectivity

One reason artists need help in all these areas is that they often lack objectivity. The manager provides objectivity.

Most people in the business are reasonably sensitive. They will never tell an artist, "I hated your last album, it stunk." A record company executive may sugarcoat remarks to an artist, but will level with the manager. Then it is the job of the manager to get the story across to the artist.

The artist who deals directly with this sort of feedback from a record company is making a serious error. Show business is an image business. A great deal of time, effort and money is spent to create the artist's image. It can be very damaging to an artist to do battle. The artist should always be the hero. The manager should always be the scapegoat. If, as sometimes happens, bad feeling is created, the artist should never suffer by it.

THE RECORDING TEAM

The manager's role in the successful negotiation of a recording contract is only the beginning. With the signing of the contract, the manager becomes the captain of an incredibly varied team of people, both inside and outside of the record company. Managers work with these people on behalf of artists.

Record Company

The most important of all the relationships an artist maintains (after his or her personal manager) is with the record company. It can be the artist's best friend or worst enemy. If the record company is not with the artist all the way, the artist's career is definitely going to suffer delays and setbacks.

A manager has to have a lot of insight concerning the people within the record company. It is important to keep them friendly and committed to furthering the artist's career.

If the president of the record company is behind a record, that album has a much greater chance of "happening." A manager must have access to the top people and be able to gain their support.

Artist Relations

The artist relations person, a creative, very important member of the team, takes the artist's part and stands up for the artist in the company (even though that person is employed by the company). The artist relations person introduces the artist and manager to other employees in the record company and acts as a general communications liaison and information resource.

Promotion Representative

The national promotion representative does all the long-distance calling to the key top-40 radio markets and has a feel for what is happening in the field. Remember, airplay is absolutely essential for success.

Sales and Marketing

The head of sales and marketing helps choose the sales tools that supplement live performances and airplay. These tools range from store displays and merchandising accessories to ads in Sunday supplements, co-op deals with leading record dealers, radio time, etc.

Relationships should be maintained with local sales and promotion representatives that can help get that important extra push.

At the appropriate time, the manager will want to work with the person in charge of international sales and promotion to help set up foreign tours and release records in other countries.

RECORD RELEASES

Normally, an album is released within 90 to 120 days after delivery of the master recordings, plus all of the information (such as writers, publishers and length of each recording), album credits (such as name of producer(s), engineer(s), musicians, vocalists, studios where the album was recorded and mixed) and personal "thanks" (such as to a manager, attorney, accountant, family members, friends and inspirational third parties). Neither the manager nor the record company will want an album of a new artist released after September, since it normally takes several months for an album to build, both at radio and retail. Once Thanksgiving arrives, the building process usually comes to a halt, and any momentum gained can be blunted during the Christmas season, when radio adds fewer records to its playlist and retailers want to concentrate their efforts on the hits of major artists. The airwaves and retailers' shelves are crowded with Christmas music. Traditionally, the "heavy" albums are released when kids are going back to school and at the beginning of the year. But except for the months of October through December, an album can be released any time of the year.

Some managers will want their artist's album to be released at the same time the record company releases albums by a number of their major artists, hoping to be carried along with the tide. Most managers, however, look for that small window when their artist's album will be the only one to be released for a period of time, so the record company can concentrate their promotional and marketing efforts on it.

With respect to "singles" or album "tracks," managers' opinions differ. Some managers will urge the record company to release the first single of their new artist a number of weeks before the album, in order for the public to become somewhat familiar with the artist and also because the single may chart, either on radio playlists or on the *Billboard* or *Radio and Records (R&R)* charts. Other managers feel that it is a waste to have a single being played on radio without the listener being able to buy the album, so they will want a single released concurrent with the album. Still others feel that it is difficult for the manager or record company to determine which is the best single, so they allow radio program directors and disc jockeys to determine what the single will be by their decisions as to what to program.

TOURING

Touring by an artist is the record company's best way to promote that artist's album. The public may buy your first album based on the music alone, but after that they want to see your face, learn about you, and equate what they hear on the album with a live human being. Your manager should know what you can handle as far as touring is concerned and find a balance between sufficient touring and your other obligations. (It should be noted that a successful artist will tour overseas, and many artists earn more by playing dates in foreign countries, and have much longer careers overseas than in the United States.)

Managers differ on appropriate times to tour. Some managers want their artists to tour extensively, even without a record deal, feeling that the artist will be building a base of fans, as well as perfecting their live performance. Other managers will want an artist to begin touring immediately after the release of an album, to support that album. Still other managers will not be anxious to have their artist tour unless and until an album is either on the *Billboard* charts or showing some sales strength in some markets. If the manager wants the record company to help defray the cost of touring with so-called tour support (making up the deficit between what it costs to have an artist on tour and the small nightly fees that are normally commanded on a first tour), an album usually has to show signs of being a winner.

At the appropriate time, the manager will meet with the record company and the agent to help put a tour together. The record company can provide the manager with sales figures showing the markets in which the album is performing the best. The manager will work with the agent in putting a tour together that encompasses those markets. (On a first tour, the agent will include spots for the artist as an opening act for major record sellers, some small theaters, colleges and clubs.)

MANAGEMENT ORGANIZATIONS

There are one-person firms and small and large organizations. A one-person organization has its limitations because a manager cannot always be supported by one talent and probably will manage other clients. But a good manager will not take on more clients than can be served effectively.

Some management companies consist of more than one person with others working for them. Selecting a large company like this can be a mistake for a young performer. An artist might think, "John/Jane Doe who runs this organization is the heaviest manager in the business and I'm going to get Doe's personal attention." Usually this does not happen. They get the services of someone who works for the firm instead of those of the top person. This is not necessarily bad if the right relationship is established with this person, and the muscle of a large organization is behind the artist.

But if you sign a contract thinking that Ms. A will be representing you, only to find after six months or so that you are dealing with Mr. B, you should be able to terminate the contract.

Again, it depends on feelings. Many performers enter the offices of a large organization and immediately turn and walk out. They do not feel comfortable and do not want to get involved with a machine, no matter how well oiled.

MANAGEMENT CONTRACTS

If something is important to you, get it in the contract. If a manager will not put a provision in writing, then the manager probably has no intention of living up to it.

Term of Contract

Management contracts vary in term from one to five years. What is important here is for the artist to decide what goals should be reached and in what time frame. Some contracts state that if the artist does not have a recording contract in one year, he or she can terminate; another might require two network variety performances in the first year. If the manager agrees, those terms should be put into the contract. It is also quite common to gear the term of the contract to a number of album cycles. An album cycle is defined as "an album release and all touring in support of that album." Some agreements will have a term of two album cycles, others will be three. Some may grant the manager an option for one additional album cycle and others may grant two. The length of an album cycle is usually between one and two years. One yardstick in determining the end of a cycle is when an artist commences recording the next album.

The artist should understand that a manager needs a fair length of time to help an artist towards success. It sometimes takes two years or more before an artist starts to make any real money. It would be unfair for a hardworking, honest and reasonably effective manager to be terminated at the end of a year after laying the groundwork and not be around to collect the rewards. Artists must be realistic about the time in which they can expect to reach their goals.

Unfortunately, there are rarely outs in contracts for someone who no longer loves their manager. Personal relationships are so important, yet quite hard to define on paper. It is very difficult to frame a contract that states, "Notwithstanding the fact that we have a five-year contract, if at any time during that contract I don't like you, I can terminate."

Power of Attorney

In standard management contracts, managers are given a blanket power of attorney, meaning that they can sign and approve anything regarding the artist's career without the consent or knowledge of the artist. Certainly, artists should work to limit that power if they are available to sign; or at least specify the circumstances under which the manager has that power, e.g., not being able to sign for engagements longer than a certain period of time or for a certain amount of money. At the very least, artists can have clauses requiring consultation and approval, if only verbal, before the manager signs anything on their behalf.

Normally, a manager makes day-to-day decisions, but leaves major ones open for discussion and consultation. But artist and manager should develop a modus operandi, and an understanding of what can be done without consultation.

Percentages and Expenses

Manager percentages usually fall between 15% and 20%, although there are exceptions. For instance, a manager who invests large sums of money in an artist, at a risk, might receive 25%.

In standard contracts, the manager is not specifically obligated to advance or lend money, but many artists expect it. If a manager does advance money, the artist must repay it.

Sometimes a manager is excluded from receiving percentage commissions on publishing, songwriting or monies from ASCAP, BMI or recording, etc. My feeling is that managers promote all their artists' causes and, if you limit their income, you may find it detrimental in the long run.

Costs incurred on behalf of the artist by the manager (other than normal overhead) should be paid by the artist. These include travel, phone calls, publicity photographs, etc.

Many artists include clauses in their management contracts limiting the circumstances and amounts that a manager can spend without their consent.

CONCLUSION

The results of a manager's efforts are not realized in days or weeks, they accumulate over a period of years.

The manager's job is multifaceted: administrator, friend, salesperson, employer, negotiator and advisor. In any one day the manager may need to effectively communicate with a record company president, road manager, lead guitarist's girlfriend, lawyer, journalist, disc jockey, record producer, food caterer, etc.

Finding a competent, knowledgeable manager at the beginning of an artist's career, when he or she is most needed, is extremely difficult. Many professional managers are reluctant to sign a band until it has achieved some success in the marketplace, such as a large draw in a major city or a contract with an independent record label. Therefore, many new bands must manage themselves, sharing the tasks, until they can attract a professional manager.

All bands should enter into a written agreement among themselves when they get together as a band. Among the many elements contained in such an agreement is a provision that normally appoints a band member to act as the leader of, and spokesperson for, the band. That spokesperson is basically a quasi-manager who arranges for the band to do whatever is necessary to get a record deal, including making a tape to submit to record companies and making sure the band gives dynamite live performances. Certain other matters a band must consider are whether to attempt to obtain a publishing deal, a merchandise agreement, endorsements and the like. It can take quite a while before a band can hook up with the right manager, as it is often as difficult to obtain a good manager as it is to obtain a record deal.

Today's manager has an opportunity to be more creative than at any time in the past. It is a new music business and while the record deal, sales through traditional retail stores and performances in clubs, theaters, colleges and arenas still play a dominant role in the career of an artist, the manager has to guide the artist through a maze of new opportunities:

- Advances in Internet technology allow heretofore unheard of opportunity for record sales.

- The iPod and the downloading of iTunes play an increasingly important role in selling and promoting music.

- Mobile technology and the availability of music on cell phones (singles, albums, ringtones and ringbacks) are coming into their own.

- Tours of bookstore chains (such as Borders) can play an important role in promoting records in the early stages of careers.

- Performances in Indian casinos and private corporate events offer substantial livelihoods for artists whose mainstream careers may be on the wane.

- Cable and satellite television offer hundreds of channels. Many create original feature films and new series and the chances of getting songs and records exposed on them are on the increase.

Managers have to be on the cutting edge of these happenings and help create opportunities for their artists as never before.

Analysis of a Personal Management Agreement

BY NEVILLE L. JOHNSON AND BERNARD M. RESNICK

It is often necessary, albeit difficult, for musicians to find good personal managers. Many new artists and "baby bands" have difficulty figuring out the right time to hire a manager, and who is the right person to fill the management role. Finding a manager with a lot of motivation (but little or no experience) is easy, but such a manager may not have the requisite contacts or reputation to do much good for the artist. Established managers rarely want to work with new artists, which makes it difficult for the artist to attract a high-caliber manager. Artists want to be a high priority for their professional advisors. The difficulty for baby bands is that established managers must spend much of their time minding the business of already-established roster of clients, which gives them little time to expend on a new group. Artists may have to decide between being a big fish in a little pond or vice versa.

Personal managers serve as supervisors and coordinators of the business and career activities of professional entertainers. They act as liaison with those that do business with artists. Depending on the needs of their clients, personal managers must motivate, direct, guide, counsel, market, make demands and advise. Managers are involved in such issues as which employment to seek and accept, creation and coordination of their clients' public mystiques and images, and the marketing and promotion of artists' careers. In most instances, communications with agents, attorneys, business managers, publicists, record companies and music publishers are routed through personal managers.

Many artists are unwilling or unable to devote the time necessary to supervise and coordinate the many services required from those that build and maintain their careers. Virtually all successful recording artists have personal managers, as do many record producers and songwriters.

Some personal managers invest money, in addition to time, into the acts they represent. Their profession is risky and often costly.

Personal managers are generally considered to be independent contractors, which means they operate independent businesses separate from the talent they manage. However, they operate in a fiduciary capacity to the artist.

A fiduciary is one in whom a special trust is placed and who, consequently, owes special duties to the client. Like attorneys and accountants, personal managers must

INDUSTRY TRADE ORGANIZATIONS

Personal managers have been poorly organized as far as being an effective lobbying group. There are three industry trade groups that a manager should consider joining for networking and educational purposes.

Music Managers Forum (MMF)

The MMF was formed to further the interests of managers and their artists in the music industry, which includes the areas of live performance, recording, endorsements/merchandising and music publishing.

The MMF provides a forum for the discussion of issues and problems that face music industry managers. The British association is quite active.

Music Managers Forum (United States)

(www.mmfus.com)
P.O. Box 444
Village Station
New York, NY 10014
(212) 213-8787

Music Managers Forum (United Kingdom)

(www.musicmanagersforum.co.uk)
British Music House
26 Berners Street
London, W1T 3LR
England
+44 (0) 870 8507 800

National Conference of Personal Managers (NCOPM)

The National Conference of Personal Managers (NCOPM) is an association committed to the advancement of personal managers and their clients. Established in 1942, NCOPM members have vast experience and expertise in concerts, motion pictures, publishing, radio, recordings, television and theatre. There are only a few music personal managers in this organization, but there is an abundance of those that represent actors. Its membership is mostly on the East Coast.

National Conference of Personal Managers

(www.ncopm.com)
Eastern Division - Executive Director
Daniel Abrahamson
330 West 38th Street
Suite 904
New York, NY 10018
(212) 245-2063

Western Division - Executive Director
Candee Barshop
1440 Beaumont Avenue
Suite A2-360
Beaumont, CA 92223
(310) 492-5983

Talent Managers Association, Inc. (TMA)

The Talent Managers Association (TMA) was founded in 1991 and grew out of the National Conference of Personal Managers and then broke away. The TMA provides guidance for talent managers and supports ethical business standards and practices. It provides educational programs and services. The TMA is self-regulating and is dedicated to raising the standards of the profession of talent management. Its members represent actors for the most part.

Talent Managers Association

(www.talentmanagers.org)
4804 Laurel Canyon Boulevard
Suite 611
Valley Village, CA 91607
(310) 205-8495

subordinate their own interests to those of their clients. The client's best interests always come first: There must at all times be complete disclosure of all material information and no side-dealing of any nature, and no secret profits. Thus, the artist is always boss—but has usually engaged the manager because of his or her superior knowledge of, and capabilities in, the business arena, as well as the manager's dependability and trustworthiness.

Personal managers are the eyes and ears of their clients and must disclose completely all business dealings involving them. They must never obtain an unfair economic advantage with respect to their clients; exercise no undue influence over their affairs; and always operate with the highest standards of good faith and fair dealing. Personal managers must always use their best efforts to see that their clients have independent advice when necessary, as in, for example, a conflict of interest situation where a manager seeks to be an employer or partner with a client and thus may be biased when giving advice. To prevent such bias personal managers should retain their own attorneys to consult with, which in turn helps better serve the needs of their clients. Sometimes the same attorney will represent the artist and the manager when the management agreement is negotiated. In such instances, the parties will sign a "conflict of interest" waiver. Though legal, we do not recommend that an artist or manager agree to let the same lawyer act on behalf of both. It is safer for all parties, including the lawyer, to see that each party has counsel or has been afforded the right to counsel.

The personal manager relationship is the business equivalent of a marriage. It must be entered into with sobriety, intelligence and forethought. Successful artists understand, appreciate and supervise the myriad duties of their personal managers. They understand and fulfill their own obligations in those relationships. Many artists incorrectly perceive that a manager will be the answer to all of their problems; and that the appointment of a manager will allow them to abdicate any knowledge of their business affairs. Nothing can be more dangerous to an artist's financial affairs than to be so lazy as to willfully ignore his or her own business. Successful artists know the ins and outs of their business deals; discuss them at length with management and empower management to carry out their wishes. Doing business any other way can seriously hamper an artist's goals of financial success and independence.

In recent years, due to mergers between multinational corporations, there has been a great reduction in the number of major record companies. This naturally means that the number of available record deals for managers to shop for their artist clients has been significantly reduced. Additionally, the proliferation of illegal file sharing and digital download sites has reduced legitimate sales of recordings, putting further pressure on the major record companies. The end result is that many artists that would have been eligible for major record deals in years past have either been passed over for deal consideration or even dropped from major label rosters. As if writing, recording and performing music were not enough to do, artists must now set up their own Internet Web sites to promote themselves; and more often than not artists must also sign up with digital companies in order to sell their music directly to the public. With increasing regularity, artists are demanding that their managers handle this on their behalf.

Managers of today thus find themselves acting like record companies in earlier eras, as they are placed in charge of sales of music on behalf of their artist clients. Additionally, since the reduction of record deals has created a wealth of independent artists, managers need to hustle on behalf of their clients to create additional income.

One such source of additional income for artists is in the arena of endorsements and merchandising. Good managers maximize their artist clients' income by making T-shirt (and other licensed merchandise) deals; finding placements for the artists' music in films, television programs, video games, commercial advertising, etc.; and finding other creative methods to supplement artists' income.

MANAGERS AT PERIL

Although the personal manager is the chief executive responsible for the promotion and marketing of the artist, procuring of labor for a musician can be a difficult and treacherous area for all personal managers that operate in California. (The other state where procurement of labor is a problem is New York.) California's Labor Code sections 1700–1700.47, called the Talent Agencies Act, regulate the offer, promise, procurement or attempted procurement of employment for entertainers. There has been much controversy about this law over the years. Except with respect to the procurement of recording agreements or acting directly under the supervision of a licensed agent, personal managers are not allowed to so act without a state license giving them permission to operate as a talent agency. Most personal managers have refused to obtain such licenses because of various state rules and union regulations. For example, the American Federation of Television and Radio Artists (AFTRA), which is an actors union, allows union members to terminate agency agreements if work is not secured within a specified period of time. Many managers cannot operate within these strictures. There have been sporadic attempts over the last 25 years to produce a workable arrangement that is satisfactory to all parties, but the matter has yet to be resolved and it is unlikely that it ever will. A personal manager may not solicit a live engagement or any other engagement (except a record deal) for an entertainer unless he or she possesses a talent agency license. The main difficulty between the law and reality is that the law restricts managers from doing the core tasks that most artists need them to do! Early in the artist-management relationship, many artists are perfectly willing to turn a blind eye to their managers' actions that are outside of those allowed by law. However, when a dispute arises between artist and manager, resulting in the artist wanting to terminate the management agreement, artists generally have no reservation with empowering their attorney to allege that the manager violated this law. Most talent agencies and established personal managers are not interested in musical acts that do not have record agreements with major labels. Thus, personal managers that represent talent in that position are effectively required to seek such employment and deal with offers that come in, but they may be violating state law if they do so. Even if the manager takes no commission, his conduct is unlawful. Personal managers are allowed to solicit recording agreements, but without the opportunity to solicit live engagements to secure showcases and build the act, they are hamstrung.

Be forewarned! We have seen many cases where managers were unceremoniously fired once a deal was obtained and a "heavy" manager was willing to come on board. Do not count on loyalty if you are a manager. Very few managers have found it to exist. For example, the former manager of The Deftones alleged in a lawsuit that he was fired

CONTINUED ON NEXT PAGE

CONTINUED FROM PREVIOUS PAGE

by the band even though he had fought for them when they were playing to empty clubs and successfully solicited a major recording contract. The A&R executive who signed the band wanted a different manager for The Deftones. The former manager could not collect any money from the group and lost the lawsuit because the group successfully argued that notwithstanding his hard work, he had violated the California Talent Agencies Act by obtaining live engagements for them when no talent agent would consider booking them, even though he took no commission. *(Park v. Deftones*, 71 Cal. App. 4th 1465 [1999].) Similar stories abound with artists such as Green Day, Aerosmith and countless others. The actress, Connie Stevens, was permitted to walk out of her management agreement in *Styne v. Stevens,* 26 Cal. 4th 42 (2001) because her manager had solicited work. Another manager on the losing end involving a former member of The Platters is found in *Yoo v. Robi,* 126 Cal. App. 4th 1089 (2005).

As this book goes to press, the California Supreme Court is deciding *Marathon Entertainment v. Blasi.* In this case, a manager engaged in unlicensed talent agent activities by obtaining engagements for his artist. The court of appeal ruled he was still permitted to recover commissions from the portion of the contract that was lawfully performed based on the legal theory of contract "severability." The manager provided professional and personal advice and other services that are not regulated by the Talent Agencies Act, so the court was willing to "sever" the contract and permit recovery for these lawful activities.

New York law allows managers to book if they do so incidentally, as just a small part of the overall managerial services. Any manager who has an act that can maintain a claim under the Talent Agencies Act in California is vulnerable, so beware if you are an out-of-state manager and seek employment for your acts in the Golden State. Despite the recent development in the *Marathon* case, it is still best to be licensed in California if you plan on performing any talent agent related activities. Remember the other moral of the case of The Deftones: loyalty in the entertainment business is virtually nonexistent. Managers must watch their backs at all times.

PERSONAL MANAGEMENT AGREEMENT

1. TERM

Manager is hereby engaged as Artist's exclusive personal manager and advisor. The agreement shall continue for three (3) years (hereinafter the "initial term") from the date thereof, and shall be renewed for one (1) year periods (hereinafter "renewal period[s]") automatically unless either party shall give written notice of termination to the other not later than thirty (30) days prior to the expiration of the initial term or the then current renewal period, as applicable, subject to the terms and conditions hereof.

Many personal management agreements have a short, initial term of one to three years, although some can last up to five years, at the manager's discretion. Since a manager's earnings are on a percentage/commission basis, managers (not artists) have the option to renew the agreement for up to six years. A deal that a manager obtains for an artist may take several years to become profitable. Therefore, the theory is that if the manager plants the seeds for the artist, the manager should be around to reap the harvest. Artists sometimes insert provisions that provide for a minimum of earnings that the artist must earn during the period before any option period may be exercised. Most personal management agreements with newer acts provide that if a recording agreement is not secured within a period of up to 18 months after commencement of the term, then either party may terminate the management agreement. What "secured" means should be specified.

If the personal manager is in negotiation with a record company but a recording agreement has not actually been signed, the agreement should not be terminated if the material terms of an agreement have been negotiated and agreed upon. Additionally, the artist could be prohibited from signing to such label for an additional period of time after the end of the term of the personal management agreement, or would otherwise have to pay a management commission.

2. SERVICES

(a) Manager agrees during the term thereof, to guide, advise, counsel and assist Artist in connection with all matters relating to Artist's career in all branches of the entertainment industry, including, without limitation, the following:

   (i) in the selection of literary, artistic and musical material;
   (ii) with respect to matters pertaining to publicity, promotion, public relations and advertising;
   (iii) with respect to the adoption of proper formats for the presentation of Artist's artistic talents and in determination of the proper style, mood, setting, business and characterization in keeping with Artist's talents;
   (iv) in the selection of artistic talent to assist, accompany or embellish Artist's artistic presentation, with regard to general practices in the entertainment industries;
   (v) with respect to such matters as Manager may have knowledge concerning compensation and privileges extended for similar artistic values;
   (vi) with respect to agreements, documents and contracts for Artist's services, talents, and/or artistic, literary and musical materials, or otherwise;
   (vii) with respect to the selection, supervision and coordination of those persons, firms and corporations that may counsel, advise, procure employment,

or otherwise render services to or on behalf of Artist, such as accountants, attorneys, business managers, publicists and talent agents; and

(b) Manager shall be required only to render reasonable services, which are called for by this Agreement as and when reasonably requested by Artist. Manager shall not be required to travel or meet with Artist at any particular place or places, except in Manager's sole discretion and following arrangements for cost and expenses of such travel, such arrangements to be mutually agreed upon by Artist and Manager.

(c) Notwithstanding anything to the contrary contained in this Agreement, Manager's commission in respect of Gross Income generated in connection with commissionable products or services which is received *after* the term hereof shall be as follows:

1. Fifteen percent (15%) during the first year following the end of the Term;
2. Ten percent (10%) during the second year following the end of the Term;
3. Five percent (5%) during the third year following the end of the Term;
4. Three percent (3%) during the fourth year following the end of the Term; and
5. Zero percent (0%) after the expiration of the fourth year following the end of the Term.

The foregoing details what services managers provide to artists. Travel requirements should be negotiated on a case-by-case basis. An artist might resist paying for travel and long-distance phone charges when the manager chooses to live in a location remote from the residence of the artist. Travel should be necessary and the cost reasonable. An artist may also require an allocation of costs if the manager, when traveling, does other business unrelated to the artist.

As far as "guidance, advice and counsel," although it is a vague job description, this is as far as most agreements go. Further, it is difficult to articulate the efforts that may be required.

Some artists find it frustrating that the manager's obligations are so vaguely defined. There is no reason why an artist cannot require the manager to specify in further detail the services required. For example, artists could require their managers not to represent a certain number of other acts and require their manager to meet with them in person, on a regular basis, to create or present strategies and goals for the artist. An artist should require that all material information about his or her business be provided as soon as it is obtained or learned.

There should be a specific provision where the manager acknowledges that a fiduciary relationship (one of special trust) exists. An artist should never agree that no such relationship exists.

What are the obligations of the manager after the term of the agreement? One of our cases involves a manager who claims to own music publishing rights of the artist. We had to sue him to get him to turn over all documents relating to the same. Thus, the artist should insert provisions that require the manager to keep the artist informed at all times of all activities of the manager and of all rights in which the manager claims an interest, and certainly upon request of the artist or the artist's representative. It is also common to insert a "sunset clause," known also as a "post-term compensation" clause, into management agreements. The sunset clause discusses and defines the manager's commission AFTER the end of the contract for deals which artist enters into DURING the contract. For the manager, the clause encourages the manager to continue to seek deals for the artist up to the end of the agreement, as there is a chance for compensation afterwards. For the artist, the sunset clause allows the artist to afford to hire and pay a new manager, while preventing a lag in deals (and income therefrom) as the end of the original management contract approaches.

3. AUTHORITY OF MANAGER

Manager is hereby appointed Artist's exclusive, true and lawful attorney-in-fact, to do any or all of the following, for or on behalf of Artist, during the term of this Agreement:

(a) approve and authorize any and all publicity and advertising, subject to Artist's previous approval;

Artists will want to have written approval; managers will want a reasonable time for approval, such as 72 hours after delivery to the artist.

(b) approve and authorize the use of Artist's name, photograph, likeness, voice, sound effects, caricatures, and literary, artistic and musical materials for the purpose of advertising any and all products and services, subject to Artist's previous approval;

(c) execute in Artist's name, American Federation of Musicians contracts for Artist's personal appearances as a live entertainer, subject to Artist's previous consent to the material terms thereof; and

(d) without in any way limiting the foregoing, generally do, execute and perform any other act, deed, matter or thing whatsoever, that ought to be done on behalf of the Artist by a personal manager.

The key words "subject to Artist's written approval" should be inserted at the end of subparagraph 3(d), though managers would balk at the "written" aspect as being too restricting and impractical, but in this age of faxes and e-mails, there is no reason why the artist should not approve and supervise the manager in all aspects. However, the manager should not be micromanaged. It is a team effort and trust is an integral aspect of the relationship and each must be allowed to perform his or her job without too much interference. An artist will usually want to delete any clause that gives the manager the right to execute agreements on behalf of the artist. The intelligent artist always supervises and understands his contractual relations. Too much control—and the possibility of abuse—reside in any manager that has unchecked freedom to bind the artist.

Managers should only be appointed to execute AFM agreements as noted in subparagraph 3(c) and only when the artist is not reasonably available to do so.

4. COMMISSIONS

(a) Since the nature and extent of the success or failure of Artist's career cannot be predetermined, it is the desire of the parties hereto that Manager's compensation shall be determined in such a manner as will permit Manager to accept the risk of failure as well as the benefit of Artist's success. Therefore, as compensation for Manager's services, Artist shall pay Manager, throughout the full term hereof, as when received by Artist, the following percentages of Artist's gross earnings (hereinafter referred to as the "Commission"):

(i) Fifteen percent (15%) of Artist's gross earnings received in connection with

Artist providing their services as a recording artist for the recording of master recordings to be manufactured and marketed as phonograph records and tapes during the term hereof. Manager shall receive said Commission in perpetuity on the sale of those master recordings recorded during the term hereof. In no event shall the term "gross earnings" be deemed to include payments to third parties (which are not owned or controlled substantially or entirely by Artist), in connection with the recordings of master recordings prior to or during the term hereof;

Managers in the music business usually take a 15% to 25% commission of an artist's earnings. The specific amount of commission depends on the relative strength of the parties to the negotiation. If a new manager is being hired to represent an established artist who already has achieved significant sales and success, the lower commission percentage is appropriate. If on the other hand a baby band is hiring an established manager and wishes the manager to use not only her contacts and reputation but her financial resources to assist the artist, the higher commission percentage is appropriate.

(ii) Fifteen percent (15%) of the Artist's gross earnings from live performances;

The artist should seek to, and generally does, limit the manager's compensation on live engagements to the artist's "net" derived from such engagements, i.e., after the deductions of travel, lights and other out-of-pocket payments that an artist makes to third parties, including agents and musicians.

(iii) Fifteen percent (15%) of the Artist's gross earnings derived from any and all of Artist's activities in connection with music publishing, or the licensing or assignment of any compositions composed by Artist alone or in collaboration with others (it being understood that no commissions shall be taken with respect to any compositions that are the subject of any separate music publishing agreement between Artist and Manager).

Some managers seek to administer the compositions of their artists and/or take a higher percentage from music publishing royalties. Although nothing is inherently wrong with such practices, the personal manager will be subjected to extra scrutiny as to the fairness of the agreements if the artist has no independent advice or unless the circumstances otherwise dictate that the arrangement is fair. Publishing can be very lucrative and it is something the artist should usually maintain for him or herself. Managers have been sued for abusing publishing rights. See Parsons. v. Tickner, 31 Cal. App. 4th 1513 (1995). See discussion after paragraph 12.

(b) The term "gross earnings" as used herein shall mean and include any and all gross monies or other consideration which Artist may receive, acquire, become entitled to, or which may be payable to Artist, or on Artist's behalf, directly or indirectly (without any exclusion or deduction) as a result of Artist's activities in the music industry, whether as a performer, writer, singer, musician, composer, publisher, or artist.

Note that virtually all aspects of entertainment are covered. Artists can and do limit the authority of a manager and his or her compensation in certain areas. This must be decided on a case-by-case basis. For example, if an artist has a thriving jingle or soundtrack business or is an established actor, then the artist may desire to exclude these areas from the manager's commission. Further, the manager will want to ensure that "other consideration" includes stock and any other inducements that may be offered to the artist. If the artist is offered the opportunity to participate in deals, then the manager should have a pro rata right to likewise participate.

(c) Manager shall be entitled to receive his full commission as provided herein in perpetuity on Artist's gross earnings derived from any agreements entered into during the term of this agreement, notwithstanding the prior termination of this agreement for any reason. Artist also agrees to pay Manager the commission following the term hereof upon and with respect to all of Artist's gross earnings received after the expiration of the term hereof but derived from any and all employments, engagements, contracts, agreements and activities, negotiated, entered into, commenced or performed during the term hereof relating to any of the foregoing, and upon any and all extensions, renewals and substitutions thereof and therefore, and upon any resumptions of such employments, engagements, contracts, agreements and activities which may have been discontinued during the term hereof and resumed within one (1) year thereafter;

This is a tricky area. In the music business, many personal managers are limited to a commission derived from activities performed during the term of the agreement, and not with respect to activities performed after the personal management agreement but pursuant to agreements that were entered into during the term of the management agreement. For example, should the manager get a commission on records recorded after the management term pursuant to a record deal entered into during the term? There are two views. The manager will argue that if he or she is responsible for building up the career of the artist, the fruits of the manager's labor should be enjoyed for as long as that "contractual tree" bears fruit and it would not be fair to build up an artist's career over a five-album period, so that the artist was about to "break" on a major scale, only to be excised from the deal on the next album when the artist achieves major success. The artist will attempt to limit the compensation to only employment activity by the artist rendered to third parties during the term of the management agreement. Artists will argue that they will be forced to pay two commissions: one to the previous manager and one to a new manager, which would be unduly onerous. Moreover, what if the failure to achieve success theretofore was in some part the manager's fault? Possible compromises are a reduced percentage for the manager, an override that extends for a limited period, or that the parties will negotiate a fee or override at the end of the term, and if they cannot agree, a third party can decide a fair buyout.

There was major litigation and a trial in 1994 over the relationship between the personal manager of blues-great Willie Dixon and his estate. The personal manager helped Dixon obtain reversions of various copyrights and was paid up to a third of the revenue stream earned from various compositions, all written before the commencement of the personal management agreement. Such work is generally outside the traditional artist-manager relationship, but if the contract is not specific enough, the personal manager might be entitled to share in such revenues.

Some managers are so heavy, they operate without written agreements. We recommend against any oral agreements. It can be very difficult to establish and prove an oral contract in a court of law.

"Negotiated" could use more definition, and most times the parties will agree that this include that the material (basic) terms have been agreed upon and the final contract is executed within 90 days after the expiration of the term of the management agreement.

(d) Manager is hereby authorized to receive, on Artist's behalf, all "gross monies and other considerations" and to deposit all such funds into a separate trust account in a bank or savings and loan association. Manager shall have the right to withdraw from such account all expenses and commissions to which Manager is entitled hereunder and shall remit the balance to Artist or as Artist shall direct. Notwithstanding the foregoing, Artist may, at any time, require all "gross monies or other considerations" to be paid to a third party, provided that such party shall irrevocably be directed in writing to pay Manager all expenses and commissions due hereunder.

This is a subject near and dear to both parties. The manager wants to be assured of getting paid; the artist needs to be sure of a fair count. In the early days of a career, when there is little to be made, most managers collect and disburse revenue. Any artist who becomes successful should have an accountant or business manager to supervise the financial activities of the artist. The artist must have the absolute right to audit the books of the manager at reasonable intervals.

It is also a good idea to have the manager acknowledge there is a fiduciary relationship to the artist, particularly with respect to the financial aspects of the relationship. (The penalties are much stronger for one who violates a fiduciary relationship, as opposed to a mere contractual relationship. If a fiduciary breaches a relationship, punitive or exemplary damages may be claimed—they may not in an ordinary breach of contract situation. Most managers, however, will balk at such a provision, even though that is the true nature of the agreement.)

(e) The term "gross monies or other considerations" as used herein shall include, without limitation, salaries, earnings, fees, royalties, gifts, bonuses, share of profit and other participations, shares of stock, partnership interests, percentages music related income, earned or received directly or indirectly by Artist or Artist's heirs, executors, administrators or assigns, or by any other person, firm or corporation on Artist's behalf. Should Artist be required to make any payment for such interest, Manager will pay Manager's percentage share of such payment, unless Manager elects not to acquire Manager's percentage thereof.

Sometimes artists are offered deals that, for example, would include a stock purchase at a reduced price in return for services. The manager may want to—and should have the right to—get in on the deal.

5. LOANS AND ADVANCES
Manager will make loans or advances to Artist or for Artist's account and incur some expenses on Artist's behalf for the furtherance of Artist's career in amounts to be determined solely by Manager in Manager's best, good faith business judgment. Artist

hereby authorizes Manager to recoup and retain the amount of any such loans, advances and/or expenses, including, without limitation, transportation and living expenses while traveling, promotion and publicity expenses, and all other reasonable and necessary expenses, from any sums Manager may receive on behalf of Artist. Artist shall reimburse Manager for any expenses incurred by Manager on behalf of Artist, including, without limitation, long-distance calls, travel expenses, messenger services, and postage and delivery costs. Notwithstanding the foregoing, no travel expenses and no single expense in excess of two hundred fifty dollars ($250.00) shall be incurred by Manager without the prior approval of Artist. Manager shall provide Artist with monthly statements of all expenses incurred hereunder and Manager shall be reimbursed by Artist within fourteen (14) days of receipt by Artist of any such statement. Notwithstanding the foregoing, any loans, advances or payment of expenses by Manager hereunder shall not be recoupable by Manager hereunder until Artist has earned revenue in the entertainment industry and there is sufficient such revenue to so recoup, repay and compensate Manager without causing Artist hardship or leaving insufficient funds for Artist to pursue his career.

> *This is another area of controversy. The artist must be careful to see that the manager is not sending them to the poorhouse. A cap on expenses, such as $250 per transaction is the best type of insurance. It does cost money to promote and further the career of an artist, however, so it makes sense that managers should be reimbursed for their out-of-pocket expenses incurred on behalf of an artist. Most publicists, attorneys, accountants and business managers charge and obtain reimbursement for out-of-pocket expenses.*

6. NONEXCLUSIVITY

Manager's services hereunder are not exclusive. Manager shall at all times be free to perform the same or similar services for others, as well as to engage in any and all other business activities.

> *The artist may wish to insert a clause that guarantees that the manager will have sufficient time to devote to the career of the artist or a "key-person" clause that guarantees that the manager, not some employee, will be primarily rendering day-to-day services to and on behalf of the artist may be inserted instead.*

7. ARTIST'S CAREER

Artist agrees at all times to pursue Artist's career in a manner consistent with Artist's values, goals, philosophy and disposition and to do all things necessary and desirable to promote such career and earnings therefrom. Artist shall at all times utilize proper theatrical and other employment agencies to obtain engagements and employment for Artist. Artist shall consult with Manager regarding all offers of employment and inquiries concerning Artist's services. Artist shall not, without Manager's prior written approval, engage any other person, firm or corporation to render any services of the kind required of Manager hereunder or which Manager is permitted to perform hereunder.

> *The manager/artist relationship is built on trust and mutual agreement. All major decisions should be mutually agreed upon, especially concerning those who will work closely with the manager and artist.*

8. ADVERTISING

During the term hereof, Manager shall have the exclusive right to advertise and publicize Manager as Artist's personal manager and representative with respect to the music industry.

Managers have businesses too, which may benefit from promotion. Artists will want to approve any advertising or publicity in which their names are used.

9. AGENT

Artist understands that Manager is not licensed as a "talent agency" and that this agreement shall remain, in full force and effect subject to any applicable regulations established by the Labor Commissioner of California, and Artist agrees to modify this agreement to the extent necessary to comply with any such laws.

See the sidebar, Managers at Peril regarding this subject.

10. ENTIRE AGREEMENT

This constitutes the entire agreement between Artist and Manager relating to the subject matter hereof. This agreement shall be subject to and construed in accordance with the laws of the State of California applicable to agreements entered into and fully performed therein. A waiver by either party hereto or a breach of any provision herein shall not be deemed a waiver of any subsequent breach, nor a permanent modification of such provision. Each party acknowledges that no statement, promise or inducement has been made to such party, except as expressly provided for herein. This agreement may not be changed or modified, or any covenant or provision hereof waived, except by an agreement in writing, signed by the party against whom enforcement of the change, modification or waiver is sought. As used in this agreement, the word "Artist" shall include any corporation owned (partially or wholly) or controlled (directly or indirectly) by Artist, and Artist agrees to cause any such corporation to enter into an agreement with Manager on the same terms and conditions contained herein.

11. LEGALITY

Nothing contained in this agreement shall be construed to require the commission of any act contrary to law. Whenever there is any conflict between any provision of this agreement and any material law, contrary to which the parties have no legal right to contract, the latter shall prevail, but in such event the provisions of this agreement affected shall be curtailed and restricted only to the extent necessary to bring them within such legal requirements, and only during the time such conflict exists.

12. CONFLICTING INTERESTS

From time to time during the term of this agreement, acting alone or in association with others, Manager may package an entertainment program in which the Artist is employed as an artist, or Manager may act as the entrepreneur or promoter of an entertainment program in which Artist is employed by Manager or Manager may employ Artist in connection with the production of phonograph records, or as a songwriter, composer or arranger. Such activity on Manager's part shall not be deemed to be a breach of this agreement or of Manager's obligations and duties to Artist. However, Manager shall not be entitled to the commission in connection with any gross earnings derived by Artist from any employment or agreement whereunder Artist is employed by Manager, or by the firm, person or corporation represented by Manager as the package agent for the entertainment program in which Artist is so employed; and Manager shall not be entitled to the commission in connection with any gross earnings derived by Artist from the sale, license or grant of any literary rights to Manager or any person, firm or corporation owned or controlled by Manager. Nothing in this agreement shall be construed to excuse Artist from the payment of the commission upon gross earnings derived by Artist from Artist's employment or sale, license or grant of rights in connection with any entertainment program, phonograph record, or other matter, merely because Manager is also employed in connection therewith as a producer, director, conductor or in some other management or supervisory capacity, but not as Artist's employer, grantee or licensee.

Many managers also act as producers or packagers of television shows and live concerts or operate production companies, record companies or music publishing companies. For this reason, a manager might be in a partnership with a client, or the employer of a client. There is nothing inherently wrong with this, but because the manager may have control in excess of that ordinarily granted to them in the management agreement, or greater compensations than ordinarily would be paid in his or her capacity as manager, it is incumbent upon the manager to insure that the artist is provided for fairly. First, the manager should not obtain "double commissions"; that is, a fee and percentage as a producer or employer, in addition to a management commission from the artist from the same activity for which the manager is compensated as an employer or partner. Actor/comedian Garry Shandling was embroiled in ugly litigation with his personal manager, Brad Grey, in 1999, over the manager's participation as a manager and producer in the television show in which Shandling starred. Shandling claimed various conflicts of interests incurred by Grey, including that he favored himself in various deals emanating therefrom.

Second, an independent third party should negotiate the artist's participation. Sometimes, the artist and manager will have the same attorney. This kind of situation can create conflicts so artists should hire their own attorneys. Further, the manager exposes himself to risk if he does not see to it that his client has independent counsel.

ARTIST UNDERSTANDS THAT THIS IS AN IMPORTANT LEGAL DOCUMENT PURSUANT TO WHICH PRODUCER GRANTS TO MANAGER CERTAIN RIGHTS FOR A PERIOD OF YEARS SPECIFIED HEREIN. ARTIST HEREBY REPRESENTS AND WARRANTS THAT SHE OR HE HAS BEEN ADVISED OF HER OR HIS RIGHT TO RETAIN INDEPENDENT LEGAL COUNSEL IN CONNECTION WITH THE NEGOTIATION AND EXECUTION OF THIS AGREEMENT, AND THAT ARTIST HAS EITHER RETAINED AND HAS BEEN REPRESENTED BY SUCH LEGAL COUNSEL OR HAS KNOWINGLY AND VOLUNTARILY WAIVED HER OR HIS RIGHT TO SUCH LEGAL COUNSEL AND DESIRES TO ENTER INTO THIS AGREEMENT WITHOUT THE BENEFIT OF INDEPENDENT LEGAL REPRESENTATION. ARTIST FURTHER ACKNOWLEDGES THAT SHE OR HE HAS READ THE TERMS AND CONDITIONS OF THIS AGREEMENT AND THAT SHE OR HE BELIEVES THAT IT IS IN HER OR HIS BEST INTERESTS TO EXECUTE SAID AGREEMENT.

It is foolish for managers to try to act as employers and managers, as inherent conflicts of interest are created. Managers that sign artists to their own production companies and music publishing companies will have a hard time arguing that as artists' managers they fought hard for the artists against the managers' own interests. Clint Black was in a very expensive and unpleasant litigation in the mid-1990s over this very issue; the case ultimately settled.

In the last few years, we have been embroiled in several lawsuits concerning managers that claim to represent a "group" and take positions adverse to a particular member of that group, including even terminating a musician or partner/member. From an artist's perspective, this is very troubling—any artist should demand that any personal manager and any lawyer for the group not be allowed to take sides should such problems develop.

13. SCOPE

This agreement shall not be construed to create a partnership between the parties. Each party is acting hereunder as an independent contractor.

Manager may appoint or engage any other persons, firms or corporations, throughout the world, in Manager's discretion, to perform any of the services which Manager has agreed to perform hereunder except that Manager may delegate all of his duties only with Artist's written consent. Manager's services hereunder are not exclusive to Artist, and Manager shall at all times be free to perform the same or similar services for others as well as to engage in any and all other business activities. Manager shall only be required to render reasonable services that are provided for herein as and when reasonably requested by Artist. Manager shall not be deemed to be in breach of this agreement unless and until Artist shall first have given Manager written notice describing the exact service that Artist requires on Manager's part and then only if Manager is in fact required to render such services hereunder, and if Manager shall thereafter have failed for a period of thirty (30) consecutive days to commence the rendition of the particular service required.

This provision has important tax ramifications. It may be necessary for the artist to consult not only with an attorney, but also an accountant, prior to signing a management contract with such a provision to ensure that a true independent contractor is created so that the artist is not required to treat the manager as an employee for tax purposes, which would entail withholding income to comply with tax codes.

14. ASSIGNMENT

Manager shall have the right to assign this agreement and any and all of Manager's rights hereunder, or delegate any and all of Manager's duties to any individual, firm or corporation with the written approval of Artist, and this agreement shall inure to the benefit of Manager's successors and assigns, provided that Manager shall always be primarily responsible for rendering of managerial services, and may not delegate all of his duties without Artist's written consent. This agreement is personal to Artist, and Artist shall not assign this agreement or any portion thereof, and any such purported assignment shall be void.

The artist will want the manager to be always personally responsible and liable, notwithstanding any assignment or delegation of any rights and duties, and as noted previously, this responsibility can and should be provided. See also the discussion of key-man clauses earlier in this article.

15. NOTICES

All notices to be given to any of the parties hereto shall be addressed to the respective party at the applicable address as follows:

("Artist") _____ and _____ ("Manager")

All notices shall be in writing and shall be served by mail or telegraph, all charges prepaid. The date of mailing or of deposit in a telegraphy office, whichever shall be first, shall be deemed the date such notice is effective.

16. ARTIST'S WARRANTIES

Artist is over the age of eighteen, free to enter into this agreement, and has not heretofore made and will not hereafter enter into or accept any engagement, commitment or agreement with any person, firm or corporation which will, can or may interfere with the full and faithful performance by Artist of the covenants, terms and conditions of this agreement to be performed by Artist or interfere with Manager's full enjoyment of Manager's rights and privileges hereunder. Artist warrants that Artist has, as of the date hereof, no commitment, engagement or agreement requiring Artist to render services or preventing Artist from rendering services (including, but not limited to, restrictions on specific musical compositions) or respecting the disposition of any rights which Artist has or may hereafter acquire in any musical composition or creation, and acknowledges that Artist's talents and abilities are exceptional, extraordinary and unique, the loss of which cannot be compensated for by money.

17. ARBITRATION

In the event of any dispute under or relating to the terms of this agreement or any breach thereof, it is agreed that the same shall be submitted to arbitration by the American Arbitration Association in Los Angeles, California in accordance with the rules promulgated by said association and judgment upon any award rendered be entered in any court having jurisdiction thereof. Any arbitration shall be held in Los Angeles County, California. In the event of arbitration arising from or out of this agreement or the relationship of the parties created hereby, the trier thereof may award to any party any reasonable attorneys' fees and other costs incurred in connection therewith. Any litigation by Manager or Artist arising from or out of this agreement shall be brought in Los Angeles, County, California.

An alternative is the "Rent-a-Judge" program, a type of arbitration, which provides that controversies be heard by retired judges. Litigation via the courts is expensive and time consuming. A typical case in the Superior Court of California may take two to three years and cost hundreds of thousands of dollars. Arbitration or Rent-a-Judge is private, swift and generally less expensive than our court trial system, but many people do not like these programs because they believe that the best form of justice is that meted out in the court system, and there is no right to appeal an arbitration. It is a good idea to specify in the agreement what "discovery"—information and documents—can be obtained prior to the arbitration. Notwithstanding any arbitration clause, the Labor

Commissioner will have exclusive jurisdiction over any dispute where the Talent Agencies Act is alleged to have been violated.

IN WITNESS WHEREOF, the parties hereto have signed this agreement as of the date hereinabove set forth.

_____   _____
("ARTIST")   ("MANAGER")

Business Managers

BY MARGARET ROBLEY

Business managers oversee all financial aspects of their clients' lives. They take an active role in the collection of income, prepare budgets and monitor expenditures, actively participate in their clients' investment decisions, oversee insurance coverage, assist in the purchase and sale of assets, initiate and participate in estate planning and constantly monitor the tax consequences of all transactions. While accounting is universal for all businesses, business management, as described herein, is unique to the entertainment industry.

There are no credentials, licensing or educational requirements to become a business manager. Since the problems business managers deal with are very complex, most are certified public accountants (CPAs), attorneys or business people with varied financial backgrounds.

SELECTING A BUSINESS MANAGER

Artists usually do not engage business managers until after they have attained a certain level of monetary success in the music industry. Until that time, accountants can be hired on an hourly basis to prepare tax returns and for advice on tax and business matters.

When searching for business managers, artists should ask colleagues and advisors for referrals and check out the firms (i.e., professional references, etc.) before setting up appointments. It is very important for business managers to have experience in dealing with music clients and the expertise to handle any specific problems or situations that artists have. Artists should consider interviewing small local companies and international accounting firms, which have worldwide networks of services available, before deciding which is best for their specific needs. Artists should feel comfortable and have good rapport with their business managers. It is very important that artists be able to communicate openly and easily with their business management team. Normally, engagement letters are the only contracts between artists and business managers, so good personal relationships are very important and it is imperative that all parties feel free to sever their relationships at any time.

Business managers are generally the last members added to management teams, and artists should consult with the other members of their team (i.e., personal manager, talent agent and attorney) before engaging one, as it is crucial that they all work together cohesively.

DUTIES OF BUSINESS MANAGERS

Business managers perform many functions in overseeing the financial affairs of their clients. A synopsis of some of these functions follows.

Bookkeeping and Collection of Income

In business management firms, the bookkeepers and account managers (under the supervision of managers and partners) are responsible for reviewing invoices, verifying their validity and processing them for payment; preparing payroll checks for clients' employees; preparing incoming checks for deposit; and monitoring bank accounts to make sure there are sufficient funds to cover checks and clients' withdrawals from ATM machines and debit card transactions. Any excess funds that will be needed in the near future are transferred to short-term investments to earn interest.

Many artists have one or more contracts (i.e., recording, merchandising, product sponsorships, music downloading, telephone ringtones, publishing, various foreign subpublishing, etc.) that the business managers are responsible for monitoring to ensure that all contractual amounts are received. They must have monitoring systems that keep track of the various types of income due and the projected due dates. All receipts are verified to ensure that all income is received in a timely manner. If monies are not received when due, business managers pursue collection of delinquent amounts. They also monitor sales, music download information and advances to make sure that income is properly reported and paid and determine if artist royalties are being escalated properly and whether any cross-collateralization is contractually allowed.

When artists control their own publishing, the process of monitoring income becomes more difficult, as there may be many subpublishing deals and synchronization licenses for which to account. Business managers will maintain continuous income schedules to monitor the publishing and subpublishing royalties earned and will keep in close contact with the music publishing administrators to make sure that monies are received for all CD sales, music downloads and synchronization and mechanical licenses granted.

Financial Reporting

Most business management firms use computerized systems for bookkeeping that generate statements that show all cash receipts and disbursements, cash balances and financial statements that reflect monthly and cumulative year-to-date income and expense figures. The monthly financial statements are reviewed by the accountants that use them to prepare tax projections, budgets, annual meeting packages and special reports prior to presentation to their clients.

Based on projected income and conversations with their clients, business managers prepare budgets that reflect projected expenditures. Budgets include capital items (which may be a large portion of client spending) and their clients' personal discretionary spending—an area that is hard to control due to the ease of using debit and credit cards. Business managers prepare budgets for personal expenditures, but it is their clients that make the decision either to stay within those budgets and maintain long-term financial security or not. Periodically, budget-to-actual comparisons are prepared to show clients any discrepancies.

Tax Services and Estate Planning

Tax planning for clients is a constant process for business managers. This entails determining which type of entity (i.e., sole proprietorship, partnership, corporation,

S-corporation, limited liability company) is best; whether a pension plan or medical reimbursement plan is desirable; whether to buy or lease an automobile; which investment strategies to pursue; etc.

Business managers are responsible for tax compliance and prepare payroll tax, sales tax, gift tax, city or local tax and income tax returns for filing with the appropriate authorities. They represent clients in examinations by tax agencies, including the Internal Revenue Service. Since the establishment and enforcement of the Internal Revenue Service's e-filing requirement the number of examinations of tax returns has increased substantially.

Business managers interact with attorneys and other advisors in preparing estate and retirement plans for clients. They compile information on assets and liabilities and assemble information on future goals with an emphasis on financial security of their clients and their clients' beneficiaries. Once the life insurance trusts, living trusts, wills, and other estate planning vehicles are in place, business managers assist their clients in obtaining life insurance, which will pay any projected estate taxes.

Touring Services

Before artists agree to U.S. or foreign tours, their business managers work with their personal managers to project income and expenses. Touring can be an effective method of promoting artists' current recordings. Even though tour support is recoupable by record companies, tours may generate sufficient CD sales or music downloads to pay any excess costs and still be profitable to some artists. Business managers monitor income and expenditures, ensure that adequate insurance (including nonappearance insurance, if applicable) is in place, ensure compliance with multistate and foreign taxing authorities, prepare budgets, negotiate to minimize tax withholding in various states and overseas, review all third-party contracts, obtain social security clearances for applicable foreign countries, monitor budget-to-actual income and expense and resolve discrepancies, and prepare tax returns for all necessary jurisdictions.

The business management staff reviews tour settlements, and staff members or partners may accompany clients to assist in box office settlements with promoters and venues.

Insurance, Investments and Asset Administration

Adequate insurance coverage is a must to protect clients' long-range security. Business managers are responsible for ensuring that their clients have sufficient insurance coverage for employees, businesses, autos, real estate, to protect assets in case of lawsuits, cover medical bills, furnish income in case of disability and provide for their families in case of death.

Due to the Federal Deposit Insurance Corporation regulations and the low interest rates offered, a minimum amount of money should be kept in bank accounts. All excess cash should be invested.

Artists and business managers should jointly develop investment policies that are comfortable for the artists. A conservative approach, which preserves capital and avoids risk, could be investing in U.S. Treasury securities and insured municipal bonds. A slightly more aggressive profile would be investment in blue chip stocks; if a client wants more growth potential with higher risk, investment can be made in more volatile securities.

Depending on the age of a client, any funds in an Individual Retirement Account

(IRA) or pension plan may be invested for growth rather than income. Growth funds are best for clients that still have at least several years before they reach retirement age.

Business managers advise and assist their clients in the acquisition, sale and improvement of residences or other real estate. This assistance includes working with loan brokers and direct lenders to acquire financing or refinancing of mortgages that take advantage of the most favorable plans and rates. Business managers also deal with the purchases and sales of other assets (such as automobiles) and are instrumental in obtaining asset appraisals to ensure that adequate insurance coverage is in place.

Royalty Examination

Some business management firms have separate royalty examination or audit departments that perform examinations of U.S. record and publishing companies and their foreign distributors to determine if there have been underpayments of royalty income. These examinations may be conducted for individual artists, writers and licensors of rights. The royalty examination department may also perform examinations on merchandisers and other licensees and on the distribution records of television shows and motion pictures for profit participation clients. The royalty department can also perform due diligence/rights valuations for clients interested in purchasing a copyright or other investment. In firms where business management and royalty examination/audit departments fall under the same roof, clients have the advantage of constant monitoring of royalties, which can result in substantially more income.

Music Publishing Administration

Some business managers have the capability to copyright, license and administer songwriter clients' musical compositions. Music publishing administration consists of analyzing domestic, foreign and performing rights societies' royalty statements and issuing royalty statements to other writers and publishers; issuing synchronization licenses, issuing mechanical licenses and issuing print/reprint licenses. Some business management firms also assist in structuring and administering foreign subpublishing deals throughout the world and can perform computations to establish catalog valuation.

Most artist/songwriters will need to secure the services of a music-publishing administrator due to the complexity of the agreements, the substantial amount of time necessary to administer the various licenses and the potential for royalties to slip through the cracks. It is very important that music-publishing administrators work very closely with business managers to ensure that the artists/songwriters receive all of the royalties due them.

THE BUSINESS MANAGER AS PART OF THE MANAGEMENT TEAM

Artists have talents and skills that must be marketed to make them successful. It is the responsibility of management teams to do that marketing.

Since business managers account for their clients' money once it has been earned, they are an important part of the management team, which consists of the personal manager (controller of the artist's life, including their recording contract, touring activities, public relations profile and their entire career plan); the talent agent (whose primary job is to work with promoters to book and promote live performances and to negotiate roles on television shows or in movies); and the attorney (who is involved in structuring deals and shaping the artist's career in addition to providing routine legal advice).

These four parties work together to help further their clients' careers and maintain their financial stability. Management teams make recommendations, but it is the clients that have the final say in all aspects of their lives and careers.

Although their total fees may range from 25% to 30% of gross income, the financial stability provided is generally worth the cost.

For most creative artists, taking care of business is not the most effective use of their time. For that reason, it is important they choose business managers that have specialized knowledge of taxes, royalties, investments and touring to handle these technical and complex matters.

In the business management firm, the bookkeepers and account managers function as their clients' bookkeeping and accounting departments. The accountants act as assistant controllers, the supervisors or managers act as treasurers or controllers, and the partner acts as the vice president or chief financial officer of their clients' businesses. Personal managers act as general managers or chief operating officers and the clients act as presidents or CEOs and are the final decision makers.

Since the careers of most artists are of limited duration, they must put their yearly income in perspective and spend accordingly. When artists are successful and money is pouring in, overspending is not noticed. When income drops, however, this overspending can lead to bankruptcy. Artists need to control spending and operate in an efficient manner so they can generate more after tax dollars and have brighter futures. Musicians' strengths lie in their musical talents, and it is the function of capable business managers to ensure that artists are prepared for the likelihood of lean years.

BUSINESS MANAGEMENT FEES

Accounting and professional fees are traditionally billed on an hourly basis. In the business management field, however, the general billing rule is a percentage fee (usually 5%) of the client's gross income. In some cases, a maximum and minimum is placed on the total yearly fee. Some business managers charge a monthly retainer fee instead of percentage billing.

GENERAL FINANCIAL ADVICE

Artists must consider how recording and publishing contracts are structured. Recording budgets or recording funds are outlined in their recording contracts to provide funds to cover all production costs with any balance going to the artists. Since artists ultimately pay all of the costs for recordings, it is very important that these costs be minimized as much as possible. The record companies recoup all recording costs before artists receive any royalties. Even if an artist's attorney has negotiated a fantastic royalty rate, the initial royalties must cover the recoupment of recording costs, free goods, packaging; and a holdback for reserves, tour support, video costs and recoupable promotion costs. Thus, there are often no royalty payments until substantial sales or music downloads take place. Artists may also receive publishing advances, which must be recouped before any publishing royalties are payable to them. Often, much of the balance from the recording budgets and publishing advances are spent on ordinary living expenses during the recoupment period and the meager royalties received after recoupment may be quite shocking to the musician.

Artists should prepare budgets (with their business managers) and make every effort to stay within their guidelines. Whenever income is received, the amount that will be necessary to pay income taxes should be segregated so that it will not be available for personal expenses. Artists should not overextend finances when purchasing real estate, autos, equipment and other assets. If possible, they should pay cash so there will be no payments due if money gets tight. Adequate insurance coverage should be maintained (including life, disability and medical) to protect against lawsuits and catastrophes. Artists should establish retirement plans in which investments of after tax dollars will accumulate. Additionally, estate planning should be a priority in order to minimize the effect of estate taxes.

Cost-cutting measures implemented now will result in more security in the future. To live comfortably later, it is necessary for artists to conserve money in their peak years.

CONCLUSION

By overseeing all financial aspects of their clients' lives, business managers strive to maximize earnings, plan for the future and preserve and expand asset bases. Although it is difficult for some artists to entrust their business and personal finances to someone else, no matter how highly regarded, it is necessary to do so in order to focus on furthering their careers. Once this happens, artists can build for the future secure in the knowledge that their finances are being handled properly.

Because of the trust that is placed in them by their clients, business managers must have integrity and be able to make sound decisions. Since most business management clients are not experienced business people, business managers must be able to explain transactions, situations and laws in language that their clients can understand. Business managers will deal closely with their clients' personal managers, attorneys, agents and personal assistants; however, their loyalty is to their clients and they must protect them in all matters.

Talent Agents: New Thinking on an Old Business

BY MATTHEW BURROWS

The purpose of this chapter is to provide an understanding of talent agents and their relationships with artists. While the touring industry is global, the focus of this chapter is on the United States.

WHAT A TALENT AGENT DOES

Talent agents procure (i.e., negotiate and book) employment and engagements for musicians, singers and other types of performers. Most talent agents work for companies that have a team of talent agents, all working from the same roster of artists. Depending on an agency's size, it will perform one or more of the following tasks:

- Negotiate bookings. These include club gigs, concerts, shows and tours. For the purposes of this chapter, each of these is referred to as an engagement. The agreement negotiated by the agent is between the artist (or their loan-out company) and the promoter of the engagement. A loan-out company is a business entity, frequently a limited liability company, which is formed by the artist for tax and liability purposes. In the engagement agreement, the loan-out company furnishes the services of the artist and grants all rights of the artist applicable to the engagement. Sometimes, in order to ensure the validity of the entity, the promoter will require that the artist sign an inducement, which is a promise by the artist that the loan-out company is legitimate and is authorized to furnish their services and grant specific rights.

- Package artists with other artists. Sometimes, this will be as a support or headline act for a tour; other times it will be as part of a festival.

- Collect deposits and settlements. Each engagement requires that a promoter pay a deposit (i.e., a portion of the total guarantee) in advance of the engagement. Depending on the financial standing and reputation of a promoter and the agent's relationship with that promoter, deposits run from 10% to 100% of the guarantee. Established promoters (for domestic engagements) typically pay 10%, while less established promoters (and foreign-based promoters) generally pay a 100% deposit. Deposits are typically paid to the agent 30 days prior to the start of the engagement or, in the case of international engagements, prior to the artist leaving the United States. The significance of the deposit to the agent and artist is that, if the promoter cancels the engagement and refuses to pay the balance of the guarantee, the deposit is frequently all that they will receive.

- Work with artists' managers and record companies to further artists' careers.

- Deal with such legalities as cancellations or postponements, ticket refunds, security issues and granting of rights (in the case of an engagement that is filmed or recorded). In a full-service agency, these areas are handled by the business affairs executive. In a smaller agency, these areas are typically handled directly by the agent or the artist's attorney. If litigation results or a lawsuit is likely from an engagement, it is handled by the artist's litigation counsel.

- Negotiate endorsement deals for the use of an artist's name and image.

- Negotiate tour sponsorship agreements.

- Obtain recording agreements for artists to be featured in movie soundtracks.

- Secure agreements for an artist's acting services for movies and television.

- Book promotional appearances on television shows.

- Help build artists as a "brand."

TALENT AGENT LEGALITIES

Many states regulate the employment and hiring of talent; however, California and New York have the most restrictive regulations and the most developed laws in this regard. This is due to these states having a large number of working artists (and unions and guilds that support and lobby for them). These states have set up a variety of regulations, including the requirement that talent agents be licensed.

Since the bulk of the major talent agencies are located in California and New York, this chapter will focus on regulations by those states. The most important thing for an artist to know about state licensing requirements is that, in California and New York, artist managers that are not licensed as agents cannot legally procure employment or engagements for an artist (though, in California, managers may be able to render services at the direction of the talent agent and in New York may be able to do so on an incidental basis). This means that if, for example, a manager in California booked an engagement and a dispute arose between the artist and the manager, the manager could be required to return all commissions and any other monies received during the term of the artist's management agreement (including not only the monies from booking engagements but monies for management services). In addition, the artist could use the manager's lack of a talent agent's license as a basis for a claim to terminate the management agreement. A well-known case in this area involved Arsenio Hall, who sued his former manager for having procured employment for him without a talent agent's license. The California State Labor Commissioner ruled in favor of Hall and, as a result, ordered the manager to return more than $2 million in commissions. One way for a manager to avoid these legal pitfalls is to be licensed as a talent agent in California or as a theatrical employment agent in New York. One distinction under California law is that the negotiation of recording agreements is specifically carved out as an exclusion from the definition of services covered by talent agents, which leaves managers free to negotiate such agreements.

As a general rule, managers can legally procure employment for artists in states other than California and New York, though they will still be subject to various business practice statutes.

While the law in California governing talent agents has been on the books for some time, it may be subject to further revision. There is an ongoing debate between lobbyists for managers and agents about whether there should be changes to California law that would expand the rights of managers to procure employment for their artist clients.

Further, managers that are also licensed as talent agents are subject to restrictions by the Screen Actors Guild (SAG) on the amount of commissions they may charge and on their ability to act as producers. For the manager who represents clients that are both musicians and actors, this might dissuade the manager from also being licensed as a talent agent.

Because laws regarding the relationships of managers, talent agents and artists are subject to change from time to time, artists should consult with attorneys regarding legalities in any given state.

TYPES OF TALENT AGENCIES

The general distinction between talent agencies is between boutique and full service. Boutique agencies generally only book live engagements. Typically, they specialize in particular genres of music and may limit their activity to particular markets. Full-service agencies attempt to procure employment for artists in all areas of the entertainment business (e.g., personal appearances, endorsements, sponsorships, soundtracks, merchandising, and acting). Examples of full-service agencies include the William Morris Agency and Creative Artists Agency. Some agencies that are multifaceted but have less of an involvement in crossover areas (such as television and motion pictures) include Monterey Peninsula Artists/Paradigm and The Agency Group. Full-service agencies operate globally, while boutique agencies tend to be more limited in territory. Still, many larger or more sophisticated boutique agencies that operate nationally in the United States, have either affiliates or close relationships with other agencies in other parts of the world (these are typically based in London).

Excellent individual agents operate at all levels of the talent agent business. The awards given each year at the *Pollstar* Awards and the *Billboard* Touring Conference attest to this. Therefore, artists should not assume that because an agent is part of a boutique agency they will be less effective. However, if they are looking for soundtrack or acting work, in addition to touring, they will be better off with full-service agencies.

Within the smaller agency, an artist typically works with the same agent in all areas of representation. At a full-service agency, the artist will have one or two overall agents (known as "RAs" or responsible agents) that will assign others within the agency to be responsible for booking shows for particular regions and to handle specialized areas such as television appearances or endorsements. While full-service agencies view the artist as their client, the day-to-day work for that client generally revolves around one RA.

Full-Service vs. Boutique Agencies

Artists want to know whether it is best for them to sign with a full-service or a boutique agency. The answer to this is that it depends on the particular goals of an artist and where they are in their career. Artists frequently start out with boutique agencies and if they become more popular and desire to expand into other areas of entertainment, switch to full-service agencies. Still, many artists will stay with boutique agencies even after the peak of their career (e.g., Aerosmith, which has a long history of being represented by Monterey Peninsula Artists/Paradigm). A key attraction of full-service agencies is that they have the resources to exploit the full spectrum of an artist's career in areas other than touring, such as soundtracks, endorsements and acting.

For the baby band or new artist that has just been signed to a major record label after a bidding war, the label may have ambitious plans for the artist to work in all areas of entertainment. In that case, the label and artist will typically be best suited to work with a larger agency in order to develop their overall brand. A prime example of this is the Pussycat Dolls (currently represented by William Morris Agency), which are involved in almost every aspect of the entertainment business.

One criticism of full-service agencies is that an artist can become a so-called small fish in a big pond. This is a risk that artists take and, for some, is a reason why they leave large agencies and go with smaller ones (or why they start with a small agency and stay there).

An additional benefit of larger agencies is that they either own or have affiliations with marketing companies that can be used to enhance the artist as a brand by providing marketing opportunities.

Both boutique and full-service agencies will try to build their artists' popularity by packaging them with more well-known artists. This could include being added as a support act on a tour by a major act represented by the same agency or by a competing agency. In the case of two-act bills, the "package" will frequently consist of other artists that are on the same roster at the talent agency because the agency has a vested interest (apart from the artist) in maximizing their commissions by booking two artists concurrently. With festivals or other large multiact events, it is more difficult for this to occur, as larger events require artists with bigger draws, and these artists are often not at one agency. While a festival may be booked by one agency, artists that perform at it (and are hired by the festival) are invariably represented by different agencies.

COMMISSIONS

Generally, a talent agency will collect a 10% commission on the gross income received from engagements. For example, if a promoter or club owner pays $1000 for an artist's performance plus 70% of the net box office receipts, then the artist will receive $900 and the agent will receive $100 (and divide the overages by the same proportion). Some managers of superstar acts, because of their leverage, can negotiate smaller percentages (e.g., 5% or less, or cap the total commission that the agency can earn). This is not well publicized because agencies have a vested interest in maintaining their market as a "ten-percent" business. It is worth noting that the American Federation of Musicians (AFM) has agreements with all of the major full-service and boutique agencies. These agreements currently allow agencies to commission artists up to 20% (for one-offs) and 15% (for two or more consecutive shows). Nevertheless, as a matter of practice (and to be market competitive), the norm remains at 10%. In areas that are more niche-oriented, such as operatic, theatrical and classical concert arenas, commissions frequently exceed 10%.

In the television and book publishing areas, commissions can range from 10% to 20%. This higher commission is attributed to the principal U.S. agent having to split commissions with a foreign agent for foreign syndication (e.g., the U.S. agent charges 20% and pays half of this to a subagent in Europe to handle an artist in that market). For many of the larger agencies, the U.S. book publishing rate is 15%.

In general, talent agencies pay artists within 30 days after the settlement of engagements. The more sophisticated agencies are automated and can transfer funds to an artist shortly after settlement. The key term here is "settlement," which is a process that occurs initially at the engagement (typically in the office of the venue manager). Sometime towards the latter part of a performance, the artist's tour accountant will meet with the promoter and venue representatives (including the box office manager) to go over the receipts and expenses for the engagement. Depending on the sophistication and forth-rightness of the people involved, this can either be a short process or a long one (sometimes not completed until several days after the show). Invariably, when a settlement is lengthy, it is due to disputes between the promoter and the tour accountant over the amount and legitimacy of expenses and the number of tickets sold. If an engagement is a "flat date" (i.e., a guarantee without overages) then the settlement is obviously short. If the engagement involves a percentage of net ticket sales (i.e., gross ticket sales less expenses), the process can take longer. As a general rule, the gross that an artist is paid on is limited to ticket sales and, in the case of festivals, a percentage of event merchandising sales and does not include other revenue streams kept by the promoter, such as concessions and parking. This sum does not include monies received by the artist (or their merchandising company) from artist merchandise sold at the engagement (from which the venue will receive a percentage of sales, typically between 30% to 40%). While it is not the purpose of this chapter to discuss the nuances of concert promotion, suffice it to say that agents and promoters are frequently at odds over settlement.

WHEN TO LOOK FOR A TALENT AGENT

When beginning artists are just playing clubs and are trying to get signed by a label, they or their manager will have to book themselves until they become attractive to an agency. However, as stated earlier, the manager who does this, depending on the state in which they operate, may risk losing the commissions earned and having their management agreement voided. Nevertheless, for the manager of an artist without an agent, this is reality.

Regional artists that book themselves or work with local talent agencies need to move beyond their initial markets as they increase in popularity. This means seeking a larger boutique agency or a full-service agency. Further, a manager of a baby band who is acting as the de facto talent agent will want to delegate the booking duties to an agent as the band progresses so that the manager can handle the other matters of the band's career.

Managers look for full-service agencies when they are interested in expanding artists' careers beyond touring. Nevertheless, the manager of an artist who is currently focused only on touring will research both boutique and full-service agencies to find a great agent who is passionate about their artist.

WHAT TALENT AGENTS LOOK FOR IN ARTISTS

Talent agents make money from commissions on the sums their artists receive based on the talent agents' work. As they help build artists' careers, they try to increase the amount of money the artist earns and thereby increase the commissions they earn. For that reason, agents want artists that are passionate about building long-term careers and, in the case of full-service agencies, artists that are multifaceted (i.e., have appeal for endorsements, acting and soundtracks).

While an agency may be passionate about an artist's music, the financial viability of an artist is an essential component to an agency agreeing to represent an artist (particularly for full-service agencies, which have a larger overhead to cover). An artist's career has to be at the level where an agency believes it can make enough in commissions to cover their overhead and make a desired profit (hopefully increasing during the term) to warrant signing and servicing an artist.

Traditionally, the larger agencies have limited their signings to artists that were also signed to major record labels. One reason for doing so was that the label would provide tour support (i.e., money to offset transportation and production costs) and pay for marketing. While these costs were recoupable by the record label from artist's record sales, agencies benefited by being able to expand tours and add to their production value, which they would not otherwise be able to do due to the economics involved. Since major record labels are now signing fewer artists and cutting back their rosters, the old rule of an artist needing to be signed by a major label in order to be represented by a major agency does not always apply. Still, full-service agencies will require that an artist be signed to a reputable label (or a reputable manager) in order to indicate present and future value.

WHAT ARTISTS LOOK FOR IN TALENT AGENTS

Artists and managers look for agents that can get artists the right engagements in terms of money, billings, promoters and venues and to help further their other career goals.

The most successful agents are passionate about their clients' music. Agents must be able to work well with managers, record companies and attorneys to help plan how to further artists' careers. This is especially important when artists release new records and have to synchronize airplay, reviews and gigs in particular markets.

Talent agents should be able to provide new and creative ideas to nurture an artist's career. For example, an agent might know of an upcoming tour by another artist that would be perfectly timed to help expand their client's audience. However, top agents sometimes put superstar artists in small venues in order to maintain core audiences, even though this may not be, in the short run, as lucrative as playing large venues. Creative Artists Agency's recent work with Bruce Springsteen is a good example of this (where the agency booked him into small theatres). Some established artists, such as Tom Waits, may avoid playing large venues because they see greater artistic value to playing in small ones, due to matters of crowd intimacy and acoustics.

Artists want agencies that are able to book them with compatible artists, whether by genre, popularity or temperament. Artists should look at the other acts that agencies represent to get an idea of what genres and types of artists the agency values and the possible touring packages for the artist.

Since packaged tours are becoming the norm for larger venues (because there are fewer headliners to fill them), the bigger agencies have more opportunities for packaging artists. The concept is that artists with a lower draw can fill larger venues by appearing on multiact bills with other artists that have a similar draw.

HOW TO FIND A TALENT AGENT

At the beginning of artists' careers, artists and managers generally rely on word-of-mouth information from other artists, managers and attorneys to research talent agents. Other sources for information are trade associations and conferences. These include the Concert Industry Consortium (CIC), South by Southwest and the *Billboard* Touring Conference and Awards. Niche area organizations, such as Folk Alliance, can also be useful.

Several directories list booking agents and talent buyers and these can be purchased in print or as digital files. The major ones are the *Billboard International Talent and Touring Directory (www.orderbillboard.com)*; and the *Pollstar Booking Agency Directory* and *Pollstar Talent Buyer Directory (www.pollstar.com* or *www.pollstaronline.com)*.

Additionally, information can be garnered on an ongoing basis from *Pollstar* and *Billboard* magazines.

As an artist's career develops to the point where they are courted by major record companies (or reputable independent labels) the nature of finding talent agents changes. The entertainment business is one of interlocking relationships among professionals that should work together to develop artists' careers; each has a specialized role to play. Many managers and agents have rosters of people they work with that are at varying levels of career development. Sometimes, a manager or a record company executive asks a favor of a talent agency and this can lead to an agency signing an artist.

CONTRACTS BETWEEN ARTISTS AND TALENT AGENTS

Most agencies require that there be written agreements between the artist and the agency. This is done to confirm and clarify the understanding between the parties concerning key terms (such as commission and length of term), requirements set by state labor commissions and to restrict an artist from leaving the agency once they become successful (or from being enticed away by a competing agency).

Here are the essentials that are generally covered by an agency agreement:

Commissions

All artists have an interest in having their agency commissions rate be based on their net income (i.e., gross revenues less expenses). However, commissions are generally based on gross because of leverage held by agents (sometimes diplomatically referred to as the "custom and practice" of the agency). Still, from an equity argument, artists can make the claim that some third-party payments (as described below) should be deducted from the gross. If an agent will not agree to a net deal, then the artist should try to set a threshold so that their income reaches a certain amount before the agent takes the full commission, or that there are caps put on the amount that the agency is able to commission. Whether the agent agrees to this point is a matter of leverage. The ideal commission agreement is a "win win" for both parties (i.e., one in which the artist maximizes income and the agent has sufficient financial incentives to do the work).

Deductions

When negotiating agreements with talent agents, artists have the incentive to reduce the commissionable amount. Typically, artists will be able to exclude the cost of support acts and production (i.e., sound and lights) from the commissionable sum. For example, an artist's agreement with a promoter may call for the artist to receive money for support acts and production, apart from the guarantee. Since these are truly out-of-pocket costs that do not directly lead to a net increase in the artist's profit, these costs are frequently excluded from the sum commissionable by the agent. What artists cannot typically deduct are other hard costs, such as the cost of road managers and other touring support staff and fees paid to business managers and attorneys. Another area where an artist can seek deductions includes any portion of the artist's touring income that is paid to their record label as a result of an agreement by the artist to allow the record label to receive a portion of that income.

Term

From an agent's point of view, the longer the contract period, the more favorable the agreement. This provides the agent with an incentive to work harder for an artist and take more risks because the artist will not have the contractual right to leave the agency until the completion of the extended term, unless there is a separate termination clause. For example, an agency that has a three-year agreement with an artist may elect to book him or her in an eclectic music festival in order to expand their market, even though it pays less than if the artist performed a solo show. Other risks the agent may take could include booking an artist in a foreign market where the artist has less exposure. If the artist is signed to a short-term deal (e.g., one year), these risks are not likely to be taken.

A shorter term is more favorable from an artist's point of view because it allows for negotiation of a better deal after the term expires (if their career escalates); lets the artist move to a competing agency; and provides an exit strategy if the relationship is just not working. Also, since agency agreements do not actually guarantee minimum levels of performance by agents (unless so negotiated), artists need to be protected against agents that underperform.

When negotiating an agency agreement, the artist should request that certain tiers of revenue be earned as the basis for extending the term of the agreement (or as a basis for termination if those tiers are not met).

Termination

Regardless of the term of the agreement, artists should always try to have termination provisions that give them the right to terminate the agreement prior to the end of the term. Once such approach is to require that, unless the agent regularly submits (e.g., every few months) reasonable offers to the artist, the artist has the right to terminate. Another approach is to allow the artist the right to terminate particular areas of representation, if such offers are not submitted for those areas.

Some agencies make contract termination issues moot by saying that artists are free to terminate whenever they feel that they are not receiving the service due. Those agencies have enough confidence in their services to believe that artists will stay with them for so long as they are delivering—and some artists are attracted to them for this reason. A downside with this approach for those agencies is that their artists are open to poaching by other agents.

Duties of Agents

As a general rule, artist agency agreements do not guarantee artists anything—short of them getting paid if agents collect from promoters or other third parties. Agents do not guarantee that they will, in fact, further the artist's career or earn them a minimum sum of money. At most, they agree to use "reasonable" or "best efforts." In practice, short of the courtroom, these assurances are hollow. At the end of the day, the key is performance. That is why it is important, from artists' points of view, to provide "outs" in contracts to protect themselves if agents do not deliver as expected.

Agents have fiduciary relationships to their artists. This means that they must, as a legal matter, act in their artists' best interests. As a practical matter, however, what they contract to do and what the law requires are often different. For example, when a promoter cancels a show because of low ticket sales, it is not considered a valid excuse under the artist-promoter agreement; therefore, an artist would be within their rights to claim breach of contract by the promoter. An agent would, in theory, be obligated to communicate this position to the promoter.

However, there may be other issues at play that prevent this from occurring. For example, an artist may value his or her relationship with a promoter and, therefore, either forego seeking payment of the full guarantee or agree to a settlement for a lesser amount (including an opportunity to replay the show at a later date). Even if the artist is interested in pursuing collection of the full guarantee, the agent may have his or her own relationship with the promoter to protect. To maintain a good working relationship with the promoter (and provide an incentive for the promoter to continue to buy shows from the agent), the agent may elect to forgo collection or demand a lesser amount than the artist might otherwise be able to collect. In this instance, the agent may be violating their fiduciary duty to the artist. The artist, who is not privy to all of the agent's communications with the promoter, may never know all of the facts and, as a result, may agree to forgo collecting the guarantee or take a lesser settlement amount, without having evaluated all of the information. The agent would say that they were acting in the artist's best interests, by preserving the artist's long-term relationship with the promoter.

It should be noted that it is not a breach of a fiduciary duty for an agent to take on multiple clients or even clients of the same genre. While it is possible that an agent may recommend one artist over another for a festival slot, the agreement between the artist and the agent will inevitably have a provision waiving any claim by the artist that this is a breach of the agent's duty to the artist.

Power of Attorney

The contracts that are negotiated by agents with promoters and other third parties are on behalf of their artists. Thus, anything in those agreements, such as the right to use artists' names, voices or likenesses, are grants by the artists and not by the agents. Therefore, it is incumbent on artists to read their agreements prior to executing them.

For this reason, it is always recommended that an artist not give an agency the power of attorney to execute agreements on the artist's behalf. At most, such a power of attorney should only be given in order to allow the agency to cash checks on the artist's behalf. In that case, the agency acts as a quasi-trust agent for the artist. The agency gets checks for gigs, as payable either to the agency (for the benefit of the artist) or to the artist. The agency then cashes these checks, even the ones payable to the artist, and puts them in the agency's own account—with a line item referencing the artist. Once the date plays, the agency withdraws its commission and then cuts a check to the artist.

Scope of Services

Agents, particularly those at full-service agencies, want to represent artists exclusively in as many areas as possible (e.g., touring, sponsorships, endorsements and acting).

From artists' points of view, this only makes sense if agents can deliver in the particular areas of representation. It makes no sense, for example, to sign an exclusive agreement for soundtracks if an agency is weak in that area. If an agency wants to sign an artist in areas outside of the agency's expertise, then the artist should require that the agent provide offers to the artist on a regular basis or for set minimum amounts; otherwise, the artist should be able to terminate that part of the agreement (or to make such representation nonexclusive). The more sophisticated boutique agencies sometimes contract with subagents in areas in which they are not strong so they can maintain overall exclusivity with their artists.

Territory

Full-service agencies and boutique agencies with foreign affiliates generally require that an artist sign with them worldwide. It is important that the artist receive assurances from the agency that they have the capability of acting globally (and are successful at doing so) prior to signing an agreement for worldwide representation. The alternative to this is for the artist, for example, to have a U.S. agent and then a separate agent for Europe or other territories.

Key Man

The agent that brings an artist to an agency and is most passionate about the artist will be the one that works hardest on the artist's behalf. This same person (the key man) is the one that the artist counts on to deliver what is promised by the agency. If the key man leaves the agency, the artist may no longer have the passionate support that first attracted them to the agency.

A key-man clause provides the artist with the right to terminate the agreement in the event that the key man is no longer with the agency. Agencies do not like this clause because they say that artists are signing with the whole agency and they have reputations for hiring people that will work hard for their artists. Whether or not an artist will be able to obtain such a clause is a matter of leverage. As such, while a superstar may be able to get a key-man clause, a developing artist will typically not be able to do so. A compromise on this issue is to have several agents be listed as key men and that the termination right would only occur if, for example, two out of three of the agents left the agency.

Other Agreements

The artist should be sure to include in the agency agreement, any verbal promises made by the agent to induce the artist to sign. Meaning, for example, if the agent promised to deliver a certain tour or to earn the artist a minimum amount of money, it is essential that these inducements be placed in the agreement if the artist is to rely upon them. Agency agreements invariably include provisions that exclude any verbal agreements or promises, unless they are expressly memorialized in writing.

PRACTICAL ISSUES
Business Affairs

Full-service agencies have business affairs departments (which are frequently staffed by attorneys). Artists should rely upon their agency's business affairs department for contract review and related matters. In a full-service agency, business affairs executives are available to the artist as part of the overall services package with the agency (meaning their services are part of the commissions). Services provided by the business affairs department include negotiating long-form agreements (apart from key deal points such as compensation and engagement dates, which are handled by the agent), including insurance, liability and cancellation issues.

Nonappearance Insurance

For a major tour, an agent should discuss nonappearance insurance with the artist or the artist's business manager. This type of coverage is intended to pay for an artist's expenses or lost profits in the event that a show or a tour is cancelled for reasons beyond the artist's control. Because of the unique nature of this risk, coverage is typically handled by a carrier associated with Lloyd's insurance syndicate in London.

Generally, only major artists acquire nonappearance coverage due to its cost (which is based on a percentage of the sum insured, less a deductible). Areas that are typically not covered by this type of coverage include intentional acts (e.g., an artist, who in a rage, smashes their hand into a wall and can no longer play guitar on a scheduled tour), reckless acts (e.g., skydiving), illegal drug use, terrorism and, sometimes, flying in noncommercial aircraft. If an artist is paid on a nonappearance policy, it should be the artist's position that none of the insurance proceeds are commissionable by the agency since the agency did not contribute to the purchase of the policy. The agent should not have a strong objection to this, particularly if they, too, obtained separate coverage for lost commissions due to a cancellation.

FUTURE TRENDS

Thus far, this chapter has focused on the key factors of the artist-agent relationship. Because the marketplace is ever changing, it is useful to anticipate changes that might impact this relationship. The following are some trends going forward.

Deduction of Monies Paid to Labels

One trend in the record industry is lower overall CD sales and increasing digital sales. An immediate impact of this has been that record labels have been forced to seek alternative revenue streams through new business models. One approach is for record labels and artists to act more like business partners. This means a greater sharing of risk and reward. Recent examples of this include deals involving Korn and Robbie Williams. In both of these deals, the record company recoups some of its recording and marketing costs by taking a portion of the artist's touring and merchandising revenue. Deals like this will put pressure on talent agents to allow artists to deduct those monies paid by the artist to record labels in connection with touring from commissionable monies.

Agents as Promoters

Another possibility is for full-service agencies to morph into traditional promoter businesses. An early example of this was Lollapalooza, which was partly owned by the William Morris Agency. Talent agencies could commission an entire package (similar to packaging for a motion picture or television production) and not commission each artist individually. The agency, in turn, would assume a financial risk, as a promoter would, by being liable to pay the artist the applicable guarantee. However, in California, there are restrictions on an agency's ability to act as both agent and producer/promoter. It is expected that talent agencies will continue their lobbying efforts to be able to act more as promoters and producers.

Venture Capital

Agents may seek third-party venture capital money and use this to offset the loss in tour support from record labels, to enhance the production of a show or to help finance ancillary revenue streams (such as funding the production of a concert film). Because of the value added to the artist and the increased financial risk to the agency, this might justify a higher commission (or the agent taking a production fee "off-the-top" prior to calculating the sum from which their commission is paid). For some superstar acts, the opposite scenario could play out, whereby the artist takes on investors (for a similar purpose) and then uses this as leverage to argue for either a reduced commission or a greater payout from a promoter.

Greater Involvement by Promoters and Managers

Artists may reduce their dependency on agents and shift those dealings to major management companies or promoters (e.g., Live Nation and AEG). This would likely call for a further review of the talent rules in California and New York, as these large media companies are not, as a general rule, licensed as talent agents. Still, an artist's agreement with a large management firm or a promoter that goes beyond the artist's services may take the agreement out of the realm of employment or engagements. Instances of this might include, the licensing of an artist's name or image (where services are not required) or where the artist acts as a producer of an event where, as part of their agreement, they agree to have their loan-out company provide certain services.

Consolidation

While the agency business is likely subject to further consolidation, a different scenario could be the merger of agents and managers. Under this scenario, the artist could get the benefit of receiving all services in exchange for paying one percentage. However, the restrictions, mentioned above concerning caps on talent agents' commissions, and licensing issues, may dissuade managers from going down this path.

Artists with long careers must expect to have dealings with the large promoters including Live Nation and AEG. This applies on a global level. Since Live Nation and AEG control the bulk of the world's midsized to large venues, if artists are to be successful, they will invariably play in venues operated by these promoters. Further, since Live Nation is now in the ticketing, retail and merchandising business, the synergies generated by working directly with artists are even greater. In theory, a company such as Live Nation may be able to offer the artist lower transaction costs (i.e., one deal rather than many), lower deal costs to Live Nation (due to economies of scale), and the key players would be operating as a team since they are part of the same company. However, touring is not the only element in an artist's career. The other components at play (e.g., soundtracks, acting and endorsements) would still need to be handled.

Expanded Role of Agents

Larger agencies traditionally have done well with soundtracks and endorsements; however, they have done a poor job with merchandising (or simply have avoided representing artists in this area). Typically, the merchandising deal is done between the manager and the merchandising company and involves each party's attorney. Going forward, the larger talent agencies may strengthen their resources to do merchandising deals as a means to capture additional revenue streams. Since an agent would then be commissioning an artist for merchandising, this might result in resistance from managers that have traditionally retained control over these types of agreements.

New Revenue Streams

With the advent of the iPod and the use of digital media in general, along with cost reductions, more and more concerts will be recorded, filmed and exploited on different platforms. For the artist, this will provide additional revenue streams, which, depending on their agency's involvement, may or may not be commissionable by the agent. Traditionally, agencies do not commission recordings from concerts. More likely, recordings such as concert films will remain the domain of record labels, and agencies will continue their traditional role in negotiating one-off deals for motion picture and television soundtracks. However, an aggressive agency could certainly enhance its clout with artists by bringing in deals of these sorts.

Do it Yourself

While the Internet has increased artists' ability to connect with their fans, this should not be seen as setting a trend for artists to book themselves (at least long term). An artist will always need someone to handle the services of talent agents (i.e., pitch the artist, get the offer, negotiate the deal, service the date and handle settlement) for the engagement. While some artists have successfully been able to book themselves (The String Cheese Incident and Grateful Dead being the best examples), a downside of doing so is that the artist does not get the benefit of cross-pollination with other acts on a large and diverse roster or, in the case of full-service agencies, the benefit of working with other areas of an agency. So, while a do-it-yourself world seems attractive because it offers artists more control (i.e., they are their own agents), there is real value to outsourcing this work to an outside agent. Another practical limitation is the cost of overhead. In order for artists to maintain full-scale business structures, they need to pay for the overhead. To do this requires a steady flow of cash, which most artists are not able to achieve.

Connecting with Fans

One area that artists and agents agree upon is that young fans want community, and artists want direct relationships with their fans. The Internet provides a great opportunity for this (the best example being MySpace). In the live entertainment business, the agents that are best able to tap into the MySpace-type community experience will be the new success stories and provide some of the best opportunities for developing artists.

Club Contracts

BY EDWARD (NED) R. HEARN

Many bands get their start playing in clubs. There are several types, for example, draw clubs, clubs with walk-in trades and lounge act clubs. A club or hotel room that has been booked by a private party for a special occasion, such as a wedding, anniversary or industrial convention, etc., is called a "casual."

The draw clubs book name acts to attract an audience. They could be national recording acts or local acts that have followings. Sometimes these clubs hire opening acts to reinforce the lead act's draw and help ensure a full house.

The walk-in trade club depends on a regular crowd that frequents the club. It normally hires club bands that play Top 40 and maybe some original material. Lounge act clubs focus on groups that do highly polished performances of popular music (copy music). They are prevalent in major cities' hotels, casinos and in resort areas.

As some clubs are signatories of agreements with the American Federation of Musicians (AFM), you must find out if you need to be a member of the AFM before a club can book you.

Sometimes bands or managers book their acts into clubs for showcase purposes to show the group's talents to industry people that have promised to attend. Showcases are also used to generate enthusiasm for a group. For example, members of a Midwest group that has a huge regional following book themselves into a Los Angeles club for almost no pay to showcase for record companies, publishers or even prospective managers. Or a record company may fill (paper) a club when a new record is released, to generate enthusiasm for the particular group being pushed by the record company, or the club may be filled by a group's personal manager or talent agency to influence record companies into developing an interest in the group.

APPROACHING THE CLUB

You should study the various kinds of clubs where you could perform and decide which best suit your act. Make presentations to clubs that most fit your style of music. It is important that you understand the reputation of the club and the makeup of the audience that is likely to enjoy your performance.

Club owners want bands that are professional and pleasing to their audiences. They want to know that the artists will work as promised, show up on time and make money for their clubs.

The more clubs you perform in and the more reliable a track record you develop, the easier the bookings should become, particularly if you show a consistent (and growing) draw.

Most club owners also expect you to have publicity materials that they can use to help promote the performance.

Some clubs have implemented a "pay-to-play" policy, by which you, as the performing artist, guarantee that a certain number of patrons (e.g., 50) will come to the club and pay to see you for some predetermined aggregate amount (e.g., $500), which the club owner will split with you (e.g., fifty-fifty). In that example, if less than 50 friends show up and pay a total of $300, the club owner will keep the first $250 and you get the balance. If less than $250 is generated, you have to pay the club owner the difference; hence pay to play. This approach has raised much protest and indignation by local bands and their supporters. In an area where there are many clubs in which to choose to play, boycotting a pay-to-play club may have an effective influence. In locations where the clubs are fewer in number, that tactic may not prove to be an effective remedy. You need venues in which to perform to develop your craft and your following and to get record industry attention, in which event you may have to be forced to play the game and pay.

CLUB CONTRACTS

When dealing with clubs, you should understand that even a casual agreement to show up and play for free, to see what happens, is a contract. This section focuses on the various points you should review with the club owner in order to arrive at a performing contract. These same points are relevant for standard AFM contracts that are used when bands are booked into clubs that are affiliated with the AFM.

Remember that the contractual relationship with a club is only as good as the relationship between the club owner and the group. You should determine whether the owners of a club are people with whom you really wish to deal. Counterbalancing that, if they are not people with whom you wish to deal, but playing their club is an important milestone in the development of your band and its credibility to the music industry, then that point has to be given consideration.

The contract with a club should be in writing. With an oral contract, in the event of a dispute, it is difficult to prove what terms the club owner and the band agreed to. When the contract is written the agreed-to points are documented. Rather than treating the written contract as an awesome legal document, consider it a checklist

A CHECKLIST OF THE IMPORTANT ITEMS IN A CLUB CONTRACT

- Identity of the performer and club owner.
- Dates and times of the performance.
- Number of sets to be performed and the length of those sets.
- Duration of the breaks between the sets.
- Special arrangements that need to be made in terms of equipment, stage settings, space for performance, and lighting.
- Refreshments (the house policy on drinks and food).
- Setup time and the time for sound checking.
- Whether any recording or broadcasting is to take place, and who controls the product of that effort.
- The advertising image of the group to be displayed by the club.
- What happens if the gig does not take place?
- What is your compensation?

of important points that should be covered by the club owner and the group. Look at the contract as a way of clarifying the relationship between the club and you by bringing to light all of the issues that are important to both parties. This way, everyone will focus on those issues at the very beginning, hopefully eliminating any later surprises. Contract discussions are an indication of your professionalism to a club owner.

Compensation

Your compensation could come in a number of forms. It could be from door receipts, in which case you should determine, with the club owner, the number of tickets to be sold, the prices of those tickets and the number of freebies for the owner and the performers. With that information, you will have some idea how much to expect based on the percentage of the door receipts you have agreed to accept. Your compensation could be a flat sum, in which case the door receipts are not a problem. Reach an agreement on the form of compensation (i.e., cash or cashier's check). The norm is cash, but insist on at least a cashier's check. Part of the money should be paid, if not at the beginning, then at least part way through the performance with the balance due, if any, immediately at the conclusion of the performance.

Sound and Lights

An audience's perception of how good a performance is often depends on the quality of sound and lights. Make sure that the club has equipment that is adequate for your needs and that the club owner understands what those needs are.

If you (or the club) wish to supplement the club's system with your own (or rented) equipment, work out the additional expense as part of your contract and arrange for a load-in time. If you are using an acoustic piano, your contract should state that it be tuned prior to performance. A simple performance contract is printed at the end of this chapter. Even if you do not use the contract, it is a good checklist that can be used during negotiations with the club owner.

If the club has a resident sound engineer whose job is setting up and operating the house sound reinforcement system, establish a harmonious relationship by providing a plot plan of how the stage looks when your equipment is set up. Communicate your priorities regarding sound and provide the sound person with a set list. Ask whether your sound person can sit with the club sound engineer and provide direction about the mix.

AFM UNION CONTRACTS

Certain clubs have signed collective bargaining agreements with the AFM that establish the scale and working conditions that the club must pay and provide union musicians that perform at that club, based on the amount of time they play and the number of sets they perform. Union contracts are most prevalent with hotels, pit orchestras, house bands and major clubs in large cities.

The musician members of the AFM also sign a contract with the AFM that requires its members to deal only with clubs that meet AFM contract requirements. AFM musicians should not play in nonunion clubs for less than union scales, since to do so is a violation of the contract.

It is not uncommon for clubs that have signed with the AFM to file, with the union local, what is known as a "dummy contract" between the performer and the club by which the club commits to pay at AFM scale, but the musician and the club owner agree (verbally) that the musician will perform at a lower price. This is done so that the AFM will not bother the club or the musician and the musician can get the work. The net effect is, the musician gets the short end.

Another common problem is that union clubs are barred by the AFM contract from hiring nonunion musicians. There is a provision in the AFM booking contract that says, "All employees covered by this agreement must be members in good standing of the Federation." Musicians that are engaged by the club and are not members of the union must become members of the union no later than the 30th day following the beginning of their employment or the effective date of the agreement, whichever of the two is later. Consequently, if you are not a union member when you start performing with a union club, you may find yourself in a situation where you must become a member of the union if you are going to continue to play in the club over a period of time—depending on the extent to which the AFM or the particular club enforce this provision.

Many of the points raised in the following checklist can be made a part of the AFM contract with the club.

Many smaller clubs do not sign contracts with the union and have no obligation to pay union scale. Union musicians, however, often perform in nonunion clubs on the q.t. or they file a dummy contract so the AFM can get its cut. If you are a union member and, on performing in a nonunion club, elect to file a dummy contract with the AFM, it means you or the club owner must submit a payment to the union for its fees on the performance. Since the club owner is not union, it is highly unlikely that the club will make that payment, which leaves it up to you to pay it from your fees, or build that cost into your fees to the club for performing. Most union members in that situation, especially outside of the major cities, just try to "fly below radar" and not pay, and hope it does not become an issue. The majority of times it does not, but there are occasional exceptions when it does and that may result in having to pay a fine to the relevant union chapter.

When a club has no contract with the AFM the only leverage union musicians have is to refuse to perform in that club unless union scale is paid. The economic realities of the business, however, are such that musicians frequently have no bargaining power to force clubs to pay union scale. Generally, musicians are glad to get any kind of work regardless of pay scale.

WHO SIGNS THE CONTRACT?

As a practical matter, one of the members of the group should be given authority to sign on behalf of all of the members of the group. Performing groups are, for all practical purposes, partnerships (unless its members have incorporated the business or formed an LLC) and one partner has the power to bind the other partners. Sometimes, a manager will be authorized to sign contracts on behalf of a group, although managers are better advised not to sign performance contracts if the state in which the band or manager is based requires talent agents to be licensed, as is the case in California. (See the chapter, "Talent Agents: New Thinking on an Old Business.") The extent of that authority depends on the agreements reached between the manager and the group and is another point to be considered carefully.

TAXES

Remember your tax obligations on your compensation. Generally, club owners will treat you as an independent contractor and you will be responsible for your own

OTHER POINTS THAT SHOULD BE CONSIDERED IN YOUR RELATIONSHIP WITH A CLUB THAT USES THE AFM CONTRACT

- The wage should be at least union minimum scale. Consider the costs that have to be paid from that wage, such as sound system, special instruments and lighting.

- The customary union procedure is to pay half of the agreed-to wages in advance of the engagement and the remaining amount prior to the performance on the evening of the engagement. The AFM may demand that the entire amount be paid in advance or that a bond be posted.

- The union contract gives the club owner complete control, supervision and direction over the musicians, including the manner, means and details of the performance. This is more often than not a matter of bargaining power and the more popular the group, the less power the owner has over the group. As a practical matter, most club owners prefer not to be involved in decisions about a group's performance or the kind of materials to be performed. Presumably, if you have properly identified your style, the club owner has decided that you are the kind of act desired and is expecting that kind of performance.

- Any disputes between the club owner and the musician under a union contract are, usually, resolved by an AFM arbitration proceeding and the results can be enforced by a court.

- If the performance is to be recorded or broadcast, the contract requires AFM approval. The AFM may demand additional compensation for the musicians in that event. At the same time, the club owner may insist on additional compensation for use of the club if the performance is to be recorded by a record company or broadcast over a radio station. These are points that should be negotiated in advance.

federal income tax and social security payment as well as any state, unemployment or workman's compensation insurance that must be paid. The IRS may impose the responsibility on the club owner for withholding if it determines that there was an employer/employee relationship, but you should take responsibility for setting aside a portion of your payment so that you can pay the IRS when the time comes.

WHEN THE CLUB DOES NOT PAY YOU

If the club owner owes you money and refuses to pay, you have recourse to the courts (and to your AFM local if it is a union club). Going to court, however, can be an expensive proposition and is not one to be pursued lightly. California law provides that if the claim is no more than $5000 or if you are willing to limit your claim to that amount, you can bring your own action in the small claims court in the county where you reside or where the club is located. Generally, you have to file the small claims action in the jurisdiction where the club is located, which can be an aggregation of time and further expense if you do not live in the same area. While you can try to file in your local court, if the club has no presence in that area, e.g., it does not advertise in the area or promote events with other promoters located in your area, it will be difficult to get jurisdiction over the club's owner. The owner could move to dismiss the case or move to transfer the case to a court in the club's jurisdiction or if you get a default judgment, challenge its enforceability for lack of jurisdiction. Less than reputable club owners can rely on this distant location situation as a way to avoid the obligation to pay you. The small claims court procedure requires you to go to the county clerk for your local court system and pay a small fee for filing, stamping and serving the complaint. The sheriff then serves the complaint on the defendant, which sets forth a date, time and place for a hearing. The defendant can file a counterclaim within 48 hours of the hearing, but it has to be verified or sworn to. (Your complaint does not have to be sworn to.) At the appointed date, time and place, both parties must appear at the court and explain their stories to the judge. The judge can then order the club to pay you. If the judge does rule in your favor, the club owner can appeal to a higher level court. If you lose, you cannot appeal, and that is the end of the case. Similar small claims procedures are in effect in most states.

CONCLUSION

Making arrangements for performing in clubs deserves special consideration and planning. You should keep in mind that your ability to get gigs will be enhanced by getting your business act together.

PERFORMANCE AGREEMENT

Agreement made as of _____, 20_____, between the parties identified below. In consideration for the following covenants, conditions and promises, the Purchaser agrees to hire the Artist to perform an engagement and the Artist agrees to provide such performance services, under the following terms and conditions:

1. Artist _____

2. Purchaser _____

3. Place of engagement

_____
NAME
_____
STREET ADDRESS
_____
CITY, STATE, ZIP
_____
TELEPHONE

4. The dates, time, duration of show and sound check time are as follows:

Dates _____ Time _____AM/PM
Number of Sets _____ Duration of Each Set _____
Sound Check Time _____

5. The consideration to be paid shall be
    (a) Guaranteed Fee of $_____
    (b) Percentage _____ (gross/net of door)
    (c) Workshop Fee of $ _____
    (d) Meals/Lodging _____
    (e) Transportation _____
        (i) Air _____
        (ii) Ground _____
    (f) Materials _____
    (g) Total _____
    (h) Advance Payment of $ _____ due on _____(Date)
    (i) Balance of Payment of $ _____ due on _____(Date)

6. Further consideration to Artist by Purchaser is provided in the Rider of Additional Terms attached to this Agreement.

7. Sound and/or lighting equipment to be provided by Purchaser shall be as described in the separate Sound Reinforcement and Lighting Agreement.

8. This Agreement and the attached Riders and Sound Reinforcement and Lighting Agreement, which by this reference are incorporated into and made a part of this Agreement, constitute the entire agreement between the parties and supersedes all prior and contemporaneous agreements, understandings, negotiations and discussions, whether oral or written. There are no warranties, representations, and/or agreements

among the parties in connection with the subject matter of this Agreement, except as specifically set forth and referenced in this Agreement and the attached Riders. This Agreement shall be governed by [insert your State's name] law; is binding and valid only when signed by the parties below; and may be modified only in a writing signed by the parties. If Artist has not received the deposit in the amount and at the time specified in subsection 5(h), then Artist thereafter at any time shall have the option to terminate this Agreement.

9. The persons signing this Agreement on behalf of Artist and Purchaser each have the authority to bind their respective principals.

10. If you have any questions, please contact our home office at _____

AGREED TO AND ACCEPTED

PURCHASER	ARTIST
BY DATE	BY DATE
NAME AND TITLE (AN AUTHORIZED SIGNATORY)	NAME AND TITLE (AN AUTHORIZED SIGNATORY)
FEDERAL I.D./SS#	FEDERAL I.D./SS#

PERFORMANCE AGREEMENT RIDER *

1. BILLING

Artist shall receive one hundred percent (100%) sole exclusive billing in any and all advertising and publicity when appearing as the sole act. When Artist is accompanied by other musicians, Artist shall receive prominent billing and shall close the show at each performance during the engagement unless specifically provided otherwise. When headlining, Artist shall have the right of approval of any and all other acts in the show, their set times, and set lengths.

2. PAYMENT

All payments provided hereunder shall be made by Money Order, Cash, Cashier's, Certified or School Check, made out to _____ unless otherwise specified.

When a percentage figure is made a part of this Agreement, the Purchaser agrees to have on hand at the end of the engagement the ticket manifest and all unsold tickets for verification by Artist or Artist's representative.

(a) If the Artist is paid according to a percentage of the gross admissions, the following applies:

(i) Purchaser must have all tickets printed by a bonded printer.

(ii) All tickets must be consecutively numbered.

(iii) Each set of tickets for a given price, and, if more than one performance is

---

* *(Riders to performance agreements specify additional requirements and working conditions that are essential and necessary for a quality performance. They can be extremely elaborate.)*

contemplated, each set of tickets for each performance must be printed on a ticket stock of contrasting color.

(iv) A bonded printer's manifest showing number, color and price of all tickets printed for the performance must be available for inspection by Artist's representative on afternoon of concert.

(v) All gross admission receipts shall be computed on the actual full admission price provided on each ticket, and, in the absence of prior written agreement by Artist, no tickets shall be offered or sold at a discount or a premium.

(vi) A representative of the Artist shall have the right to be present in the box office prior to and during the performance and intermission periods and such representative shall be given full access to all box office sales and shall other- wise be permitted to reasonably satisfy himself as to the gross receipts (and expenditures if required) at each performance hereunder.

(b) Purchaser warrants that tickets for the engagement will be scaled in the following prices:

_____TICKETS AT _____ DOLLARS.

_____TICKETS AT _____ DOLLARS.

_____TICKETS AT _____ DOLLARS.

If the scale of prices shall be varied in any respect, the percentage compensation payable to Artist shall be based upon whichever of the following is more favorable to Artist: the scale of prices as set forth above or the actual scale of prices in effect for the engagement.

(c) In the event that compensation payable to Artist hereunder is measured in whole or in part by a percentage of receipts, Artist shall have the right to set a limit on the number of free admissions authorized by Purchaser.

3. WITHHOLDING

If Purchaser is required by state or local law to make any withholding or deduction from the Artist fee specified in the attached contract, the Purchaser shall furnish to Artist a copy of the pertinent law governing said deduction when returning the Agreement to Artist or Artist's agent.

4. LIMITATIONS ON RECORDING

No performance during the engagement shall be recorded, copied, reproduced, transmitted or disseminated in or from the premises in any manner or by any means now known or later developed, including audio and video, without the prior written permission of Artist.

5. PUBLICITY PHOTOGRAPHS

Only photographs sent to the Purchaser by Artist or Artist's representative shall be used in publicizing the engagement.

6. DRESSING ROOM

Purchaser shall provide one (1) clean, lockable dressing room. Purchaser agrees to be solely responsible for the security of all items in the dressing room area and shall keep unauthorized people from entering said area.

7. ARTIST'S PROPERTY

Purchaser shall be responsible for any theft or damage to the equipment of Artist that may occur during the time that the equipment is located on Purchaser's premises.

8. SECURITY

Purchaser will make a diligent effort during the performance to maintain a quiet listening audience. Audience shall be seated prior to the performance. Purchaser is responsible for the conduct of its audience and shall provide adequate supervision of minors attending the performance. Any damage resulting from activities of the audience shall be the responsibility of Purchaser.

9. COMPLIMENTARY TICKETS

Purchaser agrees to make (_____) complimentary tickets available to Artist or Artist's representative, the unused portion of which may be placed on sale the day of perform-ance with the permission of Artist or Artist's representative.

10. BACKSTAGE ACCESS

Purchaser shall provide (_____) backstage passes for Artist on Artist's arrival at venue.

11. MERCHANDISING

Artist shall have the option to sell albums, videos, books and/or merchandising material at the performance and shall retain the proceeds of such sales.

(a) Artist has sole right to merchandise any and all products pertaining to Artist at no expense to the Artist, excluding normal hall and vending fees agreed upon in advance by Artist in writing. Purchaser will not, nor will Purchaser allow any other party to sell or distribute merchandise bearing name, likeness or logo of Artist, before, during or after concert date.

(b) Purchaser will provide at its expense, (_____) persons to sell Artist's products.

(c) Purchaser will provide the following equipment for merchandising:
  (i) One (1) cash box with fifty dollars ($50.00) starting change (ones and fives).
  (ii) Six-foot (6') table (to hold records and other Artist products).
  (iii) Two (2) chairs (for the persons selling the products).

(d) Merchandise shall be displayed in a prominent area of the foyer or lounge leading from the facility entrance to the performance area.

(e) Person who is to vend Artist's products shall be available from time of stage call to receive product and set up merchandise area. Artist or Artist's representative will conduct and set up merchandise area with Purchaser's designated sellers. Artist or Artist's representative will conduct inventory of merchandise prior to start of sale.

(f) After close of show (all audience will have left the facility) the vendor will close the merchandising booth and return all unsold product and receipts from sale to Artist or Artist's representative for final accounting.

(g) Purchaser is responsible for all product and monies from sales as signed for by the Purchaser's merchandising representative. Fifty dollars ($50.00) starting change is to be deducted from total receipts.

12. GROUND TRANSPORTATION

Unless otherwise indicated, Purchaser, at its expense, shall provide ground transportation to and from place of engagement, airport and hotel. Artist requires a large station wagon or van. Please send directions to concert site from the airport, or, if mode of travel is arranged other than by automobile, please send directions (and time tables) from airport, train station, etc., to hotel, then from hotel to concert site. Copies of highlighted street maps are very much appreciated.

13. FOOD
Food and beverages appropriate for time of day for (_____) people shall be provided by Purchaser.

14. LODGING
If Purchaser is to provide lodging, it shall be at a hotel of Holiday Inn quality or better, four (4) quiet, nonsmoking rooms, in the vicinity of the venue, away from highway noise, with king-size beds in each room.

15. OUTDOOR VENUE
In the event the engagement is outdoors, there must be a covering over the stage area that will protect the Artist and equipment from the elements.

16. SEATING
House lights should be dimmed starting ten (10) minutes before the start of the concert to facilitate audience being seated on time.

17. BACKGROUND MUSIC
No background music, taped or otherwise, is to be played before the start of or after the concert without the approval of the Artist, unless the music is from Artist's albums.

18. STAGE
Stage must be accessible to performers in a manner other than through the audience. Stage and curtains must be in clean, good condition. Whenever possible, stage should be no further than fifteen feet (15') from the audience.

19. PROMOTION
Purchaser agrees to promote the scheduled performance(s) on television, radio, newspapers and other print media and will use its best efforts to obtain calendar listings, feature articles, interviews of the Artist, reviews of the performance and Artist's records in local major and alternative newspapers, radio and television programs. Purchaser shall be responsible for all matters pertaining to the promotion and production of the scheduled engagement, including but not limited to venue rentals, security and advertising.

20. CLIPPINGS
As a special request, Artist asks that Purchaser please forward clippings, reviews, advertising and posters to Artist at _____ . If there are any questions or suggestions, please direct them to _____ .

21. FORCE MAJEURE
This agreement of Artist is subject to the unavailability of Artist because of sickness, accidents, riots, strikes, acts of God or other conditions beyond Artist's control.

22. CANCELLATION
In the event Purchaser cancels the performance for any reason less than five (5) weeks before the date of such performance, Purchaser will pay Artist, as liquidated damages,

one-half ($^1/_2$) of the guaranteed fee agreed to be paid for such performance in subsection 5(a). In the event Purchaser cancels the performance for any reason less than two (2) weeks before the date of such performance, Purchaser will pay Artist, as liquidated damages, the full guaranteed fee agreed to be paid for such performance, unless Artist subsequently agrees in writing to waive all or any part of that payment.

23. ATTORNEYS' FEES

In the event of any dispute arising under this Agreement that results in litigation or arbitration, the prevailing party shall be paid its reasonable attorneys' fees and costs by the losing party.

24. INSURANCE

Purchaser agrees to obtain any and all necessary personal injury and property damage liability insurance with respect to the activities of Artist on the premises of Purchaser or at such other location where Purchaser directs Artist to perform. Purchaser agrees to indemnify and hold Artist harmless from any and all claims, liabilities, damages, and expenses for injury, damages, or death to any person, persons, or property, including attorneys' fees, demands, suits, or costs of whatever nature, arising from any action, activity or omission of Purchaser or third parties, except for claims arising from Artist's willful misconduct or gross negligence. At least ten (10) days prior to the date of performance, Purchaser shall provide to Artist a copy of Purchaser's policy of insurance indicating coverage in the sum of at least _____ dollars for personal injury and property damage, naming Artist as an additional insured for the date of the performance.

SOUND REINFORCEMENT RIDER

This Rider for Sound Reinforcement Services is entered into as of _____ , 20__, between the parties identified below.

1. NAME OF PURCHASER _____

_____
PURCHASER ADDRESS

_____
CITY/STATE/ZIP

_____
TELEPHONE

2. NAME OF ARTIST_____

3. PLACE OF ENGAGEMENT _____

4. DATE OF EVENT _____

5. NUMBER OF SETS AND DURATION _____

6. TYPE OF EVENT _____

7. MAXIMUM AUDIENCE EXPECTED _____

8. LOAD-IN
Hall is available for load-in and set up at (time)_____ (date) _____
(a) Purchaser agrees to provide a safe and proper 20-foot "A" type ladder (with wheels), at time of load-in and until all of Artist's equipment has been removed from venue.
(b) Purchaser agrees to provide (_____) number of drum risers at a height of (_____) above the stage floor.
(c) Ladder and drum risers are to be in place at time of load-in.

9. SOUND CHECK
Hall is available for sound check at (time)_____ (date) _____
(a) Artist requires a (_____) hour sound check and technical setup period. Purchaser shall not allow the audience to enter the place of performance until such time as sound check and technical setup has been completed. Artist shall complete the setup and sound check (_____) hour(s) prior to the time of performance, provided that Purchaser makes the place of performance available for said setup at least (_____) hours prior to time of performance.

10. SOUND SYSTEM
Purchaser agrees to provide a complete sound system consisting of:
(_____) Number of amplifiers at (_____) kilowatts of power
(_____) Number of main house speakers
(_____) Number of monitor speakers
A main mixing board with (_____) number of input channels
A monitor mixing board with (_____) number of input channels
(_____) Number of microphones and stands

Other special equipment _____

Any alterations or deviations from the above items involving extra cost of equipment or labor or substitutions of equipment, are subject to written agreement.

11. PERSONNEL

Purchaser agrees to provide the following personnel to operate the equipment:

_____
_____

12. POWER

Purchaser agrees to provide at least _____ amps single phase and _____ volts of power.

13. SPEAKER SPACE

Purchaser agrees to provide adequate space for placement of loudspeakers. The space needed for the speakers will be _____ feet by _____ feet. This area must be capable of supporting the weight (_____ lbs.) of the speakers safely.

14. MIXING PLATFORM

Purchaser agrees to provide a safe platform or space in the audience within 50 to 100 feet of the stage in order to set up mixers to mix the sound for the show. Platform or area should be _____ feet by _____ feet.

15. SECURITY

Purchaser agrees to hire adequate security for stage area and accepts full liability for any stolen articles and/or destruction of Artist's equipment.

SAMPLE OF SPECIFICATIONS FOR SOUND REQUIREMENTS (SOUND REINFORCEMENT RIDER, CLAUSE 10)

(a) Purchaser shall provide a minimum of ten (10) high-quality monitor speakers. These monitor speakers shall be capable of providing at least 120 dB of clear, undistorted sound between 100 and 10,000 cycles per second (plus or minus 4 dB) at a distance of ten (10) feet. The monitor speakers shall be placed as follows:

    3–stage center
    1–down stage left
    1–up stage right
    2–monitors behind drummer
    1–monitor behind keyboards
    2–side fill monitors

(b) There shall be a minimum of ten (10) boom stands, six (6) short stands, two (2) gooseneck-type attachments, and ten (10) regular stands for the microphones.

(c) If the performance area of the engagement is outdoors or semioutdoors, all microphones shall be covered with filter windscreens.

(d) Purchaser further agrees to provide a six- (6-) station intercom hookup between the following—

    stage right or left
    both spot lights
    sound console
    monitor mixer console
    dimmer board
    house lights and curtain

All intercoms are to be headphone type with microphone and two earpieces.

Music Unions

BY JAMES A. SEDIVY AND GREGORY T. VICTOROFF

Unions have greater negotiating strength than individuals. A labor union is a group of people that have joined together to demand better pay and working conditions. A music union is a labor union whose membership is comprised of musicians. This chapter discusses many of the rules and benefits of the two major U.S. music unions, the American Federation of Musicians of the United States and Canada, AFL-CIO, CLC (AFM) and the American Federation of Television and Radio Artists, AFL CIO (AFTRA). The American Guild of Musical Artists (AGMA) represents vocalists in the fields of opera, classical music and ballet. The Screen Actors Guild (SAG) represents vocalists that sing in theatrical motion pictures. These unions will not be reviewed in this chapter, although their addresses and phone numbers are included in the resource directory at the back of this book.

AFM

The AFM is one of the largest unions of performing artists, with over 250 Locals and more than 100,000 members.

AFM members are instrumentalists, leaders, contractors, orchestrators, copyists, music librarians, arrangers and proofreaders. They work in all mediums of music including live performance, television, movies, etc.

AFTRA

AFTRA members are singers, sound effects artists, actors, announcers and narrators that work in radio, television and phonograph recording.

LOCALS

The AFM and AFTRA are comprised of local unions and governing organizations known as the International Executive Board (AFM) and the National Board (AFTRA). They grant charters to "locals" in certain geographic areas, like Los Angeles, Detroit and Nashville. AFTRA locals are usually referred to by the name of the community, whereas AFM locals are given numbers. Each local is basically autonomous and independent from other locals and the International Board or National Board, so some pay rates, such as live performance rates, and benefits vary from local to local.

SIGNATORY COMPANIES

Music employers, such as record companies and television and movie producers, negotiate contracts (agreements) with the AFM, AFTRA and SAG at two- to five-year intervals. A music employer who signs an agreement promises to hire only union members and provide at least the minimum pay and working conditions set forth in the agreement. The employer signing the agreement is called a signatory company. If you are a union member and are employed by a nonsignatory company, such as a small record label or nonunion bar or restaurant, you may be violating union rules and receiving less than union approved pay or scale. In so doing, you undermine the bargaining strength of the union and its members. Union locals can tell you whether or not your employer is a signatory company.

MEMBERSHIP BENEFITS

No union can promise professional success, especially in the highly competitive music industry, which is subject to ever changing tastes and trends. Nevertheless, union membership does offer certain opportunities for career advancement and some very real benefits, the most important of which is your eligibility for employment by signatory companies.

The benefits you get by joining a union depend on the strength of the particular union and local. For example, AFM Local 47 in Los Angeles provides job referrals for professional bands and musicians; death benefit group insurance; legal counsel and representation in grievance and arbitration proceedings; credit union membership; notary public service and business discounts; scholarship and awards programs; listings and information on agents, managers, record companies, casual leaders, nightclubs, studio contractors and community orchestras; club memberships, social activities and monthly membership meetings; a disabled musicians' fund; subscription to Local 47's monthly newspaper and *International Musician*, the AFM newspaper; a 24-hour telephone assistance line; contract preparation and consultation in areas concerning your musical career; free help wanted and audition notices; rehearsal space; and low-cost instrument insurance. If a person fails to pay you for your services, the union will attempt to collect your money without any cost to you. Also, through the Booking Agent Agreement, commissions charged by booking agents are limited to 15% to 20%. AFM signatory booking agents that have negotiated an AFM Personal Management Agreement are allowed an additional commission of 5%.

RECORDING CONTRACTS

Another good reason to join a music union is a common provision in recording contracts between musicians and record companies that are signatories to AFM or AFTRA Agreements:

> *Artist represents that during the term of this recording agreement, Artist is and will remain or will promptly become and remain a member in good standing of any applicable guild and/or union to the extent that Company may legally require such membership. All applicable provisions of the collective bargaining Agreement to which Company is a party shall be deemed a part of this Agreement and shall be incorporated herein by reference.*

This provision obligates a signatory record company to pay you at least minimum union pay or scale for recording sessions (as well as providing other benefits), after you become a union member.

AGREEMENTS

The AFM and AFTRA regularly negotiate agreements that control sound recordings, movies, television, commercials and live performance. In calculating your minimum scale be sure to refer to the correct and current agreement. Also, the different payments for recording, production, sideline musicians, contractors, leaders, instrumentalists and vocalists are found in each agreement. Although these scales change periodically, many of the "terms of art" have the same meaning from one agreement to another. When an agreement expires and is not extended, the expired terms and conditions are usually followed until a new agreement can be negotiated and signed.

Much of the current information can be found online at *www.afm.org* and *www.aftra.org.*

Funds

In addition to pay scales, some union agreements also require employers to pay money to various funds. Depending on the particular fund, the money is used for pension, welfare and retirement benefits, payments to recording members, to members that perform in videos and to members that perform free live concerts in parks, veterans' hospitals, schools and other public places.

Terms of Art

As with all professions, union musicians share certain terms of art: ordinary words that have special meanings, which derive from the various union agreements discussed in this chapter. Common terms of art used throughout the AFM Agreements follow:

Contractor

A contractor's duties are to locate and hire musicians for particular jobs. The contractor will prepare the contracts and make sure that they are filed with the union. A contractor need not be a musician but must attend the engagement. Contractors may also be responsible for rehearsals.

Leader

When a musical group is hired one of the members is designated as the leader. The leader is responsible for the group and is the person who deals directly with the employer. The leader must file the contracts with the union and collect payment from the employer. If the leader fails to collect payment and fails to report the uncollected payment to the union, the leader is personally liable to the other union members for the uncollected amount.

Arranging

This is the art of preparing and adjusting an already written composition for presentation in other than its original form. This includes reharmonization, paraphrasing and development of a composition to fully present its melodic, harmonic and rhythmic structure.

Orchestrating

The orchestrator is the person who writes the musical score (a written musical composition that indicates the part to be performed by each voice and instrument) of an arrangement without changing or adding to the melodies, countermelodies, harmonies and rhythms.

AFM SCALE: RECORDINGS

One of the fundamental things a union does is establish minimum pay rates for its members. Remember that these rates are minimum and you are free to negotiate higher pay. Called "scales," "rates," "union fees" or "minimums," they all mean money paid to you (the member), at a variable minimum rate established in the applicable agreement. Always consult your local for current scale.

The AFM Sound Recording Labor Agreement sets scale for instrumentalists, leaders, contractors, arrangers, orchestrators and copyists working in the phonograph recording industry. Vocalists are paid according to scales set by AFTRA. If you sing and play an instrument, you should join both unions.

Session Scales

For instrumentalists, leaders and contractors the AFM sets basic scale and overtime scale for recording sessions. The rates are different for symphonic and nonsymphonic work.

Low-Budget Recordings

For full-length phonograph albums but not including soundtrack or cast albums, with a recording cost budget of $99,000 or less (not including producer or artist advances or travel expenses, rework and mastering costs), the minimum scale is at a lower rate.

Doubling, Cartage and Electronic Instruments

Additional payments may be paid if you play more than one instrument during a session. This is called doubling. If you play an electronic device to simulate sounds of instruments in addition to the normal sound of the instrument to which the electronic device is attached or applied, such use is treated as a double. What is or is not considered doubling is specified in the AFM agreement.

You are also entitled to compensation for cartage (hauling) if an employer requires you to bring a heavy instrument to a session.

Orchestrators, etc.

Arrangers', orchestrators' and copyists' scales are set according to a detailed pay schedule based on the extent of the work done, per page or per line or sometimes hourly. For example, page rates for orchestrators depend on what they do. There are different rates for transcribing a melody from voice, instrument or mechanical device, including chords, symbols and lyrics. Arrangers usually negotiate their own rates, which are to be no less than orchestrators' rates. Copyists get paid per hour or per page, according to certain detailed criteria set forth in the agreement.

Dubbing

The AFM discourages dubbing (using recordings not originally released in phonograph records [such as a film soundtrack] in a phonograph recording or using a recording made at an earlier time in a present recording). These rules relate to recordings that contain performances by persons covered by any AFM Phonograph Record Labor Agreement since January 1954. Dubbing is allowed where the record company notifies the union and pays the current scale to the artist who made the original recording that is being used.

Royalty Artists

When it comes to overdubbing, tracking, sweetening or playing multiple parts there are special provisions for "royalty artists." The AFM considers you a royalty artist if you record pursuant to a recording contract, which pays you royalties of at least 3% of the suggested retail price of records sold, or you are a member of a self-contained group of two or more, performing together in fields other than phonograph records under a group name (like a band or orchestra that performs live) and the group is under a recording agreement, which provides for a royalty payment of at least 3% of the suggested retail price of records sold. As a royalty artist, you receive the basic session rate per song for the first session at which you perform in respect to each song. This applies whether or not you play multiple parts, double, overdub or sweeten.

Sampling

Under certain circumstances, the AFM collects fees for its member musicians when a record company uses a sample of a preexisting recording in a new recording. When a portion of a recording containing the performance of an AFM member, who is a "nonroyalty artist" (i.e., a musician who plays on the recording but does not receive record royalties), not a self-contained royalty group or symphonic musician, is sampled under the following AFM definition, the company owning the recording that is being sampled makes a one-time lump sum payment of $400 for the first sample (regardless of how many times it is used in the new recording) and a one-time lump sum payment of $250 for each additional sample from the same recording, plus 2% of the gross revenue received by the company in excess of $25,000, less the lump sum payments that have already been made. These payments are made to the Sound Recording Manufacturers' Special Payments Fund and then distributed to the musician members. The AFM's definition of sampling is "a recording encoded into a digital sampler, computer, digital hard drive storage unit or other device for subsequent playback on a digital synthesizer or other playback device for use in another song (but not a remix or reedit of the new song)." Note that the definition includes not only samples embodied in traditional tapes and CDs but also includes samples embodied on computers, digital hard drives, digital synthesizers, samplers and other playback devices.

Personal Services Contract

The AFM bylaws do not allow you to enter into any personal services contract (such as a recording contract) for any period of more than five years without the approval of the AFM. This is true even in states such as California, where the law allows the maximum length of a personal services contract to be longer.

Recoupable Payments

Most recording agreements allow record companies to recoup recording costs from artists' royalties. A record company may seek to include all payments made to the AFM as recoupable recording costs. However, payments made by the record company under the Sound Recording Trust Agreement and Sound Recording Special Fund Agreement, which are based on record sales, are not properly recoupable as recording costs.

Music Performance Fund

The Sound Recording Trust Agreement requires signatory record companies to pay the trustee of the agreement a small percentage of the suggested retail price of records and tapes that are sold. This money is used for the presentation of free live concerts in parks, veterans' hospitals, schools and other public places. During 2003, the Music Performance Fund paid union musicians over $15 million to perform these concerts, making the AFM the largest employer of musicians in the world.

Sound Recording Special Payments Fund Agreement (SRSP Fund)

This agreement requires record companies to pay a small percentage of the price of each record sold to the SRSP Fund. The money in this fund is automatically paid to members annually in amounts determined by the number of union recording sessions each has played during the year. For example, during a recent fiscal year the Special Payments Fund distributed more than $12 million among recording musicians.

Video Promo Supplement

The Sound Recording Labor Agreement also provides that musicians that appear in music videos be compensated when the video incorporates a recording produced by a signatory record company.

Musicians other than royalty artists that perform on camera are entitled to payment.

If the record company receives money from the licensing, sale or leasing of the video, the company pays the AFM a small percentage of revenues received after the company has recouped an agreed amount. This is distributed among all the musicians involved in producing the recording used in the video.

If the record company sells the video as a videodisc or videocassette in the consumer market, it must make a payment to the AFM after the company has received a set amount in revenues from sales.

AFM SCALE: MOVIES

The AFM Theatrical Motion Picture Agreement defines and sets different scales for recording, production and sideline musician members.

Recording Scale

If you play on the recording of a movie soundtrack, you are entitled to receive recording scale. The scale depends on the number of musicians employed. There are separate rates for single sessions (three hours or less) and double sessions (six hours or less) with overtime rates as well. You are also entitled to additional pay if you are asked to double.

Production Scale

Musicians are paid production scale when they perform at rehearsals for a movie. These musicians do not record on the soundtrack or appear on camera and are paid either single session or double session scale. Scales are quoted in the agreement for longer rehearsal periods of 30 or 40 hours per week.

Sideline Scale

Sideline musicians appear on camera but do not record. The basic scale is for up to eight hours. You are also paid extra for time spent in costume fittings, interviews, wardrobe and makeup and overtime in excess of eight hours.

Orchestrators, etc.

Scale for orchestrators, copyists, proofreaders and music librarians, per page, hourly and weekly, are set forth in the Theatrical Motion Picture Agreement.

Music Sound Consultant

If you are not a conductor, leader or contractor and are assigned by a producer to advise on the sound quality of the music being recorded you are entitled to an hourly pay rate.

Overscale Employees

By individual negotiations between you and a producer, it can be agreed that any payment you receive, which is in excess of the minimum scale, be applied to any of the minimum payments, premiums, allowance, doubling, penalties, overtime or other minimum requirements of the agreement.

Film Musicians Secondary Markets Fund

This agreement requires a signatory movie producer to make residual payments to the AFM on behalf of musicians that perform on the film soundtrack. The producer must pay a small percentage of the accountable receipts from the exhibition of the motion picture on free television and supplemental markets (i.e., videocassettes, pay-type CATV, pay television and other technologies) to the Film Musicians Secondary Markets Fund. The administrator of the fund then pays members a percentage of these receipts based on a detailed formula set forth in the agreement.

AFM SCALE: TELEVISION

The AFM Television Videotape Agreement sets scale for network and syndicated television, both live and taped.

Types of Programs

In this agreement, the AFM sets rates according to the type and length of the television program. Signatory producers of 30-, 60- or 90-minute television programs, classified as variety programs, strip variety programs, non–prime-time children's variety shows and other types, pay different rates to AFM members.

Recording Scale

You are entitled to recording scale if you actually play on the recording of the television program soundtrack. Scale is set according to the length of the program and session.

Production Scale

If you play for rehearsals only and do not record on the program's soundtrack and do not appear on camera, you are entitled to production scale at an hourly rate.

Orchestrators, etc.

Orchestrators and copyists are entitled to the per page or hourly scale set forth in the agreement.

Reuse Fees

The AFM Television Videotape Agreement also requires employers to pay reuse fees for reruns of programs. If a program is rerun in the United States or Canada, the instrumentalists, leader, contractor and music sound consultant receive 75% of the original scale payment for the second and third run; 50% for the fourth, fifth and sixth runs; 10% for the seventh run and 5% for each additional run. There are separate schedules covering payments for foreign broadcasts.

AFM SCALE: OTHER TELEVISION AGREEMENTS

There are several additional AFM agreements that provide musicians with scale payments for services including recording, production, orchestrating, arranging, etc., depending on the type of program or exhibition, those being: movies made for television, basic cable, pay television and national public television.

Supplemental Market Fees

All of the various television agreements call for supplemental market fees (i.e., cassettes, pay-type CATV, pay television and in-flight [commercial airlines, trains, ships and buses] exhibitions) and reuse fees.

Reuse payments must be made by signatory producers, to the AFM, for subsequent broadcast cycles. If a producer elects to pay the instrumentalist under the higher of two wage scales, the program may be exhibited for a longer initial release period. Following the initial release, the producer must pay reuse fees to the AFM on behalf of the musicians. The exact amounts are calculated according to a formula set forth in the agreements.

AFM SCALE: COMMERCIALS

The AFM Television and Radio Commercial Announcements Agreement sets scales, which are usually paid by the signatory advertising agency making the commercial.

Session Scale

The Commercials Agreement calls for a minimum session for instrumentalists, leaders and contractors of one hour, during which three different commercial announcements may be recorded, the total length of which may not exceed three minutes. The maximum rate varies as to the number of musicians at the session.

Reuse Fees

The initial scale payment allows the commercial's producer to broadcast the commercial by television or radio, but not both, during a period of 13 weeks from the date of first broadcast. Thereafter, you should be paid reuse fees for each additional 13-week cycle.

AFM SCALE: LIVE PERFORMANCE

The AFM represents instrumentalists and vocalists when they perform live concerts. The individual locals set minimum wage scales and working conditions for nightclubs, hotels and other venues where live music is performed.

Booking Agents Agreement

The AFM Booking Agents Agreement sets limits on the commissions agents may charge members for securing live performance engagements. Approved agent commissions range from 15% to 20% depending on the duration of the employment secured by the agent, provided your net pay, after deducting the agent's commission, is never below scale.

Union Form Contracts

Members are required to use union approved form contracts for their live performances. One advantage of using the union form contracts is the union contract provision that requires the concert promoter or venue owner to pay you interest and attorneys' fees in addition to other damages if you are not paid for your services or the contract is otherwise violated. In California, if you bring an action against a promoter for a breach of the contract and you lose, you will have to pay the promoter's attorneys' fees.

Recording or Broadcasting Prohibited

You are entitled to additional payments if your live performance is recorded (either on audio or video or both) or transmitted on television or radio. For this reason, no live performances may be recorded, reproduced or transmitted without making prior arrangements with the AFM.

Casuals

Casual engagements are one- or two-night performances. The locals negotiate minimum scale for rehearsals and various types of shows including, dance only; dance with an incidental act; show and dance; cocktail hour, tea dance, fashion shows; show with accompanying act; casual concert where admission is charged; and park concerts.

The scale is based on the number of musicians and length of show and includes payment by the employer to the union pension and welfare funds.

Continuous/Extended Engagements

The locals negotiate scale for musicians that are hired for extended live performances. There are separate scales for hotel nightclubs, freestanding nightclubs and beer and wine establishments. Within each of these scale structures the pay is based upon the number of days per week you perform, the length of each performance and the number of musicians.

Arbitration

The union form contract provides that if any dispute or claim arises out of the engagement covered by the contract, the parties shall submit the matter to either the local's trial board or to an arbitrator who is picked by the parties. In a California lawsuit between Bill Graham, a concert promoter and Leon Russell, a performer, the court ruled that union arbitration provisions must provide the parties with an opportunity to obtain an unbiased and neutral arbitrator.

AFM: NEW TECHNOLOGIES

The AFM has addressed the services of its members in new technology formats in several ways. As a side letter to the Sound Recording Labor Agreement, the AFM and signatory companies have agreed to negotiate any disputes relating to payments that are due to musicians with respect to recordings that are digitally distributed (e.g., downloaded) via online computer services, the Internet, satellite or otherwise.

AFM MEMBERSHIP

If you play a musical instrument of any kind or are a vocalist or render musical services for pay, you are classified as a professional musician and you are eligible for membership in the AFM. You may apply for membership in any local in the area where you live.

Initiation Fees

You must pay initiation fees to both the AFM local and to the International Federation. Each local sets its own initiation fee and the International Federation's fee varies according to the amount of the local's fee. You pay the total initiation fees to the local.

Indoctrination

When you apply for AFM membership you must participate in an indoctrination procedure administered by the local. This will introduce you to the rules and benefits of the AFM. The local also holds an examination meeting in which the applicant will be asked for further information about his or her musical education and proficiency. No auditions are required.

Periodic Dues

You are required to pay annual or semiannual dues to the local and the Federation. For some locals, their dues include the Federation dues and other benefits provided by the local.

Work Dues

You must pay work dues based on your total earnings for all musical services performed. Upon joining the AFM, you must authorize all employers to deduct from your pay the work dues owed and to remit that amount to your local.

Work dues are based on a percentage of scale wages depending on the type of service rendered, such as live performances or recording sessions for sound recordings, television, motion pictures or commercials.

If the musician is a traveling member (member of another local), the work dues are paid to the AFM, not to the local where the work takes place.

Health and Welfare Funds

Locals use Health and Welfare Funds to provide health insurance benefits for members. To be eligible for these benefits, your employers must contribute a set dollar amount to the Fund every six months.

Employers Pension and Welfare Fund, Strike Fund

Members can also participate in an Employers Pension and Welfare Fund. The AFM also maintains a strike fund for its members, should it be necessary for the union to call a strike.

Defaulters List

Members are not allowed to render services for an employer on the AFM's Defaulters List. It is also improper for members to record or perform for a company that is not a signatory to the AFM Agreement. The union feels that musicians that play for defaulters condone unfair practices and undermine the bargaining power of the union and its members. Also, an AFM member is not permitted to render musical services outside of Canada or the United States or their territories or possessions, without the approval of the union.

AFTRA SCALE: RECORDINGS

AFTRA Code of Fair Practice for Sound Recordings sets the scales for the recording industry.

Hourly and Side Scale

Under this agreement, scale is determined per hour or per side, whichever is greater. A side is defined as a track (each overdub or multitrack is an additional side) that does not exceed three and one-half minutes.

Solo and Group Scale

The individual scale is the same for soloists and duos but is lower for groups of three or more singers. If, however, as a singer in a group of three or more vocalists, you step out and sing 16 or more cumulative bars on a particular side, you are paid at a higher scale. There are separate scales for vocalists that make classical recordings or original cast show albums.

Dubbing

Under AFTRA rules dubbing is allowed when the record company notifies AFTRA and pays scale to the artists that were involved in making the original recording. The company must also obtain the written consent of any star, featured or overscale artist.

Royalty Artists

The minimum rates mandated by AFTRA are payable even if you are a royalty artist. AFTRA considers you a royalty artist if your recording contract pays you record royalties. As a royalty artist you are not entitled to more than three times the minimum scale per side.

AFTRA SCALE: TELEVISION

AFTRA National Code of Fair Practice for Network Television Broadcasting Agreement sets rates for AFTRA members' services in the television industry.

Solo or Group Scale

The AFTRA Code sets different wage rates for soloists, duos and chorus singers. The scale increases for programs with longer running times. Another variable that affects scale is whether the program is a single performance or multiple performances during a calendar week. The specific scale varies for work that is done on camera and off camera and whether or not the program is a dramatic prime-time program.

AFTRA members are also entitled to replay fees and supplemental market fees.

AFTRA SCALE: TELEVISION COMMERCIALS

Signatories to the AFTRA Television Recorded Commercials Agreement pay the following fees for commercials:

Session Scale

Session scale is based on an eight-hour day. Scale varies for soloists and duos and groups of different sizes when you work on or off camera.

Use Scale

Scale for use of program commercials is divided into classes, according to the number of cities in which it is telecast. Use payments for each class have separate scales for principal performers and group performers and within each of those scales are different rates for on-camera and off-camera performances, each time the commercial is used.

AFTRA SCALE: RADIO COMMERCIALS

Signatories to the AFTRA Radio Recorded Commercials Agreement pay for recording sessions. Reuse fees under this agreement are affected by many variables, including special scale for wild spots, dealer commercials, network program commercials, regional and network program commercials, single market commercials and foreign uses. Scales are determined according to complex formulas set forth in the agreement.

AFTRA MEMBERSHIP

You are eligible for AFTRA membership if you have performed or intend to perform as a singer in the fields of radio, television or phonograph recording. AFTRA does not regulate the musical services of its members outside the United States.

Initiation Fees

AFTRA imposes a uniform initiation fee of $1,300, however, this need not be paid when you first work. You have 30 days from your first engagement before the initiation fee and dues are payable.

Dues

Dues are payable semiannually. Each member pays base dues of $63.90 every six months plus additional amounts based on the performer's gross earnings under AFTRA's jurisdiction for the previous year.

Other AFTRA Benefits

Benefits of the AFTRA Health Fund are available for an individual if you have $10,000 in earnings within AFTRA's jurisdiction, during four or fewer consecutive calendar quarters. This fund includes life insurance, accidental death insurance and medical insurance. There are higher earnings requirements to be eligible for a family health plan.

The AFTRA Pension Fund provides benefits determined by the number of years you are active with AFTRA and your earnings during those years.

A credit union is also available to AFTRA members.

Discipline

As an AFTRA member, if you violate union rules, you may be disciplined by means of fine, suspension or expulsion from the union.

AFTRA: NEW TECHNOLOGIES

In keeping pace with ever changing technology, AFTRA has negotiated an agreement relating to services rendered in the production of interactive programs, on CD-ROM and the Internet, the AFTRA Interactive Media Agreement.

CONCLUSION

For a union to be successful, its members must respect its rules. By reporting unfair practices and conscientiously participating in union activities and elections you help protect other union members and, to an extent, you exercise a degree of control over how the union represents you and protects your interests. The complex array of union scales and payments for royalties, reuses and supplemental markets, were not guaranteed to musicians by employers out of friendship. Unions organized and fought for these payments. As long as enthusiastic and ethical professionals are involved in unions, they will help to ensure fair treatment for all musicians.

Recording

Practical Aspects of Securing a Record Deal with a Major Label

BY NEVILLE L. JOHNSON AND BERNARD M. RESNICK

Artists need three things to succeed in the record business: talent, luck and contacts—but not necessarily in that order. Talent alone does not guarantee a record deal; and seeking one can be one of the most discouraging parts of the business. After all of the hard work of writing songs, putting live shows together and recording demos, the people that actually sign artists are neither easier to reach nor more willing to listen to the music. Due to the intense competition between record companies, the consolidation of the bulk of retail sales into four major record companies, the erosion of sales from illegal file sharing and other industry factors, only a few hundred major record deals are offered to artists each year. However, for talented musicians, success may be just around the corner.

TODAY'S REALITY: CREATE YOUR OWN BUZZ

Four dominant record companies, Sony/BMG, Universal, EMI and WEA, generate over 75% of all worldwide retail music sales. The Internet's retail sites and fan sites are the main gateways for today's music fan to discover and purchase new music. Even hip-hop, which until recently was fundamentally a "street promotion" business, has turned to the Internet as a major source of grassroots promotion. Major record companies are loathe to develop the image and fan base of an artist—the days of a group having several LPs to "find its audience" are a thing of the past. Therefore, to have a realistic chance of getting signed to a major record deal, artists have to do what record labels used to do—create an image and a fan base. This involves getting the ball rolling by any means necessary, including but not limited to (a) release of a debut LP on the artist's own or through an independent label; (b) achievement of regular radio airplay, hopefully, in more than one market; (c) successful concert performances, which sell large amounts of tickets; (d) use of the artist's music on television programs, films, video games or downloadable telephone ringtones; (e) appearance of the artist on "mix tape" CDs; (f) launch of the artist's music and image through the artist's own Internet Web site; and (g) placement of the artist's music and discussion of the artist on fan Web sites, commercial Web sites and blogs. In all of these instances, artists need to register with companies that use technology to verify and track sales, such as SoundScan (which, via bar coding, measures the sales of recorded music in the United States),

BDS (which measures radio airplay) and Internet statistical tracking services, which measure page views and hits of Web sites. Artists and repertoire (A&R) staff at record companies regularly research and track such information and use it to contact local acts and their representatives when they sense artists are hot or when regional breakouts are occurring.

THE MUSIC PACKAGE

The music package, also known as the press kit, consists of the most important physical elements that show artists' potentials for profitable sales. Although many different elements can be included, most A&R representatives are concerned with materials that answer three questions: (1) What do the artists sound like? (2) What do they look like? and (3) What is their story?

A demonstration sound recording (demo) is necessary for most acts that have not had a record deal prior to the time of the presentation. A demo must contain music that is unique, creative and—most importantly—commercial. The majors want music that will sell in large quantities. Record companies are not in business to entertain the public—they exist to make a profit for their owners and shareholders. The styles of music that record companies sell change from year to year. The major record companies stay in business by supplying the public with music to consume that fits current trends. Record company talent scouts, known as A&R executives, seek acts that will provide significant sales and airplay, as their jobs depend on the profitability of the artists they sign. Although one function of an A&R executive is talent acquisition, most are primarily busy with, and responsible for, the talent that is already signed to their label. Therefore, new artists have a tough time getting the attention of A&R staff.

EPK (Electronic Press Kit) is an acronym commonly heard in the entertainment business. It is a cost-effective way to promote an act, but it is not recommended when submitting to a label for a deal: many A&R executives are not very computer savvy and it is easier to skip an EPK than a more inviting physical package.

Artists should bear in mind that ultimately sales will be to the public, not to record companies. Music executives evaluate music, in large part, on the basis of its sales potential.

Many artists choose to e-mail industry executives in order to invite them to view Web sites and hear their music as a way to solicit interest. Although this is a good starting point, artists that are serious about looking for a major label record deal still need to create a physical press kit for solicitation purposes, for several reasons. First, the music will sound better coming out of the executive's fancy stereo, rather than tiny, tinny-sounding laptop computer speakers. Second, the visual image will be better reproduced on high-quality glossy photograph paper than on a computer screen. Third, many older A&R executives are not as facile with a computer as they are with paper and CDs. Fourth, a physical press kit is easier for record company executives to share with each other and to present to committees in boardroom meetings. Fifth, a first-class physical press kit shows the A&R executives that artists are serious and professional about their work and its promotion.

What Do Artists Sound Like?

Artists need to create high-quality demonstration recordings (demos). Successful demos have the following characteristics.

- **Good Performance.** Artists must prove they are ready to cut tapes of master quality. The recordings must provide the basic structure of the songs, including their rhythm, melody, lyric, harmony, arrangement, mix and production. Listeners need to hear the "hook," chorus or most memorable part of the song within no more than a minute or two of pushing the play button. Demos must include songs that A&R executives can promote for public sale, so artists need to select the most commercial songs from their repertoires, which means those that are most likely to be chosen as singles or videos and be played on the radio.

- **Best Songs First.** Record company personnel that listen to demos are very busy and listen to many in a day's work. The best songs should come first and only a few selections should be provided. Self-produced and released albums may get A&R attention, however, artists should indicate the most commercial cuts on their albums. Otherwise, A&R executives will listen to the first and maybe the second song, before moving on to another demo. Aggressively self-edited demos have the best chance to gain favorable reactions. If your music cuts across several styles, choose tunes in one consistent style. Resist the temptation to include everything—leave listeners hungry for more. Demos should be underproduced since A&R executives are paid to assist artists in creating slick, full sounds, and they know how to imagine a fully-realized master when they hear a bare-bones demo.

- **Container Information.** The name of each selection and the order of performance should be clearly written or typed on the demo box and the CD. Make it easy for listeners to name the songs they like. Include the person to contact about the demo (personal manager, attorney, band leader). List the name, address, phone and fax numbers, and e-mail of the contact person for the demo on the package and the CD, not just on the accompanying materials. Many A&R executives separate the CD from the press kit, to make it more convenient to carry around. Including contact details on every part of each music package makes it easy for A&R people to contact artists if they like the music.

    The other components of the physical package, listed below, can significantly enhance the listener's evaluation and should accompany the demo.

Photographs/Videotape

The record company should know about artists' looks and images. Professional and attractive appearances are valuable assets in today's music industry. Still photographs, standard eight by ten inch size, whether color or black and white, of artists clothed as they would appear on stage or in videos, are essential to transmit part of the image artists will sell to the public. Attractive or unique visual appearances are just as important as the sounds contained in the demos—remember, the record companies "package" artists' sounds, looks and images as part of their sales promotions. Take great care in the selection of photographers and the images to be used in press kits. Record companies are interested in artists' visual impacts due to music videos and the growing interrelationship between motion pictures, television and records. Some acts have been signed on the strength of a video of their live performance sent in lieu of, or in addition to, a demo. If your act has significant visual appeal, a video demo should be considered.

Be mindful, however, of the expense of creation of a video demo and the chances it may quickly be rendered useless by changes in fashion and band member personnel.

Biographical Information

Succinct, factual statements of artists' credentials, influences and background help provide important information. Bios are analogous to résumés: they inform readers of the qualifications of the applicants. Several paragraphs on one page are all that is necessary to tell the story to A&R executives. Check carefully for spelling and grammatical errors and do not be afraid to list artists' accomplishments and achievements.

Lyric Sheets

Lyric sheets help to involve listeners in the music, especially when artists want to convey deep meanings in the messages of their music. Hip-hop artists, however, rarely include lyric sheets in their press kits.

Reviews and Itinerary

Favorable reviews indicate that artists have stage experience and are enjoyable to hear. If artists can excite audiences and have followings, record companies will want to know about it because live performance is an important method of promoting records. Some Internet review sites, such as *www.pitchforkmedia.com,* have been very influential in helping acts get noticed by record labels. A lot of attention or friends on a networking site such as *www.myspace.com* may also open doors.

If a number of impressive gigs have been played or the artists are regularly working, itineraries should be enclosed to communicate that the acts are stage wise and experienced on the road and have reliable sources of income.

By paying attention to details, artists can project professionalism to record companies. Clever, enticing press kits will merit special attention by their recipients.

THE HUMAN PACKAGE

Most successful artists are members of a team. A critical issue in a record company's decision whether to sign an act is who will carry the ball after a record is released. Who besides the A&R executive will be awake late at night, worrying about how to promote this artist? If an act has inexperienced or incompetent management or is without professional advisors for support and direction, the record company's job of selling records will be much more difficult. Artists will substantially improve their chances of securing recording agreements if they are part of functioning, well-organized business machines that can work with record companies toward the common goal of generating income. Important aspects of people that work with artists are whether they are credible, have track records and are respected throughout the industry.

Personal Managers

Personal managers are the most important members of the human package. If would-be recording artists are brought to record companies by highly regarded managers, the record companies may be more easily swayed to invest resources. Record company executives feel secure when well-regarded professional managers coordinate artists' careers, recording duties, public performances, songwriting and other professional activities on a day-to-day basis.

Artists must be extremely selective in choosing personal managers. Some managers are objectionable because of their pushy and demanding demeanors, unsavory reputations, unrealistic expectations or sheer incompetence. Most established personal managers are not interested in unsigned acts, but they do have their antennas up and can be wooed with the right approach.

Talent Agents

The human package can also include talent agents that are successfully booking artists in live engagements. Artists that have talent agents offer record companies added inducements for making deals, because they will be able to rely upon skilled professionals to book artists into live engagements before, during and after the release of albums. This will promote record sales and relieve some of the pressure on record companies to financially support artists.

Attorneys

Attorneys can be important members of the human package because of their contacts at record companies and elsewhere in the industry, through the clients they represent. Managers, music publishers, agents, lawyers, DJs and record producers are the primary persons that shop record deals to the major labels. Artists should have the guidance of professionals to assist them with legal needs and to help select the other members of their human packages. Sound advice—get a lawyer and someone else who has influence with record companies to work for you, check the lawyer's reputation to ensure that the lawyer is well-regarded throughout the industry, and make sure you and your lawyer have a clear understanding of your financial relationship. Have a clear understanding as to who is expected to do which task in the shopping process and how much you will have to pay your lawyer to do his or her assigned tasks.

Business Managers

Business managers that have strong relationships with executives at labels are also part of the human package. Business managers are different from personal managers. They specialize in financial, taxation and investment issues for artists.

Record Producers/Production Companies

Record producers and production companies (entities that help artists create demo recordings and finance and shop record deals) are other routes to deals. Be careful, however, in exclusively engaging a record producer or production company. Record companies may be unimpressed with a particular producer's talent, business ethics or track record. If artists are required contractually to work with producers/production companies, it removes any flexibility for the artists and the potential labels and could possibly ruin deals.

Artists that are signed to production companies will generally make less money than if signed directly to labels because the producers and production companies will take shares of the revenue. That being said, major record labels understand that producers are the true talent scouts and are primarily responsible for artist development in today's environment, especially in the genres of rap and R&B. Major labels in these genres rely heavily on the opinions of producers in determining which artists to promote or sign, so going through a producer or a production company may be the only viable alternative. Reducing artists' share of the profits may be necessary to achieve realistic chances for success. It is better to have a small percentage of something than a large percentage of nothing.

Anybody with Influence

The music business is very insular. Other musicians or even those outside the music industry that have personal relationships with A&R people may be willing to go to bat for the artist. A network of well-connected people is essential for any artist's eventual success. Artists should regularly attend industry conferences, seminars and lectures. There are various professional organizations where artists can meet and learn from professionals. In New York and Los Angeles, there are the Association of Independent Music Publishers and the California Copyright Conference. The National Academy of Recording Arts and Sciences (NARAS), which awards the GRAMMYs each year, has chapters in many major cities across the United States. Local songwriter associations, music support groups, universities and performance rights organizations (ASCAP, BMI and SESAC) all provide regular and inexpensive opportunities for artists to meet and learn from each other and from industry executives. The Nashville Songwriters Association International (NSAI), with over 100 chapters, is the largest nonprofit trade organization dedicated to serving songwriters. The National Association of Record Industry Professionals (NARIP) is an educational, networking group that holds seminars and events in Los Angeles, New York, Las Vegas, San Francisco and other cities.

WRITE A HIT SONG

Write a hit song for or with another artist—there is no faster entrée into the major label world.

TOTAL PACKAGE

There are three ways of presenting total packages to record companies. The first is to have representatives of record companies see artists perform live; the second is to present or send demos to record companies; and the third (and most risky) is to let record companies approach artists.

Showcases and Live Performances

Record companies, especially those in the genres of rock, country, jazz, classical and R&B, want to sign artists that perform well on stage. Performing live, by showcase (an act performed primarily for representatives of record companies) or other engagement, can be an effective way of attracting the attention and interest of a record company. If an artist's performance is a knockout, it will enhance the prospects of a record deal or a future demo at the company's expense.

It is not easy to induce record executives that are involved with talent acquisition to attend a gig or showcase. If the artist is performing in, say, Phoenix, Arizona, the chances of getting a record company person to attend are poor. New York City, Los Angeles and Nashville are the main cities where record companies are located, and it is still very tough to get executives to turn out for shows there. Virtually all country signings are made by Nashville-based record companies or by the Nashville offices of national companies.

Invitations to attend a showcase or gig should be in writing or e-mail. Multiple follow-up telephone calls in the days shortly before and on the day of the performance are the best reminders. Be certain that the names of all invited executives are on the guest list so they do not have to pay admission charges to attend. Offer to add executives "+ 1" to the guest list. This allows them to bring a date or a colleague to the show and is a small price to pay in order to increase the chances of being heard by someone in a position to offer a deal. Not only will this increase the slim chance that executives will actually attend, but it will provide them with trusted, objective opinions right there. Spare no expense in putting on a showcase, as it may be the only chance to perform in front of people that have the ability to sign artists. Do not, however, alter the fundamental character of the performances just because A&R executives might be in the crowd. The artists should perform their acts in the same way (and with the same energy and enthusiasm) as they would in their hometown bars. Executives want to see that artists can grab the attention of their audiences, sell drinks for the venues, win over new fans and most importantly, perform as professionals—on time, in tune and able to "wow the crowds."

Presenting Demos to Record Companies

The most effective way of presenting demos is through personal meetings with the individuals to whom they are to be given. If this cannot be arranged, concise, clearly typed letters that state the purpose for which the demos are sent, together with press kits and listings of the members of the human package should accompany the demos.

Because of the problems with live engagements and showcases (such as getting record company executives to attend), artists that are in search of deals should provide record companies with both demos and invitations to subsequent performances.

Occasionally, a record company will request other material or that the artist return with subsequently written material. Some companies will pay for recording sessions to make additional demos.

Letting Record Companies Approach Artists

This is the most risky method of securing record deals. This approach will fail if artists and their professional teams are not aggressive, effective self-promoters. If they are successful in promoting, they will have already generated verifiable sources of sales and uses of their artists' music. This would include, for example, BDS spins on radio stations, SoundScan reports of thousands of sales, proof of thousands of downloads, rave reviews in newspapers, magazines, e-zines and blogs, use of their artists' music in television programs, films or video games and inclusion of their artists' music in well-respected DJs' mix tapes.

In such situations, artists are bound to be noticed by the A&R staff researchers at major record companies that will then reach out to the artists' professional representatives in order to inquire about their availability for recording contracts. This will turn the tables from artists begging record companies for deals and give the artists' entertainment attorneys more leverage in negotiating the business points of recording contracts to benefit their artists. Having been in this enviable position, the authors of this article can confirm to the readers how much easier our jobs became.

Good artist Web sites are an essential way to market unsigned artists. These sites must be regularly maintained and updated, so that executives and fans know the latest news about artists' upcoming performances and most recent accomplishments. The better the Web sites, the better artists' chances are of getting signed.

SHOPPING THE PACKAGE

When the total package is presented to record companies to solicit an offer of a recording contract, it is known as "shopping a deal." Artists must decide who will perform this function, who will be approached and how to approach them. If individuals that are unknown to the record companies send invitations to showcases, they will probably be ignored. If artists send their demos directly to record companies, the probable responses will be rejection and returning them to the senders as "unwanted unsolicited material." If a record company accepts a demo, in most cases it will be referred to listeners in the A&R department. These people listen to thousands of demos each year, and most demos get less than two minutes' listen prior to rejection. This is not necessarily a reflection on artists' talents, rather a matter of sheer numbers, as there are literally thousands of artists chasing only a few hundred deals each year.

Where possible, artists should bypass individuals on the lower rungs of record companies and attempt to get their packages presented to presidents, chairmen of the boards or heads of the A&R departments—those that have the authority to commit companies to signing artists. Products should "flow downhill." Many companies work on a committee basis, and most signings occur via the A&R department. Other members of the A&R hierarchy and employees in other departments, such as promotion or marketing, may also be approached. The chances for serious consideration by the A&R department or other executives involved with talent acquisition are improved based upon the source of the intake of the music. That being said, many acts have been signed as a result of recommendations from local or regional promotion people that noticed them in cities other than New York or Los Angeles.

The best avenue of reaching people at record companies that wield substantial influence or are in decision-making positions to sign artists is personal contact. Invitations to showcases or gigs will be favorably answered and demos will get serious consideration only if they are sent or referred by people that are recognized and respected by the persons receiving such invitations and demos. This does not mean that people sending such invitations or demos need be famous within the music industry; they simply need to be credible. The adage that it is not what you know but who you know, definitely applies to the music business.

A number of personal managers, producers, lawyers, artist, writers and publishers can, because of their success, power and clientele, induce high-ranking record company executives to review press kits. Each member of the human package should be called upon to present packages to those at record companies with whom they are acquainted. Because personal contacts are so important in the industry, artists should attempt to get to know as many people in the music business as possible. The young promotion man at a record company today may be the head of the A&R department tomorrow. Artists that are friendly with promoted people may have both friends and business acquaintances that will be helpful in advancing careers.

It is essential to coordinate the shopping process through one person on each team. Anyone who presents press kits to record company executives should report the dates, times, locations, recipients and details of the presentations to the coordinator. This prevents confusion and makes certain that all parties are aware of who is supposed to approach which people at what companies. Coordinating and streamlining the shopping process maximizes the chances for artists to be offered deals.

A number of music attorneys are well connected throughout the industry. Many of these attorneys will "run a demo." Most attorneys that represent top talent in the industry will not shop deals because it is difficult, time consuming and requires them to act as agents when they would rather confine themselves to negotiating, drafting and advising on agreements. However, some will do so for a flat fee, percentage of the deal or a "partial contingency" arrangement, which may vary from a percentage of the initial advance to a continuing interest in royalties, advances and revenues earned from compositions that are recorded pursuant to any such agreement. (Any agreement for a percentage to be paid to any attorney should be reviewed for fairness by a third-party attorney.) The success ratio of attorneys shopping deals is not high, but there are success stories. Research various lawyers. Ask about their successes and methodologies and their game plans for the products to be shopped. With whom are they connected? How many other acts have they shopped and how many are they shopping presently? Be patient with any attorney that is shopping a deal, as record deals do not happen overnight. (See the chapter, "Music Attorneys," for details on fees, pricing arrangements and responsibilities.)

The human package must show the same level of professionalism as the music package. People that present total packages must have good relationships with, and be passionately enthusiastic about their artists; know and understand the music; be aware of the long-term career goals of their artists; and most importantly, be able to communicate with, and be credible to, the companies that are approached. Artists and their marketing teams must be aggressive, but never rude, when approaching those that have influence or signing ability. They must be relentless, patient, cunning and charming, and be able to distinguish their products from others, to make sure they are heard.

CHOOSING RECORD COMPANIES

Record companies all press, distribute and promote records, but the similarity ends there. Artists must carefully investigate the business structure, the standing in the industry and the marketing philosophy of any record company pursued. Artists need companies that are committed to them, have the organization to support that commitment and have shown themselves to be successful in the genres in which the artists perform.

Most artists want companies that are, or are part of, strong and successful worldwide enterprises. This does not mean however, that artists need pursue only the big companies. Look for capable companies that have the organization and financial wherewithal to exploit records successfully throughout the world.

In today's business environment, it may be just as financially rewarding to skip traditional U.S. record deals altogether. There are labels overseas that may be interested. Artists should attend MIDEM *(www.midem.com)*, the annual music business convention in Cannes, France, where music publishers and record executives congregate at the end of each January. We know of dozens of U.S. artists that have foreign deals and whose records are imported into the United States. There are many other conventions where artists can network and make contacts. The biggest is South by Southwest *(www.sxsw.com)*, which is held every March in Austin, Texas, but there are conventions in many other cities that should also be considered.

READ THE TRADES

Billboard is the industry magazine that charts the events of the music business on a week-to-week basis. Artists that want to obtain record deals in today's competitive music business should read it to become aware of the trends and developments in the industry and to keep track of key executives. *Music Connection,* based in Los Angeles, is an excellent source of information for artists. Twice a year, it publishes a list of all A&R executives, major publishers, managers and attorneys. In addition, there are many other industry trade journals, in print or online that provide useful information as to what music is being played, where and when it is being played, who is hot and which artists and musical styles are rising in popularity. Knowledge is power—successful artists and the members of their respective teams all keep current on industry trends.

CONCLUSION

The individuals that evaluate music at record companies are asked to make extremely difficult decisions. They must gamble on their instinct and ability to predict the fickle nature of the public's taste to determine what music will be commercially viable. No amount of hype can sell a demo or a performance that does not have it "in the grooves," yet no reliable definition of this phrase has ever been articulated.

Moreover, artists should seek record deals only if they are ready, dedicated and willing to spend years in the studio and on the road. The efforts necessary to launch careers are enormous, the rewards far from guaranteed.

However, with enthusiasm, hard work and perseverance, talented artists can achieve record deals. Sure, rejections are commonplace, but the only people that really matter are the executives that say, "Yes." Those executives want to find artists as much as artists want to find them. Keep at it!

Analysis of a Recording Contract

BY LAWRENCE J. BLAKE AND DANIEL K. STUART

> *Important:* *An updated copy of this chapter by Lawrence J. Blake and Daniel K. Stuart can be downloaded for free at http:www.danielkstuart.com*

The recording agreement is probably the most important document a singer or a band will sign during their career. If an artist's first recording agreement is poorly negotiated the consequences that may be suffered by the artist can be significant and long lasting. Recording artists should resist the temptation to sign anything that is presented to them as a "standard recording contract." They should hire competent counsel to negotiate on their behalf and do their own reading to make themselves aware of the issues that may affect them for the rest of their careers.

While a recording contract certainly does not guarantee success, it does often permit the recording artist to devote more attention to career development. The release of successful recordings can lead to substantial royalties; valuable exposure on radio, television, the Internet; and significant income from performing at live concerts. Further, if a recording artist writes or cowrites his or her own songs, the sale of their records and the public performances of their songs can generate publishing royalties, which often exceed the royalties they receive as a performer.

Recording agreements vary significantly from company to company and genre to genre. Agreements developed by major labels are far more lengthy and comprehensive than agreements developed by smaller independent labels. During this era of label consolidation and corporate downsizing, the legal departments within record companies have less manpower available to devote to drafting and negotiating recording agreements. Consequently, major labels try to maintain as much standardization among their agreements as possible. However, there should still be ample room in every negotiation for recording artists to obtain concessions from the record labels that can result in significant increases in earnings and career flexibility as the artist's career unfolds.

While this chapter discusses several issues that the artist and his or her counsel should raise and seek to improve during the course of negotiations, no artist should expect a label to concede to all of his or her demands. The degree to which a record company will improve upon its first draft depends in large measure on how badly the label wants to sign the artist. Typically, if a major label is willing to sign an artist, it has made the determination that it is willing to invest significant sums in developing and promoting the artist's records and the artist should bear in mind that the record company would probably not be offering a contract if it did not believe that there was a reasonable chance that it will earn substantial revenue from the exploitation of the artist's work.

Many unsigned artists underestimate their bargaining power. At the same time, it is important that an artist not overestimate his or her bargaining power at the risk of blowing the deal altogether. An artist should always bear in mind that the record company may, at any time, decide to terminate negotiations with or without any justification. If an artist is involved in a bidding war, in which more than one record label is vying for his or her services, the artist has significantly more leverage and can usually extract significant improvements and concessions. If an artist is only negotiating with one record company, he or she should adopt a measured strategic approach to negotiations to avoid losing the deal.

The negotiation of a recording contract may involve heated discussions between the attorneys for the artist and the record company. The artist's manager may also engage in negotiation discussions with creative personnel at the record label. The artist should be well insulated from having direct adversarial conflict with label personnel during negotiations but should be kept apprised of all developments and read all drafts of the recording agreement and all of the attorney's comments regarding those drafts to make certain he or she understands what issues are being fought over.

Recent developments in recording agreements include the conversion by most major labels from a complex retail-based royalty structure to a simplified wholesale-based approach, and the grappling over how to distribute the proceeds generated by emerging technologies such as music subscription services and ringtones.

THE INDUSTRY DEBATE OVER RINGTONES

This chapter would not be complete without a discussion of ringtones, which now reportedly generate in excess of $2 billion per year and are the focus of vigorous debate within the music industry itself. The first generation of ringtones consisted mainly of polyphonic tones that reproduced (sometimes poorly) popular songs. These early ringtones did not use master recordings owned by the record companies, so music publishers earned most of the early ringtones dollars. When someone purchased a polyphonic ringtone of a popular song, the artist and the record company would not receive any money, but the publisher of the composition would collect whatever fee they negotiated. Savvy publishers negotiated deals with ringtone providers that paid publishers on a percentage basis (reportedly up to 10% to 12% of retail), rather than using the decades-old mechanical royalty approach used by record companies.

The publishers' and record companies' interests met in a head-on collision with the advent of the next generation of ringtones, sometimes called "mastertones." While few consumers use the word mastertones, within the industry the term refers to the use of master recordings as ringtones on consumers' cell phones. So, instead of hearing a polyphonic performance of Kelly Clarkson's "Since U Been Gone" every time your phone rings, you actually hear Kelly's vocal performance in the context of her fully produced master recording. Further, ringtones providers and record companies successfully launched "ringbacks," which are specific audio clips (usually music, but sometimes other types of audio clips) that consumers can assign to specific incoming callers so, for example, when your crazy cousin calls you, he might hear a clip of Gnarls Barkley's "Crazy" in his cell phone earpiece instead of the traditional sound of a phone ringing. For the purpose of

CONTINUED ON NEXT PAGE

CONTINUED FROM PREVIOUS PAGE

this discussion, ringbacks are considered to be ringtones. Once the record companies' property had become an essential part of the ringtones framework, the issue of publishing royalties became a source of contention, as every penny (or fraction of a penny) that the publishers collect is one less penny for the record companies. The early deals negotiated between the music publishers and the ringtone providers often yielded fees to the publisher that exceeded the current minimum statutory rate for the reproduction of compositions on phonorecords, so the RIAA petitioned the Register of Copyrights who, in October of 2006, published a memorandum opinion that stated that ringtones are phonorecords made and distributed for private use (more on that below). This opinion, if implemented, would probably make ringtones subject to the same compulsory mechanical licensing terms as traditional phonorecords.

The Register of Copyright's memorandum, if followed, has several substantial effects. From the artist's perspective, it confirms the record companies' position that the dissemination of ringtones are "sales" (as opposed to licenses) and, accordingly, artists would receive standard record royalty rates instead of 50% of net licensing revenues (unless the recording agreement provided for a separate royalty structure for ringtones). Artists signing new contracts would face an uphill battle on this issue, although because ringtones are so new, artists should not be shy about pushing for better terms for ring-tones revenue (e.g., artists might ask for a unique royalty rate for ringtones to avoid the application of the single records rate). From the record companies' perspectives, the implementation of this opinion would seem to improve their profit margin, although the compulsory mechanical licensing requirements impose certain administrative burdens (i.e., monthly accountings, etc.). From the music publishers' perspective, the implementa-tion of this opinion would seem to reduce their profit margin, at least at current ringtones pricing, although if that pricing decreases, the implementation of the compulsory rate could prove to be better than a fixed percentage of retail. Finally, from the perspectives of the public performance societies (ASCAP, BMI and SESAC), the opinion is troubling as the use of the phrase "for private use" could be interpreted as negating their long-held position that the playing of ringtones when a phone rings constitutes "public performance" in much the same way as playing a song on the radio. (An interesting distinction might ulti-mately be drawn between ringtones that are essentially performed for all within shouting distance to hear and ringbacks that are privately heard in the earpiece of a caller, but that is a different discussion for a different article.) The public performance societies have reportedly been receiving about 4% of ringtones revenue as compensation for these public performances, and they are expected to fight hard to retain this revenue stream. Suffice it to say that the various stakeholders, the artists, record companies, publishers, public performance societies and ringtones providers, will probably continue to slug it out until some consensus of industry norms takes shape. Meanwhile, the ringtones revenue stream itself may prove vulnerable to emerging technologies and services. There is now consumer software on the market (e.g., Xingtones) that allows consumers to create their own mastertones from their personal music libraries for use with certain cell phones, and the proliferation of free bootlegged ringtones via Internet peer-to-peer networks may already be upon us.

Many small labels, production companies and indeed some major record companies have, in recent years, attempted to secure an interest in revenue streams other than record sales when negotiating their recording agreements. For example, record companies may seek to participate in an artist's earnings derived from song publishing, the sale of merchandise and even endorsements and touring revenue. The record companies argue that during this era of easily pirated CDs and ongoing illegal downloads they need to participate in these additional revenue streams to have a reasonable chance of generating a profit. Fortunately, at this time, most major labels still do not insist on participation in such revenue streams. While it is in the best interests of the recording artist to avoid granting such participation rights to their record companies, in some circumstances, such issues may truly be deal breakers and the artist must carefully consider whether or not to make some compromises in order to move forward in what would otherwise be a potentially lucrative business relationship. Each of those scenarios must be analyzed on a case-by-case basis and this article should not be construed as encouraging or discouraging recording artists to accept or reject any such proposed terms to any recording agreement. With the foregoing in mind, let us turn our attention to the careful analysis of a major record company's initial proposal and long-form agreement.

What follows is the text of an actual long-form recording agreement from a major record company, the name of which has been redacted. Our running commentary to the language in the agreement is italicized, as are certain key words in the agreement. If the reader is a recording artist negotiating a recording agreement, this article may be useful for helping you understand the issues as you discuss them with your attorney, but this article is not intended to be a substitute for legal counsel. Each negotiation between a recording artist and a record company is unique, and experienced competent music attorneys are trained to analyze each set of circumstances and to use their relationships and powers of persuasion to help their artists get the better overall deal.

EXCLUSIVE ARTIST'S RECORDING AGREEMENT

AGREEMENT made and entered into as of this _____ day of _____,200___ by and between _____ , Major Record Company Inc., 123 Anystreet, Anytown,ZZ 99999 ("<u>Company</u>") and _____ , ("<u>you</u>").

1. EXCLUSIVE SERVICES

Company hereby engages your *exclusive* services for the making of Recordings and Records and you hereby accept such engagement and agree to *exclusively* render such services to Company in the Territory during the Initial Period of this agreement and all applicable extensions and renewals (the "<u>Term</u>"). (You are sometimes called "<u>Artist</u>" herein; all references in this agreement to "<u>you</u>," "<u>Artist</u>," "<u>you and Artist</u>," "<u>you or Artist</u>," and their possessive forms and the like shall be understood to refer to you alone.)

> *The key word here is "exclusivity." There's no getting around it—when an artist signs a recording agreement, the record company owns everything the artist records for the duration of the contract.*

2. TERM

(a) The Term shall commence on the date hereof and shall continue for an initial period (the "<u>Initial Period</u>") ending on the last day of the ____ th complete month following the date of Delivery of the last Master constituting the Recording Commitment for such Initial Period.

> *The "term" of a recording agreement means the period of time during which the artist is under contract exclusively to the record company. During the term, the artist cannot record for any other company without the record company's approval. However, certain rights and obligations extend beyond the term. For example, the company's right to sell the artist's records is usually perpetual (although in rare instances might be limited for a number of years) and its obligations to account and pay royalties to the artist are perpetual. The term of this recording agreement is not measured by years but instead expires a certain number of months after the master recordings comprising the "Recording Commitment" (usually one album) are "Delivered." In some recording agreements, the expiration date is defined as a certain number of months after an album is commercially released. Because the artist cannot control the date on which the record company releases his or her album, the artist should try to have the term measured from the date of "Delivery" as opposed to the retail street date. Some record companies prefer to measure the term from the retail street date so they can have an opportunity to evaluate the commercial performance of the artist's album before having to decide whether to exercise their option to extend the term for another album.*
>
> *Pay careful attention to the use of capitalized words in the agreement. The capitalization of the word "Delivery" is not a typographical error but instead refers to a special definition of the word "Delivery" which in this case, appears in clause 22(n). Many of these "initial capped" terms are defined in a special "definitions" section of the recording agreement (in this case, paragraph 22) but in some cases are defined within the text of other paragraphs (e.g., see the definition of "Option Warning Notice" in the next*

paragraph). In contracts where the expiration of the term is measured from "Delivery," it is essential that the artist know how "Delivery" is defined and takes all necessary steps to ensure that the conditions of "Delivery" under the contract are satisfied and, whenever possible, have the record company acknowledge the date "Delivery" occurs in writing. Record companies have been known to take the position that "Delivery" under the recording agreement has not occurred, even months after the recordings in question were actually released as commercial albums.

Nearly every record company now defines the term of its recording agreements by the delivery of albums and not by the passage of time. Under California law, personal service contracts cannot be enforced for a term longer than seven years so, arguably, a recording artist cannot be prevented from recording for another company after his current contract has been in effect for seven years. However, this same California law gives the record companies the right to recover damages in cases where the artist fails to complete his or her recording commitments under the agreement by the time the seven years have expired. This provision has never been conclusively interpreted in the courts. Although lawsuits have been filed that involve certain high-profile artists (Metallica, Don Henley) neither artists nor record companies are particularly anxious to set a precedent in this regard, and the cases have settled.

(b) You hereby irrevocably grant to Company _____ (___) consecutive separate options to extend the Term for further periods (the "Option Periods"), each upon the same terms and conditions applicable to the Initial Period, except as otherwise specifically set forth herein. Each Option Period for which Company has exercised its option shall commence upon the expiration of the immediately preceding Contract Period and shall continue until the last day of the ____th complete month following the date of *Delivery* of the last Master constituting the Recording Commitment for that Option Period. Each option shall be exercised, if at all, by notice to you at any time prior to the date the Term would otherwise expire. As used herein, the term "Contract Period" shall mean the Initial Period or any Option Period of the Term, as such may be suspended or extended as provided herein.

In most new artist recording contracts, the minimum recording commitment for the initial contract period is one album, but the record company typically retains the right to extend the agreement to include additional albums. The right to extend a contract on this basis is typically called an "option," and the additional contract periods under this agreement are referred to as "Option Periods." The number of options in a recording agreement is often the subject for serious negotiations, as the record company will want to obtain as many as possible and the artist will want to grant as few as possible. A major label will rarely accept fewer than five options and will sometimes insist on as many as seven. Independent labels, however, generally require one to three options and sometimes will enter into contracts for one album with no options (these are sometimes referred to as "one-off deals"). Generally, when a new artist signs with an independent label, he or she wants to use the independent label to generate buzz and build an audience base so the artist can later sign with a major label for more money. The best way to achieve this goal is through an agreement with a small number of options and/or with a clause that gives the artist the right to buy out of the contract.

(c) Notwithstanding anything to the contrary contained in paragraph 2(b), if, as of the date when the then-current Contract Period would otherwise have expired, Company has not exercised its option to extend the Term for a further Contract Period, then: (i) you shall immediately send a notice to Company specifically referencing this paragraph 2(c) and stating that Company's option has not yet been exercised (an "Option Warning Notice"); (ii) Company shall be entitled to exercise its option at any time before receiving the Option Warning Notice or within _____ (__) Business Days thereafter; and (iii) the current Contract Period shall be deemed to have continued until Company exercises its option or until the end of such _____ (__) Business Day period (whichever shall occur first).

No record company attorney wants to be surprised by a letter from an artist's lawyer stating that the artist's recording agreement has expired and that the artist is signing a deal elsewhere. Record companies hate surprises. Therefore, to protect themselves, record companies try to shift as many administrative burdens to the artist as possible. What this clause does is essentially suspend the expiration of the current Contract Period until the artist has given the company a written warning that the period has expired and, upon receiving such notice, the company is given a certain period of time (usually five to ten business days) to decide whether or not to extend the contract for another period. If the artist has enough clout during negotiations, the record company will sometimes accept the responsibility of exercising its option before the expiration of the current term. If the record company makes this concession, then if the company fails to exercise its option on time, the contract will automatically terminate. Artists should seek this concession during negotiations, while bearing in mind how much clout they actually have.

3. RECORDING COMMITMENT AND DELIVERY

(a) During each Contract Period you shall Deliver a sufficient number of Masters to constitute the required number of Albums specified in the following schedule (the "Recording Commitment"):

CONTRACT PERIOD	RECORDING COMMITMENT
Initial Period	One (1) Album (the "First Album")
First Option Period	One (1) Album (the "Second Album")
Second Option Period	One (1) Album (the "Third Album")
Third Option Period	One (1) Album (the "Fourth Album")
Fourth Option Period	One (1) Album (the "Fifth Album")
Fifth Option Period	One (1) Album (the "Sixth Album")
Sixth Option Period	One (1) Album (the "Seventh Album")

All this means is that during each contract period, the artist is required to deliver one album. Be careful though! Occasionally a record company may pull a fast one and try to insert language that gives them the discretion to require two albums during a contract period instead of one. Major labels typically will not try to do anything that sneaky, but smaller labels can sometimes push the envelope.

(b) You shall Deliver each Album constituting the Recording Commitment to Company within _____ ( ) months following commencement of the applicable Contract Period. Each such Album of your Recording Commitment is sometimes referred to herein as a "<u>Committed Album.</u>" The applicable date that each Committed Album is required to be Delivered is sometimes referred to herein as the "<u>Delivery Date.</u>" You shall not commence recording any Album earlier than _____ ( ) months following Delivery of the immediately preceding Committed Album. You shall not Deliver any Album earlier than _____ ( ) months following Delivery of the immediately preceding Committed Album.

These clauses set forth the timetable for artist's delivery of the album required during each contract period and are generally quite negotiable. The record company wants to have a steady flow of product. The artist, however, sometimes needs additional time to create new material and therefore needs to be protected from the record company having the right to terminate the agreement abruptly if the delivery schedule is not met. In some genres, these timetable clauses are virtually ignored and bear no relationship to a record company's true business practices. For example, if the contract applies to a big budget pop or R&B album by a new artist, the record company will typically try to control all aspects of the recording process, including the scheduling and coordination of recording sessions and, in those circumstances, the recording process can extend for months or even years beyond the contractual time frame. If an artist has the experience and wherewithal to coordinate the recording of his or her own album within the contractual time frame, he or she should try to negotiate terms that reinforce and clarify the recording process and, beyond that, should be prepared to take the bull by the horns and control and direct the recording process in compliance with the letter of the contract.

4. RECORDING PROCEDURE

(a) Prior to the commencement of recording sessions in each instance, you and Company shall *mutually* agree on each of the following before you proceed further provided, however, *in the event you and Company shall not be able to reach an agreement, Company's decision shall be final:* (i) selection of producer and the financial terms of your agreement(s) with such producer(s); (ii) selection of material, including the number of Compositions to be recorded; and (iii) the dates and locations of recording and mixing and the studios where recording and mixing are to take place.

Creative control is usually of prime importance to recording artists. The selection of producers and songs to be recorded are at the creative core of any recording project. If the company and artist already have a producer in mind, have language inserted into the contract confirming that the producer is preapproved by both parties. Record companies will usually try to include language that provides that, if the artist and the company cannot agree on such matters, the company's decision will be final. That, of course, essentially transfers creative control to the record company. However, from a practical standpoint, it may be difficult for a record company to force a recording artist to sing songs he or she does not want to sing or to work with an unacceptable producer, although it does happen. If the artist has enough leverage, the company may agree to mutual approval without the company retaining veto power, but the company may insist on "reasonableness" language that would prevent the artist from "unreasonably" withholding approval of any producer or songs. Another type of compromise to balance the creative approval rights between artist and company would be to provide that the artist shall have the right to select the producers of his or her material, subject to the record company's approval, which shall not be unreasonably withheld, provided that producer agrees to render services in exchange for fees consistent with the artist's recording budget. Such an approach still effectively requires mutual agreement, but does not allow the record company to be unreasonable in its decision not to approve any given producer. In practice, the artist or the artist's manager will select the producer or producers and the record company will be consulted, but it will generally defer to the artist's choice, unless it has had a negative experience with a particular producer.

Creative control issues can often be best dealt with by the artist taking an assertive role in guiding the recording of his or her album. This can be done by proactively submitting demos and budgets for company approval in compliance with the "recording procedure" language of the contract. Following the letter of the contract (to the maximum extent possible) can enhance the artist's control over the project and discourage the company from wresting control of the project.

(b) In addition, you shall obtain prior to commencement of each applicable recording session and deliver to Company within forty-eight (48) hours following each such recording session, executed Certificates of Employment for all producers, mixers and remixers in Company's then-standard form, and all necessary W-4 and other withholding tax forms for all personnel rendering services in connection with the recording session concerned.

The artist's manager should be able to handle these administrative tasks. Timely compliance with these technical requirements can only enhance an artist's control over his or her project.

(c) In addition, at least fourteen (14) days prior to the proposed date of the first recording session for the applicable Masters, you shall submit to Company in writing a proposed recording budget setting forth, in itemized detail, all anticipated Recording Costs. Upon receipt of Company's written approval of such recording budget (the "<u>Authorized Budget</u>"), you shall commence such sessions. Company's payment of Recording Costs for any recording sessions prior to Company's approval of the applicable budget shall not constitute Company's waiver of its right to approve such budget. All Recording Costs in excess of any Authorized Budget shall be your sole responsibility and you hereby agree to forthwith pay and discharge all such excess costs. If Company agrees to pay any such excess costs on your behalf, you shall, upon demand, reimburse Company for such excess costs or, in lieu of requesting reimbursement, Company may deduct such excess costs from all monies payable under this agreement or any other agreement.

Preparing a budget is an important skill. Again, an artist's manager should be able to handle this in a professional manner but, if the manager is inexperienced in this area, the artist should consider hiring an administrative person with experience in this area to help prepare budgets and collect required documentation. Further, you should try to add language to the agreement that provides that you will not be responsible for any excess costs caused by company's acts or omissions.

(d) Nothing in this agreement shall obligate Company to continue or permit the continuation of any recording sessions, even if previously approved hereunder, if Company *reasonably* anticipates that the Recording Costs for the applicable Masters shall exceed the Authorized Budget or that Masters constituting the applicable Committed Album shall not be *technically and/or commercially* satisfactory.

This clause gives the company significant power to shut down recording sessions if costs are escalating beyond the budget or if the material coming out of the sessions does not please the company. If the artist has sufficient clout, the company may agree to remove the word "commercially" from the satisfaction standard so that, provided the music coming out of the sessions is "technically" satisfactory the company cannot shut down sessions that are otherwise within budget. For debut artists making their first album, companies may agree to include a clause that specifies that the creative content of the artist's demos are deemed commercially satisfactory. Such a clause would tend to prevent a company from trying to force an artist to reinvent himself or herself to suit the whim of a company executive.

(e) It is of the essence of this agreement that you obtain prior to each applicable recording session and deliver to Company within forty-eight (48) hours following each such recording session, a duly completed and executed Form I-9 (or such similar or other forms as may be prescribed by the United States Immigration and Naturalization Service or other government agency regarding citizenship, permanent residency or so-called documented worker status) in respect of each individual (including Artist) engaged in connection with the applicable recording session. You shall obtain and promptly deliver to Company true and complete copies of all evidentiary documents relating to the contents or subject matter of such forms. If you fail to comply with any of the foregoing requirements, Company may deduct any resulting penalty payments from all monies payable under this agreement or any other agreement.

Again, these boring administrative details are important. Having a manager or a professional administrator handle these mundane tasks in a timely manner will make the artist appear professional and will improve his or her clout should any legal issues arise during the relationship.

(f) As and when reasonably required by Company, you shall allow Company's representatives to attend any and all recording sessions hereunder at Company's expense.

Some artists do not like "suits" showing up and hanging out at their recording sessions. However, unless the artist has significant clout, the company will insist on some reasonable access to its artists' recording sessions. Often, companies will agree to limit access to one company representative at a time and will further agree to pay all costs (on a nonrecoupable basis) incurred in connection with such access (i.e., the label rep's travel and accommodation costs). In special cases, the company might agree to allow the artist to designate two or three company representatives that would be welcome to attend sessions.

(g) Unless an authorized signatory of Company consents otherwise in writing, which consent Company may withhold in its unrestricted discretion, each Master Delivered as part of the Recording Commitment: (i) shall only contain newly-recorded studio performances of previously-unrecorded Compositions *made specifically for the applicable Album* (e.g., with respect to each Committed Album after the First Album, the Masters embodied thereon shall be recorded in their entirety after the date on which you Deliver the immediately preceding Committed Album to Company); (ii) shall embody performances featuring *only* all members of Artist; (iii) shall have been recorded by Artist in its entirety during the Term in a first-class recording studio; (iv) shall have a playing time of not less than *three (3) minutes;* (v) shall not embody solely an instrumental performance unless Artist is solely an instrumentalist; (vi) shall embody solely Artist's featured performances of a single Composition which is not a medley; and (vii) shall not contain any Composition designed to appeal to a specialized or limited audience (e.g., gospel, opera, Christmas or children's music).

This clause is designed to prevent artists from using nonstandard recordings to satisfy their recording agreements, so it excludes old recordings not made for a particular album, short recordings, instrumentals and "specialty" recordings. If an artist wishes to record with another artist, and that other artist is under contract to another label, then the two labels will have to reach an agreement regarding the use of the "guest" artist. Be careful when negotiating the language regarding "specialized" audiences—as if the artist actually appeals to a specific segmented audience (i.e., children's music, religious music, holiday music) that should be specified in the contract and this clause should be tailored so that the artist's normal recordings are not excluded from satisfying his or her delivery requirement. Further, the three-minute rule is not a good standard, as there are plenty of successful pop songs that clock in at less than three minutes (a good recent example is "Crazy" by Gnarls Barkley). Companies should not object to reducing that standard to two-and-one-half minutes.

(h) During the Term, you shall not record and/or Deliver a Multiple Record Set without Company's prior written approval, which approval may be withheld by Company's in its sole discretion.

Multiple record sets raise complex issues regarding manufacturing costs, consumer pricing and publishing obligations (i.e., the duty to pay royalties to the writers of songs on the album) so record companies almost always insist on approval rights. Just be certain to check the definition of what constitutes a "Multiple Record Set" because since the compact disc holds so much more music than its predecessors (the vinyl record), current customary CDs packed to the gills with music could overlap into some older definitions of "Multiple Record Sets."

5. GRANT OF RIGHTS

(a) All *Recordings* embodying the performances of Artist recorded during the Term or submitted hereunder from the inception of the recording thereof, and all reproductions derived therefrom, together with the performances embodied thereon, shall be the property of Company in perpetuity for the Territory free from any claims whatsoever by you, Artist or any other Person. Company shall have the exclusive right throughout the Territory to copyright those Recordings in Company's name as the author and owner of them and to secure any and all renewals and extensions of copyright throughout the Territory. Each of those Recordings shall be considered a *"work made for hire"* for Company; if for any reason any one (1) or more of those Recordings is determined not to be a "work made for hire," then you and Artist hereby irrevocably grant, transfer, convey and assign to Company the entirety of the rights, titles and interests throughout the Territory in and to all of those Recordings, including the copyright, any and all renewals and extensions of copyright, and the right to secure copyright registrations therefor. You and Artist hereby irrevocably and unconditionally waive any and all so-called droit moral and like rights that you and Artist have in the Recordings and in the performances embodied thereon and hereby agree not to make any claim against Company or any Person authorized by Company to exploit those Recordings based on such moral or like rights. Without limiting the foregoing, Company and all Persons authorized by Company shall have the exclusive and unlimited rights to own, control and exploit Artist's services as a recording artist during the Term and to all the results and proceeds of such services. You agree to execute and deliver to Company, and to cause each Person rendering services in connection with such Recordings to execute and deliver to Company: (i) all documents required to apply for and obtain, and on obtaining same (if applicable), to assign to Company, all copyrights and renewals and extensions thereof with respect to such Recordings, including written assignments to Company (in a form satisfactory to Company) of all sound recording copyright rights (including renewal and extension rights) such Person may have; and/or (ii) such other instruments as Company deems necessary to effectuate and/or record ownership of rights hereunder with the U.S. Copyright Office or elsewhere. You and Artist hereby irrevocably grant to Company a power of attorney, as your agent and attorney-in-fact, to execute such documents and instruments in your name, and the name of Artist and/or all other Persons rendering services in connection with such Recordings and to dispose of such documents and instruments, which power of attorney may only be exercised if you or Artist fail to execute and deliver to Company any document which Company may reasonably submit to you or Artist for execution within seven (7) Business Days after such document is submitted to you or Artist. You acknowledge that Company's agency and power are coupled with an interest. As between Company and you and Artist, Company shall be the owner in perpetuity for the Territory of all *Artwork.*

This is fairly standard language that grants to the record company all rights to records, videos and artwork, which are created under the recording agreement. (Always check the definitions of initial-capped terms. In this agreement, the definition of "Recording" includes all recordings of sound, whether or not coupled with a visual image.) In some cases, when an artist has enough clout, he or she may carve out and retain certain rights to artwork developed for use as album art or promotional art, but it is unusual for a debut artist to have enough clout to secure those rights.

The primary reason why recording contracts include "work made for hire" language is that current copyright law gives the author a right to terminate the grant of rights of works that are not "works made for hire" 35 years after the grant was made, but if a work is deemed to be a work made for hire it would never be subject to termination.

The term of copyright protection for works made for hire is 95 years from their first publication, whereas the term of copyright for recordings that are not "works made for hire" is the life of the author plus 70 years. So, if sound recordings made under a recording contract are deemed to be works made for hire, the result could be decades of exploitation rights that the record company may not otherwise have. That being said, the question of whether recordings made by a recording artist under a typical recording contract such as this are truly works made for hire within the meaning of the United States Copyright Act is not entirely clear. In other words, just because a contract says that recordings are works made for hire does not necessarily make it so, as copyright law ultimately defines what is or is not a work made for hire. Accordingly, record companies will typically include clauses that provide that, even if the recordings are not works made for hire, all the rights therein are nonetheless transferred and assigned to the record company by this agreement for the maximum allowable duration under copyright law.

(b) Company and each Person authorized by Company shall have the perpetual right, without cost or any other liability to you or any other Person, to use and to authorize other Persons to use the names (including any professional names heretofore or hereafter adopted), and any likenesses, whether or not current (including photographs, portraits, caricatures and stills from any Artwork or Videos made hereunder), autographs (including facsimile signatures) and biographical material of or relating to Artist, to any producer and to any other Person performing services in connection with Recordings hereunder, on and in the packaging of Records, and for purposes of advertising, promotion and trade and in connection with the marketing and exploitation of such Recordings and Records and general goodwill advertising, without payment of additional compensation to you, Artist or any other Person.

This is fairly standard language, although there is some room for improvement. Record companies must have the right to use an artist's name and likeness in connection with the marketing of records. However, this language is overly broad as it would allow the company to use any picture or likeness of the artist even if it was created years before or years after the term of the agreement, and it would also allow the company to use "professional names" (i.e., stage names) that the artist did not adopt until years after the term of the contract. In most cases, companies will be reasonable enough to limit their rights to include only photos and likenesses taken during the term of the contract that the artist approves and biographical material that the artist approves. Autographs and facsimile signatures should be excluded whenever possible.

(c) (i) Company shall have the exclusive right throughout the Territory during the Web Site Term, free from any claims whatsoever by you, Artist or any other Person: (A) to establish and maintain a site (the "Company-Artist Site," which term shall include the content of such site) on the Internet having the address (i.e., Uniform Resource Locator, or "URL") "[Artist].com" or any similar designation based on or containing Artist's professional name as you and Company shall mutually approve; provided that, you shall be obligated to approve at least one URL which is available and which contains Artist's professional name (the "Artist URL") and to utilize Artist's professional name in connection with such Artist URL; (B) to couple the Artist URL with any such other appropriate suffixes (e.g., top-level domains such as .com, .net, .co.uk, etc.), which Company determines in its sole discretion are necessary or desirable and to register the Artist URL and any such suffixes in Company's name in any and all territories with the appropriate entities and to secure any and all renewals and extensions thereof on your behalf, it being understood that you and Artist hereby appoint Company as your attorney-in-fact for such purposes; (C) to refer to the Company-Artist Site as the "official" site relating to Artist; and (D) to include the Artist URL on Records embodying any Recording hereunder and in advertising and marketing materials therefor.

We have broken this agreement's Web site provisions into subsections to make it easier to discuss the issues involved. This first subsection is fairly standard and necessary language. The Internet is such a fundamental and vital part of today's marketplace that it would be foolish not to allow the company to make some meaningful use of the Internet to promote the artist and his or her music. That being said, whenever possible, it is important that the company agree that the use of key domain names be owned by the artist and licensed to the company for a specific term. For example, an artist named John Doe might already own the URL www.johndoe.com and he should not be forced to turn over ownership of his URL, but it may be appropriate for the artist to license his URL to company during the term of the agreement or, perhaps, for a slightly extended term (see the definition of "Web Site Term" below). Ideally, the artist would retain ownership and control over www.johndoe.com and the company would be required to use an alternate URL such as www.johndoemusic.com or www.company.com/johndoe and the artist would simply be required to include a link on his personal page to the company's page. Sometimes record companies need to be reminded that their contracts are limited to making and selling records, and artists may well be involved in touring, merchandise, acting, athletics and other activities, so it is important for artists to maintain as much ownership and control over their primary Web sites as possible.

(ii) Company shall be the sole and exclusive owner of the Company-Artist Site and the operation and content thereof shall be controlled by Company.

If the Company-Artist Site is not www.johndoe.com and is, instead, a site whose URL includes the company's main URL (e.g., www.company.com/johndoe), and the company agrees to allow artist to maintain his own broad-based Web site, then there is no practical problem with allowing company to own the Company-Artist Site. However, if the URL of such a site is tied solely to the artist (e.g., www.johndoe.com) then it is best if the artist retains ownership of the site but licenses it to the company for the duration of the Web Site Term.

(iii) Notwithstanding the foregoing, during the Web Site Term: (A) at your request, Company shall consult with you or Artist regarding the *initial* design of the Company-Artist Site and shall give due consideration to any reasonable request made by you or Artist relating to the content of the Company-Artist Site; (B) unless you or Artist shall *consent* thereto, Company shall not include on the Company-Artist Site: (I) any musical material that does not embody Artist's performances; or (II) any advertisements or endorsements for products or services other than Recordings embodying Artist's performances or Artist's services (provided that Company shall have the right to place on the Company-Artist Site advertisements for any seller of Records designated by Company and/or advertising in or in connection with Company's browser frames which reside outside of the Company-Artist Site and which are common to one or more of Company's main Web pages).

While it is best that the artist have approval rights, unless the artist has great leverage, most companies will try to limit the artist's rights to consultation. However, companies should agree to give the artist approval rights regarding the inclusion in any Web site any material that is not embodied on their commercially available records including outtakes, live performances, interviews and pictures. Further, the artist's consultation rights should not be limited to just the "initial" design but should include all redesigns and where the artist's consent is required, the language should provide for "separate prior written consent in each instance."

(iv) Provided that you and Artist comply with the material terms and conditions of this paragraph 5(c), nothing set forth in this paragraph 5(c) shall be construed to restrict you from establishing or maintaining (or authorizing other Persons to establish or maintain) additional web sites relating solely to goods and services other than Artist's Recordings or recording services (including fan club sites and sites relating to Artist's merchandising and touring activities).

This language is a bit heavy handed. Obviously, any recording artist would want there to be references to his or her music on his or her Web site. However, the company will want the artist to direct all music-related Web traffic to the Company-Artist Site, so this type of language should be modified to allow some reasonable use of the artist's music provided that the artist's site provides a link to the official Company-Artist Site where more robust music content would reside.

(v) You may elect to terminate Company's exclusive right and license in the Artist URL by notice to Company at any time after the date which is three (3) months after the release of the last Single in connection with the final Album Delivered by you during the Term. (The period commencing on the date of this agreement and ending thirty (30) days following the date on which you provide such notice to Company is referred to in this agreement as the "<u>Web Site Term.</u>")

This type of language is problematic, as it may be difficult to determine which Single is the last Single with respect to any Album. It would be better if the company tied the end of the Web Site Term to the release date (or, better yet, the Delivery date) of the Album (e.g., the date that is 15 months after the Delivery of the final Album required to be Delivered by you during the Term).

(vi) After the expiration of the Web Site Term, Company shall have the nonexclusive right to continue to maintain one (1) site of Company's choice established or maintained by Company during the Web Site Term or to establish and maintain one (1) new site on the Internet, the URL of which may use Artist's professional name, in connection with Company's distribution of Records subject to this agreement. In this connection, Artist hereby grants to Company the exclusive right to an alternate URL embodying Artist's professional name (e.g., [Artist]cds.com) (the "Alternate URL"), which Alternate URL: (A) shall be chosen by Company in its *sole discretion* after consultation with you to ensure that the Alternate URL does not conflict with any URL you are then using; and (B) shall be owned in perpetuity by Company and used exclusively by Company, at Company's election, at any time during or after the Web Site Term.

This is fairly standard language that exists to protect the company's interest in using the Internet to promote and sell an artist's records after the contract has expired. The artist should try to have such language modified so that the Alternate URL is subject to both the artist's and company's reasonable approval.

(vii) Company shall have the right to establish links to and from Company's sites with all other sites relating to Artist that you or Artist control, in which you or Artist have an interest or to which you or Artist have granted a Person the right to operate or administer, including fan club sites and sites relating to Artist's merchandising and touring activities. You shall have the right to establish links to and from the Company-Artist Site with all *"first-class"* sites relating to Artist that you control; provided that, in Company's reasonable, good faith opinion, such other sites or material embodied on such sites do not constitute an invasion of any Person's rights (including copyright infringement, libel or slander) and do not violate Company's standards of decency or any applicable rules, regulations, statutes or laws. You and Artist shall coordinate with Company with respect to the establishment of such links.

This is fairly standard language, but is slightly off-balance. Note that the company has sought the right to establish links to and from all of Artist's sites, but the right for artist to establish reciprocal links is limited to "first-class" sites. First-class site is not defined and that language could be used by the company to undermine the artist's reciprocal linking rights. The artist should try to make the cross-linking rights between artist and company truly mutual, so either the first-class standard should apply to all links or none of the links.

(viii) Upon Company's reasonable request during the Web Site Term, you and/or Artist shall provide Company with information obtained about users of and/or visitors to any sites which you or Artist control, including e-mail lists obtained or derived from any such site; provided that, in no event shall you and/or Artist be required to provide any information you or Artist reasonably believes would violate any applicable rules, regulations, statutes or laws. At your reasonable request, Company shall provide you with information obtained about users of and/or visitors to the Company-Artist Site during the Web Site Term; provided that, in no event shall Company be required to provide any information which Company reasonably believes would violate any applicable rules, regulations, statutes or laws or the privacy policies, guidelines or practices of Company or any of its affiliates, subsidiaries or parents.

This language deals with user data collected from Web sites. This data can be extremely useful and valuable as the e-mail addresses alone form a powerful marketing tool. This particular language is reciprocal, meaning that the company must share its Web data with the artist and vice versa. This would normally be a fair exchange. However, if the artist came into the deal with a preexisting fan base (i.e., through exposure as an actor, athlete or celebrity), the right to this data becomes much more valuable and, in some cases, it might not be appropriate to turn it over to the company without some additional consideration and/or limits on how and when the data can be used.

(ix) Company shall be responsible for and pay all costs in connection with the establishment, registration and maintenance of the Artist URL at its non-recoupable expense.

If the Artist intends to maintain ownership of the Artist URL and license it to Company, it might be worthwhile for the Artist to incur the nominal costs associated with establishing and maintaining the URL.

6. CREATIVE AND MARKETING MATTERS

(a) During the Term, with respect to Phono Records manufactured for sale in the United States, all photographs of Artist and biographical material concerning Artist which Company uses for the purposes herein stated shall be subject to your approval. Promptly following the execution of this agreement, you shall furnish Company with a reasonable number of photographs of Artist and biographical material concerning Artist. All photographs and biographical material concerning Artist furnished by you to Company shall be deemed approved by you. Any *inadvertent failure* by Company to obtain your approval pursuant to this paragraph 6(a) shall not constitute a breach of this agreement by Company. You shall cooperate with Company's efforts to promote throughout the Territory any Records released hereunder. Without limiting the foregoing, you shall cause Artist to be available, at *Company's request:* to appear for photography, poster and cover art and the like, under the direction of Company or its designees; to appear for interviews anywhere in the Territory with representatives of the communications media, including representatives of the domestic and international press and Company's publicity personnel; to appear for in-store promotional events; to make personal appearances anywhere in the Territory on radio and television and elsewhere and to record taped interviews, spot announcements and trailers; and to perform for the purpose of recording for promotional purposes by means of film, videotape or other audiovisual media performances of Compositions embodied on Masters, provided Videos produced pursuant to paragraph 18 shall be subject to the terms of such paragraph. You shall also cause Artist to be available upon Company's reasonable request to appear for exclusive on-camera interviews, so-called online "chats," webcasts and other promotional activities, and you shall provide Company with a reasonable amount of additional exclusive promotional material therefor *upon Company's request.* Neither you nor Artist shall be entitled to any compensation for such services; provided that, Company shall reimburse you for the reasonable travel and living expenses incurred by Artist pursuant to a budget approved by Company in advance in connection with the rendition by Artist of services rendered at Company's direction pursuant to this paragraph 6(a).

Here the company seeks to secure artist's commitment to participate and cooperate in promotional activities. The language is quite broad and should be narrowed a bit before closing the deal. The language should make clear that all promotional activities are to be at the company's expense. The artist should not have to come out-of-pocket for travel and accommodations but, instead, those costs should be advanced by the company pursuant to a budget approved by both the company and artist. Further, if the artist contemplates other professional activities during the term of the agreement, such as touring and acting, the artist's obligations to participate in promotional activities should be made reasonably subject to the artist's other professional obligations. Also, the artist should bear in mind to what extent he or she wants to be available for all manner of promotional appearances. Some artists and managers believe that a few high-level interviews are preferable to marathon press junkets where the artist is interviewed by dozens of fan magazines in addition to the legitimate press. If strategically limiting the scope of media activities is important to the artist, some limiting language should be negotiated. Take note the sentence that reads "any inadvertent failure by Company to obtain your approval pursuant to this paragraph 6(a) shall not constitute a breach of this agreement by Company." If the company will agree, the word "nonrepetitive" should be inserted after "inadvertent" to discourage the company from recklessly disregarding its obligations to obtain the artist's approval.

(b) Provided you and Artist have fulfilled all of your and Artist's material obligations under this agreement, during the Term and solely in respect of Phono Records manufactured by Company for sale in the United States, Company shall not, without your approval: (i) license for coupling more than two (2) Masters on any particular Record, which Record embodies Recordings that do not embody the performances of Artist. Notwithstanding the preceding sentence, the restriction provided in this paragraph 6(b)(i) shall not apply to Sampler Records, uses on transportation carriers, Consumer Compilations or Joint Label Compilations; (ii) release any Committed Album as a Mid-Price Record prior to nine (9) months or as a Budget Record prior to twelve (12) months following Company's initial United States release of that Album. If Company so releases any such Committed Album prior to the expiration of such nine (9) or twelve (12) month period, as applicable, without your approval, your sole remedy shall be that the royalty rate to which you are otherwise entitled for any units of such Committed Album sold prior to the expiration of such nine (9) or twelve (12) month period shall not be reduced pursuant to the provisions of paragraph 9(c)(i) relating to Mid-Price Records or Budget Records, as applicable; (iii) sell Records hereunder as Premium Records; (iv) initially release a Committed Album hereunder other than on one of Company's then-current top line labels (e.g., currently "_____" or the "_____" label).

This clause sets forth some commonly granted marketing restrictions. Normally, these are not contained in a first-draft recording contract for a new artist. However, since these are relatively minor concessions, this company has granted them in advance in order to show that it is artist oriented and to reduce the need for negotiation. That being said, the 9-month holdback for Mid-Priced Records should be expanded to 12 months and the 12-month holdback for Budget Records should be expanded to 18 months. There are a whole host of additional marketing restrictions that are commonly granted if requested, the most prevalent of which are restrictions on synchronizing the artist's masters in motion pictures, television programs or commercials without the artist's consent. Record companies may not grant full consent rights across the board, but they may agree to grant consent rights for potentially controversial uses, such as uses in adult films, political media and advertisements for personal hygiene or pharmaceutical products. Other restrictions that the artist should ask for are to limit or prohibit the company's rights to sell artist's records as "cut-outs" (i.e., deeply discounted records that have been deleted from the record company's current catalog), exploit outtakes or live recordings, sell artist's records through record clubs, license the use of masters as samples, or remix or otherwise alter master recordings as delivered by artist. This particular contract contains a defined term called "Development Record," which is a record sold at a discount price and that carries a significant royalty rate reduction. The artist should seek consent rights for Development Records. Further, the artist should try to have all consent clauses regarding marketing matters apply both during and after the term. If the artist has significant clout, he or she might be able to persuade the company to insert language requiring the company to consult with the artist regarding the marketing plan and the selection of singles.

(c) Provided you and Artist have fulfilled all of your and Artist's material obligations under this agreement, Company agrees to commercially release each Committed Album in the United States within one hundred twenty (120) days following Delivery of the Album concerned (the "U.S. Release Deadline Period"). If Company shall have failed to so release any such Album in the United States, you shall have the right, *within thirty (30) days following the expiration of the U.S. Release Deadline Period* to send Company a notice of Company's failure specifically referencing this paragraph 6(c) and stating your desire that the Term be terminated if Company does not, within ninety (90) days after Company receives such notice from you ("U.S. Release Cure Period"), commercially release the Album concerned in the United States. If Company then fails to release the Album concerned in the United States during the U.S. Release Cure Period, notwithstanding anything to the contrary contained herein, Company shall have no liability whatsoever to you or Artist, and your only remedy shall be to terminate the Term by notice to Company *within fifteen (15) days following the expiration of the U.S. Release Cure Period.*

This is a very typical first draft of a release commitment for a new artist. It is limited to albums only; it does not provide a guaranteed release of any singles. The rationale for this is that the company has all the necessary incentive to release singles and will release them when it believes it is going to be helpful to promote the artist. Additionally, it is difficult to craft a remedy for the failure to release a single that would be fair and appropriate. On the other hand, if the company fails to release any album of the artist's recording commitment in the United States and fails to cure that after written notice, the customary remedy is that the artist has the right to terminate the contract. As discussed previously, special attention should be paid to the contractual definition of "Delivery." An inexperienced artist may make the mistake of believing that "Delivery" has occurred when he or she has simply delivered the master recordings to the label. This is often not the case. In these so-called release commitment clauses the artist should, of course, try to reduce the time frames. However, perhaps more importantly, the language giving an artist a narrow time frame during which to notify the company of its failure to release the album *must be modified. As drafted, the artist must object to the company's failure to release the album within 30 days of company's failure to release the album within 120 days of "Delivery" and, if the artist does not object within that time frame, his or her right to object is deemed waived. Part of the problem is that, in the absence of a written acknowledgement from the company confirming the "Delivery" date, the artist cannot be certain of when the clock starts (or if it has even started). Further, this language gives the company a second bite at the apple. If the company fails to release the album after 120 days after delivery, and the artist objects within 30 days of that date, then the company still has 90 days to cure its failure by releasing the album and, if they still fail, the artist must object a second time, this time within a narrow 15-day window, or the artist's rights to object are waived. What the artist should try to do is eliminate the deadlines for the artist to object altogether. So, for example, if "Delivery" occurs on a certain date and the album is then not released after 120 days (or perhaps a shorter time frame if the company will agree), the artist should really have the right to object to the nonrelease of his or her album at any time after the company's failure. The purpose of this clause is to give an artist some rights to escape from a contract if his or her album is held in limbo indefinitely, so it would seem unfair and counterintuitive for the artist to forfeit his or her right to object to the nonrelease of the album. If the artist has sufficient clout, he or she may be able to persuade the company to include specific buy-out language that defines the terms under which the artist may exploit unreleased masters recorded under the contract after the contract has been terminated for company's failure to release the album.*

(d) The running of the U.S. Release Deadline Period and the U.S. Release Cure Period shall be suspended (and the expiration date of each of those periods shall be postponed) for the period of any suspension of the running of the Term under paragraph 13(c). For purposes of calculating the U.S. Release Deadline Period and U.S. Release Cure Period, the number of days during either such period which fall during the period from October 15 to and including the following January 15 shall not be counted. An Album shall be deemed released, for the purposes of paragraphs 6(c) only, when Company *has announced its availability* for sale in the territory concerned.

Paragraph 13(c) allows the company to suspend the contract during periods of force majeure, which typically applies only when things like natural disasters or acts of terrorism disrupt the company's ability to conduct business. That is fairly standard language. The remainder of this paragraph deals with the recording industry's habit of "freezing" calendars over the holiday period and the definition of what constitutes the "release" of a record. The "holiday calendar freeze" is fairly common, but companies will usually agree to limit it to November 15 through January 15. The definition of release should be scrutinized and negotiated carefully. As drafted here, the company could claim that an album has been released even if no records have been shipped and no records have been sold. Simply "announcing the availability for sale" of a record should not be sufficient to satisfy a record company's duty to "commercially release" an album. The language defining release should, at the very least, refer to an album's "retail street date" and perhaps refer to a minimum number of unit shipments.
One issue that has not yet been addressed in this draft, because the company omits it from its first draft, is the requirement that an album be released in major foreign

territories. Depending on the company involved and the artist's potential for international appeal, you may expect to see terms in an agreement whereby the company will commit to release the artist's album in certain foreign territories. Sometimes a company might agree to release an album in certain territories, but only if the album achieves a certain chart status in the United States. The remedy for company's failure to do so is generally limited to allowing the artist to negotiate with third-party licensees to release the record outside of the United States. In such event, the licensee generally pays the advances and royalties to the label, which will then apply half (50%) to the artist's account and keep the other half (50%) for itself. If the foreign release language is not broad enough, the artist will not be able to license the recordings to companies in countries that are not specifically set forth in the agreement without the label's consent. Further, if such foreign release obligations are made contingent on the success of the album in the United States and such contingencies are not met, the artist will not be able to license the recordings for distribution outside of the United States without the label's consent.

7. ADVANCES AND RECORDING COSTS

(a) Upon receipt of invoices therefor, Company shall pay directly all Recording Costs actually incurred in the production of Masters comprising each Committed Album, provided such costs have been incurred in accordance with the Authorized Budget. Such Recording Costs shall be deducted from, and shall not exceed, the applicable Advances for Committed Albums set forth below (the "Recording Funds").

In nearly all record deals with major record companies today, the company's financial commitment to the artist is made by way of an all-inclusive recording fund. This replaces the older approach of an allocated recording budget for each album and agreement to pay a separate, specified cash advance to the artist for each album. In the recording fund, the budget for recording costs and the artist's advance are combined, which achieves the company's objective of having a fixed production cost for the album. It also gives the artist an incentive to minimize the recording costs, since the unspent portion of the recording fund is paid to the artist as a cash advance. However, the downside for the artist is that if the entire recording fund is spent on recording costs, there will be no cash advance to cover the artist's personal living expenses during the period of time from the delivery of the album until royalties have begun to be earned, which, even with a successful album, may take many months from the commercial release of the album. Even worse, if the recording costs exceed the recording fund, the artist may be required to repay the excess to the company or, in any event, the company will have the right to deduct the excess from other monies, which may include mechanical royalties and future advances as well as artist royalties that become payable to the artist.

Fundamentally, the entire amount of the recording fund is recoupable solely from royalties payable to the artist. This is one of the most basic principles of recording contracts and it is rarely varied in any significant way. Accordingly, before the artist receives any royalties from the sale of an album, the company repays to itself the entire cost of recording the album, as well as any cash advances it paid to the artist. This recoupment is not achieved by deducting the recording costs off the top, out of the company's gross receipts, as would be the case if the company and the artist split net profits, but is instead accomplished by deducting those recording costs and advances solely from the artist's royalties. Because the company's profit margin per unit will typically be much higher than the artist's royalty per unit, the company will often enjoy a profit long before the artist receives any royalties. The higher the artist's royalty rate, the more quickly recording costs will be recouped.

(b) With respect to the First Album, the Recording Fund shall be _____ Dollars (\$_____). Such Recording Fund shall be payable as follows: (i) *ten percent (10%)* of such Recording Fund shall be paid to you, following the full execution of this agreement; and (ii) the balance, if any, of such Recording Fund shall be paid to you after deducting all Recording Costs and other Advances paid or incurred by Company in connection with the First Album, following Delivery of the First Album and receipt by Company of all union session reports and all invoices for all Recording Costs incurred in connection therewith.

This is fairly standard language defining how the Recording Fund for the first album is to be disbursed. The most critical issue is the portion of the fund to be made available for the artist's living expenses. Because record companies have a habit of involving themselves in the recording process and running up recording costs, there is a very real chance that the fund will be exhausted (and then some) during the recording process. Therefore, the artist's representative should try very hard to persuade the company to allocate a reasonable amount for the artist's personal expense. In today's market, record companies frequently agree to pay a fixed amount each month for a certain number of months in order to ensure that the artist has regular income to pay living expenses.

(c) (i) With respect to each subsequent Committed Album, if any, a Recording Fund shall be payable in an amount equal to sixty-six and two-thirds percent (66 2/3%) of *the lesser of* (A) the amount of net royalties credited to your royalty account hereunder in respect of USNRC Net Sales of the immediately preceding Committed Album or (B) the average of the amount of net royalties credited to your royalty account hereunder in respect of USNRC Net Sales of the two (2) immediately preceding Committed Albums.

(ii) For the purposes of making the computations pursuant to this paragraph 7(c): (A) Company shall refer to accounting statements rendered to you through the end of the accounting period following the earlier of: *(I) the date twelve (12) months following Company's initial release in the United States of each of the applicable Committed Albums; or (II) the earlier of: (aa) the date upon which the Album for which the Recording Fund is being computed is Delivered; or (bb) the date when such Album is required to be Delivered pursuant to paragraph 3(b);* and (B) reserves shall be deemed to be the greater of: (I) twenty percent (20%) of the number of units of each of the applicable Committed Albums shipped during the applicable period; or (II) the number of units of each of the applicable Committed Albums shipped in the United States during the applicable period less the number of units of each of such Committed Albums sold in the United States during such period as reported by SoundScan or any other similar industry-accepted reporting system. Notwithstanding the foregoing, the Recording Fund for each Committed Album other than the First Album shall be no less than the applicable minimum amount and no more than the applicable maximum amount set forth below:

These clauses that define how recording funds are to be calculated for second and subsequent albums are fairly standard. The two major variables at issue are (1) the fraction that is applied to the earned royalties to determine the fund and (2) the number of months of sales that are applied to the formula. Two-thirds is a fairly standard fraction, but if the artist has enough clout, the record company can sometimes be persuaded to use three-fourths or more. Please note that, in this draft, the label has included language that sets the Recording Fund at two-thirds of the lesser of the royalties generated by the preceding album or the average of the royalties generated by the preceding two albums. This obviously serves no purpose other than to give the company the means to reduce the Recording Fund and, with sufficient clout, the artist should be able to persuade the company to remove this clause. With respect to the applicable sales period, some labels will seek to apply as few as six months of sales, but the artist should always try to have 12 full months of sales included in that formula. In this draft, the company seeks to have the sales period end upon the earlier of 12 months postrelease, the date the album subject to the Recording Fund is actually delivered or the date the album subject to the Recording Fund is required to be delivered. These earlier dates are no good for the artist because if the company picks up its option for a subsequent album early enough, the Recording Fund might be based on fewer than six months of sales. The artist should seek a clause that provides that if the company exercises an option before the full period of sales used in calculating the recording fund has run its course, that the initial recording fund will be based on a good faith estimate of sales during such period and that at the conclusion of such period, the final recording fund shall be recalculated so that the artist gets the full benefit of sales during the full negotiated period.

Additionally, the artist should try to have the formula include so-called pipeline royalties (e.g., royalties earned by the label but not yet credited to the label's account). The use of SoundScan data in determining recording funds is not preferred because SoundScan often underreports actual sales.

The provision that "reasonable reserves for overturns and credits" should be deducted from the 12-months sales figure is normal and generally appropriate, but the artist should try to secure a firm cap on such reserves of 15% to 20% in order to protect against the record company deducting an unreasonable amount of reserves from its sales figures. This draft allows reserves to exceed 20% if actual shipments of albums subject to the contract less SoundScan-reported sales exceed 20%. This is not an appropriate standard for several reasons. First of all, SoundScan often underreports actual sales, so by deducting SoundScan sales figures from the total of actual shipments, the estimated number of returns is artificially increased. Second, SoundScan is a private company, its methods of determining sales change frequently and are protected trade secrets, so there is some risk in tying recording funds to SoundScan's sales data. The artist should fight hard for a firm reserve cap of no more than 20%, but if the label insists on having the flexibility to raise the cap if actual returns exceed 20%, they should use their actual internal returns data.

As discussed above, the fund for the first album is a fixed amount, and the fund for all subsequent albums is determined by multiplying a fraction by the gross amount of royalties earned by the artist from the sales of the prior album or albums. Under this "mini-max" structure, the fund always has a minimum, which generally escalates modestly from album to album and a maximum, which is generally twice the minimum.

ALBUM	MINIMUM	MAXIMUM
Second Album	$	$
Third Album	$	$
Fourth Album	$	$
Fifth Album	$	$
Sixth Album	$	$
Seventh Album	$	$

(d) The Recording Funds for each Committed Album other than the First Album shall be payable as follows: (i) *ten percent (10%) of the applicable minimum Recording Fund* for each Committed Album shall be paid to you, following your compliance with all of the terms of paragraph 4, including your receipt of Company's written approval of the Authorized Budget and Company's receipt of notice from you, and verification by Company that, recording of Masters to comprise the applicable Committed Album has commenced, and is scheduled to proceed, without interruption, to completion, provided that, such amount shall be reduced to the extent it would reduce the balance of the Recording Fund applicable to the Album below *one hundred fifteen percent (115%) of the Recording Costs* for the immediately preceding Committed Album; and (ii) the balance, if any, of the applicable Recording Fund shall be paid to you after deducting all Recording Costs and other Advances paid or incurred by Company in connection with the applicable Album, following Delivery of the applicable Album and receipt by Company of all union session reports and all invoices for all Recording Costs incurred in connection therewith.

The artist should try to increase the percentage used to calculate the initial payment to at least 15% to 20%. The clause allowing the reduction of that payment if it would reduce the balance of the Recording Fund to less than 115% of the Recording Costs for the prior album should be modified so that the required remainder is 100% to 105% of such Recording Costs.

(e) With respect to payments to be made pursuant to paragraph 7(b)(ii) and paragraph 7(d)(ii) in connection with Delivery of a Committed Album, Company shall have the right to withhold a reasonable portion of such payments to provide for anticipated Recording Costs which Recording Costs have not yet been paid by Company. Provided that Company shall have received all invoices relating to all such costs, and all union session reports, Company shall not withhold such sums for a period of more than forty-five (45) days following Delivery.

The withholding period should be reduced to no more than 30 days whenever possible.

(f) All monies paid to you or Artist or on behalf of you or Artist or to or on behalf of any Person representing you or Artist, other than royalties payable pursuant to paragraphs 9 and 12, shall constitute Advances, unless Company shall otherwise consent in writing.

The artist should try to persuade the company to make unrecoupable any costs incurred solely as the result of the acts or omissions of company's employees. This is a rare concession, but it could become significant in cases where a company executive runs up recording costs without authorization.

(g) All Recording Funds paid by Company pursuant to this paragraph 7 and all Advances paid by Company pursuant to paragraph 18, as applicable, shall specifically include the prepayment of session union scale, as provided in the applicable union codes, and you agree to complete any documentation required by the applicable union to effectuate the terms of this paragraph.

(h) Fifty percent (50%) of all expenses paid or incurred by Company in connection with the independent promotion, marketing and/or publicity of Masters by Persons other than regular employees of Company, including independent retail marketing services, shall constitute Advances.

(i) Any cost incurred by Company in connection with a trademark and/or service mark search to confirm Artist's right to use any professional name shall constitute an Advance.

If the artist has already had his or her professional name(s) trademarked, this language should be revised. Further, if the artist desires to control the process and expense of trademark and service mark searches, this language should be modified to create a budget for such services and permit the artist to engage third parties to conduct such searches under his or her supervision.

(j) Company shall not be required to make any payments hereunder unless and until you have furnished Company with a fully-completed "Affiliation Exhibit" in Company's then-standard form and a fully-completed IRS Form W-9 or W8-BEN, as applicable. If you fail to timely comply with the preceding sentence, Company may deduct any resulting penalty payments from all monies payable under this agreement or any other agreement.

7A. CALIFORNIA PROVISION

(a) This paragraph 7A is intended to be construed and implemented in such a manner so as to comply with the provisions of California Code of Civil Procedure, Section 526, and California Civil Code, Section 3423 concerning the availability of injunctive relief to prevent the breach of a contract in writing for the rendition or furnishing of personal services. You acknowledge that this paragraph is included to avoid compromise of Company's rights by reason of a finding of applicability of California law, but does not constitute a concession by Company that California law is actually applicable.

(b) For the purposes of this agreement, the following definitions shall apply: (i) "Contract Year" – each of the first seven (7) separate, consecutive twelve (12) month periods during which the Term of this agreement is in effect; (ii) "Annual Threshold" – (A) Nine Thousand Dollars ($9,000) for the first Contract Year, (B) Twelve Thousand Dollars ($12,000) for the second Contract Year; and (C) Fifteen Thousand Dollars ($15,000) for each of the third through seventh Contract Years. If the aggregate amount of the compensation paid to you under this agreement in any Contract Year is in excess of the Annual Threshold or any other payments specified in Section 3423 for such Contract Year, the excess shall be applied in reduction of the Annual Threshold and any other payments specified in Section 3423 for any subsequent Contract Year.

(c) If you have not received compensation equal to the Annual Threshold for any Contract Year, Company shall have the right to pay you the amount of any shortfall before the expiration of the applicable Contract Year. At least sixty (60) days before the end of each Contract Year, you shall notify Company if you have not received compensation equal to the Annual Threshold for such Contract Year and of the amount of any shortfall. Each payment made by Company pursuant to this paragraph 7A shall constitute an Advance and Company shall have the right to deduct each such payment from all monies payable under this agreement or any other agreement.

The purpose of this clause is to reflect the content of California Civil Code Section 3423, which requires the employer in a personal service contract to pay minimum amounts to the employee during each year of the contract or else the employer forfeits its rights to injunctive relief to prevent the employee from rendering his or her services to another company. Since the minimum payment applies to each member of a group, the company may be put to a difficult choice as to whether it should guarantee the minimum compensation to all members of a group that is newly signed to a label and therefore has no track record of sales or perhaps only to the key member or members, or whether it should forego entirely the possibility of injunctive relief. In this regard it is important for the artist to realize that even if the company is not entitled to injunctive relief to prevent the artist from recording for a new label in breach of the artist's recording contract, the company would be entitled to recover damages, which could be greater than the entire amount of royalties the artist may be paid by the new record company.

8. PRODUCER SERVICES

Without limiting Company's right of approval under paragraph 4, you shall be solely responsible for the engagement of each producer and for the payment of all monies becoming payable to each producer. Subject to the terms of paragraph 4, at your request, Company shall accept a letter of direction from you in a form approved by Company pursuant to which Company, on your behalf, shall pay to producers approved by Company (other than you, Artist or any employee or principal of you or Artist) the advances and royalties payable by you to such producer. Notwithstanding anything to the contrary contained herein, Company's acceptance of letters of direction hereunder shall constitute an accommodation to you and/or Artist alone and no other Person shall be deemed to be a beneficiary thereof (nor shall Company otherwise have any obligation to you and Artist or any other Person as a result of Company's acceptance of any such letter of direction) and you and Artist shall indemnify Company with respect thereto in accordance with the provisions of this agreement. If Company elects to pay any such producer (including any Staff Producer) directly, Company may deduct or recoup such payments from all monies payable under this agreement or any other agreement.

This section reconfirms the obligation of the artist to engage his or her own producers but provides that the company will honor artist's letters of direction to the company that instruct the company to pay producers on the artist's behalf.

Normally, producers are paid a fee for their services in producing the masters, which is usually treated as a fully recoupable advance against their royalties. Some savvy producers require that only a portion of their fee be deemed advances against royalties with the remainder deemed simple recording costs, which would be recoupable just like any other recording cost but not recoupable against the producer's advance. Producers' fees are normally paid half upon commencement of their services and half upon completion of the album. This is paid out of the recording fund and is one element of the recording costs of the album. Most commonly, producers are paid a royalty rate of approximately 3% of the royalty base price. Generally, producers' royalties are paid retroactively to the first record sold after recoupment of the recording costs of the album at the net artist's rate. This means that if the record is not successful enough to recoup its recording costs, the producer will not be paid any royalties in addition to the fee paid to him, but if it is, the producer will be paid royalties on all records sold. The net artist's rate means the all-in rate payable to the artist, which would be the rate set forth in this agreement, less the producer's rate, e.g., 13% less 3% equals 10%. If the record is successful enough that the recording costs have been recouped at the net artist's rate, then the producer will be credited with royalties on all records sold, not merely those sold after recoupment. Of course, those royalties will be reduced by the portion of the producer's fee deemed to be an advance against royalties.

9. ROYALTIES

Company shall credit to your royalty account royalties as described below. Royalties shall be computed by applying the applicable royalty rate specified herein to the applicable Royalty Base Price in respect of Net Sales of the Record concerned:

During the past few years, most major record companies have abandoned the archaic practice of calculating record royalties based on the retail list price and a long list of deductions for things like packaging, automatic free goods (a ghost of an era when a certain percentage of vinyl records would break during shipping) and even for manufacturing records in the compact-disc format. Instead, they have migrated to a more transparent wholesale-based royalty methodology, which typically just multiplies the wholesale price by the royalty rate and applies limited reductions for things like actual free goods used in specific retail discount programs. During the transition, record companies would sometimes claim that the "points" (i.e., the percentage of the applicable "royalty base price" used to calculate royalties) were roughly equal under their prior archaic retail-based approach and the current more transparent wholesale-based approach. Our own analysis, undertaken while negotiating recording agreements during the period of transition between methodologies, revealed that one point under the new methodology was worth somewhat less than one point over the old methodology. Depending on one's view of so-called standard terms, a "new" point is worth anywhere from 5% to 15% less than an "old" point. So, a "12% deal," using the new methodology, is actually worth between 10.2% and 11.4% using the old methodology.

The initial album royalty rate for a typical new artist deal with a major label using the new royalty basis ranges from 12% to 15%. Those rates typically increase over the life of the contract and are typically subject to escalations but, since historically escalations were based on 500,000 royalty-bearing units, and usually at least 15% of units did not bear royalties, today's escalations are sometimes triggered at higher thresholds (e.g., 600,000), although this is subject to negotiation. Also, the value of the escalations, which historically had been half points or full points, are sometimes subject to more negotiation because of the variable impact the new royalty bases have on calculations.

(a) (i) The royalty rate (the "Basic U.S. Rate") on USNRC Net Sales of Records consisting entirely of Recordings made hereunder during the applicable Contract Periods specified below shall be as follows:

TYPE OF RECORD	CONTRACT PERIOD	BASIC U.S. RATES
EPs in Phono Record form	Any	_____%
Singles and Maxi-Singles in Phono Record form	Any	_____%
Any other Audio Record	Initial Period and First Option Period	_____%
	Second Option Period and Third Option Period	_____%
	Fourth Option Period and Fifth Option Period	_____%
	Sixth Option Period	_____%
Value-Added Record	Any	_____%
Audiovisual Record	Any	_____%

(ii) The royalty rate (the "Escalated U.S. Album Rate") solely on USNRC Net Sales of each Committed Album in excess of the following number of units shall be the applicable rate set forth below rather than the otherwise applicable Basic U.S. Rate or any prior and otherwise applicable Escalated U.S. Album Rate:

RECORDING COMMITMENT	USNRC NET SALES	ESCALATED U.S. ALBUM RATES
First Album & Second Album	600,000 units 1,200,000 units	_____% _____%
Third Album & Fourth Album	600,000 units 1,200,000 units	_____% _____%
Fifth Album & Sixth Album	600,000 units 1,200,000 units	_____% _____%
Seventh Album	600,000 units 1,200,000 units	_____% _____%

(b) The royalty rate (the "<u>Foreign Rate</u>") for Net Sales of Records sold for distribution in the following territories outside the United States by Company or its Principal Licensees shall be computed at the applicable percentage of the royalty rate (without regard to any applicable Escalated U.S. Album Rate) that would otherwise apply to Net Sales in the United States of the Record concerned, as follows:

TERRITORIES	PERCENTAGE OF APPLICABLE U.S. RATE
Canada	85%
United Kingdom	80%
Japan, Australia, New Zealand & the EU other than the United Kingdom	75%
Rest of the World	60%

These foreign rate deductions are fairly typical, although the reduction for the "rest of the world" can sometimes be edged upward to 70%.

(c) (i) The royalty rate for Net Sales of the following categories of sales of Records by Company or its Principal Licensees shall be computed at the applicable percentage of the U.S. royalty rate (without regard to any applicable Escalated U.S. Album Rate) or Foreign Rate that would otherwise apply to such Net Sales:

CATEGORY	PERCENTAGE OF APPLICABLE U.S. ROYALTY RATE OR FOREIGN RATE
Government & Educational Institutions	50%
Premium Record	50%
Development Record & PX	75%
Mid-Price Record	66 2/3%
Compilation Record	75%
Budget Record	50%

Record companies argue that their profit margins for the aforementioned categories of records are less than their margins for normal full-priced retail albums so they seek reductions in the royalty rates for records in such categories. Of course, this functions as a sort of double-reduction, because since the royalty is tied to the wholesale price, the dollars-and-cents credited to the artist's account would naturally be less for a discounted product even with a rate reduction, but record companies insist that such reductions are necessary. The figures in the above chart are conservative, and with some persuasion, some labels may increase the factor for government and education to 66 ²/₃%, Mid-Price up to 75%, and Compilation Records up to 100%.

(ii) The royalty rate on Net Sales of: (A) any Record sold by Company or a Principal Licensee through any direct mail or mail order distribution method other than a Club Operation; and (B) any Record sold in conjunction with a substantial television advertising campaign, during the royalty accounting period in which that campaign begins and the next such period, shall be fifty percent (50%) of the otherwise applicable royalty rate set forth in this agreement.

This clause leaves considerable room for improvement. Companies may agree to improve the rate for records sold through television campaigns to 66 ²/₃%, and they may further agree that any reductions for such records be capped at 50% of their expenses incurred in connection with such a campaign. Further, the artist should seek a very specific definition of "substantial television advertising campaign" and the reduction should be limited to records sold within no more than 30 to 60 days after the end of such campaign.

(iii) The royalty rate on Net Sales of any Multiple Record Set (other than a Value-Added Record) shall be the otherwise applicable royalty rate set forth in this agreement multiplied by a fraction, the numerator of which shall be the PPD for such Multiple Record Set and the denominator of which shall be: (A) the number of Records in the Multiple Record Set multiplied by (B) the PPD applicable to the majority (or plurality) of Company's or its Principal Licensee's top line single Albums in the same format.

This is the standard formula to calculate royalties for multiple record sets. That being said, depending on the artist's clout and the circumstances surrounding the development of a multiple record set, it may be possible to negotiate a better rate at the time he or she seeks consent for the set from the company.

(d) (i) The royalty rate on Net Sales of Phono Records which are derived from Recordings hereunder, which Phono Records are licensed by Company or a Principal Licensee for sale through any Club Operation, shall be fifty percent (50%) of Net Receipts. No royalties shall be payable with respect to Phono Records received by members of any Club Operation in an introductory offer in connection with joining it or purchasing a required number of Phono Records including Phono Records distributed as "bonus" or "free" Phono Records, or Phono Records for which the Club Operation is not paid.

The artist should try to have language inserted that provides that no fewer than one-half of all records sold through club operations shall be deemed to bear royalties.

(ii) The royalty rate for any Recordings hereunder licensed by Company or a Principal Licensee for use in the distribution of Records (other than for

On-Demand Usages) shall be fifty percent (50%) of Net Receipts; provided that, such credit to your royalty account shall not exceed the royalty amount that would otherwise be credited to your account hereunder for such use if Company or a Principal Licensee had distributed the Records concerned. The royalty rate for any Recordings hereunder licensed by Company or a Principal Licensee for use in synchronization with motion pictures, television programs or any form of commercials shall be fifty percent (50%) of Net Receipts.

This is fairly standard language. However, it would help the artist to remove the clause that limits the artist's share of net receipts to that which the artist would have received if the company had sold the records instead of a licensee.

(iii) The royalty rate for any Recordings hereunder licensed by Company or a Principal Licensee for On-Demand Usages shall be a percentage of Net Receipts equal to one hundred twenty percent (120%) of the Basic U.S. Rate for the Record concerned; provided that, such credit to your royalty account shall not exceed the royalty amount that would otherwise be credited to your account hereunder for such use if Company or a Principal Licensee had distributed the Records concerned.

The new revenue streams being developed through new Internet-based technologies and systems have created an interesting set of issues. Traditionally, record companies pay a certain royalty for albums, reduced royalties for all other types of records and split the net receipts for all licenses. For example, if an artist's record gets licensed for use in a film, television show or commercial, the label and the artist usually split the net fee. However, legitimate music subscription services have shaken up this tradition. Those who represent artists would argue that the net proceeds generated from such services should be split fifty-fifty just like any other license. However, record companies argue that subscription services, unlike licenses for commercials, film and television, are viewed by some consumers as the replacement of traditional record sales—instead of buying tangible records or even purchasing and downloading songs from legitimate services like iTunes, consumers pay a monthly subscription fee and, for that money, can basically listen to what they want. So, if you buy the record companies' argument, the royalty rate for subscription revenue should be more like traditional record royalties. Many record companies have sought to simply apply the album royalty rate to the division of net receipts for such services. So, for example, if an artist has a 12% royalty rate for album sales, he or she would get 12% of the net receipts for subscription revenue. However, that analysis is badly flawed, since the 12% royalty rate for album sales does not reflect the allocation of net receipts, it simply establishes a dollars-and-cents royalty rate for the sale of albums. Because of the possibility, however remote or likely it may be, that subscription services may become the "next big thing" in the music business, the artist's royalty therefor is something that requires a fair amount of attention on two levels: (1) establishing an equitable royalty rate, and (2) understanding how the royalties are to be determined. For example, if a record company licenses 1,000 songs to a subscription service for a $100,000 fee for a fixed period, does that mean that each song is deemed to have generated $100? Or, should the royalty for each master recording be based on "spins"? So, for example, if an artist has a huge hit song that accounts *for 5% of the spins on the subscription service, should the master be deemed to have generated $100 as one of 1,000 license songs, or $5,000 as the song that got 5% of the spins among those songs licensed for $100,000? As a practical matter, for a new artist negotiating a recording agreement, the company will want to avoid getting bogged down in discussions of subscription services which, to date, are not huge money makers. That being said, artists should start the bidding by asking for a fifty-fifty split of the net receipts, just as they would receive for any other license; insist on a meaningful discussion of the issues with the company; request some concessions such as most-favored-nations status against a majority of new artists signed during the Term of the contract; and provisions to reopen the issue to adapt to developing industry norms at the artist's request. If all that does not work, just try to get the applicable factor up as high as possible.*

(e) Notwithstanding anything to the contrary contained herein, for sales by Company or a Principal Licensee of: (i) Records in now widely distributed compact disc forms including Enhanced CD and CD Extra formats, the royalty rate shall be one hundred percent (100%) of the otherwise applicable royalty rate set forth in this agreement; and (ii) Phono Records in any form, format or technology not herein described, which is now known but not widely distributed or which hereafter becomes known, including Super Audio CD and DVD Audio ("New Technology Formats"), the royalty rate shall be seventy-five percent (75%) of the otherwise applicable royalty rate set forth in this agreement; provided that, if in any calendar year the revenues generated from the sale of Records in a particular New Technology Format exceed twenty percent (20%) of total United States recorded music revenues (as reported in a reputable published industry source such as IFPI's *The Recording Industry in Numbers*), then, with respect to sales of Records hereunder in any subsequent calendar years, such particular New Technology Format shall no longer constitute a New Technology Format and the royalty rate with respect to such particular New Technology Format shall be one hundred percent (100%) of the otherwise applicable royalty rate set forth in this agreement rather than seventy-five percent (75%).

This language allows companies to reduce royalties for developing and emerging technologies until such technologies generate 20% of the industry's annual revenue. Artists should try to reduce that threshold as much as possible. Due to the growing fragmentation of the industry through emerging technologies, the chances of any new technology growing to comprise 20% of industry revenue seems remote (although you never know) and a 10-year-old technology with a strong foothold in the industry that consistently generates 5% of industry revenue should not be subject to a "new technology" reduction. Artists should try to have that threshold reduced to 10% of industry revenue during any one year or 5% of industry revenue for any three years. Any technology that succeeds at that level should no longer be considered "new." That being said, royalty reductions for new technologies are not important enough by themselves to sour an otherwise good deal. Record companies may dig in their heels on these issues and, once the issue has been raised and amply discussed, it should not be considered a deal breaker.

(f) With respect to Electronic Transmissions, the royalty rate shall be one hundred percent (100%) of the otherwise applicable royalty rate set forth in this agreement. (g) The royalty rate on any Record embodying Recordings hereunder coupled with other Recordings shall be computed by multiplying the otherwise applicable royalty rate by a fraction, the numerator of which is the number of Recordings hereunder embodied on such Record and the denominator of which is the total number of Recordings embodied on such Record; however, the royalty rate on a Video which is coupled with Recordings by other artists on Audiovisual Records shall in no event exceed the royalty rate that would apply if such royalty were computed by apportionment based on the actual playing time of each Recording embodied in the Audiovisual Record concerned.

(h) As to any Recording hereunder embodying the performances of Artist together with the performances of any other artist(s), the royalty rate otherwise payable hereunder with respect to sales of any Record derived from such Recording shall be computed by multiplying such royalty rate by a fraction, the numerator of which shall be one (1) and the denominator of which shall be the total number of artists whose performances are embodied on such Recording.

This language states the default position for calculating royalties for master recordings of more than one royalty-bearing artist. Artists would be well-advised to seek a simple clause that clarifies that such automatic fractional division of royalties applies only in the absence of a written agreement between the featured artists to the contrary. Often, guest artists will accept a one-time fee or, if they are important enough, a one-point or two-point side artist royalty. They will not always demand half of the applicable royalty.

(i) Notwithstanding anything to the contrary expressed or implied in this agreement, this paragraph 9 shall not be deemed to apply to any payments received by Company pursuant to any statute or other legislation or collective bargaining agreement or industry agreement including payments for the public performance of Recordings or royalties payable for the sale of blank cassettes or for the sale of recording equipment. Notwithstanding the foregoing if: (A) legislation or a collective bargaining agreement or industry agreement applicable to Company requiring the payment of copyright royalties for the public performance of sound recordings or for sales of blank tape is or has been enacted in any country of the Territory; (B) such legislation or collective bargaining agreement apportions such royalties into a recording artist share and a record company share; (C) you do not receive or waive the right to receive (e.g., fail to make a timely application to receive) the applicable recording artist share of such royalties; and (D) Company actually receives in the United States a recording artist share of royalties attributable to you; then Company shall credit your royalty account hereunder with such recording artist share of royalties directly attributable to Recordings hereunder.

Songwriters and publishers already receive monies directly from public performance societies like ASCAP and BMI for the public performance of their compositions. From time to time, some aspiring legislator tries to create a parallel revenue stream for recording artists so that, when an artist's songs are played on the radio (or otherwise performed publicly), moneys are collected and ultimately disbursed directly to the artist. These efforts are usually shot down, as lobbyists for those interests that would pay the license fees carry great influence and, so far, have outgunned the recording artist lobby. However, as CD piracy and illegal downloads continue to change the landscape of the music industry, there is a reasonable chance that there will be renewed efforts to create some sort of public performance royalty system for recording artists. Under this clause, if a public performance system were created and the artist's public performance royalties somehow made it into the record company's coffers (instead of directly to the artist), the record company would be able to credit the artist's royalties against his or her unrecouped balance! That would defeat the whole purpose of making sure that artists received direct payment for the public perform-ance of their works. This clause should be modified to require the label to pass through the artist's portion of any such moneys received by the company regardless of whether or not the artist's account is recouped.

(j) The royalties payable pursuant to this agreement include all royalties payable to you, Artist and any other Persons with respect to the Record concerned including, with respect to audiovisual materials embodied thereon, all music publishing royalties payable to you, Artist and any other Persons.

(k) If the performances embodied on any Recording hereunder enter the public domain in any country of the Territory so that such Recording may be repro-duced and/or exploited in such country without license from and payment to Company, then, notwithstanding anything to the contrary contained herein, no monies shall be payable hereunder to you and/or Artist with respect to such Recording sold in such country on and after the date such Recording enters the public domain.

This clause seems a bit unfair. If and when any of the artist's recordings enter the public domain in any country, third parties may be able to duplicate and sell the artist's recordings without payment to the company. However, the demand for the original or official releases may well be greater than the demand for freelance duplications of public domain works so, because the company may continue to sell the artist's records even after the masters have entered public domain, the artist should try to persuade the company to agree to account for and pay royalties to the artist even after the recordings in question have entered the public domain. Record companies are unlikely, however, to back away from this point, but it should not be a deal breaker.

(l) If any Artwork is sold separately in connection with the sale of a Record, Company shall credit your royalty account hereunder with a percentage of Net Receipts derived from the sale of such Artwork which is equal to the Basic U.S. Rate applicable to the sale of such Record if such Record were sold in the United States. If any Artwork is sold or licensed separately in connection with the license for use in the distribution of a Record, Company shall credit your royalty account hereunder with a percentage of Net Receipts derived from the sale or licensing of such Artwork which is equal to the percentage of Net Receipts applicable under paragraph 9(d)(ii) or (iii) to the license for use in the distribution of such Record.

Referencing the prior discussion regarding the royalty for On-Demand Uses, if Artwork is sold separately, there are good arguments that the artist and company should split the net proceeds. In fact, if the artist has sufficient clout, he or she should seek language that provides for the artist to own the Artwork and license it to the company for use solely in connection with the sale of records.

10. STATEMENTS AND PAYMENTS

(a) Within ninety (90) days after June 30 and December 31 of each year during which applicable Records are sold, Company shall render a statement of accrued royalties earned under this agreement during the preceding calendar semi-annual period. Concurrently with the rendition of each statement, Company shall pay you all royalties shown to be due by such statement, after deducting all Advances made prior to the rendition of the statement. Notwithstanding the foregoing, Company shall not have the right to recoup from royalties payable hereunder with respect to a given calendar semi-annual period Advances expressly set forth in this agreement which are paid by Company hereunder to you or Artist or to third parties on your or Artist's behalf after the close of such calendar semi-annual period unless: (i) the date of a payment has been delayed due to your or Artist's acts or omissions or (ii) you or Artist have requested that a payment scheduled to be made prior to the close of such calendar semi-annual period be delayed until after the close of such calendar semi-annual period. No statements need be rendered by Company for any such calendar semi-annual period after the expiration of the Term for which there are no sales of Records derived from Recordings hereunder. All statements and payments shall be made to the order of _____ and shall be sent to _____ at the following address: _____.

While the timing of payments is generally not negotiable, the artist should try to limit the waiting period for semiannual payments to six weeks from the end of the period as opposed to three months as provided for in the agreement.

(b) Company shall be entitled to maintain a single account with respect to all Recordings subject to this agreement or any other agreement.

This contract is typical in that all recordings made under this agreement are treated as part of a single, consolidated account. For example, if the artist's first album is quite successful, but the artist's second album is costly and unsuccessful, the recording costs and advances attributable to the second album will offset the royalties earned from sales of the first album, on a dollar-for-dollar basis, so that there may be no net payment due to the artist. This concept of consolidating the recoupable advances and charges and the earned royalties associated with one project with the recoupable advances and charges and the earned royalties associated with another project is known as cross-collateralization. Cross-collateralization limited to the recordings made under a single agreement is almost universally accepted. However, this agreement goes beyond that to cross-collateralize any other agreement to which the artist may be a party with the company, e.g., a prior or subsequent recording agreement. This is always a point to be negotiated. It becomes particularly contentious when the company requires cross-collateralization with mechanical royalty payments or with a publishing agreement with the company's affiliate. While it is very difficult to persuade a record company to not cross-collateralize accounts for separate albums under the agreement, the artist should negotiate aggressively to prevent the label from cross-collateralizing record royalty accounts with mechanical royalty accounts. An artist should not be penalized for composing or cocomposing his or her own recordings and a label that insists on the right to deduct unrecouped recording expenses from mechanical royalties is doing just that. In this case, while the agreement provides for a "single account" the intent is probably not to cross-collateralize against mechanical royalties, but that should be clarified.

(c) Company may withhold a reasonable reserve against returns, exchanges, refunds, credits and the like.

It is typical for a recording contract to allow a company to maintain reserves against anticipated returns of records. Often, there is no limit on the amount of reserves that a company can maintain, except that they will be "reasonable." Such a provision makes it very difficult for the artist to do anything if the company is maintaining levels of reserves that the artist believes to be unreasonable in view of the company's actual returns experience with respect to the artist's records. In this contract, reserves are limited in paragraph 7(c)(ii) but that paragraph should be referenced here to erase any ambiguity regarding company's flexibility to establish reasonable reserves. Although this draft is silent on the matter, generally, the company will agree to liquidate the reserve within three or four semiannual periods, i.e., 18 months to 24 months, after it has been established. This means that the reserve will either be used up by applying returns against it, or it will be paid out in the form of royalties to the artist if it is not used up.

(d) You shall be deemed to have consented to all accountings rendered by Company hereunder and such accountings shall be binding upon you and not subject to any objection by you for any reason unless specific objection, in writing, stating the basis thereof, is given to Company within two (2) years after the date Company is deemed to have rendered the applicable statement, and after such written objection, unless suit is instituted within three (3) years after the date Company is deemed to have rendered the applicable statement. Company shall be deemed conclusively to have rendered each statement on the date prescribed in paragraph 10(a) unless you notify Company otherwise with respect to any particular statement within sixty (60) days after the date that Company is required to render that statement pursuant to the first sentence of paragraph 10(a).

This is fairy typical language. An artist should make sure that he or she has at least two years to object to a statement and three years to file a lawsuit regarding such statement.

(e) (i) You shall have the right at your sole cost and expense to appoint a certified public accountant who is not then currently engaged in an outstanding audit of Company to examine Books and Records as same pertain to sales of Records subject hereto; provided that, any such examination shall be for a reasonable duration, shall take place at Company's offices during normal business hours on reasonable prior notice and shall not occur more than once in any calendar year. You may examine Books and Records with respect to a particular statement only once. Notwithstanding anything to the contrary, if Company notifies you that the certified public accountant designated by you to conduct an audit under paragraph 10(b)(i) is engaged in another outstanding audit of Company on behalf of another Person, you may nevertheless have your audit conducted by such accountant, and the running of the time within which such audit may be made shall be suspended until such accountant has completed such other audit, provided: (A) you shall notify Company of your election to that effect within fifteen (15) days after the date of Company's such notice to you; (B) your accountant shall proceed in a reasonably continuous and expeditious manner to complete such other audit and render the final report thereon to you and Company; and (C) your audit shall not be commenced by your accountant before the delivery to Company of the final report on such other audit, shall be commenced within thirty (30) days thereafter, and shall be conducted in a reasonably continuous manner. The provisions of this paragraph shall not apply if Company elects to waive the provisions of paragraph 10(b)(i) that require that your accountant shall not be engaged in any other audit.

Recording contracts typically place specified time limits upon the artist's right to audit the company's books and records. These time periods are generally shorter than those that are otherwise allowable under state law. The company justifies such limitations because of the tremendous amount of record keeping involved and the cost associated therewith. Generally, companies try to limit the audit and objection period to one year, whereas artists' representatives seek to make it as long as possible, but two years is a fairly typical compromise.

(ii) If Company agrees that there has been an undercrediting of royalties to you exceeding ten percent (10%) of the total royalties reported as credited by Company to your account hereunder for the period covered by such examination or if an undercrediting of royalties exceeding such amount is established by a court of competent jurisdiction, Company shall reimburse you in the amount of all reasonable fees paid by you to the auditors concerned in connection with such audit, up to a maximum amount of Twenty-Five Thousand Dollars ($25,000) per audit. Company shall pay interest to you on the payable portion (i.e., the portion in excess of any then-unrecouped Advances) of any agreed upon or so-established undercrediting of royalties hereunder at the prime rate as quoted in the "Money Rate" section of *The Wall Street Journal* or any other similarly-reputable published source, calculated on the basis of a 365-day year.

Traditionally, record companies seldom agree to reimburse artists for auditing costs and rarely agree to pay interest on recovered sums. However, this clause protects the artist in the event that an audit reveals a substantial underpayment.

(f) Company shall compute your royalties in the same national currency in which Company's licensee pays Company for that sale, and Company shall credit those royalties to your account at the same rate of exchange at which the licensee pays Company (or credits Company in recoupment of an advance made to Company by such licensee, as reflected in a royalty accounting statement received by Company). For purposes of accounting to you, Company shall treat any sale outside of the United States as a sale made during the same royalty accounting period in which Company receives accounting and payment (or credit to Company in recoupment of an advance made to Company by such licensee, as reflected in a royalty accounting statement received by Company) for that sale from the applicable licensee. If Company cannot collect payment in the

United States in U.S. Dollars, Company shall not be required to account to you for that sale, except that Company shall, at your request and at your expense, deduct from the monies so blocked, and deposit in a foreign depository, the equivalent in local currency of the royalties which would be payable to you on the foreign sales concerned, to the extent such monies are available for that purpose, and only to the extent to which your royalty account is then in a fully-recouped position. All such deposits shall constitute royalty payments to you for accounting purposes. To the extent possible, Company shall allow you to select the foreign depository referred to in this paragraph 10(c).

This provision clarifies how revenues for foreign sales are applied to the accounting provisions in the agreement. This agreement provides that if the label does not receive payments for foreign sales in the United States in U.S. dollars that it is not required to pay the artist for that sale. This is fairly common language, and it is important that the language be further clarified to provide that if the label does receive payment but not in the United States and not in U.S. currency, that the label will nonetheless convert such payment into U.S. currency and deposit it into the artist's account. The language of this agreement takes a step in that direction but with some additional negotiating, the label would likely agree to such clarifying provisions.

11. NOTICES

Except as otherwise specifically set forth herein, all notices under this agreement shall be in writing and shall be given by courier or other personal delivery, by overnight delivery by an established overnight delivery service (e.g., Federal Express, Airborne Express, UPS, etc.), or by registered or certified mail (return receipt requested) at the appropriate address below, or at a substitute address designated in a notice (made in accordance with this paragraph 11) sent by the party concerned to the other party hereto.

TO YOU: The address shown above

TO COMPANY: The address shown above
                   Attention:
                   Major Record Company Inc., 123 Anystreet, Anytown,
                   ZZ 99999, Attention: Senior Vice President, Business
                   and Legal Affairs and also to 123 Anystreet, Anytown,
                   ZZ 99999, Attention: Chief Financial Officer

A copy of each notice to Company shall be sent simultaneously to the attention of Company's Chief Financial Officer. *Company shall undertake to send a copy of each notice to _____, but Company's failure to send any such copy shall not constitute a breach of this agreement or impair the effectiveness of the notice concerned.* Notices shall be deemed given when mailed or deposited into the custody of an overnight delivery service for overnight delivery, or, if personally delivered, when so delivered, except that a notice of change of address shall be effective only from the date of its receipt. Company may send royalty statements and payments to you by first class mail.

This is fairly typical "notice" language and artists must be very careful to comply with the precise letter of this provision when sending any type of formal notice to the company. Also, the italicized clause that lets the company off the hook if it fails to send the notice to artist's designee should be improved through negotiation. If the artist must notify the company's CFO in order for his or her notice to be valid, company should notify the artist's designee in order for the company's notice to be valid.

12. LICENSES FOR MUSICAL COMPOSITIONS

The minimum statutory rate for records made and distributed as of January 1, 2006 is 9.1¢. When the current copyright act became effective on January 1, 1978 the minimum statutory rate was 2.75¢. As you can see, it has risen quite dramatically and it is anticipated that it will continue to rise in the future. However, under this provision the mechanical royalty rate on a master delivered will never increase regardless of increases in the statutory rate.

(a) For the purposes of this agreement, the following definitions shall apply:
 (i) "<u>Controlled Compositions</u>" - any Composition or material recorded pursuant to this agreement which, in whole or in part, is written or composed, and/or owned or controlled, directly or indirectly, by you and/or any individual member of Artist and/or any producer of a Master and/or anyone associated or affiliated with you, Artist or any such producer;
 (ii) "<u>Effective Date</u>" - the earlier of: (A) the date on which you Deliver the first Master which embodies the Controlled Composition concerned; or (B) the date on which you are required to Deliver such Master;

Most of the definitions in 12(a) are standard and not subject to negotiation. However, the "Effective Date" can actually be very important and could be ripe for negotiation under certain circumstances. The minimum license rate set by U.S. Copyright Law increases every so often, so the artist should negotiate for the latest possible "Effective Date." The best "Effective Date" for the artist would be the date each Record embodying a Controlled Composition was manufactured, but record companies are unlikely to agree to that. The next best date would by the first date a Record embodying a Controlled Composition is sold in the U.S. If that idea does not fly, eliminating the (B) clause in the above definition is a reasonable compromise.

 (iii) "<u>U.S. 75% Rate</u>" - seventy-five percent (75%) of the United States minimum per Composition compulsory license rate applicable to the use of Compositions on phonorecords under the United States Copyright Law (without regard to playing time) in effect as of the Effective Date, or, if there is no statutory rate in the United States as of the Effective Date, seventy-five percent (75%) of the per Composition rate (without regard to playing time) generally utilized by major record companies in the United States as of the Effective Date;
 (iv) "<u>Canadian 75% Rate</u>" - seventy-five percent (75%) of the Canadian statutory per Composition rate (without regard to playing time) in effect as of the Effective Date, or, if there is no statutory rate in Canada as of the Effective Date, seventy-five percent (75%) of the per Composition rate (without regard to playing time) generally utilized by major record companies

in Canada as of the Effective Date;

(v) "<u>U.S. 100% Rate</u>" - the United States minimum per Composition compulsory license rate applicable to the use of Compositions on phonorecords under the United States Copyright Law (without regard to playing time) in effect as of the Effective Date, or, if there is no statutory rate in the United States as of the Effective Date, the per Composition rate (without regard to playing time) generally utilized by major record companies in the United States as of the Effective Date; and

(vi) "<u>Canadian 100% Rate</u>" - the Canadian statutory per Composition rate (without regard to playing time) in effect as of the Effective Date, or, if there is no statutory rate in Canada as of the Effective Date, the per Composition rate (without regard to playing time) generally utilized by major record companies in Canada as of the Effective Date.

(b) Controlled Compositions shall be and are hereby irrevocably licensed to Company and its licensees: (i) for the United States, at a royalty per Controlled Composition equal to the U.S. 75% Rate; and (ii) for Canada, at a royalty per Controlled Composition equal to the Canadian 75% Rate.

(c) Notwithstanding the foregoing, regardless of the total number of Compositions embodied on the Record concerned, the maximum aggregate mechanical royalty rate which Company shall be required to pay in respect of: (i) any Single hereunder shall not exceed two (2) times the U.S. 75% Rate or the Canadian 75% Rate, as the case may be; (ii) any Maxi-Single hereunder shall not exceed three (3) times the U.S. 75% Rate or the Canadian 75% Rate, as the case may be; (iii) any EP hereunder shall not exceed five (5) times the U.S. 75% Rate or the Canadian 75% Rate, as the case may be; (iv) any Album (and any Value-Added Record) hereunder shall not exceed ten (10) times the U.S. 75% Rate or the Canadian 75% Rate, as the case may be.

This clause establishes the mechanical royalty cap or budget for each configuration of Record. A 10-song cap for an album by a debut artist is fairly common, although the cap can often be increased to 11 with some persuasion. To determine the amount of money available to pay the songwriters and publishers of songs embodied on the album, simply multiply the cap by the mechanical rate.

(d) Notwithstanding the foregoing, if the Album concerned embodies solely non-Controlled Compositions, or if the Album concerned embodies both Controlled Compositions and non-Controlled Compositions, the maximum aggregate mechanical royalty rate shall not exceed the U.S. 100% Rate or the Canadian 100% Rate times the number of Masters embodying such non-Controlled Compositions (but not more than ten (10)), plus the U.S. 75% Rate or Canadian 75% Rate times the number that is equal to ten (10) minus the lesser of ten (10) or the number of such non-Controlled Compositions; and (v) any Multiple Record Set hereunder (other than any Value-Added Record) shall not exceed the otherwise applicable maximum aggregate mechanical royalty rate set forth in this paragraph 12(c) multiplied by a fraction, the numerator of which shall be the PPD for such Multiple Record Set and the denominator of which shall be the PPD applicable to the majority (or plurality) of Company's or its Principal Licensee's top line single Albums in the same format.

This is an unusual clause that requires the company to make additional money available in the event that some of the compositions on a particular record are not written by the artist. Artists should always ask for this type of clause, sometimes called a "mechanical protection clause."

(e) If the aggregate mechanical royalty rate for any Record exceeds the applicable maximum aggregate mechanical royalty rate provided in paragraph 12(c), the aggregate mechanical royalty rate for Controlled Compositions contained thereon shall be reduced by the amount of that excess. Additionally, Company (and/or Company's Principal Licensee in Canada) shall have the right to deduct the amount of that excess from all monies payable under this agreement or any other agreement. Mechanical royalties shall be paid on 100% of Publishing Net Sales. No mechanical royalties shall be payable with respect to nonmusical material, Compositions that are two (2) minutes or less in duration, *Compositions embodied in "hidden" Recordings* (i.e., Recordings which are not listed in the primary track listing on the liner notes for the Record concerned), or "intros," "interludes," "extraludes," or similar Compositions. Company may maintain *reserves* with respect to the payment of mechanical royalties.

Be careful if a company tries to exclude mechanical royalties for so-called hidden tracks. Usually a songwriter and his or her publisher will expect to receive mechanical royalties for any song placed on an album whether hidden or not. Also, any reserves taken against mechanical royalties should be handled on the same basis as record royalty reserves. The agreement should be clarified to reflect that.

(f) If Company (or its applicable Principal Licensee) makes an overpayment of mechanical royalties in respect of Compositions recorded under this agreement, you shall reimburse Company for same, failing which Company may recoup any such overpayment from all monies becoming payable under this agreement or any other agreement. Mechanical royalty payments on Records subsequently returned are considered overpayments. Notwithstanding anything to the contrary contained herein, mechanical royalties payable in respect of Controlled Compositions for Publishing Net Sales other than from USNRC Net Sales shall be seventy-five percent (75%) of the otherwise applicable U.S. 75% Rate or Canadian 75% Rate, as the case may be. Mechanical royalties for Controlled Compositions which are arranged versions of any Compositions in the public domain shall be paid in the same proportion as the appropriate performing rights society grants performing credits to the publisher of such Controlled Composition, provided you have furnished Company with a copy of the letter from such performing rights society setting forth the percentage of the otherwise applicable credit which the publisher shall receive. Any assignment of the ownership or administration of copyright in any Controlled Composition shall be made subject to the provisions hereof and any inconsistencies between the terms of this agreement and mechanical licenses issued to and accepted by Company shall be determined by the terms of this agreement.

(g) If any Record contains Compositions which are not Controlled Compositions, you shall obtain for Company's benefit mechanical licenses covering such Compositions on the same terms and conditions applicable to Controlled Compositions pursuant to this paragraph 12.

This language is fine to the extent that the artist controls what songs are included on the album. If the company selects songs that are not "Controlled Compositions" then the company should be responsible for obtaining the license.

(h) You hereby agree that all Compositions shall be available for licensing by Company and Company's licensees for reproduction and distribution in each country of the Territory outside of the United States and Canada through the author's society or other licensing and collecting body generally responsible for such activities in the country concerned. You shall cause the issuance of effective licenses, under copyright and otherwise, to reproduce each Composition on Records and distribute those Records outside the United States and Canada, on terms not less favorable to Company or Company's licensees than the terms prevailing on a general basis in the country concerned with respect to the use of Compositions on comparable Records.

Same comment as 12(g).

(i) In respect of all Controlled Compositions, Company and its licensees are hereby granted the irrevocable perpetual right throughout the Territory, at no cost, to reprint the lyrics on and/or in connection with the jackets, sleeves and other packaging of Records derived from Recordings hereunder, and to transmit, broadcast, or otherwise reproduce such lyrics on, or cause the transmission, broadcast or other reproduction of lyrics by means of Records containing audio-visual material, and on websites, in connection with the exploitation and promotion of Recordings hereunder. Company shall provide appropriate copyright notices and writer and publisher credits with respect to such reprinted lyrics; provided that, Company's inadvertent failure to do so in any instance shall not constitute a breach of this agreement. You also grant to Company and Company's licensees an irrevocable license under copyright to reproduce each Controlled Composition in Videos and in advertisements for Recordings hereunder (including so-called EPKs) or Artist's recording services in any and all media (including television, radio and the Internet), to reproduce, distribute and perform those Videos and advertisements in any manner (including publicly and for profit, and including use of such Videos and advertisements in Records containing audiovisual material and in webcasts), to manufacture and distribute Audiovisual Records and other copies of those Videos, and to exploit such Videos and advertisements otherwise, by any method and in any form known now or in the future, in per-petuity and throughout the Territory, and to authorize others to do so. Company and Company's licensees shall not be required to make any payment in connection with those uses, and that license shall apply whether or not Company receives any payment in connection with any use of any Video or advertisement. If any exhibition of a Video and/or advertisement is also authorized under another license (such as a public performance license granted by ASCAP or BMI), that exhibition shall be deemed authorized by that license instead of this agreement. In all events, Company and Company's licensees shall have no liability by reason of any such exhibition. You also grant to Company and Company's licensees at no cost an irrevocable license under copyright to reproduce, distribute and perform each Controlled Composition or any portion thereof for promotional purposes on websites maintained by Company or its licensees or affiliates throughout the Territory.

The company should agree to pay a publishing royalty for the use of compositions in Videos to the extent that the Video production costs have been recouped. A common rate is 8¢ per composition subject to an aggregate cap of 6% of the royalty base price for the Audiovisual Record.

(j) Notwithstanding anything in the foregoing provisions of this paragraph 12 to the contrary, if a particular Controlled Composition recorded hereunder is embodied more than once on a particular Record, Company shall pay mechanical royalties in connection therewith at the applicable rate for such Controlled Composition as if the Controlled Composition concerned were embodied thereon only once. For purposes of this paragraph 12, a Composition and all adaptations thereof (e.g., remixes, etc.), if any, shall be deemed to be one (1) Composition.

13. EVENTS OF DEFAULT

(a) If you do not timely fulfill any portion of the Recording Commitment hereunder or any of your other material obligations hereunder in accordance with all of the terms and conditions of this agreement, then, in addition to any other rights or remedies which Company may have, Company shall have the right, upon notice to you at any time prior to the expiration of the then-current Contract Period: (i) to terminate the Term, in which event Company shall be entitled to require you to repay to Company the unrecouped amount of any Advance previously paid to you and not specifically attributable under paragraph 7 to an Album which has actually been Delivered, except as otherwise specifically set forth in the next sentence, unless your default is due solely to the death or disability of Artist and/or (ii) if the applicable Album is not Delivered within thirty (30) days following the Delivery Date, to reduce the Advance or Recording Fund (as applicable) for such Album by an amount equal to ten percent (10%) of such Advance or Recording Fund (as applicable) for each thirty (30) day period (or portion thereof) elapsing after the Delivery Date prior to Delivery of such Album. You shall not be required to repay any such Advance to the extent to which you furnish Company with documentation satisfactory to Company establishing that you have actually used the Advance to make payments to Persons not affiliated with you and in which you do not have an interest for Recording Costs incurred in connection with the Album concerned prior to Company's demand for repayment. Company may exercise any or all of its rights pursuant to this paragraph 13(a) by sending you the appropriate notice. No exercise by Company of its rights under this paragraph shall limit Company's right to recover damages by reason of your default or to exercise any of its other rights and remedies.

This first draft of the default clause is way over the top in many respects. First of all, if the artist is in default, the company must provide the artist with written notice of the default and give the artist the opportunity to cure the default. Second, the penalty for termination should not be the reimbursement of the unrecouped balance unless artist's conduct is truly egregious (such as the deliberate misappropriation of recording funds). Third, the notion that the Recording Fund should be reduced by 10% every 30 days that an album is not delivered is not an appropriate way to motivate a creative person to perform.

(b) If Company refuses without cause to allow you to fulfill the Recording Commitment for any Contract Period and if, not later than sixty (60) days following that refusal, you notify Company of your desire to fulfill such Recording Commitment, then Company shall permit you to fulfill such Recording Commitment by notice to you to such effect within sixty (60) days following Company's receipt of your notice. Should Company fail to give such notice, or if Company notifies you of its refusal to allow you to fulfill the applicable Recording Commitment, your sole remedy shall be that you shall have the option to terminate the Term by notice given to Company within thirty (30) days after the expiration of the latter sixty (60) day period. On receipt by Company of such notice, the Term shall terminate and all parties shall be deemed to have fulfilled all of their obligations hereunder except those obligations which survive the end of the Term (e.g., warranties, representations, indemnities, Re-recording Restrictions and Company's obligation to pay royalties), at which time Company shall pay to you, in full and complete settlement of Company's obligations to you (other than such royalty obligations) under this agreement, an Advance equal to the difference between: (i) the minimum Recording Fund with respect to such unrecorded Album, as set forth in paragraph 7 less any sums paid by Company in connection with such unrecorded Album; and (ii) the Recording Costs incurred in connection with the immediately preceding Committed Album; provided that, such Advance shall not exceed twenty percent (20%) of the minimum Recording Fund for the unrecorded Album less any sums paid by Company with respect to such unrecorded Album. If Masters sufficient to constitute the First Album have not been completed, then the amount of the Advance payable to you under the preceding sentence shall be the amount equal to the minimum union scale compensation for the portion of the First Album that Company refused without cause to allow you to fulfill, assuming that the First Album would have consisted of eleven (11) Masters less any sums paid by Company in connection with the First Album. If you administered Recording Costs with respect to part or all of the applicable immediately preceding Committed Album, then an amount equal to the greater of: (A) eighty-five percent (85%) of the minimum Recording Fund; or (B) the Recording Costs incurred by Company with respect to such Album, shall be treated as Recording Costs for the purposes of paragraph 13(b)(ii).

The first part of this section establishes a timetable and a method for the artist to terminate the agreement in the event the company refuses to fund the recording of the then-current album commitment. If possible, the artist should try to have removed that portion of the paragraph that requires notification to the label of his or her intent to fulfill such recording agreement within 60 days of that refusal. Depending on how things unfold, there might be some debate about when such refusal actually occurs. Ideally, an artist ought to be able to initiate the process of terminating the agreement at any time if the record company is refusing to fund the project. The second part of this section is the so-called pay-or-play provision of the agreement. This requires the record company to pay a specified sum to the artist in the event that the company is obligated to fund the recording of an album but refuses to do so. The amount of the payment is typically the amount of the minimum recording fund less the anticipated recording costs or, in other words, the amount of money that the artist would expect to pocket upon completion and delivery of the album in question.

(c) Company reserves the right, at its election upon notice to you, to suspend the operation of this agreement for the duration of any force majeure event (including any of the following contingencies), if by reason of any such contingency, it is materially hampered in the performance of its obligations under this agreement or its normal business operations are delayed or become impossible or commercially impracticable: Act of God, fire, catastrophe, labor disagreement, acts of government, its agencies or officers, any order, regulation, ruling or action of any labor union or association of artists, musicians, composers or employees affecting Company or the industry in which it is engaged, delays in the delivery of materials and supplies or any other cause beyond Company's control. Any such suspension due to a labor controversy which involves only Company shall be limited to a period of six (6) months.

This is a typical force majeure clause, which absolves the company from performance of its obligations if performance is prevented by an act of God or similar occurrence. Typically, the artist's representative will seek to limit the duration of any suspension period due to a cause that only affects the particular company and will try to clarify that accounting statements will be rendered and royalty payments will continue to be made except to the extent that the company is rendered unable to do so.

(d) Each of the following shall constitute an event of default hereunder: (i) if Artist's voice or Artist's ability to perform should be permanently impaired or otherwise materially impaired for a period of ninety (90) days or longer *or an aggregate period of ninety (90) days during any one (1) year period;* (ii) if you or Artist commences a voluntary case under any applicable bankruptcy, insolvency or other similar law now or hereafter in effect or consents to the entry of an order for relief in any involuntary case under such law or consents to the appointment of or taking possession by a receiver, liquidator, assignee, trustee or sequestrator (or similar appointee) of you or Artist or any substantial part of your or Artist's property or you or Artist makes an assignment for the benefit of creditors or takes any act (whether corporate or otherwise) in furtherance of any of the foregoing; or (iii) a court having jurisdiction over the affairs or property of you or Artist enters a decree or order for relief in respect of you or Artist or any of your or Artist's property in an involuntary case under any applicable bankruptcy, insolvency or other similar law now or hereafter in effect or appoints a receiver, liquidator, assignee, custodian, trustee or sequestrator (or similar appointee) of you or Artist or for any substantial part of your or Artist's property or orders the winding up or liquidation of your or Artist's affairs and such decree or order remains unstayed and in effect for a period of fifteen (15) consecutive days. Upon the occurrence of any of the events described in this paragraph 13(d) or in paragraph 19, in addition to any other rights or remedies which Company may have, Company shall have the right, upon notice to you, to suspend the running of the Term and/or Company's obligations to you hereunder (including all payment obligations other than payment of royalties) and/or to terminate the Term (whether or not during a period of suspension based on such event or based upon any other event), and thereby be relieved of all liability other than any obligations hereunder to pay royalties in respect of Masters Delivered prior to such termination.

This is fairly typical first-draft language but should be improved before closing. Specifically, the clause about the artist's voice being impaired for 90 days in the aggregate during any one-year period should come out, and the language that allows the company to terminate the contract if the artist files bankruptcy is too one-sided and heavy handed. Record companies do not like their artists to file bankruptcy because the bankruptcy court has the power to nullify recording contracts. However, an artist who has no desire to terminate his recording agreement but otherwise has legitimate reasons to seek bankruptcy should not have to put his or her entire recording agreement at risk. The record companies will insist on some level of protection.

14. INJUNCTIVE RELIEF

You expressly acknowledge that Artist's services hereunder are of a special, unique intellectual and extraordinary character which gives them peculiar value, and that in the event of a breach or threatened breach of any term, condition, representation, warranty, agreement or covenant hereof, Company shall be caused immediate irreparable injury, including loss of goodwill and harm to reputation, which cannot be adequately compensated in monetary damages. Accordingly, in the event of any such breach, actual or threatened, Company shall have, in addition to any other legal remedies, the right to injunctive or other equitable relief.

This is a standard clause, which states that the artist's services are unique. The purpose of this clause is to establish the company's entitlement to obtain an injunction against the artist should the artist attempt to breach the agreement by recording for another record company. However, this alone is not enough to entitle the company to obtain an injunction. The company will still be required to prove its entitlement according to the standards that have been developed in the case law. Additionally, for contracts governed by California law, which may include not only those that specifically state that California law is applicable but may also include those that the artist signed before becoming a resident of California, there are specific guarantees that must be made by the company in order to entitle it to injunctive relief.

15. WARRANTIES AND REPRESENTATIONS; INDEMNITIES

(a) You warrant, represent and agree that:

(i) You and Artist have the right and legal capacity to enter into, execute and implement this agreement, and you and Artist are not subject to any prior obligations or agreements, whether as a party or otherwise, which would restrict or interfere in any way with the full and prompt performance of your obligations hereunder. You and Artist shall fulfill all of your obligations under this agreement in a timely manner;

If an artist uses a loanout company, he or she should make doubly certain that the company is in good standing before the contract is signed.

(ii) No Person other than Company has any right to use, and during the Term no Person other than Company shall be authorized to use, any existing Recordings embodying Artist's performances for making, promoting or marketing Records;

(iii) Company shall not be required to make any payments of any nature for or in connection with the acquisition, exercise or exploitation of any of Company's rights hereunder, except as otherwise specifically set forth in this agreement;

(iv) The Materials or any use thereof shall not violate any law or infringe upon or violate the rights of any Person (including contractual rights, copyrights, rights of publicity and rights of privacy); and each track-by-track list identifying the performers on and timings of (and titles, writers and publishers of each Composition embodied on) each Master hereunder and describing their performances which you furnish to Company is and shall be true, accurate and complete. "Materials" as used in this paragraph 15(a)(iv) means: Recordings hereunder (including any Samples embodied therein); all Compositions; each name used by Artist, individually or as a group, in connection with Recordings hereunder; all photographs and likenesses of Artist; and all other musical, dramatic, artistic and literary materials, ideas and other intellectual properties contained in or used in connection with any Recordings hereunder or their packaging, sale, distribution, advertising, publicizing or other exploitation. Company's acceptance and/or utilization of Recordings, Materials or track-by-track lists hereunder shall not constitute a waiver of your representations, warranties or agreements in respect thereof or a waiver of any of Company's rights or remedies;

(v) No changes in the personnel comprising Artist will be made without Company's prior written consent. Neither you nor Artist shall, during the Term, assign or otherwise permit Artist's professional name set forth on Page 1 (the "Artist Name"), or any other professional name(s) utilized by Artist, to be used by any other individual or group of individuals without Company's prior written consent, and any attempt to do so shall be null and void and shall convey no right or title. You hereby warrant and represent that: (A) Artist is and shall be the sole owner of the Artist Name and all other professional names used by Artist in connection with Recordings hereunder; (B) no Person other than Company has, or shall have, the right to use such names and Artist's likenesses or to permit such names and Artist's likenesses to be used in connection with Records or Recordings at any time during the Term; (C) you and Artist have the authority to and hereby grant Company the exclusive right to use such names in the Territory in accordance with all of the terms and conditions of this agreement; and (D) you will not permit Artist to use (and Artist shall not use) any professional name other than the Artist Name during the Term without Company's prior written consent, which may be withheld for any reason. If any Person challenges Artist's right to use a professional name (including the Artist Name) or if Company determines in its reasonable good faith discretion that any such professional name (including the Artist Name) is not available for use by Company hereunder in any portion of the Territory or that its availability in any portion of the Territory is in question, then you and Artist shall, at Company's request, promptly designate another professional name to be used by Artist, such other professional name to be subject to Company's prior written consent; upon Company's written consent of any such professional name, such name shall be deemed to be the Artist Name for purposes of this agreement. Notwithstanding anything to the contrary contained in this paragraph 15(a)(v), Company's failure to object to Artist's use of any professional name (including the Artist Name) or Company's approval of Artist's use of any such name, shall not constitute a waiver by Company of any of your or Artist's warranties and representations hereunder;

This clause is designed to protect the company in the event that the artist's professional name proves to be unavailable. Any recording artist preparing to enter into a recording agreement should run a trademark search to identify and avoid any problems involving the artist's use of his or her professional name.

(vi) During the Term, Artist shall not perform for, and neither you nor Artist shall authorize or knowingly permit Artist's performances to be recorded and/or transmitted by, any Person for any purpose, without an express written agreement with such Person for Company's benefit that: (A) prohibits the use of such performance and/or Recording for: (I) making, promoting, or marketing Recordings or Records (provided that this paragraph 15(a)(vi)(A) shall not preclude Artist from performing for *analog* television broadcasts and no rights are granted with respect to such performances other than analog television broadcast rights); (II) digital broadcasts or other transmissions, distributions or other communications now or hereafter known, including webcasts; and (III) any form of transmission or broadcast of Recordings by any means which permits the consumer to access the Recording concerned (whether in isolation or with other Recordings) on demand or via repetitive broadcast enabling the consumer to choose the approximate time at which to access the Recording concerned, including television broadcast, cable transmission and/or transmission via the Internet; and (B) specifically provides that, if a Recording is made of Artist's performance, such Recording is made for the benefit, and is the exclusive property, of Company. You shall furnish Company with a fully-executed copy of each such agreement promptly following the execution thereof;

(vii) Artist shall not perform or render any services and neither you nor Artist shall authorize the use of Artist's name, likeness or other identification for the purpose of distributing, selling, advertising or exploiting Records for any Person other than Company during the Term in the Territory;

Under certain circumstances, a record company will agree to allow an artist to place a recording or two in a film or television episode without the company's separate consent. If the artist has a particular connection to the acting industry or otherwise reasonably anticipates the need to record anything for any entity other than the company, the artist should consider raising that issue during negotiations to determine if the company is willing to allow the artist to place a certain number of recordings in film or television without the company's consent. Further, in the hip-hop and R&B genres, there could be considerable opportunities to make additional money by appearing as a featured or guest artist on another artist's record. Occasionally, artists are able to persuade labels to agree to allow a fixed number of such guest performances during specific time frames without separate consent.

(viii) Artist shall not perform for the purpose of recording any Composition, or any adaptation of any Composition, recorded hereunder for any Person other than Company for use in the Territory on Records (including in radio or television commercials or otherwise for synchronization with visual images), before the later of: (A) five (5) years after the date of Delivery of all Recordings made in the course of the same Album (or other recording project) as the last Delivered Recording of the restricted Composition concerned or adaptation thereof; or (B) two (2) years after the expiration or other termination of the Term (the "<u>Re-recording Restriction</u>"); and further, Artist shall not at any time within ten (10) years after the expiration of the period referred to in the preceding sentence, re-record for inclusion on a particular Record more than four (4) Compositions recorded hereunder and embodied on a particular Record hereunder;

The first part of this clause is a standard rerecording restriction designed to prevent artists from undermining the company by rerecording their hits for other companies after the contract has expired. The second part of this clause is designed to prevent the artist from recording several songs from the same record to be embodied on a single record for 12 years after the term of the agreement. This second part should be stricken if the company can be so persuaded, but as more and more artists rerecord their popular works after the expiration of their contracts, record companies are likely to fight harder for these types of provisions.

(ix) All Persons rendering services in connection with Masters or Videos shall fully comply with the provisions of the Immigration Reform Control Act of 1986; and

(x) All members of Artist are United States citizens and are at least eighteen (18) years of age;

(b) You shall and do hereby indemnify, save and hold Company and its parent, affiliates, divisions, successors, licensees and assigns and/or the officers, directors and employees of any of the foregoing (collectively, the "<u>Company Indemnitees</u>") harmless from any and all loss, damage and liability (including court costs and reasonable attorneys' fees) arising out of, connected with or as a result of: (i) any act or omission by you or Artist (or any of your respective agents) or (ii) any inconsistency with, failure of or breach or threatened breach by you of any warranty, representation, agreement, undertaking or covenant contained in this agreement including any claim, demand or action by any third party in connection with the foregoing, which has resulted in a judgment or which has been settled with your consent, it being agreed that such consent shall only be required for settlements in excess of Ten Thousand Dollars ($10,000). In addition to any other rights or remedies Company may have by reason of any such inconsistency, failure, breach, threatened breach or claim, Company may obtain reimbursement from you, on demand, for any payment made by the Company Indemnitees at any time after the date hereof with respect to any loss, damage or liability (including anticipated and actual court costs and reasonable attorneys' fees) resulting therefrom. Such amounts may also be deducted from all monies becoming payable under this agreement or any other agreement to the extent to which they have not been reimbursed to Company by you. If the amount of any such claim or loss has not been determined, Company may withhold from monies otherwise payable under this agreement or any other agreement an amount consistent with such claim or loss pending such determination unless you post a bond in a form and from a bonding company acceptable to Company in an amount equal to Company's estimate of the amount of the claim, demand or action. If no action is filed within one (1) year following the date on which such claim was first received by Company and/or its licensees, Company shall release all sums withheld in connection with such claim, unless Company, in its reasonable business judgment, believes that such an action may be instituted notwithstanding the passage of such time. Notwithstanding the foregoing, if after such release by Company of sums withheld in connection with a particular claim such claim is reasserted, then Company's rights under this paragraph 15(b) shall apply in full force and effect. Company shall give you notice of any third-party claim, demand or action to which the foregoing indemnity applies and you shall have the right to participate in the defense of any such claim, demand or action through counsel of your own choice and at your expense; provided that, Company shall have the right at all times, in its sole discretion, to retain or resume control of the conduct thereof.

This is a fairly typical indemnification clause, which has been stepped up a bit from normal first-draft language, but still has some room for improvement. What an indemnification clause does is provide that if a third party files a claim that the company considers to be inconsistent with the artist's representations and warranties (e.g., a claim that a song on the artist's album infringes the copyright of a third party's composition), then the company shall have the right to pass the buck to the artist, who would then be ultimately responsible for resolving the claim. What the artist wants to do in the indemnification clause is to retain as much control over such claims as possible. Here, the record company has allowed the artist to participate in the defense of any claim through his or her own attorney but has retained the right to retain control over the conduct of the defense. The artist will want to have the right to handle the defense. The record company will typically insist on the right to withhold payments of monies payable to the artist in an amount reasonably related to the claim unless the artist posts a bond to cover the potential judgment, which would be difficult for most artists to do. Such language is difficult to negotiate, but the artist should at least request that mechanical royalties be exempt from such withholding. What the artist will want to do here is reduce the settlement threshold so that the label cannot settle a claim for more than $5,000 without the artist's consent, unless the label is willing to soak up the amount in excess of $5,000. Major labels will typically insist on making any maximum settlement amount contingent upon the artist posting a satisfactory bond. A label does not want to find itself in a position where an artist refuses to accept a reasonable settlement offer and thereby exposes the label to a large claim without the financial resources to compensate the label in the event the third party prevails on the claim. On the other hand, artists are understandably reluctant to give record companies the right to settle claims that the artist may consider to be without merit and to charge the artist for the settlement and attorneys' fees.

16. APPROVALS

Except as otherwise specifically set forth in this agreement, as to all matters designated herein to be determined by mutual agreement or selection, or as to which any approval or consent is required, such agreement, selection, approval or consent shall not be unreasonably withheld. You agree that any approvals (including creative or marketing approvals) to be exercised by you and/or Artist hereunder shall apply only during the Term, except as otherwise expressly provided herein. Your agreement, selection, approval or consent, whenever required (including your written agreement, selection, approval or consent), shall be deemed to have been given unless you notify Company otherwise within five (5) Business Days following the date of Company's request to you. You shall not hinder or delay the scheduled release of any Record subject to this agreement. In the event of your disapproval or no consent, the reasons therefor shall be stated. Each of your then-current attorney and manager is hereby deemed an authorized agent to give approval on your behalf.

> *It should be made clear that the company's requests for the artist's consents or approvals must be in writing and sent pursuant to the notice provisions of this agreement, and the artist should have at least 10 business days after receiving such written request to reply.*

17. COLLECTIVE BARGAINING AGREEMENTS

You hereby warrant and represent that, during the Term, Artist shall become and remain a member in good standing of any labor unions with which Company may at any time have agreements lawfully requiring such union membership. All Recordings hereunder shall be produced in accordance with the rules and regulations of all unions having jurisdiction. Those provisions of any collective bargaining agreement between Company and any labor organization which are required, by the terms of such agreement, to be included in this agreement shall be deemed incorporated herein.

> *This is a standard provision, provided that the company is a signatory to the applicable union or guild agreements.*

18. VIDEOS

With respect to any Video requested by Company: (a) the Master to be embodied in such Video, the concept for such Video, the creative aspects of the production of such Video (including preparation of the script and storyboard), and the dates and locations for the shooting of such Video shall be mutually selected by you and Company; provided that, in the event of a dispute with respect to any of the foregoing elements, Company's decision shall be final, and provided further that each Master released as a Single and/or promoted by Company to radio stations as a "Single," "radio single," or "emphasis track" shall be deemed approved by you for inclusion in a Video; (b) the director shall be mutually selected by you and Company and such director shall engage the other production personnel for such Video. You and Artist shall fully cooperate with the director and all other production personnel in the production of such Video. The production budget submitted by the director shall be mutually approved by you and Company; and (c) Company shall pay all Video Production Costs incurred in connection with such Video consistent with the production budget approved by Company. All Video Production Costs in excess of the approved budget that have been incurred *due to your or Artist's acts or omissions shall be your sole responsibility and you hereby agree to forthwith pay and discharge all such excess costs.* If Company agrees to pay any such excess costs on your behalf, you shall, upon demand, reimburse Company for such excess costs or, in lieu of requesting reimbursement, Company may deduct such excess costs from *all monies payable* under this agreement or any other agreement. If Artist fails to appear at locations and/or on dates which have been mutually approved by you and Company, without reasonable excuse as determined by Company, the costs of cancellation of the shoot shall be your responsibility, and if Company agrees to pay such cancellation costs on your behalf, such cancellation costs shall be fully deductible from *all monies payable* under this agreement or any other agreement. All Video Production Costs paid or incurred by Company shall constitute additional Advances, one hundred percent (100%) of which shall be recoupable from royalties derived from the commercial exploitation of Videos credited to your account pursuant to this agreement and fifty percent (50%) of which shall be recoupable from *all other royalties* credited to your account pursuant to this agreement. Notwithstanding the preceding sentence, you acknowledge and agree that any Video Production Costs in excess of Two Hundred Thousand Dollars ($200,000) per Video shall be one hundred percent (100%) recoupable from all royalties credited to your account pursuant to this agreement. Notwithstanding anything to the contrary contained in this agreement, Company shall have the right to use, and to allow others to use, each Video and any portions thereof for advertising and promotional purposes, without payment of additional compensation to you, Artist or any other Person.

> *This video clause leaves a lot of room for improvement. First of all, excess costs should not constitute a direct debt for the artist unless the excess costs were caused* solely *by the artist's* negligent *acts or omissions and, even then, excess video costs should not be deducted from mechanical royalties. The $200,000 figure, found toward the end of the section, should be modified to reflect whatever budget is established for each video. For example, if the company wants to spend $500,000 on a video, then the company should adopt a proportionately increased risk.*

19. INTENTIONALLY OMITTED

20. GROUP PROVISIONS

    (a) (i) For the purposes of this agreement, the following definitions shall apply: (A) "<u>Leaving Member</u>" - (I) each individual member of Artist who refuses, neglects, fails or ceases for any reason (including dying or becoming disabled) to perform together with the other individuals comprising Artist in fulfillment of the obligations described in this agreement or who leaves the Group; (II) each individual member of Artist if Artist disbands or (III) each individual member of Artist with respect to whom Company exercises the option described in paragraph 20(a)(ii)(B)(I); (B) "<u>Leaving Member Event</u>" - the occurrence of any one (1) or more of the following events: (I) any one (1) or more individual members of Artist refusing, neglecting, failing or ceasing for any reason (including dying or becoming disabled) to perform together with the other individual members comprising Artist in fulfillment of the obligations under this agreement or leaving the Group; or (II) the disbanding of Artist; (C) "<u>Reunion Member</u>" - (I) each individual member of Artist who desires to recommence performing in a group of at least fifty percent (50%) of the members of Artist for the purpose of making Records; or (II) each member of Artist desiring to perform under any group name of Artist used by Company hereunder; and (D) "Reunion Event" - at least fifty percent (50%) of the individual members of Artist desiring to recommence performing together for the purpose of making Records or one (1) or more of such members desiring to perform under any group name of Artist used by Company hereunder.

(ii) Notwithstanding paragraph 1, as used in this agreement, the term "Artist" refers jointly and severally to the individuals first mentioned herein as comprising Artist and to such other individuals who during the Term shall comprise Artist. You warrant, represent and agree that, throughout the Term, Artist shall perform together as a group (the "Group") for Company. Artist's obligations under this agreement are joint and several and all references herein to "you" or "Artist" and their possessive forms shall include all members of the Group collectively and each member of the Group individually, unless otherwise specified. If any Leaving Member Event occurs during the Term, then: (A) you and each member of Artist shall give Company prompt notice thereof (the "Leaving Member Notice") specifically referencing this paragraph 20(a); and (B) Company shall have, and each individual member of the Group hereby irrevocably grants to Company, the option, exercisable by notice ("Company's Leaving Member Notice") to you within three (3) months after Company's receipt of the Leaving Member Notice: (I) to deem any or all members of Artist as Leaving Members in accordance with this paragraph 20; (II) to obtain the individual and exclusive services of any or all Leaving Members; (III) to terminate the Term with respect to any or all Leaving Members; and/or (IV) to terminate the Term in its entirety without any obligation as to unrecorded or un-Delivered Masters. For the avoidance of doubt, each member of Artist who is not deemed to be a Leaving Member, as well as each Leaving Member with respect to whom Company does not terminate the Term, shall remain bound by this agreement. If Company deems any one (1) or more members of Artist as Leaving Members, then Company's Leaving Member Notice shall specify whether Company requires you to cause such Leaving Member(s) to record and Deliver Demos of at least four (4) completed, fully-mixed and previously-unreleased Masters (the "Leaving Member Demos"), to perform for a personal audition, or to record and Deliver Masters sufficient to comprise one (1) Album, all in accordance with paragraph 20(b); provided if Company's Leaving Member Notice does not so specify, then Company shall be deemed to have required you to cause such Leaving Member(s) to record and Deliver the Leaving Member Demos. Company shall have no liability or obligations to any Leaving Member unless Company elects to exercise its rights to the recording services of such Leaving Member in accordance with paragraph 20(b). If Company terminates the Term with respect to a particular Leaving Member, then you shall be solely responsible for and shall pay all monies required to be paid to such Leaving Member in connection with any Recordings theretofore or thereafter Delivered for which royalties are payable to such Leaving Member and you shall indemnify and hold harmless Company against any claims relating thereto pursuant to the terms of paragraph 15(b). No Leaving Member (whether or not his or her engagement is terminated by Company) shall, without Company's prior written consent: (I) perform for any Person other than Company for the purpose of recording any Composition as to which the applicable Re-recording Restriction has not yet expired; or (II) use the professional name of the Group in any commercial or artistic endeavor other than for Company. The person, if any, engaged to replace any Leaving Member shall be mutually agreed upon by Company and you. Each person added to Artist, as a replacement or otherwise, shall become bound by the terms and conditions of this agreement and shall execute this agreement and any other documents required by Company as a condition precedent to being so added. Neither Company nor you shall unreasonably withhold agreement with regard thereto; and, if agreement cannot be reached, Company may terminate this agreement by notice to you.

(b) If Company exercises its option for the individual and exclusive services of any or all Leaving Members pursuant to paragraph 20(a)(ii)(B)(II), you and the Leaving Member(s) referred to in Company's Leaving Member Notice shall be deemed to have entered into a new and separate agreement (the "Leaving Member Agreement") with Company with respect to each such Leaving Member(s)' exclusive recording services upon all the terms and conditions of this agreement except that:

(i) If Company requires the applicable Leaving Member(s) to record the Leaving Member Demos, then you shall cause such Leaving Member(s) to record same in accordance with a budget approved by Company in writing and you shall Deliver the Leaving Member Demos. If Company requires that the applicable Leaving Member(s) perform for a personal audition, then you shall arrange for same at such place and time as Company may approve. Nothing in this paragraph 20 shall be deemed to require that Company request the Leaving Member Demos or a personal audition if pursuant to paragraph 20(a)(ii) Company elects to require such Leaving Member(s) to record and Deliver Masters sufficient to comprise one (1) Album;

(ii) By the later to occur of ninety (90) days after Company's receipt of the Leaving Member Notice or sixty (60) days after Company's receipt of the Leaving Member Demos or the date of the personal audition, as the case may be, Company shall have the option by notice to require you to cause the Leaving Member(s) concerned to record and Deliver Masters sufficient to comprise one (1) Album (the "Leaving Member Recording Commitment"). Without limiting the foregoing, if Company's Leaving Member Notice requires the applicable Leaving Member(s) to record and Deliver Masters sufficient to comprise one (1) Album, then Company's Leaving Member Notice shall be deemed to constitute the notice required by the preceding sentence. Company shall thereafter have the right to increase the Leaving Member Recording Commitment and the right to extend the term of the Leaving Member Agreement for option periods so that Company shall have the right under the Leaving Member Agreement to the same number of Albums (including optional Albums, i.e., Albums to be Delivered during optional Contract Periods) remaining un-Delivered under this agreement, provided that, notwithstanding anything to the contrary herein, Company shall have options for no fewer than three (3) Albums under the Leaving Member Agreement. (The first Album of the Leaving Member Recording

Commitment pursuant to each Leaving Member Agreement is referred to in this paragraph 20 as the "First Leaving Member Album," the second such Album is referred to as the "Second Leaving Member Album," etc.);

(iii) The Recording Fund for the First Leaving Member Album shall be seventy-five percent (75%) of the minimum Recording Fund set forth in paragraph 7 for the immediately preceding Committed Album Delivered under this agreement ("Preceding Group Album"), provided if you have not yet Delivered the First Album hereunder, then the First Album shall be deemed the "Preceding Group Album" for purposes of paragraphs 20(b)(iii) and 20(b)(iv) only. With respect to each subsequent Album of the Leaving Member Recording Commitment, the Recording Fund shall be calculated in accordance with the provisions of paragraphs 7(c); provided that, "net royalties credited to your royalty account hereunder" as used in paragraph 7(c), shall mean net royalties credited to such Leaving Member's royalty account with respect to units of the particular Album of the Leaving Member Recording Commitment; the minimum Recording Fund applicable with respect to each subsequent Album of the Leaving Member Recording Commitment shall be the minimum Recording Fund for the immediately preceding Album of the Leaving Member Recording Commitment plus five percent (5%); and the maximum Recording Fund applicable to each such Album shall be two (2) times the minimum Recording Fund for such Album;

(iv) Company's royalty obligation in respect of Recordings constituting the First Leaving Member Album shall be seventy-five percent (75%) of the otherwise applicable rate set forth in paragraph 9 of this agreement for Recordings constituting the Preceding Group Album. The royalty rates with respect to all subsequent Albums of the Leaving Member Recording Commitment shall be seventy-five percent (75%) of the royalty rates applicable to the comparable Committed Album hereunder (e.g., for the Second Leaving Member Album, the Basic U.S. Rate shall be seventy-five percent (75%) of the Basic U.S. Rate applicable to the Committed Album immediately following the Preceding Group Album, provided if such comparable Album would be subsequent to the final Album of the Recording Commitment under this agreement, the royalty rates for each subsequent Album of the Leaving Member Recording Commitment shall be seventy-five percent (75%) of the royalty rates applicable to such final Album);

(v) Company shall only be entitled to recoup the Leaving Member Portion of the unrecouped balance of your royalty account hereunder as of the date of Company's Leaving Member Notice from royalties otherwise payable under the Leaving Member Agreement concerned and the unrecouped balance of the royalty account under the Leaving Member Agreement concerned from the Leaving Member Portion of the royalties otherwise payable hereunder in respect of Recordings made prior to the date of Company's Leaving Member Notice. As used in the preceding sentence, the term "Leaving Member Portion" shall be calculated by multiplying the unrecouped balance concerned by a fraction, the numerator of which shall be one (1) (or, if more than one (1) Leaving Member is performing together, such number of Leaving Members as are performing together) and the denominator of which shall be the total number of royalty-earning members constituting Artist as of the date of

Company's exercise of its option with respect to such Leaving Member; provided that, if as of such date Artist has disbanded, the numerator and denominator shall both be deemed to be one (1);

(vi) Recordings by a Leaving Member shall not be applied in diminution of the Recording Commitment or Delivery obligations described in paragraph 3; and

(vii) If there shall be more than one (1) Leaving Member for whom Company has exercised its option as provided in this paragraph 20(b) and two (2) or more of such Leaving Members shall, with Company's consent, elect to perform together as a duo or group, then (except as otherwise specifically set forth in paragraph 20(b)(v)), Company shall have the right to treat such Leaving Members collectively as if they were one (1) Leaving Member for the purpose of this paragraph 20(b), including royalty rates, advances and other monies payable in respect of their joint Recordings pursuant to this paragraph 20(b).

(c) Notwithstanding anything to the contrary contained in this paragraph 20, if any Reunion Event occurs within five (5) years after Company terminates the Term with respect to any or all member(s) of Artist based on Company's receipt of a notice claiming, or Company's good faith determination that, Artist has disbanded, then: (A) you and each of the Reunion Members shall give Company prompt notice that such Reunion Event has occurred (the "Reunion Notice"), specifically referencing this paragraph 20(c); and (B) Company shall have the option, exercisable by notice to you within thirty (30) days after Company's receipt of the Reunion Notice, to require you to produce and Deliver within thirty (30) days of Company's notice Demos comprised of at least four (4) completed, fully-mixed and previously-unreleased Masters featuring the performances of the Reunion Members, which Demos shall be recorded in accordance with a budget approved by Company in writing. Company shall thereafter have the right to reinstate this agreement with respect to the Reunion Members by notice to you on or before the later to occur of ninety (90) days after Company's receipt of the Reunion Notice or thirty (30) days after Delivery of the above-described Demos. If this agreement is so reinstated, Company hereby nevertheless acknowledges and agrees that its subsequent leaving member rights pursuant to paragraph 20(b) with respect to each Reunion Member whose services Company had previously terminated shall be subject to any agreement then-currently in force relating to such Reunion Member's solo recording services which was executed by such Reunion Member during the period in which his or her services hereunder had been terminated.

(d) Company shall have the right, in its sole discretion, to rely on notice from you or any member of Artist that a Leaving Member Event or Reunion Event has occurred. In addition, your or any such member's failure or refusal to send any Leaving Member Notice or Reunion Notice shall not be deemed to limit Company's rights pursuant to this paragraph 20 if Company determines in its good faith judgment that a Leaving Member Event or Reunion Event, as applicable, has occurred. Company shall have no liability to you, Artist or any member thereof (including any Leaving Member or any Reunion Member) by reason of Company's acts or omissions based upon Company's receipt of any notice that a Leaving Member Event or Reunion Event has occurred or Company's good-faith determination that a Leaving Member Event or Reunion Event has occurred.

(e) If you or any individual member of Artist wishes to record performances of any one (1) or more of the individual members comprising Artist, which such individual(s) remains a member of Artist and continues to perform his or her obligations hereunder, you and Artist shall give Company prompt notice thereof. Company shall thereafter have the irrevocable option to permit such member(s) of Artist to record such Recordings, and if exercised, such Recordings shall be acquired upon all of the terms and conditions set forth herein; provided that, if Company exercises such option, the financial terms set forth in paragraph 20(b) shall be applied with respect to such Recordings and all references in that paragraph to a Leaving Member shall be deemed to be references to such individuals. If Company shall decline to permit you to make any such Recordings, then you and Artist hereby warrant, represent and agree that such Recordings shall not be made.

An important part of any recording agreement for a group artist is the section that deals with changes in the group membership, the so-called leaving member provisions. In the typical first-draft agreement, if any member leaves the group, the company has the right to terminate the agreement. This could be disastrous and unfair to the group, particularly if the member is not a key member. Accordingly, artist's representatives should negotiate to restrict this clause to situations where a specified key member has left the group. Of course, this is a tricky subject for the artist's representative to address, since merely discussing who is key and who is not key can cause strains in relationships among group members and their representatives, but to protect the interests of the group it is important to deal with the subject even though it may ruffle a few feathers. All bands and groups should negotiate and document an agreement among themselves that sets forth the roles of each member prior to shopping for a deal, but the details of such an agreement are beyond the scope of this chapter.

Another primary function of these provisions is to provide that the individual who leaves the group is still bound by the agreement in certain respects. For example, the leaving member is bound by the rerecording restrictions and is prohibited from using the group name in connection with their own activities thereafter. This section also provides that the remaining group members are solely responsible for making any payments due to the leaving member. Where a member has been thrown out of the group by the rest of the members, there is a likelihood of litigation over the right of that leaving member to share not only in income derived by the group from the member's activities with the group, e.g., albums on which the departed member performed but also on future income of the group. Courts have found there is goodwill in the group name, for which the remaining members must pay the departing member his or her allocable share of the value thereof at the time the departed member left the group. In the case of a superstar group, this can be an enormous sum of money. In this contract, the company is stating that this is the group's problem, not the company's. This issue, and many of the other issues touched on by this section, are best addressed in a written partnership agreement among the group members. Ideally, a written partnership agreement should exist for every group, and it should be created as soon as the group is able to afford it, preferably at the same time they make their first recording agreement. However, the various issues that relate to how the group members share in money, who makes the decisions for the group, and what happens if a member voluntarily leaves the group or if the other members want to force a member out of the group are extremely emotional and sensitive, and many groups simply do not wish to confront them legally. They prefer instead to work out informal rules. The downside of this approach is that if the group becomes successful and these issues have not been addressed in a written agreement, the consequence can be years of litigation that costs tremendous amounts of time, money and emotional distress.

Finally, the company takes the right to approve replacement members and requires that they become a party to this agreement. In most instances, record companies do not take an active role in the process of selecting replacement members, although in certain situations, e.g., the replacement of the lead singer of a superstar act, a company will exercise this right if it has it. Also, if an original member of a superstar act leaves the group for any reason, it is common not to make the replacement an equity member of the group, but merely a paid employee of the rest of the members or their affiliated corporation, in which event that replacement member would not have all of the rights of the original members and would not be a party to the recording agreement, although the company might insist on having the member sign an inducement letter whereby the member would give the company certain rights and agree to some or all of the same restrictions placed on the equity members, e.g., rerecording restrictions.

The warranties and representations regarding the artist's ownership of the group name are quite important. If there are concerns at the time of signing the agreement that the artist's group name may infringe upon someone else's name, a resolution of the competing claims ought to be worked out quickly, or a new name should be picked before the stakes escalate, which will happen if the artist has a hit record.

Perhaps the most important consequence of a member leaving the group or the group disbanding is that the company has the option to retain the services of the leaving member or, if the group disbands, of any individual member(s). However, record companies are usually not content to obtain the services of the leaving member(s) on the same terms as would have been applicable had the group stayed together. Instead, contracts often require the leaving member(s), in effect, to go back to square one, i.e., be compensated on the same basis as for the first album of the contract. Sometimes the terms are even less favorable than that. For example, in this contract, the leaving member is obligated to record demos and there is no recording fund or advance payable in connection with albums by the leaving member. Instead, the company merely allocates a recording budget. Royalty rates are reduced to two-thirds of what the group's royalty rate would have been for its next album. Moreover, in this agreement the company is allowed to cross-collateralize all or at least a pro rata portion of the unrecouped balance of the group's royalty account against the leaving member's royalty account and is allowed to use a pro rata portion of the group's account to recoup recording costs and charges under the leaving member's agreement. Accordingly, although a group breakup may be the furthest thing from the members' minds at the time they are being signed to a recording contract, it is important that they be aware of these provisions and negotiate the best possible terms.

21. ARTWORK

    (a) (i) For the purposes of this agreement, the following definitions shall apply: (A) "<u>Album Packaging</u>" – the packaging for an Album in all formats (including any inserts or other special elements or materials); (B) "<u>Production Costs</u>" – all costs of production of Album Packaging and the components thereof including production of Artwork; (C) "<u>Development Level Albums</u>" – Albums that are Development Records, Mid-Price Records or Budget Records; (D) "<u>Premium Level Albums</u>" – Albums the PPD of which is at least one hundred fifty percent

(150%) of the then-prevailing PPD of the majority (or plurality) of Company's or its Principal Licensee(s)' Top Line Records in such format and configuration; (E) "Standard Level Albums" - Albums other than Development Level Albums and Premium Level Albums; and (F) "Excess Packaging Costs" - costs in excess of the amounts applicable to the respective Album category as follows:

	Development Level Albums	Standard Level Albums	Premium Level Albums
Production Costs of Album Packaging	$10,500	$15,000	$30,000
Inlay Cards	Costs of a four (4) color digipak with no inlay card	Costs of inlay card with four (4) colors on one (1) side and one (1) color on one (1) side	Costs of inlay card with four (4) colors on each side
CD Booklets	Costs of a four (4) color digipak with no booklet	Costs of an eight (8) page booklet with four (4) color outside cover and all other pages one (1) color	Costs of a sixteen (16) page booklet with all pages four (4) color

(ii) You or Artist shall prepare or cause the preparation of the Artwork for Album Packaging and shall deliver production-ready copies thereof to Company not later than currently with Delivery of the Masters associated with such Artwork.

(iii) If Company incurs Excess Packaging Costs, then you shall, upon demand, reimburse Company for the Excess Packaging Costs, or, in lieu of requesting reimbursement, Company may deduct Excess Packaging Costs *from all monies otherwise payable under this agreement or any other agreement.*

Excess Packaging Costs should not be deducted from mechanical royalties. The artwork language could be improved to provide that if the artist desires special packaging in connection with a particular album that the artist would request the company's support and the company would consider the request in good faith and, only if the company rejected the artist's request, would excess packaging costs become a debt recoupable from the artist's next Advance under the contract.

(iv) At any time after initial release of an Album, Company shall have the right to modify Album Packaging if: (A) the costs of using the original packaging on a continuing basis increase on a per-unit basis as a result of changes in size of fabrication runs or otherwise; or (B) the Album moves into a different category and the manufacturing costs associated with the original packaging exceed the Excess Packaging Costs for the newly-applicable category of such album.

(b) All Artwork for Album Packaging: (i) shall contain all such materials, information, logos, stickers and other items (including a "parental guidance" or similar legend in a form and location specified by Company) as Company then-currently customarily includes on its packaging for other Albums, with the placement of any such materials, information, logos, inserts, stickers and other items to be determined by Company in its sole discretion; and (ii) shall not, in Company's reasonable, good faith opinion, constitute an invasion of any Person's rights (including copyright infringement, libel or slander) or violate Company's standards of decency or any applicable rules, regulations, statutes or laws.

22. DEFINITIONS

For the purposes of this agreement, the following definitions shall apply:

(a) "Advance" - a prepayment of royalties. Company may recoup Advances from royalties to be paid or accrued to or on behalf of you or Artist pursuant to this agreement or any other agreement. Advances paid under paragraph 7 shall not be returnable to Company except as otherwise specifically set forth in this agreement or in other circumstances in which Company is entitled to their return by reason of your failure to fulfill your obligations. Mechanical royalties shall not be chargeable in recoupment of any Advances except those Advances which are expressly recoupable from all monies payable under this agreement or any other agreement;

(b) "Album" - a Record having no less than forty (40) minutes of playing time and which embodies at least eleven (11) Masters each containing a different Composition sold in a single package;

(c) "any other agreement" - any other agreement with Company relating to Artist's Recordings or relating to Artist as a recording artist or as a producer of Recordings of Artist's own performances;

(d) "Artwork" - all material embodied in, or supplied by you or Artist for use in, the packaging of Records (including any inserts or other special elements or materials), or created, commissioned or acquired by Company or supplied by you or Artist, for use in publicity, promotion or marketing or as part of Videos, EPKs, or any other Records, including all drawings, photographs, logos, calligraphy, images, paintings or other visual or audiovisual material;

(e) "Audio Record" - a Record which embodies, reproduces, transmits or communicates primarily audio-only (as opposed to audiovisual) material, including any Master;

(f) "Audiovisual Record" - a Record which embodies, reproduces, transmits or communicates primarily audiovisual (as opposed to audio-only) material, including any Video;

(g) "Books and Records" - that portion of Company's books and records which specifically reports: (1) sales and other distributions of Records embodying Recordings hereunder; (2) Net Receipts; and (3) Recording Costs and Video Production Costs incurred in connection with Recordings hereunder and any other sums specifically charged against royalties hereunder. Upon your written request in connection with any audit hereunder, Books and Records shall also include Company's standard summary inventory report for Phono Records reflecting the following information on a title-by-title basis and on a format-by-format basis: units manufactured, units shipped, returned units (both returns to inventory and defective returns), current inventory and any adjustments thereto (e.g., "shrinkage");

(h) "<u>Budget Record</u>" - (1) in the United States, a Record in a particular format which is sold by Company or through Company's distributors at a PPD which is less than sixty-six and two-thirds percent (66²/₃%) of the then-prevailing PPD for the majority (or plurality) of Company's Top Line Records in such format and (2) outside the United States, a Record in a particular format which is sold by Company, Company's Principal Licensees or their distributors at a PPD which is less than fifty percent (50%) of the applicable Principal Licensee's then-prevailing PPD for the majority (or plurality) of such Principal Licensee's Top Line Records in such format;

(i) "<u>Business Day</u>" - any day other than a Saturday, a Sunday, a day on which banks in New York City or Los Angeles are authorized or obligated by law to close or a day on which Company's headquarters is officially closed;

(j) "<u>Club Operation</u>" - a business which is primarily engaged in the direct marketing to consumers on a membership basis of audio and audiovisual products in Phono Record form;

(k) "<u>Compilation Record</u>" - a Record embodying Recordings hereunder together with other Recordings, but excluding motion picture soundtrack Albums which are released by record companies other than companies owned or controlled by Major Record Company;

(l) "<u>Composition</u>" - a musical composition or medley consisting of words and/or music, or any dramatic material and bridging passages, whether in the form of instrumental and/or vocal music, prose or otherwise, irrespective of length;

(m) "<u>Consumer Compilation</u>" - a Compilation Record embodying Recordings that are individually selected and/or sequenced by the consumer (via systems such as musicmaker.com, digital on-demand kiosks, the now-defunct "Personics" system and similar systems);

(n) "<u>Delivery</u>," "<u>Deliver</u>" and "<u>Delivered</u>" - the actual receipt by Company of a completed, fully-edited, mixed and equalized two-track stereo tape, in the format customarily used by Company for the manufacture of Records at the time of Delivery (currently 2.0 DDP file set masters in Yellowbook CD-ROM, 8mm Exabyte or DVD-R for audio-only Records) for each format (e.g., compact disc and cassette) of each Master comprising the applicable Committed Album, which tapes shall in all respects be in the proper form for the production of the parts necessary for the manufacture or creation of Records, together with: (1) the Producer's Package; (2) all Artwork and all required consents, approvals, licenses and permissions in respect of each such Master and Artwork; and (3) using Company's then-standard form therefor, a complete and accurate summary regarding all Samples embodied in each Master, and all consents, licenses and documentation in connection with such Samples. Your Delivery obligation shall include all union session reports and the delivery of a track-by-track list identifying the performers on and timings of (and titles, writers and publishers of each Composition embodied on) each Master (including any "hidden" Recordings on any Record) and shall describe such performers' performances. Each Master shall be subject to Company's approval as *technically and commercially satisfactory,* and shall not be deemed Delivered *unless and until such approval is given.* Without limiting the preceding sentence, no Master shall be deemed Delivered if, in Company's reasonable, good faith opinion, such Master or material embodied in such Master would constitute an invasion of any Person's rights (including copyright infringement, libel or slander) or would violate Company's standards of decency or any applicable rules, regulations, statutes or laws. Upon the request of Company, you shall cause Artist to re-record any Composition until a technically and commercially satisfactory Master shall have been obtained. Only Masters Delivered in full compliance with the provisions of this agreement shall be applied in fulfillment of the Recording Commitment and no payments shall be required to be made to you in connection with any Masters which are not in full compliance. Each Master shall be delivered to Company at Major Record Company Inc., 123 Anystreet, Anytown, ZZ 99999, or such other place as Company may notify you. In addition, you shall maintain or cause to be maintained in Company's name all Recordings of Artist's performances made during the Term, including session tapes, alternate mixes and outtakes (but excluding Masters Delivered hereunder and the Producer's Package) in good condition at a location selected or approved by Company and Company shall own such Recordings as provided in paragraph 5 whether or not such Recordings are Delivered. Notwithstanding the preceding sentence, Company may elect to send you notice of the date upon which Company has determined that Delivery has occurred. If Company sends you such a notice, and if you do not notify Company within five (5) Business Days of the date of such notice of any alternate date upon which you believe Delivery has occurred, Delivery shall be deemed to have occurred, solely for purposes of calculating the duration of the then-current Contract Period, on the date set forth in Company's such notice. The preceding two sentences shall not be construed to derogate from any of your Delivery obligations. Any payments made by Company following the physical delivery of Masters herein but prior to Delivery shall not constitute a waiver of your Delivery obligations hereunder or of Company's right to approve Masters as technically and commercially satisfactory;

The definition of "Delivery" is an important part of the agreement. If an artist has sufficient clout, he or she should seek a delivery standard of "technically satisfactory" as opposed to "technically and commercially satisfactory." Ideally, the company will agree to respond promptly to artist's delivery of any master recording with a declaration of whether the master was accepted or rejected as "Delivered" and, if rejected, specify the reasons why. Some artists are put in a terribly unfair position when they submit materials for "Delivery" and the company simply fails to respond for weeks or months on end. Some improvements in the definition of "Delivery" should help protect artists from that type of difficulty.

(o) "Demo" - a so-called demonstration Recording;

(p) "Development Record" - a Record which is sold by Company or its distributors or by Company's Principal Licensees or their distributors at a PPD which is below the then-prevailing PPD for the majority (or plurality) of Company's or its applicable Principal Licensee's Top Line Records in such format, which PPD is consistently applied by Company or its applicable Principal Licensee to developing Records or in some like-denominated sales category and which Records are sold by Company or its applicable Principal Licensee(s) as developing Records or in some like-denominated sales category;

(q) "Electronic Transmissions" - Records sold by Company or through Company's distributors in the United States or by Company, Company's Principal Licensees or their distributors outside the United States other than as Phono Records including via telephone, satellite, cable, point-of-sale manufacturing, transmission over wire or through the air, downloading and any other methods now or hereafter known;

(r) "EP" - a Record embodying thereon between five (5) Masters and ten (10) Masters; provided that, if more than one (1) of such Masters contains the same Composition, such Record shall be deemed to be a Maxi-Single for the purposes of this agreement;

(s) "EU" - Austria, Belgium, Denmark, Finland, France, Germany, Greece, Ireland, Italy, Luxembourg, the Netherlands, Portugal, Spain, Sweden and the United Kingdom;

The contract should provide that the definition of EU should be deemed automatically updated as new nations are accepted into the European Union.

(t) "Gross Receipts" - all monies actually received by Company in the United States which are directly and identifiably attributable to the exploitation of particular Recordings or Artwork hereunder. For the purposes of determining Gross Receipts, any royalties credited to Company's account but charged in recoupment of a prior advance made to Company and retained by the payor by reason of that charge shall be deemed paid to Company and received by Company when Company receives the accounting reflecting the credit and charge concerned. Notwithstanding anything to the contrary contained in this agreement, Gross Receipts shall not include advances or so-called "flat-fee" amounts received with respect to any so-called "blanket licenses" between Company and a licensee under which the licensee is granted access to all or a significant portion of Company's catalog of Recordings nor any profits received by Company, any Principal Licensee or their affiliates as a joint venturer in a Club Operation;

(u) "Gross Royalty Base" - the PPD applicable to the Record concerned less Program Discounts;

(v) "Internet" - the wide area cooperative network of university, corporate, government, private computer networks, Internet Service Providers (ISPs), ISP-like services and any successor, parallel or spin-off network of the foregoing and any current or future proprietary, private, subscription online networks or services communicating through Transmission Control Protocol/Internet Protocol (TCP/IP);

(w) "Joint Label Compilation" - a Compilation Record with respect to which two (2) or more labels are profit participants, e.g., the "Totally Hits" or "Now" series;

(x) "Master" - a Recording embodying a performance by all the members of Artist of one (1) Composition which consists of sound only and is used or useful in the recording, production, manufacture and/or exploitation of Records;

(y) "Maxi-Single" - a Record embodying thereon four (4) Masters;

(z) "Mid-Price Record" - (1) in the United States, a Record in a particular format which is sold by Company or through Company's distributors at a PPD which is at least sixty-six and two-thirds percent (66 2/3%) but not more than eighty percent (80%) of the then-prevailing PPD for the majority (or plurality) of Company's Top Line Records in such format and (2) outside the United States, a Record in a particular format which is sold by Company, Company's Principal Licensees or their distributors at a PPD which is at least fifty percent (50%) but not more than seventy-five percent (75%) of the applicable Principal Licensee's then-prevailing PPD for the majority (or plurality) of Company's Principal Licensee's Top Line Records in such format;

(aa) "<u>Multiple Record Set</u>" – a Record consisting of two (2) or more Records packaged and/or marketed as a single unit;

(bb) "<u>Net Receipts</u>" – Gross Receipts after deduction by Company of all direct expenses, third-party payments, taxes and adjustments related thereto. With respect to Videos, Net Receipts shall be determined after also deducting a marketing and distribution fee equal to: (1) twenty percent (20%) of the applicable Gross Receipts in respect of any broadcast, telecast, cablecast or other similar exploitation (excluding the sale of Audiovisual Records) within the United States if an affiliate of Company arranges for such exploitation; and (2) thirty-five percent (35%) of the applicable Gross Receipts in respect of any broadcast, telecast, cablecast or other similar exploitation (excluding the sale of Audiovisual Records) outside the United States if an affiliate of Company arranges for such exploitation;

(cc) "<u>Net Sales</u>" – one hundred percent (100%) of Records sold by Company or through Company's distributors in the United States or by Company, Company's Principal Licensees or their distributors, as applicable, to independent third parties (including consumers), for which Company's distributor, Company's Principal Licensee or its distributor, as applicable, has been paid or credited, less Records returned for credit at any time for any reason, including at Company's request, and less all credits, cancellations, exchanges or other adjustments. Net Sales shall not include: (1) Records given away or sold at below the applicable PPD for promotional purposes to disc jockeys, reviewers, radio and television stations and networks, motion picture companies, music publishers, Company's employees, you, Artist or others or for use on transportation facilities; (2) Records sold as scrap, salvage, overstock or "cut-outs;" (3) Records sold below cost; and (4) Sampler Records;

(dd) "<u>On-Demand Usages</u>" – licensed usages of Records other than Phono Records as part of a service containing a functionality which permits a consumer to access a particular Recording or Recordings on a so-called "on-demand" basis including Subscription;

(ee) "<u>Online Store Compilation</u>" – a Compilation Record embodying Recordings that are individually selected and/or sequenced by an online retail store (such as amazon.com, listen.com, towerrecords.com, CDnow.com, pressplay.com and similar stores);

(ff) "<u>Person</u>" – any natural person, legal entity or other organized group of persons or entities. All pronouns, whether personal or impersonal, which refer to Persons include natural persons and other Persons;

(gg) "<u>Phono Record</u>" – a Record distributed in a physical Record format (e.g., vinyl LPs, cassettes and compact discs);

(hh) "<u>PPD</u>" – the published price to dealers utilized by Company or its distributors,

THE MUSICIAN'S BUSINESS AND LEGAL GUIDE

as applicable, in the United States and by Company, Company's Principal Licensee or its distributors in each country outside the United States. Company's principal distributors in the United States and Company's Principal Licensee in Canada both currently refer to the published price to dealers as the "Base Price." For Premium Records the PPD shall be deemed to be the amount actually received by Company;

(ii) "Premium Record" - a Record produced for use in promoting the sale of merchandise other than Records, and which bears the name of the sponsor for whom the Record is produced;

(jj) "Principal Licensee" - Company's licensee for the majority (or plurality) of Records sold on behalf of Company in the territory concerned including Company's affiliates and nonaffiliated Persons;

(kk) "Producer's Package" - for each Master comprising the applicable Committed Album, Company's then-standard "producer's package" currently composed of each of the following elements: (1) "flat master" mix reels (i.e., two-track master mixes on 1/2" analog tape, 30 i.p.s., no noise reduction), recorded and compiled at the mixing studio (i.e., prior to mastering); (2) analog and/or digital multitracks (masters and slaves) with accompanying tone reels; (3) computer-based recording storage formats (e.g., ProTools session and audio data files, Exabyte reels, magneto-optical discs, CD-Rs, hard discs, etc.); (4) sample and automation discs; and (5) all existing documentation (e.g., console strips, outboard settings, session notes, etc.). In addition, for one (1) of the Masters comprising the applicable Committed Album (such Master to be designated by Company), one (1) set of remixes (comprised of a radio mix, a TV mix, an instrumental mix and an a cappella mix with timecode, unless Company notifies you otherwise);

(ll) "Program Discounts" - discounts given by way of price breaks or so-called "free goods" to "one-stops," rack jobbers, distributors or dealers, whether or not affiliated with Company, which are not Standard Discounts;

(mm) "Proportionate Deductions" - proportionate amounts of: (1) any sums deducted by a licensee from its payments to Company pursuant to any law, any government ruling, or any other restriction affecting the amount of the payments which a licensee can remit to Company; and (2) any taxes deducted by a licensee from its payments to Company;

(nn) "Publishing Net Sales" - Net Sales less the "free goods" unit equivalent of 100% of Standard Discounts and 100% of Program Discounts included within such Net Sales;

(oo) "Record" - any form of reproduction, distribution, transmission or communication of Recordings (whether or not in physical form) now or hereafter known (including reproductions of sound alone or together with visual images) which is manufactured, distributed, transmitted or communicated primarily for personal use, home use, institutional (e.g., library or school) use, jukebox use, or use in means of transportation, including any computer-assisted media (e.g., CD-ROM, DVD Audio, CD Extra, Enhanced CD) or use as a so-called "ring tone;"

(pp) "Recording" - any recording of sound, whether or not coupled with a visual image, by any method and on any substance or material, whether now or hereafter known, which is used or useful in the recording, production and/or manufacture of Records or for any other exploitation of sound;

(qq) "Recording Costs" - wages, fees, advances and payments of any nature to or in respect of all musicians, vocalists, conductors, arrangers, orchestrators, engineers, producers, copyists, etc.; payments to a trustee or fund based on wages to the extent required by any agreement between Company and any labor organization or trustee; union session scale payable to Artist; all studio, tape, editing, mixing, re-mixing, mastering and engineering costs; artist development costs including physical training, vocal conditioning, cosmetic enhancement and other similar costs, authoring costs; all costs of travel, per diems, rehearsal halls, non-studio facilities and equipment, dubdown, rental and transportation of instruments; all costs occasioned by the cancellation of any scheduled recording session; all amounts paid in connection with the production, conversion, authoring, mastering and delivery of audiovisual materials prepared for or embodied on Audio Records or Value-Added Records; all expenses of clearing and licensing any Samples embodied on Recordings hereunder; and all other costs and expenses incurred in the production, but not the manufacture, of Recordings and Records hereunder or otherwise made in connection with Artist, which are then customarily recognized as recording costs in the recording industry. If Company furnishes any of its own facilities, materials, services or equipment for which Company has a standard rate, the amount of such standard rate (or if there is no standard rate, the market value for the services or thing furnished) shall be deemed Recording Costs. Payments to the American Federation of Musicians' Special Payments Fund and the Music Performance Trust Fund based upon Record sales (so-called "per-record royalties") shall not constitute a Recording Cost and shall not be recoupable from your royalties or reimbursable by you;

(rr) "Royalty Base Price" - the Gross Royalty Base applicable to the Record concerned, less excise taxes, duties and other applicable taxes included within the Gross Royalty Base and less Proportionate Deductions, if any;

(ss) "Sample" - any copyrightable work which is owned or controlled by any Person other than you, embodied on a Recording hereunder, but not Artist's newly-recorded performance hereunder of an entire Composition previously recorded by other recording artist(s) and theretofore released;

(tt) "Sampler Records" - promotional Records on which Recordings hereunder and other Recordings are included, which such Records are given away or sold at a substantially lower PPD than the then-prevailing PPD for the majority (or plurality) of Company's Top Line Records in such format;

(uu) "Single" - a Record embodying thereon three (3) or fewer Masters;

(vv) "Staff Producer" - a producer who is an employee of Company or any affiliate of Company;

(ww) "Standard Discounts" - discounts reflected in the PPD;

(xx) "Subscription" - transmission of Records other than Phono Records to consumers, either by Company or through its distributors, its Principal Licensees or their distributors or another Person, in return for a subscription or other fee paid by the consumer to obtain access to such Recordings for a limited period of time and/or a limited number of uses or any other method of exploitation commonly recognized as a subscription service;

(yy) "Territory" - the universe;

(zz) "Top Line Record" - a Record bearing the same PPD as the majority (or plurality) of the new Record releases in the same format and configuration by Company's best-selling artists;

(aaa) "<u>USNRC Net Sales</u>" - Net Sales of Top Line Records consisting entirely of Recordings hereunder through normal retail channels in the United States;

(bbb) "<u>Value-Added Record</u>" - a Multiple Record Set which is sold by Company or its distributors or Company's Principal Licensees or their distributors at a PPD which is no more than one hundred twenty percent (120%) of Company's or the applicable Principal Licensee's then-prevailing PPD for one (1) of the Records comprising such Multiple Record Set;

(ccc) "<u>Video</u>" - a Recording embodying an audiovisual work primarily featuring the audio soundtrack of one (1) or more Masters hereunder; and

(ddd) "<u>Video Production Costs</u>" - all amounts paid or incurred in connection with the production, conversion and delivery of Videos. Video Production Costs include flat-fee payments to the publishers of musical works, unreimbursed costs and expenses incurred in the duplication and delivery of copies of Videos to licensees, and all direct out-of-pocket costs (such as for rights, artists including Artist, producers and other personnel, travel, per-diems, facilities, materials, services and use of equipment). If Company furnishes any of its own facilities, materials, services or equipment for which Company has a standard rate, the amount of such standard rate (or if there is no standard rate, the market value for the services or thing furnished) shall be deemed Video Production Costs.

23. MERCHANDISING

You and Artist warrant that you and Artist are not currently subject to any contract that grants to any Person the right to manufacture and sell products that embody Artist's name and/or likeness (such rights being herein referred to as "<u>Merchandising Rights</u>"). If, during the Term, you or Artist desire to grant Merchandising Rights to a third party and if at such time Company (or one of Company's affiliates) is actively involved in the merchandising business, then prior to commencing negotiations with any such third party with respect to any such Merchandising Rights, you and Artist shall notify Company thereof and Company and you and Artist shall promptly begin good faith negotiations regarding the material terms and conditions of an agreement relating to such Merchandising Rights (a "Merchandising Agreement"). If, after such good faith negotiations, Company and you and Artist are unable to agree on the material terms of such Merchandising Agreement, then you and Artist shall not have the right to enter into a Merchandising Agreement with any Person with respect to such Merchandising Rights unless you and Artist first: (1) notify Company of the basic terms of the proposed agreement between you and Artist and the applicable third party regarding Artist's Merchandising Rights (the "Outside Proposal"); and (ii) offer to enter into an agreement with Company (or Company's merchandising affiliate, as applicable) on terms no more favorable to you and Artist than those set forth in the Outside Proposal. If Company does not agree to enter into an agreement with you and Artist on the same terms as the Outside Proposal (i.e., to "match" the Outside Proposal) within thirty (30) days of Company's receipt of your and Artist's notice of such proposal, then you and Artist may enter into an agreement with the third party concerned on terms no less favorable to you and Artist than those set forth in such Outside Proposal.

As the music industry has changed and the sale of records has reportedly become less profitable, record companies have sought to get involved in artists' other revenue streams. This clause is an example of a major label's efforts to get a toehold on artists' merchandising rights. Artists should remain free to enter into merchandising deals with third-party companies without interference from their record companies and should, therefore, aggressively negotiate against the inclusion of such terms in their recording agreements. While this agreement only provides the company with a matching right, it undermines the artist's freedom to make deals, and that should be discouraged.

24. MISCELLANEOUS

(a) This agreement constitutes the entire agreement between the parties hereto with respect to the subject matter hereof and supersedes and cancels any and all previous and contemporaneous discussions, negotiations, covenants, agreements, commitments, representations, warranties and writings of any kind with respect thereto, all of which have been and are merged and integrated into, and are superseded by, this agreement. No modification, amendment, waiver, termination or discharge of this agreement shall be binding upon Company unless confirmed by a written instrument signed by an authorized officer of Company, or binding upon you unless confirmed by a written instrument signed by you or your representative. A waiver by either you or Company of any term or condition of this agreement in any instance shall not be deemed or construed as a waiver of such term or condition for the future or of any subsequent breach thereof. Except as otherwise specifically set forth in this agreement, all rights, options and remedies in this agreement shall be cumulative and none of them shall be in limitation of any other remedy, option or right available to Company or to you. Each and every provision of this agreement shall be considered severable, and if for any reason any provision or provisions herein are determined to be indefinite, invalid, contrary to any applicable existing or future laws or otherwise unenforceable, that shall not impair the operation or effect of any other portion of this agreement, and this agreement shall be deemed modified, but only to the extent necessary to make the provision enforceable. The headings of the paragraphs hereof are for convenience only and shall not be deemed to in any way affect the scope, meaning or intent of this agreement or any portion thereof. The terms "include," "including" or "e.g." wherever used in this agreement shall mean "include without limitation" or "including without limitation" unless expressly otherwise indicated. All accountings and payments required herein, all recoupments permitted herein, and all grants and all warranties made herein, shall survive and continue beyond the expiration or earlier termination of this agreement. You shall not be entitled to recover damages or to terminate the Term by reason of any breach by Company of its material obligations, nor shall Company otherwise be deemed in default or breach of this agreement by reason of any such breach, unless Company is given notice thereof and same is not cured within thirty (30) days after receipt of such notice. You shall not be deemed to be in default or breach of this agreement unless you are given notice thereof and same is not cured within thirty (30) days after such notice; provided that, the foregoing shall not be applicable to any breach, alleged breach or threatened breach of the exclusivity provisions of this agreement, to your or Artist's failure to timely Deliver any Masters required to be Delivered hereunder, to the provisions of paragraph 15(a)(viii) of this agreement, or to any breach, alleged breach or threatened breach for which a cure period is already provided in this agreement. If you claim that additional monies are payable to you hereunder, Company shall not be deemed in material breach of this agreement unless such claim is reduced to a final judgment by a court of competent jurisdiction. In entering into this agreement, and in providing services pursuant hereto, you and Artist have and shall have the status of independent contractors. Nothing herein contained shall contemplate or constitute you or Artist as Company's agents or employees, and nothing herein shall constitute a partnership, joint venture or fiduciary relationship between you and Company. The parties hereto acknowledge and agree that: (i) each party and its counsel reviewed and negotiated the terms and provisions of this agreement and have contributed to its revision; (ii) the rule of construction that any ambiguities are resolved against the drafting party shall not be employed in the interpretation of this agreement; and (iii) the terms and provisions of this agreement shall be construed fairly as to all parties, regardless of which party was generally responsible for the preparation of this agreement.

The default rule of thumb in contract interpretation is that if any provision of an agreement is deemed to be ambiguous, it will be interpreted in favor of the nondrafting party, which in this case would be the artist—by including clause (ii), the record companies hope to prevent the implementation of that rule in the event of a legal dispute. The artist should try to have clause (ii) removed if possible, but this should not be the subject of heated debate.

(b) You and Artist recognize and acknowledge that the sale of Records is speculative and agree that the judgment of Company (and its affiliates, licensees and distributors) in regard to any matter affecting the sale, marketing, promotion, distribution and exploitation of such Records shall be binding and conclusive upon you and Artist. Without limiting the preceding sentence, you and Artist recognize and acknowledge that Company has not made, and does not hereby make, any representation or warranty with respect to the quantity (if any) of sales of Records embodying Masters. You warrant, represent and agree that neither you nor Artist shall make any claim, nor shall any liability be imposed upon Company or Company's affiliates, licensees or distributors based upon any claim, that more sales could have been made or better business could have been done than was actually made or done by Company or Company's affiliates, licensees or distributors.

This clause is specifically designed to protect record companies in the event they are sued for failing to properly promote records. If an artist can get this type of language removed or weakened, it is a good idea but not worth fighting for beyond the second draft.

(c) Company shall have the right to secure insurance with respect to Artist for Company's own benefit. In this connection, you shall cause Artist to be available for physical examinations by a physician as and when reasonably requested to do so and to complete such questionnaires and other documents which Company or any insurance carrier may from time to time require in connection with securing and maintaining such insurance. Company shall keep such information confidential, except that Company may disclose such information to the applicable insurance carrier(s) or as required by law. Neither you, Artist nor Artist's estate shall have any right to claim the benefit of any such policy obtained by Company.

Companies want the right to carry life insurance on their artists. Artists should try to have this language tailored so that they are only required to visit a doctor of their choosing and that the insurance company be required to maintain the confidentiality of artist's medical records. The company should be entitled to know whether or not the insurance company will insure the artist, but it should not be privy to an artist's private medical history.

(d) Company may assign this agreement to: (i) any parent, subsidiary, sister corporation, joint venture partner or affiliate thereof, or other affiliate of Company; (ii) a Person acquiring all or substantially all of the Record-related assets of Company; or (iii) an entity merged into or consolidated with Company. The foregoing shall not prohibit or in any way restrict Company from assigning or licensing any of its rights hereunder in the ordinary course of business. This agreement is personal to you and Artist, and neither you nor Artist shall have the right to assign this agreement or any of your or Artist's rights or obligations hereunder; provided that, you may assign your rights under this agreement to a corporation, all of whose capital stock is owned solely by you or Artist, provided: (A) you have delivered to Company an instrument signed by you and Artist and any other required Person satisfactory to Company in its sole discretion effecting the assignment and the assignees assumption of your obligations, and Company has executed that instrument to evidence Company's approval of it; (B) no such assignment relieves you or Artist of your or Artist's obligations under this agreement; and (C) such assignee agrees that any further assignment is subject to the same conditions as set forth in this paragraph.

This clause should be modified to permit the artist to assign his or her right to receive money to third parties, as artists often do via letters of direction, to insure timely payment to their business managers, managers, attorneys and so forth.

(e) THIS AGREEMENT SHALL BE DEEMED TO HAVE BEEN MADE IN THE STATE OF CALIFORNIA AND ITS VALIDITY, CONSTRUCTION, PERFORMANCE AND BREACH SHALL BE GOVERNED BY THE LAWS OF THE STATE OF CALIFORNIA APPLICABLE TO AGREEMENTS MADE AND TO BE WHOLLY PERFORMED THEREIN. You agree to submit yourself to the jurisdiction of the federal or state courts located in Los Angeles County in any action which may arise out of this agreement and such courts shall have exclusive jurisdiction over all disputes between Company and you or Artist pertaining to this agreement and all matters related thereto. In this regard, any process in any action or proceeding commenced in the courts of the State of California arising out of any claim, dispute or disagreement under this agreement may, among other methods, be served upon you by delivering or mailing the same, via registered or certified mail, addressed to you at the address provided herein for notices to you; any such delivery or mail service shall be deemed to have the same force and effect as personal service within the State of California. Nothing contained in this paragraph shall preclude Company from joining you or Artist in an action brought by another Person against Company in any jurisdiction, although Company's failure to join you or Artist in any such action in one instance shall not constitute a waiver of any of Company's rights with respect thereto or with respect to any subsequent action brought by a third party against Company. Nothing contained herein shall constitute a waiver of any other remedies available to Company.

(f) This agreement shall not become effective until executed by all parties.

IN WITNESS WHEREOF, the parties hereto have executed this agreement as of the day and year first above written.

MAJOR RECORD COMPANY INC.

BY: _____

[ARTIST]

BY:_____
SOCIAL SECURITY #:_____

BY:_____
SOCIAL SECURITY #:_____

BY:_____
SOCIAL SECURITY #:_____

BY:_____
SOCIAL SECURITY #:_____

p/k/a "Name of Artist"

How to Read and Evaluate Artist Royalty Statements

BY JACK PHILLIPS

Suppose you are, or represent, a newly successful artist who has a hit album. In September, *Billboard* shows the album has been certified "gold," which means "...sales of 500,000 units or more." In early October the first royalty statement is received, which seems to add up to only about 100,000 album units. Is something amiss? Not necessarily.

REPORTABLE ARTIST ROYALTY UNITS

First of all, the 500,000-unit criterion includes sales plan and special program free goods that can range from 15% to 25% of the units counted for certification, although royalties by agreement are not normally paid on them. Additionally, gold album criteria include record club sales, bonus and free units (if the album has been out long enough), which may be communicated from the club to the record company for certification purposes well before the record club remits the money due on the sales. Even then, all

or at least a portion of the club bonus and free units are usually royalty free by agreement. Also, by agreement, artist royalties may only be payable on a percentage of net sales, say 85% or 90%. Usually, these "royalty reducers" are offset by a royalty rate that is higher than a record company would pay in their absence. The typical artist contract also allows for a reserve for returns in calculating royalties, which can amount to 25% or more. Royalties will eventually be received on units held in

---

EXAMPLE OF GOLD ALBUM VS. REPORTABLE UNITS

Release Date	January 15, 200X
Certification Date	September 15, 200X
Certified Units	500,200
Record Club Distribution	(99,950)
Record Company Distribution	400,250
Standard Free Goods - 15%	(60,038)
Special Program Free Goods - 10%	(34,021)
90% Unit Base Adjustment	(30,619)
30% Reserve Adjustment	(82,672)
Units Distributed After June 30	(89,250)
Units Reported on June 30, 200X Statement	**103,650**

reserve to the extent returns do not deplete them. Lastly, some of the 500,000 units could be from the period between the June 30th royalty statement period end and the certification date in September.

Similar situations can occur with the reporting of royalties on foreign sales. Suppose a friend or colleague from London has mentioned what a big hit the album is there and nil royalties for the United Kingdom show on the statement. The problem is probably a matter of time lag. The English affiliate or licensee record company has a normal accounting period to accumulate, process and report the sales and royalties to the record company in the United States, which should report them on the next royalty statement.

ARTIST ROYALTY STATEMENT FORMAT

Each record company's royalty statements are different, and the statements of the individual labels of a record company may differ. Often, preceding the details is a summary of the various types of earnings, including domestic that may or may not include Canada, domestic licensee sales such as record clubs and foreign licensee (that may actually be affiliates) sales. The summary will give the previous statement balance and payment, if any, reserves currently held and prior reserves released, recording costs and advances deducted, charges (including session costs), video costs, producer royalty deductions, miscellaneous adjustments and an ending balance.

RCX RECORD COMPANY ARTIST ROYALTY STATEMENT EXAMPLE OF A ROYALTY STATEMENT SUMMARY

Period 07/01/0X to 12/31/0X

Balance Forward	267,246.03
Royalty Payments	(267,246.03)
Prior Reserves Held	76,812.82
Beginning Balance	**76,812.82**

Earnings

Domestic Sales	1,093,863.74
Digital Download Sales	2,380.46
Military Sales	20,932.38
Licensee Sales	474,509.67
Licensee Club Sales	6,982.52
Digital Downloads by Tune	8,046.40
Licensee Miscellaneous	1,250.00
Subscription	2,120.80
Total Earnings	**1,610,085.97**

Charges

Advances	(300,000.00)
Session Charges	(348,790.18)
Miscellaneous Charges	(94,512.88)
Total Charges	**(743,303.06)**

Reserves	(392,411.31)
Balance Payable	551,184.42
Producer Deduction (Album #2)	(251,546.07)
Ending Balance Payable	**299,638.35**

DOMESTIC ROYALTIES

The common thread among record companies in reporting domestic royalties is the presentation of selections, units, royalty rates and amounts. A number and title usually identify each recording. Presently, there is one dominant physically distributed configuration of an album, i.e., the compact disc (CD.) There may also be sales of cassette tapes, abbreviated as TCs for tape cassettes. They may also be identified by the addition of a prefix or suffix letter or number, for example 2 = CD, and 4 = TC. Seven-inch 45-RPM singles, if available, may be identified by a 7 prefix. Or, a configuration code (Cfg) may be given, such as AQ for a CD album, SS for a 45-rpm singles. Generally you can tell the difference between the products by the royalty cent rate. Compact discs should have the highest rate to correspond with their higher prices. Forty-fives generally have the lowest rate. To confuse things, however, there may be 12-inch vinyl singles, CD singles and cassette singles at prices in between. Ultimately, the record company may have to be consulted to identify some or all of the selections, particularly if titles are not given.

Our example record company, RCX, discloses all the elements used to calculate royalties for normal domestic sales. This information includes the catalog number, title description, configuration code, royalty percentage rate, packaging deduction percentage, suggested retail list price (SRLP), and the royalty cent rate. It also includes the quantity base (if other than 100%), the quantity of royalty units, the royalty amount for each configuration and the total for the catalog number. Since it would be beyond the scope of this chapter to cover all the variations between record companies, we will utilize RCX as an example for further discussion. To calculate the domestic sales royalty for album #2 AQ, you multiply the retail price, $18.98 by 100% minus the packaging percentage (i.e., 100% - 25% = 75%), multiplied by the royalty percentage rate, 16%, to arrive at $2.2776. This unit rate multiplied by the quantity of units gives the royalty amount.

Simple? Not exactly, as you will see.

Prices

RCX negotiates contractually to pay royalties on a suggested retail list price basis. Other companies may use a wholesale price basis or variation thereof.

For new releases in 2006, RCX's SRLPs for full-priced normal retail channel sales were $18.98 for CDs and $12.98 for TCs. Compact disc singles were $4.98, cassette singles $3.49 and 45s were $1.98. Most albums are released primarily on prerecorded CDs and often on TCs. However, this is changing as DVDs and digital downloads from the Internet continue to gain popularity.

Videos, even at record companies such as RCX that have primarily SRLP based royalties, have royalties calculated usually based on their wholesale price, also known as the published price to dealers (PPD).

Currently, there appears to be a standard retail price for digital downloads from Napster, iTunes, Liquid Audio, etc., of $.99 per single tune and $9.99 per album. However, instead of starting with an album base price of $7.49, which is the $9.99, less the $2.50 (25%) packaging allowance, RCX is starting with wholesale prices that range from $6.24 to $7.01, with no packaging deduction. Artist representatives will undoubtedly address this issue. Some are already questioning whether the transactions between the record company and Napster et al., should be treated as licensing revenue that is normally split evenly with the artist.

For new product configurations the contract may provide that royalties are based on the CD "penny" rate, at least for some time period. If older releases remain popular, they are usually sold at midprice levels, such as $12.98 for CDs and $8.98 for TCs.

Care must be taken to assure that price changes are properly reflected in the calculation of royalties. Suppose, unlike RCX that retains a "dollar" reserve for returns, a record company has held a "unit" reserve on the first album released. Two years, and two albums later, the first album is reduced to midprice. Any reserves still held on the first album relating to sales at the higher price should be reported at the higher royalty than the current midprice sales. For another illustration, a few years ago CDs went from $17.98 to $18.98. To the extent that there were any returns after the price increase that relate to sales at the old price they should have been segregated and charged back at the old, lower royalty rate.

Packaging Deductions

Packaging allowances are customarily deducted to arrive at a royalty base price on which your royalty percentage rate is applied. Generally, they are 20% for TCs and 25% for CDs or any new album-length configuration. Many contracts even allow a 25% deduction for albums that are delivered digitally over the Internet. Actually, the packaging deduction is more like a distribution fee. Everyone knows it does not cost anywhere near as much as $4.75 ($18.98 x 25%) to package a CD. However, it is generally a nonnegotiable royalty reducer in every recording agreement.

Royalty Percentage

Typically, for the succeeding albums of an artist's commitment there are higher rates. There may also be increases of royalty percentage rates (escalations) for reaching plateaus of sales levels.

Artist agreements usually allow the record company royalty relief for albums sold at midprices. Often, an artist receives 75% of the normal royalty rate for such albums, which may be defined as selling at a price between 66.6% and 80% of the normal full price. For budget-price sales, which are defined as selling for less than 66.6% of the normal top price, an artist generally receives 50% of the normal royalty rate.

The recording agreement may also state that approval must be obtained for the record company to lower the pricing or that a certain amount of time must have passed since the initial full-priced release.

PX sales are often paid at a reduced royalty percentage rate, as are singles, record club and foreign sales. One needs to summarize the differing percentages from the contract and compare them to what is shown on the statement. For record companies where just a cent rate is presented, it is more difficult to check. In this case, knowing the contractual royalty percentage rate and packaging percentage, one can check if the price is reasonable. For example, if the agreement specifies a 16% rate and 25% packaging for the CD version of an album and the royalty statement simply shows a royalty cent rate of $2.1576, which divided by 16%, divided by 75% (100% less the 25% packaging allowance) equals $17.98. If, however, when the album was on the charts, *Billboard* showed a SRLP of $18.98 (shown right after the album title, label and selection number on the Top 200-album chart) that discrepancy would deserve a phone call to the record company.

Quantity

Since only net units payable are shown on the statements, not much can be done to check the quantities reported without access to the record company's internal records. Primarily, one can check reasonableness and make inquiries about an omission of product known to be out in the market. Considering all possible reasons, if quantities still appear too low, consideration should be given to a royalty examination by professionals.

FOREIGN ROYALTIES

Record companies vary widely in their presentation of foreign royalties. While some simply report the total amount due for each territory, some give a substantial amount of detail. RCX first has a summary of total royalties earned by territory and all the details of the royalty calculation for each selection sold in each territory in a foreign detail attachment. Generally, record companies show only a U.S. dollar equivalent base price, i.e., the local currency suggested retail list price or constructed price (if there is no SRLP) has already been reduced by taxes and packaging allowances and a conversion rate has been applied. The conversion rate may have been adjusted for withholding taxes in the territory. All these actions are probably permitted by the recording agreement. However, you cannot tell if they have been done correctly. For example, the constructed retail price may have been based on an incorrect wholesale price or calculated using an incorrect markup. The sales or value added tax (VAT) deducted might also be incorrect. Suppose the contract calls for the royalty to be calculated on a wholesale price basis defined as 50% of the territory's marked up retail price. Suppose further that the foreign VAT was calculated applying the correct percentage incorrectly to the marked up price. Since the VAT is imposed on the wholesale price, we have an overdeduction. The packaging deduction may also have been calculated at the correct percentage but on the price including tax. Further deductions may have been made that conform to the local copyright society's allowances but may differ from the artist's agreement.

Unfortunately, it would require prohibitively detailed statements to give all the necessary information to check all of these concerns. However, you can check for reasonableness and inquire about what looks really odd. For example, you would expect a higher rate for CDs than TCs corresponding to their higher price. Prices generally are higher in foreign territories, so you should not see a significant number of albums being sold at an equivalent U.S. price that is notably lower than on domestic sales, although sales could be in a territory that has runaway inflation. Older albums may be mid or budget priced, if allowed by the artist's contract. Nevertheless, foreign sales of the older albums that are being reported at the contractually reduced midprice rate must fit the price criterion required by contract, just like domestic sales.

One can also check that the rates specified in the recording contract are being correctly utilized in reporting. If the record company is supposed to report 75% of the normal 16% domestic rate for major foreign territories you would expect to see 12% for the United Kingdom, Germany, etc., as major is defined in the agreement. Also, if the particular artist's recordings are generally successful overseas, inquiries should be made about significant missing territories for any selections.

RECORD CLUB AND OTHER DOMESTIC LICENSEES

RCX has a summary section that gives the total of royalties earned for each licensee club's sales whether a domestic or foreign record club. Details of RCX's domestic record clubs' reporting will be found among the other foreign record clubs in the foreign detail attachment. Artists usually receive 50% of their normal domestic album royalty rate or 50% of the record company's receipts from the club as their share of royalties. Sometimes the recording agreement calls for the artist to receive a one-half share of the record club's reporting of excess bonus and free units distributed, i.e., units, in excess of sales, distributed to club members at no charge for joining or purchasing a certain number selections. The clubs, at the end of a three-year or more contract period, usually report the excess units to the record companies. Some record companies will share this income only if an audit is performed.

If there is a provision for a percentage of record club receipts in the artist agreement, it might allow club royalties to be paid on less than 100% of net sales. Often clubs pay on a reduced unit basis, for example, 85%.

Special product licensing arrangements may also have occurred on which the record company reports a reduced royalty. These may be compilation albums, which

RCX RECORD COMPANY ARTIST ROYALTY STATEMENT
EXAMPLE OF ROYALTY STATEMENT DOMESTIC DETAIL AND LICENSEE SUMMARY

Period 07/01/0X to 12/31/0X

OPENING BALANCE AND ADJUSTMENTS	AMOUNT
Balance Forward 06/30/0X	267,246.03
09/30/0X Payment of Royalty	(267,246.03)
Reserve Held 06/30/0X	76,812.82
Opening Balance and Adjustments	**76,812.82**

DOMESTIC EARNINGS

Domestic Sales

LABEL	CAT. NO.	DESCRIPTION	CFG	RETAIL PRICE	PACK%	PPD	ROY BASE	ROY RATE%	PER UNIT RATE	UNITS	AMOUNT	NET PAYABLE
7 RCX	10001	Single #1	SS	1.9800				16.0000%	0.3168	41	12.99	
7 RCX	10001	Single #1 - Producer	SS	1.9800				-4.0000%	-0.0792	41	(3.25)	
2 RCX	10001	Single #1	S3	4.9800	25.00%			16.0000%	0.5976	15	8.96	
2 RCX	10001	Single #1 - Producer	S3	4.9800	25.00%			-4.0000%	-0.1494	15	(2.24)	
4 RCX	10001	Single #1	TC	3.4900	20.00%			16.0000%	0.4467	10	4.47	
4 RCX	10001	Single #1 - Producer	TC	3.4900	20.00%			-4.0000%	-0.1117	10	(1.12)	19.81
7 RCX	10002	Single #2	SS	1.9800				16.0000%	0.3168	220	69.70	
2 RCX	10002	Single #2	S3	4.9800	25.00%			16.0000%	0.5976	23	13.74	
4 RCX	10002	Single #2	TC	3.4900	20.00%			16.0000%	0.4467	46	20.55	103.99
2 RCX	20001	Album #1	AQ	12.9800	25.00%			12.0000%	1.1682	32,106	37,506.23	
2 RCX	20001	Album #1 - Producer	AQ	12.9800	25.00%			-3.0000%	-0.2921	32,106	(9,376.56)	
4 RCX	20001	Album #1	TC	8.9800	20.00%			12.0000%	0.8621	895	771.56	
4 RCX	20001	Album #1 - Producer	TC	8.9800	20.00%			-3.0000%	-0.2155	895	(192.89)	28,708.34
2 RCX	20002	Album #2	AQ	18.9800	25.00%			16.0000%	2.2776	418,324	952,774.74	
4 RCX	20002	Album #2	TC	12.9800	20.00%			16.0000%	1.6614	67,566	112,256.86	1,065,031.60
		Total Domestic Sales										**1,093,863.74**

Digital Download Sales

LABEL	CAT. NO.	DESCRIPTION	CFG	RETAIL PRICE	PACK%	PPD	ROY BASE	ROY RATE%	PER UNIT RATE	UNITS	AMOUNT	NET PAYABLE
6 RCX	20001	Album #1	IA			6.2400	6.2400	16.0000%	0.9984	393	392.37	
6 RCX	20001	Album #1 - Producer	IA			6.2400	6.2400	-4.0000%	-0.2496	393	(98.09)	294.28
6 RCX	20002	Album #2	IA			7.0100	7.0100	16.0000%	1.1216	1860	2,086.18	2,086.18
		Total Digital Download Sales										**2,380.46**

Military Sales

LABEL	CAT. NO.	DESCRIPTION	CFG	RETAIL PRICE	PACK%	PPD	ROY BASE	ROY RATE%	PER UNIT RATE	UNITS	AMOUNT	NET PAYABLE
2 RCX	20001	Album #1	AQ	12.9800	25.00%			12.0000%	1.1682	1,166	1,362.12	
2 RCX	20001	Album #1 - Producer	AQ	12.9800	25.00%			-3.0000%	-0.2921	1,166	(340.53)	
4 RCX	20001	Album #1	TC	8.9800	20.00%			12.0000%	0.8621	35	30.17	
4 RCX	20001	Album #1 - Producer	TC	8.9800	20.00%			-3.0000%	-0.2155	35	(7.54)	1,044.22
2 RCX	20002	Album #2	AQ	18.9800	25.00%			12.0000%	1.7082	10,275	17,551.76	
4 RCX	20002	Album #2	TC	12.9800	20.00%			12.0000%	1.2461	1,875	2,336.40	19,888.16
		Total Military Sales										**20,932.38**

CONTINUED ON NEXT PAGE

CONTINUED FROM PREVIOUS PAGE

LICENSEE EARNINGS

Licensee Sales

COUNTRY	REPORTING PERIOD (YEAR-QUARTER)	AMOUNT	NET PAYABLE
Australia	0X-02	30,699.25	
Australia	0X-03	14,074.28	44,773.53
Canada	0X-02	16,425.37	
Canada	0X-03	6,782.67	23,208.04
RCX Special Products	0X-03	62.21	62.21
Others	0X-02	294,668.26	
Others	0X-03	111,797.63	406,465.89
Total Licensee Sales			**474,509.67**

Licensee Club Sales

Australia R/C	0X-02	288.84	288.84
BMG Record Club	0X-03	1,233.66	1,233.66
BMG R/C Free Goods	0X-02	972.96	972.96
Others	0X-02	4,487.06	4,487.06
Total Licensee Club Sales			**6,982.52**

Digital Downloads by Tune		8,046.40	**8,046.40**

Licensee Miscellaneous

RSP Sync3125 Commercial		1,250.00	
Total Licensee Miscellaneous			**1,250.00**

Subscriptions		2,120.80	**2,120.80**
Total Earnings			**1,686,898.79**

Charges

Session - 999999		(648,790.18)	
11/05/0X Transfer of video costs		(94,512.88)	
Total Charges			**(743,303.06)**

Adjustments and Reserves

Royalty Reserve		(392,411.31)	
Total Adjustments and Reserves			**(392,411.31)**
Ending Balance Payable			**551,184.42**

RCX RECORD COMPANY ARTIST ROYALTY STATEMENT
EXAMPLE OF ROYALTY STATEMENT ARTIST COST DETAIL

Period 07/01/0X to 12/31/0X

TRAN CODE	SESSION NO	INVOICE CONTRACT	INV/CON DATE	LEDGER NO	DESCRIPTION	NONRECOVERABLE	RECOVERABLE
SC	999999	26096	11/13/0X	5220-00	Sunset Sound		(1,400.00)
SC	999999	26097	11/14/0X	5220-00	Sunset Sound		(1,400.00)
SC	999999	26098	11/15/0X	5220-00	Sunset Sound		(1,400.00)
					Others		(36,400.00)
					Studio Time		**(40,600.00)**
SC	999999	C/R088	11/15/0X	5224-00	Mr. Producer		(100,000.00)
					Producer Fee/Advance		**(100,000.00)**
SC	999999	A7505	11/15/0X	5226-00	Mr. Engineer		(4,500.00)
					Others		(31,115.00)
					Engineers Fees		**(35,615.00)**
SC	999999	1344	11/15/0X	5227-00	Limousine connection		(80.73)
SC	999999	60299	11/15/0X	5227-00	Hotel Sofitel		(1,276.06)
					Others		(22,943.55)
					Travel and Living Expense		**(24,300.34)**
					Miscellaneous Other		**(148,274.84)**
SC	999999	C/R087	07/15/0X	5267-00	The Artist		(300,000.00)
					Recording Advance		**(300,000.00)**
Artist Total							**(648,790.18)**

usually have an intense media advertising campaign and a short life. Normally the royalties are prorated among the tracks included based on their share of the total number of tracks. Our example record company has its affiliate, RCX Special Products, administer and collect from licensees for these uses. If artist approval was contractually required one can check for unreported product. However, the approval may have been obtained and then the track may not have been included or the product never released. One can check the All Music Guide on the Internet *(www.allmusic.com)* to see if they list any selections that are not being reported.

LICENSEE MISCELLANEOUS

The record company, through its foreign affiliate may have licensed the artist's recordings through a foreign record club. Likewise, the domestic record company or its foreign

RCX RECORD COMPANY ARTIST ROYALTY STATEMENT
EXAMPLE OF ROYALTY STATEMENT FOREIGN DETAIL

Period 07/01/0X to 12/31/0X

CATALOG PRE	NO. TITLE	SELECTION	ARTIST ROY%	QTY%	RATE	QUANTITY	UNIT PRICE	RECEIPTS	ROYALTIES EARNED
		Australia-RCX	0X-02						
2	20001	Album #1	12.0000%	100.0000%	1.27642	32,068	10.63686		40,932.34
2	20001	Album #1 - Producer	-3.0000%	100.0000%	-0.31911	32,068	10.63686		(10,233.08)
									30,699.26
		Australia-RCX	0X-03						
2	20001	Album #1	12.0000%	100.0000%	1.24747	15,043	10.39559		18,765.70
2	20001	Album #1 - Producer	-3.0000%	100.0000%	-0.31187	15,043	10.39559		(4,691.43)
									14,074.27
		Australia R/C							
2	20001	Album #1	50.0000%					770.24	385.12
2	20001	Album #1 - Producer	-12.5000%					770.24	(96.28)
									288.84
		BMG Record Club							
2	20001	Album #1	50.0000%					3,289.76	1,644.88
2	20001	Album #1 - Producer	-12.5000%					3,289.76	(411.22)
									1,233.66
		BMG R/C Free Goods							
2	20001	Album #1	50.0000%					2,594.56	1,297.28
2	20001	Album #1 - Producer	-12.5000%					2,594.56	(324.32)
									972.96
		Canada-RCX	0X-02						
2	20001	Album #1	13.6000%	100.0000%	1.30632	10,059	9.60531		13,140.29
2	20001	Album #1 - Producer	3.4000%	100.0000%	0.32658	10,059	9.60531		3,285.07
									16,425.36
		Canada-RCX	0X-03						
2	20001	Album #1	13.6000%	100.0000%	1.33761	6,761	9.83535		9,043.56
2	20001	Album #1 - Producer	-3.4000%	100.0000%	-0.33440	6,761	9.83535		(2,260.89)
									6,782.67
2	20001	Others-RCX	0X-02						294,668.26
2	20001	Others-RCX	0X-03						111,797.63
									406,465.89
2	20001	Others-R/C	0X-01						1,122.90
2	20001	Others-R/C	0X-02						3,364.16
									4,487.06
		RCX Special Products	0X-03						
2	21401	Rock 2000 - Song Title		100.0000%	0.06500	957			**62.21**
Artist Total									**481,492.18**

affiliates may sell digital downloads for individual tunes. If allowed in the recording agreement, the record company may have licensed an album master for use in a commercial or motion picture or TV show for a flat fee. Record companies may also license artist recordings to be streamed by third-party subscription services, such as Listen.com, Touchtunes.com, or Streamwaves.com. Generally, artist contracts require 50% of receipts for such uses to be reported as a royalty.

PREVIOUS STATEMENT BALANCE

Surprisingly, sometimes the amount labeled "Previous Balance Forward" on your current statement does not agree with the balance on the previous statement. Perhaps an undetailed adjustment has been made and it should be queried.

Payment dates for the statement balance are contractually specified, normally within 60 or 90 days of the royalty statement period end. If late, someone should call the record company. The large record companies are generally reliable in getting their statements and payments out on time.

RESERVES

A record company can withhold the normally allowed reserve for returns and credits in two ways—in units or in dollars. In the former instance, the royalty statement may or may not show the quantities held in reserve. If not, the record company should supply this information, if requested, at least for domestic sales.

Sometimes record companies withhold a percentage of "royalties otherwise payable..." as a reserve. This will usually be shown on the royalty statement. The recording contract should limit the percentage of allowable reserves and specify a time schedule for release. With the necessary information at hand, one can readily see if the limits are being exceeded or that the release schedule is not being adhered to.

Many contracts permit the record company to hold reasonable reserves in their best business judgment. If the artist is new and the record company has pushed product into the stores, expect a high reserve percentage. About all one can do is reason with the company for a reduction. Perhaps delivery of another album is imminent. Also, if there have been several releases that are cross-collateralized, i.e., negative royalties from net returns on one are offset against positive royalties otherwise payable on another, there is a good deal less justification for a high reserve percentage. High reserves on foreign royalties are a possibly objectionable area as well. Returns are not as readily accepted overseas. Normally, 5% to 10% is the maximum actually accepted. If reserves have been held in a foreign territory, the domestic record company has no reason to hold reserves on that income.

CHARGES AGAINST ROYALTIES

Session charges, other recording costs and advances are usually the largest charges on royalty statements, at least on the royalty statements immediately following a release. Combined with producer fees and advances and some miscellaneous charges, these elements usually make up the recording fund as defined in the recording agreement.

It is important to remember that record companies desire to foster artists' good will by cooperating and providing explanations and reasonable support for any significant charges they have questions about. The amount of details involved with sessions will prohibit total disclosure in the royalty statement. If any detail is given on sessions, it is likely to be invoice dates, descriptions or just the vendor's name and amounts.

About all you can do with this information is to look for familiar company and individual names.

The record company is normally contractually allowed to charge all recording costs up to the point where the recording is ready for manufacture. One may also notice miscellaneous charges for hotels and per diems, limos, gold record copies, etc. Despite the erroneous assumption that these items are being given free, it is normal for them to be charged against artist royalties.

The recording fund for an album, after the first album's release, may be based on the results of the previous album. For example, the agreement may say that the current recording fund will amount to 66.6% of the net royalties earned on the last album. Producer fees and advances, along with the recording costs and artist advances, will normally equal the current fund, i.e., the delivery advance will be adjusted to make it so.

Promotional videos, because of their high cost and modest independent earning power in the past, have developed their own customary treatment. Typically, 50% of the cost is chargeable against artist royalties from audio recordings. If you are aware of the budget and actual costs, you can check that no more than 50% is charged to the audio royalty account, unless contractually permitted.

Currently, even with a commercially exploited video for home viewing, it is not unusual for the video earnings to be less than production costs. The artist agreement may or may not allow the record company to apply 100% of earnings to the 50% share of costs not charged to audio royalties. In other words, the earnings, however modest, should be shared fifty-fifty from the first dollar unless the contract allows the record company to first recoup its share. Also, one might question how the record company distributes the earnings between the videos submitted to MTV, VH1, etc. For example, record companies may receive large catalog guarantee advances periodically, with no identification of the airplay of individual videos and simply apportion a share equally to all videos submitted, which would be detrimental to an artist whose video received a great deal of airplay.

Producer Royalty Deductions

Producer royalty deductions are shown on the artist royalty statement in one of three ways: (1) the producer's royalty cent rate is deducted from the artist's and just a net rate shown; (2) the producer deduction is shown by a repetition of a line showing the unit sales, etc., but using the negative producer cent rate to calculate the amount to be deducted; or (3) the total producer royalties payable are deducted in a lump sum on the summary page. In the last case, a copy of the producer's statement that gives the details of the calculation can be requested. The producer may be receiving a higher percentage rate than appropriate. The producer royalty calculation may not be reflecting the same royalty reductions as the artist, as is often contractually required. Finally, the artist royalty may be reduced for the producer royalty on both a line item and lump sum basis.

There is the concern about when the producer royalty starts to be payable. The artist's agreement should be reviewed as to whether the producer royalty should commence only when the costs are recouped and whether the costs and advances should be recouped at rates inclusive or exclusive of the producer's rate and whether the producer is then paid from record one or just after recoupment. In addition, if the recording costs charged to the artist's account include producer advances, then the artist should not see any producer royalty deductions until the producer advance is recouped from the producer's royalties. At that point, only royalties in excess of this advance should be deducted from the artist.

Miscellaneous Adjustments

On succeeding royalty statements, adjustments may be made that correct errors made by the record company on previous statements rendered. If, for example, a rate is being corrected, the applicable quantities adjusted should agree with those on the previous statement. Analyzing the rate should reveal if the correction is appropriate.

Another adjustment, if the artist writes songs, may be for the deduction of excess mechanicals. The recording agreement may have a controlled composition clause that states, for example, artist royalties may be charged for the excess of mechanical royalties the record company must pay over ten times 75% of the minimum statutory rate at time of release of the album. In other words, if you have cowritten one or more songs with individuals not in your recording group, and there are ten or more songs on the album, you are likely to be charged excess mechanicals. This is generally because the outsider will have to be paid at the full statutory rate. Multiple cowritten songs, statutory rate changes and escalations of the maximum based on reaching sales levels can complicate this calculation. It may be best to simply request the record company to provide support for their calculation.

There may also be charges for costs of special packaging or artwork, which exceed contractually allowed amounts and are therefore deductible from artist royalties.

ROYALTY EXAMINATIONS

If all of the procedures discussed herein have been applied to the artist royalty statements, either some comfort has been gained that there are no glaring improprieties, or a royalty examination is being considered. If an examination appears warranted, and routine periodic examinations are usually warranted after several releases/royalty statements, the artist agreement should be checked concerning any limitation on the time period to object to statements rendered. Record companies put a great deal of effort into making timely and accurate royalty accountings. However, errors do occur and contracts often contain language that can be interpreted in various ways.

When we review artist royalty statements on behalf of clients, we ask ourselves the same questions and apply the same procedures heretofore described. However, we often find that the royalty statements do not supply enough information. To get satisfaction, we need to actually see the details available only at the record company.

Royalty examinations, when preceded by thorough analysis, usually have cash benefits that exceed their cost. They just make good business sense. Otherwise, you may never know the record company has, for example, exceeded the contractual limit of nonroyalty bearing free goods, has not reported a share of income received from a licensee or has not correctly applied a VAT in calculating royalties on foreign sales.

Royalty Statements: Audits and Lawsuits

BY STEVEN AMES BROWN

Perhaps the most perplexing part of a musician's career centers around royalties and control over how works are exploited.

Under typical writer and artist agreements, ownership of the copyrights in compositions and sound recordings are transferred in exchange for a right to receive contractual royalties.

The conventional wisdom is that publishers and labels own the copyrights free and clear of all claims, except for conduct that violates specific terms of the contract. While such agreements do provide for an express right of audit, it is generally limited to a short window; there is no express right to receive interest in the event of under-reporting and neither audit nor attorneys' fees are reimbursed. The company is usually relieved of any obligation to actually exploit the material and has the right to delete songs and recordings at will and without recourse.

Musicians are at a decided disadvantage when it comes to self-protection, and enforcing their rights requires constant vigilance and resourcefulness.

ROYALTY STATEMENTS

Royalty statements are, for the most part, vague and confusing.

The first thing to do is compare the statements with goods available to the public. Numerous Web sites exist that sell recorded music. Many of these sites list sufficient information to determine if all configurations in the market are reflected on the statements. Unofficial fan sites and some label sites may also contain this information.

Wherever in the world there are sales or airplay chart activity on a title, there is likely to be a Web site that lists its local catalog number for that particular country's release. This information should be compared with the numbers on the royalty statements.

An important market now exists in "compilations," where tracks of various artists are included on a single release. Not only do labels release their own compilations, a substantial business is done in licensing between different companies. This compounds the possibility of royalties being underreported.

Comparing catalog numbers and licensing activity on royalty statements with goods available around the world can identify substantial discrepancies.

Nothing takes the place of conducting your own preliminary investigation. Even if you ultimately engage an auditor or file suit, you simply cannot accumulate too much information on your own.

Understanding the financial calculations for artist royalties is always problematic.

Historically, labels combated rising artist royalty rates by introducing corresponding deductions and reductions. Many years ago, it was assumed that 10% of records shipped were lost, broken or stolen. Therefore, many labels simply declared that only 90% of records shipped were "sold" and multiplied the artist rate against the published retail price for each of those sold units.

Armed with modern computing facilities, many labels now pay royalties on only those units they deem as sold, which by definition excludes regular "free goods" or records shipped as gratis under "special" sales plans (some of which inexplicably last for years at a time) and apply either a multitude of base prices instead of a "retail" price or reduce the royalty percentage under a variety of conditions.

To make matters worse, labels seldom reveal the details on the statements, which results in royalty rates that are nearly impossible for a musician to decipher without assistance. There is no easy means to determine whether the number of units sold was accurately reported or whether the correct rate was applied.

Writer statements are, generally, not quite as difficult to understand. The bulk of income comes from mechanical (records, CDs, etc.) and synchronization (movies and commercials) licenses where the writer receives half the income. Verifying most income on writer statements is simpler than with recording artist statements.

Most publishers delegate their domestic licensing to The Harry Fox Agency (www.harryfox.com). It is a relatively simple matter to match up income reported by Fox to what is reported on writer statements. More difficult to verify is foreign income. Even though mechanical licensing income in most major territories is collected by local collection societies, foreign subpublishers rarely include copies of those reports with their statements, although they should be available when the foreign subpublisher is owned or controlled by the domestic publisher.

AUDITS

Experienced auditors are the professionals best equipped to verify the accuracy of statements. The question of whether to conduct a formal audit is really one of cost versus expected benefit.

Statements for a title that sells millions of units should be audited, but it is a tougher decision for sales of less than 500,000 units.

At the very least, if more than a few hundred thousand units are reported, an auditor should be engaged to perform a simple "bench audit" to determine whether discrepancies on the face of the statement can be identified and other issues clarified.

Artist statements really cannot be accurately verified without a detailed review of the label's business records.

Complicating matters are provisions in most writer and artist agreements that prohibit the musician from engaging an auditor who is engaged in another audit of the company or from compensating the auditor on a contingent fee basis (i.e., paying the auditor a percentage of what is recovered instead of hourly or guaranteed fees).

Further roadblocks are in the form of restrictions on the type of information that is available in an audit. For instance, record companies limit documents to those relating to sales and will not produce inventory or manufacturing documents.

By limiting access to auditors (e.g., to those musicians that can afford to pay up-front fees) and by restricting the information available to verify the accuracy of statements on an industry-wide basis, labels present significant obstacles to royalty verification.

SUING

The most efficient way to level the playing field in a royalty dispute is to file suit. Once a dispute is in court, the labels and publishers lose the advantage of contractual restrictions.

Should You Sue?

Many artists are understandably nervous about suing a label or publisher. After all, some 90% of the world's recorded music business is in the hands of only four conglomerates. However, the risks of suing are more apparent than real.

Artists of all stature and levels of success have sued to enforce their rights. And if the company believes it can make money from the artist's creative talent, the existence of a dispute will not change its insistence that future product be delivered.

It is not unusual for active lawsuits to be temporarily stayed while the parties release new material; nor is it unusual for companies to settle disputes by signing new agreements.

As a general rule, the only tragedy is where an artist tolerates a company underpaying royalties or releasing material in a way that disparages the creator.

Retaining an Attorney

In general terms, entertainment attorneys either practice transactional law (deal making) or litigation (deal enforcing).

Each of these subspecialties has a different purpose and seems to require a different approach.

By the nature of their practice, transactional attorneys generally maintain the best of relations with labels and publishers. Persuading, cajoling and enticing companies to pay large advances and higher-than-average royalties seems to require a fraternal and salesperson-like approach, whereas pushing companies into doing something they do not want to do through the brute force of litigation seems to require dogged determination and an indifference to being liked.

Yet, there are music lawyers that have demonstrated effectiveness at both subspecialties. Some very aggressive attorneys are successful at making deals and some very low-key litigators obtain perfectly acceptable recoveries from recalcitrant companies.

The point is that neither a transactional nor litigation attorney should be selected based on stereotype or personality.

It is very important to have a candid talk with an attorney about his or her preferences and track record.

The artist should ask pointed questions, like how does the attorney feel about the prospect of souring his or her own relationship with the company, should that be necessary to advance your claim?

Executives at competing companies can be surprisingly good sources of information about attorneys. It could be well worth the effort to ask which music litigation attorneys produce good results for clients and have a reputation for being honest. Be sure to distinguish between the attorneys executives like and those that are effective. The most important factors are consistent success and truthfulness, not whether an executive would like to have a particular litigator as a friend or coworker.

Attorneys are generally compensated by either guaranteed or contingent compensation. Most attorneys charge an hourly fee for services. Other forms of guaranteed fees, although less frequent, are flat fees for an entire case or a reduced hourly fee plus a flat or percentage bonus based on results.

The other system of compensation is a pure contingent fee, where the attorney is paid a percentage of the winnings but nothing if the case is lost.

Each system has its merits and should be carefully evaluated.

An hourly fee can become an open-ended expense item, depending on the complexity of the action and the defendant's recalcitrance. In a protracted battle, most artists simply cannot match the resources of a major adversary.

Some attorneys will accept a reduced hourly fee with a bonus either in the form of fixed sum(s) or a percentage of the recovery. That could be a boon or bust for the artist, depending on the recovery and the amount of attorney services it takes to obtain the settlement or judgment.

Flat fees are more theory than reality. They are rarely available since the attorney would be underwriting a substantial risk with only a fixed fee at the end of the road.

A pure contingent fee eliminates all risk to the artist, but generally at a price. The attorney is paid only out of a recovery, but the percentage is rarely small and if the attorney reinstates a royalty stream or increases the royalty rate, the contingent participation lasts as long as the reinstated or increased royalty stream itself.

The precise percentage varies among attorneys and is also affected by whether the attorney or the client advances third-party expenses, such as deposition transcripts and expert witness fees.

However, a purely contingent fee means the artist bears none of the risk that the litigation will be protracted or lost. The artist can hold out against the largest and best-heeled adversary. The ultimate price paid for attorneys' fees under a contingent arrangement could equate to a very high or very low hourly rate, but the artist cannot be starved out of a claim and for that reason, the company should be advised of that fact at the earliest stage, since it effectively levels the playing field.

Whom to Sue

The choice of whom to sue is an easy one if the artist has a contract with a large company and that company handles the money.

More difficult choices are faced where the artist has an agreement with a smaller company that transferred the masters/songs to another company and agreed to be responsible for paying the artist.

For instance, "production deals" for recording artists commonly involve an artist signing with a producer who then sells the masters to another company but continues to handle the artist's royalties.

A production company with few assets or hard-to-find executives is a hard target when it comes to satisfying a judgment.

Most states follow the "common law," which states that a party who accepts the benefits of a contract, must also bear its burdens. Thus, if a record company accepts the benefits of the grants of rights to the masters and the authorizations to use the name and likeness that are embodied in an artist agreement, it becomes responsible for the royalties that are due under the agreement.

In practical terms that means (unless the artist signed a specific agreement waiving the right to sue third parties), the company that actually ends up with the copyrights can be directly sued for any unpaid royalties, even if the company and the producer agree otherwise between themselves. The company may have a claim against the producer for failing to pay the artist royalties, but that has no bearing on the artist's right to sue the company.

This affects how much money is due the artist. The prevailing practice for third-party income (such as from compilations and synchronization) is that an artist receives 50% of the earnings. The question is 50% of whose income? Is the artist's 50% share calculated at the level of the owner of the master or at the lower level of the royalty paid by the owner to the producer?

In cases where the artist sells the master to a producer or a company and that transferee in turn sells the master to another, the artist's share is properly calculated at the source of income received by the party that owns the master at the time the income accrued to that owner.

Moreover, a successor company is responsible for royalties that a prior owner failed to pay.

None of this works a hardship on successive purchasers of copyrights since as part of their acquisition they routinely perform due diligence reviews and hold reserves to cover any claims.

Theories of Recovery

Lawsuits are initiated by the filing of a "complaint" that sets out the nature and theories underlying the claim.

The most obvious complaint is a claim for breach of contract; that the defendant committed a material breach by failing to timely and accurately pay the full royalties due.

Since the general nature of the relationship between an artist/writer and a label/publisher would be one of contract, it is often assumed that the claims have to be limited to damages that flow from the breach of contract.

However, there are more theories that should be considered.

One remedy is to ask that the copyrights or at least the income be put into the hands of a receiver. That need not be as disruptive as it might sound. For instance, virtually all publishers use The Harry Fox Agency to handle mechanical licensing. It is a very simple matter for a court to order the Agency to pay over the writer's share to the writer's own company.

Just seeking such a remedy will get the company's attention since control over the administration and the float from holding royalty income for six months at a time are a company's financial lifeblood. A single successful artist or writer claim can result in similar attacks by others; it is a powerful incentive to a company to pay any underreported income without delay.

The ultimate remedies are "rescission" and "restitution." If successful, the artist not only ends up getting the copyrights back but possibly the entire gross royalty received by the record company as well.

These remedies are generally reserved for instances of very serious company breaches, such as the total or near total failure to pay royalties.

The most famous case involved The Kingsmen's recording of "Louie, Louie." As with most artists, The Kingsmen signed an agreement transferring ownership of the master to a record company in exchange for the right to receive royalties. Even though the masters changed hands several times, nobody ever paid royalties to the artists. Decades later The Kingsmen sued to rescind the original agreement and asked that ownership of the master be returned to them.

The appellate court affirmed the judgment in favor of the artists and the artists were awarded ownership of the master again. Left unsettled in that case was how total the failure to pay royalties must be (how substantial must the breach be) before an artist can rescind an agreement. However, the court did hold that the statute of limitations on the right to rescind starts anew with every accounting period. Thus, the artists were able to sue for rescission because within the four years preceding their lawsuit (California has a four-year statute of limitations for disputes over written contracts) the artists had not been paid.

Interestingly enough, The Kingsmen waived their right to seek restitution (the money earned by the defendant for the four years prior to the time they gave notice that they were rescinding). There may indeed have been a good strategic reason why they waived that claim, but it does not appear to be a requirement in any state.

Elsewhere in this book are discussions of additional theories, such as a label licensing a recording for use in commercials or movies that are objectionable to the artist. Issues concerning who has the right to approve such uses should not be overlooked when drafting a lawsuit.

Discovery of Information

Under federal discovery rules and the practices of most states, all relevant information is discoverable, not merely that allowed under the agreement.

Among the most important documents are the intracompany agreements by which record companies and publishers have access to the catalogs of foreign affiliates and vice versa. These agreements provide a road map to how affiliates report sales and income information to each other. Although there is nothing inherently proprietary or confidential about these agreements, virtually no company will disclose these documents without a court order.

Modern pretrial discovery also affords an easy way to track royalties. For little more than the cost of postage, a plaintiff can send written questions to a defendant, asking such things as how many copies of a recording have been manufactured; the names and addresses of all those who have been given licenses to exploit a particular work; and the amounts, dates and sources of all income pertaining to a particular title. The defendant is obligated to sign the responses under oath.

Defendants often seek confidentiality orders, to restrict the artist from discussing with others the material turned over in discovery.

It is generally not in a plaintiff's interest to consent to a confidentiality order since it drastically curtails the artist's ability to communicate with others and swap useful information. It is precisely this sort of information pooling that companies seek to prevent.

As the information available in discovery basically revolves around the exploitation of an artist's work and since a company has no greater expectation of privacy concerning the exploitation than the royalty artist, it is hard to justify restricting a plaintiff from discussing the success of his own works.

Virtually no writer or artist agreements contain a provision that awards attorneys' fees to the prevailing party in a dispute over royalties. The conventional wisdom is that such a clause would only encourage artists to pursue claims, since if successful they would be repaid their legal fees.

Most jurisdictions have a discovery device that requires the defendant to admit or deny the truth of matters in dispute. The sanction for the failure to admit a fact generally shifts the costs of proving the matter to the party that failed to admit it was true.

In practical terms, an artist can ask a company to admit or deny that the royalty statements in dispute report lower sales than were actually made. If the company wrongly denies the fact and the artist proves there was underreporting at trial, the costs associated with proving that fact can be assessed against the company, even if the artist loses the lawsuit. The policy behind this procedure is to discourage people from unreasonably running up the costs and length of a trial by failing to eliminate issues on which there really is no dispute.

Proving the Claim

At trial or in a motion for summary judgment, the artist is responsible for proving that he has sustained damage at the hands of the defendant, i.e., that the defendant breached some legal duty it owed to the plaintiff and that as a result of the breach, the plaintiff has sustained a quantifiable loss.

The most difficult issue to prove is damages. There are rarely disputes over who signed what contract and which party is liable for any underpayment. The problem is proving the amount of underpayment.

This is particularly true in the case of modern recording artist agreements that subject royalty calculations to numerous adjustments and reductions.

Worse still, are the cases where the defendant either refuses to produce adequate documentation or simply does not have the necessary documents.

Withholding such information has turned out to be a fools paradise at best. The seminal dispute involving inadequate and otherwise missing financial information involved B. J. Thomas, Gene Pitney and The Shirelles. There, the record company kept very sketchy documentation and much of what it did have, it sent to a state where it was beyond discovery through a subpoena.

Undaunted, the artists' expert witness simply created a chart with estimates of the income and then to resolve any doubts in favor of the artists and against the company (that had caused the information vacuum), he upped the estimate by 30%. The judgment in favor of the artists was affirmed on appeal.

The lesson to be learned is simple, no artist need be afraid of a company that hides documents; that only leaves the artist free to estimate the income and then up the estimate to resolve any lingering doubts.

The appellate court was quite specific in holding that when a defendant fails to maintain and produce the documents necessary to calculate damages it cannot at the same time complain that the plaintiff did not prove the underpayment with certainty. All that is required is that the plaintiff's expert demonstrate a stable basis for making the estimate. That could come from market share projections; income earned by comparable recordings, etc.

The artist could end up with a judgment that exceeds the amount of royalties that were actually due; that is the risk a company assumes when it hides financial documents.

Should You Settle?

Over 90% of all cases settle before the first witness is called at trial. Therefore, all parties should be talking about settlement from the moment the complaint is filed with the court. Only a fool refuses to discuss a reasonable resolution at every stage of the proceedings.

A litigant should always consider the risks of forcing a case to judgment and the quality of the other side's position. If there is some merit to the other side's view, it should be taken into account when valuing the case.

Litigation is not a moral battleground; it is not a place for making statements or punishing people.

Ultimately, obtaining a satisfactory result and eliminating risk is the best outcome and if that point is reached before judgment, it is time to settle; if it cannot be reached, then and only then should the case proceed to trial.

Analysis of a Record Producer Agreement

BY LINDA A. NEWMARK

The record producer is one of the most important individuals involved in creating recordings. Certain producers are sought out by recording artists because the artists believe that those producers can assist them in creating the sound that will help them achieve record sales at platinum or multiplatinum levels.

This chapter focuses upon the situation in which the producer is engaged to produce a master recording for use on an album by an artist who already has a recording agreement with a major record company.

PRODUCER COMPENSATION

The producer of master recordings for an artist with a record deal generally receives an advance payment that is recoupable from the producer's future royalties. Generally, the artist's recording agreement with the record company will provide that the artist receives an "all-in" royalty on net sales of the artist's records. An all-in royalty means that the artist must pay the producer out of the artist's royalty. However, in certain genres, such as country music, the recording agreement may provide for the artist to receive a net artist royalty, with no payment obligations to the producer. In most cases, the record company will agree to pay the producer directly, after receiving a "letter of direction" from the artist requesting the record company to do so. Thus, if the artist's all-in royalty rate is 12% of the retail selling price (after deduction of a packaging charge) on net sales of records sold through normal retail channels in the United States, and the producer's royalty rate on such sales is 3% of the retail price (with appropriate reductions), the royalty rate that the artist is really entitled to is 9% of the retail price. However, the artist and the producer must both bear in mind that they will not receive royalties from the moment the first record is shipped from the record company to the record store (or other purchaser), and they will not receive royalties from the first sale of a digital download of the recording. The record company only pays royalties on "net sales," which are some portion of the records that are sold and not returned, with no royalties payable on "free goods." (See the chapter, "Analysis of a Recording Contract," for an explanation of free goods.) Furthermore, the artist and the producer will not receive royalties until they have recouped recording costs and advances from the royalties earned in connection with the sales of records embodying the relevant master recordings. The artist and the producer will have to recoup different sums at different royalty rates. The concept of recoupment for record producers is discussed below in paragraph 6 of the sample Producer Agreement.

WHO CHOOSES THE PRODUCER?

Generally, when an artist receives an all-in royalty, the recording agreement will specify that the artist is responsible for engaging (i.e., entering into an agreement to engage) the producer; however, the record company usually retains the ultimate control over determining which producer will be engaged. The artist's attorney should always attempt to obtain the right for the artist to approve the producer. Nevertheless, recording agreements for new artists generally provide that the record company and the artist will mutually approve the producer and if the record company and the artist disagree, the record company's decision will prevail. As the artist becomes more successful, the record company will probably allow the artist to have more control over creative decisions, including the selection of a producer.

In some cases, a producer who is on the staff of the record company will produce the album. Many recording agreements contain provisions relating to the minimum compensation (for example, a $2,000 advance per master or $20,000 advance per album and a 3% of retail royalty) that would be payable if the record company's staff producer produces any master recordings for the artist. The artist's attorney should require that a provision be included in the recording agreement stating that a staff producer can only be engaged with the artist's consent and that the advances and royalties that are payable to the staff producer will be prorated if there are coproducers on the master recordings or if there are other master recordings on the album that are produced by someone else.

When the producer is not an employee of the record company and is not the artist, a producer agreement is prepared, either by the artist's attorney or by the record company. The producer agreement provided below was prepared by an attorney for a record company. With slight modifications, it could easily be an agreement between an artist and a producer.

Since most producer agreements favor the artist or the record company, I will review the provisions of the following agreement from the perspective of the attorney who is negotiating on behalf of the producer.

PRODUCER AGREEMENT

The subject matter of this Agreement is your services to us as the producer of _____ (insert #) master recording(s) ("Master[s]") embodying performances by _____ ("Artist"). You and we agree as follows:

1. The term of this Agreement ("Term") shall commence as of the date hereof and shall continue until the Master(s) are completed to our satisfaction and delivered to us or until we terminate the Term upon written notice to you. During the Term, you shall render your services as the producer of the Master(s) in cooperation with us and Artist, at times and places designated or approved in writing by us. You shall produce the Master(s), and you shall deliver the Master(s) to us or our designee promptly after the Master(s) are completed. All elements for the creation and production of the Master(s), including, without limitation, the compositions to be recorded in the Master(s) and other individuals rendering services in connection with the production of the Master(s), shall be designated or approved by us in writing. We shall pay or cause to be paid all costs to produce and record the Master(s) in an amount not to exceed a recording budget therefor, which is designated or approved by us in writing. If the costs to produce and record the Master(s) exceed the recording budget for reasons within your control or which you could have avoided, then you shall, upon our demand, pay to us the amount of those excess costs, and we may, at our election, deduct the amount of those costs from any royalties or other monies payable to you under this Agreement.

The agreement should contain a more definite completion standard than "completed to our satisfaction." The producer's attorney should attempt to obtain a "technically satisfactory" delivery standard (i.e., the masters must be of suitable sound quality from a sound engineer's perspective); however, if (as most current recording agreements provide) the artist's recording agreement contains a "technically and commercially satisfactory" delivery standard, the artist's or record company's attorney should not provide a more favorable provision to the producer than "until the completion of technically and commercially satisfactory Masters as determined by the record company."

Generally, the artist and/or record company will retain rights of approval over the elements for the creation and production of the masters. If the producer intends to use his or her own studio, a statement that the studio is approved for recording the masters should be included in the agreement to avoid any doubt about what studio will be used. The titles of the musical compositions to be recorded, if known, should be included as well.

This agreement provides that the record company will pay the recording costs. (In some instances the producer's agreement provides that the producer will receive an all-in advance, which is a lump sum that may be paid in two or three installments during the recording of the masters, which includes the money to pay the recording costs and the producer's advance.)

The producer should be certain to find out the amount available to record the masters before agreeing to take on the project. If the recording costs for the masters exceed the amount of the authorized budget, those excess costs may be charged against monies payable to the producer and; accordingly, the producer could lose part of the advance or be delayed or prevented from receiving royalties.

Many agreements provide that any excess recording costs will constitute a direct debt from the producer to the artist or record company, which must be repaid on demand. The producer's attorney should attempt to delete the record company's and artist's right to direct repayment from the producer and should limit the rights of recovery to the excess costs caused only by situations that were within the producer's control. Furthermore, those excess costs should be recoverable only from any royalties or advances payable to the producer under the specific agreement. In any event, the producer should know at the beginning of the project how much money is available to record the masters and should bear that figure in mind while working. Although the record company may pay excess recording costs, the producer should make every effort to complete the masters within the originally approved budget.

2. From the inception of the recording of the Master(s), we shall own the entire worldwide right, title and interest, including, without limitation, the copyright, in and to the Master(s), the performances embodied therein and the results and proceeds of your services hereunder, as our employee for hire for all purposes of the applicable copyright laws, free of any claims by you or any person, firm or corporation. Alternatively, you grant to us the entire worldwide right, title and interest derived from you, including, without limitation, the copyright, in and to the Master(s).

This language is very standard in producer agreements and would not be subject to negotiation by the producer's attorney. The artist and record company want the masters created by the producer to be "works made for hire" as defined in the United States Copyright Act of 1976, as amended. The benefit to the artist and record company of this is the creator of a work made for hire has no right to terminate the transfer of the work and reacquire the copyright at a later date. Nevertheless, since there is some question as to whether the masters that are created as the result of the producer's services qualify as works made for hire, the agreement also contains language stating that the producer grants all rights in the masters to the artist or record company. To protect the artist's or record company's interests better, this agreement should state that the last sentence of paragraph 2 would apply only if the masters were determined not to be works made for hire.

If the producer will write all or part of any of the musical compositions embodied in the masters, those musical compositions should be specifically excluded from the provisions of paragraph 2. The agreement would also contain a provision (that is often referred to as a "controlled composition clause") that requires the producer to grant a reduced rate mechanical license, giving the record company the right to reproduce the compositions on records (in all configurations) in exchange for payment to the producer/songwriter of mechanical royalties at 75% of the minimum statutory rate on a specified date (which could be the date of the commencement of recording, the date of delivery of the master to the record company or the date of initial commercial release in the United States of the master—the later the date the better for the producer because the mechanical royalty rate has tended to increase every few years and a later date may wind up occurring after an increase in the rate). The producer's attorney should attempt to revise this provision to provide for payment of mechanical royalties based on 100% of the minimum statutory rate in the United States (as of January 1, 2006 that rate is 9.1¢ for each record sold that embodies one use of a musical composition that is five minutes or less in length); however, many record companies refuse to negotiate on this issue unless the producer has some clout. This provision may also contain a requirement that the producer/songwriter issue a free "synchronization license" to the record company. A synchronization license is an agreement that grants the right to synchronize or use a musical composition in the soundtrack of an audiovisual work (e.g., a music video or television program). The producer should only be required to grant a free synchronization license for MTV-type free promotional videos. The terms that relate to the licensing of musical compositions written by a producer, can be very complex. Accordingly, those terms should be reviewed very carefully by the producer and his or her attorney. Also, if the producer has assigned to a music publisher rights to musical compositions that he or she writes, the producer or the producer's attorney should make certain that the controlled composition clause is provided to the producer's music publisher so that the publisher can review, comment on and approve the clause before the producer signs the producer agreement.

3. You hereby grant to us and our designees the worldwide right in perpetuity to use and to permit others to use, at no cost, your name, likeness and biographical material concerning you in connection with any and all phonograph records and other reproductions made from the Master(s), the advertising in connection therewith and institutional advertising. We shall accord you appropriate production credit on the jackets, labels or liner notes of all records embodying the Master(s), which you agree may be in substantially the following form: "Produced by _____." Any failure to comply with the provisions of this paragraph shall not be a breach of this Agreement. Your sole right and remedy in that event shall be to notify us of that failure, after which we shall use reasonable efforts to accord that production credit to you on records manufactured after the date we receive that notice.

The producer should have a right of approval over all photographs, likenesses and biographical material concerning him or her that are used under this paragraph. "Institutional advertising" should be limited to the record company's institutional advertising. Producer credit should be placed on all record labels and on jackets or liner notes on all records in all configurations (including compact disc and tape packaging). The producer should receive credit in all one-half page or larger trade and consumer advertisements featuring a master produced by the producer. The producer's attorney should attempt to obtain a provision relating to credit so that the producer's credit will be of similar size and placement as any other producer's credit on the album and will appear in advertising relating to the album if another producer is credited (unless the advertisement features a master that is produced by another producer). The agreement should state that the credit will be in the following form: "_____," not "may be in substantially the following form."

The failure to provide the credit should not be a material breach of the agreement provided that the record company and/or artist use their best efforts to cure the failure on records (in all configurations) manufactured after receipt of the notice of the failure from the producer and in advertisements authorized after the receipt of such notice.

4. In full consideration for your entering into and executing this Agreement and your fulfilling all of your obligations hereunder, you shall be paid _____Dollars ($_____), payable one-half (¹/₂) promptly after the later of the execution of this Agreement or the commencement of recording sessions for the Master(s) and one-half

(¹/₂) promptly after the later of the completion and delivery to us of all Master(s) or our determination of the aggregate costs to record the Master(s). Those monies payable to you shall be an advance recoupable from royalties earned by you hereunder.

The producer's attorney may wish to delete the word "full" in the first sentence since the possibility of the producer receiving royalties under the agreement is also consideration to the producer. ("Consideration" is a legal concept that requires that in order for a contract to be binding upon the parties, one party must give or do something of value in exchange for receiving something of value from the other party.) Additionally, the word "material" should be added before the word "obligations" because the producer should still receive his or her advance even if there is some kind of failure to fulfill a minor, nonmaterial obligation under the agreement. The agreement should specify that the advance is nonreturnable once it is paid.

The amount of the advance is based upon the experience and reputation of the producer. As the status and role of the record producer has expanded over the last several years, it has become more difficult to provide generalizations about the level of advances that a producer should receive. Accordingly, any discussion of the amount of advance payments to producers needs to include a disclaimer that each situation is different and the actual advances that a producer may obtain will be influenced by a number of factors. The advance for a single master could range from a few thousand dollars to $25,000 or more. Of course, there are always exceptions (both at the high end and the low end), including certain superstar producers who receive very significantly higher advances. The amount of the producer's advance can depend on both the producer's status and the status of the artist. The advances paid by independent labels are generally smaller than the advances paid by major labels. Also, the advances paid in connection with certain genres of music (for example, traditional jazz) can be significantly less than other genres (such as pop or rock). As mentioned previously, this agreement presents the situation where the record company pays the recording costs and pays a separate advance to the producer.

In the all-in advance situation, the producer would receive a sum of money from which the recording costs would be paid and any remaining monies would be retained by the producer. This works best for a producer who has his or her own studio and can keep recording costs down. But, in this case, the producer may have a real need to obtain the advance monies more quickly than as set forth in this agreement. One method of payment of the all-in advance could be 50% upon the commencement of recording, 25% upon the producer's delivery of a rough mix of the master and 25% upon delivery of the completed master. An all-in advance for producing a master for a new rock artist on a major label could be $25,000 or more. A more established producer producing a master for a more established rock artist might receive an all-in advance of $50,000 or more. Again, bear in mind that the actual numbers could vary widely from the numbers presented here, and the top level producers can receive signifi-cantly higher advances. The amount of the recording fund available to the artist from the record company will have a strong impact on the amount of the advance available to the producer (whether the producer's advance is an all-in advance or not).

The producer's attorney should try to limit the time that the artist or the record company has to determine the aggregate costs to record the masters to no more than 30 days after delivery. I am aware of at least one situation where a record was released and on the charts for several months and the record company's attorney still claimed that the recording costs had not yet been determined, notwithstanding the fact that all recording was conducted in the artist's own studio.

5. Conditioned upon your full and faithful performance of all the terms hereof, you shall be paid a royalty on reproductions and exploitations of the Master(s) at the following rates in accordance with the following terms:

The word "material" should be inserted before the word "terms" in the first sentence of this paragraph. The producer should request to be paid directly from the record company rather than from the artist. The artist should sign a letter of direction to that effect, which would be attached to the agreement as an exhibit.

(a) (i) On sales of full-priced, top-line long-playing phonograph records embodying solely Master(s) (in the form of conventional vinyl-discs and cassette tapes), which are sold through normal retail distribution channels in the United States ("Base Rate") of _____ percent (___%) of the suggested retail list price ("SRLP") of those Base Rate Records (or the equivalent). Your Base Rate on Base Rate Records shall be prorated, calculated, adjusted and paid on the same percentage of net sales of Base Rate Records as Artist's royalty rate on sales of Base Rate Records is prorated, calculated, adjusted and paid under the recording agreement between us and Artist ("Artist Agreement"). On sales in and outside of the United States of all records other than Base Rate Records, you shall be paid a royalty at a rate equal to the Base Rate but which is prorated, calculated, proportionately reduced, adjusted and paid on the same percentage of net sales as Artist's base royalty rate on sales of Base Rate Records is prorated, calculated, proportionately reduced, adjusted and paid under the Artist Agreement; and

A producer royalty rate generally ranges between 3% and 4% of the suggested retail list price of Base Rate Records (as defined in the producer agreement), with top producers receiving 5%. If two producers coproduce a master they might each receive a royalty at the rate of 1.5% or 2% of the retail price of records embodying the master. If the artist's royalty is computed on the basis of the wholesale price of records, rather than the retail price, then the producer's royalty would be computed based on the wholesale price of records. In that event, the producer's royalty rate would be approximately double (e.g., approximately 6% of wholesale rather than 3% of retail). Many producers receive increased royalties if the record they produce sells a certain number of units. A typical royalty rate structure is a 3% of retail royalty rate escalating to 3.5% on sales in excess of 500,000 units and escalating to 4% on sales in excess of 1,000,000 units.

The producer's royalty is generally paid on the same basis as the artist's. In the situation where the artist has a recording agreement with a production company and the production company has an agreement with the record company whereby it agrees to provide the artist's services to the record company, the producer's attorney should attempt to have the producer's royalty paid on the same basis as the production company's. Note that this agreement states that the producer's royalty is to be prorated on the same basis as the artist's royalty but this is not technically correct: the producer's royalty is prorated based on the number of masters produced by the producer that are on the particular record, and the artist's royalty is prorated based upon the number of masters recorded by the artist on the record. For example, if the producer produced five of 10 masters on Artist A's most recent album and the producer's basic royalty rate was 3% of the retail price of records comprised entirely of masters produced by the producer, the producer's royalty on Artist A's album would be reduced from 3% to 1.5% because the producer only produced half of the masters. The artist's royalty rate would not be reduced in this fashion since the entire album was comprised of masters embodying the artist's performance.

When singles are sold that have two recordings on them (an A-side and a B-side), many established producers have a special exception to one of the proration provisions in their producer agreements. This is known as "A-side protection" and it applies only to singles where the A-side is produced by one producer and the B-side is produced by another. When a producer who does not have A-side protection produces only the A-side of a single, that producer's royalty rate is cut in half. The producer with A-side protection does not receive this royalty rate reduction on singles where that producer's master appears on only the A-side, because the vast majority of people who buy a single do so because of the A-side. Since few people were buying a single for the B-side, the theory has been that the royalty of the producer of the A-side should not be reduced because of the B-side. In most instances, the producer of the B-side of a single would still be entitled to a prorated royalty on the B-side of the single, even if the producer of the A-side of the single has A-side protection. At present, a single song download that does not present proration issues is more common than a commercial sale of a single that has an A-side and a B-side.

(ii) On exploitations of the Master(s) for which Artist is paid a percentage of our net royalty or net flat fees under the Artist Agreement, you shall be paid a royalty equal to _____ percent (_____%) of our net flat fees or net royalties on such exploitations. On exploitations of the Master(s) embodied in audiovisual devices (such as videodiscs and videocassettes), however, you shall be paid a royalty equal to _____ percent (_____%) of our net flat fees or net royalties on those exploitations;

When the artist is paid based on a percentage of the record company's net royalty or net flat fee, then the producer should be paid a percentage of the amount received by the artist computed by dividing the producer's basic royalty rate (without regard to escalations) by the artist's basic all-in royalty rate (without regard to escalations). For example, if the producer's basic royalty rate is 3% of retail and the artist's basic all-in royalty rate is 12% of retail, the producer would receive 25% of any monies that the artist received as a percentage of the record company's net royalties or net flat fees. On net receipts from the exploitation of audiovisual devices, the producer would generally receive 50% of the otherwise applicable net receipts royalty.

Accordingly, in the foregoing example, the producer would receive 12.5% (rather than 25%) of the monies the artist received from the record company for the exploitation of audiovisual devices. Again, if the artist is signed to a production company instead of directly to the record company, the producer's attorney should attempt to have the producer's royalty calculated based upon the royalties payable by the record company to the production company rather than on the royalties payable from the production company to the artist; however, the producer's attorney should be aware that this may be a difficult concession to obtain.

In any event, subparagraphs 5(a)(i) and 5(a)(ii) make it clear that in order to know what royalties may be payable on a particular project, the producer must know the royalty provisions of the artist's recording agreement. Accordingly, a copy of the royalty provisions relating to the applicable album and the definitions provisions of the artist's (or, if applicable, the production company's) recording agreement should be attached, as an exhibit, to the producer agreement.

(b) Your royalty rate on records and other devices embodying Master(s) and other master recordings shall be the otherwise applicable royalty rate multiplied by a fraction, the numerator of which is the number of Master(s) embodied in that record or other device and the denominator of which is the total number of master recordings (including Master[s]) embodied in the record or other device;

This paragraph sets forth the appropriate proration of the producer's royalty. The words "royalty-bearing" should be inserted after the words "total number of" towards the end of the sentence.

(c) Your royalty rates hereunder shall not be increased due to increases in Artist's royalty rates under the Artist Agreement based on record sales; and

The producer does not generally share in sales escalations received by the artist; however, as discussed in subparagraph 5(a)(i), the producer or the producer's attorney can sometimes negotiate for escalations based on sales, which would be separate from the sales escalations received by the artist.

(d) Your royalties hereunder shall be reduced by the royalties payable by us for the services of any other person to produce or complete the production of the Master(s) until they are satisfactory to us.

The producer's attorney should request that the producer be accorded the first opportunity to do any mixing, remixing, editing or other material altering of the masters produced by the producer. If any other person performs these services, the producer should have the right, at the producer's sole discretion, to remove his or her name from the master. Also, if another person is engaged to perform production work on the master, the producer's royalty should not be reduced unless the producer is in material breach of the agreement. The producer's attorney should require that if a mixer is engaged to mix the masters, the artist or the record company should bear any royalties payable to the mixer. If the producer's attorney is not able to obtain this protection for his or her client, the producer should not have to bear more than one-third, or at most one-half, of the royalty payable to the mixer (but as noted above, the best situation would be for the producer to not have to bear any portion of the royalty payable to a mixer).

6. No royalties shall be credited to your account hereunder unless and until the aggregate of recording costs of the Master(s) and advances and fees payable to you for the Master(s) are recouped from royalties on reproductions and exploitations of the Master(s) at the "Net Artist Royalty Rate." The term Net Artist Royalty Rate shall mean the aggregate royalty rate payable to Artist and the producers on reproductions of the Master(s), less the aggregate royalty rate payable to the producers on reproductions and exploitations of the Master(s). After that recoupment, your royalty account shall be credited with royalties earned by your hereunder on all exploitations

of the Master(s) retroactive to the first record sold. We shall account for and pay royalties earned by you hereunder within ninety (90) days after the end of each of our then-current six-month accounting periods, currently ending on June 30 and December 31. Accountings and statements for royalties earned by you on reproductions and exploitations of the Master(s) shall be based upon our receipt in the United States of an accounting and payment or final credit for the actual reproductions and exploitations of the Master(s) in the accounting period for which a statement is rendered. We shall have no obligation to account for or pay to you any royalties unless and until we receive in the United States an accounting for and payment of or final credit for royalties on actual reproductions and other exploitations of the Master(s). All statements and accountings rendered to you shall be binding and not subject to any examination, audit or objection for any reason unless you shall notify us in writing of your specific objection thereto within one (1) year after the date the statement is rendered or was to be rendered. No action, suit or proceeding regarding any royalty statement or accounting rendered to you may be maintained by or on behalf of you unless commenced in court within one (1) year after the date the statement is rendered or was to be rendered. We may deduct from any amounts payable to you hereunder that portion hereof required to be deducted under any statute, regulation, treaty or other law, or under any union or guild agreement.

The first three sentences of this paragraph deal with recoupment of the recording costs and the producer advance and fees. The producer will not receive royalties until the recording costs incurred by the record company and the artist and all advances and fees paid to the producer in connection with the masters produced by that producer are recouped from royalties earned at the Net Artist Royalty Rate (i.e., the artist's all-in royalty rate minus the producer's royalty rate) from sales of records embodying the masters produced by the producer. The producer's attorney should attempt to exclude any advances or fees to the artist from the recording costs for the purposes of determining recoupment with respect to the producer. Furthermore, the advances to the producer should be excluded as well since paragraph 4 states that the advance to the producer will be recouped from royalties payable to the producer. A failure to exclude the producer advance from this provision may result in double recoupment of the producer advance and, accordingly, may delay or prevent the producer's receipt of royalties.

Once the appropriate costs are recouped at the Net Artist Royalty Rate, the producer's royalty account is credited with all royalties earned from the first record that was sold. These royalties will be paid to the producer after deduction of the producer's advance. This provision is favorable to the producer. The artist receives royalties "prospectively" after recoupment of all recording costs for the album at the artist's all-in rate. This means that if the appropriate costs are recouped after sales of 200,000 units, the artist will receive royalties for the 200,001st unit and future units sold, as long as the artist's royalty account remains in a recouped position; however, the artist will not receive any royalties on the first 200,000 units sold prior to recoupment.

If the producer is entitled to receive royalties "retroactively from the first record sold" and the costs chargeable against the producer's account are recouped after sales of 100,000 units, the producer's account would be credited with the producer's royalty on units one through 100,000 and these royalties would be paid to the producer after deduction of the advance previously paid to the producer. The producer would then be paid royalties on all sales in excess of 100,000 units. In some cases the producer agreement specifies that the producer is only to be paid royalties prospectively after recoupment of the recording costs. In that event, the producer's attorney should request that the producer be paid retroactively from the first record sold after recoupment of the appropriate costs at the Net Artist Royalty Rate. This is an important deal point that should not be overlooked in any producer agreement.

The producer should be paid directly from the record company. Accounting statements and any royalty payments that may be due should be sent to the producer at the same time that accounting statements are sent to the artist. If the record company fails or refuses to send accounting statements directly to the producer, the artist should be required to send such statements and any royalty payments that are due within 30 days after the artist receives them. The producer should have a minimum of two years after the date a statement is rendered (delete "or was to be rendered") to audit the artist or record company and to object to that statement, and two and one-half to three years from the date the statement was rendered in which to file a lawsuit based on that statement (a longer time period is better for the producer).

7. You warrant, represent, covenant and agree as follows:
   (a) You have the right and power to enter into this agreement, to grant the rights granted by you to us hereunder and to perform all the terms hereof; and
   (b) No materials, ideas or other properties furnished or designated by you and used in connection with the Master(s) will violate or infringe upon the rights of any person, firm or corporation.

This is a standard provision in producer agreements. Subparagraph 7(b) should be limited to elements "furnished" by the producer, not "designated" by the producer. The producer's attorney should require that a warranty from the artist or record company be included in the agreement similar to subparagraph 7(b) stating that all elements not furnished by the producer will not violate or infringe on the rights of others.

8. You hereby indemnify, save and hold us and any person, firm or corporation deriving rights from us harmless from any and all damages, liability and costs (including legal costs and attorneys' fees) arising out of or in connection with any claim, demand or action by us or by any third party that is inconsistent with any of the warranties, representations, covenants or agreements made by you in this Agreement. You shall reimburse us, on demand, for any loss, cost, expense or damage to which the foregoing indemnity applies. Pending the disposition of any claim, demand or action to which the foregoing indemnity applies, we shall have the right to withhold payment of any monies payable to you hereunder and under any other agreement between you and us or our affiliates.

This paragraph is called an indemnity provision. If the artist or record company is sued (or sues the producer) based on any facts (or purported facts) that are inconsistent with any of the promises made by the producer in the producer agreement, the record company and/or artist could look to the producer to pay all costs incurred in connection with that lawsuit or claim.

The producer's attorney should limit the producer's indemnity of the artist and record company to claims reduced to final judgment by a court of competent jurisdiction or to settlements with the producer's consent. The word "reasonable" should be inserted before the words "attorneys' fees" in the first sentence of this paragraph. This provision should also state that monies will not be withheld in an amount exceeding the producer's probable liability under the producer agreement, would be held in an interest bearing account, and would be released if no action was taken on the claim during a one-year period. The following phrase at the end of the paragraph should be deleted: "and under any other agreement between you and us or our affiliates." The artist or record company should indemnify the producer with respect to materials not furnished by the producer to the same extent that the producer indemnifies the artist or record company pursuant to this paragraph.

9. The respective addresses of you and us for all purposes hereunder are set forth on page 1 hereof, unless and until notice of a different address is received by the party notified of that different address. All notices shall be in writing and shall either be served by certified mail return receipt requested or by telex, in each case with all charges prepaid. Notices shall be deemed effective when mailed or sent by telex, all charges prepaid, except for notices of a change of address, which shall be effective only when received by the party notified. A copy of each notice to us shall be sent to: _____(Attorney's name and address).

This is a standard provision. If the producer is represented by an attorney, the attorney should receive a copy of any notice sent to the producer so that the attorney can advise the producer whether any action needs to be taken on any notices received by the producer.

10. We may, at our election, assign this Agreement or any of our rights hereunder or delegate any of our obligations hereunder, in whole or in part, to any person, firm or corporation. You may not delegate any of your obligations hereunder.

The record company's right to assign its rights or obligations under the producer agreement should be limited to a person, firm or corporation that acquires all or substantially all of its stock or assets. If the agreement is with the artist, the artist's right to assign his or her rights under the agreement should be limited to assigning it to the record company. Any assignment by the artist or record company should not relieve them of liability for their obligations to the producer under the producer agreement.

11. During the Term and for three (3) years thereafter, you shall not produce or coproduce any recording for any person, firm or corporation other than us embodying, in whole or in part, the musical selections recorded in the Master(s).

This provision is called a rerecording restriction. The restriction period should be reduced from three years to two.

12. You acknowledge and agree that your services hereunder are of a special, unique, intellectual and extraordinary character which gives them peculiar value, and that if you breach any term hereof, we will be caused irreparable injury which cannot adequately be compensated by money damages.

This language assists the artist and/or record company in obtaining an injunction against the producer should the producer engage in activities that violate the terms of the producer agreement. An injunction is a court order that demands that an individual or firm stop doing something. An injunction could prevent the producer from working for someone else. Since issuing an injunction is such a drastic action, a court will not issue an injunction in the situation where a person is rendering personal services unless there is a showing that the person's services are unique and that the injured party would not be made whole by the payment of money. The language contained in paragraph 12 is almost always found in the artist's recording agreement, but is not as common in a producer agreement. The producer's attorney should attempt to delete the paragraph or, at a minimum, insert the word "material" before the word "term" and substitute the word "may" for "will" and the words "may not" for the word "cannot."

13.   (a) This document sets forth the entire agreement between you and us with respect to the subject matter hereof and may not be modified except by a written agreement signed by the party sought to be bound. Except as expressly provided herein to the contrary, you are performing your obligations hereunder as an independent contractor;

(b) In the event of any action, suit or proceeding arising from or based upon this Agreement brought by either party hereto against the other, the prevailing party shall be entitled to recover from the other its attorneys' fees in connection therewith in addition to the costs of that action, suit or proceeding;

(c) The validity, construction, interpretation and legal effect of this Agreement shall be governed by the laws of the State of California;

(d) Nothing contained in this Agreement or otherwise shall obligate us or any other person, firm or corporation to reproduce or exploit the Master(s) in any manner or media;

These provisions are all very standard. In subparagraph 13(b), the word "reasonable" should be inserted before the words "attorneys' fees."

(e) We may terminate the Term for any reason, with or without cause, on the date of our notice to you terminating the Term;

This subparagraph should be deleted. If the subparagraph is not deleted it should be limited to the situation in which the producer is in material breach of the producer agreement and has failed to cure that breach within 30 days after the artist or record company provides written notice to the producer of that breach. In any event, the producer should receive the advances and royalties that he or she is otherwise entitled to under the agreement.

(f) We shall not be in breach of any of our obligations under this Agreement unless and until you notify us in writing in detail of our breach or alleged breach and we fail to cure that breach or alleged breach within thirty (30) days after our receipt of that notice from you; and

This subparagraph should be made mutual (i.e., the artist or record company should have to provide notice and a 30-day cure period to the producer prior to the producer being placed in breach of the agreement). The cure period for the artist or record company should be reduced to 15 days if the artist or record company fails to pay any monies owing to the producer.

(g) You have been represented by independent counsel or have had the unrestricted opportunity to be represented by independent counsel of your choice for purposes of advising you in connection with the negotiation and execution of this Agreement. If you have not been represented by independent legal counsel of your choice in connection with this Agreement, you acknowledge and agree that your failure to be represented by independent legal counsel in connection with this Agreement was determined solely by you.

This paragraph is a standard provision in producer agreements. Due to the complexity of the issues involved in the negotiation of a producer agreement, the producer is advised to seek an attorney's advice in the negotiation and execution of any agreement.

If the foregoing sets forth your understanding and agreement with us, please so indicate by signing in the space provided below.

Very truly yours,

AGREED TO AND ACCEPTED:

BY: _____   BY: _____

FEDERAL I.D./SS#: _____   FEDERAL I.D./SS#: _____

Recording and Distribution Contracts with Independent Labels

BY EDWARD (NED) R. HEARN

An alternative to seeking a major label recording contract or raising funds to produce your own recording is to approach independent record companies. Many independent record labels have become very successful in reaching and developing niche markets. By researching these labels, you may find one that successfully markets music that fits your style and is interested in producing, manufacturing and distributing your record. Some of these independent labels have been very successful and have become subsidiaries to major recording labels, such as Def Jam (Universal), Aftermath (Interscope/Universal), Maverick (Warner Bros. Music), and LaFace and Zomba (Sony BMG), or have developed affiliations with major label branch distribution, such as Rounder Records and Concord Records.

SMALL LABEL ADVANTAGES

The chief advantages of releasing your album with independent record labels are similar to the reasons for signing with major labels. They generally have a distribution mechanism in place. They are organized to handle the time and costs of financing and administering the production, manufacture, marketing and distribution of records. They can better absorb the financial risks and have more leverage in collecting money from the wholesalers and retailers of records. In addition, the company may have developed a reputation in the music community for a certain style of music and can move a great volume of records in a wide geographical territory.

Bear in mind, however, that if a small label invests time and money in your career and is successful in generating a reasonable level of income for you, you should carefully weigh the benefits of signing with a major label if asked (where you probably will be one of many)—against staying with the smaller one (where you may be the star!). Far too often, the benefits of a smaller label are discovered only after an unhappy relationship with a major recording label occurs. Much depends on the style of music involved, for example, pop and rock may get more attention from a major label than music aimed at more narrow and focused audiences, such as jazz, new age, children's music, or Yiddish folk songs. Both small and large labels have demonstrated effectiveness at marketing heavy metal, dance, hip-hop and rap music.

CONTRACTS

Although contracts with independent labels can be very similar to those negotiated with major labels, smaller independent companies sometimes work out arrangements that do not mirror these standards. These companies may be willing to step away from obtuse and confusing language to create a contract in plain English that is balanced between the interests of the record company and those of the artist to more equitably share the economic benefits realized from the skills and talents of the artist and the business expertise and mechanisms of the recording company, either by paying a respectable royalty or perhaps even agreeing to a profit split. Smaller labels, however, increasingly are reflecting the contractual style and approach of the major labels, perhaps because of the investment costs and financial risks incurred in developing an artist and the desire to be secure that the contract with the artist is sufficiently strong so that a larger label will not be in a position to tempt the artist to switch labels without the smaller label participating in the benefits of that switch. Many smaller labels also insist on participating in some or all of the music publishing of the artist. That is an issue that needs to be carefully examined and should be the subject of a separate deal.

Here are some options with smaller labels not usually available to musicians signing with major labels:

Distribution Deals

In this type of deal, you deliver an agreed amount of packaged compact discs to a record company. Some labels only distribute your product, while you do the marketing and promotion; others do everything.

In a distribution only deal, the record label will either contract directly with stores or deal with networks of independent distributors or both, selling to them at wholesale prices.

If the company only distributes your record, you will receive a sum equivalent to the wholesale price, minus a fee of 20% to 30% and other direct expenses that you authorize the company to spend, but you pay for all the manufacturing costs and all associated marketing and promotion costs. A standard contractual agreement is that you will receive money only on records actually sold and paid for, and even then reserves against returns will be held for up to two years, and sometimes longer.

These types of deals often result after bands release recordings for a regional audience, find themselves with growing popularity and use the added leverage to make a deal that will broaden their audiences.

Unlike major recording labels, independent labels sometimes encourage the sale of compact discs at performances or to fan mailing lists. In this case, a clause can be added to the standard recording contract that will state that the musician can buy product at a low wholesale price. This inventory may be provided as an "advance" against the royalties or other fees that will be owing. This practice is actively discouraged by most major recording labels.

Pressing and Distribution (P&D) Deals

In P&D deals, you deliver a fully mixed recording master and artwork to the record label, which then assumes the responsibility of manufacturing and distributing your records, cassettes or compact discs. If the label advances the manufacturing costs, it will reimburse itself out of the sales proceeds of your recordings, plus, perhaps, some value for the use of its money, in addition to the distribution fee.

If the record label also picks up promotion, publicity and marketing, then the deal is usually structured as a royalty deal that will leave the record label with a sufficient margin to cover all of its costs and make a reasonable profit. The royalty is sometimes higher than in standard recording contracts because you have already invested the costs of recording and producing. That is not always the case, however. When negotiating this type of deal, ask that any royalty percentages be specified as net cents per unit for each configuration for both physical product and digital deliveries.

As an alternative, if providing marketing and promotional duties by the company are involved, these expenses could be deducted as direct costs also, along with the distribution fee and manufacturing costs, with the balance paid to you, but more likely the deal will be structured on a royalty basis, with a royalty of anywhere from 10% to 18% of retail, plus mechanical royalties on the music.

Production Deals

In this type of deal, you sign as an artist with a production company. The company is responsible for recording your music and for obtaining distribution through independent distributors or a record company. In many cases, contracts for these deals are structured similarly to record contracts because the production company will typically make a pressing and distribution deal with a record label that also includes marketing and promotion and then contract with you for a percentage of the royalty paid to it by the record company.

For example, a production company may have a deal with a record company that pays 14% to 18% of the retail selling price on records sold, depending in part on whether the recording costs are paid by the production company or advanced by the record company. The production company might then have contracted with the artist to pay a royalty from between 6% and 10% of the retail selling price or 50% to 60% of the royalty paid to the production company by the record company.

Net Profits Deals

There are some smaller labels that have adopted a policy of doing fifty-fifty shares of their "net income" with the artists in lieu of paying a royalty per unit. In other words, once the label has recovered all of its costs of recording the album and its publishing royalties, marketing, promotion and publicity costs, as well as manufacturing, art design, and distribution costs, and perhaps a percentage of income attributed to overhead, for example, 10%, then it splits the remaining "net" one-half to itself and one-half to the artist. Whether this is a better deal for the artist will depend on the attitude and values of the people running the record company and how the term, "net income" is defined. At the end of the day, unless the record sells very well, it will mean that the artists will not see any money on the sales of their records if there are no net profits. Of course, that often can be the case under the more traditional way of paying an artist a royalty per unit as discussed elsewhere in this article and in related articles in this book, given how labels recoup the costs of recording, and even some, if not all, of promotion and publicity and sometimes marketing costs out of just the artist's royalty as opposed to the full dollars that come in. By way of illustration, the profile below gives a comparison of income of an artist on a fifty-fifty split and a 15% of retail royalty assuming equal costs to the label for the project.

Total recording costs – $20,000

Total manufacturing costs for 10,000 units – $10,000

Art and design costs – $4,000

Marketing budget – $5,000

Promotion budget – $6,000

Publicity budget – $5,000

Mechanicals (9.1¢ x 75% x 12 per unit x 10,000 units) – $8,190

Distribution and shipping – $2,000

Miscellaneous – $2,000

Overhead (10% of $75,000 in sales at $7.50 per unit for 10,000 units) – $7,500

Total costs – $69,690

Assuming that all 10,000 units are sold and paid for with an average wholesale price of $7.50, the aggregate income is $75,000. After expenses of $69,690, on a fifty-fifty split, the artist would see one-half of $5,310, which is $2,655. In addition, if the artist owned all of the publishing, and his or her share of mechanicals was not included in the 50% split, the artist would get an additional $8,190 for mechanicals.

On a 15% of retail ($15.98) per unit royalty, which, with standard packaging deductions and other take-aways, would generally net down to approximately 9.5% of retail, the artist would see an aggregate royalty of $15,181 (9.5% x $15.98 x 10,000) (assuming no free goods). After applying that amount to recoupment of recording costs of $20,000, and 50% of marketing, promotion and publicity costs, which equals $7,500, it leaves an unrecouped balance of $12,319, i.e., $15,181 – ($20,000 + $7,500). Obviously, the fifty-fifty split is preferable. Even in this example, if the artist is getting the more traditional master royalty, the artist generally would still be getting his or her mechanicals from the first unit sold since mechanicals are not usually used to recoup recording costs and other recoupable expenditures. Those mechanicals would be $8,190 as computed in the above illustration.

An example of a fifty-fifty clause from a label, which provides some likelihood that the artist may actually see a 50% share of net follows:

Royalty. On paid-for phonorecords of the Album sold by Company under this Agreement, Company shall pay Artist an all-in master royalty (i.e., inclusive of Artist, producer, and any other person providing services and for any samples used on the Masters), at the rate of fifty percent (50%) of Company's Net Receipts as defined below ("Master Royalty") consisting entirely of phonorecords of Masters subject to this Agreement and based on the payments received by Company from its Net Sales of phonorecords of the Album and other uses of the Masters. Company will pay Artist a Master Royalty prospectively after Company has recovered from all income from the Masters its recoverable costs as further described below. It shall be the responsibility of Artist to pay producers, and all third party royalty participants, including for samples, from Artist's all-in Master Royalty described in this Agreement. No Master Royalty shall be paid to Artist under this Agreement until Company has recouped from all income received by and derived from sales of phonorecords of the Masters and other uses of the Masters a sum equal to all of Company's costs for recording and mastering all of the Masters under this Agreement, as well as all of the costs incurred and paid to third parties from time to time for independent promotion and publicity support; special marketing procedures, such as, for example only, audio interview tapes and electronic press kits; retail store listening posts; videos; and travel costs, accommodations, and meals of Artist in connection with fulfilling public relations and promotion activities; album packaging, manufacturing, mechanical royalties for Non-Controlled Compositions, and all other out-of-pocket costs. Artist's mechanical royalties for Controlled Compositions will be included in Artist's fifty percent (50%) share of Net Receipts. The term "Net Sales" shall mean one hundred percent (100%) of sales for which Company has been paid, less returns, credits, and reasonable reserves against anticipated returns and credits, and less free goods as from time to time prescribed by the policies of Company or its primary distributors. The term "Net Receipts" shall mean all money paid to and received by Company for its sales of phonorecords and other uses of the Masters minus all of Company's out-of-pocket costs incurred in connection with the Masters.

In the above example, the 50% allocation to the artist is a true split of net, and if the label does not overspend on marketing relative to paid-for sales, there is a greater likelihood that there will be some net for the label and artist to share at the end of the day.

An example of a fifty-fifty clause from a label, which provides little likelihood that the artist will see any 50% share of money follows:

Net Profits: We shall pay you the following Net Profits:
(a) "Gross Income" is hereby defined as all income received by us from all sources in connection with our commercial release of records embodying the Masters or any other exploitation of the Masters, prorated if applicable (but not including any shipping or handling type charges received by us) and including any synchronization fees paid in respect to the Masters in the Territory, except as otherwise provided for herein.
(b) Unless otherwise specified herein, "Gross Expenses" is hereby defined as: (i) $1.10 per unit manufactured by us in Jewel Box 6 panel 4/1 folder, 4/0 tray card 3 colors on compact disc (other configurations to be marked up at similar ratios); and (ii) all expenses incurred by us related to all sales and marketing hereunder, including, but not limited to, artwork/packaging, photographs, shipping/mailing/courier service and supplies, phone costs, advertising, point-of-purchase displays and related costs, publicity, promotion, video production, additional manufacturing costs/overruns, taxes (e.g., sale and VAT, but excluding income tax), licensing costs and expenses and collection fees, etc. Notwithstanding the foregoing, you shall be charged the so-called published rates by companies with which we have procured discounts. Further, notwithstanding the foregoing, you hereby acknowledge that the cost of administration of certain expenses (e.g., postage and supplies) would exceed the actual cost or expense of such materials, and therefore our estimate of such Expenses shall be conclusive and binding upon you. Prior to the release of each Album, you shall have reasonable approval of the total expenses to be deducted hereunder for each sales level, provided, however, in

the event of a dispute between you and us in connection with such expenses, our decision shall be controlling.

(c) "Net Profits" (e.g., your share of Net Profits) is hereby defined as: (i) 45% of the first $350,000 of Gross Income in any one calendar year; and (ii) 60% of Gross Income which exceeds $350,000 in any one calendar year; (iii) after deducting any and all Gross Expenses, returns, and reserves from such 45% or 60% share.

This means that all expenses are taken from the artist's share of Gross Income.

(d) Product sold to you for your resale: We hereby agree to sell to you, solely for your resale at live concerts, a reasonable number of copies of any of your physical Albums distributed by us at a per unit price equal to $4.50 plus any shipping and credit card (if applicable) charges. All invoices must be prepaid. Any monies received by us in connection with this subparagraph shall not be included in Gross Income.

(e) Your share of Net Profits shall include all royalties and other monies payable to any producers, mixers, third party publishers, or any other persons entitled to royalties and other monies payable in connection with the sale and other exploitation of the Masters (including, without limitation, mechanical and synchronization royalties). You hereby agree that your share of Net Profits as described in this paragraph is in lieu of all other royalties with respect to the sales of records embodying the Master(s), including, without limitation, any mechanical royalties which would otherwise be due and owing to you, and any other exploitation of the Masters hereunder.

In this example, all of the gross expenses incurred by the label are deducted from only the artist's share of gross income rather than from the total gross income. So, while this deal is described by the label as a share of gross, all of the expenses are charged to the artist's share, and the computation is much different than that provided in the first illustration, which is a true equal share of net.

ARRANGEMENTS ON DIGITAL RIGHTS

Most independent labels, when entering into a deal with the artist, as is the case with major labels, will insist on the right to handle the artist's product not just in the physical medium, but also will want to have the right to distribute and sell the artist's recordings in the digital medium through such outlets as Apple's iTunes, Napster, MusicNet, Yahoo!, and the like, including downloads to computers and over-the-air downloads to mobile devices for both full track downloads (OTAs), ringtones, ringbacks, and other wireless uses. Most labels that work on a royalty basis will try to maintain the payment of just a royalty to the artist in the same way that a royalty is paid on a physical sale, but generally without factoring in packaging deductions and free goods, since those elements are not relevant. The labels obviously get a good advantage on this approach as they have no manufacturing, warehousing, shipping or distribution costs. Payment of a 15% royalty on a 99¢ download (i.e., 15¢), plus statutory mechanicals (namely, 9.1¢, at the rate in effect as of January 1, 2006), leaves a nice margin for the label, with the digital music service downloader paying the label 70¢ on the download. If the label goes to an aggregator, like IODA, DRA, or The

Orchard, then that label likely will pay the aggregator about 15% as a fee for providing the "middle person" service (which is actually a very reasonable charge). Even with an aggregator as part of the picture, the label on a 15% royalty to the artist is still doing very well, netting approximately 36¢ (70¢ minus 9.1¢ mechanical, minus 15¢ to the artist, minus 10¢ to the aggregator).

If the artist's deal with the label, however, is for a fifty-fifty split of net, the artist will do much better than a royalty deal of 15%. On a fifty-fifty split of the net, even with an aggregator, the artist will see about 25¢ (70¢ minus 15% or 10¢ to the aggregator, minus 9.1¢ mechanicals, divided by 2), plus mechanicals at 9.1¢, for a total of 34.5¢, whereas with the royalty deal, the artist will see just 15¢ against a 99¢ retail download, plus the 9.1¢ for mechanicals if the song is the artist's, for a total of 24.1¢.

The other consideration to keep in mind is whether the label will account on a fifty-fifty split separately for the digital downloads or whether it will apply its receipts from that distribution mechanism against its costs in the physical medium. There also are some labels that have taken the approach that they will only distribute product digitally and leave rights to sell the masters in physical media, such as CDs (physical rights), at least to some extent, to the artist, and then reassume physical rights if the artist gets sufficiently established so that the costs of being in the physical market are more likely to be covered by receipts from that market.

Contracts and Relationships Between Independent Labels and Major Labels

BY BARTLEY F. DAY AND CHRISTOPHER KNAB

The new millennium brought with it significant changes in the way recordings are made, marketed, sold and distributed. These changes have shaken the music industry to the core and forced record companies to completely reexamine the commercial viability of the traditional business model. Indeed, several commentators have suggested that if a record company were created today from the ground up, it would look nothing like the traditional record business.

Many of the major industry changes in the past—such as converting record formats from vinyl to cassette to CD—brought to mind Alphonse Karr's maxim, "The more things change, the more they remain the same." But that maxim hardly applies to the revolutionary changes brought by the current state of affairs. With the advent of digital distribution, streaming audio, ringtones and other digital music products, the essential underpinning of the traditional business model—namely the need for expensive physical distribution systems and infrastructures—has been seriously challenged.

Music distribution is no longer completely dependent on those few large companies that could afford to create and maintain huge distribution systems. Now, distribution can happen with a few clicks of a mouse. As a result, small labels can survive and prosper today without access to an expensive physical distribution system, especially if they are savvy about how to effectively promote their music online.

However, there will continue to be business relationships and contracts between major labels and independent labels for a long time to come. What is unknown is exactly how those relationships and contracts will evolve.

Over the years, a complicated relationship has developed between major labels and independent labels. In many instances they are business competitors. Yet, they have also found that there can be a valuable synergy between them. They have often concluded that a business relationship—whether for only certain artists, or for an independent label's entire catalog—could be mutually beneficial.

For independent labels, affiliation with major labels can provide greater levels of media exposure, distribution and financial stability than are otherwise normally available. For major labels, an affiliation with an independent label can provide access to some or all of the independent label's artists. The owners of most successful independent labels are good talent spotters and often find talented artists before they are on the major labels' radar screens. In addition, many independent labels have focused on specific cutting edge genres of music and the audiences for those specific genres, and as a result have been much better at spotting future trends in recorded music. Independent labels provide artists with development assistance, market and promote them, and develop name recognition and fan bases so that the artists are ready to move to the next level of their careers.

Independent and major labels have formulated various kinds of contracts and relationships in order to provide business and legal structure to their working relationships. Sometimes it is only a distribution relationship—the major label (more specifically, a distribution company affiliated with the major label) provides the independent label with record distribution. In other scenarios, the independent label and major label are more entangled, such as in a joint venture relationship, where the major label provides the funding for a label owned jointly by the major label and the independent label. The parties' respective needs determine which one of the various kinds of business and legal relationships is the most appropriate.

TRENDS AFFECTING MAJORS AND INDIES

Since the early 1990s, two specific trends have had an impact on the relationships between major labels and independent labels: (1) a sharp decline in artist development at major labels; and (2) the advent of the Internet and new technology applications, such as digital distribution, audio streaming, podcasting, and ringtones. These concurrent trends have changed the music business on a general level and have altered the natural synergies and balance of power between major labels and independent labels.

The Decline of Artist Development

Until the late 1980s, artist development was a well-established practice at major and independent labels alike. (Artist development refers to any and all support tactics and strategies labels use to enhance a recording artist's musical skills and appeal. For example, a recording artist's songwriting skills may need to be improved, or their onstage presence and overall image may need enhancement. Artist development also involves the slow and gradual building of a strong and loyal fan base that will buy the artist's records.)

By the early 1990s, major labels increasingly became subsidiaries of huge publicly traded corporate conglomerates. With that change came increasing pressure on the major labels from their parent companies to provide faster and greater financial returns. Consequently, artist development—a process that by definition requires substantial investment and a long-term view—quickly fell into disfavor. Artists whose first or second albums showed slow sales were dropped. The major labels began looking for talent whose recordings were already selling before giving them a shot at the big time. And even then, if those acts did not catch on quickly, they too were dropped.

And so, major labels today do relatively little artist development. Given the pressures of Wall Street, it is simply too costly and time consuming. Today, artist development is the domain of independent labels, and the major labels increasingly rely on them to develop new artists. Whenever a recording artist, signed to an independent label, demonstrates considerable popular appeal, as well as substantial CD sales and downloads and an increasing fan base, a major label that wants that artist will have to deal with that artist's label.

By abandoning artist development, major labels have saved themselves substantial development costs. But, they have empowered independent labels to become the predominant gatekeepers to the record industry. This has shifted the balance of power away from the major labels and toward the more successful independent labels.

New Technologies

The advent of the Internet and digital distribution has revolutionized the record industry.

In addition, there have been numerous other developments that have weakened the power and business viability of major labels. Examples of these are the growth of alternate entertainment forms such as computer games and the exponential rise in illegal downloading.

The net effect of all of these developments has been to substantially reduce the power of major labels and make it more necessary for them to enter into business relationships with strong, well managed independent labels, and they must partner innovatively with various businesses outside the record industry, such as telecommunications and Internet companies.

Summarized below are the main types of deals and business relationships that exist today between independent and major labels. An understanding of the various possible relationships with major labels, and the advantages and disadvantages of each, can help an independent label determine the best strategy for attaining its long-term objectives. And for those independent labels presently being courted by one or more major labels, an understanding of the ramifications of the various types of relationships can enable them to negotiate more knowledgeably and effectively.

Before getting into the intricacies of the various types of contracts and relationships, it is important to emphasize that any independent label or entrepreneur that seeks major label affiliation must first have a very substantial track record. While major labels have a growing need for business relationships with independent labels today, those same major labels are in a weakened financial position. They have a greater aversion to risk than in the past when they were flush with profits. Major labels are only interested in entering into relationships with independent labels that have successful track records and management that is experienced in the record industry.

ADVANTAGES AND DISADVANTAGES OF MAJOR LABEL AFFILIATION

There are numerous advantages and disadvantages of affiliating with a major label. Some of the main advantages are as follows:

- Major label affiliation may enable an independent label to increase its artists' exposure in commercial media and to expand its distribution networks by increasing its access to major retail record chain stores and rack jobbers.

- It can provide an independent label with a substantial cash infusion, eliminating the need to continually focus on day-to-day survival issues, which allows more effective operation. The major label may also take on manufacturing and promotion.

- Affiliation may permit an independent label to expand and upgrade its artist roster or enter a mainstream, mass market genre where developmental and promotional costs are much higher than for niche market music.

- Affiliation may also increase the likelihood of the independent actually getting paid for records sold.

The disadvantages of affiliating with a major label follow:

- An association with a major label makes the independent label vulnerable to events completely out of its control, such as internal corporate power struggles and firings at the major label and corporate mergers.

- If an independent label has several independent distributors, it can likely survive a late payment or lack of cooperation from one or two of its distributors. But, if distribution is through a single distributor, the lack of payment or cooperation can be seriously damaging.

- There can be a high degree of bureaucracy in major labels. This can affect an independent label's ability to sign an artist quickly enough when other labels are interested and can affect the independent label's ability to get a promising recording into distribution quickly enough to fully capitalize on a particular trend or to react quickly to the fast-changing developments in the digital distribution realm.

ISSUES TO CONSIDER

When an independent label is considering an affiliation with a major label, there are many issues to consider. Here are some specific questions that will help to focus your research and analysis:

- What are the independent label's present sales volumes and what are they likely to be in the next few years (i.e., with major label affiliation, versus without)?

- Would the major label effectively distribute to the mom-and-pop stores and nontraditional channels (i.e., gift shops) that carry the independent label?

- What are the major label's strategies for developing its online retailing and distribution capabilities, and for taking advantage of Web marketing opportunities? Are the major label's Internet strategies compatible with the independent label's?

- Would the independent label's existing deals with retailers and online distributors be violated by the terms of the deal between it and the major label?

- Are the digital distribution and digital marketing opportunities afforded by an association with a major label, equal to or better than any existing business affiliations that the independent label already has? Would a major label affiliation give it better visibility and positioning on sites like iTunes?

- Is the major label demanding exclusive digital distribution rights, or will the independent label retain the right to strike its own digital distribution deals or enter into relationships with online aggregators such as the Independent Online Distribution Alliance (IODA)? If striking its own distribution deals, is the independent label willing to accept the responsibility and burden of managing and monitoring multiple relationships with multiple online retail sites?

- Would the major label be responsive to regional demands and the demands of niche markets?

- What kind of reputation and support does the independent label have among its fans? Would a major label affiliation jeopardize this? Would the independent label's core fans be best served by the major label's distribution system?

- Would an affiliation with a major label create an unhealthy pressure on the independent label to sell more records than it can comfortably or realistically sell? Would it prevent the independent label from developing the market for an artist at a slow, grassroots pace?

- What is the present financial status of the independent label, and what is its access to additional resources without major label affiliation?

- Assuming affiliation, what would the cash infusion (if any) be used for?

- How could the independent label's existing staff—promotion, marketing and administrative—be best utilized after affiliation?

- How would the long-term business objectives of the independent label be served by affiliating with a major label?

- Do the owners of the independent label really want the responsibilities and financial burdens of operating a fully-staffed record company and overseeing the promotion and marketing of records? Or are they only interested in the creative process of signing artists and producing recordings?

- Is there good personal chemistry between the managers of the major label and the independent label?

- Does the major label's management have a collaborative style, or do they have a more "top down," unilateral style?

- What is the personal style of the independent label's owner(s)? Do they place a high value on being able to operate independently? Are they willing to take input and direction from a large corporate entity? Are they comfortable with the culture of large music corporations, where the focus is more on "product" than "music?"

- What is the major label's real motivation for entering into the relationship? Is it to use the independent label as an "indie front" or to take over the label's strongest artists? Does it view the relationship as a mutually beneficial long-term strategic alliance?

- Would a relationship with a major label serve the best interests of the independent label's artists? (A major label might not have the same degree of commitment to the independent label's artists.)

- What is the corporate direction of the major label? Is there sound long-term vision?

- Are there any indications that the major label's management team is about to change in the near future or that the major label is about to be acquired by (or merged into) another conglomerate?

To get the best possible answers to the above questions, it is a good idea to discuss areas of concern with the major label's management and with other independent labels that have current or recent experience with the major label in question.

TYPES OF DEALS

There are numerous types of deals between independent and major labels, the most common of which are as follows: (1) pressing and distribution (P&D) deals; (2) multi-tiered pressing and distribution deals; (3) distribution only deals; (4) fulfillment deals; (5) piggyback deals; (6) incubator deals; (7) production agreements; (8) joint ventures; (9) equity deals; (10) licensing out (licensing of recordings by independent labels to major labels); (11) licensing in (licensing of recordings by independent labels from major labels); and (12) rights buyouts.

In general, the type of contract offered by a major label, its specific terms and the degree of flexibility in the major label's bargaining position, are dictated by the extent to which the independent label has strong artists, a healthy and ever-improving sales record and the confidence of the major label in the independent's key personnel. There are a number of independent labels that resisted the repeated entreaties of major labels until they achieved sufficient bargaining power to obtain acceptable terms.

The type of contract signed will determine exactly what kind of company the relationship will be with. For example, in the case of distribution agreements with major label conglomerates, the agreements are with *distribution companies* owned by the major label conglomerates, e.g., WEA Distribution (which is part of the Warner Music Group conglomerate) or UMVD Distribution (part of the Universal Music conglomerate). The other types of agreements are typically with the *record companies themselves*—for example, Warner Bros. Records, EMI Records, etc. However, record companies and their affiliated distribution companies are all referred to below by the general term "major label."

There can be several types of deals in place at the same time between a particular major label and a particular independent label. For example, an independent label might have a joint venture agreement with a major label for certain artists and a distribution agreement for other artists. Or, the independent label might have agreements with several major labels, each covering a particular artist or territory.

These multifaceted situations most often occur when an independent label has savvy and experienced management that structures its relationships with major labels in the most advantageous and strategic ways.

Whenever an independent label plans to have multiple agreements in effect with various other labels at the same time, it must ensure that its obligations under one contract do not conflict with the terms of any of the other contracts. Otherwise, it will face the ongoing risk of litigation from one or more of those labels, based on claims that the independent label has breached its contractual obligations.

PRELIMINARY CONSIDERATIONS

Before entering into a contract with a major label, it must first be determined whether such arrangements are permissible under the terms of the independent label's existing recording contracts with its artists. Do the contracts limit or prohibit assignment of artists' rights to a major label? Are there clauses that entitle artists to review or reject any affiliation?

Even if there is no contractual limitation on the assignment of rights, the independent label should find out how its artists feel about major label affiliation. Some artists perceive it as a wonderful windfall, while others view it as an abandonment of principles. Such considerations should be addressed prior to entering into any contracts.

The independent label should also examine its existing royalty and other obligations to its artists, to determine whether the terms offered by the major label make economic sense.

Listed below are the various types of deals between major and independent labels and the essential features of each.

PRESSING AND DISTRIBUTION (P&D) DEALS

In the typical P&D scenario, the independent label signs recording artists to recording contracts, produces the recordings and the graphics and delivers the master to the major label. The independent label is financially responsible for these tasks.

The major label then presses the records and distributes them through its distribution system. After records are sold, the major label deducts its pressing costs and a distribution fee from the monies it receives from its distributors and pays the balance to the independent label. The independent label is responsible for handling (and paying for) all advertising, promotion and publicity, including exposure in commercial and noncommercial media.

Pressing and distribution deals used to be the most common kind of deal between independent and major labels. However, major labels often found themselves involved with numerous independents, many of which were selling only a relatively small number of records.

Major labels eventually concluded that it was not worth clogging their distribution pipelines with low-selling records merely to receive a distribution fee, and today P&D deals are more difficult to obtain. Now, the relationship is more likely to involve a production deal or equity deal (described in more detail below) or the licensing of the independent label's recordings, because these types of deals are potentially more profitable for the major labels. Even so, an independent label in strong financial condition with high sales volumes may still be able to secure a P&D deal.

Two Kinds of Major Label-Affiliated Distribution Companies

In addition to their own distribution companies, each of the four current major label conglomerates—i.e., Sony BMG, Warner Music Group, Universal Music and EMI—has in recent years created or acquired substantial financial interests in separate distribution companies that act and look like independent distribution companies. These ostensibly independent distribution companies have names that do not use any part of a major's name to avoid suggesting any connection with major labels. At present, the companies are Fontana (affiliated with Universal), RED (affiliated with Sony BMG), Alternative Distribution Alliance (ADA, affiliated with the Warner Music Group) and Caroline (affiliated with EMI). They are sometimes referred to as the FRAC distributors.

The reasons why major labels created such distribution companies are simple. Every developing new sound originating from the street is initially championed by a devoted fan base, which tends to be anticorporate and buys its records from independent record stores and other nontraditional retailers that are normally serviced by independent distributors. By having companies that are active in the independent distribution world, major labels are much better able to keep their "ears to the street," keep current on new music trends and have street credibility ("street cred") with the generally anticorporate fans of new kinds of music.

Most independent labels distributed by a major-affiliated distributor are serviced by one of those independent-looking distributors and not by a major company. There are only a few independent labels, namely sizeable ones such as Disney Records, Concord Records, Curb Records, Razor & Tie, Roadrunner, Rounder and Univision, that are distributed by the major distribution companies.

MAIN DEAL POINTS OF A P&D AGREEMENT

The main "deal points" of a distribution agreement are as follows:

Artistic Control

The independent label usually retains control over the content of songs, the design and copy of artwork and the content of promotional and advertising materials. However, the major label may require a right to screen the content for any extreme language.

Ownership of Masters

Typically, the independent label retains ownership of master recordings. However, the major label will have the right to use those masters as collateral for the financial obligations of the independent to the major label. The major label is entitled to be reimbursed its manufacturing costs from the income generated by its sales of the independent label's records. But sometimes those records do not sell in sufficient quantities to do this. In anticipation of this possibility, P&D contracts generally grant to the major label a security interest in the independent's masters and the records manufactured.

Bonds and Letters of Credit

As an additional means of assuring that it will be fully paid for its manufacturing costs, a major label often requires that the independent provide a bond or letter of credit from a financial institution.

Exclusivity

Most P&D agreements require that the independent label's records be distributed to retail record stores, chains and rack jobbers only through the major label's normal distribution system (or through an ostensibly independent distributor owned by the major label).

However, P&D agreements sometimes provide for one or more of the following exceptions:

1. The independent label may be allowed to sell a limited number of records directly or through its own independent distributors to certain retail outlets

not serviced by the major label—for example, health food stores, specialty book and record stores and nonprofit organizations.

2. The independent label or the bands on the label may be allowed to sell records at gigs and by direct mail-order sales.

These special sales channels will be specified in the contract, and the number of records that the independent label will be allowed to sell may be limited. In most cases, the independent will be entitled to buy product from the major at a price determined by a formula specified in the contract. The price is determined by one or a variation of the following: the actual manufacturing cost, calculated on a per recording basis; the manufacturing cost per recording plus an additional amount per recording; the regular wholesale price; or some percentage of the regular wholesale price.

Divided Distribution

Sometimes the agreement will provide that a separate distribution company (which may or may not be affiliated with the major distributor) will handle distribution to niche markets. For example, in the Christian music world, distribution to the Christian Booksellers Association (CBA) market is usually handled by a separate distribution company that specializes in the Christian bookstore market.

Term of Agreement

Typically, a P&D deal will be for an initial term of one to three years (most often two or three), with the major label then having the unilateral right to extend the term of the agreement for an additional two to four years. Usually, these options are exercisable on a year-to-year basis by the major label. Quite often, a P&D agreement will provide for a total possible term (the initial period, plus extensions) of five years.

Territory

Sometimes the territory will be worldwide, but sometimes it is limited to any one of several countries. While it may be more time consuming for an independent label to manage multiple distribution relationships, many experienced independent label owners prefer to select their distribution partners on a territory-by-territory basis.

When an independent label has multiple distribution agents for various territories, consideration needs to be given to determining how online sales will be handled, i.e., will a distributor in one territory have the right to sell downloads or records to consumers residing in other territories?

Distribution Fees and Manufacturing Costs

The most significant fees and costs deducted by the distributor are as follows:

1. The manufacturing costs (i.e., for the duplication of records, printing of artwork, etc.). The manufacturing prices are itemized in a price schedule attached to the P&D contract.

2. A distribution fee, which in most P&D contracts is defined as being a percentage of the wholesale price. This fee can range from 15% to 35%, but is most often in the 18% to 25% range. (A 22% to 23% fee is typical at the major distribution companies.) The exact percentage will depend on the particular distributor

involved and the negotiating leverage of the independent label, as well as the general cyclical changes in the record industry.

3. Sometimes the distributor will provide the services of its in-house promotion and marketing staffs, and possibly its sales staff and in some instances coordinate radio airplay. If so, it may receive an additional fee (10% or more) on top of the distribution fee. The contract will normally provide that the major label will be reimbursed for its out-of-pocket costs (e.g., the costs of hiring independent promotion companies to promote records to radio programmers), sometimes up to a certain specific dollar limit per recording. The contract should provide that the independent label will have the right to approve (or at least the right to be consulted about) the marketing and promotion strategies involved and the way in which money will be spent.

The major label will deduct these fees and costs from the money it receives from record buyers (chain stores, rack jobbers, etc.) and pay the balance to the independent label. In most P&D deals, these fees and costs are calculated on the full wholesale price. Distribution monies are calculated on *wholesale* receipts, but artist royalties are calculated as a percentage of the *retail* price.

Reserves for Returns

Pressing and distribution agreements often include a reserve clause that allows the major label to temporarily withhold a percentage (20% to 35%) of the sums that may be otherwise owing to the independent label. This reserve is to avoid overpayments that might result from returns of unsold records.

The reserves are generally released to the independent label within 12 to 24 months after each reserve period, as established in the contract.

The independent label should seek the lowest possible reserve percentage. A low reserve percentage is especially warranted now because of the new SoundScan technology that allows distributors to efficiently monitor sales patterns and reduce the oversupply of records in the marketplace. In addition, many distributors penalize retailers that return more than a specified percentage (for example, 20%) of records purchased. As a result, the actual percentage of records being returned today is lower than in the past.

Vague terminology, such as "reasonable reserves," should be avoided, since it gives the major label considerable leeway about what percentage of sale proceeds can be reserved. The independent should also try to avoid provisions that require a letter of credit or bond against reserves.

Free Goods

The major label may wish to provide its wholesale and retail accounts with free goods. For example, a distributor might give a store 15 records as free goods for every 100 records purchased, as a sales incentive.

The independent label should seek a clause that limits what percentage of manufactured records can be distributed as free goods.

Key-Person Clause

The contract may include a key-person clause, which gives the major label the right to terminate the agreement if one of the principals of the independent label dies, becomes incapacitated or ceases to be actively involved.

Major labels will not normally agree to a reciprocal key-person clause that allows the independent label to terminate the agreement if and when a key executive at the major label leaves. Major labels will argue that they will be fully able to perform their contractual obligations with or without the presence of a particular executive, whereas the continued presence of key personnel at the independent label is essential.

Digital Rights

Distributors want exclusive digital distribution rights in addition to the right to sell traditional physical records (CDs, etc.). The degree of pressure applied for this will vary from one distributor to another and will depend in part on the negotiating leverage held by the independent label.

In instances in which the distributor is willing to forego exclusive digital distribution rights, it may insist on a higher distribution percentage on the sale of physical records.

Advances

The amount of money (if any) to be advanced by the major label will depend on the leverage and negotiating ability of the independent label. Some distributors are more inclined to give advances than others.

The major label will be entitled to recoup any such advances from future monies owed by the major label to the independent label.

Sometimes the advance, particularly if it is large, will be a "rolling advance," meaning that the advance is paid in installments. For example, once the distributor has recouped the first installment of the advance, then it will pay the second installment.

Incidentally, many experienced independent label owners are more interested in getting top quality service from the distributor and a lower percentage for the distribution fee, than they are in getting a large advance.

MULTITIERED P&D DEALS (UPSTREAMING)

It can be advantageous to market and distribute a new musical group first through the major label's independent distribution company. Then, as the group's sales increase and its fan base becomes broader and certain sales benchmarks are reached, their records can be distributed to a more mainstream audience through the traditional major distribution system. This is referred to as upstreaming. (The term "upstreaming" is also used to refer to a change of *record company*, i.e., switching an artist from an independent label to a major label.)

In order to maintain long-term control over how their records are marketed and distributed, independent labels today often seek to avoid signing a contract that permits upstreaming solely at the major label's option and without the independent label's prior consent.

DISTRIBUTION ONLY DEALS, FULFILLMENT DEALS AND PIGGYBACK DEALS

There are three other types of contracts—distribution only deals, fulfillment deals and piggyback deals—which are similar to P&D deals but are distinguishable in certain important respects.

Distribution Only Deals

Here the independent label itself (not the distributor) manufactures the records and then delivers them to the major label, for distribution through its system. In all other important respects, a "distribution only" contract is identical to a P&D contract.

Fulfillment Deals

The major label manufactures the records and ships them to the independent label's usual independent distributors, rather than to the major label's own distribution system (as is the case with a P&D deal). The major label will collect from the independent distributors, deduct the manufacturing costs and a distribution fee and pay the balance to the independent label. The deal may also include the major label's collection of previous monies owed to the independent label by those independent distributors with whom the major label has an existing business relationship. Major labels generally have more leverage than independents to collect from distributors. Once sales warrant, the parties to a fulfillment deal may agree to change to the major label's own distribution system.

Some independent labels enter into more limited fulfillment deals. For example, the major label might be authorized to fulfill sales only to certain large chains (such as Best Buy and Wal-Mart).

Piggyback Deals

Independent labels that do not have sufficient leverage to obtain a distribution deal with a major label can try to piggyback onto another independent label's existing deal.

In a piggyback deal, the independent label with the existing relationship will deduct a separate and additional distribution fee for itself, then pay the balance to the piggybacked label. For example, the major label may first deduct an 18% distribution fee from the wholesale proceeds and pay the balance to the independent label with which it has a relationship. That independent label may deduct another 7% from the wholesale price as its own distribution fee, before paying the piggybacked label the balance of the monies. In that situation, the piggybacked label is being charged a total combined distribution fee of 25%.

Typically, the piggybacking label will depend on accountings and payments from the independent label. Therefore, before entering into this type of deal, it should fully understand the exact terms of the relationship between the other independent label and the major.

INCUBATOR DEALS

Some major labels have started or support, so-called incubator labels. These labels are designed to nurture and develop young musical talent relatively inexpensively and at a slower pace than is normal for new artists signed to major labels.

Incubator labels come in two varieties. Some incubator labels are in-house subsidiaries of major labels. Others are independent labels not owned by a major label, but they are given a certain amount of support and nurturing by a major label.

In-House Incubator Labels

These labels are owned by the major label but are operated differently than the usual major label. In effect, these labels are designed to find artists that are in the early stages of their careers and are less developed than is typically the case with artists signed to major labels, but the major label believes they have great long-term potential. Generally, the advances and recording budgets given by these major label incubator labels are much less than are normally given by major labels, with the idea that the artist will be allowed to grow their career more slowly, without the major label expecting an immediate financial return on the artist.

Examples of this kind of incubator label would be East-West and Asylum, which are subsidiaries of the Warner Music Group.

Independent Incubator Labels

These labels are usually founded by young record producers or entrepreneurs whom a major label believes to be adept at finding strong new musical talent.

These incubator deals tend to be hybrids of some of the various kinds of deals discussed elsewhere in this chapter. Most often, these deals are essentially P&D deals with the major label, and they often provide a certain agreed upon amount of marketing and promotion support to the incubator label (in exchange, sometimes, for the major label receiving an increased percentage of sales income).

Certain other features may be added. The major label might have the right to upstream an artist from the incubator label to the major label, in which case the artist will become a major label artist, though the incubator label would still continue to share to a certain extent in any success of the artist.

With incubator label deals, the major label may also have the right in the future, under certain circumstances and on certain predefined terms, to acquire ownership of some or all of the incubator label's master recordings.

In contract negotiations, the independent incubator label will usually seek to restrict as much as possible the major label's unilateral rights to force upstreaming and to acquire rights in master recordings.

PRODUCTION DEALS

Production companies (imprints) find and sign talent and produce recordings. Many are owned by producers that have reputations for turning out commercial hits. Others are vanity labels, owned by successful recording artists that have been rewarded by their labels with production deals.

In some instances, the production deal is for only one artist. In other instances, the deal is for multiple artists.

The production company signs artists to recording contracts and agrees to pay royalties at a specified rate. The production company also signs a separate production agreement with the major label. This agreement provides for a somewhat higher royalty rate to be paid by the major label to the independent, than the royalty rate that the independent label has agreed to pay to the artist. The production company's profit is based on the difference between the rate it receives from the major label and the rate that it pays its artists.

The production company delivers master recordings to the major label, which manufactures, distributes, markets and promotes them directly or through its subsidiaries.

Often, these production companies have names and logos that make them look like record companies, and their names and logos will appear on records next to the major labels'.

Term of Agreement

A production deal will typically have an initial term of two or three years, with the major label having options for an additional one to three (or more) years.

Signing of Artists

If the production deal is for multiple artists, the agreement will typically limit the total number of artists the production company may sign over the entire term of the agreement or for each year during the term. The more established and successful the production company is, the more artists it will be entitled to sign. The major label may or may not have approval rights over which artists are signed. This depends on the outcome of the negotiations between the production company and the major label. In many instances, the production company will be entitled to sign a certain number of artists without the major label's consent but will be obligated to obtain the major label's consent for any other artists signed.

The contract will also specify the total number of recordings the production company is required to supply from each artist. The production company (and its artists) will be obligated to ultimately deliver that number of recordings for each such artist, even if the term of the production agreement expires before that happens. As a result, the production deal may end in regard to some artists earlier than others.

Usually, production agreements are "first look" agreements, which give the major label the first rights to recordings delivered by the production company, but the major label will not be obligated to commercially release any recordings delivered by the production company. For example, the major label might reject a recording or artist it considers lacking in commercial potential. Therefore, the production agreement should allow the production company the right to offer any rejected artists or masters to other labels.

Incidentally, a production company, when signing artists, should be careful about what approval rights it guarantees to artists (e.g., approval rights over the use of master recordings in film and television projects, and on compilation records). Before granting any particular approval rights, the independent label should make sure that those rights are specifically provided for in the production agreement with the major label. Otherwise, the independent label may be guaranteeing rights to artists that the major label will not honor.

Royalties

A production deal provides for the major label to pay royalties to the production company, based on a percentage of the retail price. The typical range is 16% to 22%, less the same packaging and other deductions that are standard in most recording agreements. (For more information, see the chapter, "Analysis of a Recording Contract.") Out of this royalty the production company must pay artist and producer royalties. Typically the artist/producer will together receive in the range of 50% to 75% of the royalties paid by the major label to the production company (more often, 75%).

Advances

The major label may advance monies to the production company for salaries, administrative costs and other overhead costs not necessarily attributed to any specific recording project; and may advance the recording costs for each recording produced. If so, recording budgets for each project will be specified in detail in the contract.

The major label will have the right to recoup some or all of those costs before it pays any royalties to the production company.

From a production company's perspective, recording costs should be recouped only on an artist-by-artist basis; a production company should avoid any cross-collateralization clause that allows the major label to recoup recording costs for all artists from the total amount of royalties owing for all artists. Otherwise, the monies paid by the major label to the production company may not be sufficient for it to cover its royalty obligations to those artists that are commercially successful.

If the production company does not have the clout to avoid cross-collateralization, then it should at least try to obtain a clause providing that if, because of cross-collateralization the production company does not receive sufficient monies from the major label to pay successful artists, the major label will pay such monies to the artist. In such situations, though, the amount of such payments will normally be recoupable by the major label from any monies due in the future to the production company.

Ownership of Masters

Typically, the major label, not the production company, owns the masters of any recordings released and sold.

Because the production company is not acquiring any ownership interest in the masters, unlike the situation with joint venture agreements (discussed below), production deals are sometimes referred to as "the poor man's joint venture."

Some production companies, however, have been successful in negotiating for a reversion of that ownership to occur sometime after the end of the term of the agreement (for example, seven to ten years). If, as of the date of reversion, the major label has not yet recouped all recoupable sums, then the independent label may not be entitled to reversion until the major label is fully recouped. In some deals, the independent label can obtain reversion by paying the major label the unrecouped amount.

JOINT VENTURES

Joint ventures are usually between a major label and one of the following: an existing independent label; an established music business entrepreneur; or a successful artist who wants to have his or her own label.

When the joint venture is with a successful artist, it is normally set up to record and promote other artists.

Under the terms of a joint venture agreement, the major label fronts all or most of the operating costs (overhead costs, money needed to sign artists, recording, manufacturing and marketing costs). The parties to the joint venture then share the net profits of the joint venture on the terms set forth in the joint venture agreement. The master recordings will be owned either by the joint venture entity or by the major label.

Many joint ventures are unsuccessful, particularly joint ventures with successful artists, which fail because the successful artist lacks the skill set or time availability to successfully manage his or her share of the joint venture responsibilities.

Joint ventures have fallen largely out of favor with the heads of major labels. The reasons are simple. Not only have joint ventures often proved unsuccessful, but major labels find unappealing the idea of fronting all or most of the funding of the joint venture, then having to share a large share (typically 30% to 50%) of profits if the joint venture is successful.

Many deals that, in the past, would have been joint venture deals, are today production deals, since production deals allow the major label to keep a much larger share of the profits from successful records.

Joint ventures do still happen to a limited extent. However, the terms of joint venture agreements today are more favorable to the major label than in the past.

Calculating the Joint Venture's Net Profits

Normally joint venture agreements contain complex provisions regarding how the net profits or net receipts will be calculated.

To compute the net, the major label typically deducts a fee off the top of approximately 10% of the gross receipts from sales, to pay the distribution fee charged by the distribution company affiliated with the major label and approximately another 5% to 10% to compensate the major label for managing the relationship with the distributor. And so, a total of approximately 15% to 20% will be deducted in connection with distribution, part of which goes to the affiliated distribution company, with the other part going to the major label. With substantial clout, the joint venture partner can get that total percentage of 15% to 20% reduced slightly.

In addition, the major label will be entitled deduct (and reimburse itself) for 50% to 100% of all actual out-of-pocket costs it incurs and 50% to 100% of the monies previously advanced for the independent label's operating costs. The exact percentages will be as negotiated.

The major label may also be entitled under the parties' agreement to deduct another 5% to 10%, as compensation for overseeing marketing and promotion of the joint venture's records.

After all of these costs and fees are deducted from the joint venture's gross sales receipts, the parties will divide the remaining amount in whatever proportions their contract says. (Traditionally, fifty-fifty, but now it is often sixty-forty or seventy-thirty in favor of the major label.)

Related Profit Split Considerations

The major label will duplicate and distribute the joint venture's records and charge the joint venture for duplication costs and distribution fees. In fact, the major label receives a profit from those duplication and distribution activities, however, the joint venture will not be entitled to share in any of that profit.

Scope of Agreement

Sometimes the joint venture will apply to the sale of records in only certain territories (e.g., North America), in which case only one of the partners will have the right to sell such records in other territories, outside the scope of the joint venture.

In some instances, the joint venture will be limited in scope to certain named artists, in which case the independent label will be entitled to continue operating outside the scope of the joint venture as a stand-alone label with respect to its *other* artists.

The agreement may also include a clause that states that after an artist sells a specified amount of records on the joint venture's label, the major label will have the option to release any new recordings by that artist exclusively under the major's name (another version of upstreaming).

Employment Agreement

Usually the person heading up the joint venture will sign an employment agreement, containing complex compensation provisions. The term of the employment agreement is normally for at least the term of the joint venture and often beyond that.

The Signing of Artists

Normally the joint venture agreement will provide that a certain number of artists may be signed each year, sometimes by the joint venture partner without the major label's consent, up to a certain number of signings each year.

There will be caps on the amount of advances, royalty rates, the number of masters to be recorded, etc.

The Dropping of Artists

More often than not, the independent label will not be allowed to drop an artist without the major label's consent.

Letter of Credit

In some instances, the major label and its joint venture partner will each pay a predefined share of artist advances. In such situations, the major label will require that its joint venture partner provide a letter of credit from a financial institution, to guarantee that the joint venture partner will follow through on its obligation to pay its share of such advances.

Marketing and Promotion Issues

Depending on the independent label's bargaining power, it may be able to obtain the right to oversee all marketing and promotion decisions, and perhaps the right to spend up to a certain specified amount each year for that marketing and promotion. However, since the major label holds the purse strings (not to mention being much better able to absorb the costs of possible future litigation between the parties), the independent typically will have little practical recourse if the major label later decides to provide less funding than originally agreed.

That being said, the independent may, when negotiating the terms of the joint venture agreement, seek to have certain clauses inserted into the agreement that would penalize the major for breaching its financial commitments, and thereby possibly reduce the likelihood of such problems. For example, the agreement might provide that if the major fails to meet such commitments, the independent will be entitled to terminate the joint venture and to keep certain joint venture assets to which it would not otherwise have been entitled at the end of the joint venture. The independent might also seek a "stipulated damages clause," that would entitle it to a predetermined amount of damages in the event that the major breaches its financial commitments.

As a practical matter, the independent will need substantial bargaining power in order to obtain such clauses.

Term of Agreement

The agreement will provide that the joint venture will last for a certain period of time, often two to five years (with two or three being the most common). The major label will usually have the right to later extend the term of the agreement for a specified number of years.

Often, the major label is entitled to terminate the agreement early if the joint venture's losses reach a certain amount (stop loss termination).

There are a number of methods for determining how assets will be allocated between the parties once the joint venture is terminated, several of which follow: (1) The agreement might contain buy-sell provisions, which state that each party will have the right to buy out the other's rights in the joint venture, and specify which party has the first right and priority to do so; (2) the agreement may provide that the joint venture assets will be divided equally upon termination; or (3) there will not be a buyout or division of assets as such, but the major label will be obligated to continue paying its joint venture partner a share of all income earned after the end of the joint venture from the recordings made during the joint venture.

An important issue is determining which of the parties will have first dibs on the acts that are still signed to the joint venture as of the date of its termination.

From an independent label's point of view, it is crucial that the agreement contain clearly defined termination provisions. History has shown that many major labels are enthusiastic about a joint venture at its beginning, but quickly lose interest if profit expectations are not met or if there are changes in corporate management.

EQUITY DEALS

In an equity deal, the major label will either purchase an independent label outright or buy a part interest in it, rather than merely receiving rights to sell its records.

Terms of Purchase

Often, the major label's buyout rights will have been originally negotiated between the parties as part of a P&D or joint venture deal, whereby the major label receives an option to buy part or all of the independent label. Sometimes the major label will exercise its buyout rights incrementally.

When a major label purchases an independent outright, the price is heavily negotiated. As a rule of thumb, independent labels generally sell for either six to ten times annual net earnings or two and one-half times annual gross revenues.

In many instances, there will be a timing issue, i.e., *when* to sell. If the label is for sale prematurely, the independent label owner will get a lower price. If the label waits too long, the potential buyer may lose interest.

Allocation of Costs and Income

When a major label wants to buy only a partial interest in an independent label, there are other issues that will be as heavily negotiated as the price. For example, the major label may agree to pay all of the independent's operating costs, and the parties must resolve the specific terms regarding how future income will be allocated.

The Future Role of the Independent Label's Owners

Normally, the major label will want the original owners of the independent label to remain active because they had the vision to make it a success in the first place.

If the original owners of the label will continue to be involved, there must be contractual arrangements for determining how the label's operations will be shared. Also, those original owners may sign an employment agreement as part of the overall deal, typically for a two- to five-year employment term.

Certain questions arise when original owners of an independent label try to decide whether they want to remain active in the label. For example—

- How much autonomy (if any) will they have with regard to the signing of new artists?

- Who will have the direct day-to-day relationship with artists?

- How much say will they have in marketing, promotion and other operational decisions?

- Who will be making the day-to-day decisions about how money is spent?

- Will the major label commit to spend a certain amount of money each year on marketing, promotion, tour support, etc.?

- Would the original owners be primarily responsible for promotion and marketing activities on a day-to-day basis? If not, who will be?

- Do the independent label's original owners have a clear contractual right to terminate the relationship if the major label does not meet its commitments?

There are no standard answers to these questions. The terms of an equity deal must be customized to fit the specific needs of the parties involved.

LICENSING OUT (THE LICENSING OF RECORDINGS BY AN INDEPENDENT LABEL TO A MAJOR LABEL)

The independent label may license recordings of one or more of its artists to a major label, generally in exchange for a specified royalty. The independent label might license only certain existing recordings or agree to license certain future recordings.

Often this licensing is done on an artist-by-artist basis. For example, an independent label might license the recordings of Artist #1 to one major label and license the recordings of Artist #2 to a different one. This can happen when a major label does not want to acquire the rights to all of the independent label's artists. It can also happen when an independent label feels that it wants to find the major label most interested in, and most committed to, each particular artist.

Term of Agreement

These agreements are normally for three to seven years (most often five years) and often are for only certain specified territories.

The agreement may contain a clause stating that the licensor may have the right to terminate the deal if certain sales levels are not met or if the licensee fails to make timely payment of licensing royalties.

Royalties

The licensing royalty rate for records sold in the United States is typically 15% to 20% of the retail price. But from this 15% to 20%, the independent label must pay artist/producer royalties of usually 10% to 14% of the retail price or a percentage (often 50%) of the licensing receipts.

For the licensing of recordings to be sold outside the United States, the royalty rate is generally 12% to 26% of the wholesale price, often referred to as the published price to dealers (PPD).

LICENSING IN (THE LICENSING OF RECORDINGS BY A MAJOR LABEL TO AN INDEPENDENT LABEL)

An independent label can license particular recordings from a major label. The recordings may be either new or previously released.

New Recordings

New artists are sometimes licensed to an independent label when that label has credibility and marketing strength in a specific genre of music and will help build a fan base for the artist. The major label will usually provide marketing and promotion funds to enable the independent label to effectively promote the artist's records. This type of deal resembles a joint venture in some respects, since the parties often agree to split the net profits after all costs have been paid.

They may agree that the major label will have the right to take back the artist once recording sales reach a certain level. When that happens, the independent label's financial participation may change—for example, from a share of profits to a royalty structure, which may be substantially less rewarding.

Previously Released Recordings

Licensing by a major label to an independent label can also occur in connection with an independent label's reissue of recordings that are no longer available to the public. This can happen when the major label feels that the market for the reissued recording is too small (for example, under 10,000 units).

This kind of licensing is usually on a royalty basis, with a prepayment of royalties to the major label for a certain number of units, typically 5,000 to 20,000 units.

To avoid legal problems, it is crucial that the independent label acquiring the reissue rights be certain that the party with whom it is dealing is the true owner of the masters being licensed. That is often the label that had previously handled the product. However, the ownership of the masters may have been sold, or the rights may have reverted to the artist. In any event, ownership must be clearly determined, and the licensing agreement should contain all appropriate ownership warranties, as well as an indemnification clause. (For an explanation of indemnification clauses, see paragraph 15 of the recording contract in the chapter, "Analysis of a Recording Contract.")

RIGHTS BUYOUTS

If an artist's career is breaking faster than an independent label's financial and promotional capacities can handle, the independent label may enter into a one-artist agreement with a major label, whereby the independent label assigns to the major label its rights in that one artist.

In return, the major label agrees to pay a substantial "recoupable but nonrefundable" cash advance to the independent label against future "override royalties" on the major label's future sale of some or all of the artist's recordings. (The term override royalties, as used here, means royalties paid by the major label directly to the *independent label* on sales of the artist's records. These royalties are separate from and in addition to the artist royalties paid by the major label to the *recording artist*.)

Often, the override royalty rate is in the range of 2% to 4% (sometimes more) of the retail price of records sold. The major label customarily pays such royalties at the same intervals as artist royalties (usually semiannually).

Sometimes, an independent label will have an artist who is the subject of a major label bidding war. In that situation, the independent label may have the bargaining power to demand that part of the cash payment from the major label will be considered *nonrecoupable* by the major label from future override royalties.

A LOOK AT THESE DEALS FROM THE ARTIST'S PERSPECTIVE

An artist's career may be substantially affected by a new affiliation between the artist's independent label and a major label or by the independent label's assignment of the artist's contract to another label (major or independent). Therefore, artists should consider various issues before entering into a recording agreement, or, if already signed, before consenting to a new agreement between the artist's label and another label, including the following:

An artist should seek a clause in his or her recording contract that prohibits the label from assigning the contract to another label without the artist's prior written consent.

Also, a key-person clause should be inserted that permits the artist to terminate the contract if certain key personnel leave the label (the key personnel being those particular individuals at the label whose presence caused the artist to have confidence in the label in the first place).

If an artist's recording contract with an independent label contains such clauses, and the independent label later undertakes to establish a relationship with another label, it is important that the artist immediately review the nonassignment and key-person clauses in his or her contract and take all contractually required procedural steps to preserve their rights.

Whenever the artist's independent label assigns rights to an online retailer or aggregator, the artist should determine whether the original artist-label contract in fact allows the assignment of such rights. For example, the terms of many older recording contracts are not broad enough to allow the independent label to assign *digital* distribution rights to a third party.

An artist who signs a contract with an independent label that already has a relationship with a major label, should clearly understand how that relationship works and how responsibilities are allocated between the two labels. The artist should determine how the major label treats the calculation of royalties on online sales by companies like iTunes, i.e., does it treat such income as *sales* income, versus as *licensing* income? (If treated as sales income, the artist's share of that income will be much less.)

The artist should also determine how the new relationship will affect the payment of artist royalties and how the artist's royalty audit rights are affected.

If the major label will be handling the marketing and promotion, the artist needs to determine how the relationship will work, in terms of coordinating the artist's own activities with the major label's release dates and marketing and promotion activities.

If another label is coming into the picture, the artist should consider meeting with key personnel at the label to try to determine whether the new label has a sincere commitment to promoting the artist's records and whether the proposed relationship will be a boost or a hindrance. This evaluation process is particularly relevant when there are multiple offers.

CONCLUSION

A clear understanding of the possible relationships between independent labels and major labels will help an independent label to take the best advantage of any such opportunities that come its way. However, it is also important to remember this: Even though you may now have a basic understanding of the issues and possible ramifications of these deals, many of the everyday activities involved with working these deals are about cultivating and building personal relationships. The music business ends up being about people and the personal relationships you develop as you go along.

Resources

INDUSTRY DIRECTORIES

All Music Guide
(www.allmusic.com)
1168 Oak Valley Drive
Ann Arbor, MI 48108
(734) 887-5600

Billboard Directories
(www.orderbillboard.com)
P.O. Box 15158
Hollywood, CA 91615
Billboard AudArena International Guide
Billboard International Buyer's Guide
Billboard International Talent & Touring Guide
Billboard Record Retailing Directory
Billboard Musicians Guide to Touring and Promotion

Festivals Directory Northwest
(www.festivalsdirectory.com)
P.O. Box 7515
Bonney Lake, WA 98391
(253) 863-6617

The Music Business Registry
(www.musicregistry.com) or
(www.recordxpress.com) (digital edition)
7510 Sunset Boulevard
Suite 1041
Los Angeles, CA 90046
(818) 995-7458
A&R Registry
Film & Television Music Guide
International Showcase, The Music
  Business Guide
Music Attorney, Legal and
  Business Affairs Guide
Music Publisher Registry
Producer & Engineer Directory

Music Directory Canada
(www.musicdirectorycanada.com)
Norris-Whitney Communications Inc.
23 Hannover Drive, #7
St. Catharines, ON L2W 1A3
Canada
(905) 641-3471

The Music Phone Book
(www.musicphonebook.com)
631 S. 70th Street
Omaha, NE 68106
(402) 932-1456

Music Week Directory
United Kingdom music and media listings
(www.musicweekdirectory.com)
CMP Information Ltd.
Ludgate House
245 Blackfriars Road
London, SE1 9UR
United Kingdom
+44 (0)20 7921 8353

The Music Yellow Pages
(www.musicyellowpages.com)
NewBay Media, LLC
810 Seventh Avenue
27th Floor
New York, NY 10019
(212) 378-0400

The Musician's Atlas
(www.musiciansatlas.com)
Music Resource Group
38 Porter Place
Montclair, NJ 07042
(973) 509-9898

New On The Charts
(www.notc.com)
70 Laurel Place
New Rochelle, NY 10801
(914) 632-3349

Pollstar Directories
(www.pollstar.com)
Pollstar
4697 W. Jacquelyn Avenue
Fresno, CA 93722
(559) 271-7900
Artist Management Directory
Booking Agency Directory
Concert Support Services Directory
Concert Venue Directory
Record Company Directory
Talent Buyer Directory

The Songwriter's Market
(www.writersdigest.com)
Writer's Digest Books
4700 E. Galbraith Road
Cincinnati, OH 45236
(800) 258-0929

GOVERNMENT AGENCIES

Copyright Royalty Board (CRB)
(www.loc.gov/crb)
P.O. Box 70977
Southwest Station
Washington, DC 20024
(202) 707-7658

National Endowment for the Arts
(www.arts.endow.gov)
1100 Pennsylvania Avenue NW
Washington, DC 20506
(202) 682-5400

United States Copyright Office
(www.copyright.gov)
Register of Copyrights
Library of Congress
James Madison Memorial Building
101 Independence Avenue, S.E.
Washington, DC 20559
(202) 707-3000 (Information)
(202) 707-9100 (Forms hotline—use this number
if you know which form[s] you need.)

United States Patent and Trademark Office
(www.uspto.gov)
(800) 786-9199
See Web site for the appropriate
address for your needs.

United States Securities and Exchange Commission (SEC)
(www.sec.gov)
SEC Headquarters
100 F Street, NE
Washington, DC 20549
(202) 551-6551
See Web site for additional locations.

United States Small Business Administration (SBA)
(www.sba.gov)
SBA Answer Desk
6302 Fairview Road
Suite 300
Charlotte, NC 28210
(800) 827-5722
See Web site for additional locations.

World Intellectual Property Organization (WIPO)
(www.wipo.int)
WIPO Coordination Office
2 United Nations Plaza
Suite 2525
New York, New York 10017
(212) 963-6813

World Trade Organization (WTO)
(www.wto.org)
Centre William Rappard
Rue de Lausanne 154
CH-1211 Geneva 21
Switzerland
+41 22 739 51 11

AGENCIES, ORGANIZATIONS, TRADE ASSOCIATIONS AND CONFERENCES

Academy of Country Music
(www.acmcountry.com)
4100 W. Alameda Avenue
Suite 208
Burbank, CA 91505
(818) 842-8400

The Agency Group Ltd.
(www.theagencygroup.com)
1880 Century Park East
Suite 711
Los Angeles, CA 90067
(310) 385-2800
See Web site for additional locations.

Alliance of Artists and Recording Companies (AARC)
(www.aarcroyalties.com)
700 N. Fairfax Street
Suite 601
Alexandria, VA 22314
(703) 535-8101

American Arbitration Association
(www.adr.org)
335 Madison Avenue
10th Floor
New York, NY 10017
(800) 778-7879 or (212) 716-5800

American Bar Association
(www.abanet.org)
321 N. Clark Street
Chicago, IL 60610
(800) 285-2221 or (312) 988-5522

American Federation of Musicians (AFM)
(www.afm.org)
1501 Broadway
Suite 600
New York, NY 10036
(212) 869-1330
See Web site for additional locations.

American Federation of Television & Radio Artists (AFTRA)
(www.aftra.com)
260 Madison Avenue
New York, NY 10016
(212) 532-0800
See Web site for additional locations.

American Guild of Musical Artists
(www.musicalartists.org)
1430 Broadway
14th Floor
New York, NY 10018
(212) 265-3687

American Music Conference
(www.amc-music.org)
5790 Armada Drive
Carlsbad, CA 92008
(760) 431-9124

American Society of Composers, Authors and Publishers (ASCAP)
(www.ascap.com)
One Lincoln Plaza
New York, NY 10023
(212) 621-6000
See Web site for additional locations.

Arts Resolution Services
National Mediation Hotline
(800) 526-8252

Association of Independent Music Publishers (AIMP)
(www.aimp.org)
P.O. Box 69473
Los Angeles, CA 90069
(818) 771-7301
See Web site for additional locations.

Atlantis Music Conference & Festival
(www.atlantismusic.com)
Barrett Parkway
Suite 1200; PMB 342
Marietta, GA 30066
(770) 499-8600

Audio Engineering Society (AES)
(www.aes.org)
60 East 42nd Street
Room 2520
New York, NY 10165
(212) 661-8528

Beverly Hills Bar Association
(www.bhba.org)
300 South Beverly Drive
Suite 201
Beverly Hills, CA 90212
(310) 601-2422

***Billboard* Events**
(www.billboardevents.com)
(646) 654-4660
Information on numerous *Billboard* events and conferences, including the *Billboard* R&B Hip-Hop Conference and Awards, *Billboard* Dance Music Summit, *Billboard* Touring Conference and Awards and many more.

The Blues Foundation
(www.blues.org)
49 Union Avenue
Memphis, TN 38103
(901) 527-2583

Broadcast Music, Inc. (BMI)
(www.bmi.com)
320 West 57th Street
New York, NY 10019
(212) 586-2000
See Web site for additional locations.

Bug Music
(www.bugmusic.com)
7750 Sunset Boulevard
Los Angeles, CA 90046
(323) 969-0988
See Web site for additional locations.

California Copyright Conference
(www.theccc.org)
P.O. Box 57962
Sherman Oaks, CA 91413
(818) 379-3312

California Lawyers for the Arts (CLA)
(www.calawyersforthearts.org)
Fort Mason Center
Building C, Room 255
San Francisco, CA 94123
(415) 775-7200
See Web site for additional locations.

Canadian Academy of Recording Arts and Sciences (CARAS)
(www.carasonline.ca)
355 King Street West
Suite 501
Toronto, ON M5V 1J6
Canada
(416) 485-3135

Canadian Conference of the Arts
(www.ccarts.ca)
804 - 130 Albert Street
Ottawa, ON K1P 5G4
Canada
(613) 238-3561

Canadian Country Music Association (CCMA)
(www.ccma.org)
626 King Street West
Suite 203
Toronto, ON M5V 1M7
Canada
(416) 947-1331

The Canadian Independent Record Production Association (CIRPA)
(www.cirpa.ca)
30 St. Patrick Street
2nd Floor
Toronto, ON M5T 3A3
Canada
(416) 485-3152

Canadian Music Reproduction Rights Agency Ltd. (CMRRA)
(www.cmrra.ca)
56 Wellesley Street West
Suite 320
Toronto, ON M5S 2S3
Canada
(416) 926-1966

The Canadian Recording Industry Association (CRIA)
(www.cria.ca)
85 Mowat Avenue
Toronto, ON M6K 3E3
Canada
(416) 967-7272

Chamber Music America
(www.chamber-music.org)
305 Seventh Avenue
New York, NY 10001
(212) 242-2022

Children's Entertainment Association (CEA)
(www.kidsentertainment.com)
271 Madison Avenue
Suite 200
New York, NY 10016
(212) 545-9559

Concert Industry Consortium (CIC)
(www.pollstaronline.com)
(Click on Concert Industry Consortium Special Features/CIC Archive.)
4697 W. Jacquelyn Avenue
Fresno, CA 93722
(559)-271-7900

Copyright Clearinghouse, Inc.
(www.copyrightclearinghouse.com)
21122 Erwin Street
Woodland Hills, CA 91367
(818) 558-3480

Country Music Association (CMA)
(www.countrymusic.org)
One Music Circle South
Nashville, TN 37203
(615) 244-2840

Creative Artists Agency
(www.caa.com)
9830 Wilshire Boulevard
Beverly Hills, CA 90212
(310) 288-4545

Creative Commons
(www.creativecommons.org)
543 Howard Street
5th Floor
San Francisco, CA 94105
(415) 946-3070

Creative Musicians Coalition
(www.creativemusicianscoalition.com)
P.O. Box 6205
Peoria, IL 61601
(309) 685-4843

Digital Rights Agency LLC (DRA)
(www.digitalrightsagency.com)
1550 Bryant Street
Suite 305
San Francisco, CA 94103
(415) 864-1756

Electronic Industries Alliance (EIA)
(www.eia.org)
2500 Wilson Boulevard
Arlington, VA 22201
(703) 907-7500

The Fischoff National Chamber Music Association
(www.fischoff.org)
303 Brownson Hall
University of Notre Dame
Notre Dame, IN 46556
(574) 631-0984

Folk Alliance
North American Folk Music and Dance Alliance
(www.folkalliance.org)
510 South Main
1st Floor
Memphis, TN 38103
(901) 522-1170

The Foundation Assisting Canadian Talent on Recordings (FACTOR)
(www.factor.ca)
355 King Street W
5th Floor
Toronto, ON M5V 1J6
Canada
(416) 351-1361

Future of Music Coalition
(www.futureofmusic.org)
1325 13th Street NW
Suite 34
Washington, DC 20005
(202) 518-4117

Gospel Music Association (GMA)
(www.gospelmusic.org)
1205 Division Street
Nashville, TN 37203
(615) 242-0303

The Harry Fox Agency, Inc.
(www.harryfox.com)
711 Third Avenue
New York, NY 10017
(212) 370-5330

Home Recording Rights Coalition
(www.hrrc.org)
P.O. Box 14267
1145 19th Street NW
Washington, DC 20044
(800) 282-8273

Independent Music Conference
(www.indiemusicon.com)
304 Main Avenue
PMB 287
Norwalk, CT 06851
(203) 606-4649

Independent Online Distribution Alliance (IODA)
(www.iodalliance.com)
539 Bryant Street
Suite 303
San Francisco, CA 94107
(415) 777-4632

Intercollegiate Broadcasting System (IBS)
(www.ibsradio.org)
367 Windsor Highway
New Windsor, NY 12553-7900
(845) 565-0003

International Association for Jazz Education (IAJE)
(www.iaje.org)
P.O. Box 724
Manhattan, KS 66505
(785) 776-8744

International Bluegrass Music Association (IBMA)
(www.ibma.org)
2 Music Circle South
Suite 100
Nashville, TN 37203
(615) 256-3222 or (888) 438-4262

International Federation of the Phonographic Industry (IFPI)
(www.ifpi.org)
IFPI Secretariat
54 Regent Street
London, W1B 5RE
United Kingdom
+44 (0) 20 7878 7900
See Web site for additional locations.

International Music Products Association (NAMM)
(www.namm.com)
5790 Armada Drive
Carlsbad, CA 92008
(800) 767-6266 or (760) 438-8001

International Recording Media Association (IRMA)
(www.recordingmedia.org)
182 Nassau Street
Suite 204
Princeton, NJ 08542
(609) 279-1700

International Trademark Association (INTA)
(www.inta.org)
655 Third Avenue
10th Floor
New York, NY 10017
(212) 642-1700

LACBA Lawyer Referral and Information Service
(www.smartlaw.org)
Los Angeles County Bar Association
P.O. Box 55020
Los Angeles, CA 90055
(213) 243-1525

Los Angeles Music Network (LAMN)
(www.lamn.com)
P.O. Box 2446
Toluca Lake, CA 91610
(818) 769-6095

Los Angeles WoMen in Music
(www.lawim.com)
P.O. Box 1817
Burbank, CA 91507
(213) 243-6440

MIDEM
(www.midem.com)
U.S.A. Reed MIDEM Inc.
360 Park Avenue South
14th Floor
New York, NY 10010
(212) 284-5142

Millennium Music Conference
(www.musicconference.net)
P.O. Box 1012
Harrisburg, PA 17108
(717) 221-1124

Monterey Peninsula Artists/Paradigm
(www.montereypeninsulaartists.com)
509 Hartnell Street
Monterey, CA 93940
(831) 375-4889
See Web site for additional locations.

Music and Entertainment Industry Educator's Association (MEIEA)
(www.meiea.org)
1900 Belmont Boulevard
Nashvile, TN 37212
(615) 460-6946

Music Managers Forum – UK
(www.musicmanagersforum.co.uk)
British Music House
26 Berners Street
London W1T 3LR
United Kingdom
+44 (0) 870 8507 800

Music Managers Forum – U.S.
(www.mmfus.com)
P.O. Box 444
Village Station
New York, NY 10014
(212) 213-8787

Music Publishers' Association
(www.mpa.org)
243 5th Avenue
Suite 236
New York, NY 10016
(212) 327-4044

Nashville Songwriters Association International
(www.nashvillesongwriters.com)
1710 Roy Acuff Place
Nashville, TN 37203
(800) 321-6008 or (615) 256-3354

National Association of Music Merchants (NAMM)
see International Music Products Association (NAMM)

National Association of Recording Industry Professionals (NARIP)
(www.narip.com)
P.O. Box 2446
Toluca Lake, CA 91610
(818) 769-7007

National Association of Recording Merchandisers (NARM)
(www.narm.com)
9 Eves Drive
Suite 120
Marlton, NJ 08053
(856) 596-2221

National Federation of Community Broadcasters (NFCB)
(www.nfcb.org)
1970 Broadway
Suite 1000
Oakland, CA 94612
(510) 451-8200

National Music Publishers Association (NMPA)
(www.nmpa.org)
101 Constitution Avenue NW
Suite 705 East
Washington, DC 20001
(202) 742-4375

NEMO Music Festival
(www.nemoboston.com)
312 Stuart Street
4th Floor
Boston, MA 02116
(617) 348-2899

North by Northeast (NXNE)
(www.nxne.com)
189 Church Street
Lower Level
Toronto, Ontario M5B 1Y7
Canada
(416) 863-6963

The Orchard
(www.theorchard.com)
100 Park Avenue
2nd Floor
New York, NY 10017
(212) 201-9280
See Web site for additional locations.

Pacific Music Industry Association (PMIA)
(www.musicbc.org)
#501 – 425 Carrall Street
Vancouver, BC V6B 6E3
Canada
(604) 873-1914

Rap Coalition
(www.rapcoalition.org) or *(www.rapcointelpro.com)*
3000 Alabama Road
Suite 119-171
Alpharetta, GA 30022
(404) 474-1999

The Recording Academy (GRAMMY Awards, GRAMMY Foundation and MusiCares)
(www.grammy.com)
3402 Pico Boulevard
Santa Monica, CA 90405
(310) 392-3777

Recording Industry Association of America, Inc. (RIAA)
(www.riaa.com)
1330 Connecticut Avenue NW
Suite 300
Washington, DC 20036
(202) 775-0101

The Royalty Network, Inc.
(www.roynet.com)
224 W. 30th Street
Suite 1007
New York, NY 10001
(212) 967-4300
See Web site for additional locations.

Screen Actors Guild (SAG)
(www.sag.org)
5757 Wilshire Boulevard
Los Angeles, CA 90036
(323) 954-1600
See Web site for additional locations.

SESAC, Inc.
(www.sesac.com)
55 Music Square East
Nashville, TN 37203
(615) 320-0055
See Web site for additional locations.

Society of Composers, Authors and Music Publishers of Canada (SOCAN)
(www.socan.ca)
41 Valleybrook Drive
Toronto, Ontario M3B 2S6
Canada
(416) 445-8700
See Web site for additional locations.

Society for the Preservation of Bluegrass Music of America (SPBGMA)
(www.spbgma.com)
P.O. Box 271
Kirksville, MO 63501
(660) 665-7172

Society of Professional Audio Recording Services (SPARS)
(www.spars.com)
9 Music Square South
Suite 222
Nashville, TN 37203
(800) 771-7727

The Songwriter's Guild of America (SGA)
(www.songwritersguild.com)
6430 Sunset Boulevard
Suite 705
Hollywood, CA 90028
(323) 462-1108
See Web site for additional locations.

SongwriterUniverse
(www.songwriteruniverse.com)
11684 Ventura Boulevard
Suite 975
Studio City, CA 91604

Sound Recording Special Payments Fund
(www.sound-recording.org)
570 Lexington Avenue
21st Floor
New York, NY 10022
(866) 711-3863 or (212) 310-9400

SoundExchange, Inc.
(www.soundexchange.com)
1330 Connecticut Avenue NW
Suite 330
Washington, DC 20036
(202) 828-0120

**South by Southwest Music and Media
Conference and Festival (SXSW)**
(www.sxsw.com)
P.O. Box 4999
Austin, TX 78765
(512) 467-7979

TAXI
(www.taxi.com)
5010 N. Parkway Calabasas
Suite 200
Calabasas, CA 91302
(800) 458-2111 or (818) 888-2111

Volunteer Lawyers for the Arts
(www.vlany.org)
1 East 53rd Street
6th Floor
New York, NY 10022
(212) 319-2787, ext. 1

William Morris Agency (WMA)
(www.wma.com)
1325 Avenue of the Americas
New York, NY 10019
(212) 586-5100
See Web site for additional locations.

Contributors

STEPHEN BIGGER is a graduate of Yale Law School and a partner in the New York law firm of Fross Zelnick Lehrman & Zissu. He has for many years authored the "International Notes" column in *The Trademark Reporter,* the official publication of the International Trademark Association.

LAWRENCE J. BLAKE is a Counsel in the Los Angeles office of the law firm of Manatt, Phelps & Phillips, LLP, which has one of the largest music industry practices in the United States. They represent a broad and diverse clientele in the music industry, including recording artists (from those about to sign their first deal to superstars), songwriters, composers, music publishers, record producers, independent record labels and some of the leading companies engaged in the distribution of music over the Internet. Mr. Blake represents clients in all of these areas of the music business. His practice consists of structuring, negotiating, drafting and reviewing the entire gamut of contracts that pertain to the music industry and related areas, such as merchandising. He also advises clients with respect to related intellectual property matters, such as copyright, trademark, rights of publicity and entertainment-related dispute resolution. Representative clients for whom Mr. Blake provides services include Anschutz Entertainment Group (AEG), which is presently the second largest concert promoter in the United States, Cher, The Eagles, Don Henley, The Pixies, The Rolling Stones and Barbra Streisand.

Mr. Blake also serves as the Sr. Vice President, Business Affairs and General Counsel for Concord Music Group, Inc., which is one of the largest independent record companies in the world, boasting a huge catalog of outstanding music in the jazz and R&B genres on such legendary labels as Prestige, Riverside, Milestone, Pablo, Stax, Volt and Specialty, as well as rock and contemporary music on the Fantasy and Concord labels. Concord won GRAMMYs in 2005 for Best Album of the Year and Best Record of the Year for Ray Charles' *Genius Loves Company* and Ray's duet with Norah Jones "Here We Go Again," respectively.

Mr. Blake has written various articles about the music business and has testified as an expert witness in connection with music industry matters. He has also taught a course for industry professionals at the UCLA Extension entitled "Understanding Contracts in the Music Industry." Mr. Blake is cofounder of the Beverly Hills Bar Association (BHBA)'s Committee for the Arts, which originated this book. He served as President of the Barristers (Young Lawyers Division) of the BHBA from 1983–84 and they later created the Lawrence J. Blake Award in his honor, which is presented annually to a young lawyer in recognition of service to the community. Mr. Blake received his law degree from Harvard Law School in 1976 and has practiced with Manatt, Phelps & Phillips, LLP since 1978.

STEVEN AMES BROWN practices both litigation and transactional entertainment law in San Francisco. He specializes in enforcing the rights of performers and authors in the areas of music, film, rights of publicity, unfair competition and royalty collection. He is a graduate of the University of Michigan with a degree in mass communication and clinical psychology. He was an undergraduate teaching fellow and earned teacher certification. He is a graduate of the University of California, Hastings College of the

Law, where he was Associate Editor of *COMM/ENT, A Journal of Communications and Entertainment Law*. He was a law clerk to the California Court of Appeal, First District; U.S. District Court, Northern District of California; and the San Francisco District Attorney. He was a broadcast journalist and produced public radio programs in Michigan. He also taught radio and television production and performance.

His client roster has included the estates of Fred Astaire, Judy Garland and Orson Welles, and actors such as Ginger Rogers, Annette Funicello, Shelley Fabares, Celeste Holm and James Darren. His roster has also included pop stars such as the Supremes, Mary Wells, Dion, Sam the Sham and the Pharaohs, Nina Simone, Tommy James, Little Anthony and the Imperials, Barbara Lewis, Peaches and Herb, the Flamingos, Jean Knight, Fontella Bass, the Marvelettes, the Capitols, Little Eva, the Weather Girls, Joan Jett and the Runaways, Billy Paul, Evelyn "Champagne" King and the estates of Frankie Lymon and Thurston Harris.

MATTHEW BURROWS is an entertainment and technology attorney based in California. Mr. Burrows has extensive experience negotiating agreements for the live entertainment industry and has been involved in major tours and events throughout the world. Mr. Burrows was previously Head of Music Business Affairs for the William Morris Agency. Mr. Burrows received a BA from the University of California, Berkeley in 1987 and a JD from Loyola Law School, Los Angeles in 1991.

BARTLEY F. DAY has been an entertainment attorney since 1977. He currently divides his time between Los Angeles (where he serves as Vice-President of Legal and Business Affairs for Media Creature Music, a music publishing company) and Portland, Oregon, where he has an entertainment law practice. In his law practice, he represents numerous nationally known recording artists, songwriters, record producers, independent labels, personal managers, music publishers, authors, independent television and film producers and e-commerce companies. In addition, he provides legal counsel on music law and copyright matters to Vivendi Universal Games, the computer games unit of Universal Studios. Mr. Day lectures and writes extensively on entertainment industry issues and is the coauthor (with Christopher Knab) of the book *Music Is Your Business* (3rd ed. 2006). From 1998 to 2002, Mr. Day served two terms as an elected member of the Board of Governors, Pacific Northwest Chapter, of The Recording Academy, the presenter of the GRAMMY Awards.

ROBERT M. DUDNIK is Of Counsel c/o the law firm of Mitchell, Silberberg & Knupp, which has offices in Los Angeles and Washington, DC. Mr. Dudnik is a graduate of Cornell University and the Yale Law School, where he was a member of the Order of the Coif and graduated cum laude.

Mr. Dudnik practiced and taught law in Cleveland, Ohio from 1964 to 1969. Since moving to Los Angeles in 1969, his practice has been primarily related to the handling of entertainment litigation matters and providing prelitigation counseling to clients in all areas of the entertainment industry. He has handled numerous cases involving claims of copyright infringement with respect to musical compositions and recordings.

MARK HALLORAN, a graduate of UCLA and Hastings College of Law, is the principal of Halloran Law Firm, specializing in film, television and music law. Previously, he was a founding partner of Erickson, Halloran & Small; and Alexander, Halloran,

Nau & Rose. Mark also served as Vice President, Feature Business Affairs, at Universal Pictures and Business Affairs Counsel at Orion Pictures. He specializes in representing independent film producers in their development, financing, production, distribution and music matters, and he has served as expert witness for Muhammad Ali and Kim Basinger, among others.

Mark has coauthored two nationally published books on the music business, *The Musician's Guide to Copyright* (with Gunnar Erickson and Edward [Ned] R. Hearn) and the current *The Musician's Business and Legal Guide,* as well as numerous articles on entertainment business and legal issues. His most recent book is *The Independent Film Producer's Survival Guide* coauthored with Gunnar Erickson and Harris Tulchin.

Mark is Adjunct Professor of Law at Southwestern University of Law in Los Angeles and cochair of the USC/Beverly Hills Bar Association Institution on Entertainment Law and Business. He has two daughters, Ashley and Jessica and resides in Santa Monica, California.

EDWARD (NED) R. HEARN is in private law practice. His principal office is in San Jose, California *(www.internetmedialaw.com).* Mr. Hearn's practice concentrates on the entertainment, Internet and computer software industries and their convergence in the digital media market. These matters include recording, production and publishing; multimedia production; licensing, distribution and marketing in traditional and digital media markets; copyright and trademark matters; merchandising, sponsorships, film and television scoring and soundtracks; content syndications; clearances for use of intellectual property in all forms of media; talent services negotiation and contracting; business start-ups and development; strategic alliances, content catalog sales and purchases; and private financing, private mergers and acquisitions. His clients include record labels; music publishers; traditional and Internet-based media, production, technology and content development and distribution companies; webcasting companies; recording artists, producers, writers, managers, software designers; and developers of multimedia products, media technology, and Web sites.

He is a director of the California Lawyers for the Arts, an organization that provides legal assistance to musicians and other artists; Board President of the West Coast Songwriters Association; and coauthor of *The Musician's Guide to Copyright* and *The Musician's Business and Legal Guide.* Mr. Hearn also lectures on music business and related legal issues.

E. SCOTT JOHNSON is Chair of the Intellectual Property Practice Group of Ober|Kaler, a law firm with offices in Maryland, Virginia and Washington, DC. He has diverse experience in copyright, trademark, licensing, technology, Internet, entertainment and media law matters. Mr. Johnson is immediate past-president of Maryland Lawyers for the Arts and immediate past-chair of the Mid Atlantic Arts Foundation. He currently serves as Secretary-Treasurer of the Maryland State Arts Council, is a member of the Copyright Society of the U.S.A., and the National Academy of Recording Arts and Sciences. A former working musician and record producer, Mr. Johnson has written and lectured extensively on copyright, trademark and music industry legal matters. He is recognized in *The Best Lawyers in America* in the fields of Intellectual Property Law and Entertainment Law. His clients include regional and national nonprofit organizations, publishing companies, production companies, recording artists, authors, artists and others in the entertainment and media fields.

NEVILLE L. JOHNSON is an attorney with Johnson & Rishwain LLP *(www.jrllp.com),* in Beverly Hills, California. He is a Phi Beta Kappa graduate of the University of California at Berkeley, where he was the music critic for *The Daily Californian.* He obtained his law degree from Southwestern University School of Law, graduating near the top of his class. Mr. Johnson has practiced as a music industry attorney since 1975, representing such clients as Yoko Ono Lennon and the estate of John Lennon, the Academy of Country Music, Bug Music, Nancy Sinatra, and numerous independent labels, publishers, managers and artists. He has extensive litigation experience in music industry-related matters, including class actions on behalf of songwriters, publishers and recording artists. He was nominated for 2005 Trial Lawyer of the Year by the Consumer Attorneys Association of Los Angeles and voted a "Super Lawyer" (top 5%) by his peers for the years 2006 and 2007.

Besides being an expert in entertainment law and domestic and international copyright, Mr. Johnson is a nationally recognized expert in the law of privacy and defamation. *Editor and Publisher* magazine named him one of the top six plaintiff media attorneys in the United States; Privacy Torts, a treatise on privacy, contains a special dedication to him.

He is the author of a definitive law review article on California law applicable to personal managers and talent agencies, as well as *The John Wooden Pyramid of Success, The Biography of the Greatest Coach in the History of Sports,* and the *Ultimate Guide to Life, Leadership, Friendship and Love* (Second Edition, 2004). Mr. Johnson has spoken on music business issues at many universities and to music industry groups.

He thanks print music publishing expert Ronnie Schiff for advising him on the print aspects of the chapter, "Music Publishing" and Peter Primont, CEO of Cherry Lane Music, for reviewing and commenting on that chapter. Mr. Johnson especially acknowledges the late Don Biederman, former Executive Vice-President and General Counsel of Warner-Chappell Music and subsequently the Director of, and a law professor at, the Biederman Entertainment and Media Law Institute at Southwestern University School of Law, who read and commented on all the chapters for the previous edition.

CHRISTOPHER KNAB is the owner of FourFront Media and Music, a consultation service dedicated to helping independent musicians promote, market and sell their music. He has been involved with the business side of independent music for over 30 years.

He is a former president of the Northwest Area Music Association; Station Manager of alternative radio station KCMU (now KEXP 90.3 FM); and cofounder and Vice President of 415/Columbia Records. He retired in 2005 from the faculty of the Audio Production Program at the Art Institute of Seattle after 18 years of teaching music business related courses. He released the 3rd edition of his book *Music Is Your Business* in the fall of 2006. It is coauthored by entertainment law attorney Bartley F. Day. In addition, his Web site, *www.4frontmusic.com,* posts many useful articles and resources for the independent musician.

He can be reached to arrange consultations at (206) 282-6116; by e-mail, Chris@Knab.com; and by regular mail, 1245 S. 128th Street, Seattle, WA 98168.

EVANNE L. LEVIN graduated with honors from UCLA and Loyola Law School in her native Los Angeles. Since 1974, she has specialized in the music and entertainment law fields and she has been associated with the law firm of Mason & Sloane, where she has represented clients such as Motley Crue, Olivia Newton-John, Kenny Rogers and Sammy Hagar. Ms. Levin worked with Ervin, Cohen & Jessup as attorney to the California Jam II that attracted 250,000 concertgoers. Her in-house legal and business affairs experience includes Twentieth Century Fox, Orion Pictures, Paramount and ABC. Additionally, she has served as outside counsel to MTM, International Family Entertainment, The Family Channel, Hanna Barbera and Warner Bros. TV. She currently maintains her own practice in Los Angeles where she continues to specialize in entertainment, music and related corporate matters. She married Al Gerisch in 2005, however, continues her professional career as Evanne Levin.

Ms. Levin was a founding member and Cochair of the Beverly Hills Bar Association Committee for the Arts. She chaired its annual symposium that produced the written materials, subsequently edited and now published as *The Musician's Business and Legal Guide* that you are currently reading. She has also served on the board of directors of the Hollywood Women's Coalition, was a founding board member of Los Angeles Women in Music and was a member of the Executive Committee of the Los Angeles County Bar Association Intellectual Property and Entertainment Law Section.

In addition to offering personal management, music publishing, television and general entertainment law courses at institutions including UCLA, Ms. Levin is a senior lecturer for UCLA's acclaimed Attorney Assistant Training Program (AATP), the only paralegal school to earn American Bar Association accreditation. She has generously shared her knowledge and experience as a panelist and speaker and as a contributor to numerous music and entertainment publications.

Ms. Levin's civic activities have included board membership on the fundraising arm of The Wellness Community, a nonprofit organization that provides free-of-charge counseling, psychological support and education to those diagnosed with cancer, as well as fundraising for higher education and sociopolitical causes. Her biography appears in numerous editions of *Who's Who in America, Who's Who of American Women, Who's Who in American Law* and other compilations.

LINDA A. NEWMARK is Executive Vice President, Acquisitions and Strategic Projects, for Universal Music Publishing Group. She obtains opportunities for Universal Music Publishing Group to acquire rights to musical compositions and music publishing catalogs; evaluates and negotiates acquisition, administration and subpublishing agreements; and promotes the general business development of the company. Prior to joining Universal Music Publishing Group, Linda was Vice President, Business Affairs for PolyGram Music Publishing and handled the drafting and negotiation of songwriter and copublishing agreements, as well as other legal and business affairs matters for PolyGram. Previously, she was a music attorney with the law firm of Cooper, Epstein & Hurewitz in Beverly Hills. Linda earned her law degree from Stanford Law School. She serves on the Music and Entertainment Industry Executive Committee for the City of Hope Medical Center, and is a member of the Board of Directors of the Association of Independent Music Publishers (AIMP) and the Board of Managers of The Leonard Bernstein Music Publishing Company, LLC. Linda is based in Universal Music Publishing Group's Los Angeles offices.

JACK PHILLIPS, as the former partner-in-chargeand now part-time consultant, has directed auditing activities at the Los Angeles office of Gelfand, Rennert & Feldman, LLP since 1979. He has specialized in royalty and profit participation examinations on a worldwide basis. He also has many years of experience in conducting financial due diligence reviews of record company and music publisher potential acquisitions and valuations of intangible assets, such as recording and music publishing catalogs. Mr. Phillips has testified in judicial proceedings and has authored several articles and lectured on the subject of royalties.

Mr. Phillips has a graduate degree in finance and several years of prior financial auditing experience with Price Waterhouse & Co., and internal audit experience with CBS, Inc. He is a member of the American Institute of Certified Public Accountants, the New York and California State Societies of CPAs and several entertainment industry organizations. Now retired, he remains available for occasional projects. He can be reached by phone at (310) 266-0647 and by e-mail at jphillips1j@aol.com.

DIANE SWARD RAPAPORT is the founder of Jerome Headlands Press, a company that produces and designs books for musicians and artists. Our current catalog includes *A Music Business Primer; How to Make & Sell Your Own Recording;* and *The Musician's Business & Legal Guide.* The books are published by Prentice Hall.

Diane is a pioneer of music business education. She began offering courses for musicians in music business management and publishing in 1974, after working for seven years as an artist's manager for Bill Graham's Fillmore Management. Her goal was to help musicians and songwriters make a living from their art. In 1976, she cofounded, edited and published *Music Works—A Manual for Musicians,* a magazine that the *San Francisco Chronicle* hailed as a "bible for musicians." It was the first magazine to feature music business and technology news.

In 1979, Putnam published her first book, *How to Make and Sell Your Own Record,* which was called the "bible and basic text" that helped revolutionize the recording industry. It provided information about setting up independent record labels. Diane's second book, *A Music Business Primer,* was published by Prentice Hall in 2002.

BERNARD MAX RESNICK, ESQ. is a Philadelphia-based entertainment and sports attorney and manager. Before forming Bernard M. Resnick, Esq., PC in 1999, Mr. Resnick served as counsel to Zane Management, Inc., where he was involved in the representation of entertainers including Grover Washington, Jr., Charles Fambrough, and Pieces of a Dream, as well as numerous NFL, NBA and MLB athletes, professional boxing champions and Olympic medalists.

Mr. Resnick received his BA from Colgate University and his JD from the Villanova University School of Law. He has taught college classes and has lectured widely on entertainment law and related issues at bar association sponsored continuing legal education seminars and at entertainment industry conferences such as MIDEM, the *Billboard Magazine*/American Urban Radio Network's Hip Hop/R&B Conference and Awards, the Independent Music Conference, the Philadelphia Music Conference, the Music and Entertainment Industry Educators Association, the Independent Music Conference and the Millennium Music Conference. He has also served as an expert witness in several lawsuits.

Mr. Resnick produced and performed on the CD *Classical Requests,* released on BMP Records. He owns both ASCAP and BMI-affiliated publishing companies and is a voting member of the National Academy of Recording Arts and Sciences. For the past three years, Mr. Resnick has been awarded "Super Lawyer" status by *Philadelphia Magazine.* He manages and comanages several recording artists. He is a shareholder of The Athenaeum, a member of the Musical Fund Society and a double bassist in the Main Line Symphony. Mr. Resnick practices law with his wife, the beautiful and vivacious former Hollywood filmmaker Priscilla J. "Sally" Mattison.

Representative clients (past and present) include Trina, Bun B., UGK, Us3, Peedi Peedi, Beenie Man, The Rembrandts, Timbaland, Pink, Chris Brown, Dave Mason, Pornosonic, Nina Storey, Complete Music, Ltd., The Estate of Linda Creed, The Philadelphia Orchestra, Jae Staxx, Rugged Ness, Quran Goodman, Infinite Arkatechz, Jim Beanz, Simon Illa, and many other recording artists, record producers, songwriters, record labels, music libraries, filmmakers, managers, booking agencies, photographers, fine artists, Web sites and publicly traded corporations.

Mr. Resnick can be contacted at Bernard M. Resnick, Esq., PC, Two Bala Plaza, Suite 300, Bala Cynwyd, PA 19004; phone (610) 660-7774; fax (610) 668-0574; e-mail, BMResnick@aol.com; and on the Web at *www.bernardresnick.com*.

MARGARET ROBLEY, CPA, EA is the president of R & R Business Management located in Woodland Hills, California. Margaret has a MBA from Chapman College in Orange, California and a Masters of Science in Taxation from California State University Northridge. Margaret has worked in all phases of business management for almost 20 years but has specialized in the music industry.

GERALD ROSENBLATT is in the private practice of transactional entertainment law with an emphasis on music in Century City, California. He was of counsel to the entertainment firm of Mason, Sloane and Gilbert for 12 years. Prior entertainment company legal and business affairs experience includes Vice President, Business Affairs, 20th Century Fox Records and Music (Hollywood); Assistant General Counsel, Capitol Records (Hollywood); Senior Attorney, Motown Records/Jobete Music (Hollywood); Records, Music and Publishing Attorney, CBS Records (New York); attorney for antitrust enforcement and national distribution of motion pictures, Columbia Pictures Corporation (New York).

Mr. Rosenblatt is a graduate of the University of Michigan Law School, a member of the New York and California Bar Associations, the American Bar Association (Forum Committee on Entertainment and Sports), Beverly Hills Bar Association, past President of the California Copyright Conference and a 25-year member of The Recording Academy (GRAMMYs).

He currently represents rock, pop, country, jazz, R&B and classical performers, producers, arrangers, labels, artist managers and film, stage and television actors.

Mr. Rosenblatt administers publishing catalogs for songwriters and independent music publishers. He has spoken at American Bar Association, RIAA, NARAS and ASCAP seminars and at universities and professional music schools.

ALFRED SCHLESINGER has been a music business attorney for over 45 years. Prior to becoming an attorney, he had his own record and music publishing companies. His entire practice is now, and has been, in the field of music, representing record companies, music publishing companies, recording artists, record producers, songwriters, personal managers, talent agents and disc jockeys.

In addition to his activities as an attorney, he was the personal manager of the recording and performing group Bread, from its inception in 1968 to its dissolution in 1978.

Alfred Schlesinger has written articles for the Beverly Hills Bar Association Journal, the National Academy of Songwriters (of which he is a founding member), the Association of International Entertainment Attorneys (of which he is a charter member) and various educational institutions throughout the United States. He has also taught courses on the music business and has been a guest lecturer and panelist for many educational institutions and music-oriented organizations. He currently teaches a one-week music business course six times per year at Full Sail Center for the Recording Arts in Winter Park, Florida.

Mr. Schlesinger is a past president of the California Copyright Conference, a past president of the Los Angeles Chapter of the National Academy of Recording Arts and Sciences (NARAS) and past two-term national chairman of the board of said academy. He served as president of the Society of Singers for four years and then chairman of the board of said organization for four years. He is also a past recipient of *Billboard Magazine's* award as Entertainment Attorney of the Year.

JAMES A. SEDIVY is an attorney who has worked in both Los Angeles and Las Vegas representing artists and companies in the areas of music, film, television, e-commerce, copyright and trademark. In addition to his experience with entertainment transactions, Mr. Sedivy has a background of litigating disputes arising out of entertainment industry agreements along with copyright and trademark infringement actions. He also assists in the formation and maintenance of businesses in California and Nevada. A past president of the Beverly Hills Bar Association Barristers and Cochair of the Committee for the Arts, Mr. Sedivy is currently associated with the firm of Gersh Kaplan, LLP, in Encino, California.

MADELEINE E. SELTZER, formerly a practicing attorney, is a partner in Seltzer Fontaine Beckwith, a legal search firm based in Los Angeles *(www.sfbsearch.com)*. She received her JD from the University of Southern California Law School in 1975. She was a volunteer mediator for Arts Arbitration and Mediation Services, a program of California Lawyers for the Arts, and she is a member of the Docent Council of the Los Angeles County Museum of Art.

DANIEL K. STUART is a Senior Associate in the Los Angeles office of the law firm of Manatt, Phelps & Phillips, LLP, which has one of the largest music industry practices in the United States. Mr. Stuart received his law degree from Loyola Law School in Los Angeles in 1996 and has practiced with Manatt, Phelps & Phillips, LLP since 1999.

Mr. Stuart represents a broad range of recording artists, producers, songwriters, production companies and management companies. The main focus of his practice is negotiating and drafting recording, producer and publishing agreements and his special areas of expertise include negotiating all manner of concert tour agreements, conducting due diligence reviews of publishing and sound recording catalogs in connection with the negotiation of major acquisition agreements, and he advises clients regarding the intricacies of entertainment contracts with minors. Mr. Stuart coauthored "Children As Chattels," an article about the shortcomings of the old California Coogan Law and later played a key role in the drafting and passage of the improved California Coogan Law that took effect in 2000. Mr. Stuart has appeared on a variety of panels at conferences for *Billboard* and *Remix* magazines and Eat'M (Emerging Artists and Technology in Music). He has also been a guest on KPCC's *AirTalk* hosted by Larry Mantle.

Prior to becoming an attorney, Mr. Stuart covered the music industry as a print and broadcast journalist, wrote dozens of articles for such magazines as *Billboard,* served as the managing editor of the nationally broadcast program *RadioScope* for several years and created and helped launch the first nationally broadcast rap music countdown show, *The Hip-Hop Countdown & Report.* Mr. Stuart was a successful club DJ in the 1980s and his "mixes" were broadcast on LA's seminal hip-hop radio station KDAY, where he served as the personal assistant to the music director.

GREGORY T. VICTOROFF is a partner in the Los Angeles law firm of Rohde & Victoroff. Since 1979 his law practice has involved negotiating intellectual property, publishing, movie, recording and fine arts contracts and handling trials and appeals in state and federal courts.

Mr. Victoroff received a BA in theater and a teaching credential from Beloit College in 1976. In 1978, he transferred to the UCLA School of Law to study copyright and entertainment law with the late Melville Nimmer and art law with Monroe Price and he received his JD degree from Cleveland-Marshall College of Law in 1979. He is the editor and coauthor of *The Visual Artists' Business and Legal Guide* (1995 Prentice Hall) and author of *Poetic Justice: Delivery of Legal Services to Artists and Authors,* published by the American Bar Association in conjunction with his live and video ABA art law presentations in the U.S. and Canada. Mr. Victoroff is a former Associate Editor of *Art Calendar* magazine and a contributor to the *Graphic Artist Guild Handbook, Pricing and Ethical Guidelines* (GAG 1999–2004). His entertainment law articles have been published in the *Hastings Communications and Entertainment Law Journal, Whittier Law Review, Entertainment Law Review, Loyola Entertainment Law Journal, Beverly Hills Bar Association Journal, Los Angeles Lawyer Magazine, Los Angeles Daily Journal; 1990 Entertainment, Publishing and the Arts Handbook; The Musician's Business and Legal Guide* (Prentice Hall 1996), *How to Make and Sell Your Own Recording* (Prentice Hall 1999), *The Visual Artist's Manual,* and *The Writer's Manual.* His entertainment law interviews have appeared in *USA Today, Los Angeles Times, LA Daily Journal, Art and Business News, Long Beach Press-Telegram* and *Keyboard Player* magazine. He is the past president of the Beverly Hills Bar Association Barristers and a founder of its Committee for the Arts. He serves on the statewide advisory board of California Lawyers for the Arts and on the board of directors of Through Children's Eyes, a gifted children's photography program. He has lectured on copyright, photography, digital filmmaking, Internet film distribution, art law, censorship and publishing contracts for the Yale Entertainment and Sports Law Association, American Bar Association, American Law Institute, State Bar of California, American Association of Museums, Honolulu Academy of Art Center, Claremont College, UCLA Anderson School of Management, California Institute of the Arts, Hollywood Film Festival, Otis/Parsons College of Art and of Design, California State Northridge, Art Center College of Design, Ringling School of Art and Design, Chaffee College, College of the Desert, Los Angeles International Contemporary Art Fair and Art Expo New York. Mr. Victoroff has served as a legal consultant to documentary films including *Bombing LA,* about Los Angeles graffiti; *Kamikaze Hearts,* about the San Francisco and Los Angeles adult movie business; and NBC's *Midnight Caller.* He is an arts arbitrator and mediator with California Lawyers for the Arts. For his pro bono volunteer legal services, Mr. Victoroff has received awards from the American Bar Association, the Beverly Hills Bar Association, the Boy Scouts of America, the Urban League and former Los Angeles Mayor Tom Bradley. In addition to his private practice, Mr. Victoroff is editor-in-chief of Law Arts Seminars™, a Division of Parker and Barrow Law Publications, an intellectual property publisher and continuing legal education (CLE) provider. As an orchestra musician, Mr. Victoroff has backed artists such as Santana, Huey Lewis and the News, Bobby McFerrin, Journey, Jefferson Starship and Graham Nash.

THOMAS A. WHITE is a consultant in the record and music publishing industries. He is based in Beverly Hills, California and is the author of "The Crisis of A&R Competence and Record Industry Economics" and other analytical articles. Mr. White headed the Artist Development Department at CBS Records (Epic, Portrait and the CBS Associated Labels), West Coast and was president of the European label CBO Records Inc., and president of Harmony Gold Music Inc.

KATHLEEN WILLIAMSON is a practicing partner at Williamson and Young, PC, with offices in New York City and Tucson, Arizona. She received a BA with high distinction in Humanities from Northern Arizona University; a JD with distinction from the University of Arizona; a PhD in Cultural Anthropology from the University of Arizona; and an LLM in Intellectual Property Law from the Cardozo School of Law at Yeshiva University in New York City. She has taught law as an adjunct professor at the College of Law at the University of Arizona. A former judge pro tempore and seasoned criminal litigator, she now focuses her practice exclusively on arts and entertainment law and intellectual property rights (copyrights and trademarks). Kathleen has contributed to numerous periodicals and books in the areas of law, anthropology and music, including her essay in *My Generation: Rock 'n' Roll Remembered, An Imperfect History* (Lilliput Press, Dublin). Her law Web site is *www.williamsonandyoung.com*. Kathleen is also an award-winning performing songwriter and has played all over the world since the 1970s. She cofounded and was legal counsel for several indie labels and helped manage numerous artists' careers. She self-produced and published two award-winning CDs of her original music and is now developing her own new label, Sacred Spud® Productions.

Index

About Jerome Headlands Press, Inc.

Jerome Headlands Press, Inc., based in Hines, Oregon, designs and produces business books for professionals that work in entertainment and the arts. The company was founded in 1988 by Diane Rapaport with the goal to provide artists with access to business information and training to help them make a living and avoid costly mistakes. All books are published by Pearson Education/Prentice-Hall.

Current titles include *A Music Business Primer* by Diane Rapaport, which is an introductory textbook for music business classes in colleges, universities and private schools and *The Musician's Business and Legal Guide,* 4th Edition.

Previous titles include *How to Make and Sell Your Own Recording* by Diane Rapaport, *The Acoustic Musician's Guide to Sound Reinforcement and Live Recording* by Mike Sokol and *The Visual Artist's Business and Legal Guide,* edited by Gregory Victoroff.

Jerome Headlands Press, Inc.
P.O. Box 398
Hines, OR 97738
jhpress@centurytel.net
www.dianerapaport.com